PARENT-CHILD RELATIONS
An Introduction to Parenting

EIGHTH EDITION

PARENT-CHILD RELATIONS

An Introduction to Parenting

JERRY J. BIGNER
Colorado State University, Emeritus Professor

Merrill
Upper Saddle River, New Jersey
Columbus, Ohio

Library of Congress Cataloging-in-Publication Data

Bigner, Jerry J.

   Parent-child relations: an introduction to parenting / Jerry J. Bigner.—8th ed.

     p. cm.

   Includes bibliographical references and index.

   ISBN-13: 978-0-13-500219-3

   ISBN-10: 0-13-500219-2

   1. Parenting. 2. Parent and child. 3. Child development. 4. Family.

I. Title.

   HQ755.8.B53 2010

   306.874—dc22

                                2008043242

Vice President and Editor in Chief: Jeffery W. Johnston
Acquisitions Editor: Julie Peters
Editorial Assistant: Tiffany Bitzel
Production Manager: Wanda Rockwell
Creative Director: Jayne Conte
Cover Design: Bruce Kenselaar
Cover Photo: Getty Images
Media Project Manager: Rebecca Norsic
Printer/Binder: Hamilton Printing Company
Vice President, Director of Sales & Marketing: Quinn Perkson
Marketing Manager: Erica DeLuca
Marketing Coordinator: Brian Mounts
Manager, Rights and Permissions: Carol Sykes
Manager, Visual Research & Permissions: Karen Sanatar
Image Permissions Coordinator: Sandy Schaefer
Full-Service Project Management/Composition: Anupam Mukharjee/Aptara®, Inc.

Pearson® is a registered trademark of Pearson plc
Merrill® is a registered trademark of Pearson Education, Inc.

Pearson Education Ltd., London
Pearson Education Singapore, Pte. Ltd.
Pearson Education Canada, Inc.
Pearson Education–Japan
Pearson Education Australia PTY, Limited

Pearson Education North Asia, Ltd., Hong Kong
Pearson Educación de Mexico, S.A. de C.V.
Pearson Education Malaysia, Pte. Ltd.
Pearson Education Upper Saddle River, New Jersey

Merrill
is an imprint of

www.pearsonhighered.com

10 9 8 7 6 5 4 3 2
ISBN-13: 978-0-13-500219-3
ISBN-10:   0-13-500219-2

To All Who Have Influenced Me . . .

   My Family of Choice, Teachers, and Friends

Who Have Taught Me by Their Example,

   Nurtured My Development,

Given Support and Encouragement,

   And Showed the Meaning of Unconditional Love.

But Most Especially for Duane . . .

Preface

Welcome to the eighth edition of *Parent-Child Relations: An Introduction to Parenting*! This text was first conceived in 1972 but was not published until 1979 as the beginning edition of this long series. After many attempts to put my thoughts into written form, I was able to initiate the very first academic textbook aimed at undergraduate college students on this topic. What initially was a short but concise examination of this topic (the total length of the first edition was 273 pages with no photographs) has become more detailed and interesting, as I hope you will discover as you read the material.

In 1978, when the draft of the first edition was completed, there was little research available on parenting, mostly a limited collection of studies based on samples of mothers. We were just beginning to see the first quantitative data published on fathers and fathering in that year. The United States had changed following the Vietnam War, and the enormous social upheavals started in the late 1960s. The Women's Movement had taken hold, causing many adjustments in gender roles that were reflected in equally numerous adjustments in family life. The median family income that year was slightly over $15,000 and homelessness as we know it today was practically nonexistent. Marriages and births continued to occur at levels we still observe today for the most part. Divorces, however, had begun to soar in frequency and the single-parent family headed by a woman started to become more observable in society. Remarriages and stepfamilies also began to occur with greater frequency.

All this has changed today, as you will read in Chapter 2. However, some things remain constant over this 30-year history of writing about parent-child relations: (1) We now have greater detail in our explanations, more comprehensive and elaborate theory, and considerably more-complex research studies addressing issues that have evolved over these past years; (2) we still lack a definitive answer about how to raise children to become effectively functioning adults; (3) parents continue to bear the major responsibilities of socializing children for their lives as adults, but they do so with the uncertainties that began to be encountered some 30 to 40 years ago.

This text will not provide you with all the answers to the questions you may have about parenting and parenthood. It will not resolve all the problems your parents faced in preparing you for your adulthood, nor will it do so for all the work you will do as a parent in preparing your own children for this life stage. It will, most likely, raise questions that you will need to critically examine about your own experiences in being parented as well as how you might conduct your own experiences as a parent. Examine as well your own opinions, beliefs, and attitudes about this significant family relationship and then decide what you want to keep and if you need to adapt and change in light of what is likely to be new information on this topic.

FEATURES OF THE TEXT

This eighth edition of *Parent-Child Relations* has been revamped to retain the significant pedagogical features of previous editions with the addition of new features. Based on comments from reviewers, these retained features include: (1) a sharper focus on parenting per se throughout the text as basic child development information is assumed to be held by students using this text; (2) an emphasis on family systems theory as a means for understanding and explaining parent-child relations over a number of years in families as children are reared toward adulthood; (3) continued application of the concepts of nurturance and structure as a means for understanding how parents shape their behavior and practice in raising children to adulthood; (4) continued application of the *Frequently Asked Questions* feature that allows students to see parenting concerns and issues through the eyes of a parent as well as those of a therapist who consults with the parent; (5) continued application of *Parenting Reflection* material, which raises significant questions related to material being discussed that are designed to promote critical thinking; (6) continued use of the *Focus On* feature to highlight information being discussed in the text body; and (7) continued emphasis on the Systemic Family Development Model that describes multigenerational family adjustments.

NEW TO THIS EDITION

New to this edition are the following features: (1) updated research information on all topics discussed in the text; (2) a sharper focus on the ecological, social, and cultural contexts in which parent-child relations occur that are examined in each chapter of the text; (3) an extended discussion of attachment between parents and children that is addressed in multiple text chapters; (4) expanded discussions of ethnic diversity and family structures in the United States; (5) additional sections that address how various theories are applicable in parent-child relations; (6) discussions on particular parenting styles at appropriate junctures in several chapters; (7) reorganization of certain topics to ensure reader comprehension; (8) additional Systemic Family Development Snapshots in several chapters that serve as case studies; and (9) an additional chapter discussion that examines parenting in high-risk families where an adult is affected by an addiction or dependency. Unfortunately, it continues to be impossible to cover all topics that reviewers suggested for inclusion in this new edition due to space limitations set by the publisher. However, instructors will be pleased that their favorite topics may be included during lectures to supplement what could not be addressed in these limited pages.

SUPPLEMENTS TO THE TEXT

The following online supplements are available for downloading by instructors at www.pearsonhighered.com:

- **Online Instructor's Manual.** This manual provides professors with a variety of resources supporting the text, including notes from the author regarding each chapter, suggestions for supplementary lecture topics, and a listing of audiovisual materials which illustrate chapter concepts.
- **Online Test Bank.** The *Test Bank* features an array of items for evaluating student comprehension, such as matching, true-false and multiple choice items, designed to assess student understanding.
- **Online PowerPoint Slides.** PowerPoint presentations are provided to accompany each chapter of the text. Professors may customize these slides by adding their own comments and points to what is presented from the text.
- **Computerized Test Bank Software.** Known as TestGen, this computerized test bank software gives instructors electronic access to the *Test Bank* items, allowing them to create and customize exams. TestGen is available in a dual Macintosh and PC/Windows version.
- **Course Management.** The assessment items in the Test Bank are also available in WebCT and Blackboard formats.

ACKNOWLEDGMENTS

Although it is my name that appears as the author of this text, it would not be possible to provide the information here without the efforts of many others. I am especially indebted to my colleagues who conducted the research I discuss here. Students and colleagues have provided feedback, which is helpful in making improvements and changes. I am especially grateful to Nathan Cottle, University of North Texas; Vonda Jump, Utah State University; Jane Lanigan, Washington State University; Beth Magistad, University of Minnesota; Leo R. Sandy, Plymouth State University; Margaret A. Smedley, Cleveland State University and John Carroll University, who provided comments specifically for this edition. I am especially grateful to Julie Peters at Pearson/Merrill, who has guided and supported my work on this edition with sensitivity, astuteness, and candor. The production and editorial staff at Pearson/Merrill have been superlative as well.

My work on this project was made possible as well through the support and understanding of my family of choice and especially my partner. I am indeed fortunate to be connected with these individuals as part of my life.

Jerry J. Bigner, PhD
Emeritus Professor

Email: bigner@lamar.colostate.edu
Web site: http://lamar.colostate.edu/~bigner

Brief Contents

Contents

CHAPTER 10
Parenting Adolescents and Young Adults   219

PART III
Challenges for Contemporary Parents and Children   247

CHAPTER 11
Parenting in Single-Parent Family Systems   249

CHAPTER 12
Parenting in Stepfamily Systems   271

CHAPTER 13
Homosexuality and Parent-Child Relations   288

CHAPTER 14
Adolescent Parents   309

CHAPTER 15
Parent-Child Relations
in High-Risk Families   328

REFERENCES   345

INDEX   369

Note: Every effort has been made to provide accurate and current Internet information in this book. However, this Internet and information posted on it are constantly changing, so it is inevitable that some of the Internet addresses listed in this textbook will change.

Photo Credits

PARENT-CHILD RELATIONS

An Introduction to Parenting

PART I

Parent-Child Relations in Social Context

The role of a parent is a complex combination of many different but related behaviors. Parents today consciously define what their role is, which behaviors are acceptable and appropriate in their role, and how their particular role functions in their family system. However, in developing and conducting their parenting role, people generally have little guidance other than the model they observed from their own parents.

The caretaking relationship an adult creates with children in a family has only recently come under the scrutiny of behavioral scientists. Until modern times, our culture viewed parenting and parent-child relationships as something of a sacred cow. The belief was that this family relationship was beyond reproach and too basic to the survival of society to warrant scientific study. Until recently, it was thought that people did not need training in parenting skills or in preparation to become a parent. The idea was that parenting skills were acquired naturally from living in a family and that these skills were handed down successfully from one generation to the next.

These ideas are changing in relation to other social changes taking place in our society today. Many people question the ability of parents to give children the attention and guidance they need to become effectively functioning adults. The prevalence of violence in homes, delinquency and crime, drug use, pregnancy, and poorly developed academic, interpersonal relationship, and life skills among children and youth today are often cited as results of the inability of parents and schools to perform adequately as teachers. Regardless of the source of such problems, it becomes increasingly obvious that people who are parents today or who desire to become parents need assistance, education, and information in learning how to conduct this family role, how to interact effectively with children, and how to teach their children skills to become effectively functioning adults in society.

Contemporary families differ in their structure and functioning from those of the past. Because of significant changes in family life, what we learned as children in our families about how to be a parent may not be applicable when forming our own families today. The diversity observed among family forms today also creates challenges for effective parenting that differ considerably from what families of the past encountered in the process of raising children to adulthood.

This part of the text focuses on this family role and the rich social contexts in which parenting takes place. To understand parenting and parent-child relations, we must establish the significance of this role within a family system. We must understand how the contexts in which a family functions shape parenting roles and interactions with children. Exploring the origins of and influences on parental behavior establish the foundation, even in these uncertain times, for studying parent-child relations.

CHAPTER 1

Ecology of Parent-Child Relations

Focus Questions
■ ■ ■ ■ ■ ■ ■ ■ ■ ■

1. Why is it important to learn about parenting?
2. What attributes describe the nature of parenthood?
3. Why has the relationship between parents and children traditionally been viewed as unidirectional? How is this relationship seen differently today?
4. How have our ideas about parenthood and childhood changed as a result of social evolution over the years?
5. What factors significantly influence the contexts of parenting behavior and parent-child relations?

■ ■ ■ ■ ■ ■ ■ ■ ■ ■

One of the fundamental questions most of us have, particularly when looking back on our childhood, is: Why did our parents behave as they did? Behavioral scientists interested in human development have devised myriad theories in attempting to answer the broader question of why we experience developmental changes over our lifetime. Some of these theories are applicable in addressing that fundamental question just mentioned about parental behavior and will be discussed in a later chapter of this text. To begin understanding the contexts of the relationship between parents and children, we must examine the complexity of this relationship from an ecological perspective.

Ecology is an interdisciplinary branch of biology that examines the interrelationships between organisms and their environment (Barry, 2007). Behavioral scientists have adopted this view in putting an ecological perspective into human development and social behavior. When applied in this manner, developmental changes in individuals as well as in families and other social groups take place within the context of interactions with changing environmental systems (Bronfenbrenner, 1979). In examining the nature of parent-child relations, we take this perspective as well. To understand this relationship, we must examine the context of the various environments, both past and present, that influence and shape not only the behavior of adults as parents but also that of their children. This chapter explores the basic nature of parent-child relations and identifies the particular influences that influence the role as well as behaviors that adults assume as parents.

THE NEED FOR PARENTING EDUCATION

One of the most significant and intimate relationships among humans is that between parent and child. The parent-child bond is unique both in its biological foundations and in its psychological meanings. For a child, this essential relationship ensures survival and helps to shape his or her destiny. For an adult, it can be one of the most fulfilling of human experiences and a challenging opportunity for personal growth and development.

Contemporary ideas about the nature of parent-child relations are the result of years of social evolution and artifacts of many historical changes. Our concepts of the relationship between a parent and child carry numerous complex meanings and implications. These perceptions influence an adult's decision to become a parent and shape his or her parenting behavior. Our understanding of this significant family relationship has improved over the years with increased knowledge in the behavioral sciences. However, experts continue to study parent-child interactions in the hope of gaining a clearer understanding of how this relationship changes over time and in relation to certain social contexts. Researchers seek to determine how interactions influence relations among all participants, what can be learned about competent parenting behaviors, and how children's actions influence their parents' behavior.

Serious events occurring in families and in our society today point to the need for preparing people to perform competently as parents. It is becoming clearer how the nature of this relationship can harm or benefit a child's development. The widespread prevalence of various addictions to substances, behaviors, and relationships among adults today are traced to early family of origin experiences in which poor and ineffective parenting is thought to play a major role (Coontz, 2006). Similarly, awareness and concern are increasing about the effects of sexual, emotional, and physical abuse perpetrated upon children by parents. Many family experts and practitioners believe these situations result partially from poor preparation for parenthood, inadequate social support, and lack of adequate skills for coping with the stresses of parenting (Cheal, 2007).

For many years, few people saw the need for formal training or education for parenthood. However, many people who work closely with parents today concur that such training is sorely needed. Our society goes to great lengths to train people for most vocational roles. A license indicating training and preparation is required to drive a car, possess a firearm, pilot a plane, and sell insurance or real estate, for example. However, no state or federal statute requires people to have training or preparation to become a parent.

The media sometimes depict parenthood in unrealistic ways. People may be influenced by such depictions and hold idealistic, unrealistic expectations about parenting and parent-child relations. For example, one may gain an impression that parents and children have smooth interactions generally; that children improve their parents' marriage; that children will turn out well if they have good parents; that children generally are compliant with parents' requests or demands; or that parents are solely responsible for their child's character, personality, and achievements upon attaining maturity. Learning what parenting is all about in classes, observing parents and children interact in natural settings, and hearing parents share their experiences may help to deconstruct these stereotypes and myths.

Although most parents would agree they could profit from learning new ways to be effective in their role, we lack concise, clear guidelines about what qualities or behaviors make someone a competent parent. Perhaps we will never achieve complete agreement in our society about this issue. However, researchers continue to make much progress in helping parents to find more effective ways to perform their tasks in raising children to become competent adults.

The relationship between parents and children is complex and is characterized in a variety of ways that are explored in this chapter and throughout this text. Contemporary and historical perspectives of this interactional relationship are discussed. Parenthood is described as a developmental role that changes over time, usually in response to changing developmental needs of children. Factors that significantly influence an adult's behavior as a parent are identified and described.

Clearly, people can learn how to be effective in raising children to adulthood and may be able to improve their behavior as parents. By studying the research, theories, issues, and approaches that have been developed and examined by practitioners and investigators, it is possible to develop a better understanding of parent-child relations.

Parenting Reflection 1–1

Suppose you are in charge of developing a parenting course for first-time, new parents. What are some topics you would include in the course (even before you have studied parent-child relations)?

Focus Point.   It is important for parents to learn how to raise children, to understand their developmental needs, and to become more effective in their role.

CONCEPTS OF PARENTHOOD

The parenting role is associated with several different concepts or ideas in our society. Originally, the idea of parenthood referred singularly to the reproduction aspect that is so prominent in this role. Our society, like all others, values the function of reproduction within a family setting because this is the only way that the population has been sustained until recently.

Although advances have been made in medical technology that allow for reproduction to take place in the laboratory and embryo transfers to be successfully performed, the usual mode of reproduction is generally preferred, followed by careful supervision by adults until children attain maturity.

Other ideas are also embedded in our society's concepts of parenthood. These include the notion that parents are responsible for nurturing, teaching, and acting as guardians for their children until the age of legal maturity (see Figure 1–1). This long period of providing care for children is unique among most species found on Earth. Human infants and children have a long period of dependency on adults due in part to the immaturity of their brains and the length of time it takes for maturity in all aspects to be attained (Stiles, 2008). The brain of a human infant, unlike the brain of offspring of most other species of mammals, is not completely functional at birth and for many years following. Infant humans' survival is dependent on being protected by adults. In contrast, infants of many other species walk within hours of birth and are capable of running to escape danger. Human infants do not master these same motor functions until many months following birth. Differences in brain size and function account for such disparities between humans and other species.

Parents were also originally considered to be a child's principal teachers. This instruction function related to the responsibility given to parents by society to

FIGURE 1–1.   Our society conceptualizes parent-child relations in a variety of ways. It is best understood in relation to the various contexts in which parenting takes place.

prepare children for adulthood by teaching them how to behave appropriately, what rules they must follow, what values to hold, and how to make decisions, for example. This process is referred to as **socialization,** or learning how to conform to the conventional ways of behavior in society.

In the past, parents also served as educators for their children by teaching them the essential skills needed to survive in society, such as reading, writing, and calculation. They helped children learn the job skills necessary to provide a living upon attaining adulthood. These functions today are accomplished by schools and other agents in society, but parents are expected to help children learn the basic rules of social functioning and to impart values that are held in esteem by their family to guide their behavior and decisions.

●●●●●●●●●●●●●●●●●●●●●●●●●●●●●●●●●●●●●●●

Parenting Reflection 1–2

Try to imagine yourself as the best parent you could possibly be. What characteristics would you have? What are some things you would always try to do and always try to avoid doing?

●●●●●●●●●●●●●●●●●●●●●●●●●●●●●●●●●●●●●●●

●●●●●●●●●●●●●●●●●●●●●●●●●●●●●●●●●●●●●●●

Focus Point.   A number of concepts are embedded in the role of a parent. These concepts act to define the different meanings associated with the role.

●●●●●●●●●●●●●●●●●●●●●●●●●●●●●●●●●●●●●●●

CHARACTERISTICS OF PARENTHOOD AND PARENT-CHILD RELATIONS

The relationship between parents and children can be characterized in several ways. This relationship has been taken for granted and assumed to be the most natural and ubiquitous of all human associations, largely because of the biological basis upon which it is founded. It is considered to be a bastion of our culture, for society could not continue if new members were not produced and socialized.

Our contemporary ideas and philosophies about the nature of parent-child relations are derived from diverse

cultural and historical influences. Until recently, the relationship between parent and child was described as based upon a **unidirectional model of socialization.** In this model, the relationship traditionally patterns the role of the adult as a teacher who is responsible for inculcating appropriate behavior patterns, values, and attitudes that prepare children for effective participation in society upon reaching maturity. The child's role is that of being an active learner. According to this model, the flow of information is solely from parent to child. Clearly, this model features the adult as having a significant power, effect, and influence on the child; however, the child is not seen as having influence on the adult, due to his or her subordinate role and lack of social power. Until recently, this basic notion about parents and children received strong support culturally and within the scientific literature on parenting (Ambert, 1994).

Today, our ideas about the nature of parent-child relations are shaped by the new information gained from research that reframes this bond as being **bidirectional** in nature (Ambert, 1994). By this, we mean that both adults and children influence one another as their relationship experiences developmental changes over time. Characteristic traits and qualities about this relationship are summarized briefly here and discussed in more detail in later chapters.

1. *The relationship between parents and children is a subsystem of the larger social system we call a family.*   One of the most salient models for understanding how family groups function is family systems theory, an explanation that is ecological in context (Becvar & Becvar, 1998). We discuss this model in detail in Chapter 3. **Family systems theory** describes how a family functions in ways that resemble other systems found in nature, such as the solar system and ecological systems. The model explains how everyday functioning takes place in a family, how rules evolve to govern the behavior of members, how roles are assigned to regulate behavior, and how these relate to goals the family group seeks to accomplish. It also explains how a family group strives to maintain its stability over time and to adapt or make changes in rules, behaviors, roles, and goals. The model recognizes that family members experience developmental changes, resolve interpersonal conflicts, or confront crises that challenge effective, continued functioning.

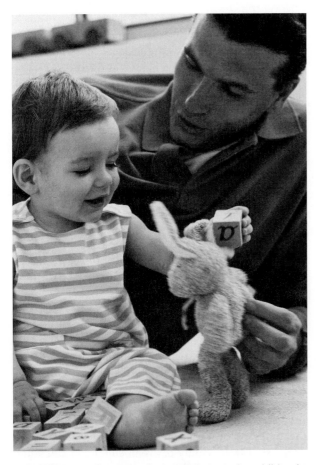

FIGURE 1–2. Parenting focuses on nurturing children's growth and development to facilitate learning to become an effectively functioning adult.

Several other subsystems exist simultaneously within a larger family system, such as the committed relationship or marriage between adults and the relationships between siblings. A subsystem is a microcosm of the larger family system that mirrors the functioning of this group. The same principles and concepts that explain the functioning of the larger family system relate to how subsystems, including the parent-child subsystem, function (Figure 1–2).

The main priority of the relationship between parents and children is to nurture children so that they may learn to become effectively functioning adults upon reaching maturity. However, the family systems model describes the parent-child relationship as being bidirectional in nature. The flow of influence goes both ways.

Children's behavior and development are strong factors that contribute to the quality and scope of interactions with parents. As children experience developmental changes, parents change their behavior and adapt by changing rules, the ways they interact with children, and their goals of child-rearing. In this manner, interactions between parents and children evolve in tandem with children's developmental changes. Similarly, children respond to changes in parenting behavior in ways that help them to achieve specific developmental tasks appropriate for the particular stage they are experiencing in their life span.

2. *Parenthood is a developmental role.*   Unlike most adult social roles, parenting behavior and interactions must adapt in congruence with developmental changes in children as they grow. Similarly, changes arising from a parent's own personal development affect his or her caregiving behavior. The age and developmental status of both parent and child affect the nature and context of this relationship at any particular point in time.

The parental role is sensitive and responsive to changes within the family system. For example, when one adult is removed from the family through divorce or death, the remaining adult's quality and style of parenting change. The parenthood role is also heavily influenced by factors arising from what is known as the *family ecology,* the influences of the larger environments within which a family system exists.

3. *Parenthood is a social construct.*   The parental role is a social institution based on a complex of values, beliefs, norms, and behaviors that focus on procreation and the need to care for young (LaRossa, 1986). As unlikely as it may seem, people who are not parents can experience this role vicariously just as parents experience it directly. The role is universally understood throughout cultures on the planet. Despite the ubiquitous understanding of parenthood, its meanings largely require explanation in a particular historical time. A visit to a nearby bookstore to examine the numerous titles on parenting illustrates this point. Every society, culture, and subculture defines what is appropriate behavior in this role. In addition, people who assume this role may be considered by a particular society or culture to be of higher moral stature than those who do not. In other words, people who are not parents may be devalued by societies in which parenthood is valued.

....

Focus Point. Parent-child relations were traditionally described as unidirectional; that is, the adult had complete jurisdiction, power, and control of the relationship. Today, however, we describe this relationship as bidirectional, meaning that a child is acknowledged as an active participant and contributor to the relationship. Each person influences the behavior of the other. The parent-child relationship is unique to family systems and can be described in various ways.

....

HISTORICAL CHANGES IN PARENT-CHILD RELATIONS

Contemporary ideas about the nature of parent-child relations are very different from those of the past. Current ideas have evolved from earlier beliefs and concepts. The nature and quality of parent-child interactions are influenced significantly by cultural values and by the historical time in which individuals actively conduct themselves in this role (Coontz, 1998, 2006).

Many people believe that our culture values the well-being of children and supports this notion by providing numerous social institutions—the family, schools, social service agencies, and so on—to meet children's needs. Others, however, strongly disagree with this view. We tend to think of our society as child centered. We see childhood as a special time in one's life span, a time of preparation and education for functioning in the later years of life and a time for happiness and freedom from anxiety. We believe children have special needs that are met first by those in their family system and later by institutions, groups, and agencies outside their family system.

Our current concerns and ideas about the unique nature of childhood developed only as a result of many years of social change and transformation in Western culture (Coontz, 1998, 2006). Contrary to what we may assume, the ideas of childhood, parenthood, and the family are viewed differently now than during the Middle Ages, or even during the Colonial period of the United States. Our current ideas about what children need and how adults can conduct their parenting effectively are characteristic of contemporary times. These notions are thought to be particularly related to the manner in which family systems function and how this has changed over the years.

Most social historians agree that the basic contextual nature of parenting children probably has not changed over time. However, changes are noted in the ways adults define and conduct appropriate parenting behavior. In other words, although parenting always has had a strong nurturing context, the specific ways adults define and express nurturing have changed in culturally approved ways at particular points in history. Child-rearing practices have changed throughout history in accordance with changing ideas about what children need from adults to prepare them for their future as adults. Studying the evolution of these ideas will help us understand why we have the particular beliefs and attitudes today about the nature of parent-child relations, parenthood and childhood roles, and the proper way to conduct this relationship. A brief review of this evolution follows, beginning with the ancient cultures that influenced contemporary Western societies.

Ancient Greece and Rome

In ancient times, only two stages of the human life span were recognized: childhood and adulthood (Greenleaf, 1978). Adulthood was considered to be the culmination of childhood experiences. Childhood was the time for preparing to become an adult. Achieving this status was the primary goal of an individual's developmental progress. The boundary between childhood and adulthood was distinct. Childhood commenced at birth and usually ended between the ages of 5 and 7 years, at which time individuals assumed adult status, along with the associated responsibilities, behaviors, and traits expected of an adult.

The ancient cultures of Greece and Rome recognized that the experiences of childhood gave rise to the adult's character. However, the artistic works of these eras suggest that adulthood was considered to be of higher value and the epitome of human development (Greenleaf, 1978). Infancy and late adulthood apparently did not receive similar degrees of interest, assuming artistic attention is a valid indicator of social concern. Child sacrifices, infanticide, and slavery were common during these historical eras. On the authority of the father, infants who were deformed, weakly, or of an undesired sex (usually female) could be left to the elements, drowned, or suffocated.

There was, however, concern during these times for children's preparation for their future adulthood roles.

Although schools taught a wide range of subjects, parents were responsible for teaching their children basic skills and knowledge of the cultures. Education was considered ultimately to benefit the well-being of the community and state rather than an individual's welfare. In these cultures, a formal education was a privilege restricted to males. Females were expected to acquire only domestic skills related to home management and child care.

The family was recognized as the core element in both of these early civilizations. The father was considered to be the family leader and the mother was regarded as a child's first teacher. Women and children had very few rights in these cultures and were considered to be the property of an adult male. Children could be sold into slavery or even abandoned by their father (Bossard & Boll, 1966). By the fifth century A.D., rewards were given to families who gave asylum to orphaned or deserted children. Conditions changed, however, during the Middle Ages.

The Middle Ages to Renaissance

The Middle Ages (400–1400 A.D.) were a time in which Western societies functioned in a rural, primitive manner. Formal education was minimal and generally restricted to the clergy of the Roman Catholic Church. Families were generally structured according to a form known as the extended family, involving several generations living together. Family life during this period centered primarily on an agricultural lifestyle.

In these premodern times, children were raised in a manner that we would interpret today as being indifferent to their special needs. During the Middle Ages and for some time afterward, the nature of an infant was taken for granted by adults. There was no idea that infants needed to learn to trust their caregivers. Assimilation into the adult world came early, usually between the age of 5 and 7 years. A child's education—probably his or her only schooling—came from observing and imitating adult models. A parent in the Middle Ages probably had the notion that children needed adult supervision and care, but apparently this did not include close emotional ties with adults. Parents did not appear to provide warm nurturance to children, since many died in infancy and childhood from diseases that are preventable today. During this period, parenting was only one of many functions individuals performed in families, and it did

not seem to have a high priority. What most concerned family members were the production of food, clothing, and shelter to ensure daily survival.

The prevailing attitude during the Middle Ages was that children were miniature adults. They were dressed in adult-type clothing and given responsibilities in the family at an early age. The lives of children and adults were closely parallel. Children mingled with and were exposed to much adult behavior and living conditions. For example, most children of commoners in Europe were apprenticed to learn a particular skill or trade once they reached age 7.

Infants began to be featured in artwork during medieval times. During the early part of this era, the poses shown in artwork depicted a rather detached way of holding infants, with little direct eye contact between mother and child. Infant mortality rates were particularly high at this time because greater numbers of infants died from disease and unsanitary living conditions. The advent of medical care, and especially the availability of antibiotics, was centuries away in preventing such deaths. Because life was uncertain, adults probably did not develop a close attachment to infants and young children for fear of a disastrous, premature end to their relationship. This would change, however, in the years that followed.

Over the next two centuries that followed the Middle Ages, that is, 1400–1600 A.D., Europe experienced a period of cultural revitalization that was marked by the exploration of newly discovered lands, scientific discoveries, and an explosion of artistic activity. It was a time of great intellectual ferment as adults explored their inner environments or personalities in an attempt to discover the nature of their true selves. However, this time of social and cultural expansion generally did not result in equally great strides in ideas about the nature of children and parenting. The focus clearly was on the adult, as illustrated by the concept of the "Renaissance Man": that is, someone who was well rounded in almost all areas of development—intellectual, artistic, social, and physical.

It was common practice among Italian Renaissance nobility to send their infants to live with "wet nurses"—peasant women who had infants of their own. The wet nurse usually cared for the nobility's infant for about 2 years. Apparently, the biological parents were not particularly concerned about the quality of care given to their infant during this time (Greenleaf, 1978).

Nevertheless, the artistic works produced during this period show a greater interest in children than in earlier times. Fra Fillipo Lippi was among the first of the Renaissance artists to portray infants in accurate body proportions. In the artwork of this period, babies were usually drawn as cherubs, which was considered to be the position in the angelic hierarchy of Heaven to which infants and children who died were assigned. A new sentimentality about children began to emerge during this era. This contributed to changes in existing attitudes about the nature and status of children in society. Artists increasingly gave more attention to children in their works during the late 1500s. Another indication of greater concern and attention given to children at the end of the Renaissance was the creation of special clothing styles just for children. Until this time, children had been dressed in replicas of adult costumes. This change in clothing style would appear to indicate that children (at least those of nobility) were now seen as distinct and separate entities from adults (Greenleaf, 1978).

By the late 1500s, additional distinctions between the worlds of adults and children could be observed. Recreational activities, stories, and types of medical care began to differ between the two groups. Also, advice emerged at this time on how to provide discipline and guidance in child rearing (Greenleaf, 1978). Over the next 200 years, however, the rate of social change would accelerate, bringing new adjustments to the ways people viewed parenthood and childhood.

Colonial America: 1600–1800

The cultural and religious conditions that existed at the time America was being colonized contributed to a unique view of the nature of children and the role of parents in providing for their care. Children were seen as having an inherently depraved nature. Adults thought that children were basically bad or evil. It was thought that parents could overcome or change this by providing particular child-rearing experiences. Many parents believed that if they administered stern discipline through hard labor or work experiences, children would become self-denying, pious adults upon attaining maturity. Adults prized children for their usefulness in the colonization process and for being a good source of cheap labor to their families. Their value in the colonies increased because of the high rate of infant deaths in those times.

The notion that the nature of children was evil or sinful stemmed primarily from the rigid Puritan religious orientation of the colonists (Mintz, 2006). These views are illustrated in the *Day of Doom*, a catechism learned by almost every child in Puritan New England. Puritan parents were responsible for providing rigorous moral and religious training for children, which also included stern discipline in learning appropriate everyday behaviors. These parents believed an essential responsibility of their child rearing was to bring children to religious salvation or conversion. This was accomplished when children were able to recognize and admit their own sinful nature and become Christians. The earlier in their age this occurred, the better, from many parents' point of view. To help children achieve religious conversion, they were taught that they must always obey their parents unquestionably, especially their father. They were taught to curb their so-called natural inclinations to commit sins. Aspects of childhood that are considered today to be acceptable and developmentally appropriate were viewed then in Colonial times as satanic manifestations. Play was considered to be sinful, and children were kept occupied by memorizing scripture and religious songs. This approach to child rearing placed total authority over children's lives and welfare squarely in the hands of parents. It is from this approach that the unidirectional model of parent-child relations became sanctioned as the primary acceptable model on how to rear children properly in the United States.

Adults approached their parenting role in Colonial times in ways that we would label today as being overinvolved in children's lives and bordering on abusiveness. This was a distinct adaptation in parent-child relations from the indifference that characterized the relationship in the previous era of the Renaissance. During Colonial times, there was a heavy emphasis on religious matters and use of harsh disciplinary methods to achieve children's salvation and obedience to parents. Despite the punitive image that this invokes, parents evidently had great affection for their children and showed concern for their welfare in ways that were thought to be appropriate at that time in history.

Industrial Revolution Era: 1800–1860

The nineteenth century in the United States involved a serious internal conflict: The War Between the States. Prior to this event, however, several major views about the nature of parenthood and childhood emerged that, in association with the ideas of authoritarianism that originated during the Colonial period, continue to influence our ideas today.

Three different and contradictory philosophies as to how to rear children appropriately emerged during this era. These depicted different approaches in prescribing appropriate parental roles and behaviors as well as child outcomes.

Calvinism.   The strongest approach, which received the most attention, was inspired by the Calvinist religious movement. This view advocated stern, harsh use of physical punishment and strict moral instruction for children—essentially a strong, authoritarian child-rearing style. It reflected a belief in a cause-and-effect association between the manner in which a child was trained by his or her parents and the outcome that was observed in the nature of the child's personality or character that became manifested in adulthood. This approach could be thought to be based on the Biblical admonition to parents, "Train up a child in the way he should go: and when he is old he will not depart from it" (Proverbs 22:6).

The Industrial Revolution produced dramatic changes in family life and roles. During the Colonial period, the father's central role in a family system consisted of providing the economic support and moral and religious education for children and acting as disciplinarian—as such, authoritarianism and fatherhood became intertwined. During and following the Industrial Revolution, fathers began to be employed in nonfarm jobs, which placed them away from their families for long periods of time. To compensate, mothers assumed increasing responsibilities for the character development and socialization of children. The mother came to be considered to be the best instructor and the central family figure in a child's life. Because of this shift within parenting roles and responsibilities, a shift eventually took place from the harsh Calvanist use of physical punishment with children as a means for molding their character to a greater emphasis on nurturance, perhaps because of mothers' increasing involvement in all aspects of child rearing.

Environmentalism.   As the Calvinist approach began to wane, a second approach to child rearing emerged that was influenced by the writings of John Locke

(1699). Locke was known for his theory of development known as *tabula rasa*. In this view, children were believed to be born with their minds and personalities empty like blank slates (tabula rasa), and the child-rearing experiences provided by parents wrote in the traits that became manifested in their adult personalities. This is a cause-and-effect view of child rearing as well, but was a departure from the Calvinist-inspired approach to child rearing in that it was less harsh in prescribing what parents should do to raise children properly. It emphasized that the model of behavior presented by parents to children played an important role in children's future character development. The strength of a child's character also was thought to come from being exposed to a wide range of experiences while growing up.

Early Developmentalism.   The third approach to child rearing that emerged during the nineteenth century is similar to views that have emerged in more contemporary times. Stemming in part from the movement in Europe that advocated early childhood education via nursery schools and kindergartens, this approach held that children were "ignorant of right rather than bent to wrong" (Sunley, 1955). Parents were advised not to be so concerned about breaking a child's will or to be fearful of indulging their child. Obedience was valued, but it could be obtained from children in more humane ways such as by being firm, using persuasion, and giving rewards rather than physical punishment (Mann & Peabody, 1863). This view can be considered to be the first type of developmental attitude toward children in modern times because it emphasized: (1) the role of meeting children's developmental needs; (2) the role that parents play in shaping children's personalities; and (3) the effects of neglect and harsh punishment as well as gentle care and nurturance on children's developmental progress.

Twentieth-Century Era and Current Trends

The 20th century has witnessed a vast array of attitudes about children and child rearing that range from the promotion of permissiveness, encouraged by the writings of Sigmund Freud (1856–1939) and Benjamin Spock (1903–1998), to the restrictive, authoritarian, and stern approaches advocated by John Watson (1928) and others (Bigner & Yang, 1996). As scientific information increased in respectability, numerous child-rearing experts offered copious, often conflicting advice to parents on how child rearing should best be conducted. With the advent of the child-rearing expert, the emphasis in disciplinary practices shifted to those that were more psychological in nature. Behavior modification based on parental use of positive reinforcement or reward gained over reliance on physical punishment as the recommended method of socializing children. In general, increasing emphasis has been observed on encouraging parents to use methods of guidance based on psychology rather than on the use of physical punishment to shape children's behavior.

During this period, changes took place in expectations of fathers' involvement with their children. One of the means that may have been responsible for this shift was the significant acceptance of prepared childbirth approaches, such as Lamaze (1958). These approaches promote an active role for a father in preparing and in participating in the birth of his children and in bonding with the child during infancy and later years. Another factor in promoting men's greater involvement in family life was the emergence of the Women's Movement during the late 1960s and early 1970s. This produced widespread and significant social changes in ways that both women and men participated in all aspects of life: family, work, and community involvement.

Even more significant during this period were the gains made by the Civil Rights Movement that changed the ways that our society approached the granting of equal rights for all citizens, regardless of racial or ethnic origin. This movement gained momentum in the 1960s with a myriad of legislative acts at federal, state, and local levels that gave muscle to the shift in social attitudes about race and ethnic origin. Many federal programs were forged during this period, with the War on Poverty program playing a significant role on many community levels. One of these programs remains in effect today as Project Head Start, a proven educational approach to prepare children for public school participation as well as enhance family life, physical well-being, and parental involvement. Other programs too numerous to mention here were a part of the War on Poverty that impacted the lives of many poverty-level, inner-city families in the United States.

Another trend that has affected parent-child relations is the dramatic increase in the number of women who are employed outside the home who are also parents of at least one child. This trend was first noticed during World War II, when large numbers of women took the place of men in the war effort to produce the goods and services needed by the military services. Following the war, with the movement of many families from cities into the suburbs, many women forsook their employment opportunities. However, economic conditions coupled with the rise of the Women's Movement forced many families to revise ideas about gender roles that involved working mothers. A two-income family has become the norm today as the vast majority of women are employed for part or for the entirety of the years when children are being produced and growing up.

Teen pregnancy reached a peak during the years following World War II. As with any social phenomenon that becomes more prevalent in society, attitudes shifted from stigmatizing adolescent parenthood to accepting this but not necessarily condoning it. Many teen mothers relinquished parental rights when their child was born, creating a large source of children to be placed for adoption. However, as the numbers of teen mothers grew and families became more willing to support the young mother and her child, fewer children became available for adoption. Teen fathers failed to receive the high degree of attention and acceptance afforded to teen mothers, although in more recent years this has reversed. In addition, changes took place in policies of public school systems that allowed teen parents to continue their educational programs both before and after a child was born.

During this period, the American public became more aware of the insidious and increasingly pervasive presence of incest and sexual abuse of children by parents and other family members. This was prompted in part by a number of well-known public figures and celebrities sharing the news of their own victimization via various media sources. The extensiveness of family violence and addictions also became more better known, particularly when figures became available showing the dramatic increases in the number of children who have been placed in the foster care system. While alcohol and recreational drug addictions, for example, methamphetamine and cocaine, continue to account for the most frequent causes of dependency problems, the number of parents who became incarcerated due to these addictions has also climbed dramatically in recent years. This has accounted for the concomitant increase in the number of grandparents who have custody of grandchildren and are actively raising these children.

Changes in laws and attitudes led to less stigmatization and greater acceptance of divorce. This, in turn, led to the emergence of the single-parent family as the predominant family type. Changes in American society following World War II also contributed to the demise of the traditional nuclear family. Increases in divorce were accompanied by a rise in the numbers of remarriages and stepfamilies in the United States. By the end of the 20th century, diversity in family forms and structures became the norm rather than the exception. Today, a variety of family forms are considered functional, healthy, and effective in meeting the needs of their members. The insidiousness of poverty and homelessness was never eliminated during this century and continues to affect families, children, parent-child relations, child rearing, and society at large.

A number of other contemporary social issues impact parent-child relations directly or indirectly. What occurs in the larger society affects all individuals and families to some degree, and vice versa. Some of these issues are controversial and can be divisive in nature. A brief listing of these might include:

■ the continuing influence of the events that took place on September 11, 2001, at the World Trade Center in New York City. This was a significant turning point in American culture, after which many believed that we could no longer feel immune and distanced from the effects of international terrorism.
■ the effects currently taking place in the Middle East, in which the United States has been playing a major role since the invasion of Iraq and the toppling of that government in 2003.
■ the continuing debate surrounding abortion and right-to-life issues.
■ the continuing debate surrounding same-sex marriage, adoption rights, and general civil rights issues of gay, lesbian, bisexual, and transgender (GLBT) individuals and their families.
■ the current legislative issues relating to legal and illegal immigration into the United States, especially regarding Mexican citizens, and the impact on work and jobs in the United States and on other social issues, including poverty.
■ the complicated problems with public education reforms, especially with federally backed programs such as No Child Left Behind and the promotion of programs involving faith organizations with public funding.

■ the government's ability to react to large-scale public disasters effectively, such as Hurricane Katrina in 2005.
■ the continuing effects of gang violence and large-scale substance-abuse issues, for example, methamphetamine abuse by an increasing number of youth and young adults.
■ the enormously increasing presence of the Internet in many homes via personal computers and other electronic devices, such as iPods and cell phones with cameras and text-messaging capability.

All these issues are discussed in greater detail in other chapters of this text.

Parenting Reflection 1–3
Why don't all parents raise their children using the same methods, styles, and approaches? How would such standard uniformity in child rearing result in what people are like as adults?

Focus Point.   The concepts of parenthood and childhood have experienced many changes in the last 2,000+ years. Contemporary ideas of these roles and of this relationship are derived from these past notions. In many ways, contemporary ideas reflect the changes in cultural values about these roles.

CONFIGURING THE PARENTHOOD ROLE

We now have the opportunity to integrate what has been presented and discussed thus far in this chapter and extend the discussion about the nature of the parenthood role. Let's examine the significant factors that contribute to the arrangement or configuration of people's master blueprint for their parenthood role and their resulting behaviors.

A variety of factors contribute to the nature and context of people's notions of how to act as a parent and conduct themselves in this role (see Figure 1–3). Several variables are known to contribute to the way adults

FIGURE 1–3. Parental role behaviors are configured according to the interaction of a variety of factors.

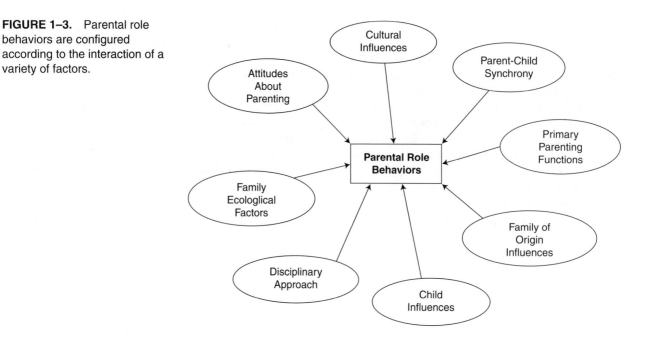

configure their parenting role. By configuring one's parenting role, an individual combines a variety of factors or parameters into a workable blueprint that guides behavior. A good metaphor for this process is what happens when someone takes pieces of a puzzle, manages to perceive how they all fit together, and accomplishes a complete solution to the task of puzzle making.

Some factors that contribute to an adult's configuration of parenting behavior come from past experiences, and new ones are added as the person gains experience in parenting children. Certainly the contribution of a child to the configuration of parenting roles is apparent. Family ecological factors, attitudes about discipline, and an individual's past experiences all influence parenting style.

These predisposing factors that combine to influence parenting style and form a parenting blueprint include the following:

■ **Cultural influences** such as social class or peer value systems
■ The **developmental time** in which adults and children are actively engaged in the child-rearing process
■ **Primary parenting functions** that fall into two basic categories of actions that serve as the basis for parenting behaviors: providing structure and nurturance to children

■ **Family of origin influences** such as the role model one observed as a child from one's own parents
■ **Child influences,** or the myriad ways in which children can impact parental behavior
■ **Disciplinary approach,** or the program of discipline adopted in tandem with a child's developmental level
■ **Family ecological factors** such as the particular structure of a family system and the trends that have affected family form
■ **Attitudes and parenting styles** or beliefs that influence how one should behave as a parent

Cultural Influences

Much research conducted over the past 60 years related to the assumption that cultural variations in child-rearing patterns result in personality and behavioral differences in children. In theory, differences in social class value systems cause corresponding differences in the ways children are reared. The patterns in child rearing found in the social class groupings are thought to be perpetuated from one generation to the next, although individual parents interpret them in different ways.

Numerous studies reported considerable differences among socioeconomic groups in the ways that children are reared and in the values that are promoted

(Coontz, 1998). For example, middle-class families were believed to use more psychologically harsh methods in attempting to control children's behavior than lower-class families. Middle-class families were thought to teach children to delay the immediate gratification of their needs, while lower-class families tended to promote gratifying needs as conveniently as possible. Lower-class families also appeared to place greater emphasis on children's conformance to parents' values than did middle-class families.

Generally, however, differences between families of different socioeconomic class backgrounds have diminished over the years. There are perhaps more similarities than differences in the child-rearing patterns in the family systems of society today. This has been attributed in part to the ubiquitous presence of television in most homes, which offers many programs portraying middle-class values and to the fact that more families can achieve a middle-class lifestyle due to the increased availability of education and better-paying jobs.

Although the general differences in child rearing among social groups have diminished, differences in certain values and patterns in children's behavior persist. For example, the learning styles and ability to process information of children from disadvantaged families differ drastically from those of children from middle-class families (Coontz, 1998). This suggests that the potential for children's mental growth may be strongly influenced by the differences in language and the teaching styles of mothers from these two social groups. The value placed on education and academic achievement among middle-class family systems may result in patterns of interaction that promote children's problem-solving skills.

A parent's behavioral style is guided in part by the value system of the social class with which he or she identifies. Each group maintains essentially the same common objective in child rearing—that is, to support children's growth and development. However, the style of each group in interactions with children differs considerably. For example, as compared to lower-class parents, middle-class parents tend to value social achievement of children, to encourage children to acquire knowledge, and to expect independence early in their children's lives. These differences in values translate to differences in parents' child-rearing styles and what they teach their children (Coontz, 1998).

Synchrony of Parental Style and Child Development

Parenting style should be congruent, or synchronized, with children's developmental level. For example, parenting style at the infancy stage focuses on nurturing and providing the tremendous amounts of physical caregiving infants need. When families have a broad age range of children, parenting styles must be mixed, in general, while continuing to focus on being congruent with a particular child's developmental level.

Further complicating this situation are the developmental experiences that parents are involved with at the time they are raising their children. Parents must attend to the developmental needs of their children while attempting to meet their own developmental demands. For example, interactions with children may be tempered by the pressures on working parents who must juggle family and work roles.

Primary Parenting Functions

Parents' behavior and ways of interacting with children are usually purposeful attempts to meet what they perceive children's needs to be (J. I. Clarke & Dawson, 1998), which in turn relate strongly to the goals adults wish to accomplish in their socialization of children for adulthood. Two broad categories describe parenting behavior aimed at meeting children's needs in preparing them for their future: **structure** and **nurturance** (J. I. Clarke & Dawson). These constitute two principal functions parents perform in socializing children and are discussed in later chapters of this text.

Structure describes those aspects of parenting behavior aimed toward providing children with the means to regulate their lives and to lay the foundation upon which a child's personality is formed and expressed. Structure involves teaching children about personal boundaries, teaching them the limits to which they may go in their behavior so that they do not infringe on others' needs and rights, providing the experiences that promote their acquiring a healthy sense of self-worth, and providing a sense of safety and security so that they will learn to be appropriately trusting of others. Structure also involves helping children to develop healthy habits in thought and behavior; learn values and ethics; acquire healthy character traits such as honesty, integrity, and personal honor; and develop personal responsibility for their actions. Structure helps to provide a child with a healthy, strong sense of self-esteem that permits growth toward meeting personal potential and becoming a well-differentiated individual who is valued for distinct qualities and traits.

Nurturance is the second function involved in parenting children. It relates to those parenting behaviors intended to meet children's needs for unconditional love. This is necessary for children's healthy growth and well-being. By learning that he or she is lovable, a child learns that others can be loved as well. The assertive care and support that are given in unconditional ways to children form the basis of nurturance. **Assertive care** involves noticing, understanding, and responding to the behavioral cues and verbal requests that children pose to parents. It is expressed to children when adults determine children's needs and respond to those needs in loving, predictable, and trustworthy ways. **Supportive care** is expressed at those times when adults offer care to children but allow them the freedom to accept or reject the offer since parents give it in terms of unconditional love. Adults provide structure to children by teaching them rules and skills, which in turn allow children to accept nurturing more willingly. These two aspects of parenting are explored more fully in the later chapters that describe child rearing at each stage of children's development.

Family of Origin Influences

Because humans become parents without the assistance of instinct to guide our behavior, we rely on other means to help us learn how to care for a dependent child. One of the major influences comes from the observation of our own parents. Essentially, we appear to use our parents as models for how to act as a parent (Marsiglio, Hutchinson, & Cohan, 2000). This statement may be an oversimplification, however. The reactions, perceptions, and feelings we have about how we were raised also influence how we approach our own children when we become parents. Generally, people who are satisfied about how they were raised and how they feel about themselves as adults will probably duplicate the methods and attitudes of their parents upon assuming a parenting role (Clarke & Dawson, 1998). Conversely, people who are dissatisfied with their parents' methods may try to be just the opposite when acting as parents. Another type of response is the feeling that one's parents did not provide enough love or physical affection, in which case the reaction may be to overcompensate with one's own children.

The experiences we have as children provide a blueprint for a number of interactional patterns manifested when we grow up and become parents ourselves (Marsiglio et al., 2000). There are several sources of this blueprint: (1) the goals our parents had for our growth and development, (2) the model of parenthood we observed from our parents' behavior, and (3) the influence of parenting models that have been handed down from one generation to another. For these reasons, the blueprint we assimilate for how to act as a parent may not be especially helpful when the time comes to assume the role ourselves. It may be outmoded, inappropriate, and unrealistic based on the particular circumstances in which we conduct ourselves as parents.

Additionally, not every family system is healthy or functions in healthy ways. For example, one or both adults can be affected by addictions to substances, mental or emotional disturbances can thwart effective and healthy functioning, and living conditions can hamper one's ability to parent. Most such families attempt to hide the emotional pain that results from their inability to function healthily. When this occurs, the adults often adopt certain parenting behaviors (possibly learned from the models of their parents) and assign children certain roles that mirror their own family's dysfunction. This illustrates the concepts of wholeness and interrelatedness in family systems theory: What affects one person in a family system affects everyone to some degree. Patterns for coping with the stress of an unhealthy family of origin tend to carry over into future generations.

Based on observations of numerous adults acting as parents, several models of parenting behavior have been developed that illustrate how an unhealthy family of origin influences a person's own patterns or styles of parenting (Framo, Weber, & Levine, 2003). There is never a pure assimilation of one particular model into a person's potential parenting behavior; rather, a mixture or composite of behaviors usually resembles several aspects of the various models.

Influence of Children on Parents

Our culture traditionally ascribes to children the role of learner. Children and adolescents are thought to need numerous learning experiences to prepare them for adulthood. They are the objects of adults' intensive socialization efforts. The relationship between parents and children focuses in many respects on the configuration of the adult as teacher and the child as learner. From this viewpoint, there is support for maintaining the unidirectional model of socialization.

Our culture also constructs the concept of children as people who are in need of adults' protection. Children obviously need assistance in learning the many skills considered necessary to their effective functioning as adults. Today, children are dependent on parents for a longer time than they were earlier in history. The relationship between parent and child has become one of the last human interactional relationships in which the use of social power by an adult is largely unquestioned. Because of the inherent teacher-student quality of this relationship, the power of adults is accentuated in interactions with children. In addition, the greater physical size and strength of adults also contribute to the greater use of their power over children. According to many psychologists and sociologists, this has caused the child to become something of a victim.

Power may not be the culprit, but rather the way in which it is used. Some adults use power to control and manipulate, rather than to facilitate, children's growth and development. This causes difficulty in the relationship, especially as children grow older (Ambert, 1992).

With the advent of family systems theory, which describes interactions within family relationships as having a reciprocal effect upon participants (discussed in Chapter 3), researchers have begun to acknowledge that children have an impact upon their parents' behavior (Ambert, 1992). Initial work points strongly to the effects that children can have upon adults' lives in at least 11 areas: (1) parental health; (2) adults' activities; (3) parental employment status; (4) use and availability of family financial resources; (5) parents' intimate relationship; (6) parents' interactions; (7) parent's community interactions; (8) parental personality development; (9) parents' values, attitudes, and belief systems; (10) parents' life plans; and (11) adults' feelings of having control over their lives.

These effects are perhaps even more broad than are outlined here. We may wonder why it has taken so long for behavioral and social science to acknowledge the impact of these kinds of influence by children on adults' lives. Perhaps this is because it has not been socially proper for adults to admit that children can influence them (Ambert, 1992).

Disciplinary Approach

The approach parents take in teaching their children the values and beliefs their family hold will shape parenting style in a variety of ways. Goals that parents hold for their children's growth and development usually arise out of altruism. What adults desire for children and how most people shape their parenting activities and behavior relate to what they believe children need to become effective adults. Ordinarily, most parents want their child: (1) to have a happy and fulfilling life, (2) to become a person who functions independently and gets along well in work and in relationships with others, and (3) to acquire the skills and competencies that permit effective functioning as an adult in society (Elkin & Handel, 1989).

Parents think about those behaviors and social competencies they feel are important for children to acquire to become effectively functioning adults. These constitute another aspect of what adults believe children need, and parenting behaviors may be directed toward shaping these as part of children's behavior repertoire. **Social competence** usually refers to a group of attributes that are believed to be essential in assisting a person to make full use of his or her personal resources to cope productively with the circumstances of life. The ways that parents provide structure for children in their child rearing or disciplinary program are usually shaped to help children acquire these essential social skills.

The goals that parents establish for their child rearing or disciplinary approach are influenced by both personal and societal sources. Adults' perceptions of what children need are based on complex personal opinions but also reflect the realities of what life presents as part of a family experience. Parents' general opinions about what children need are based on their past experiences, the values the parents were taught by their own families of origin, the philosophies of parenting they have developed since becoming adults, and so on. However, these perceptions can be tempered by specific situations, such as when one has a child with some type of physical or mental disability or when divorce changes one's status to that of a single parent.

Adults also come to understand that what children need changes with age and developmental stage, and they adapt their parenting behavior accordingly. As they establish goals, most parents come to understand they must change how they relate and interact with children if children are to attain the new goals. It is not unusual for parents to seek out sources of information and assistance in learning how to adapt and change their behavior in response to developmental changes taking place in children as they grow (Bigner & Yang, 1996). This constitutes one of the major challenges to effective parenting behavior.

Family Ecological Factors

The influence of various environmental systems on the functioning of the parent-child microenvironment can be observed in a variety of ways, but they are often difficult to anticipate completely or measure accurately. Each of us is influenced in our behavior by a number of environmental factors. Our past experience with children is one factor. Our behavior can be influenced by internal factors, such as blood sugar levels, hormone balances, sleep deprivation, and emotional states. Sociocultural factors that affect our behavior include value systems and beliefs about appropriate role behavior. Other factors are more physical; for example, where we live (in an apartment or in a single-family residence, in the city or in a rural area) may affect parent-child interactions. Even the time of day that interactions occur can be an important consideration. All these factors from the past and present tend to influence and cause variability in parents' behavior and affect the way interactions take place between parents and children.

Family ecological factors such as the level of family income (poverty-level vs. middle-class income), ethnic identity, or type of family structure can influence parenting styles in a variety of ways. These factors affect a family's ability to provide equipment and services such as medical or dental care, clothing, and food that can influence the quality and nature of interactions between parents and children. Parents' goals in their child-rearing efforts may also be tempered by these family ecological factors.

Attitudes and Parenting Styles

Closely associated with other factors are the attitudes adults hold about children and child rearing in general. These attitudes and beliefs are the result of a person's socialization and past experiences. In many respects, they form the implicit rules, or "shoulds," that guide a person's behavior as a parent and have a significant influence on the behavioral choices a person makes in interacting with his or her child. The attitudes about how one should act as a parent may also be seen more clearly in the parenting style that expresses a program of discipline.

The range of attitudes about how to parent children appropriately and effectively may be viewed as a compilation of the attributes of parental control (what parents feel they should do or act in controlling children's behavior and development) and emotional warmth. They range from authoritarian (strict) to permissive (lenient) in combining these attributes (Baumrind, 1966). For example, an authoritarian attitude is distinctly high in parental control regarding children's behavior but also low in degree of emotional warmth felt toward children. Typically, attitudes serve to guide actual parenting behavior and can be expected to shift in tandem with the changing developmental stages of children. Some parents may adopt a particular parenting attitude and style once a child is born and never stray from it as the child grows older. Others may adopt a particular attitude and parenting style that can shift and change in relation to children's changing developmental stages and abilities. These attitudes begin to have significant influence on parenting style when children reach preschool age (see Chapter 8).

● ●

Parenting Reflection 1–4

Suppose you are a parent of a 4-year-old; you and your child are grocery shopping. Which of the factors just described will influence how you behave in public as a parent when your child misbehaves?

● ●

● ●

Focus Point. Eight major categories of factors contribute to the nature and context of an adult's potential behavior as a parent and act to influence the configuration of the parenting style that someone adopts: (1) cultural influences, such as one's social class background and associated values and beliefs systems; (2) synchrony of parental style and a child's developmental stage; (3) primary parenting objectives that guide parental behavior in achieving child-rearing goals, such as the manner in which nurturance and structure are provided to children; (4) family of origin influences, such as the model of parental behavior observed in one's own parents; (5) children's myriad ways of influencing parental behaviors; (6) the disciplinary approach adopted by parents in emphasizing the goals they wish to accomplish in their child-rearing efforts; (7) family ecological factors such as ethnic identity, level of family income, or type of family structure; and (8) attitudes about parenting behavior, such as authoritarian, permissive, and authoritative beliefs.

....

POINTS TO CONSIDER

■ Individuals in our society need training and education to be effective parents, just as they do to perform other roles in adulthood. Until recently, little preparation has been given to those who plan to become parents.

■ The parenthood role is associated with a variety of different concepts and ideas in our society.

■ Three basic traits characterize the parenthood role in contemporary society.

■ Our current ideas about the nature of parent-child relations have evolved over time. What were considered appropriate traits for this role in the past are different from what are held today about this family role.

■ Eight factors significantly contribute to the manner by which one's behavior is patterned in the parenthood role.

CHAPTER 2

Cultural Perspectives

Focus Questions
■ ■ ■ ■ ■ ■ ■ ■ ■ ■

1. What are the roles of culture and socialization in influencing parent-child relations?

2. What features characterize contemporary American families?

3. What are the principal types of forms and structures found in contemporary American families?

4. What is the nature of parent-child relations in ethnically diverse families in the United States?

■ ■ ■ ■ ■ ■ ■ ■ ■ ■

To understand how parenthood roles function within family systems, it is essential to describe the various factors that may be collectively grouped as family ecological influences. Some of these factors serve as part of the social context in which parent-child relations take place. While the topic of family ecology is discussed in greater detail in Chapter 3, we may tentatively describe this now as the various social, psychological, and physical environmental systems in which parenting operates. For example, the level of a family's income (poverty vs. middle-class income) as well as the ethnic identity of a family system can influence parenting style or behavior. For all practical purposes, these systems comprise a larger phenomenon known as culture, which is relative to each particular group.

This chapter discusses a variety of issues that expand on the topics introduced in Chapter 1. More specifically, this chapter first presents information about how culture is influential in parent-child relations. We then examine how a range of family systems are defined, structured, and characterized in contemporary American society. Finally, we explore the ecological factors of ethnicity and background from an ethnographical perspective as these influence parent-child relations.

THE ROLE OF CULTURE IN PARENT-CHILD RELATIONS

Culture

Perhaps the most significant context in which parent-child relations take place is the cultural context. This social construct defines what families value and believe to be important that guides behavior of all members. Culture shapes the rules or social norms that outline appropriate behavior of people in a variety of other contexts such as the roles they fulfill, the notions of what are acceptable and unacceptable actions, and the individuals, agencies, and institutions that transmit these values and beliefs. For some, these values are derived from the larger ethnic group with which they identify; for others, these values come from religious beliefs and philosophies, for example. Regardless of the origin of the values, parents are charged with transmitting these to children; in effect, parents typically are viewed as teachers and transmitters of culture to their children.

Culture is a difficult concept to define. It is a construct that has been described as: (1) the accepted, standardized ways of acting, thinking, and feeling that are shared by the members of a society (Wainryb, 2004); (2) the standardized skills, beliefs, values, symbols, meanings, and concepts held in common by a group of people (Greenfield, Suzuki, & Rothstein-Fisch, 2006); or (3) those lifeways that distinguish one social group from another that include the various ecological settings that define and give meaning to roles, behaviors, and customs (Kagitecibasi, 1990). Applied here, culture serves as the lens through which parenting behavior may be observed regarding the proper ways to raise children to maturity in accordance with cultural values and beliefs (Derbort, 2006). More specifically, each culture is likely to have its own particular ways of defining the proper ways of child rearing. Taken from this vantage, culture becomes a worldview possessed and practiced in unique ways by each culture or subculture we may examine (Figure 2–1).

Large societies, such as the United States, often consist of a variety of subcultures that are differentiated from the larger society according to distinct sets of behaviors, values, and beliefs. These subcultures may be based upon features held in common with others such as ethnic group, nationality of origin, sexual orientation, age, gender, political affiliation, religious belief, geographic location, and so on. It is entirely possible that individuals may ascribe to more than one subculture based on these factors. In the United States, where the population has been derived from immigration of many different groups over

FIGURE 2–1. Family events such as Thanksgiving provide ways for transmitting culture to children.

the years, multiculturalism may be seen in that various subcultures are encouraged and allowed to retain their basic features and coexist with others while living as one nation.

Individualism and *collectivism* or *sociocentrism* are two cultural conceptions of value systems (Greenfield, Trumbull, Keller, Rothstein-Fisch, Suzuki, & Quiroz, 2006). The various cultures around the world are characterized by the manner in which these two value systems are blended or balanced. Essentially, individualism in a culture values the person and what can be accomplished on one's own. Individual identity and self-expression are valued as well. Collectivism as a cultural trait places emphasis on the interdependence of the individual with the larger community. Collectivism encourages people to fit in and adapt to the characteristics of the larger community.

These two cultural conceptions have direct application in parent-child relations in that these influence how parents translate cultural values into interactions with their children. For example, parents in cultures characterized as individualistic tend to (1) encourage autonomy or independence in children; (2) promote children's self-reliance; (3) foster children's personal achievements; (4) support children's competitiveness; (5) allow children to question and explore; and (6) allow children to participate in decision making. By contrast, parents in cultures characterized as collectivist or sociocentric tend to (1) have closer emotional ties to children for longer lengths in infancy and childhood; (2) emphasize the extended family network in teaching children what is valued; (3) stress obedience to all authority, especially to parents and other older family members; (4) emphasize children learning and respecting social norms governing appropriate behavior; (5) emphasize sharing of property and belongings; and (6) shape children's behavior that demonstrates responsibility and obligations to others (Greenfield & Suzuki, 2001; Trumbull, Rothstein-Fisch, & Greenfield, 2000).

Behavioral scientists who study cultural influences warn us about the problems of ethnocentrism as we study our culture in the United States in comparison with that of others. This occurs when we use the understandings of our culture to compare, evaluate, and judge those of others. Implicit is the conclusion that our culture is superior and preferable to that of others (Rogoff, 2003). For example, the use of physical punishment by parents with children has different meanings and different values

from culture to culture and even from one subculture to another. Furthermore, American parents typically value children becoming autonomous at an early age, while this practice is viewed as unusual in other cultures.

In studying parents and children as well as families, it behooves us to strive to recognize that there are patterns that are likely to be shared across subcultures but also patterns that are distinctly unique to each, that is, recognizing the functioning of *cultural universalism* versus *cultural relativism* in influencing our perceptions. In the social science literature, this is represented by ethnographic approaches to studying cultures that stress an *emic* perspective, or that of an insider's views of a culture, as well as an *etic* perspective, or that of an outsider's views into a culture (J. W. Berry, 1999). These approaches, while appearing at first to be antagonistic with one another, are more likely complementary (Sabbagh, 2005). We will apply these approaches in a later section of this chapter to examine ethnic diversity in contemporary American families.

Socialization

The family is a ubiquitous social institution in societies around the globe. This group has the responsibility of producing and training or socializing children to become effectively functioning members of the larger society in which their family participates. Although families have always been the basic component of any society in which they live, they have changed significantly in the United States over the years in terms of composition, size, and functioning as well as in the characteristics that give them meaning.

Years of social evolution have produced changes in families and in the societies in which they participate. Family functions have changed accordingly over time as societies have changed. Of all the functions that families originally held in society, socialization of children for their future participation in society is perhaps the only principal function held by parents in contemporary families.

While there are various definitions of what comprises **socialization**, we will use this term to mean "the set of interpersonal processes through which cultural meaning is passed on and changed" (Peterson, Steinmetz, & Wilson, 2005, p. 10). In a more practical vein, socialization is what parents do to teach children to conform to social rules, acquire personal values, and develop attitudes and behaviors typical or representative of their culture at large. Socialization is the myriad ways that culture is transmitted to children by parents, the media, institutions, and agencies.

This process begins in earnest when children are toddlers and preschoolers—when parents and other caregivers begin to take an active role in teaching and instructing children in such lessons. The lessons are not always given in formal, verbal instruction; many are learned by children when they observe the behaviors of their parents and caregivers.

Depending on the nature of a particular family system, certain standards may be promoted more than others. Despite the diversity of families today, almost all teach certain kinds of behaviors and values to children. Embedded in the lessons about acceptable behaviors are lessons about those that are undesirable. All this is based on the assumption that there are shared meanings for the terms *acceptable and undesirable behaviors* that are taught by all parents and other agents in society that influence individuals and families.

This depiction of socialization is a unidirectional model that, in reality, fails to accurately describe that happens in families when parents are raising children for adulthood. More accurately, we know that the process of socialization is bidirectional in nature because children play a role in this process (Kuczynski, 2003). Parents change and shape the lessons of socialization based on a number of factors such as a child's age, developmental abilities, ability to use and understand language, gender, and so on, which are constantly changing.

••

Focus Point.   Parent-child relations are influenced by and take place within a cultural context. Socialization is the way that parents and other societal entities teach culture to children. Socialization, however, is also bidirectional in that children participate with parents in this process.

••

••

▉ Parenting Reflection 2–1

Try to predict how parenthood and parent-child relations will be conceptualized in the year 2100 or even 2200. How would you rate contemporary families in their abilities to socialize children effectively for their future?

••

FEATURES OF CONTEMPORARY FAMILIES

Characteristics

Societal changes are reflected in families. For example, an economic recession greatly affects families. Family members may lose their jobs, and the family system may find its buying power drastically decreased. Society and the families within it have a reciprocal relationship. What affects society affects families, and vice versa.

Demographic data are useful in understanding what contemporary American families are like and the conditions under which they operate that can influence parent-child relations. This information, much of it collected by the U.S. Bureau of the Census, is helpful in evaluating changes in family and population characteristics and for making predictions about American family forms. Contemporary American families exhibit trends and features that help to provide another ecological dimension that shapes parenthood and other family functions and relationships as well as represent the influences of culture and socialization in parent-child relations.

Marriage.   Americans continue to value marriage as a social institution (Thornton & Young-DeMarco, 2001). Three-quarters of all women in the United States have married by age 30 (Bramlett & Mosher, 2002). However, important changes in marriage behavior affect family formation and the assumption of parenting roles. For example, there are fewer married couples today than 30 years ago. This implies that there may be more people who choose to cohabitate prior to or in place of marriage, an increasing number of nonfamily households (consisting of people who are not related), increases in those who are not parents, and increases in the numbers of single-parent families and unmarried women who are parents.

The age at first marriage has been gradually increasing since the mid-1960s after experiencing a long-standing trend of occurring at younger ages (Fields, 2003). For example, in 1970, the median age at first marriage was 23.2 years for men and 20.8 years for women. By 2003, the median age at first marriage climbed to 27.1 years for men and to 25.3 years for women (see Figure 2–2).

FIGURE 2–2. Median age at first marriage for men and women between 1970 and 2003.

Source: Fields, J. (2003). America's families and living arrangements: 2003. *Current Population Reports, P20-553.* Washington, DC: U.S. Bureau of the Census.

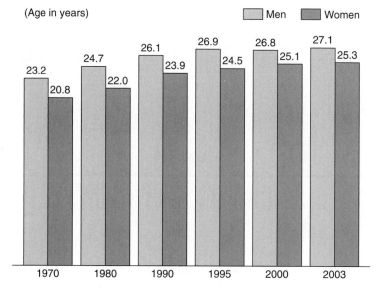

The higher median ages at first marriage appear to be related to economic and social issues. It takes longer for young people today to complete their education and training and to establish themselves in an occupational path. It is also associated with the desire of more women to complete their college education or establish their career path than in years past. The higher median age of women relates as well to women's participation in the labor force for longer periods before marriage. Later marriage has contributed to delayed childbearing, smaller families, and greater marital stability (Fields, 2003; Hobbs & Stoops, 2002).

Another indication of the delay in first marriage is the increasingly larger numbers of young unmarried adults in the population. From 1970 to 2005, the number of people who remained unmarried between 25 to 34 years of age more than tripled (U.S. Bureau of the Census, 2006). Apparently, increasingly larger numbers of both men and women are choosing to remain unmarried or to cohabitate rather than marry. Combining these data with statistics about births indicates that a sizable number of Americans are deciding whether to become parents independently of their choices about marriage.

Currently, there is significant debate taking place in many quarters of our society regarding whether same-sex couples in committed relationships should be given the right to marry as heterosexual couples do

(Rothblum, 2004; Samar, 2005). A number of states have enacted legislation as well as changes in their constitutions to limit marriage to opposite-sex couples and to either deny or permit same-sex couples to have domestic partnership or civil union arrangements. Some domestic partnership arrangements closely resemble the rights extended to heterosexual couples via marriage, while others clearly outline limited rights. Presently, only two states—Massachusetts and California—permit legally recognized marriages for all couples, regardless of sexual orientation. While there are many pros and cons to this argument, there are countless numbers of children who are affected by living in same-sex families who may experience hardship by lacking protections that are present for children of opposite-sex married couples. These include having a legal definition of parenthood and parenting rights, family leave benefits, adoption rights, and coverage under medical health plans, for example (Brewer, 2008).

Births. The number of children born in the United States has been relatively stable since about 1975, following a significant decline in births from 1958 (Martin, Hamilton, Sutton, et al., 2006) (see Figure 2–3). The number of births declined slightly between 1990 and 1997 but has increased slightly in recent

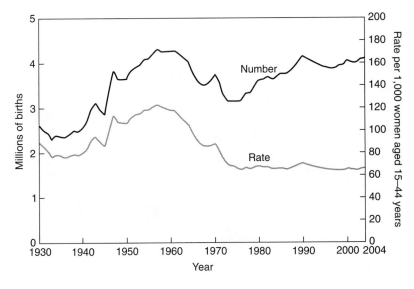

FIGURE 2–3.   Fertility rate and number of live births to women in the United States between 1930 and 2004.

Source: Martin J. A., Hamilton, B. E., Ventura, S. J., Sutton, P. D. et al. (2006). Births: Final data for 2004. *National Vital Statistics Reports, 55(1)*. Hyattsville, Maryland: National Center of Health Statistics.

years. The number of births increased dramatically among unmarried women within recent years, while those among adolescents has declined significantly. Asian and Hispanic women tend to have higher fertility rates (the number of births a typical woman will have over her lifetime) in recent years than women in other ethnic groups.

Only 10% of all American families had four children or more in 2002, a decline from 36% of all families in 1976 (Downs, 2003). This figure contrasts with 52% of all American families that had only one or two children in that same year, an increase from 31% in 1976 (Downs). The number of children who die either before birth or during infancy has declined over the last 100 years, resulting in a smaller number of conceptions and births today. Small family size produces other ripple effects observed in society, such as the overall age structure of the population, school enrollments, and social programming needs.

Divorce.   Divorce data are reported in many forms by different government agencies. This presents complicated and often contradictory information. In addition, the federal agency that is charged with collecting vital statistics on U.S. citizens discontinued collecting data on divorce in 1996. Hence, much of the detailed information about divorce is based on aged data.

The rate of divorce appears to have stabilized within the last 20 or more years, although at a level that is the highest in our nation's history (Munson & Sutton, 2006). In fact, the United States has one of the highest divorce rates of any country on the planet. More than 1 million children annually are affected by parental divorce. Predictions are that if the current rate of divorce continues, one out of every two first marriages contracted since the early 1980s will be dissolved through divorce. Interestingly, it appears that age and racial group membership at first marriage are related to the probability of divorce (Figure 2–4). Those who are 18 years of age or less at marriage and who are non-Hispanic white or black have a higher probability of experiencing divorce within 10 years. The high incidence of divorce has given rise to the prevalently observed family form in the United States called the single-parent family.

As divorce has become more common, it has lost much of its social stigma. It is difficult in these more liberal times for many couples to maintain long-term commitments to marriage for several reasons (Cherlin, 2004, 2005): (1) changes in the status and roles of women in society, (2) changes in laws that make obtaining divorce less complicated and less stigmatizing, and (3) the strong desire to achieve personal happiness. The effects of divorce on both parents and children are discussed in greater detail in Chapter 11.

FIGURE 2–4. The probability that a first marriage breaks up within 10 years by race/ethnicity and age at the beginning of marriage: United States, 1995.

Source: Bramlett, M. D., & Mosher, W. D. (2002). Cohabitation, marriage, divorce, and remarriage in the United States. *Vital Health Statistics, 23(22).* Hyattsville, MD: National Center for Health Statistics.

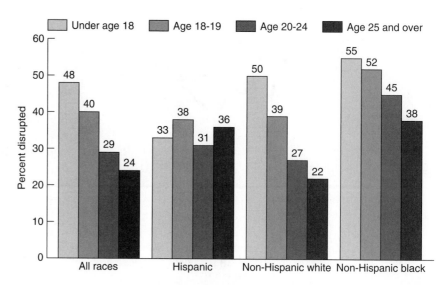

● ●

Parenting Reflection 2–2

You are the mother of a young woman who is contemplating marriage. She has only one concern that she wishes to discuss with you: Why do people continue to get married given the current likelihood of a divorce happening? What would you say to her in defense of marriage?

● ●

Remarriage. Remarriage is more likely to occur among those who leave a first marriage via divorce (U.S. Bureau of the Census, 2006), although there has

been a general decline in the rate at which remarriages occur since the mid-1960s. The median length of first marriage in the United States has remained at about 7 years since 1980. The median interval between divorce and remarriage is about 3 years. Fifty-four percent of divorced women tend to remarry within 5 years and 75%, within 10 years (Bramlett & Mosher, 2002). Racial group identity also influences remarriage rates; whites are more likely to remarry than are blacks (Figure 2–5). These relationships are considered to be at high risk of divorce, often within 6 years.

Remarriage creates stepfamilies for many individuals. The result is that many remarried adults can expect to parent children of other people as well as their own.

FIGURE 2–5. Probability of remarriage by duration of divorce and race/ethnicity: United States, 1995.

Source: Bramlett, M. D., & Mosher, W. D. (2002). Cohabitation, marriage, divorce, and remarriage in the United States. *Vital Health Statistics, 23(22).* Hyattsville, MD: National Center for Health Statistics.

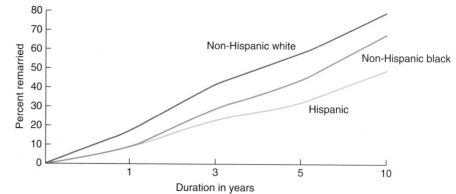

The 2000 U.S. Census reported that about 5% of all children were living in stepfamilies (Kreider, 2003). Researchers who study stepfamilies disagree about the effects of this family form on children's welfare and that of adult family members (Love & Murdock, 2004; McCarthy & Ginsberg, 2007). Issues relating to parenting in stepfamilies are discussed in greater detail in Chapter 12.

Family Income and Working Mothers.   Employment of both adults in contemporary families has become the norm in recent years. Family income may have a more influential effect on the quality of family life and on parent-child relations than other factors that have been previously discussed. When both adults are employed, challenges in family life take several forms: who does what household work, how child care is arranged and financed, how much time can be devoted to child rearing and parent-child interactions, what kinds of extracurricular activities children may participate in, how children can be assisted in schoolwork, how personal and leisure time are spent, what quality of medical and dental care may be provided, and what amount of attention can be devoted to marital relationships.

The median income of families in the United States provides an idea of how finances influence quality of life. The median income of all family types in the United States has risen considerably since the mid-1940s (DeNavas-Walt, Proctor, & Lee, 2006; U.S. Bureau of

the Census, 2006). The main reason is due to the employment of both adults in intact family homes. In 2005, this figure, representing total income prior to withholding taxes, was $46,326 (see Figure 2–6). The lowest median income ($30,650) was among single-parent families headed by a mother. This compares to a median income of $66,067 for married-couple families. These sharp differences in family income have a significant influence on quality of life experienced in these families. Quality-of-life issues play a central role in parenting and parent-child relations.

The increase in the numbers of married women in the labor force has resulted in a concomitant increase in dual-earner families. The largest segment of these are married mothers of children between the ages of 6 and 17 (U.S. Bureau of the Census, 2007a). In 2001, about 68% of all married women in the United States were employed outside their homes. Employment of both adults in an intact family produces ripple effects in other areas of family life and parenting. For example, supplementary child care must be financed and arranged, and household tasks must be shared.

Poverty and Homelessness.   Family well-being is threatened when homelessness occurs and a family exists at poverty level or below. Poverty varies considerably in the United States relative to family structure, racial group, and ethnicity. In 2005, the average poverty threshold for a family of four was almost

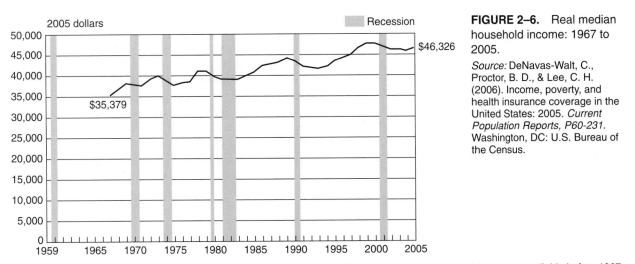

FIGURE 2–6.   Real median household income: 1967 to 2005.

Source: DeNavas-Walt, C., Proctor, B. D., & Lee, C. H. (2006). Income, poverty, and health insurance coverage in the United States: 2005. *Current Population Reports, P60-231.* Washington, DC: U.S. Bureau of the Census.

Note: The data points are placed at the midpoints of the respective years. Median household income data are not available before 1967.

$20,000 (DeNevas-Walt, et al., 2006). This accounted for slightly more than 10% of all American families living below poverty level and about 7% of all married couple families with children under 18 years. Almost 18 million children, or 18% of all American children, live in families affected by poverty. To provide a different perspective on poverty, it is estimated that a family of four needs about $40,000 annually to meet basic needs (Cauthen & Fass, 2007). This figure is tempered depending on a family's locality; if living in a high-cost, large urban area such as New York City, the figure increases to about $50,000 annually, while if living in a rural area, the figure decreases to about $30,000.

The number of individuals and families living in poverty, along with the rate of poverty, did not change significantly from what occurred in 2004 (DeNevas-Walt et al., 2006). Black and Hispanic families with children were the most likely and white families, the least likely to be poor. The higher incidence of single-parent families headed by women among minorities is a major factor in the differences in family income among racial groups. Two trends in those affected by poverty continued to be observed in recent years: (1) the feminization of poverty, as noted by the increasing numbers of women and children who are poor, and (2) an increasing number of the working poor or those who may work one or more jobs earning low wages with few or no benefits. In addition to these factors, inflation has continued to erode the buying power of the American dollar, affecting those earning minimum wages the greatest.

It is extremely difficult to estimate the number of homeless individuals currently in the United States. These are individuals who live on the streets or in public shelters. An increasingly large segment of the homeless are women and families with children. In 2003, 42% of children affected by homelessness were less than 5 years of age (National Coalition for the Homeless, 2006). In rural areas, these segments of the population account for the largest numbers of those who are homeless. Blacks and whites account for the largest ethnic groups who are homeless, while Hispanics, Asians, and Native Americans account for the smallest numbers of the homeless. Economic conditions are a leading factor in producing poverty-level incomes and the likelihood of homelessness for many families. Although it may appear

reasonable to assume that anyone who wishes to work can make an adequate income, this is not so. Other factors such as substance abuse, mental illness, unemployment, disabilities, or unstable family life may also contribute to homelessness. Domestic violence experienced by women is a leading factor, however; about half of all women who were homeless are estimated to be escaping from abusive relationships (American Civil Liberties Union, 2006).

Parent-child relations under these circumstances invoked by homelessness renders this relationship at one of its most strained perspectives. Parenting is either terminated when one adult leaves their family under these circumstances or the relationship can become stagnated because of the inability of the adult/s to provide not only for their most basic needs but especially for those of their children. Besides jeopardizing children's nutrition, health and dental care, clothing, and educational experiences, homelessness may threaten the very lives of children and their parents. The complexity of the problems leading to homelessness as well as the complexity of providing solutions to end this status challenge communities, large and small, urban or rural, to reintegrate homeless children and families into the mainstream of American culture.

• •

Focus Point. The ways that parenthood is defined, child rearing is conducted, and parent-child relations are valued vary based on how each family system experiences different ecological factors. Contemporary family life in America has certain features: (1) Both men and women are marrying for the first time at later ages. (2) One marriage in two will terminate in divorce, usually after 7 years. (3) There is a high probability of remarriage following divorce, leading to a sizable number of children who grow up in stepfamilies. (4) The birth rate has declined over the past 30 years, resulting in smaller families. (5) Family incomes have increased significantly in the years since World War II. Today, about two-thirds of all married women over 18 years of age work outside the home. (6) Poverty and homelessness affect an increasing percentage of families in the United States each year. This situation affects minority families to a greater extent than others.

• •

DIVERSITY IN CONTEMPORARY FAMILY FORMS AND STRUCTURES

The family has become more important as a source of stability in our rapidly changing and increasingly complex society. It can be a refuge when individuals feel buffeted by impersonal forces. The United States was founded on the idea that people have the right to pursue personal happiness. Since the 1960s especially, the pursuit of individual happiness has been heavily emphasized. At the same time, Americans have become more sensitive to other human rights. We are today more conscious of discrimination based on age, gender, race, sexual orientation, and ethnic group identity.

These social changes are reflected in family life. For example, a trend reported recently by the U.S. Census Bureau is an increase in the number of non-family households accompanied by a decrease in the number of family households (Fields, 2003). In 1970, 70% of all American households were family households (at least two people related by blood, marriage, or adoption), while these kinds of households accounted for 52% of all households in 2003 (see Figure 2–7).

Social conditions such as the high probability of divorce for married couples have changed the face of the American family. Families have changed in size, structure, form, and function. Today, diversity in family form and structure is the norm. The predominant types that include children are outlined briefly here. These will be discussed in greater detail in other chapters.

Two-Parent Families

Traditionally, families are thought to be composed of two opposite-sex married adults and their children. This family form has been considered for generations to be the ideal, normative family form in which to produce and raise children to their maturity. Much of the information on parent-child relations contained in this text is derived from research based on individuals living in this type of family structure. As such, it has been and continues to be the predominant family form in the United States (U.S. Bureau of the Census, 2007b). However, this family form is declining in numbers in the general population. In 2005, two-parent families accounted for

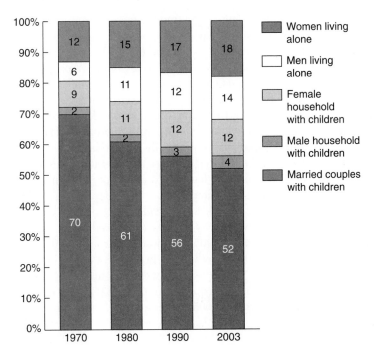

FIGURE 2–7. Percentage of different types of households in the United States between 1970 and 2003.

Source: U.S. Bureau of the Census. Households by type: 1940 to present. Released September 14, 2004 and retrieved July 9, 2007, from http://www.census.gov/population/socdemo/hh-fam/tabHH-4.xls.

52% of all American families compared with 70% in 1970. This decline is often attributed to the change in attitudes that has made adult cohabitation, or living together without marriage, and divorce less stigmatized and more acceptable throughout American society (Pinsof, 2002). In addition, the decline in two-parent families is contrasted with the increase in single-parent families in the United States.

Despite the decline in this type of family form, most children in the United States experience having two parents rather than just one or none while growing up (Scommegna, 2002). Many adult couples choose not to marry but to cohabitate while raising children of both partners or of only one. Today, however, a two-parent family does not automatically mean that there are two opposite-sex married adults who are coparenting children. Many children today are growing up in homes where the adult parents are of the same sex.

The literature is not clear regarding the effects or outcomes of cohabitating opposite-sex adults who are parenting children. Some research indicates that children growing up in homes where parents cohabitate fare no better or worse than children growing up in single-parent families (Acs & Nelson, 2002), while other work suggests otherwise (Federal Interagency Forum on Child and Family Statistics, 2006, 2007). However, it is clear that (1) The number of adults who co-habitate rather than marry is increasing yearly (Fields, 2003; U.S. Bureau of the Census, 2007a, 2007b); (2) for all practical purposes, the nature of the relationship of a cohabitating couple closely resembles that of a married couple (S. L. Brown, 2000), although it has been associated with increased risk of divorce and marital distress following marriage (Stanley, Rhoades, & Markman, 2006); and (3) cohabitation does not necessarily lead to marriage (Heuveline & Timberlake, 2004).

The need for children to have two opposite-sex parents who are married in order to grow up healthy and relatively problem free is under debate today with both sides presenting evidence in support of their positions. The evidence that is presented is largely conflicting, however. It is completely possible to find studies that appear to support both sides of this issue, leaving one to wonder which position is correct or even largely correct. For example, columnists and talk show hosts bolster the conservative position about this topic by quoting a wide variety of sources in support of the traditional two-parent, opposite-sex, married-couple family (see http://www. uexpress.com/maggiegallagher/?uc_full_date=20040127).On the other hand, those who have a more liberal position on this topic also present evidence to debunk the superiority of this traditional family form (see http://www. questia.com/PM.qst?a=o&d=34358866). Perhaps the thoughts of Judith Stacey (1998, p. 80), a sociologist at New York University, provide an objective insight to this debate:

> The most careful studies and the most careful researchers confirm what most of us know from our own lives: The quality of any family's relationships and resources readily trumps its formal structure or form. Access to economic, educational, and social resources; the quality and consistency of parental nurturance, guidance, and responsibility; and the degree of domestic harmony, conflict, and hostility affect child development and welfare far more substantially than does the particular number, gender, sexual orientation, and marital status of parents or the family structure in which children are reared.

Single-Parent and Binuclear Families

One of the more common types of families in the United States today is composed of one adult parent and one or more children under 18 years of age. Whether headed by a man or a woman (most often a woman), this is called a single-parent family. A binuclear family refers to the presence of two families shared by children, usually as a result of adults' divorcing. The single-parent family is increasing faster in number than any other family form today, not only because of divorce but because many single, unmarried women choose to have children (Federal Interagency Forum on Child and Family Statistics, 2007; Fields, 2003). The proportion of children under 18 years of age living with two parents decreased from 77% in 1980 to 67% in 2005. Of these children in 2005, 23% lived with their mother, 5% lived with their father, and 4% lived with neither parent (see Figure 2–8). Single-parent families accounted for about 31% of all families with children in 2005. Single-parent families are more prevalent among blacks as a group (U.S. Bureau of the Census, 2007a, 2007b). In 2005, about 62% of all black

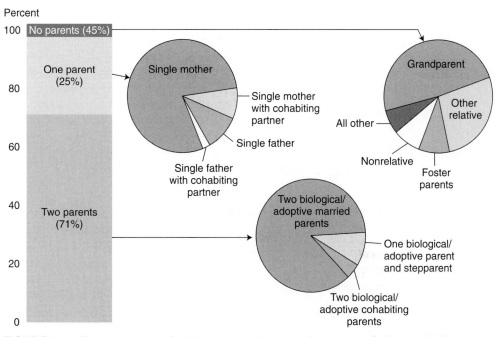

FIGURE 2–8. The percentage of children under 18 years of age living in different family structures in 2001.

Source: Federal Interagency Forum on Child and Family Statistics. (2006). *America's children in brief: Key national indicators of well-being, 2006.* Washington, DC: Author.

families, 28% of all white families, 16% of all Asian, and 36% of all Hispanic families were single-parent families (Figure 2–9).

A single-parent family is created through one of three means: (1) divorce, desertion, or separation of the adults; (2) death of one adult; or (3) having a child while unmarried. The most common means is through divorce, and generally the mother is given custody of the children. The vast majority of single-parent families are headed by women because courts typically award full or physical custody to women in the United States.

Quality of life is a major issue for many single-parent families (Hildebrand, Pheniuce, Gray, & Hines, 2008). Any type of disruption in family life can produce a crisis, and divorce is one of the most stressful experiences that one can have in adulthood. It can also be traumatic for children. Although divorce has become commonplace, it is a crisis event that forces many short- and long-range adjustments on those involved.

The experience of being a single parent is different for women and men. Women generally can expect to have financial difficulties, and there are significantly more children who live in poverty because they live in a female-headed, single-parent family (Federal Interagency Forum on Child and Family Statistics, 2007). The implications for children growing up in single-parent families, especially those headed by mothers, can be serious. While most studies report that children generally fare well when living in a single-parent family, those who live in poverty are at greater risk than those from more affluent families to experience school problems, to become teen parents, and, as adults, to earn less and be unemployed more frequently.

Life is not easy for most single-parent families. Yet many people choose to divorce rather than remain in an unhappy relationship, even though they know they will have to make a multitude of difficult adjustments. For many people, this type of family arrangement is

FIGURE 2–9. Most single-parent families are headed by women.

more efficient and harmonious than a household marked by tensions and strife between the adults. This family type is discussed in greater detail in Chapter 11.

● ●

Parenting Reflection 2–3

You have been elected mayor of a large city, running your campaign on social reform. What are some things you can do as a political figure to improve the quality of life of single-parent families headed by women in your community?

● ●

Stepfamilies

Stepfamilies are also known as blended families. Stepfamilies include an adult couple and children of one or both of them from a previous marriage or relationship. This family type is based on the remarriage of at least one of the adult partners (Hildebrand et al., 2008) or on the cohabitation of a couple. Since the vast majority of single-parent families are headed by women, the person usually filling the vacant adult family role in the new stepfamily is a man. He may or may not have been divorced and have children of his own.

Remarriage is popular today, although these relationships have a higher risk of divorce than first marriages (B. N. Adams, 2004). The median length of first marriages in the United States is about 7 years (Kreider, 2005). Most people who divorce remarry within 3 years following divorce. Second marriages tend to last about the same length as first marriages. It is unusual for an individual to have been married three times or more.

Stepfamilies by definition involve children of one or both remarried partners, although many remarried couples often have at least one child of their own. There are no recent estimates of the number of American children living in stepfamilies.

Popular perception holds that stepfamily life is highly problematic for all involved. Researchers have found that this family form may be no better or worse than other family forms, however, although the challenges are distinct (Hildebrand et al., 2008). These include the need to deal with a complicated extended family network, difficulty in establishing stepparenting roles, an uncertain developmental life career, and unique developmental tasks. This family form is discussed in greater detail in Chapter 12.

Gay and Lesbian Families

A common misconception about gays and lesbians is that they are antifamily and prefer to maintain a single lifestyle. People are often surprised to learn that many homosexual men and women form families that may include children (Figure 2–10). Gay and lesbian families are difficult to distinguish from other family types today. While many gay and lesbian individuals prefer to remain single, there are a growing number who have long-term, committed relationships that are reported to be at least healthy as those of married heterosexuals (Kurdek, 2004).

FIGURE 2–10.   Gay men and lesbian women form families that resemble other family forms but differ in many respects.

Children are a part of many gay and lesbian families. Their presence is more likely in lesbian than in gay families, probably because women generally hold sole custody of children after a divorce. Researchers have found few differences between homosexual parents and heterosexual parents (Golombok, et al., 2003; Patterson, Fulcher, & Wainright, 2002; Stacey & Biblarz, 2001; Tasker, 2002; Tasker & Patterson, 2007). Many people are surprised to learn that homosexuals are involved in something that is so heterosexual in nature as having children and parenting them. Many homosexuals became parents when they were young adults and often were denying their homosexual orientation by attempting to lead a heterosexual lifestyle. Some lesbian couples, though, choose to become parents. To accomplish this, one partner usually is artificially inseminated. In addition, adoption is a viable option in becoming parents for gays and lesbians in many states.

There are no valid research data that demonstrate unquestionably that having a homosexual parent has any significant negative effects on children (Allen & Burrell, 2002; Buxton, 1999; Golombok & MacCallum, 2003; Patterson et al., 2002; Tasker, 2002; Tasker & Patterson, 2007). In fact, gay or lesbian parents are as effective as nongay parents in raising children and may in some respects be even more efficient. Because our society continues to support heterosexist attitudes that favor het-

erosexuality over homosexuality, these facts are not widely known or accepted by the public at large.

Of course, gay and lesbian families have a different family life and different problems than other families. In many respects, however, homosexual families are like heterosexual blended families (Laird, 2003). This is particularly true among lesbian mothers, who frequently have custody of their children from past heterosexual marriages. The distinctive problems of gay and lesbian families do not make them pathological. Rather, they reflect the difficulties of conducting family life in a society that looks askance on such arrangements. This family form is discussed in greater detail in Chapter 13.

Parenting Reflection 2–4

Suppose you are a family therapist advising a lesbian couple who is contemplating having a child. What would you help them consider in this decision-making process?

Families with Renested Adult Children

Families with renested adult children are a modern phenomenon. This renested family type emerges when

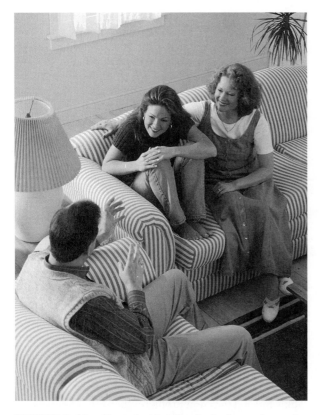

FIGURE 2–11. Renested families typically are formed when a young adult child returns to live with their family of origin for a short period of time.

children who have been launched into adult lives of their own return to the home base of their family of origin (Steinmetz, Clavan, & Stein, 1990). The young adult children are also referred to as boomerang kids (Mitchell, 2006; Mitchell & Gee, 1996). Most children who return to their parental home are males under 20 years of age. Some estimates suggest that more than 60% of all young adults between 18 and 30 years of age will at some time return to their family of origin to live temporarily (Piper & Balswick, 1997). Currently, it is estimated that about 56% of men and 43% of women between 18 and 24 years live with one or both parents (U.S. Bureau of the Census, 2006) (Figure 2–11).

The phenomenon of renested families occurs primarily when young adult children experience some type of economic or personal crisis or transitional life event, such as job loss or divorce, and turn to their family for support. Some renested families are also formed

when young adults return to their elderly parents' home to care for them (Mitchell, 2006).

Very little is known about the interaction patterns or lifestyle of renested families (Mitchell, 1998, 2006; Mitchell & Gee, 1996). This type of family system probably needs to be adaptable to respond effectively to the developmental level of a young adult. Family rules may need to be changed and new boundaries established as parents and young adult children work through interaction issues. The kind of arrangements derived will involve new definitions of parent-child relations that depend less on the social power of the parents. Parents are more likely to provide greater support when their boomerang kids reciprocate with their own support for parents and are more autonomous, for example (Bold, 2001).

Custodial (Coresident) Grandparents and Grandchildren: Kinship Families

The newest variation in family structure was first noticed in the early 1990s by researchers, public policy makers, and the media (Bryson & Casper, 1999). This new family structure typically involves grandchildren who live in grandparent-maintained households, although it also includes extended family members who are caring for related children. In 1970, there were about 2.2 million of these households involving children 18 years of age and younger living with at least one grandparent. By 1997, this number increased to about 3.9 million children and constituted about 5.5% of all American children under 18 (Bryson & Casper). By 2001, this number reached about 8% of all children in the United States living with a grandparent (Fields, 2003).

The grandmother maintains the household in the large majority of coresident grandparent/grandchildren families (Fields, 2003). Coresident grandparent/grandchild families typically are created when parents experience some type of personal problem that prevents them from performing effectively in their caregiving role. Examples of such debilitating personal problems include incarceration, drug abuse, addictions, child abuse, AIDS, chronic physical or emotional illness, or even death. Grandparents often step in to assume custody of grandchildren under such circumstances rather than having the children placed into foster care. The motivation to assume primary caregiving responsibilities is to provide their grandchildren with a stable environment.

The children in these families (1) are likely to be age 6 and under, (2) are mostly white, (3) live in poverty, (4) lack health insurance coverage, and (5) are likely to receive some form of public assistance (Fields, 2003).

Coresident families have difficult challenges not usually faced by other family structures (Edwards & Daire, 2006; M. M. Robinson & Wilkes, 2006; Ross & Aday, 2006; Smithgall & Mason, 2004). Many grandparents, while acting compassionately in the best interests of their grandchildren, find that their plans for a serene retirement must be postponed or abandoned to provide for their grandchildren. Others find it necessary to apply for public assistance upon assuming custody of grandchildren due to the increased expenses involved that tax an already-limited fixed income. The grandchildren may also arrive with multiple problems that can be traced to parental problems such as divorce, addictions and dependencies, and inconsistent parenting behavior. Additionally, grandparents in coresident households are more likely to be poor and to experience all the negative aspects associated with poverty. They are less likely to be insured and especially lack health insurance coverage for grandchildren. Furthermore, grandparents may not be able to cope with providing the educational needs of grandchildren. Many have not completed high school and may not be completely aware of how to guide children's educational experiences.

∙∙

Focus Point.   Diversity, in structure and form, is the principal characteristic of contemporary American families. Significant variations in the ways that families are defined and how they are composed reflect changes occurring in the larger society. The most commonly observed family types are (1) two opposite-sex adults with an intact marriage and their children, (2) single-parent adults and their children, (3) stepfamilies composed of two opposite-sex adults who have remarried and the children of one or both, (4) gay and lesbian families composed of two same-sex adults and sometimes the children of one or both, (5) renested families composed of adult parents and their adult children who have returned to the home base, and (6) custodial (coresident) grandparent-grandchild families. These emergent family forms do not represent a pathological or dysfunctional orientation to family life in the United States.

∙∙

ETHNIC DIVERSITY AND CONTEMPORARY FAMILIES

Cultural diversity has always been a hallmark of American society—the product of the immigration of various ethnic groups to the United States since pre-Colonial times. In recent years, ethnic identity has been reemphasized as Americans have become more curious about their family roots. Americans have always considered themselves to have a culturally diverse society. This diversity is reflected in the numerous ethnic and racial groups that have emigrated from other countries to make new homes in the United States.

Ethnic identity is a central family ecological factor that influences how most of these family systems are organized and how they function. It continues to play a role in each subsequent generation. Many ethnic minority families have created new lives and discovered new opportunities, but they have also struggled with the prejudice and discrimination that limits educational experiences, job opportunities, and the ability to function fully in communities. Because of such problems, family systems with ethnic and racial backgrounds experience problems not usually shared by those with an Anglo, or white, middle-class background.

Researchers examining family structure and functioning have tended to classify minority families according to stereotypes promulgated within the larger society. Early researchers examining Hispanic families, for example, identified the concept of machismo as the prime factor shaping the dynamics of this ethnic group's family life (Staples & Mirande, 1980). More recent research refutes this and other findings as not relevant to the contemporary Hispanic family (J. H. Skinner, 2001).

Today, we are concerned about building bridges between all families that make up American society. Diversity, and its essential importance in our society, is not just a politically correct term but a critical element that has made American society what it has become today and predicts how the future can become. Ethnic diversity is a part of the sociocultural ecological system in which we live. It encompasses the values in which people believe, how their families operate as a social system, how they teach their children to function effectively, and how resources are used to promote daily functioning. While diversity is a hallmark of family systems in American society, it is important to examine these from the perspective of discerning how each attempts to accomplish a common goal but in different ways: how to raise children in a diverse society, in the midst of great uncertainty about the future, to become effectively functioning members of this society.

This section examines issues that challenge parents and children within those cultural and racial groups representing a cross section of families in the United States. Specifically, this section focuses on the parenting and child-rearing practices of Caucasian (Anglo), African American, Hispanic, Asian American, and Native American families. We also discuss interracial, interethnic families as well as newly arrived families who have immigrated into the United States. We approach this examination using an ethnographic perspective, described earlier in the first section of this chapter. Some readers will have an *emic* view of at least one of these groups we discuss by virtue of already being a member. By studying these groups, we are enabled in developing an *etic* perspective. Both of these must be tempered by an awareness of ethnocentrism.

Caucasian (Anglo) Parents and Children

Characteristics. Our discussion of the ethnic diversity of families in the United States begins with an examination of a few of the major features of the dominant ethnic group—Caucasian (Anglo) families. People of European extraction comprise the majority of the population of the United States and have done so since the colonization process began more than 300 years ago. In 2005, slightly more than 80% of the population fit into this ethnic category (U.S. Bureau of the Census, 2007a, 2007b). These individuals and their families reside most frequently in all areas of the United States, except for three Southwestern states and the District of Columbia. Most are considered to be middle or working class, holding jobs that are based on educational achievement and earning combined household incomes ranging from $25,000 to more than $100,000 annually.

Caucasian individuals and their families have dominated American culture for a number of reasons—one being their sheer size in relation to other ethnic groups and another perhaps because of holding positions of power as well as social and financial stature in communities. The majority of individuals and families of this group settled the Colonies that became the United States as well as the frontier areas that gave rise to the other states comprising the Union. The modern-day middle class also emerged from this group following the Great Depression of the 1930s. It is this segment of the Caucasian population whose values became a dominant force in influencing the entire culture of the United States to this day.

Parenting. For the most part, we might assert that the majority of what we know about parenting and parent-child relations until recently was based on research using this group of individuals and their children. And, until recently, researchers focused on the social class configuration of Caucasians as mediating considerable differences from other subcultures in terms of the ways that parenting took place and the outcomes of children exposed to these differences.

One of the fundamental findings of research conducted in the past that examined such social class differences in parenting was that social class variations, that is, middle- versus blue-collar class, advantaged versus disadvantaged groups, resulted in corresponding differences in the ways that children were raised and the values that they were taught by parents (Lambert, Hames, & Frasure-Smith, 1979; Davidson & Moore, 1992). This position was supported repeatedly in the past by studies showing that middle-class parents differed from others in a number of child-rearing patterns such as greater use of harshness, emphasizing that children must delay the gratification of their immediate needs, the learning of a work ethic at an early age, valuing and achieving academic successes such as earning a high school diploma or a college degree, and valuing and demonstrating the value of cleanliness and neatness in one's personal life, for example. Researchers have described differences in speech, communication styles, and interaction patterns of middle-class versus lower-class parents. What may more accurately have been at work here were family ecological factors such as significant differences in family income, quality of housing, availability of health care, provision of adequate nutrition, and availability of time to devote to parenting children that produced such differences. The inherent message coming from these studies, however, was ethnocentric in pointing to the relative successfulness of middle-class parents in raising children to a supposedly equally successful adulthood.

Later researchers refuted these findings, noting that social class variations have become reduced in American society due to factors such as the increased exposure of the entire population to media sources such as television programs portraying middle-class values and the increased numbers of lower-class individuals who have become socially mobile upward into the working- or middle-class due to better-paying jobs and positions.

There is no doubt that middle-class values continue to play a major role in providing a template for what is termed success and the status to which many other groups may aspire. In some respects, however, this template may come with a price. The middle-class white population appears to be living the contemporary American Dream. The pressures to succeed, however, may not always bring about the degree of happiness imagined among middle-class Caucasian individuals and families (Drum Major Institute for Public Policy, 2006). The degree of materialism associated with middle-class success may not always grant peace of mind (Warren & Tyagi, 2004). The conspicuous consumption of middle-class Caucasian individuals and families may eventually lead to an erosion of certain moral and ethical values, ac-

cording to some critics. Regardless of these shortcomings, Caucasian families provide one model of parent-child relations that demonstrates both cultural universalism and cultural relativism in child rearing.

••

Focus Point.   Caucasians constitute the largest ethnic group represented in the United States today. Most of the research on parent-child relations has been based on this group, focusing on differences in social class subgroups.

••

Hispanic Parents and Children

Hispanic families constitute a diverse group (Figure 2–12). What all may hold in common is the use of Spanish in addition to English as a second language (Hildebrand et al., 2008). Hispanics may have the distinction of being the largest minority group in the United States (U.S. Bureau of the Census, 2007a, 2007b). The increases in this segment of the population are due largely to immigration from Mexico and other Latin American countries. Another factor accounting for the large

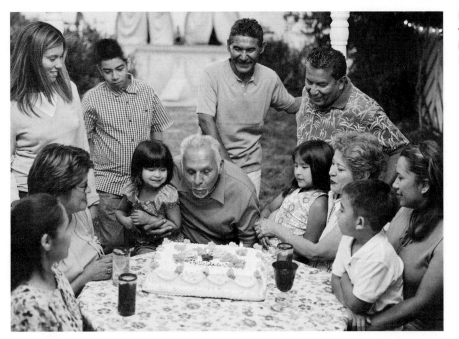

FIGURE 2–12. Hispanic families now constitute the largest ethnic minority in the United States.

increases of this ethnic group is the high fertility rate experienced by Hispanic women, the highest among all ethnic groups in the United States. Hispanics live predominantly in southwestern states such as Texas, Arizona, New Mexico, and Califormia, although they are represented in all of the United States. Most work predominantly in service occupations and earn moderately comfortable incomes. However, the poverty rate is about 21% for all Hispanic families in the United States (Fronczek, 2005).

The role of family ecological factors has a significant influence on the nature of parent-child relations in Hispanic families. While the increasing size of this group is a significant characteristic, Hispanic families may be characterized in other ways (Hildebrand et al., 2008; McLoyd, Cauce, Takeuchi, & Wilson, 2000; Therrien & Ramirez, 2000; U.S. Bureau of the Census, 2007a, 2007b):

- Hispanic families are more likely to live in large families (four or more people) as compared with non-Hispanic white families (three people or less).
- There is a greater tendency for these parents and children to experience substandard levels of education. Over half of this population group have not graduated from high school and one-quarter have less than a ninth-grade education.
- About 23% of Hispanic parents and their children live in poverty, compared to 8% of non-Latino whites.
- Religion plays a significant role in daily family life.
- Hispanics may be more family oriented than whites and use a more extensive kinship-based support network than whites.

Parenting. In matters of child rearing, Hispanic parents are challenged by the traditional scripts they learned as children themselves that may have a poor fit with the realities of raising children in a different cultural environment. For example, a generation gap problem between parents and children in differences of English and Spanish language fluency can color parent-child interactions with frustration and even resentment (Becerra, 1998). In a similar vein, the conditions produced by having low income due to lack of educational attainment tend to promote a more authoritarian-like approach to child rearing known as *hierarchical parenting*. This parenting style combines emotionally warm support for children within the context of demanding exceptional respect for parents and others such as extended family members. This approach is noted for promoting a collective value system among children as opposed to the individualism promoted among whites in their child-rearing approaches (McLoyd et al., 2000).

Within the context of hierarchical parenting, children learn the importance of the "three Rs" of Hispanic family values: personal relationships, respect, and responsibility (Hildebrand et al., 2008). Children also learn the role of cooperation (as opposed to competition) and other-centeredness (as opposed to self-centeredness) in their family relationships. Children are taught to make decisions based on the impact on others in their families. In this manner, they learn about family loyalty and the strength of family bonds in providing support, which in turn spills over into relationships outside their families. The emphasis on learning these values promotes the notion of *la familia* and the high importance placed on the family group and its ability to meet the needs of all members.

Educational achievement is highly valued among Hispanic families, often serving as a basis for the desire to immigrate to the United States from other countries because of the opportunities available to children. However, it is not unusual for educational attainment to be assigned a low priority by parents and other family members if this conflicts with a child's allegiances to the family (Hildebrand et al., 2008).

Hispanic children are socially and educationally challenged by being bilingual. Most learn Spanish as the primary language spoken at home and in the community while learning English as a second language. For this reason, bilingual education is desirable because it recognizes these children's needs rather than making them an educational liability (Olmos, Yberra, and Monterrey, 1999). The issue of bilingual education is controversial; however. Hispanic parents generally favor this approach because it appears to support their children's cultural heritage, and there is the belief that bilingual classes help to facilitate children's learning of the English language. Critics of bilingual education assert that this approach is likely to prevent a Hispanic child's full assimilation into American society. This point of view is part of a broader political movement that addresses immigration issues as well as the implications of cultural assimilation of ethnic groups into American society (see http://publicagenda.org/).

••

Focus Point.   Their family structure, values, and parenting styles give Hispanics a unique position among ethnic minority families in the United States.

••

African American Parents and Children

Family Characteristics.   African Americans now constitute the second largest minority group in the United States (U.S. Bureau of the Census, 2007a, 2007b). This group increased in size to constitute about 13% of the total population in 2005. In general, marriage is less likely between adults. Black women tend to have a higher fertility rate than whites, and there is a larger proportion of families headed by women in the black community. In 2004, the median income of black families in the United States was slightly more than $30,000, which was significantly less than the median income of whites. As such, the poverty rate was higher in that year for blacks than for whites, with about one-quarter of the black community living below the poverty rate compared with 9% of whites (Pew Hispanic Center, 2007).

Parenting.   The child-rearing practices of African American family systems are found to be similar to other groups in several aspects (Julian, McHenry, & McKelvey, 1994). When compared with Latino families, blacks tend to encourage early autonomy of children, are intolerant of wasted time, appear to practice authoritative methods of discipline based on reasoning with children, and encourage egalitarian family roles (Bluestone & Tamis-LeMonda, 1999; Wiley, Warren, & Montenelli, 2002). This approach may vary, however, depending on the socioeconomic status of the parents and other factors.

One of the greatest obstacles to effective parenting among African American families relates to economic pressures (Jones, Forehand, Brody, & Armistead, 2002) . In spite of dire financial circumstances that can exacerbate stressfulness in family life, effective African American parents use encouragement and sharing activities with children that tend to counteract the negative influences of harsh economic family conditions. In spite of the obstacles and challenges facing African American families in general, stable family systems are found throughout these communities with

the working class, nonpoor forming the backbone of support (Billingsley, 1993).

Ethnicity is a major family ecological factor in child-rearing practices. It contributes to how children are socialized in developing a personal identity considered appropriate to their ethnic background as African Americans. Because of these and other ecological factors such as low family incomes and younger ages of parents than other families, the general child-rearing style is seen as parent-centered, where children are expected to become responsible and independent at early ages (Hildebrand et al., 2008). As are children in other minority groups in the United States, black children are generally raised by parents who emphasize the importance of educational success as a means of bettering one's quality of life (Balkcom, 2002; Thompson, 2003; Trosper, 2002). When black parents consistently use authoritative methods in child rearing, their children generally perform successfully in school. However, involvement of African American parents in working with the schooling of their children is often problematic because of inconvenient meeting times with teachers, parents' own past experiences with schools that were of poor quality, and feelings of intimidation by school personnel (Abdul-Adil & Farmer, 2006; Koonce & Harper, 2005). It should also be noted that religious values and church participation play a vital role in African American family life. The church has played a central role in the socialization of African American children since the days of slavery (Billingsley, 1993).

African American parents, like other minority parents, are challenged in teaching their children to have a positive ethnic group identity while learning to cope with the problems associated with societal prejudice and discrimination (Hughes, 2003). Even being a middle-class black family does not completely protect parents and children from acts of prejudice and discrimination. Most black parents make efforts to ensure that children are prepared with the means to place such attitudes and treatment into proper perspective. The challenge is to teach children what it means to be an African American in a society that has strong racist overtones (Staples, 1999). But even the simple task of choosing toys can be problematic in this regard. For example, should children be encouraged only to choose black dolls, or is it appropriate to allow a white doll?

Other aspects of parenting are unique to African Americans. For example, it is estimated that more

African American parents spank their children in comparison with parents of other ethnic groups (Dodge, McLoyd, & Lansford, 2005; McLoyd et al., 2000). In general, these parents are described as conducting discipline of children within the contexts of warmth and acceptance while employing mild physical punishment. Spanking is not likely to be seen as negative, inappropriate parenting behavior among African American parents. Rather, using corporal punishment is more likely to be viewed as an appropriate positive parental behavior by both parents and children.

In addition, parenting frequently occurs within the context of single-parent family structure headed by women who may or may not have been married (Federal Interagency Forum on Child and Family Statistics, 2006). In addition, many of the custodial coresident grandparent-grandchild families are composed of African Americans.

Given that these family systems are characterized by low-income or poverty-level status as well as living in an inner-city environment, children are often at risk of experiencing difficulties in school, participating in high-risk behaviors such as drug use and gang involvement, pregnancies, health problems, and other difficulties. Many African American parents, however, are successful in buffering their children from these problems by monitoring their leisure time and social contacts. They may also require younger children to tag along with older siblings, who are responsible for their care (Jarrett, 1995). In addition, African American teenagers tend to view their families as a refuge from a world that is often hostile (Giordano, Cernkovich, & DeMaris, 1993). As such, their family relationships are characterized as more intimate, while peer relationships are less intense than those of white teenagers.

••

Focus Point. African American families currently constitute the second-largest number of minorities in the United States. Although many stereotypes and myths characterize these families and their members, research indicates that they are far from pathological in their nature. Most problems associated with these family systems can be traced to the insidious effects of poverty; about half are single-parent families headed by a woman. African American parents prepare their children to handle racist attitudes and their future adult roles in society by promoting education. African American parents possess many strengths that enable them to cope with adversity.

••

Asian American Parents and Children

Family Characteristics. Less information is available about Asian American and Pacific Islander families in comparison with other ethnic groups in the United States. This is perhaps because these families make up a smaller percentage of the population and are located in fewer geographic areas (Figure 2–13). In addition, these families are not likely to be viewed as abnormal nor as a problem in society (Hildebrand et al., 2008). The majority live in the western states and in Hawaii, with substantial populations in the largest northern cities such as Chicago and New York City (U.S. Bureau of the Census, 2007a, 2007b). Like Hispanics, Asian Americans are a diverse ethnic group, including people with Chinese, Japanese, Korean, and Southeast Asian heritage. Those with Chinese and Japanese backgrounds make up the largest and oldest established groups in the United States (Hildebrand et al., 2008). Those from Southeast Asia (including Cambodians, Vietnamese, Laotians, and Hmong) constitute the smallest groups, most having migrated as refugees during the last 30 years. Differences between groups of Asian Americans are due to cultural variations.

FIGURE 2–13. The diversity in family forms found among Asian Americans can be traced to different national cultures of origin.

**Parenting
FAQs 2–1**

My oldest child just entered first grade in a community elementary school. We've always taught our children to be accepting of everyone regardless of skin color, appearance, disabilities, or other kinds of differences. Recently, our first grader has heard other children make derogatory comments about minority children in his school. He's asked us how he can tell these children that it's wrong to make these comments and to stop doing this. We're not sure what to suggest that he might say when he encounters these comments from other children. Can you help us?

A: You might explain to your child that other children who tease and make derogatory remarks about minorities or others who are different may have learned these at home or from others. You are doing a good job in teaching your child not to hold prejudicial views of others based on race, ethnic background, the presence of disabilities, or other differences. You could suggest your child respond to others when hearing such remarks by saying something like, "It hurts people's feelings when you say things like that. Suppose how you'd feel if you were in their place and they were saying something like that about you. How would you feel?" or " Just because others look different from you on the outside doesn't mean that they are different on the inside, too. It hurts to hear hateful things, and it isn't right." This might be a good time, also, to encourage your child's teacher to conduct a teaching unit on diversity. Apparently, there is much consciousness-raising that can be done at your child's school about diversity, even beginning in the first grade.

Parenting.   Parenting styles among Asian American families appear to be more authoritarian and authoritative rather than permissive, with a greater reliance on verbal rather than physical means for disciplining children (Hildebrand et al., 2008). However, what appear to be very strict parenting styles to an outside observer are something entirely different to those who reside within such family systems (Gorman, 1988). These family systems typically combine nurturance with control in order to shape children's behavior to conform to the family's achievement goals (Rosenthal & Feldman, 1992).

Asian American parents can be expected to be highly involved in their children's academic activities. Educational achievement is highly valued among Asian American parents for their children (McLoyd et al., 2000). For example, more than 42% of Asian Americans have completed 4 years of college or more (U.S. Bureau of the Census, 2007a, 2007b). Some researchers attribute this high level of achievement educationally to the Asian American parenting style, which is commonly compared with authoritarianism (Greenfield & Suzuki, 2001). Other Asian American researchers have explained this as the *Confucian training doctrine*, which is similar to the hierarchical parenting concept discussed in the section on Hispanic parents and children. The Confucian training doctrine emphasizes the blending of nurturance, parental involvement, and physical closeness with strict and firm control over children (McBride-Chang & Chang, 1998).

Children of Asian American parents are expected to achieve personal maturity at early ages in comparison with those of other family systems in our society (Caplan, Whitmore, & Choy, 1989). Certain behaviors are not tolerated from children, such as acting physically or verbally aggressive, especially with siblings. Older children are expected to serve as good role models of behavior for younger siblings.

•••

Focus Point.   Asian American families may be stereotyped as the model minority since parents heavily invest in their children and in their educational achievements. These families value strong parent-child relationships and encourage children while providing a stable family life that emphasizes closeness within a strict adherence to family rules.

•••

Native American Parents and Children

Characteristics.   There may be similarities between Native American family systems and those of other minority groups (Glover, 2001), especially African Americans. These groups have long histories of being viewed as pathological and largely have been studied from a cultural deviance model. Characteristics typically describing Native American Indian family systems include high fertility rates, large numbers of illegitimate births, prevalence of female-headed households, and high rates of unemployment and substance abuse, especially alcoholism (Joe & Malach, 1992).

Problems indigenous to life on and off the reservation include high rates of adult alcoholism, homicide rates higher than the rest of the U.S. population, accidents, and suicides. These problems put some Native Indian children at a higher-than-usual risk of experiencing the loss of parents, siblings, relatives, and friends. In many tribes, the paternal uncle and male cousins, in addition to the child's father and brothers, play an important role in a child's life. Because children continually lose family members due to situations particular to their lifestyle, they are challenged to acquire coping strategies not usually found in children of other ethnic groups. Their response patterns frequently include disruptive, aggressive behaviors at school and home; emotional depression; feelings of low self-worth and self-esteem; substance abuse; developmental delays; flattened emotional affect; interpersonal distancing; self-destructive behaviors, including suicidal gestures; sexual acting out; and running away from home (Hildebrand et al., 2008).

Native American families may view children differently from other groups in the United States (Hildebrand et al., 2008). Children typically are seen as treasured gifts. Parents and other extended family members are charged with discovering the unique characteristics of a child at birth to determine her or his place within the tribe. Infants are carefully observed for several months to learn about their nature. The child's name as well as his or her sexual orientation and gender role is determined relative to the characteristics family members observe. Only then is the naming ceremony conducted, sometimes many months after birth.

Because most Native American tribes value personal autonomy and independence of members, individual differences in children appear to be tolerated and accepted as part of their nature. Children are generally reared through grooming these traits as they are encouraged to learn to make personal choices and learn by the consequences of their actions. This parenting style may appear to be permissive to outsiders since parents often ignore children's behavior that is considered inappropriate.

Parenting.   Native American parents might be thought to use more permissive styles of raising their children in comparison with other ethnic groups (John, 1998). However, some tribes may use methods that are more punitive and controlling. Like Asian American parents, Native American parents tend to combine nurturance with control in guiding children's development, especially when the children are young. Traditional styles of child rearing emphasize teaching children to maintain a sense of unity and cohesiveness with their tribal and immediate family groups and to suppress the tendency to experience conflict with others. While these practices may be useful in facilitating daily life among the people living on reservations, they may not be effective in teaching Native American children to function well in urban settings when they live in families away from the reservation.

Contemporary Native American parents usually teach their children traditional values based on practical application of personal belief systems. For example, children are taught to perceive things and people according to intrinsic rather than extrinsic traits and characteristics. Children are taught to be in touch with the rhythms of nature and to be sensitive to the needs of others. Sharing personal resources, thoughts, and knowledge is considered appropriate in smoothing interpersonal interactions.

••

Focus Point.   Native American parents and children are challenged by sociocultural factors not experienced by other ethnic minorities. These relate to reconciling traditional ways and values with the necessity of adapting and acculturating to modern contemporary society. Native American parents and children may have competing allegiances to both sociocultural worlds. The family structure and functioning of tribes may be difficult for outsiders to understand and appreciate. Native Americans appear to have a unique approach to child rearing and family life.

••

Interracial-Interethnic Parents and Children

The number of interracial and interethnic married couples has increased significantly since 1980, although only constituting about 3% of all marriages in the United States (Fields, 2003). Not long ago these relationships were against the law in the United States. As early as 1761, colonial laws prohibited marriage or sexual relations between people of different races. These laws remained in effect until 1967, when the U.S. Supreme Court ruled that these laws were unconstitutional.

The reasons why these marriages have increased in the years since 1967 are varied. First, the general desegregation of American society presents greater opportunities for people of different racial groups to mingle socially and work together. Increased socioeconomic opportunities available today encourage the upward social mobility of ethnic minorities, which increases contact between people of all racial and ethnic groups in housing, employment, school, work, and leisure activities (McLoyd et al., 2000). In some cases, upward social mobility may be a factor, especially for white women who marry black men of higher status. The increases may also reflect changes in attitudes about interracial marriages, despite the continuing threat of discrimination and even verbal abuse aimed at such couples (Kalish, 1995).

The challenges their children would face as biracial, biethnic individuals is a serious concern for many interracial, interethnic couples considering marriage (Funderberg, 1994). They fear their children will experience rejection and isolation from peers and others because of their heritage. This concern also exists for parents who adopt children of a different race. In the end, however, it appears that most biracial individuals have learned to look at their challenges due to their status with humor and a determination not to let other people's prejudices discourage them.

Research is limited on how biracial children and their parents manage and learn to cope with their situation (Byrd & Garwick, 2006). Many do not experience significant adjustments, but most must resolve issues relating to ambiguous ethnicity and their need to define their identities in a society where racial issues are prominent (Gibbs, 2003). One explanation for these children's healthy outcomes is in the efforts of parents to provide support, encourage activities that build ethnic identity, instruct children how to respond when their identity is questioned, and expose their children to effective adult role models in both racial and family groups.

Parenting Reflection 2–5

How would you explain to a child why interracial-interethnic families continue to experience discrimination in their communities and neighborhoods? What would you suggest to the child about how to react when hearing offensive remarks of this nature?

Focus Point.   Interracial-interethnic parents and children have particular challenges related primarily to identity issues and preparing children to cope with discrimination.

Immigrant Parents and Children

The United States was formed by the immigration of many different nationalities and ethnic groups over the centuries. Large numbers of people arrived in this new country to pursue their dreams of freedom, wealth, and personal happiness. Many individuals and families arrived legally and eventually assumed respected positions in their adopted communities. The amalgam of so many different ways of life, languages, family lives, parenting styles, and perspectives has given strength to the diversity of American culture.

Revisions in federal legislation in 1965 changed the criteria for lawful entry into the United States. Priority was given to those who possessed valued work skills, refugees from foreign aggressions, and those who already had relatives living in the United States. In fact, the final criteria has accounted for about two-thirds of all legal entrants into the United States (Fix, Zimmerman, & Passel, 2001; Martin & Midgely, 1999).

The number of immigrations into the United States has increased steadily since 1960 (Fix et al., 2001). Today, immigrants constitute about 11% of the total U.S. population. Most come from Latin American and Asian countries, now causing the greater metropolitan cities on the west coast to become the new Ellis Islands that receive large numbers of these individuals and families.

Many native individuals and families in the United States have become more aware of immigration issues, both legal and illegal in nature since the terrorist attacks of September 11, 2001. Restrictions are more stringent because of security issues, and immigrant families may be scrutinized more than in the past. Many families report tension associated with this heightened attitude about their presence in communities. Much debate is currently taking place in American society as Congress attempts to revise laws dealing with immigrants who have arrive in the United States illegally.

Economic difficulties are often associated with many immigrant parents and children because of language barriers and general acculturation problems. These challenges affect everyone in a family and hinder parent-child relations. For example, economic well-being of immigrant families improved only slightly between 1998 and 2001 (Capps, Fix, & Reardon-Anderson, 2003), and there was significant concern about food availability and cost. Many parents and children are reported to be living in crowded housing units, and an estimated half of a typical family's income goes toward rent or mortgage payments. Many immigrant parents and children do not have health insurance coverage, although substantial increases have occurred in Medicaid and SCHIP (State Children's Health Insurance Program) coverage for many individuals and families (Morse, 2003).

Immigrant parents encourage their children to achieve high levels of education and become good citizens of their new country (Detzner & Xiong, 1999). However, parent-child relations in immigrant families may be strained by negative family ecological factors and by discrepancies observed in parents who may have problems with acculturation (e.g., difficulties in learning a new language) and in those observed in parents of native children (Aroian, 2006). Immigrant children may also experience problems with reconciling the traditional standards and expectations of their parents with the consumer-oriented culture of contemporary American society. When immigrant families come from war-torn pasts in other countries, the entire family system is likely to be challenged even more by the posttraumatic stress resulting from these past experiences.

Parenting Reflection 2–6

What is your opinion about states or cities that enact legislation requiring English as the official language? What might be the impact of such legislation on immigrant parents and children?

Focus Point. Issues confronting newly arrived immigrants involve the marginal nature of these families. Economic difficulties, problems in acquiring and using a new language, and general acculturation issues present a special challenge for immigrant parents and children.

POINTS TO CONSIDER

■ The most significant context in which parent-child relations take place is the cultural context. Culture defines what families value and believe to be important that guides behavior of all members. Culture shapes the rules or social norms that outline appropriate behavior of people in a variety of other contexts such as the roles they fulfill, the notions of what is acceptable and unacceptable actions, and the individuals, agencies, and institutions that transmit these values and beliefs.

■ *Individualism* and *collectivism,* or *sociocentrism,* are two cultural conceptions of value systems. These cultural concepts have direct application in parent-child relations in that these influence how parents translate cultural values into how they interact with their children.

■ In studying parents and children as well as families, it behooves us to recognize that there are patterns that are likely to be shared across subcultures but also patterns that are distinctly unique to each, that is, recognizing the functioning of *cultural universalism* vs. *cultural relativism* in influencing our perceptions.

■ Socialization is what parents do to teach children to conform to social rules, acquire personal values, and develop attitudes and behaviors typical or representative of their culture at large as well as their family of origin. Socialization is the way that culture is transmitted to children by parents, the media, institutions, and agencies.

- The process of socialization also is bidirectional in nature because children play a role in this process. Parents change and shape the lessons of socialization based on a number of factors such as a child's age, developmental abilities, ability to use and understand language, their gender, and so on.
- People define their family in a variety of ways.
- Families in contemporary American society are diverse in form and structure. Single-parent families are the fastest-growing family form today.
- Stepfamilies usually are formed when a biological mother remarries. These families usually include children from the previous marriage, and remarried couples frequently have children of their own. Stepfamily maintenance requires that members rework their former family system into one that is pertinent to new participants. These families have many strengths to offer members.
- A renested family is formed when children who have been launched into adult lives of their own return to their home base to live temporarily. Very little is known about how these families function.
- Gay men and lesbians form families that resemble those of heterosexuals. These families may include children of one or both partners from a former heterosexual marriage or children who are adopted or conceived by artificial insemination. Contrary to popular belief, homosexuals do not differ from heterosexuals in their ability to parent children effectively or in their commitment to long-term relationships.
- Custodial coresident grandparent/grandchildren families are formed when an adult child cannot function in his or her parenting role. Coresident grandparents often need help and financial assistance in providing adequate care for their grandchildren.
- Families of diverse racial/ethnic origins must deal with racist attitudes and bigotry and, for many, the insidious effects of poverty.
- Hispanic parents and children come from diverse groups themselves. This ethnic group is the largest of all ethnic groups in the United States. Children are taught family values such as developing a strong sense of belongingness and loyalty, respecting other family members, and cooperation with other family members. Child rearing is characterized as hierarchi-

cal parenting, a style based on authoritarianism that combines emotional warmth with strictness. Children learn about the high value placed on family membership.
- Many African American parents raise their children based on an authoritative style. Many parents must contend with severe economic conditions but use approaches that temper this severity on family life. Educational advancement is encouraged, and children are equipped with ways for coping with societal prejudice and bigotry.
- Asian American parents and children constitute the smallest ethnic group in the United States. Asian American parents typically use a parenting style known as Confucian training doctrine.
- Native American Indian parents and children come from even more diverse groups. The notion of what constitutes a family usually is relative to a particular tribe. A variety of child-rearing approaches may be employed in different Native American Indian tribes, but children generally are taught to respect authority and their elders. Because there is a division in those who live on and those who live off of reservations, Native American Indian families are challenged by different acculturation issues than other ethnic families. Many families must cope with the insidious effects of poverty and associated problems.
- The number of interracial, interethnic marriages in the United States is increasing, with an accompanying larger number of biracial, biethnic children. Many parents involved in these marriages are concerned about their children's welfare, especially when they are rejected by other children. These children generally fare well in spite of their particular challenges.
- Immigrant parents and children face challenges unique to their situation. Many problems arise from severe economic conditions as well as difficulties in dealing with language barriers and other acculturation issues. Quality of life is at risk as well as quality of parent-child relations. Parents desire that their children become good citizens and responsible individuals. Children may experience conflict between parents pressing for adoption of traditional values in a contemporary society that does not support these values from the countries of origin.

CHAPTER 3

Theoretical Perspectives on Parent-Child Relations

Focus Questions
▪ ▪ ▪ ▪ ▪ ▪ ▪ ▪ ▪ ▪

1. How can a family be described as a social system?
2. What major concepts describe how families function as a social system?
3. How can we best describe developmental changes that occur over time within family systems?
4. How can ecological theory assist the understanding of individuals within the context of their family system?
5. How does psychosocial theory address issues in parent-child relations?
6. How do other psychological theories address issues in parent-child relations?

One of the ideas discussed in the previous chapters is that a parent is an agent of socialization and a child is the object of the adult's socialization efforts. This notion has been labeled the *unidirectional model of socialization*. Stated simply, this model focuses on the adult's behavior as a stimulus that causes or produces some particular response or outcome within a child. Interpreted more broadly, this model of parent-child relations implies that if an adult behaves well as a parent, the child will grow to become a good person. That is, adults can achieve their parenting goals if they act properly as parents by doing and saying the appropriate things at the appropriate time and in the appropriate manner, thereby providing appropriate caregiving. Following this logic, there is a formula for effective parenting based on consistently good parental performance over the years of child rearing. By accepting this model as an accurate depiction of what occurs in the relationship between parents and children, society has been able to make judgments about success in child rearing in our culture and the process by which this is accomplished.

This traditional notion about parenting makes several assumptions about the process and the factors that influence someone's parenting style and behavior. Upon more careful study and observation, behavioral and social scientists have discovered that this traditional idea about parenting and what occurs as a result in children is too simplistic and imprecise for several reasons (Ambert, 1992). First, it does not realistically address the changes that take place as both child and parent experience growth and development over time. Second, it does not recognize the complexity of interactions over a long period of time between these individuals as they experience dynamic interchanges. Third, it disregards a child's contribution to and impact on the exchange of information or the behavior and conduct of an adult as a parent. Fourth, it assumes that adults are solely responsible for the outcome of their parenting experiences as manifested in children's character, behavior, and competency upon attaining maturity. In reality, although parents have a strong and vital influence on children's development, other factors also play a part, and effective parenting cannot be judged strictly in this manner. The *bidirectional model* is suggested in Chapter 1 as a more accurate depiction of parent-child relations. This model portrays the give-and-take flow of information and influence between parents and children; each person has an influence and impact on the behavior of the other.

This chapter introduces several theoretical explanations that describe the bidirectional nature of the process involved in parenting children. These explanations describe the parenting process more realistically and provide a basis for understanding how the relationship between parents and children takes place, which factors influence how it functions, how it changes over time, and how child rearing in each family system is a unique statement of personal and family philosophy. These explanations help to describe how adults shape the nature of their parenting behavior in relation to a variety of factors. The parent-child relationship is seen as a means of providing a primary opportunity for the psychosocial development of both children and adults, especially the adults. Parents are assisted in their growth and development as adults by parenting children while children are socialized into adulthood by parents. Although the theories presented in this chapter do not directly address issues in parent-child relations, it is possible to describe how the theories and their concepts may be applied to understanding this relationship.

This chapter also describes the family as a social system and the relationship between parents and children as a subsystem within this system. From this view, the parent-child relationship mirrors the larger family process. More specifically, using this perspective on family systems, it is possible to describe how the developmental changes being experienced by all members, typically two generations or more, affect the specific individuals involved as well as all other members of the system.

FAMILY SYSTEMS THEORY

The discussion in Chapter 2 of the diversity found among contemporary American families stressed the notion that a family is a social system characterized by certain features and traits. Despite the myriad nature of forms to be found among contemporary American families, each family operates according to certain rules that govern how it performs and functions in meeting goals, making decisions, and resolving conflicts between its members.

Behavioral scientists who study families have devised various methods to describe these groups and the ways they function. For example, one of the first theoretical approaches explaining family functioning was derived from sociological thought known as *structural functionalism*. This explanation of family functioning focused on the social roles of family members and addressed the manner in which the family (as seen via the roles of its members) became integrated with other social institutions such as schools, churches, and business and service organizations (Lamanna & Reidman, 2006).

The approach that will be used extensively in this text to explain family functioning, and especially that between parents and children, employs the concepts of **general systems theory.** This theoretical approach has been applied largely in the physical sciences to explain the complex workings of naturally occurring systems such as biological ecological systems and the solar system (von Bertalanffy, 1968, 1974). As applied to humans, families are described as operating in ways that are similar to those of other systems observed in nature. This way of looking at family functioning describes the operation of a family as a social system (Becvar & Becvar, 1998; Broderick, 1993). Systems theory is useful in explaining the complex interactions of a family and the factors that influence the processes by which a family makes decisions, sets and achieves particular goals, and establishes rules that regulate behavior, for example. The model provided by systems theory describes how these processes govern daily interactions and work to maintain stability of the family group over time. The theory also explains how a family responds to change, both developmental changes in family members and external changes that challenge its ability to function effectively as a group.

Several subsystems exist as part of a family group. For example, the relationships between parents and children, between two adult marriage partners, and between siblings are recognized as subsystems that reflect the patterns observed in the larger family system. The concepts and processes that describe the functioning of a family system also describe how these smaller subsystems function.

To understand how families operate according to **family systems theory,** let's consider some basic concepts in the following sections.

Wholeness

A family is not simply a group of individuals who operate or behave independently of one another. Rather, a family operates on the principle of **wholeness.** The family group must be considered in its entirety to understand how it works. It is not possible to do so by studying only one person from the group. In other words, a family is seen as being greater than the sum of its parts.

Interdependence

Interdependence, which is related to the principle of wholeness, means that anything that affects one person in a family also affects every other person in the family to some degree. A mobile is a good way to illustrate this concept of family systems theory (see Figure 3–1). All parts of a mobile are connected, so when one part is moved abruptly, other parts are affected and respond accordingly, although to a lesser degree (Satir, 1972a, 1972b). The parts of the mobile represent different family members and the wires connecting each piece of the mobile represent the different relationships found in a family system. Thus, the mobile illustrates the interdependence of family members.

When one person in a family system experiences some type of change, such as becoming seriously ill, leaving the family, or receiving a job promotion, everyone in the system is affected to some degree by the change. Whether the change is good or bad, beneficial or detrimental, all members of a family system react and attempt to compensate for the imbalance caused by a change that directly affects just one member. The

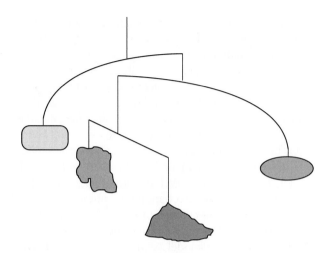

FIGURE 3–1. A mobile graphically illustrates the concepts of wholeness and interdependence in family systems theory. If one part of the mobile is moved, all other parts react by also moving, although to a lesser degree.

objective is to return to the state of balance, called *homeostasis*, that existed prior to the change that caused the imbalance.

Patterns

Within a family system, **patterns** evolve that serve to regulate the behavior of members and allow members to anticipate one another's behavior. These patterns are unique to each family system, although some patterns follow general guidelines that are common to all family systems. The patterns that usually can be found in most family systems include rules, roles, and communication styles.

Rules. A family system usually develops **rules** to govern members' behavior. Rules provide common ground for understanding which behaviors are acceptable and appropriate within each family system. In turn, the consistent application of rules helps to maintain the stability of a family system over time in general and especially in times of uncertainty or crisis. Rules govern the behavior of both adults and children in families. To be effective, rules also outline the consequences that occur when they are obeyed and disobeyed.

Each family system evolves its own rules, usually through negotiations of the adults. In many instances, the rules that become established in a family system have their roots in the adults' families of origin.

Rules can be explicit or implicit. **Explicit rules** are known, stated, and outlined clearly so that all people in the family know and understand them. Because these rules are clear to all, family members can discuss them and change them if they prove ineffective. **Implicit rules** are unspoken and are often inferred from nonverbal behavior. Explicit rules are often stated verbally, especially when transgressions occur ("You know the rule is that you must be home by 10."). Implicit rules are not usually discussed openly or otherwise acknowledged by family members, yet everyone is expected to know and obey them. For example, some family systems do not allow the expression of anger. In such families, everyone is expected to be pleasant and not to engage in open conflict with one another. When conflict is imminent, one person leaves or is told, "Don't be so silly. You're acting childish." It is difficult to discuss such rules and to change them when necessary, since they are not readily acknowledged by family members despite their strong influence on behavior. Generally, healthy family systems operate with an abundance of explicit rules and few implicit rules, while those that are unhealthy have a greater number of implicit rules (J. I. Clarke & Dawson, 1998; Richardson, 1999).

In addition to these types of rules, most family systems develop and exercise a set of rules that are considered to be **negotiable** as well as a set that are **nonnegotiable**. In the first instance, parents practice and allow flexibility in the enforcement of a particular group of rules, and children may contest these rules as well. For example, a family rule that may be negotiable relates to coming to dinner when called. A nonnegotiable rule might be requiring children to always inform parents of their whereabouts when away from home. Interesting, rules that may be negotiable in some family systems are nonnegotiable in others. Each family generates these rules initially based on those that the parents experienced as children. As time goes on and children grow older and become more mature, rules may change from being nonnegotiable (to protect younger children) to being negotiable to reflect children's increasing abilities to become more responsible for their own decisions.

Roles.   Roles are also used in family systems to outline acceptable behavior and to regulate the system's functioning. Roles generally have associated rules that estab-

lish appropriate behavior of the person who occupies that particular role. For example, a family system may be expected to evolve rules that describe and outline the role of the mother. The mother's behavior is regulated by rules that reflect family members' beliefs about how a mother should act. For example, to be a good mother, she should attend all school-related functions of her children, maintain a clean and orderly home, be employed outside the home, and so on. Rules that describe the child's role might be that the person should be a willing learner, should be able to perform some family tasks, but not as efficiently as an adult, and so on. The rules, or shoulds, provide the script enacted by the person filling a particular role in a family system.

Unhealthy families often evolve implicit roles that are largely governed by implicit rules. Because such families often cannot or do not know how to cope with stresses effectively or in healthy ways, one family member may assume—either willingly or unknowingly—a special role in which he or she acts out the stress on behalf of the family member under stress or for a particularly dysfunctional member (Becvar & Becvar, 1998). For example, a child may act as the family scapegoat by becoming depressed emotionally or acting out delinquently as a means of expressing stress in the parents' unhealthy marriage. In this instance, the child's role reflects an unhealthy implicit rule prohibiting or regulating the expression of conflict between the married spouses. In a different family system, a child's implicit role may be the "best little boy." In this system, the role carries a heavy expectation of perfectionism in the child's behavior. This child acts out the script of an implicit rule that states, "We are better than other families. We are special and are expected to achieve things that others only dream of."

Communication Styles.   Communication styles relate strongly to the nature of relationships within a family system. Three basic styles are found in most families: verbal, nonverbal, and contextual (Becvar & Becvar, 1998). **Verbal communications** relate to the words used to convey information between people in the family system. Taken at face value, verbal communication is essentially meaningless. For example, the message "It's cold outside today" simply provides descriptive information to the listener by the sender.

Nonverbal communications that accompany a verbal message include tone of voice, facial expressions, body posture, and hand gestures. The purpose of the nonverbal message is to inform the receiver about what to do with the verbal message. It hints at the intent of the message and often contains an implicit command or request. For example, the message "It's cold outside today," from a mother to her daughter, may contain nonverbal elements that communicate an implicit message such as, "Wear a sweater today." Hence, nonverbal communications relate to the way a relationship is outlined or defined.

Contextual communication is allied closely with nonverbal communication, and usually the two are considered together. The context often refers to where and under what circumstances the verbal and nonverbal communications occur. If a mother says "It's cold outside today" before the daughter dresses for school, the message has an entirely different meaning than if it occurred as the two were leaving the house.

Communication styles are unique to each family system, especially the contextual and nonverbal aspects of information exchange between members. These styles emerge as each family system evolves and develops its own meanings to communications. The more frequently members interact and exchange information with each other and the outside world, the more flexible and receptive to change the system becomes. This flexibility occurs in ways that act to stabilize rather than disrupt healthy, effective functioning.

Reciprocal Interaction and Feedback

Systems theory does not support a cause-and-effect process of interaction between members of families or between family systems. Rather, causality is seen as a **reciprocal interaction** between people and systems (Becvar & Becvar, 1998). For example, a cause-and-effect pattern is implied in a child asserting, "I behave as a child because you treat me as a child," and the parent responding, "I treat you as a child because you behave as a child." Taken from a family systems perspective, this assertion would be reframed as, "This has become a never-ending cycle: I act as a child because you treat me as a child, which makes me act in even more childish ways, which makes you continue to treat me as a child." Essentially, systems theory stresses that people in relationships or subsystems and in a family system as a whole influence one another's actions and behavior (see Figure 3–2). Behavioral interactions become intertwined as one person reacts to another, setting up a chain of interactional sequences. One person's

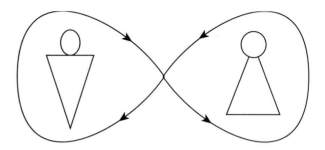

FIGURE 3–2.   Interactions between people in subsystems in families involve reciprocity and feedback. People react to one another's actions and communications; behavior serves as both stimulus and feedback in interactions.

action serves as a stimulus that elicits a reaction or response from another; this reaction, in turn, acts as a stimulus that elicits a different reaction or response from the other; and the cycle continues. Behavior serves as both *stimulus* and *feedback* to maintain reciprocal interaction between people in a relationship or subsystem.

Boundaries

Boundaries serve to establish limits that distinguish a family system from all others and differentiate between the people who are members of a particular family system (Knowles, 1997; Minuchin, 1974; Wood & Talmon, 1983). These abstract, psychological dividers are based on implicit as well as explicit rules that also outline who participates in a particular subsystem and the role that they have in that subsystem.

Boundaries assist in keeping subsystems distinct from one another as well, since a family member can be a participant in several of these within a family system (Orthner, Bowen, & Beare, 1990). In this regard, boundaries help prevent overlap between subsystems. For example, when conflicts occur within one subsystem, boundaries help prevent the conflict from overlapping into other subsystems in which family members participate. When the adults experience disagreements related to their committed relationship, boundaries help them keep the dispute from affecting the relationship with their children.

Boundaries act to regulate the degree of closeness or intimacy permissible according to a particular family system with other families and between the members of that system (Goodrich, 1990). In this respect, the

Open family system   Closed family system

FIGURE 3–3.   Families may be either open or closed systems based on the type of boundaries used to regulate interaction and information exchanges within the system and with others in the environment. Those that are open have flexible boundaries while those that are closed have rigid boundaries. Boundaries also define roles and relationships within a family system.

boundaries maintained between people and family systems assist in regulating information exchange, communication, identities, and behavior. Although boundaries can be changed and may vary by situation, families typically either have flexible boundaries, resulting in an open family system, or rigid boundaries, resulting in a closed system (see Figure 3–3). Likewise, the boundaries that delineate the different subsystems within a family system usually are closed as well. For example, healthy family systems maintain closed boundaries for the married adult couple relationship that do not allow for the participation of children in this relationship.

Family systems theory describes an *open* family as one with flexible boundaries that permit the easy flow and exchange of information and interaction between other families and individuals. When this is the case, the family system is open to input or new data from outside the system and is receptive to change. Essentially, healthy families operate as an open system. Some families, however, operate as a *closed* system; the boundaries serve to maintain the status quo of the group rather than allow external input to bring about positive changes within the system. Change is resisted rather than accepted as healthy (von Bertalanffy, 1974). When this is the case, family systems theory predicts that personal boundaries between family members in a closed system will become fused, or *enmeshed* (Minuchin, 1974). For example, children are not encouraged to differentiate themselves as individuals as part of their normal devel-

opmental process in growing toward maturity. Rather, implicit rules promote prolonged emotional attachment between family members and blurring of personal boundaries to maintain dependency between family members (Bowen, 1978).

In healthy family systems, boundaries are valued for helping to differentiate one person from the other, even though a high level of intimacy is permitted. In such families, boundaries highlight individual differences without eliciting high degrees of anxiety among other members. Personal differences are viewed positively as another means by which the family system is enriched by behavioral, philosophical, and emotional variety among its members. In these families, the implicit rules that serve as the foundation for personal boundaries promote the balance between individuation and intimacy among family members. Some unhealthy family systems, however, view differences in members as threatening the welfare and effective functioning of the family system. Such families demand lesser degrees of individuation and maintain less rigid personal boundaries that differentiate each member (Richardson, 1999). These families foster an expectation of similarity among members rather than distinct differences. They support the strong belief that everyone must hold the same beliefs, philosophies, opinions, and attitudes. Rules in these families are exceptionally strict and serve to promote the idea of sameness and maintain weak or diffuse personal boundaries between members.

Entropy

Although a family system maintains separateness from other family systems, the degree of closure is never thought to be complete (von Bertalanffy, 1968). There will always be some exchange of information between systems. **Entropy** is disorder or chaos in system functioning that results from lack of input or information from outside the system as a means of resolving a crisis or problem. A family may react to the presence of entropy in two basic ways. Positive actions involve movement of a system away from disorder and chaos by accepting and using information and energy from outside itself, such as from other family systems. Negative actions occur when movements of the system enhance the level of entropy to even greater chaos or disruption. Such actions by the system may entail dedicated efforts to maintain the status quo, refusing to allow the exchange of information between the family and other environmental systems or using denial to resist acknowledging that some problem or crisis exists.

In family systems with more open and flexible boundaries, energy and information input is accepted and used to maximize group functioning. For example, some energy in such a family system is directed toward organization and some is directed toward performing family tasks. By accepting and using information about how other family systems solve certain problems, open systems work effectively to achieve healthy solutions to their problems. In family systems that are rigidly closed, little new energy or information is allowed. This tends to promote greater family disorganization and greater expenditure of energy in random and inefficient ways. The continued maintenance of rigid boundaries enhances higher levels of entropy in such families (Becvar & Becvar, 1998).

Equifinality

All subsystems have goals that substantiate the reason for their existence. Likewise, all family systems develop goals that influence functioning and behavior. The concept of **equifinality** holds that families share common goals but reach these goals in different ways. For example, the ultimate goal of the parent-child subsystem is likely to be to raise children to become effectively functioning adults. All parent-child relationships may have this goal as the primary endeavor. However, different family systems in society accomplish this goal in diverse ways. The concept of equifinality significantly differentiates family systems theory from a unidirectional model of cause and effect.

Adaptation

A family system is challenged by both internal and external events and processes to restructure patterns to accommodate these changes. Change is a constant threat to effective functioning of a family system, because nothing is ever completely stable for families over the long term. All persons within the family system experience constant developmental changes over time. If the system is to continue to function effectively, patterns must be readjusted periodically upon discovering that they are not working properly. For example, rules developed at the beginning of a couple's parenting career may reflect a lack of experience with children more than knowledge of an infant's developmental abilities. After gaining experience, the parents' rules are **adapted,** or changed, to permit a more realistic

experience in nurturing an infant. By rigidly maintaining rules that clearly don't work to everyone's benefit, a family system risks becoming unhealthy by virtue of its inability to function adequately.

Homeostasis

The ultimate goal of family system functioning is to maintain stability, or **homeostasis,** over time. This is also known as *dynamic equilibrium.* There may seem to be a fundamental contradiction between a family system's needs for adaptation and stability. To address this seeming contradiction, two other terms are often used to illustrate the more fundamental need for stability over time. *Morphogenesis* describes the tendency of a family system to respond to variables that cause change by experiencing growth, change, innovation, and creativity and adapting its structure and patterns accordingly (Hoffman, 1973). *Morphostasis* describes the desire of a family system to remain stable over time by attempting to retain its organization, structure, and patterns. To understand these concepts, it may be helpful to visualize them as residing at opposite ends of a continuum and to view homeostasis as an attempt to achieve dynamic equilibrium between them. Healthy family systems seek continually to maintain homeostasis between the dynamic factors of change and stability. The rules of such systems allow changes in patterns, rules, and boundaries to accommodate changing situations and conditions.

During times of stress, morphogenesis is thought to be more desirable than morphostasis in allowing a system to work out means that will ensure its continued existence and functioning. However, too many and too frequent experiences in morphogenesis call for greater and more extended efforts to maintain morphostasis.

Application to Parent-Child Relations

Family systems theory has direct application to parent-child relations in several ways. First, it depicts this relationship as one of several that occur as subsystems within a family. Other relationships or subsystems include the marriage or committed relationship between adults, the relationship between siblings, the relationship within the extended family (e.g., grandparent-grandchild), and the various relationships between the family, other families, and other agencies and institutions with whom members interact (e.g., schools, churches, neighbors, and so on).

All subsystems within a family reflect the workings and configuration found in the larger group. For example, there are explicit rules, similar in nature to others found in the larger family system, that become established to guide parental behavior and that of children. These rules allow everyone to understand what is expected of each participant within their particular role and also allow predictability of behavior. Roles of both parents and children are outlined in this manner.

This relationship is affected by the variables just described. For example, what affects an adult will also affect children to some degree, and vice versa (interrelatedness). If a child develops a chronic illness, this condition alters the relationship with the parent as well as with other family members. If divorce takes place between the adults, then we can expect children to experience related effects of this event. Likewise, we cannot completely understand the nature of parent-child relations in a family just by studying a child or an adult alone (wholeness).

Boundaries also outline what are acceptable and unacceptable behaviors within this relationship. Our culture specifically prohibits sexual activity between parents and children as totally inappropriate and unhealthy for all parties. We tend, as a culture, to separate the worlds of children from that of adults. In other words, we believe that children should not become involved in the affairs of their parents and other adults in their family.

Adaptation and reciprocal interaction may be observed within this relationship as communication styles, roles, and rules are changed in accordance with the changing developmental abilities and stages of the children involved. For example, parents may have many more nonnegotiable rules in place when children are young than when they become older adolescents and young adults. Parents usually change rules when it is discovered that they are no longer effective in achieving the desired results in children's behavior. All the while, parents are often monitoring a variety of issues that are intended to maintain family homeostasis and making adaptations when necessary.

Equifinality is observed when parents learn that there are a number of equally acceptable ways and strategies to raise children into adulthood. Not everyone will agree on particular approaches as preferable, but there becomes an understanding that there is no recipe or absolute approach that can be applied in parent-child relations.

When parents seek advice, assistance, and information from outside their family system to strengthen their situations or to help with problem solving, they are actively working to avoid entropy from occurring. By showing a willingness to have an open family system in problem solving, parents demonstrate a desire to avoid maintaining the status quo as well as denial that a problem exists that needs correction. In this way, stability is promoted while chaos and disruption are avoided.

This theory as well as the next that is discussed will be highlighted in many of the chapters that follow in this text.

●●●●●●●●●●●●●●●●●●●●●●●●●●●●●●●●●●●

Parenting Reflection 3–1

What are some advantages and disadvantages of using family systems theory to explain family functioning? Could this theory have application in family therapy? How? Could this theory have application in other social situations, for example, work environments, committee participation, sports, church groups, and so on?

●●●●●●●●●●●●●●●●●●●●●●●●●●●●●●●●●●●

●●●●●●●●●●●●●●●●●●●●●●●●●●●●●●●●●●●

Focus Point. Family systems theory explains the complex interactions of a family group. It addresses the factors that influence the manner in which the group makes decisions, sets and achieves goals, and establishes patterns that govern members' behavior. It explains how these processes work to maintain the group's stability over time. Concepts central to this theory include wholeness, interdependence, patterns (rules, roles, and communication styles), reciprocal interaction and feedback, boundaries, entropy, equifinality, adaptation, and homeostasis (morphogenesis and morphostasis). The relationship between parents and children is one of several subsystems that make up a family system.

●●●●●●●●●●●●●●●●●●●●●●●●●●●●●●●●●●●

SYSTEMIC FAMILY DEVELOPMENT THEORY

Many years ago, pioneer sociologist Ernest Burgess (1926) described the family as a "unity of interacting personalities." Unity in this context alludes to the concepts of wholeness and interdependence used today in family systems theory. The reference to interacting personalities denotes Burgess's observation that interaction among family members serves a vital purpose in the functioning of a family system by promoting the psychological welfare of each family member.

A family system provides an expressive function for members. This means that each member has the opportunity for being nurtured and assisted as a developing individual by others and thus is provided with the means for realizing his or her emotional needs. The idea of unity among interacting personalities implies that a family is a dynamic system that responds to changes taking place in members and to those that come from external sources and impinge on its functioning. The inescapable reality implied in this description is echoed in the concepts of homeostasis and adaptation from family systems theory. These concepts hold that family members are dynamic, developmentally changing individuals, and hence a family system also must change over time in response.

Just as individuals follow predictable stages in their personal development, families likewise experience stages that follow a predictable course (O'Rand & Krecker, 1990). The progression of stages a family follows from its establishment to its demise (Aldous, 1978; Duvall, 1988; Duvall & Miller, 1985; Mattessich & Hill, 1987) has been labeled the **family life cycle,** although this is a misleading notion in some respects. The term *cycle* connotes an alternating repetition of some factor or pattern. Because no readily identifiable repetitious patterns are commonly observed in all families, family studies experts disagree as to whether the changes that take place in a family system over time can be appropriately considered cyclical (Aldous 1978; Mattessich & Hill 1987).

The family life cycle model presents several other problems: (1) it was based on the notion that all families experience developmental changes in the same way and in predictable stages; (2) it excludes the diversity of family structures found in contemporary American society (e.g., stepfamilies, gay and lesbian families); (3) it was first developed in the 1950s based on a white, middle-class family representation; (4) it assumes that ethnic minority families experience developmental changes in the same way that white families do; (5) it excludes families that are affected by poverty and homelessness; (6) it focuses on the notion of a progression of stages where there is only one generation in a family when in reality more than one generation is involved in family life; and (7) developmental progress is dependent on the increasing age of the first-born child through many of the stages, thus excluding those families that lack children, with the reality that many families do not include children at all.

A more realistic model that describes how families change in association with the passage of time is the **systemic family development theory** model (Laszloffy, 2002). This process-oriented model addresses the problems inherent in traditional family development theory. It uses concepts derived from family systems theory to challenge the principal assumptions of the older model: (1) all families develop in the same way; (2) there is a single generation focus at certain stages such as before children are produced and following their launching into adulthood; and (3) all families include children. Instead, the systemic model promotes the notions that families are both similar and diverse and that the concepts of wholeness and interrelatedness are strong characteristics of the complexity found in their intergenerational composition.

Common Developmental Process in Families

All families share a common process of developmental change over time, but how this occurs in a particular family varies widely. The common developmental process shared by all families according to the systemic development model is the experience of **stressors** at various times in their existence (Laszloffy, 2002). Stressors are those phenomena that force a family system to adapt, resulting in what is referred to as a **transition** (see Focus On 3–1). The transition typically produces changes in family roles and relationships.

Most transitions relieve the pressure that comes from the stressor. However, sometimes a family finds this to be a difficult task and cannot make a successful adaptation or transition. When this occurs, the group finds itself experiencing a **snag point,** or general inflexibility in the face of the pressure to make changes (Pittman, 1987). This is likely to prevent a family from using resources to cope with the stressor and the associated stress increases accordingly. The end result of the snag point is a **family crisis,** which keeps the group from progressing and making necessary adaptations to dismantle their dilemma (Joselevich, 1988).

The experience of a single stressor event usually can be dealt with by making appropriate changes or using helpful resources to reduce the stress associated with the event. For example, the birth of a child is stressful in the sense that the routine in the home is altered (e.g., adult sleep patterns are disturbed by the need to feed and care for the baby) and financial resources are strained. People make changes in their roles and routines to adapt to the

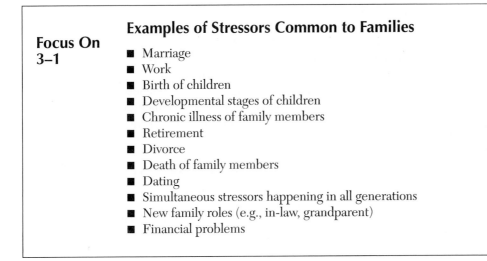

Focus On 3–1

Examples of Stressors Common to Families

- Marriage
- Work
- Birth of children
- Developmental stages of children
- Chronic illness of family members
- Retirement
- Divorce
- Death of family members
- Dating
- Simultaneous stressors happening in all generations
- New family roles (e.g., in-law, grandparent)
- Financial problems

needs of the new baby. Stressors do not become problematic unless several occur simultaneously or within a short time. When this happens, the snag point emerges because of the accumulation of higher levels of stress from each of the events.

As stress continues to pile up in the family, a crisis emerges that prevents the family from adapting and making appropriate changes. For example, suppose a family has experienced a new birth, the oldest child has begun school for the first time, and the father loses his job, all within a 2-week period. This is enough to produce a family crisis since the group is incapacitated by the cumulative stress occurring from these events within a short time and is unable to cope successfully. Taken individually and spread out over a longer period of time, the stressor events might be managed more successfully. What may help a family to avoid chaos is to use effective stress management skills or to locate and use resources that will allow the group to cope ffectively with the stressors. In this way, the family may prevent the crisis or at least head off devastating effects (Boss, 1988).

Family Systems Are Complex and Multigenerational

The systemic family developmental model also emphasizes the notion that families must be taken as a whole at any point in developmental time to understand how they function, change, and adapt. This notion comes from the concepts of wholeness and interrelatedness found in family systems theory. Unlike the stages proposed in the family life cycle model, the systemic model assumes that it is not possible to reduce a family system to only one generation at any point in developmental time. This notion also acknowledges the diversity of family structures, thereby avoiding a principal criticism of the family life cycle model.

A Metaphor

Laszloffy (2002) suggests the use of a metaphor to illustrate how the concepts of the systemic model are applied to understanding family development. She has chosen the depiction of a round layer cake as a representation of the life span of a family system (see Figure 3–4). The cake

FIGURE 3–4. A round layer cake serves as the metaphor for a family system in the systemic family development model.

Source: Laszloffy, T. A. (2002). Rethinking family development theory: Teaching with the systemic family development (SFD) model. *Family Relations, 51*, 206–214. Copyright 2002 by the National Council on Family Relations, 3989 Central Ave. NE, Suite 550, Minneapolis, MN 55421. Reprinted by permission.

represents the family boundaries or definition as well as the concept of wholeness. We view the cake in its totality just as we must view a family in its totality to understand it. The metaphor continues with comparing the individual ingredients of a cake recipe to individual family members. When mixed together and baked, the particular ingredients result in a particular type of cake; individuals form a family when brought together through the processes of marriage, birth, adoption, or choice. The different cake layers represent the different generations found in a family. The roundness of the cake represents the passage of developmental time during a family's life span. As the family metaphor revolves in a circular manner, old layers of the cake (older generations) are eliminated through death while new layers (younger generations) are being added. These changes represent a certain type of stressors commonly experienced by all families. By losing layers (generations) and adding new ones, the cake is required to make adjustments. If the cake cannot accommodate these changes, pressures increase that distort the cake. If the cake continues to be unable to adapt, the pressures increase to the point of a crisis that might cause the cake to collapse. And so it is with families.

To perceive what may be occurring developmentally in a family, we would observe the entire group for a short time. In the metaphor, we would cut a slice from the cake. What would be revealed in observing a "slice" of family life are the particular stressors being experienced by each generation (see Figure 3–5). By examining and studying the slice of the family's place in developmental time, we can determine how the family needs to adjust to the pressures produced by the stressors each generation is experiencing. Those adjustments allow the family to cope with a crisis. Family members can realign their roles, patterns, and boundaries accordingly to reestablish the degree of homeostasis that existed before the crisis or to achieve a higher degree of cohesion and balance.

Parenting Reflection 3–2

How can families locate resources to help them learn to cope with stressors before they occur? Does advance knowledge about something truly help to prepare people to react appropriately? Or does this information make people fret more?

Focus Point. Systemic family development theory makes allowances in understanding how families are highly complex and diverse. By examining a family at a particular point in developmental time, it is possible to see that families share common stressors that challenge each generation involved. This model has significant practical application in working with all families.

1st Generation: Recent death
2nd Generation: Recent divorce; retirement
3rd Generation: Couple marries at midlife for the first time; preparing for son's departure for college
4th Generation: A young adult prepares to leave home for college

FIGURE 3–5. A slice taken from the metaphorical layer cake represents a snapshot in developmental time of a family system. Stressors affecting each generation of a family (represented by each layer of the cake) and the effects of these on members of each generation may then be examined.

Source: Laszloffy, T. A. (2002). Rethinking family development theory: Teaching with the systemic family development (SFD) model. *Family Relations, 51,* 206–214. Copyright 2002 by the National Council on Family Relations, 3989 Central Ave. NE, Suite 550, Minneapolis, MN 55421. Reprinted by permission.

Focus On 3–2

Application to Parent-Child Relations: A Case Study or Snapshot

The systemic family development model can be illustrated by studying a hypothetical family periodically over three periods of developmental time (after Laszloffy, 2002). In this case, we will examine what is occurring in the family's developmental progress at an arbitrarily chosen time and then, at intervals of 2 and 4 years later. We will note the stressors each generation is experiencing that call for transitions at each point in time.

Because this model recognizes diversity in family structures, this example is useful largely in illustrating how the various stressors affect individuals within each generation and across all generations. Thus, each slice of time serves as a **snapshot** of the family's functioning and options for reacting to the stressors.

Background

The Smith family is composed of six family members from three generations: Generation 1 comprises the grandparents, Hank and Joan; Generation 2 is composed of their only child, Mark, Sr., and his wife, Karen; and Generation 3 comprises the young couple's children, Mark, Jr., and Jessica. The Smiths have lived in a Midwestern state for the past 150 years, owning the same property, which has been handed down from generation to generation. Additional homes were built on the property as needed.

Slice 1

This slice is taken at a point in developmental time when a stressor is being experienced directly by two generations. Having a child marry and leave the family of origin to begin his own family is being experienced by both adults in Generation 2 and by the children in Generation 3. Mark, Jr. (age 18), is to be married. His leaving the family of origin eases the tension between himself and his little sister, Jessica (age 15). However, this is affecting his parents (Mark, Sr., age 43, and Karen, age 40) as they are becoming less involved in his life. They must now renegotiate their relationship with their son and his wife-to-be and take on roles they have never had before: being in-laws. Mark, Jr., now will assume a new family role of spouse. With the new marriage come new responsibilities and adjustments. He and Lisa, his new wife, must negotiate how to define their spousal roles, how work will be accomplished in the new home, and how to define the boundaries for their new family. The parents in Generation 2 face another stressor: They must find a way to revitalize their marriage relationship since they focused intensely on their parenting responsibilities. Now that these responsibilities will be diminished, they will not have to direct as much energy and attention away from their marital relationship. Generation 1 is not exempt from this impending change in the family system. The grandparents (Hank, age 60, and Joan, age 58) must redefine their family roles as grandparents as they accept a new family member. All family members must devise shifts in their roles, patterns, and boundaries to adapt to the stressor of a child's and grandchild's impending marriage.

Slice 2 (2 years later)

Mark, Jr., is now 20 and has just become a father. He and his wife now have their own quarters on the family property in the form of a manufactured home they have recently acquired. They have more financial responsibilities than ever before, and the routine that was established in the marriage and in the home requires adjustments to accommodate the presence of a new baby. The birth of a child acts as the stressor in this case. And we now have a fourth generation in the Smith family. Mark's sister, Jessica, is now 17 and facing the decision about whether to attend college or become a part of the family business. The adults in Generation 2 are now older. Mark, Sr., is 45 and Karen is 42. The baby's birth affects them as they must now assume new family roles as grandparents.

Mark, Sr., has additional pressures because he is in the depths of his midlife transition experience. He questions many things in this life, such as decisions made earlier, whether he is happy in his marriage, and whether he is happy with his work. This disturbing self-examination is acting as a trigger for Karen's

(continued)

Focus On 3–2

(continued)

own midlife transition experience. She also has been thinking deeply about her own life and how it has unfolded. She questions the same issues as her husband. This introspection occasionally surfaces in heated discussions between the two as they try to reach answers and solutions to serious questions. Divorce is always a possibility, as are life-changing choices to move to a different place of residence, a different job, a different lifestyle. Generation 1 participants now must also make adjustments to add the new role of great-grandparent and determine how they will fit in with the new great-grandchild and his family. The Smiths may be brought to a crisis if they are unable to adapt successfully to these tremendous stressors. The family's resources for coping with the severity of the stressors are their willingness to help one another, to discuss issues head-on and rationally, and to seek outside assistance if necessary (through therapy, for example).

Slice 3 (2 years later)

Mark, Jr., age 22, has again become a father with the birth of his second child. His wife, Lisa, is mindful of their need for additional income and is thinking about entering the workforce in their community as soon as possible. This child was born with a birth defect that requires additional family resources in time and money. The child's grandparents from Generation 2 (Mark, Sr., now age 47, and Karen, age 44) have weathered the more severe aspects of their midlife transition experiences and have become more attached and bonded as a couple because of a rededication to their marriage relationship. What spoils the totally positive outlook at this point is a strong economic downturn in the community, which has brought a financial stressor in the form of a potential bankruptcy to the couple. This has caused much concern for Jessica, now age 19, who is in her second year at the local community college. She is fearful that the financial conditions facing her parents will jeopardize the opportunity to continue her education at the state university. The participants of Generation 1—Hank, now age 64, and Joan, age 62—face their own particular stressor of Hank's retirement. This will necessitate making adjustments in roles, finances, and quality of life for these two family members. The multiple stressors taking place in this family at this point in developmental time are critical. The manner by which each stressor affects individuals within and across generations is noticeable. How each stressor is dealt with by each and all generations will determine the stability and cohesion of the family as a whole.

FAMILY ECOLOGY THEORY AND PARENTING

The **ecological theory** proposed by Bronfenbrenner (1979, 1986, 1993) extends our attention to the role of different environments and how these affect individual and family functioning as well as parent-child relations. Bronfenbrenner focuses on the role of five distinct but related environmental settings to explain how an individual and his or her family system are influenced in his or her development, how relationships function, and how interactions take place. A person is at the center of a set of environments (see Figure 3–6). From this standpoint, an individual is not a passive recipient of interactions with other people and other environments but is actively involved in direct interactions. The first environmental setting with which he or she interacts is that comprising the environments provided by family, peers, school, or neighborhood. This is known as the **microsystem.** The next environment is known as the **mesosystem,** which encompasses the microsystem. This system involves relations between the first and all other systems that affect the person. For example, the family has relationships and interactions with the school the child attends. The child's relationships at school, then, are influenced by what takes place in the family setting, and vice versa. If one or both parents have some type of addiction or substance-abuse problem, this will affect a child's interactions and relationships within the family setting and influence interactions and relationships within the child's school setting. Academic performance as well as social relationships and interactions with peers and teachers are

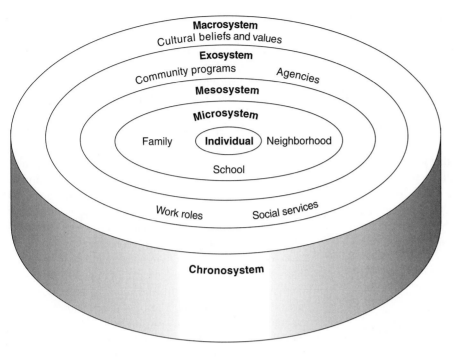

FIGURE 3–6.
Bronfenbrenner's ecological theory can be visualized as a composite of five distinct but related environmental settings that influence an individual directly and indirectly.

influenced by what happens in the child's family life and vice versa.

An **exosystem** also influences the individual. This setting may be visualized as encompassing the mesosystem (see Figure 3–6). The individual does not have an active role in this context but is influenced by it nevertheless. An exosystem may be government agencies, community programs, employment settings of parents, and so on. For example, the work responsibilities or assignments of one parent may change, requiring different and extraordinary work hours. When the parent begins to work longer hours or during the night rather than day shift, the parenting experiences of the child are affected accordingly. Another example would be how the quality of the child's life is affected by funding cutbacks to community recreation programs sponsored by local governmental agencies.

A **macrosystem** is an even larger context that affects an individual (see Figure 3–6). This environment involves the larger culture in which the individual lives and encompasses the exosystem and all others affecting the person. In this context, the person is affected by the broad, generalized beliefs, behavior patterns, and value systems deemed appropriate to be adopted by all members of a particular society. These influence how a person interacts with all other environmental settings.

The last environment is the **chronosystem,** which encompasses the entire network of other systems (see Figure 3–6). This context involves the organization of events and changes of an individual over his or her life span at a particular historical time. For example, we know that adults are influenced in their current behaviors and interactions by events and interactions that took place at earlier stages in their lives. In this regard, it is generally understood that if a person was abused as a child, the effects can last a lifetime. With therapeutic assistance, these effects can be minimized but perhaps not completely ameliorated and can continue to influence the person in various ways for years. Likewise, changes in cultural attitudes are reflected within the chronosystem to affect individuals at different historical times. Attitudes about gender roles in society are different today in many respects than what were held 100 years ago. Androgyny is more acceptable today in this context, for example, than a century ago.

Bronfenbrenner's ecological approach resembles some of the features found in family systems theory, especially with regard to the concepts of interdependence, reciprocal interaction and feedback, equifinality, and adaptation. His explanation adds another valuable dimension to understanding how individuals and families are affected by one another and the larger contexts in which they exist.

It is possible to view society as an immense collective of families. As such, what goes on in families is reflected in society and vice versa. A family system cannot function independently of the physical, social, economical, and psychological environments of which it is a part. The family ecology perspective outlined by Bronfenbrenner emphasizes the dual influence between families and societies locally and throughout the world. Essentially, what happens in one environmental aspect influences what occurs in others as well as in families that make up a society. Likewise, what occurs in families affects the various environments in which they live. The family ecology view leads to an examination of the ways that various sociocultural environments influence family form and functioning. The presence of a reciprocal feedback loop between families that make up society and the environments that impact them produce a dynamic model described by the family ecology perspective (Bubolz & Sontag, 1993).

Application to Parent-Child Relations

There is increasing alarm about the health of contemporary American families. Observers note the high incidence of family violence, child abuse, substance abuse, divorce, and other problems that disrupt family life. Some believe that the family is declining as an effectively functioning social institution. There is much discussion about basic issues relating to family life and values, including the conscious choice to become a parent, a couple's determination of when and how many children to produce, the possibility of changing careers several times in adulthood, and early retirement, for example. Family life may be different today because these kinds of choices were much less commonly observed in the past.

Some people attribute many of the social problems in contemporary America to recent changes in family structure and functioning. However, some family sociologists who have studied the issue speculate that these same changes indicate the family's ability to adapt to societal changes. They, therefore, regard these changes in family structure and functioning as healthy.

The success of family life is closely related to conditions found in the larger society. Families have changed today in size, structure, composition, and function as a response to changes taking place in the larger society. A significant portion of family life in the past was devoted to fulfilling cultural and socioeconomic functions, especially the reproduction of new members for society and the pro-

duction of necessary goods and services. Family functions today center on the expression and fulfillment of the needs of family members, especially their emotional and social needs, and on training children to become effective members of society upon reaching adulthood. In today's smaller families, members find that their interactions within the family group are intense and frequent. The survival and continuation of families may depend on how well each member's personal needs are met by the group.

Survival of the family as a social institution may also depend on how successful families are in responding to changes taking place in society. Parents today must deal with many new and difficult situations that are different from those encountered by families in the past. These include rapidly changing societal economic conditions, severe social pressures on children, restricted family size, the hazards of living in urban environments, and the need for both parents to work outside the home in occupations that are often highly stressful. Many families do not know how to react or adapt in healthy ways to these kinds of changes. Family life today is described as *asynchronous*; that is, family leaders (the adults) depend on personal past experiences to guide their current behavior and to prepare children for future functioning as adults. The problem is that there is little guarantee that the future will be anything like the past, especially if societal changes continue to occur as rapidly as they have over the last 50 years.

The ways that parenthood are defined, that child rearing is conducted, and that parent-child relations are valued will vary based on how family ecological factors are experienced differently by each family system. While almost every family system adheres to the central role expectations of parenthood, including an emphasis on nurturing, teaching, and caring for children, variations occur because of differences in the environments or culture in which each family lives. Because of such variations, it is impossible to speak of families using only one definition, one form, one structure, or one method of defining parenthood and childrearing methods.

••

Focus Point. Bronfenbrenner's ecological theory supplements some of the family systems theory concepts and explains how individuals and families are affected by a variety of interacting environments, and vice versa. An individual's family, by being part of the total environment, also is influenced by these other systems.

••

PSYCHOSOCIAL DEVELOPMENT THEORY AND PARENTING

Most modern developmental theories focus on the development of an individual child during the years between birth and the end of adolescence. Extensive abstract explanations have been formulated about how the interaction between heredity and environment influences individual development. To date, the years of childhood and adolescence have received the greatest attention. Few developmental theorists have attempted to explain or interpret what takes place in the years of adulthood and old age. The psychosocial theory of Erik Erikson (1950, 1964, 1982; Erikson, Erikson, & Kivnick, 1986) is a notable exception. Erikson's theory features developmental change as a process that continues throughout the life span between birth and death, not just during the growth years of infancy, childhood, and adolescence.

Each stage of the life span has its own developmental theme, which Erikson terms a **psychosocial crisis,** or a challenge to attain a healthy rather than unhealthy attitude or generalized feeling. Developmental change is enhanced or retarded by a person's experiences in confronting and handling each psychosocial crisis that occurs within each stage of the life span. The person must confront a central problem—a specific psychosocial crisis—at each life stage and is given the opportunity to develop strengths and skills leading toward a particular attitude that is healthy or unhealthy. Provided with a social and psychological environment that is conducive to developmental change, an individual faces each problem at that stage with the potential for healthy, normal accomplishment. If the person experiences overwhelming difficulty in accomplishing what is expected at one stage of the life span, the result will be difficulty in dealing with the psychosocial crises at future stages.

Developmental change, however, does not occur within a vacuum free of other influences and factors. The process is not structured so that a person is forced to face the challenges and trials of life alone. Developmental change usually occurs first within the context of a supportive family atmosphere, then within an increasingly wider social radius of friends, then within the school environment, and so on, as life progresses. **Significant others**—those who are singularly important to a person—assist or inhibit his or her developmental progress at each life stage. An individual proceeds to the next stage after meeting the particular requirements of biological, social, and psychological **readiness.** This readiness to progress further along one's developmental path is influenced significantly by others in one's social environment, especially by the parents in the case of a developing child.

The psychosocial crises at each stage of the life span present the individual with the challenge of acquiring what Erikson calls **psychosocial senses.** Psychosocial senses are attitudes or general feelings that result from how adequately a person can meet and master the crisis at a particular stage of psychosocial development.

Erikson describes eight stages of psychosocial change over the life span and labels each in terms of healthy or unhealthy psychosocial development. It is important to note that a person's mastery of a psychosocial attitude or sense is not an all-or-nothing matter, but is continually being weighed on a balance. It is possible to gain some measure of unhealthy, as well as healthy, feelings related to the psychosocial attitude associated with a particular life stage. In the balance of experiences, attitudes and feelings that promote healthy psychological development derive from attaining healthy experiences that outweigh those that are unhealthy (see Figure 3–7). In early childhood, for example, children are thought to experience a psychosocial stage during which they have opportunities to acquire the ability to function independently, or what Erikson calls a sense of autonomy. Positive experiences that lead children to conclude that they can function autonomously result in a healthy sense of autonomy. Negative experiences, if constituting the majority of a child's experiences or occurring with sufficient consistency and strength, lead the child to feel shame and doubt about his or her ability to function autonomously. The result is an unhealthy sense of shame and doubt. In Erikson's theory, at each of the eight stages, progress in development occurs when the healthy attitude in that stage is acquired, whereas future difficulty in psychosocial development will occur when the unhealthy attitude results from that stage.

Erikson uses a timetable to illustrate his eight stages of psychosocial development (see Table 3–1). Although the ages listed are flexible guidelines for the times at which people experience the stages, the first five occur during the growth years of infancy, childhood, and adolescence, and the remaining three occur during adulthood.

Application to Parent-Child Relations

Erikson does not specifically indicate in his theory how it might be applied to parent-child relations, but we may

FIGURE 3–7. Psychosocial development at any particular stage can be viewed as having a majority of experiences that promote one attitude (sense) or the other. Some unhealthy feelings inevitably occur at any particular stage. Healthy development results when healthy experiences outweigh those that are unhealthy.

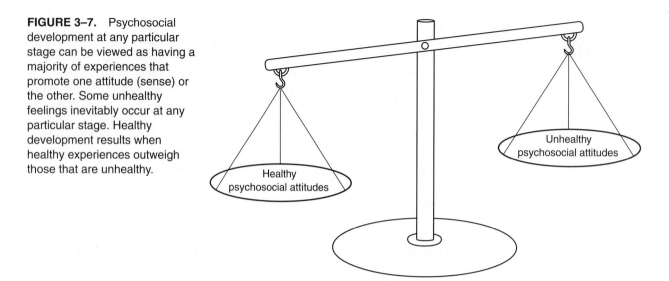

Healthy psychosocial attitudes

Unhealthy psychosocial attitudes

infer from his writings how this may be accomplished. His theory provides a basic framework for understanding the psychosocial changes experienced by an individual. A family system, however, is composed of several individuals of differing ages and developmental levels, each of whom is involved in resolving the challenges of his or her own particular psychosocial stage. The parents are at the stage of psychosocial development termed generativity versus self-absorption. If several children have been produced by a couple, they are likely to be at different developmental stages (see Figure 3–8). For example, the oldest child may be involved in accomplishing the tasks leading toward a sense of industry versus inferiority, the middle child may be addressing the tasks involving a sense of initiative versus guilt, and the youngest may be learning to accomplish the tasks of basic trust versus mistrust.

This intertwining or congruence of developmental stages being experienced by parents and children is referred to as **reciprocal interaction** in family systems theory. In the everyday interactions taking place between parents and children, each participant in this subsystem promotes the acquisition of the healthy psychosocial sense being experienced by the other. Providing appropriate parental caregiving assists the children in achieving the particular psychosocial attitude they are attempting to master at that particular developmental point in time. In turn, by providing a source for parents to provide caregiving, children assist their parents in mastering their sense of generativity.

It is also in this manner that parenting behavior becomes adapted or modified as children grow older. By passing through the various stages of psychosocial development, children's needs change and parenting styles must be adapted to meet these new needs. Using the concepts of reciprocal interaction and adaptation, homeostasis is achieved in parent-child relations when parenting behavior becomes congruent with meeting the needs of children at their different stages of growth and development. For example, a child who is striving for autonomy during the latter part of infancy prompts entirely different patterns of caregiving from parents than were called for when the child was focused on developing a sense of trust. The course of parent-child relations proceeds according to these interactional sequences: The child assists or inhibits the parents in their development of a sense of generativity, as the parents assist or inhibit the child in meeting the challenges of each developmental stage. Like the larger family system of which it is a part, the parent-child subsystem must adapt to changes in the individual participants to maintain stability and effective functioning.

Parenting Reflection 3–3

What are some ways at each stage of Erikson's theory that inappropriate and ineffective caregiving by parents could impede a child's psychosocial development and encourage their acquiring the unhealthy attitude?

TABLE 3–1. Erikson's Timetable of Developmental Stages

Stage	Psychosocial Crisis	Radius of Significant Others	Theme	Ages
I.	Trust vs. Mistrust	Maternal person	To get; to give in return	Birth to 18 months
II.	Autonomy vs. Shame/Doubt	Paternal person	To hold on; to let go	18 months to 3 years
III.	Initiative vs. Guilt	Family	To make; to make like	3 to 6 years
IV.	Industry vs. Inferiority	School; Neighborhood	To make things; to make together	6 to 12 years
V.	Identity vs. Role Confusion	Peer groups	To be oneself; to share being oneself	12 to 18 years
VI.	Intimacy vs. Isolation	Partners in friendship, sex, competition	To lose and find oneself in another	18 to 24 years
VII.	Generativity vs. Self-absorption	Partner	To make be; to take care of	24 to 54 years
VIII.	Integrity vs. Despair	Mankind	To be through having been; to face not being	54 years to death

Source: Adapted from E. H. Erikson. (1959). Identity and the life cycle: Selected papers. *Psychological Issues 1(1).*

FIGURE 3–8. Parents play an important role in facilitating children's psychosocial development and vice versa.

....

Focus Point. Erik Erikson's framework for explaining the process of psychosocial development over the life span provides another means for interpreting the relationship between parents and children. The framework focuses on developmental changes in individuals that occur in association with the passage of time. These changes are couched within the context of the social environments individuals experience throughout their life span. Parent-child relations change in response to the concept of reciprocal interaction.

....

OTHER RELATED THEORIES AND PARENTING

Learning Theory

Learning theory encompasses several different explanations of how individual behavior is modified or changed as a result of experiences and interactions with factors external to the person. These explanations discussed here include: (a) operant conditioning or behavior modification (B. F. Skinner, 1938); and (b) social learning theory (Bandura, 1977) as each relates to parent-child relations.

Operant conditioning, or **behavior modification,** is one of the most powerful tools that parents can

use to shape children's behavior. In brief, this approach (which is discussed in greater detail in Chapter 4) emphasizes the role of rewards or reinforcers that are associated with particular acts. If a parent wishes to teach a child a new skill or help him or her acquire a new type of behavior, then a reward of some type would be given immediately following the child's action or behavior. Positive rewards have been shown repeatedly in investigations to be very powerful in changing a child's behavior or in teaching new skills. Positive rewards in this regard may be social in nature such as a hug, smile, or praise, for example, "I'm very proud of you for doing that!"

Social learning theory explains how learning may occur when there is no visible reinforcer or reward. This theory is especially useful in explaining how socialization occurs or how someone learns appropriate behaviors based on family beliefs and values. According to this theory, an individual responds to a number of complex stimuli in forming associations between appropriate and inappropriate behavior. Conscious thought, rather than automatic response to a stimulus, assists in shaping behavior and actions.

This approach focuses on the importance of the role of a ***model*** or the effect of observation learning also known as imitation. Many kinds of behaviors are believed to be acquired by watching the behavior of another person and then replicating the observed behavior in one's own actions.

Research into this type of learning shows how children learn to express such social behaviors as sharing and cooperation as well as aggression and violence by watching such behaviors demonstrated by a model. Models include both real people and characters seen in media presentations. Research reveals that when children see a model being rewarded for acting aggressively, for instance, they are more likely to demonstrate that same kind of behavior in their own play.

Social learning theory also explains how people acquire social values and attitudes. Social roles also are learned in this manner. Children imitate behaviors they observe in adults and in other children they perceive as models. For example, social learning accounts for how sex-role behaviors or scripts are acquired in childhood.

Cognitive Theory

Several theoretical approaches explain how people acquire their thought processes and problem-solving abilities as well as organize and use information. One of the more useful in application to parent-child relations is that proposed by Jean Piaget. His writings (Piaget, 1967; Piaget & Inhelder, 1969) on this topic were based initially on observations of his own children.

Several concepts are central to Piaget's thoughts about the development of intellect. **Cognition** and **cognitive development** are terms that refer to the way in which humans come to know and understand the world or environments in which they live. A variety of related processes—perception, problem solving, judgment, and reasoning, for example—are involved in how people organize their mental life. Cognitive development also refers to the changes that take place as people acquire a general understanding of their environments.

Cognition is based on the acquisition of **schemes**. This refers to a consistent, reliable pattern or plan of interaction with the environment. Schemes are usually goal-oriented strategies that help a person to achieve some type of intended result from his or her behavior. For example, a rudimentary scheme is built or acquired that serves to guide a child's behavior in picking up an object that draws his or her curiosity or attention to explore by touch, sight, and even taste. This scheme acts as a script of sorts that becomes a permanent part of the child's mental abilities in learning how to manipulate objects and learn about their nature. Once the scheme is acquired with learning about one object, it can be generalized to be used in learning about all objects that a child is interested in manipulating.

As such, Piaget believed that there are two basic types of schemes that are formed throughout infancy, childhood, and adolescence: (1) **Sensorimotor schemes**, formed in infancy and childhood, are based in motor acts and serve to help the child understand how the world operates in very rudimentary terms; and (2) **cognitive schemes** are more like ideas or patterns based on symbolism and abstract reasoning, formed from early childhood into adolescence and older years, that also permit problem solving and attainment of certain goals, for example, mathematical processes such as addition and subtraction.

Schemes evolve, once formed, from basic to more advanced and complex natures. Essentially, we are able to modify existing schemes by two processes: (1) **Assimilation** occurs when new information is incorporated into an existing scheme; and (2) **accommodation** occurs when an existing scheme is altered to bring about congruence with reality. For example, an infant acquires the basic scheme for sucking on an object. After this is mastered, the baby will attempt to suck on anything that comes near its mouth, such as fingers, toes, and so on. However, it may learn from interactions with parents that sucking is appropriate only with a human or bottle nipple and not the thumb, for instance.

Piaget proposed that individuals experience a series of four stages in infancy, childhood, and adolescence in acquiring an understanding of the world. Development proceeds from a general to more specific understandings as children acquire greater experiences with their environments. The ages at which people proceed through these stages are somewhat variable but Piaget believed that the sequence of the stages is invariable. These stages and the characteristics are briefly outlined in Table 3–2.

Application to Parent-Child Relations

This theory is a comprehensive guide to understanding mental processes and how these are acquired and change as a person grows and develops from birth through the years of childhood and adolescence. Central to Piaget's explanation is the role of personal experience with one's environment, both physical and social, in influencing how we come to think and reason. Parents are an essential component of a child's experiences in the ways that they interact with a child and provide a variety of experiences both physical and social in nature. For example, parents provide physical experiences for infants through the toys given for play, the food for meals, and the destinations

TABLE 3–2. Piaget's Stages of Cognitive Development

Sensorimotor (Birth to 3 Years)

- Period of establishing sensorimotor schemes
- Through assimilation and accommodation, many schemes becomimg modified during this time
- Establishment of elementary understanding of cause-and-effect relationships
- Emergence of object permanence
- Emergence of elementary logic

Preoperational-Intuitive (3–6 years)

- Emergence of language helps to establish cognitive schemes
- Great preoccupation with classification tasks
- Thinking becomes intuitive in nature
- Development of large database of knowledge and information about the world
- Cognitive flaws include egocentrism
- Perception is based upon appearances

Concrete Operations (6–11 years)

Understanding and use of principles and relationships between events and things
Operating with objects, symbols, and concepts to acquire this understanding
Internalizing the outer environment by using mental imagery and symbolism

Other cognitive attributes:

- Centering
- Mastery of conservation problems
- Reversibility
- Black and white thinking

Formal Operations (Adolescence and Older)

- Increasing use of scientific reasoning
- Decrease in egocentricity
- Ability to empathize increases
- Emergence of personal meanings
- Higher-order moral reasoning emerges

Adapted from Piaget, J., & Inhelder, B. (1969). The psychology of the child. New York: Basic Books.

---

they take children in the community (Figure 3–9). These shape children's understanding of their physical environment and how they can operate in this setting. Parents also provide a social environment to their infants by talking with them, playing with them, and teaching them certain rudimentary social skills in late infancy. These actions by parents continue throughout the years of childhood and adolescence. For example, when parents read to their children and encourage them to look at picture books, the children learn that information can be acquired from printed materials. What parents provide as experiences for children influences the quality of their cognitive de-velopment. We discuss these implications for parent-child relations in those chapters dealing with parenting children between infancy and adolescence.

Vygotsky's Sociocultural Theory

Lev Vygotsky (1962, 1987) is a Russian psychologist who has proposed a different perspective of psychological development known as the **sociocultural** theory. This approach emphasizes the social aspects of cognitive development, that is, intellectual growth is stimulated by interactions with others, especially parents. Vygotsky also

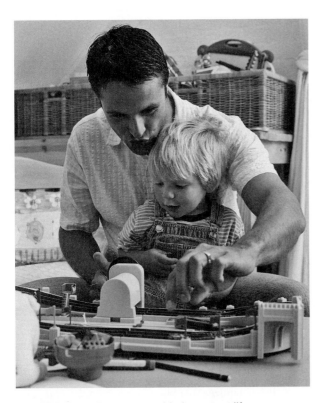

FIGURE 3–9. Parents provide important life experiences for children that stimulate their cognitive growth.

believed that (1) development during infancy and early childhood is specific to the particular historical time in which a person lives resulting in differences in development depending on when and where someone grows up; (2) development takes place when a child observes an activity taking place in group interactions and then internalizes this activity; (3) symbols such as language assist in internalizing these activities; and (4) culture is learned by interactions with others within the culture.

Vygotsky proposes that children accomplish many developmental tasks within the context of what he terms the **zone of proximal development (ZPD).** Many tasks that are too difficult for children to master alone can be accomplished successfully with the guidance and assistance of adults who are more skilled than children. The lower limit of the ZPD is what a child can accomplish in learning a task independently of adult assistance. The upper limit of this zone is what can be accomplished when assisted by an adult. The ZPD represents an idea of a child's learning potential. It emphasizes the inter-

personal context in which learning such tasks occurs for children by implying that learning is a shared experience.

Young children are assisted by parents and other caregivers by motivating their interest in accomplishing a task that appears difficult for them to achieve successfully. By providing children with verbal instruction and by helping them to learn by doing things themselves with guidance, parents and others assist children to organize the information they already possess in existing mental structures and transform these to allow them to accomplish increasingly more difficult tasks.

Application to Parent-Child Relations

Some researchers use the term **scaffolding** to refer to any parental behavior that supports children's efforts at more advanced skill acquisition until the children become competent at that behavior. In the context of this text, we refer to such assistance as *assertive* and *supportive care*, which comprise the concept of nurturance and refer to the ways parents provide this to children in appropriate, healthy ways. When parents provide this kind of instruction for their preschool-age child, it often happens in this sequence: (1) recruiting the child's interest in performing a task or activity; (2) simplifying the task to a number of steps that lead to a correct solution; (3) maintaining the child's interest in the task; (4) pointing out errors as they occur and providing guidance toward correction; (5) controlling the child's frustration by discounting the distress caused by making mistakes; and (6) demonstrating or modeling correct solutions (Astington, 1993; Rogoff, 1990). When viewed in this manner, children learn best when parents model problem-solving skills or mentor the child in ways for learning how to reach solutions to problems. In this manner, Vygotsky's views approximate that of social learning theory but are couched within the cultural context in which development is occurring.

Vygotsky's views of development incorporate the notion of interdependence as a central part of development (Rogoff, 1990). This notion runs counter to the manner and philosophy in which many parents in the culture of the United States raise children. In our society, child-rearing practices generally promote individualism as a valued trait for children to acquire. For example, infants are placed in separate sleeping quarters from parents and are expected to learn to comfort themselves while going to sleep. Children are expected to conduct their own play activities with a minimal amount of adult guidance. School performance is based on competition with others, and individualism is highlighted by the heavy emphasis on personal performance in sports and athletic activities, for example. Other cultures promote collectivism rather than independence in child rearing. The cultures of many minority ethnic groups discussed in the last chapter reflect the promotion of group, family, or community identity. In Vygotsky's views, optimal development occurs within the collectivist context of relationships between individuals.

● ●

Parenting Reflection 3–4

Has information from behavioral science improved or only served to complicate matters even more for adults who are trying to parent children effectively?

● ●

● ●

Focus Point.   Other theoretical approaches may be useful in understanding the social context of parent-child relations. Learning theory components (behavior modification and social learning) explain how parents teach children by using rewards to reinforce the behaviors they desire of children and by serving as models of behavior. Cognitive theory stresses the importance of the experiences parents provide for children that are both physical and social in nature as a means for shaping their mental life and understanding of the world in which they live. Vygotsky's views expand on social learning to explain how parents teach skills to their children.

● ●

POINTS TO CONSIDER

■ Several different but related theories can be applied to understanding and studying parent-child relations. Each provides insight into a particular aspect of this relationship. Some describe how the relationship is subject to being changed over time; others describe how the relationship functions in more general terms.

■ Systems theory has been applied to the study of families. Family systems theory is useful in explaining the processes by which a family group makes decisions, sets and achieves particular goals, and establishes methods for governing the behavior of its members. The theory is helpful in describing how these processes work to maintain the stability of a family group over time and how the family reacts to changes affecting individual members and the group. According to the theory, several subsystems often can be found within the larger family system. These are usually based on relationships between two or more members, such as the adult spouses, parents and children, or brothers and sisters. Each subsystem has its own patterns that mirror those of the larger family system.

■ Family systems theory uses several concepts to explain family functioning: wholeness, interdependence, patterns (rules, roles, communication styles), reciprocal interaction and feedback, boundaries, entropy, equifinality, adaptation, and homeostasis.

■ Systemic family development theory is an extension of family systems theory that is useful in understanding how a family group changes in response to stressors that occur as part of normal developmental processes of individuals. This realistic model of family life recognizes that families are complex and composed of several interrelated generations. By taking a snapshot or slice of developmental time being experienced by a family, it is possible to examine the stressors affecting each generation in a family and study how a family copes with these stressors in response. By making adaptations in patterns, families are able to make necessary changes in order to re-establish their stability in functioning.

■ Ecological theory proposed by Bronfenbrenner offers an additional way to understand family functioning. Bronfenbrenner suggests that five distinct environmental settings explain how an individual is influenced in his or her developmental progress and how relationships function in interaction with various environments and people in those environments.

■ Erikson proposes a theory of eight stages that describe the psychosocial development of individuals over the life span. This theory stresses: (1) the continuity of developmental changes over a person's entire life span; (2) the resolution of a central crisis or challenge at each stage; (3) the mastery or acquisition of a healthy or unhealthy psychosocial attitude at the completion of each stage; and (4) the assistance and support from significant others who assist or impede an individual's development progress. The theory may be applied to parent-child relations by examining the congruence between the psychosocial stages of parents and children. By applying the concepts of reciprocal interaction and adaptation, parenting behavior changes in response to the changing developmental needs of children. In turn, children help parents to achieve their particular psychosocial attitude by virtue of being the recipient of their caregiving behavior.

■ Other theories can also be applied to understanding parent-child relations. Learning theory stresses how behavior is modified through rewards and by observing the behavior of others. Cognitive theory described by Piaget focuses on the role of physical and social experiences provided by parents in shaping how children come to understand their world. Vygotsky's observations emphasize how parents structure learning experiences in teaching children to master skills.

CHAPTER 4

Parenting Strategies

Focus Questions

1. Why are parents considered to be teachers? What qualities characterize a competent parent?

2. How is discipline defined? What are some guidelines that help parents to be effective disciplinarians?

3. How are structure and nurturance provided to children through discipline?

4. What basic methods of discipline can be used by parents? What elements do they have in common? How are they applied to a program of discipline?

5. Why are behavior problems considered a normal aspect of children's development?

Our culture provides little preparation or assistance in training people to act as competent parents. Parental behavior may be guided by trial-and-error learning, self-education, the model provided by one's own parents, and clouded, uncertain ideas of what is to be expected of children at each stage of their developmental progress (Simons, Whitlock, Conger, & Wu, 1991). It is also influenced by those factors and variables discussed in previous chapters, such as family ecological factors.

For many years, a prevalent belief has been that people in our society do not need formal training or education to be parents. However, professionals and others who work closely with parents today believe there is considerable need for such training (C. Smith, Perou, & Lesesne, 2002).

Although most people involved in parenting would agree that they could profit from learning new ways to be effective in their role, no clear guidelines identify the qualities or behaviors that make someone a competent parent. It is possible that our culture will never reach a consensus on this issue. However, researchers continue to make much progress in helping parents find more effective ways to perform their tasks in working with children and attaining goals established for their child-rearing efforts.

Many people discover their lack of knowledge about parenting skills after serious problems have developed in their family systems. Those problems may relate to ineffective guidance and communication within the group, for example. Professionals who

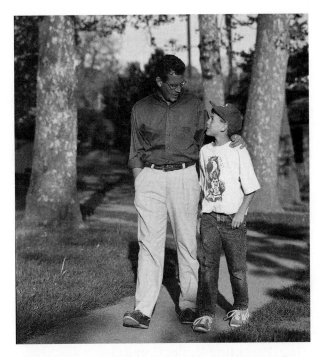

FIGURE 4–1 Parents are expected to teach discipline to their children. This does not refer to punishment for transgressions but teaching appropriate behaviors, including self-control.

promote education for parenting believe that people can be offered opportunities to learn a variety of means and methods to improve their parenting abilities (First & Way, 1995). Education is seen as a means for preventing or minimizing problems in child rearing. This is preferable to some interventionist approaches designed to deal with the aftermath of problems (Figure 4–1).

Clearly, people can learn how to be more effective parents. By studying the research, theory, issues, and approaches developed and examined by parent education practitioners and investigators, it is possible to develop a better understanding of the challenges and adventures of parenting children.

This chapter presents information about specific methods and techniques of child rearing that are recommended today by child development and family experts. These methods have emerged from changes in social attitudes about how to raise children properly and from information derived from behavioral science research on such issues as what children need and the long-term effects of child-rearing methods on personality development and self-esteem. Thus, unlike the advice

on child rearing passed down from grandmothers and great-aunts, these methods have added credibility in being derived from research and clinical study.

PARENTS AS TEACHERS

From ancient times to the present, societies have recognized that parents are their children's first and most important teachers. Long before public school systems were established in the United States, parents held the responsibility for training and teaching their children all the essential skills and knowledge for becoming an effectively functioning adult in society. While formal educational functions have been assumed by other agents, society has never relinquished the socialization responsibilities of parents in equipping children with basic skills and knowledge in order to prepare them for adulthood.

In looking back at the past and comparing what we know about what children needed to be prepared for their future, we may easily conclude that things are more complex today in what parents face as teachers for their children. The dilemma that confronts most contemporary parents is knowing what children need in order to grow and develop into healthy adults. It is practically impossible, for example, for today's parents to know what kind of occupation their children will hold in the future, for example. The uncertainties that comprise a vision of the future certainly cloud the ability of parents (or that of anyone else) to predict the nature of the world next year—much less what it will be like in 20 years or more.

Teaching and caregiving are what most people associate with parenting and what parents do in rearing children. Parents have always taught their children the skills and knowledge they believe children will need to function as effective adults in society. However, with changes in society over the years, other institutions have assumed many of the family's primary functions, so that children's socialization is the main concern of parenting today.

In our culture, people must have years of education and training to become competent in an occupation or profession, yet few are adequately prepared for the work of parenting children. Little formal education and training in parenting are offered as part of one's educational experiences. Society delegates the responsibility for socializing children to parents but does little to prepare them to meet that responsibility. Preparing the next generation to cope emotionally and to have social and interpersonal skills is usually a matter of trial and error for many parents.

It is understandable that many people may feel overwhelmed by the prospect as well as the tasks of parenting children. Often they develop feelings of frustration and disappointment and begin to wonder whether they are doing an adequate job of teaching their children the values held by their families. Parents have to determine which values are important to teach to children—values that will have meaning and usefulness to them when they are grown. Many parents believe that certain values and beliefs do not lose their applicability in a child's future, regardless of the changes that may occur in society. These are likely to include (1) having a personal integrity that will guide appropriate, contributive, law-abiding behavior; (2) using one's ability to the fullest to attain goals and objectives; (3) valuing knowledge and learning for its own sake; (4) having adequate interpersonal skills and abilities to cope successfully with the stresses of life; and (5) acting in ways that are considerate of others' needs as well as one's own (Coontz, 1992).

The childhood experiences of today's parents differ from those their children will encounter as they grow toward maturity. The isolated and differently structured nuclear family system of today has few outside supports to assist in its child-rearing efforts. Modern behavioral science has made many attempts to fill this void; however, the methods of child guidance that have been proposed can be conflicting in philosophy, content, and expected outcomes. Parents have been and continue to be bombarded by the media with diverse and often incompatible advice on how to raise children (Bigner & Yang, 1996).

When modern behavioral science appeared to be able to offer sensible solutions and methods for raising healthy children, many parents adopted the idea that if one simply followed these suggestions, all problems of child rearing would vanish. However, it has become increasingly apparent that there is not an adequate, standard, or simple recipe by which to raise children to be successful, competent, and effective adults. Experts today are unable to provide parents with detailed instructions about how to do their work in ways that will guarantee the desired results in children (Bigner & Yang, 1996). However, most parents wish to know what they can do, even in general ways, to raise healthy children to become healthy adults. A strong intuitive notion is that

parents need to provide teaching and caregiving experiences that meet those needs that are specific to a child's developmental age and abilities (McNally, Eisenberg, & Harris, 1991).

According to Kagan (1976) and others (Bronfenbrenner, 1985), children in our society generally need (1) to feel valued by parents and a few special adults, for example, a teacher or a relative; (2) to develop their own personal attitudes, values, and opinions and become autonomous in their behavior; (3) to develop and master skills and abilities that are valued by society; and (4) to accept their sexual orientation and feel successful in terms of loving others and being able to accept love from others. There is general agreement that these attributes are necessary and essential for children to learn, but many parents are unsure about how to encourage children to adopt them effectively so that they will become manifested in the children's lives and behaviors.

Parenting Reflection 4-1

Can you identify needs of children other than those mentioned in the text that can be met by parents and family members? What are the origins of these needs, for example, a family's ethnic group identity, geographic location, and so on?

Competency as a parent today requires knowledge of a variety of approaches for guiding children to adulthood. Parental love and nurturance of children is important for their healthy growth and development; however, being a competent and effective parent requires much more. Although there are a number of strategies or methods as well as parenting styles observed in child rearing, each usually focuses on fostering the emotional needs and character development of both parents and children. Some strategies are therapeutic in context, some attempt to resolve conflicts between parents and children and teach interpersonal interaction skills to both, and some propose a more humane approach to conducting parent-child interactions. These strategies for parenting are embraced eagerly by many adults who may have found the models and scripts for parenting that they learned from their own parents to be inadequate and inappropriate. Rather than offering a recipe

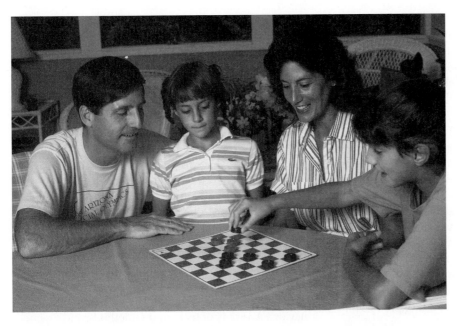

FIGURE 4–2 Competent parenting today differs from what occurred in the past. Today, competent parenting requires more than providing love and nurturance.

for child rearing, these strategies and parenting styles provide parents a repertoire of skills for raising children to be competent adults (Figure 4–2).

••

Focus Point.   There are many strategies that parents can use to become competent teachers and socializers of children. It is helpful to learn a variety of these to be an effective parent.

••

DEALING WITH DISCIPLINE

Teaching and guiding children are perhaps the greatest concerns parents have in performing adequately as care-givers to growing children. As discussed in Chapter 1, cultural ideas have evolved about what children need and how best to teach them the behaviors, values, and beliefs adults consider important for their effective future functioning. Advice on how to raise children has proliferated in modern times. Information on a variety of topics pertaining to parenting, child development, and guidance techniques is available in magazines, books, and pamphlets. Such materials tend to be used more frequently by today's parents than they were in previous generations (Bigner & Yang, 1996; Francis-Connolly, 2003). Uppermost in many parents' thinking

is the issue of how to provide adequate and appropriate discipline in guiding children's growth and development (Chamberlain & Patterson, 1995).

Some Generalizations About Discipline

The concept of **discipline** is largely misunderstood. The term is derived from an old English word meaning in-struction. A derivative of the term is *disciple*, which means pupil or student. Contrary to its definition, most people equate discipline to the use of punishment or penalties in response to children's misbehavior. For dis-cipline to be effective, however, parents need to view it in light of the term's original meaning.

First, discipline is teaching children to behave in ways considered appropriate by their parents, teachers, and other caregivers. Discipline is the means by which children are taught to internalize the rules, values, and beliefs that will help them to become effective individu-als as adults.

Second, discipline involves measures that help chil-dren learn to control their impulses so that they can learn to reason and make appropriate choices for their behavior before acting. These measures also help chil-dren learn social skills in considering others' needs as well as their own, which will facilitate their future par-ticipation in work and family life and in other interac-tions with people.

Third, to be effective, disciplinary actions of a parent must be positive, reasonable, and temperate.

Fourth, methods and strategies of discipline should be geared to a child's age and developmental level.

Fifth, to discipline a child effectively, an adult must understand the child and his or her particular needs and problems.

Finally, discipline provides structure in children's lives by means of the rules developed within their family system. Rules are found in both healthy and unhealthy family systems. These act as the means for helping everyone know the guidelines of what serves as acceptable and unacceptable behavior and the consequences of both actions. In healthy family systems, negotiable rules abound. Children in healthy families learn that the rules are for their protection and freedom. They know they can talk with their parents about making occasional exceptions to the rules. The topic of rules as applied to the practice of discipline is discussed in greater detail later in this chapter.

Children's misbehavior is often a primary focus of parental attention. This preoccupation, which may be more of a problem to the adult than to the child, can be traced to the following questions: (1) Are adult expectations too high for the child's age and abilities? (2) Are instructions to children given in a negative framework involving an excessive number of "don'ts" rather than "dos"? (3) Is the adult consistent in enforcing some rules and policies that are not negotiable and at the same time flexible to debate negotiable rules to teach the child conflict-resolution and discussion skills? (4) Is the emphasis on teaching children how to arrive at win-win solutions to problems with parental or family rules instead of on the deliberate, conscientious expression of parental power over children when problems arise in their behavior? Environmental factors discussed in Chapter 1 that influence both parents' and children's behavior and interaction also influence disciplinary actions.

Parents can learn certain skills and gain understanding and knowledge that will guide them in teaching children acceptable and responsible behavior. However, no child development or family expert can offer programs of discipline and guidance that will work effectively for all families or for all children.

Each family system must develop its own rules, policies, and values of child rearing and socialization. How these evolve in a particular family system depends on a host of factors, such as personalities, family of origin backgrounds, values, financial and social status, and the number and birth order of children. Experimentation with what works, what feels comfortable, and what is reasonable contributes to the program of discipline parents use. The ability of a family system to adapt or change rules that either don't work or are no longer functional because children have grown older is also an essential feature of a healthy program of discipline.

The concepts and possible approaches outlined in the paragraphs that follow may prove helpful to parents attempting to develop a program of discipline for their family system:

1. *Understand how the concept of equifinality applies to a program of discipline.* The equifinality concept from family systems theory implies that families attain similar goals in different and varied ways. Hence, different methods of socializing children may result in adult individuals who hold similar values, attitudes, and behaviors. A variety of techniques, methods, and practices can help accomplish similar goals of socialization. No single, correct program of discipline will accomplish these goals.

2. *Do not use abusive corporal punishment.* Contrary to popular opinion, spanking and other abusive corporal punishments do not appear to be effective means to achieve desired behavior from children (Kazdin & Benjet, 2003; Straus, 1994). Instead, such forms of physical violence model this behavior as appropriate ways to resolve conflicts and lead to habitual use of violent behavior by children (Kyriacou, 2002; Straus & Yodanis, 1996). Recent work also strongly substantiates the connection between harsh physical, abusive punishment in childhood and violence in adult romantic involvements (Swinford, DeMaris, Cernkovich, & Giordano, 2000). Many adults were spanked by their parents in attempts to control their misbehavior as children. However, researchers increasingly note that it is the consistency with which this and other punishment measures are used rather than the act itself that helps children learn to control their actions (Kazdin & Benjet). Spanking and other forms of physical punishment usually occur within the context of expressions of parental anger, which can result in overly aggressive actions that harm the child (Figure 4–3).

Considering this danger along with the negative effect on a child's self-esteem, alternatives such as positive reinforcement, time-out, and other less damaging

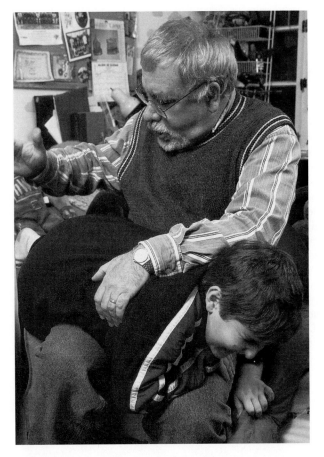

FIGURE 4–3 Many parents believe that physical punishments, such as spanking, are an appropriate way to teach children to obey family rules. What do you think about this practice?

methods are viewed as more appropriate disciplinary measures (Saadeh, Rizzo, & Roberts, 2002; see Focus On 4–1).

One study, however, reports that parental reliance on reasoning alone to shape and guide a disciplinary program for toddlers is ineffective (Larzelere et al., 1989). When the reasoning approach is combined with non-corporal, nonabusive punishment (e.g., time-out, withdrawal of privileges), then disciplinary programs become more effective and toddlers learn to comply with parental wishes. And, as all parents of toddlers learn, there are times when even this kind of procedure may not work well. In these instances, the authors recommend that parents use a nonabusive corporal punish-

ment as a backup for the reasoning and use of noncorporal punishment. A two-swat hand-slap, for example, is advocated in these circumstances. Not every parent, however, may wish to go even to this as a last resort in working with a noncompliant toddler. The authors of this study note that how parents use disciplinary tactics may be more critical than which ones they choose to use.

● ●

■ Parenting Reflection 4–2

Does anyone have the right to intervene when parents use physical punishment as a disciplinary technique with their child, especially in public? What would you say to a parent who is a stranger about what he or she is doing?

● ●

3. *Try to understand children's feelings and motivations.* Many parents consider the misbehavior of a child to be a personal attack motivated by the child's malicious intent. This is rarely the case. The child's misbehavior may be a learned response or action that is logical enough to him or her at that particular time. Parents who attempt in a loving, noncritical way to develop an understanding of their children will feel less hostile when they misbehave. As a result, the parents will be more rational in developing corrective action that teaches children to think before they act. Such an approach will also facilitate the parent's position as the child's ally in solving a particular problem. On the other hand, the parent who sees misbehavior as a personal attack with malicious intent will likely respond with anger and frustration, which will serve only to intensify the problem.

A parent has various means to gain understanding of a child's feelings and motivations for behaving in unacceptable ways. The parent can listen carefully to a child's verbal and nonverbal communications and reflect the feelings being expressed back to the child. This exercise will help the child express himself or herself and help the parent to understand the emotional aspects that underlie the child's actions. To employ this technique effectively, the adult must respect the child as a fallible human being who is by nature prone to make mistakes and errors. This attitude is based in compassion and empathy. Parents who are

Focus On 4–1

Is It OK to Spank?

Consider these issues and findings from research studies on the effects of spanking children. Draw your own conclusions as to the advisability of using spanking as a means of discipline.

■ There is a very strong association between experiencing harsh, abusive, physical punishment in childhood and being a perpetrator of violence in intimate relationships in adulthood (Swinford et al., 2000).

■ Spanking as a means of discipline appears to be strongly ingrained in certain ethnic and cultural groups (Dodge et al., 2005; Hall, 2005; McLoyd, Kaplan, Hardaway, & Wood, 2007).

■ Nevertheless, spanking appears to be a prevalent means of child maltreatment, frequently used as a last resort in gaining children's compliance to adult wishes (Buriel. Mercado, Rodriguez, & Chavez, 1991).

■ Most spankings occur when adults are angry with children (Bensley et al., 2004; Graziano & Namaste, 1990).

■ Parents who are considered abusive to children by mental health professionals and by the court system consider spanking to be an acceptable means of discipline (Kelley, Grace, & Elliott, 1990; Stafford, 2004).

■ Spanking is used frequently as a replacement for positive communications and reinforcement with children about their behavior and parent's ideas about appropriate behavior (Flora, 2004; Larzelere, Klein, Schumm, & Alibrando, 1989).

■ More boys than girls are spanked by parents (Day, Peterson, & McCracken, 1998; Lytton & Romney, 1991; Simons et al., 1991).

■ Younger children (infants through preschool age) are spanked by parents more than older children (school age through adolescent) (Day et al., 1998; Magnuson & Waldfogel, 2005; Walsh, 2002).

■ Mothers are more likely to spank children than fathers, especially if they are young (Ateah & Durrant, 2005; Day et al., 1998).

■ Children who are spanked exhibit more aggressive behaviors than children who are not spanked (Aggarwal & Verma, 1987).

■ Spanking is associated with children's negative feelings of self-esteem and personal worth (Larzelere et al., 1989; Straus, 1994).

■ Males are more likely than females to approve of spanking children (Kelder, McNamara, Carlson, & Lynn, 1991).

■ Spanking may produce a child's conformity to parental wishes in an immediate situation, but its long-term effects may include increased probability of deviance, including delinquency in adolescence and violent crime in adulthood (Straus, 1991a, 1991b).

■ Children who are emotionally disturbed (and have been physically or sexually abused) are more likely to endorse (approve of) physical punishment than nonemotionally disturbed children (Strassberg, Dodge, Petit, & Bates, 1994).

■ Parents who are members of fundamentalist Protestant religious groups prefer the use of spanking (corporal punishment) over alternate methods of discipline (Grogan-Kaylor & Otis, 2007; Wiehe, 1990).

■ Adults who spank children are likely to have been spanked by their parents as a primary means of controlling their misbehavior (Simons et al., 1991).

■ Males who exhibit Type A personalities and behavioral tendencies—perfectionism, stressful feelings about time pressures, extraordinarily high achievement expectations for self and others, and high risk of coronary heart disease—experienced more frequent physical punishment by parents as children (McCranie & Simpson, 1986).

■ Few children recommend that adults use physical punishment as a means of discipline (B. E. Carlson, 1986).

■ Individuals who are considered to be bullies have been subjected to physical punishment/abuse as children and have learned that the use of physical force is an acceptable means of resolving conflicts with others (Floyd, 1985).

■ The use of corporal punishment (including spanking) is controversial with its proponents as well as opponents. A number of countries prohibit this practice by law, however (M. Bailey, 2003; Baumrind, Larzelere, & Cowan 2002; Kazdin & Benjet, 2003).

angry and critical of a child because of misbehavior often dictate their own solution to a problem, which tends to thwart thinking and reasoning on the child's part. Such behavior serves to discount the child rather than foster an understanding of why the child acts as he or she does.

A parent might also attempt to help the child identify and rectify the cause of the misbehavior. This approach is similar to that used by a mechanic fixing a malfunctioning engine. Ordinarily, mechanics do not shout out in anger, condemn, or strike an engine because it has malfunctioned. They simply discover the cause of the malfunction and make repairs. A parent can approach a malfunctioning child in similar ways, first by attempting to identify what caused the problem behavior and then by helping the child make the necessary adjustments to his or her behavior.

4. *Facilitate children's opportunities to learn to think and reason and make choices for their actions.*   A child who is granted the right to make personal decisions and to experience the consequences, both positive and negative, of those decisions will learn to be responsible for his or her actions. Here the parent's role is to help in generating alternatives without supplying all the answers, options, or solutions all the time. The adult must determine which decisions a child can make and at what age. The parent who continually makes all the child's decisions and accepts responsibility for all the child's actions fosters dependency rather than autonomy in the child. By making their own decisions and living with the results, children learn to differentiate themselves from others and to establish personal boundaries.

5. *Learn to value the individual differences of children as interesting and positive tools for personal growth rather than require that everyone in the family system be the same.*   Some family systems value sameness or rigid conformity in all members rather than seeing the benefits of individual differences in values, opinions, ideas, or means of self-expression (Richardson, 1999). Parenting and disciplining children in such family systems is approached with a cookie-cutter mentality: Children are required to think and act like their parents and hold identical values and beliefs. The demand for sameness can kill a child's spirit and self-perception as an autonomous, unique human being who has the ability to reason and think and the right to be who he or she is.

Faced with the demand for sameness among family members, a child may react in one of several ways:

■ The child may comply with the rule of sameness by denial of his or her true self. The child will avoid conflict and seek peace at any price.

■ The child may rebel and seek self-definition by not acting as the parents wish, often in ways that are contrary to his or her own wishes.

■ The child may project blame on others rather than admit his or her own part in conflicts. A power struggle with parents is a typical result.

■ When the demand for sameness becomes overwhelming, the child may disengage emotionally from parents.

6. *Maintain a clear understanding that discipline should be based on helping children develop internal structure that is based on healthy self-esteem rather than fear, guilt, or shame.*   Structure refers to the internalized controls that people acquire through socialization experiences that guide their behavior (J. L. Clarke & Dawson, 1998). Parents provide socialization experiences to their children through care, instruction, and rules that result in children's self-disciplined actions (see Focus On 4–2). This differs drastically from the experiences of children who are raised by parents who use criticism, sarcasm, nagging, discounting, shame, and guilt to provide children with internal controls for their behavior. When parents attempt to shape and motivate children's development by instilling fear and shame about misbehavior, the children suffer a loss of self-esteem. Such children internalize what psychologists refer to as a critical parent aspect of their personality to motivate and regulate their behavior. As adults, such individuals respond to committing an error or transgression with guilt and shame. These emotions tend to block effective problem solving because the person's thinking skills become frozen and ineffective at reaching rational solutions to the problem at hand (Burns, 1999).

Rules provide an important aspect of helping children learn structure. When applied appropriately, rules provide children with a sense of protection and foster a sense of trust and security. Parents must teach children rules that are rational and serve to outline the limits to which children can go in their behavior by maintaining personal boundaries. If rules derive from parents' critical,

Focus On 4–2

Identifying Positive and Negative Structure by Parenting Style

There are six possible ways that parents provide or fail to provide structure for their children. These are arranged here from left to right in order of degree of strictness. For example, the parenting style *Rigidity* is characterized by having the highest degree of strictness, whereas the parenting style *Abandonment* has no rules. Although these two styles lie at opposite ends of the continuum, they are similar in their effects upon children. The two parenting styles *Nonnegotiable Rules* and *Negotiable Rules* are the patterns that support and facilitate children's development of healthy structure and are the most helpful to both children and parents. The other four parenting styles, *Rigidity*, *Criticism*, *Marshmallow*, and *Abandonment*, do not provide children with healthy structure and are considered negative in their effects.

Hypothetical Situation: Fifteen-year-old drank alcoholic beverages.

Rigidity	*Criticism*	*Nonnegotiable Rules*
Characteristics:		
Rigidity, supposedly for the child's welfare, springs from fear. It consists of old rules "written in concrete" sometime in the past and usually for someone else. These rules often ignore the developmental tasks of the child. It threatens abuse and/or withdrawing love to enforce compliance; doesn't believe children should have a say in working things out.	Criticism labels the person with bad names rather than setting standards for acceptable behavior. Criticism often includes global words such as "never" and "always." It negates children and suggests ways to fail. Ridicule, which issues a bitter and mocking invitation for contemptuous laughter, is a devastating form of criticism.	Reasonable, nonnegotiable rules build self-esteem in children. Nonnegotiable rules must be followed. Children come to know they can count on these rules and that there are rewards when they are followed and negative consequences when they are broken. However, even though nonnegotiable rules are firmly set and firmly enforced, they are not "rigid" and can be rewritten for the welfare of the family and its members.
Example:		
"If you ever touch alcohol again, don't bother coming home."	"You're always doing something stupid. Now you are drinking, just like your dad."	"You may not drink alcohol until you've reached legal age. There are penalties. They are …"
Underlying Messages Children Hear:		
You are not important. Don't think. Don't be. You will be abandoned if you make a mistake. Don't trust your own competence.	Don't be who you are. Don't be successful. Don't be capable. You are not lovable.	Your welfare and safety are important. Your parents are willing and able to be responsible and enforce the rules.

Negotiable Rules	*Marshmallow*	*Abandonment*
Characteristics:		
Negotiable rules teach children how to think clearly and to problem solve, helping them raise their self-esteem. These rules are negotiated and then firmly	Marshmallow parenting grants freedom without demanding responsibility in return. It sounds supportive, but it implies the child does not have to or is not	Abandonment consists of a lack of rules, protection, and contact. It tells the child the adult is not available for him. If teasing is offered when a child needs

Focus On 4–2   *(continued)*

enforced. When they are designed to support a nonnegotiable rule, they can be adjusted to match maturing skills and needs. The process of negotiating provides children an opportunity to argue with parents, learn about the relevancy of rules, and learn to be responsible for themselves in new ways.

capable of following rules. It discounts the child's ability and gives the child permission to be irresponsible and to fail, to be helpless and hopeless. At the same time, it lets the parent look good, play the martyr, or feel in control.

structure or approval, that teasing, constitutes abandonment.

Example:

"You may find yourself around kids whose number-one priority is drinking. Find other things to do so you don't spend all your free time with those kids."

"If all the kids drink, I suppose you can," or "You're too young to drink and drive, so you can have a kegger here," or "Boys will be boys!"

"I don't want to talk about it," or makes fun of pain or humiliates the child. Parent is not available (either physically or emotionally), is drunk or irrational, or ignores or teases instead of responding to the child.

Underlying Messages Children Hear:

You can think, negotiate, and initiate. Your needs are important and others' needs are important. You must deal with how things really are. You are expected to be powerful in positive ways for yourself and others.

Don't be competent or responsible. Don't be who you are. Don't grow up. You can have your way and be obnoxious and get by with it. I need to continue taking care of you. My needs are more important than your needs.

I am not willing to care for you; I don't want you. Your needs are not important; mine are. No one is here for you. You don't exist.

Rigidity

Criticism

Nonnegotiable Rules

Common Responses of Children:

Feels oppressed, distanced, angry, scared, hopeless, imperfect, discounted, mistrusted, abandoned, no good.

Feels powerless and diminished, rejected, hurt, humiliated, squashed, angry, unimportant, inadequate, scared, discounted.

Feels safe, cared for, powerful, helped, responsible, accounted for, and may feel frustrated, irritated, and resistant at times. Learns to follow rules and be responsible.

Decisions Children Make:

I am not wanted. Parents don't care about me. Rules are more important than my needs. I will let others think. I will comply, rebel, or withdraw. I will blame myself.

I have to know what I don't know. I will try harder, be strong, be perfect. If I don't do things right, I am a bad person. I can't be good enough. I am hopeless. Why bother?

There are some rules I have to follow. I can learn from my mistakes. I am a good person. I'm lovable and capable. They care about me and take care of me.

(continued)

Focus On 4–2   *(continued)*

	Negotiable Rules	*Marshmallow*	*Abandonment*
Common Responses of Children:	Feels respected, cared for, listened to, powerful, important, loved, intelligent, safe, and sometimes frustrated. Learns to evaluate rules and participate in the making of rules as well as to follow rules and be responsible.	Feels patronized and kept little, remains incompetent in order to please parent. Feels undermined, crazy, manipulated, discounted, unloved, unsatisfied, and angry.	Feels scared, terrified, hurt, angry, rejected, discounted, baffled, unimportant, upset, like a nonbeing. Perhaps suicidal.
Decisions Children Make:	It's OK for me to grow up and still be dependent at times. I can think things through and get help doing that. I continually expand my ability to be responsible and competent.	I must take care of other people's feelings and needs, or I don't need to care about anyone but me. I am not capable of learning how to value and take care of myself. If help is offered, mistrust it or at least expect to pay a price for it, but don't expect helpful structure from others.	Don't ask for or expect help. No one cares. If I am to survive, I will have to do it by myself. If help is offered, mistrust it. Help and trust are a joke.

Source: Adapted from Clarke, J. I., & Dawson, C. (1998). *Growing up again: Parenting ourselves, parenting our children* (2nd ed.). Minneapolis, MN: Hazelden.

---

judgmental, unloving positions promoted by authoritarian attitudes, the resulting discipline and structure provided for children will tend to be rigid and inflexible. Such rules and the ways parents enforce them become similar to the poisonous pedagogy of authoritarianism that causes children to acquire negative rather than positive structure.

Some parents provide implicit rules and inconsistent experiences, resulting in what is called *marshmallowing*, or abandonment of children's needs for adequate structure. Some rules will be negotiable while others, by necessity, will not. Negotiable rules will lead to healthy feelings of self-esteem in children. On the other hand, rigidity, inflexibility, having the majority of rules be nonnegotiable, and abandoning children's needs will damage children's self-esteem. An example of how these different parenting styles are applied to a hypothetical teenager's infraction of a family rule is given in Focus On 4–2. In four of these styles the structure provided for children is negative in nature and results for children. In two of these, which feature degrees of flexibility in applying rules, the structure parents provide is positive in nature and results for children.

When enforcing rules, it is wise for parents to decide how and when to use their authority, when to be lenient, and when to penalize children for misbehavior. Rules constitute a significant aspect of the patterns that govern the functioning of the family system and the parent-child microenvironment. Without some form of rules, the family system cannot function effectively for the benefit of its members. It is essential that rules for children's welfare and development be formed rationally rather than emotionally.

7. *Discipline is most effective when provided to children within an atmosphere of nurturance.* By

nurturing their children, parents show them that they are loved and are lovable unconditionally (J. I. Clarke & Dawson, 1998).

Nurturance relates to all the ways in which we demonstrate love, not only for others but also for ourselves. Nurturing another involves touching, noticing, and caring for that person in ways that are healthy. Nurturance is expressed to children in two basic forms and in many variations of these forms. **Assertive care** is expressed when a parent knows and determines what a child's needs are and responds to those needs in loving ways that generate a sense of trust within the child. Assertive care involves noticing and listening to the child and understanding the cues and requests the child offers. **Supportive care** is provided as children grow older and can make decisions for themselves about what kinds of attention and care they need from their parents. In providing supportive care, parents offer care at appropriate times, and children are free to accept or decline the care (see Focus On 4–3).

Both forms of care derive from love that is unconditional. This means that love is given freely, without expectations, without limits, and without measure. The parent's message to the child is, "I love you because you are who you are."

In reality, both assertive and supportive care can be given by parents in ways that are both positive and negative. When both assertive and supportive care are offered positively and consistently, children's growth and development as individuals are facilitated in healthy ways. When care is offered negatively or inconsistently, love is conditional rather than unconditional and manifests as conditional care, indulgence, or abuse and neglect (J. I. Clarke & Dawson, 1998). These represent harshness in relating to children, resulting in negative and harmful effects that are seen in children's unhealthy self-esteem. Parents' treatment of children when applying discipline teaches children about themselves and leads them to make conclusions about their self-worth.

Parenting Reflection 4–3

What is the difference between child abuse and disciplining children? At what point would discipline become abusive?.

Focus Point.   Many people believe that discipline is synonymous with punishment. However, discipline refers to teaching children appropriate behaviors through positive means. Parents need to discuss those ways of discipline that are acceptable to them by developing rules and boundaries that provide children with structure and teach them to internalize self-discipline.

METHODS AND APPROACHES

In Chapter 1, we noted that changes have taken place in parenting as various strategies of child rearing rose and fell in popularity. What was appropriate for one generation of parents became inappropriate for the next. Knowledge gained from studies of human development and behavior contributed to much of this vacillation. In the process of applying the various strategies to interactions with children, parents have come to realize that there is no single, adequate method for being an effective, competent parent. However, many publications on this topic continue to appear each year, and they sell very well.

A plethora of child-rearing experts has emerged within the past 75 years, each advocating a particular approach to discipline. Three strategies that have survived the tests of time and practice are discussed in this section: behavior modification and social learning, the democratic approach to child training, and Parent Effectiveness Training. The popularity of these strategies derives from their effectiveness as methods that parents can learn and apply in daily interactions with children to achieve long-range goals. Each of these strategies is representative of modern applied behavioral science. None guarantees consistent results in children's behavior or in parents' interactions with children.

Behavior Modification and Social Learning

Behavior Modification.   Using behavior modification techniques (Bloch, 2003), parents teach children acceptable behavior by weakening undesirable behavior and reinforcing desirable behavior. All behavior is a learned response, according to this view. Just as a child is taught to read, so he or she is taught to behave in a

**Focus On
4–3**

Identifying Positive and Negative Nurturance

Unconditional love for a child is generated through parental actions that represent the two facets of nurturance known as assertive care and supportive care. These lead children to experience joy, hope, self-confidence, and self-esteem. When children are loved conditionally, parental actions demonstrate that there are limits and controls to when and how a child is loved and under what conditions or circumstances. Such conditional parental actions are observed when parents abuse children physically, mentally, and/or emotionally; provide conditional care; act indulgently; and neglect children physically, mentally, and/or emotionally. Such treatment leads children to experience despair, joylessness, depression, and loneliness, all of which are damaging to self-esteem and feelings of self-worth.

Situation: School-age child has a badly scraped arm.

Abuse	*Conditional Love*	*Assertive Care*
Characteristics:		
Abuse is relating to a child by assault, by physical or psychological invasion, or by direct or indirect "don't be" messages. Abuse negates the child's needs.	Parents who use conditional care connect with the child by the use of threats and conditions. The care the parent gives the child is based on the parent's needs and expectations, not on the child's needs.	Assertive care is comforting and loving. It is freely given; it is helpful to the child, responsive to the child's needs, and appropriate to the circumstance.
Example:		
Parent does not care for wounds. Says, "Stop sniffling or I'll give you something to cry about." Parent yells at or shakes child.	Parent says: "Stop crying or I won't bandage your arm."	Parent gives loving care and a hug, cleans and dresses the wound, and says, "Your arm is scraped! I'm sorry."
Underlying Messages Children Hear:		
You don't count. Your needs don't count. You are not lovable. You don't deserve to exist. To get what you need, you must expect pain.	I matter and you don't. Your needs and feelings don't count. You can have care as long as you earn it. Don't believe you are lovable; you have to earn love.	I love you and you are lovable. You are important. Your needs are important. I care for you willingly.
Common Responses of Children:		
Pain in the heart, as well as pain in the scraped arm. Fear, terror, rage, withdrawal, loneliness, despair, shame.	Pain in the heart, as well as pain in the scraped arm. Fear, terror, anger, mistrust of own perceptions, shame, feelings of inadequacy.	Pain in the arm and warmth in the heart. Feels comforted, accepted, important, satisfied, relieved, secure, safe, loved.

**Focus On
4–3**   *(continued)*

Supportive Care	*Indulgence*	*Neglect*
Characteristics:		
Nurturing support offers help, comfort, and love. It encourages the child to think and do what he or she is capable of doing for himself or herself.	Indulgence is a sticky, patronizing kind of love. It promotes continuing dependence on the parents and teaches the child not to think for himself or herself and not to be responsible for self or to others.	Neglect is passive abuse. It is lack of attention, emotionally or physically, by parents who are unavailable or who ignore the needs of the child. These parents may be "there, but not there."
Example:		
Parent, who has already taught child how to clean a scrape, says in a concerned and loving tone, "I see you've scraped your arm. Does it hurt? Do you want to take care of it yourself or would you like some help from me?" Offers a hug.	Parent rushes to child. Says, "Oh, look at your arm, you poor thing. That really stings! I'll bandage it. Go and lie down in front of the television and I'll do your chores for you."	Parent ignores the scrape. Says, "Don't bother me."
Common Responses of Children:		
Pain in the arm and a heart filled with confidence. Child feels cared for, comforted, challenged, secure, and trustworthy.	Pain in the arm and uncertainty in the heart. Self-centered satisfaction, temporary comfort. Later on: helplessness, confusion, obligation, resentment, defensiveness, and shame.	Pain in the heart, as well as pain in the scraped arm. Feelings of abandonment, fear, shame, rage, hopelessness, helplessness, abject disappointment.

Abuse	*Conditional Love*	*Assertive Care*
Decisions Often Made by Children:		
I am not powerful. I deserve to die, or the reverse, I will live in spite of them. It's my fault, or the reverse, I'll blame everything on others. I'll be good, or the reverse, I'll be bad. Big people get to abuse, or I can abuse those smaller than me, or I will never abuse. I won't feel or have needs. Love does not exist. I am alone; I keep emotional distance from, and don't trust, others. I blame or strike or leave first.	I am what I do. I must strive to please. Big people get what they want. I can never do enough. I must be perfect. I don't deserve love. There is a scarcity of love. I must be strong. Love obligates me and is costly. I don't trust. I do keep emotional distance, run away, or blame others.	I am important. I deserve care. It's OK to ask for what I need. I belong here. I am loved. Others can be trusted and relied upon. I can know what I need. It's OK to be dependent at times.

(continued)

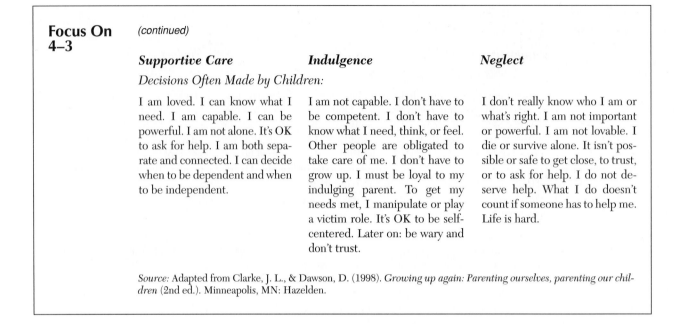

Focus On 4–3 *(continued)*

Supportive Care	Indulgence	Neglect
Decisions Often Made by Children:		
I am loved. I can know what I need. I am capable. I can be powerful. I am not alone. It's OK to ask for help. I am both separate and connected. I can decide when to be dependent and when to be independent.	I am not capable. I don't have to be competent. I don't have to know what I need, think, or feel. Other people are obligated to take care of me. I don't have to grow up. I must be loyal to my indulging parent. To get my needs met, I manipulate or play a victim role. It's OK to be self-centered. Later on: be wary and don't trust.	I don't really know who I am or what's right. I am not important or powerful. I am not lovable. I die or survive alone. It isn't possible or safe to get close, to trust, or to ask for help. I do not deserve help. What I do doesn't count if someone has to help me. Life is hard.

Source: Adapted from Clarke, J. L., & Dawson, D. (1998). *Growing up again: Parenting ourselves, parenting our children* (2nd ed.). Minneapolis, MN: Hazelden.

given manner in a variety of situations. A parent intentionally or unintentionally encourages and shapes certain behaviors in a child by responding to how the child acts. A child learns to adopt a given behavior pattern if it accomplishes a desired goal. Several publications describe how behavior modification procedures shape desired responses and acts of children by parents (Van Houten & Hall, 2001).

Basic Concepts. The basic concepts and approaches used in behavior modification are (1) all behavior is learned; (2) behavior is a function of its consequences; (3) a given behavior is encouraged and taught when it is immediately rewarded or reinforced; (4) reinforcement may be either positive or negative in nature; (5) learning may generalize from one situation or setting to another.

All approaches based on behavior modification emphasize that an awareness of environmental events as well as the context in which behavior occurs are necessary to fully comprehend the nature of stimuli that control behavior. Not only do such approaches stress that all behavior is learned, but also that whatever is learned can be unlearned, changed, or modified.

The basic premise of behavior modification theory is that individuals adjust their behavior according to its consequences. Essentially, people behave in ways that result in positive consequences and avoid behaving in ways that result in negative consequences (Figure 4–4). Stated thus, this view may seem overly simplistic. However, several factors influence the development and occurrence of behavior and the ways in which behavior can be changed or modified.

Reinforcement. The concept of reinforcement maintains that a *reinforcement* (reward) must immediately follow a particular behavior to increase the likelihood that the behavior will occur again in the future. All reinforcers are considered to be stimuli and are either positive or negative. A *positive reward* (positive reinforcer) increases the likelihood that a particular behavior will occur again. An example of positive reinforcement might be praising a child for using good table manners. It is important that the positive reinforcement (praise, in this instance) *immediately follows* the occurrence of the desired behavior. Performance of the act thus becomes associated with its reinforcement. *Negative reinforcement* occurs when an unpleasant stimulus is removed, thus increasing the likelihood that a particular behavior will occur again. An unpleasant stimulus associated with a certain type of behavior becomes reinforcing when its withdrawal is a positive or pleasurable experience. For

FIGURE 4–4 Parental responses to child behavior that are positive in nature, such as hugs and smiles, can shape future child behavior.

example, the discomfort of having something stuck painfully between one's teeth is removed by flossing. In this example, flossing is a negative reinforcer because it removes an unpleasant stimulus rather than adding one to a behavioral act.

● ●

Parenting Reflection 4–4

If positive reinforcement is so effective in producing desirable behavior from children, why do so many parents continue to use physical punishment as a means to gain the same effect with children?

● ●

Extinction.   Behavior modification includes the concept of extinction of behaviors that are undesired or unpleasant. This concept is illustrated by a teacher who ignores the whining behaviors of children. The undesirable behavior is not reinforced when the teacher's attention is not given. Likewise, undesired behaviors of children that are not reinforced by attention from parents will eventually cease. This is a difficult process for many parents, however. The number of times a behavior must be ignored is often excessive, and it may take a long time for the child to eliminate it from his or her repertoire of behaviors.

Reinforcement Schedule.   Another factor that is important to the success of behavior modification approaches is the frequency with which reinforcers are used. Researchers have discovered that continuous reinforcement of behaviors is not desirable. Rather, reinforcement that is intermittent may achieve most effective results. Two dimensions distinguish this approach to reinforcement. First, the desired behavior may be reinforced according to the number of occurrences. For example, a child may receive reinforcement only after he or she correctly pronounces five words consecutively. Second, the amount of time between behaviors may determine when reinforcement is given. For example, the child may receive reinforcement every other minute while he or she is talking, or there may be a variable amount of time between reinforcements, such as once after 1 minute, again after 3 minutes, and again after 10 minutes.

These methods involving reinforcement to teach children desirable behaviors are among the most powerful tools of discipline available to adults. However, the reinforcement process can be applied by children to adult behavior as well. Through reciprocal feedback, children also teach behavior patterns to their parents by applying their own brand of reinforcers. When an adult nags loudly, for example, a child usually tunes out the adult's unpleasant behavior by not listening, thus reinforcing the nagging behavior. Similarly, a child who wishes the attention of parents learns to act in a manner that reinforces parental attention.

Social Learning

Social learning theory explains how learning may occur when there is no visible reinforcer or reward. This theory is especially useful in explaining how socialization occurs or how someone learns appropriate behaviors based on family beliefs and values. According to this theory, an individual responds to a number of complex stimuli in forming associations between appropriate and inappropriate behavior. Conscious thought, rather than automatic response to a stimulus, assists in shaping behavior and actions.

This approach focuses on the importance of the role of a ***model*** or the effect of observation learning also known as ***imitation***. Many kinds of behaviors are believed to be acquired by watching the behavior of another person and then replicating the observed behavior in one's own actions.

Research into this type of learning shows how children learn to express such social behaviors as sharing and cooperation as well as aggression and violence by watching such behaviors demonstrated by a model. Models include both real people and characters seen in media presentations. Research reveals that when children see a model being rewarded for acting aggressively, for instance, they are more likely to demonstrate that same kind of behavior in their own play.

Social learning theory also explains how people acquire social values and attitudes. Social roles are learned in this manner. Children imitate behaviors they observe in adults and in other children they perceive as models. For example, social learning accounts for how sex-role behaviors or scripts are acquired in childhood.

Parenting Reflection 4–5

Do you think that parents truly realize that they are teaching their children certain values, attitudes, and behaviors by the behavioral example they model?

Focus Point.　Behavior modification is a highly reliable method for eliciting desired behaviors from children through the effective, conscientious application of positive reinforcement. Behaviors can be shaped by using reinforcement and paying close attention to the time when reinforcement is given. Social learning theory emphasizes the influence of modeling and observation as a means for learning a variety of social behaviors and roles.

Democratic Child Training

The democratic approach to child training is based on principles from Adlerian psychology, an approach used in family therapy. Rudolf Driekurs (1950) and his colleagues present a strategy for parenting and discipline that emphasizes democratic means of family operation such as encouragement, setting appropriate limits, practicing mutual respect for members, and collective deci-

sion making. A parent education curriculum that teaches this strategy is called Systematic Training for Effective Parenting (STEP). Some research reports that the democratic approach appears to show more consistently significant outcomes as a means of attaining parenting goals (Dembo, Switzer, & Lauritzen, 1985; Krebs, 1986; Ring, 2001). However, other work does not support this claim (P. W. Robinson, Robinson, & Dunn, 2003).

The democratic approach is based on the following assumptions (Dinkmeyer, 1979; Dinkmeyer & Driekurs, 2000; Dinkmeyer & McKay, 1981; Driekurs, 1950): (1) Behavior is purposeful and caused—it does not happen by chance; (2) it is necessary to understand behavior within its social context; (3) goals of misbehavior explain unacceptable actions of children; (4) to understand a child's behavior, one needs to understand the child's interpretation of the events he or she experiences; (5) belonging to social groups is a basic need of people, regardless of age; (6) people, including children, develop a life plan (script) that guides their behavioral decisions, even though these decisions may be based on faulty assumptions and logic.

These assumptions form the basis for parents' interactions with a child (Magen, Levin, & Yeshurun, 1991). The starting point for developing an effective, loving relationship with a child is for the adult to learn the impact of the family system in shaping the child's emerging patterns of behavior. The family system is seen as the child's model for all social interactions with others (Driekurs, 1950).

The *life plan* or *script* is the consistent pattern of decision making by which people make choices for their behavior. It is encouraged and developed first within the family system. The life plan is based on decisions about how to act, which relate to the goals one works for in his or her actions. A child discovers this plan for behavior to be effective in solving certain interaction problems within the family system and especially within the sibling and parent-child subsystems. As children grow older, they develop a personal logic to justify actions that make up the life plan. Different life plans emerge under each of the different parenting conditions outlined in Focus On 4–3: abuse, neglect, conditional love, indulgence, assertive care, and supportive care. If a parent consistently responds to children's behaviors in an indulgent manner, the child may adopt a life plan that involves being manipulative, self-indulgent, and self-centered (see section labeled "Decisions Often Made by

Children" in Focus On 4–3). When children are taught in ways that cause them to reach faulty conclusions about themselves or they draw these conclusions on their own, they develop life scripts containing behavioral choices that support these faulty conclusions.

Four basic goals of misbehavior occur from flaws in the logic of the life plan (see Table 4–1).

1. *Attention getting.* The child exhibits positive or negative behaviors that make others notice him or her, such as showing off or crying.

2. *Social power.* The child controls others by only doing what he or she wants and refusing to cooperate.

3. *Revenge.* The child retaliates for being hurt and feeling unloved by misbehaving.

4. *Displaying inadequacy.* Failure in all endeavors becomes expected and is used by the child to escape participation in interactions with others.

Democratic child training recognizes the impact of a child's sibling subsystem in influencing behavior. Driekurs believes that a child's birth order and position among siblings in the family system act to shape the life plan the child adopts. Competition for parents' attention, alliances that emerge between siblings, and different parental expectations for behavior of siblings account for differences in life plans and personalities of children from the same family system. For example, a first-born child may learn to adopt behavior patterns that work toward achieving the goal of power, or of power with revenge, first in interactions with siblings and parents and later with persons outside the family system. Being the oldest child generally brings heavy responsibilities and high expectations from parents. Competition for parental attention and affection may be intense, with the next child in the sibling constellation seen as an adversary who usurped the position of the first born in receiving the majority of attention from parents.

According to Driekurs, the second child is made to feel inferior to the older child through their interactions. The older child makes the younger child feel that he or she has to catch up with or be better than the older sibling. This child may learn patterns of behavior designed to meet goals of displaying inadequacy or power with revenge in interactions with others.

The middle child may learn power-oriented or attention-getting types of behavior to make himself or her-self noticed among siblings. The youngest child—the baby of the family—may learn patterns that achieve goals of getting others' attention or displaying inadequacy.

Logical Versus Natural Consequences. A key element of this strategy featured strongly in the STEP program is teaching children the logical consequences of their behavior as opposed to using rewards or punishment. In this guidance technique, authoritarianism is replaced with allowing the child to assume personal responsibility for his or her own actions (Ring, 2001).

A natural consequence results obviously and immediately from a given action: If you touch a hot stove, you get burned. Natural consequences are sometimes either too dangerous to be allowed or too remote in time to be effective in teaching children the results of their actions. In such cases, the parent must substitute a logical consequence, a consequence that is a rational result of a given action. For example, if a child arrives home after the evening meal has been served, the logical consequence to the child's tardiness (which should have been established and agreed to by all family members in advance) is that the child must prepare his or her own meal or else eat cold food. When this logical consequence to tardiness is administered consistently, the child eventually concludes that to avoid the unpleasant consequence of not being on time for meals, he or she must watch the time more carefully. This technique places the responsibility for both the choice of behavior and its consequences on the child, not the parent. Thus, a child learns to think, make plans, weigh consequences of decisions, and accept responsibility for those decisions.

A consequence must be experienced fully and consistently by a child before it can be an effective learning tool. Parents must resist the temptation to intervene and prevent the child from experiencing the consequence. When parents take pity on children and intervene, children learn that someone else will take responsibility for their actions. They also learn to pity themselves when they must endure the consequences of their actions.

• •

Parenting Reflection 4–6

Why do you think that many parents appear to prefer to use physical punishments rather than logical consequences to teach children appropriate behaviors?

• •

TABLE 4–1 The Goals of Misbehavior

Child's Faulty Belief	Child's Goal	Parent's Feeling and Reaction	Child's Response to Parent's Attempts at Correction	Alternatives for Parents
I belong *only* when I am being noticed.	Attention	*Feeling:* Annoyed. *Reaction:* Tendency to remind and coax.	Temporarily stops misbehavior. Later resumes same behavior or disturbs in another way.	Ignore misbehavior when possible. Give attention for positive behavior when child is not making a bid for it.
I belong *only* if I am in control or am the boss, or when I am proving no one can boss me!	Power	*Feeling:* Angry, provoked, as if one's authority is threatened. *Reaction:* Tendency to fight or to give in.	Active- or passive-aggressive misbehavior is intensified, or child submits with "defiant compliance."	Withdraw from conflict. Help child to see how to use power constructively by appealing for child's help and enlisting cooperation. Realize that fighting or giving in only increases the child's desire for power.
I belong *only* by hurting others as I feel hurt. I cannot be loved.	Revenge	*Feeling:* Deeply hurt. *Reaction:* Tendency to retaliate or get even.	Seeks further revenge by intensifying misbehavior or choosing another weapon.	Avoid feeling hurt. Avoid punishment and retaliation. Build trusting relationship; convince child that she or he is loved.
I belong *only* by convincing others not to expect anything from me. I am unable; I am helpless.	Display inadequacy	*Feeling:* Despair; hopelessness. "I give up." *Reaction:* Tendency to agree with child that nothing can be done.	Passively responds or fails to respond to whatever is done. Shows no improvement.	Stop all criticism. Encourage any positive attempt, no matter how small; focus on assets. Above all, don't be hooked into pity, and don't give up.

Source: Reprinted by permission of American Guidance Service, Publishers' Building, Circle Pines, MN. *Parents' handbook: Systematic training for effective parenting* by Don Dinkmeyer, Sr., and Gary D. McKay. Copyright (c) 1981. All rights reserved.

FIGURE 4–5 Families can gather to discuss issues, reach agreements, and develop a sense of togetherness. Mealtimes may be the most convenient time for such meetings in contemporary families.

Encouragement Instead of Reward or Punishment.   A major tenet of this strategy is that stimulation from within is more effective in producing desirable behavior than is pressure from without (Edgar, 1985). In this strategy, encouragement replaces reward and logical consequences replace punishment. Encouragement and reward are different in both timing and effect. Encouragement is given before an act takes place; a reward is given afterward. Encouragement is given not only upon success, but upon experiencing difficulty or failure; a reward is given only when one succeeds.

The Family Council.   The democratic basis of this strategy is reflected in the use of the family council or meeting as a means of reaching agreements, communicating effectively, and helping children develop a sense of participation in the family (Figure 4–5). It is suggested that these meetings occur on a regular basis, and that children be allowed an equal voice and vote in reaching family decisions. Such decisions may relate to establishing logical consequences to family rules, determining use of family resources, and resolving disputes among members.

••

Focus Point   The democratic approach to discipline strives to help children learn to become self-disciplined by experiencing the logical consequences of their behavior. Children's misbehaviors are seen to relate to the particular goal they wish to achieve through their behavior, which in turn is related to their particular life script. Encouragement is an important tool that is preferred over rewards or punishment. Family councils are recommended as a means to enable children to participate in family decision making.

••

Parent Effectiveness Training

Thomas Gordon's text *Parent Effectiveness Training* (1975/2000) represents a humanistic strategy for promoting a healthy relationship between parents and children. It is an outgrowth of a course Gordon developed to teach parents how to be more effective in their caregiving and disciplinary activities. The strategy focuses primarily on communication skills developed by the parent and a method of resolving conflicts that occur between the parent and child. As with other humanistic methods, such as those promoted by Ginott (1965), this strategy teaches the parent when to act as a counselor to children regarding their behavior. The strategy is grounded firmly in proven counseling methods developed by other professionals and applied to parenting skills by Gordon. The Parent Effectiveness Training (PET) program provides a useful battery of techniques for parents to use in their program of discipline (Wood & Davidson, 2003). Although there is a good possibility that these work well when performed appropriately by parents, their overuse may lead a child to tune out the parents, rendering their efforts ineffectual. Children of parents who have received this training exhibit greater self-reliance on problem solving and a higher degree of self-esteem. Like other strategies, PET is designed to achieve a more effective manner of communicating and interacting with children.

1.   *The parent acts as a counselor when a child has a particular problem.*   In this role, the parent engages in active listening, a common therapeutic technique used in many counseling methods. Instead of rescuing the child by offering solutions and suggestions for solving the problem for the child, the parent listens to the child and sifts through the child's statements to determine the feelings being covertly communicated. The parent then responds with what he or she perceives the problem to be as stated by the child. The goal is for the parent to empathize with the child, thus providing a nurturing response, objectively reflect back to the child the parent's perception of the problem, and allow the child to search for his or her own solution. In the following example, notice how the father uses active listening to help the child solve his problem.

DAD: Why aren't you playing with the other kids?

BOY: Nobody wants to play with me.

DAD: You feel that you don't have any friends and that makes you feel bad, huh? (*paraphrasing what is not being said but is assumed to be embedded in the message; reflecting the emotions in the message*)

BOY: Yeah. I hate Tommy and all the others.

DAD: You just hate them all. (*reflecting the emotion in the last message*)

BOY: Yeah. Especially Tommy.

DAD: He's the worst, huh? Why is that? (*reflecting the meaning and the emotion of the last message; taking an investigative stance*)

BOY: He makes fun of me because I don't always throw the ball right.

DAD: It really makes you feel bad when he teases you. (*reflecting the meaning and the emotion of the last message*)

BOY: You bet. He shouldn't do that to me. It hurts people's feelings when they get teased.

DAD: You think it's OK to make mistakes and Tommy needs to feel that way, too. (*reflecting the meaning and the emotion of the last message*)

BOY: Yeah. He calls me names. I don't like that. I don't do that to him when he goofs up.

DAD: You would get along better with Tommy if he didn't call you names when you goof up, and you wish he'd treat you like you try to treat him. (*reflecting the meaning and the emotion of the last message*)

BOY: You bet. I'm his friend, but I don't like it when he calls me names.

DAD: You think you're Tommy's friend, and friends should try to treat each other fairly and decently. Seems like you've got a problem about this. What do you think you can do to straighten things out? (*reflecting the meaning and emotion of the last message; bringing closure to the discussion by indicating that the solutions generated are the child's responsibility*)

BOY: Well, I think I need to tell Tommy how I don't want him to call me names when I goof up. Maybe I can ask him to show me how to throw the ball better. Then he won't call me names!

This hypothetical interchange allowed the father to help his son express feelings about the real issue that bothered him: being treated unfairly by his friend. The child's initial statement had many underlying feelings, implications, messages, and meanings that the father helped the child identify. The father did not offer his own solution to the child's problem ("You're bigger than Tommy. Get out there and knock his block off!"), nor did he admonish the child ("You're acting like a baby. Get used to being teased; there'll be a lot of it in your lifetime."). The father did not moralize ("You're a bigger person than Tommy. Now get out there and show him what you're made of!") or discount his son for those feelings ("You shouldn't feel like that. If I were you, I'd start practicing right now on my ball throwing so nobody could have the chance to tease me."). These responses fall into the categories of conditional love and criticism and would not promote healthy structure and nurturance. The father provided assertive and supportive care by recognizing the child's feelings of hurt and rejection and helping him reach his own solution to the problem.

Parenting FAQs 4–1

What do you think about using threats to gain children's cooperation with parents' wishes? Do these work?

A: Not really, especially in the long term. Threats usually are used when parents are feeling exasperated, tired, powerless, or otherwise at their wits' end. Sometimes they are used because a parent doesn't know of any other way to gain children's cooperation. Threats often act to stimulate children's noncompliance with parental wishes, promoting an "I-dare-you" stance between parents and children. These can develop into power plays between parents and children that are not healthy for the relationship. Instead of helping children learn about how to achieve win-win solutions to problems, threats force a no-win attitude upon children. Using forceful threats can also promote a fear of adults in children and damage their self-respect by the discounting nature of some threats.

A major problem with using threats is that they often involve hollow consequences or ones that are difficult to enforce. Imagine the reaction of a 5-year-old to hearing a mother's threat, "If you don't stop doing that, I'll slap you so hard you'll be looking backwards the rest of your life!" Such threats do not make sense to children and may instill fear and mistrust about parents to children.

Using positive alternatives such as choices rather than threats may help to gain children's cooperation with rules that have clearly identifiable consequences. For example:

Threat: This is the last time I'm telling you to stop what you're doing and come to dinner or else you'll go hungry tonight.

Alternative: It's time to stop playing and put your things away where they belong. You can have either 5 or 10 minutes to do this now.

Source: Adapted in part from A. Faber. (1995). *How to talk so kids can learn—at home and in school.* New York: Rawson Associates.

Parenting Reflection 4–7

How old should a child be when parents begin to use Parent Effectiveness Training techniques? At what age would these become ineffective with a child?

2. Parents can express their feelings to children about troublesome behavior in nondamaging ways. On those occasions when a child's behavior is a problem to a parent, the child may not know that he or she is causing a problem, or the child may be testing a parent's limits. At times, children just can't seem to resist the temptation to misbehave, even though they know they will get into trouble for doing so. In such situations, where the parent "owns" the problem (that is, the child's behavior is a problem because it is troublesome to the parent), Gordon suggests that the adult use a strongly phrased "I" message to communicate the problem to the child.

Without having learned to do otherwise, most adults phrase an initial sentence about someone's offensive behavior with a sentence beginning with *you:* "You're acting stupid," "You are doing that all wrong," or "You are driving me crazy with all that noise." Such "you" messages occur especially in cases where the adult is angry about the other person's behavior. Gordon suggests that a different sentence format be used when adults want children to pay attention and listen to what they are saying. First, Gordon proposes that rather than begin a message with "you," start with the word "I." Next, he suggests adding how the parent feels ("I get angry ..."), and then labeling the problem ("I get angry when I see you hit your sister," "I'm upset because I can't talk on the phone when you have the TV so loud," or "I feel bad when you don't listen when I'm talking to you").

According to Gordon, "I" messages differ from "you" messages in that they enable parents to effectively communicate a message to a child without damaging the child's self-esteem. Recall from the example of active listening given earlier that the father started many sentences with "you." In that context the father was acting as a counselor, so using sentences beginning with "you" was appropriate because they showed that he was listening to the child.

The "you" messages the father used did not contain content that would hurt the child's character or self-esteem, as do the "you" messages in the preceding paragraph: "You are acting stupid" or "You are doing that all wrong."

"I" messages are used to get a child to listen to what an adult has to say, to communicate facts to the child, and to help the child modify the unacceptable behavior. When parents learn to use this communication format, children also acquire the skill and begin to express their feelings to parents in nondamaging ways. "I" messages place the responsibility for changing the child's behavior on the child rather than on the parent, and they are less likely to promote resistance and rebellion in children. Additionally, these methods may be more effective with preschool- and school-age children than with adolescents.

3. *When conflicts occur that cannot be avoided, Gordon suggests that parents use the no-lose method of conflict resolution.* All too often, individuals in families believe that in resolving conflicts there must be someone who wins and someone who loses. This belief tends to promote adversarial situations in which parent and child are pitted against one another in a power struggle, each attempting to win by gaining his or her own way. In employing the no-lose strategy, parent and child strive to reach a win-win solution based on a compromise that is satisfactory to both. Neither parent nor child wins or loses in resolving the conflict; they come to an understanding that mutual needs must be satisfied to some degree in order for both people to be happy with the solution.

Gordon lists six steps for implementing this method. The steps are listed here, along with an example of a parent-child interaction.

1. Identify and define the conflict.

   PARENT: I've been very upset lately because you've been coming home late from school. I worry so much about you that I can't concentrate on my work until I know that you're home OK.

2. Generate possible solutions.

   PARENT: What can we do to solve this problem? Perhaps you should ride the bus home instead of staying after school to play.

   CHILD: I suppose I could keep better track of the time. If you would buy me a watch, I could set an alarm to let me know when to stop playing and leave for home.

3. Evaluate the solutions.

   PARENT: How much would a watch cost?

   CHILD: There are some kinds that aren't very expensive. I'd rather have a watch to remind me when to start home than not be able to stay after school and play with the kids.

4. Decide on the best solution for both parties.

   PARENT: OK, if we can find the right watch at the right price, I think that's a good idea.

5. Work out ways to implement the solution.

   PARENT: We can go to the department store after dinner tonight and shop for a watch. If you'd like, I'll help you learn how to set the alarm.

6. Evaluate how well the solution worked.

   PARENT: You've been doing a great job at being home on time now that you've got a watch. I'm proud that you learned how to do this yourself.

There are several advantages to this method: (1) Part of the responsibility for conflict resolution is placed with the child; (2) the child's cognitive skills in generating solutions are developed; (3) increased communication between parent and child results; (4) communications have no destructive emotional effects for parent or child; (5) the parent does not exert power over the child; and (6) autonomous behavior from the child is encouraged.

**Parenting
FAQs 4–2**

My partner and I often disagree about how to discipline our children. We usually get into arguments about who's right and which rules our children have to follow—hers or mine. Sometimes the kids will play one of us against the other to get what they want. How can we resolve this?

A: There are always going to be differences between parenting partners. These usually happen because we are raised by different families having different rules and different values. Many people believe that both parenting partners *must* agree on everything—every rule and every consequence to rules for children. However, it may be essential to reach an agreement about how to prioritize those rules that are more important than others and those rules that fall into the categories of negotiable and nonnegotiable, upon which both parenting partners can agree. Rather than reaching this consensus by trial and error, it is best to do so by explicit discussion and agreement. This will help everyone to know that there are some things that both parenting partners do not budge on, whereas there are other rules that are one parent's while not being an issue with the other. Such arrangements usually are not harmful to children

Gordon's strategy is significant in recognizing the influence of children's behavior on parents and in showing how to teach children to recognize the rights and needs of parents. Perhaps even more important, the strategy provides ways for parents to interact on a more equal basis with children instead of relying on power-assertive methods that damage children's self-esteem.

Gordon recognizes that there are times when active listening, "I" messages, and the no-lose method are inappropriate, as when children's safety is endangered or there are time pressures. These methods, however, generally are useful for anyone who works with children or with people in general.

Different effects are reported by researchers who have compared the behaviors of parents who attended training sessions in behavior modification and PET with those of parents who had no training in either strategy (Wood & Davidson, 2003). PET-trained parents felt that they had tools for working with children that enabled them to have a healthy relationship.

Focus Point.   Parent Effectiveness Training stresses communication between parents and children and gives specific formats for such communication. It recognizes that there are times when adults can be helpful to children by simply listening to their problems, and it recommends the technique of active listening. When a child's behavior is offensive or problematic, parents

need to communicate this to the child in nondamaging ways by using "I" messages. With the no-lose strategy for conflict resolution, parents and children learn to develop satisfactory compromises. The methods promoted in PET help parents provide structure and nurturance to children in healthy ways.

Ineffective Disciplinary Methods

A review of the research literature on parental disciplinary practices suggests that there are at least four methods that do not work well or effectively in providing structure for children and gaining their compliance (Chamberlain & Patterson, 1995). These include (1) discipline or parental behavior that is inconsistent, (2) irritable explosive practices, (3) inflexible rigid discipline, and (4) low parental supervision and involvement.

Inconsistency in parental behavior and especially that which constitutes a program of discipline serves primarily to confuse children about how they are expected to behave. For example, children receive mixed signals when a parent enforces a rule with its attendant consequences but at another time relents and does not enforce the rule or its consequences. When parents fail to agree on certain policies or rules about child behavior, children may also interpret this response as parental inconsistency.

Some parents appear to have only one type of reaction to all manner and types of children's transgressions, such as loud emotional outbursts like yelling, screaming, or using violent physical acts of aggression. The intensity of the parental reaction and the degree of punitiveness usually escalates in relation to the frequency that the child misbehaves.

When parents employ inflexible, rigid discipline, they appear to rely on one type of punitive strategy regardless of the nature of a child's transgression. No matter what a child does that is unacceptable, the parent reacts the same way. What is lacking is a hierarchy in an organization of parental reactions that links the seriousness of the offense to the nature of the parental reaction. Typically, when parents rely on this inflexible approach, they do not employ verbal reasoning with a child when transgressions occur. Rather, the parent reacts in the same manner with little assistance given to the child on how to learn from the mistake.

When parents provide poor supervision or involvement, children become abandoned and neglected emotionally. Left to their own devices under such circumstances, children become at risk for experiencing a wide range of behavior problems and poor school performance and for failing to develop effective interpersonal skills.

PARENTING STYLES AND MODELS

Parenting styles refer to those collections of child-rearing behaviors that are global in nature. They refer to an umbrella of parental behaviors rather than to specific ones alone. While being fairly abstract in nature, parenting styles characterize an overall approach to parenting, while, in reality, parents can display a variety of behaviors that change and become modified by a number of real-life circumstances. Parenting styles also reflect a philosophy of parenting that is believed to characterize what parents feel to be important in shaping children's behaviors toward their eventual maturity as adults. In addition, parenting styles encapsulate those attitudes and beliefs that form the implicit rules, or "shoulds," that guide a person's behavior as a parent. These have significant influence on the behavioral choices that a person makes in interacting and guiding the child into adulthood.

Behavioral and social scientists who have studied parent-child interactions recognize a group of basic categories of parenting styles. Initial work revealed three

basic styles: authoritarian, authoritative, and permissive (Baumrind, 1966). It is thought that parents initially adopt one particular style that strongly influences the manner in which they interact with children, but that this position shifts according to particular situations, for example, in public or private settings and in response to children's needs as they change developmentally. Thus, parenting styles show the characteristic of adaptability within family systems as parents attempt to maintain homeostasis within this relationship. For example, when a child is preschool age, a parent may feel it is necessary to practice authoritarian-style behaviors in order to provide assertive care, to promote appropriate standards for children, and to control their impulses. The parenting style shifts to more authoritative approaches when children reach their school-age years and supportive care is mixed with assertive care. Later, as children reach adolescents, parenting styles become more permissive in nature as teens learn to take increasing responsibility for decisions and actions.

Parenting styles also may vary according to ethnic group identity or social-class background. For example, middle-class parents might be more authoritative in the long run of child rearing, while working-class parents may operate within a more authoritarian approach.

Authoritarian Styles

Authoritarian styles are firmly grounded in traditional ways of child rearing. Authoritarian parenting relies predominantly on controlling children's behavior and places value on obtaining children's immediate and long-range obedience to their wishes. Such parents value "keeping a child in his place . . . restricting his autonomy, . . . and assigning household responsibilities in order to inculcate respect for work" (Baumrind, 1966, p. 889). Typically, this parenting style involves controlling children's behavior in every respect. Obedience is obtained in numerous ways, but physical punishment and other forceful means are often used to gain the child's cooperation. A typical response to a child's questioning of rules (and an authoritarian parent has many, many nonnegotiable rules) may be, "Because I said so." Usually this parenting approach evaluates, judges, and shapes the behavior of a child according to an established and often absolute standard to which the child is expected to conform. The parent's word is law for the child, who is taught to believe that the parent's actions are always in their best interest. Children raised by such standards are not encouraged to think for themselves or to think critically but to look to their parents for approval and solutions to problems.

Authoritarian styles are not considered to be especially conducive to promoting children's emotional health (A. Miller, 1990, 2002, 2006) because parents intimidate children rather than promote healthy feelings of self-worth. Rather than growing up with positive self-esteem, it is thought that children of authoritarian parents heavily incorporate the negative criticisms made by parents attempting to provide what they consider to be appropriate child guidance into adulthood. Alice Miller (1990) terms authoritarian parenting as the "poisonous pedagogy" because this style appears to promote parenting behavior that is, in effect, emotionally abusive and damaging to a child's self-esteem. Miller believes that the net result of this parenting style robs children of their human spirit, promotes the development of neuroses that are manifested in adulthood, and inhibit normal emotional development in children that is often expressed in self-hatred later in life.

Permissive Styles

A permissive parent "allows the child to regulate his or her own activities as much as possible, avoids the exercise of controls, and does not encourage him or her to obey externally defined standards" (Baumrind, 1966, p. 889). Parents who use this style believe that they should respond to their children as individuals and encourage them to be autonomous. This style typically incorporates reasoning and manipulation rather than overt demonstrations of power to gain children's cooperation. Parenting behaviors are expressed in ways that communicate these beliefs. For example, a permissive-style parent is not interested in being viewed by a child as an authority figure or as an ideal person to be imitated; rather, this parent wishes to be seen as a resource the child can use for learning about the world. People who practice permissive parenting styles allow greater latitude in children's behavior. Policies or limits to behavior are determined in consultation with children in an attempt to allow them to voice their own opinions. Children are expected to learn from their mistakes and to use the consequences of their actions as a guide for how to act in the future. However, Baumrind found that the least self-reliant, curious, and self-controlled children were being parented under this style.

Authoritative Styles

Authoritative styles combine the best features of both the authoritarian and permissive orientations. Authoritative styles emphasize the development of autonomy in children, but within reasonable limits. When using controls to achieve this end, authoritative parents may resort to whatever tactics lie within their means such as reasoning, overt demonstrations of power through mild physical punishment, or psychological reinforcement. A parent who uses such controls predominantly "encourages verbal give and take, shares with the child the reasoning behind the policies the parent establishes, and solicits his objections when he refuses to conform" (Baumrind, 1966, p. 890). Baurmind reported that children of parents using this approach were often self-reliant, self-controlled, contented, and curious about learning and exploring their environment. Later research (Baumrind, 1991, 1994, 1996) found that this parenting style is particularly effective when children become adolescents. Other researchers also report that this parenting style encourages a child's success in school, development of a healthy sense of personal autonomy, and positive work attitudes (L. Steinberg, Elmen, & Mounts, 1989). Breaking down this parenting style into dimensions of certain behaviors by parents, Gray and Steinberg (1999) report that three particular types of parenting behaviors make this style so effective with adolescents. These include (1) *acceptance and involvement* or the ways that parents respond to their children's needs and individual differences; (2) *strictness and supervision* or parental monitoring and supervision of their children's behavior in order to bring conformity to family rules; and (3) *granting autonomy* or encouraging teens expressions of individuality and permitting participation in family decision-making.

Other Classifications

Another way to classify parenting styles uses the dimensions of warmth/responsiveness and control/demandingness (Maccoby & Martin, 1983). When the basic parenting styles are viewed through these lenses, authoritative styles are seen to be high in warmth and high in control, authoritarian styles are seen to be low in warmth and high in control, and indulgent or permissive styles are seen to be high in warmth and low in control. A fourth parenting style is identified using this typology, termed neglectful, is seen to be low in warmth as well as in control.

Based on these observations, Baumrind (1991, 1994, 1996) sees that authoritative parental approaches appear to promote healthy, socially responsible outcomes for children that include

■ use of firm policies that are enforced,
■ use of acceptance rather than rejection,
■ emphasis of critical thinking skills, individuality, and self-initiative behaviors,
■ acting as models of the behaviors and attitudes parents wish children to adopt,
■ providing explanations and reasons for rules and policies.

Parenting Models

Unfortunately, not all families are healthy and attempt to parent children carefully with positive intended outcomes. Reality is that some parents can be abusive to children. Based on observations of numerous adults, several models of parenting illustrate how child rearing can unfold in unhealthy manners (Becnel, 1991; Forward, 1989; Isensee, 1991). The blueprint for these models as well as the healthy ones appears to be acquired unconsciously by way of observing the behaviors of one's parents while growing up. This is the basis of what social learning theory postulates about how many social behaviors are acquired through observation while growing up. These models can have long-lasting, long-term effects that are manifested in a child's adult years when they become parents themselves. There is often a mixture or composite of behaviors that resembles several aspects of the various models discussed here. Since we have discussed other parenting styles, we examine these models here:

The *demanding parent* often conducts child rearing using authoritarian styles. This parent requires children to believe that they must live their lives according to the adult's standards and ideas of what is acceptable and appropriate. Guilt and manipulation are often used to achieve these ends with children. Children are treated consistently as if they are totally helpless and must be dependent on their parents, regardless of their abilities or ages. Children react to such treatment over a long period of time in various ways, such as developing a high need for parental approval, lying, or practicing deception.

The *critical parent* devotes a large part of his or her interactions with children to criticizing and being

judgmental. This tactic can be used as a means to achieve control over children or as a means of coping with fears by imposing an attitude of perfectionism. Such behavior can motivate both parents and children to maintain a high degree of family secrecy, substantial personal boundaries that minimize intimacy, and rigid rules to regulate behavior. Both adults and children suffer from low levels of personal esteem because of the pervasive air of failure that permeates their relationship. In addition, children often have overdeveloped and highly sensitive feelings of guilt when mistakes occur or errors are made.

The *overfunctioning parent* sends consistent messages to children of their ineptitude that serve to substantiate the parent's overprotective behavior. Such a parent feels overly responsible for what a child does and believes it is necessary to manage almost every aspect of a child's life. Some family therapists feel that overfunctioning parental behavior arises out of a deep fear of being abandoned.

The *disengaged parent* is not emotionally involved with children or with his or her work as a parent. These individuals often appear to be too busy, tired, or sick to function adequately as a parent. There is some belief that these individuals never truly learned to love or to be loved as children and, hence, are unable to love or to be loved as parents.

The *ineffective parent* is incapable of meeting the needs of children and accepting the responsibilities of parenting. Many reasons may underlie this parenting model, such as having an addiction or a chronic illness. Children often assume roles in their family that are far beyond their abilities to perform well, such as when an older child assumes the full-time care of younger children.

The *abusive parent* harms children emotionally, physically, and even sexually. These parents often were abused themselves as children by their parents and are prone to repeat such actions as parents themselves. The emotional scars that such behavior leaves with children take much effort and time to heal when they become adults. These unhealthy parenting actions are discussed in more detail in Chapter 15 of this text.

It is important to stress that it is possible for someone to alter his or her parenting style or model by consciously becoming aware of his or her actions and learning how these impact children's growth and development. Working with a competent family therapist is one of the better ways that this can take place.

Parenting Reflection 4–8

Reflect on the parenting style and/or model of your own parents. Based on what you observed and what you remember, can you predict what model and/or style you think you will adopt when you become a parent yourself?

Focus Point.   Three basic approaches to parenting include authoritarian, permissive, and authoritative styles. Each influences child outcomes in different ways and in different effects. Authoritative parenting appears to be especially effective in child rearing. Other models of parenting behavior may be unhealthy in nature and are acquired through observation of one's own parents.

NORMAL BEHAVIOR PROBLEMS OF CHILDREN

One of the major preoccupations of many parents concerns problems in children's behavior and development. Frequently, there are conflicts that occur between parents and children over socialization tasks, relationship concerns, and gaining compliance from children. Many situations that are termed normal behavior problems are actually a problem for the adult and not the child. Similarly, many problems are simply a normal part of development as children strive to accomplish specific tasks but experience difficulties in mastering them. These may relate to the age of a child: What is normal behavior at one stage may be problematic at another and may indicate some type of developmental or emotional disturbance.

Parents need to be aware of the difference between normal behavior problems and problems that are indicative of a serious disorder that calls for professional attention. Each of the chapters that follow includes a section about the normal behavior problems that parents can anticipate as a part of the development of children. These range from sleep problems in young children to eating disorders in adolescents. For many individuals, the major sources of information on these common problems are parenting books, articles in popular magazines, and discussions with friends.

POINTS TO CONSIDER

- Parents serve as children's first teachers about life, how to interact with others, and what values are important to learn. Today, a competent parent actively acquires knowledge about child growth and development and gains experience in using a variety of methods and strategies that facilitate healthy parent-child interactions.
- One of the greatest concerns of most parents is how to provide adequate and proper discipline for children. Discipline refers to those methods used to help children learn to behave in appropriate ways, according to the patterns supported by their family system. To be effective, discipline should be positive, moderate, aimed at a child's particular age and developmental level, and based on an understanding of a particular child's needs.
- Discipline often is considered to refer to those behaviors and methods that involve punishment used to control children's misbehaviors. In truth, spanking and other forms of physical punishment are not recommended as part of any discipline program. Effective discipline aims to provide children with structure (self-discipline) and nurturance.
- Discipline is facilitated when caregivers (1) attempt to identify and understand a child's feelings and motivations; (2) discuss and adopt a consistent plan of discipline methods; (3) attempt to accomplish effective communication with children by listening to their opinions and feelings; (4) allow children to learn to make decisions as well as mistakes and to take responsibility for their actions; and (5) base discipline on the use of rules, some negotiable and others nonnegotiable, as well as assertive and supportive care.
- A variety of methods or strategies are available to contemporary parents for use in establishing disciplinary programs for children.
- The disciplinary strategies discussed in this chapter are derived from modern behavioral science and range from reward and reinforcement to ways that facilitate effective communications between parents and children. Those strategies include behavior modification, the democratic approach, and Parent Effectiveness Training.
- Four characteristics describe these discipline strategies: (1) Each seeks to reduce parental power over child behavior and fosters reacting in positive ways

that do not damage children's self-esteem; (2) children are taught to learn self-discipline in controlling their actions; (3) caregivers are provided with proven, effective means of communication that help reduce conflict and facilitate healthy interpersonal interactions; and (4) each seeks to help parents gain a better understanding of child growth and development.

■ Behavior modification involves the use of positive rewards and reinforcement of desired child behaviors by parents. Caregivers use these methods to teach children how to behave in an appropriate manner. Reinforcers must immediately follow a desired act to be effective. Caregivers may teach a complex task to children in sequential stages using reinforcement as children master progressively difficult behaviors. In addition, caregivers must be aware of the ability of children to reinforce certain parent behaviors.

■ A central tenet of the democratic approach to parenting is based on several assumptions: (1) There are reasons for children's actions; (2) parents must attempt to understand children's behavior by determining and analyzing the child's reasoning for his or her behavior; (3) everyone has a basic need to belong to a social group; and (4) people develop a life plan that guides decisions to behave in certain ways, and that life plan may be based on faulty assumptions. A child's birth order in a family has a strong influence on the kind of life plan the child develops. Goals of misbehavior may explain reasons underlying most behaviors of children. Parents are encouraged to teach children that there are logical consequences, either positive or negative, to behavior. These consequences teach children to behave in accordance with family rules and policies. Encouragement is suggested as being more appropriate in shaping children's behavior than rewards. Family councils or regular meetings of the family group are recommended to establish policies and rules, consequences to the rules, and to resolve conflicts. Children should have an equal voice with that of parents at such councils.

■ Parent Effectiveness Training focuses on enhancing communication skills between parents and children and on ways to resolve conflicts. Effective communication is thought to occur when (1) the parent acts as a counselor when a child has a problem; (2) a child's behavior is causing a problem for the adult and others; and (3) conflicts between parents and children are resolved through compromise.

■ There are three basic parenting styles: authoritarian, permissive, and authoritative. These styles may be modified when the dimensions of warmth and control are examined in relation to various combinations. Other models of parenting behavior, which may not be healthy in nature, are acquired by observing the model provided by one's own parents as a child.

PART II

The Work of Parenting

The work of parents in actively producing and socializing children into adulthood usually lasts for about 25 years. As we have seen in the first part of this text, on-the-job learning, especially regarding how to rear the first-born child, is required.

One of the distinctive characteristics of parenting children is the changing nature of the style or actual behavior that changes in tandem with children's changing developmental needs. The shifts, refinements, and adaptations made in parenting style that occur in the interactions between parents and children are examined in the chapters of this part. For example, as a child matures and grows, parents must change from being physical helpers to psychological helpers and assist the child in coping with cultural as well as family expectations of how to behave appropriately.

Other expressions of caregiving also change as parents adapt their ways of providing structure and nurturance to accommodate the needs of growing children. When children are young, physical expressions of nurturance dominate parenting styles with increasing emphasis on experiences that teach structure. As children grow older, these are replaced by verbal methods such as encouragement, reassurance, and listening to their problems. Parents change their methods of controlling a child's behavior as part of the adaptation of providing structure. Physical means of control that are used frequently with young children are replaced with psychological and verbal guidance methods when children enter their preschool, school-age, and adolescent years.

This part of the text first examines the issues that adults consider in deciding to become a parent or not. We discuss pregnancy and childbirth as important aspects of parenting children and providing for a healthy start in life. Next, we focus on parenting infants and toddlers and then young children. The focus shifts to a discussion of parenting strategies, which become a major issue as children grow into their preschool years and into middle childhood and adolescence. The remaining chapters discuss parenting issues involved in rearing school-age children, adolescents, and young adults. Portions of some chapters examine slices of family developmental time (using the Systemic Family Development model from Chapter 3) as a means for understanding what is taking place in an entire family system when children are of particular ages.

CHAPTER 5

The Transition to Parenthood

Focus Questions

▪ ▪ ▪ ▪ ▪ ▪ ▪ ▪ ▪ ▪

1. What major factors influence a person's decision to become a parent?
2. Is first-time parenthood a crisis experience for many adults?
3. How does first-time parenthood affect a couple's committed relationship? What other factors may influence someone's adjustment to becoming a parent?
4. What new medical technologies assist people with reproductive difficulties in becoming parents?
5. What major factors and issues relate to adopting children? What are the different types of adoption? Should adopted children be informed of their birth circumstances?
6. What is foster care? Why are children placed into the foster care system?
7. What are some characteristics of foster children? What are foster parents like, and why does someone become a foster parent? What particular challenges face foster parents?
8. What are some outcomes for foster children? What can be done to improve the foster care system?
9. What kinds of support are available for new parents?

▪ ▪ ▪ ▪ ▪ ▪ ▪ ▪ ▪ ▪

DO I WANT TO BE A PARENT?

Before the advent of modern contraceptives, it was taken for granted that married couples would have children if they were biologically able. Circumstances are different today. People have greater freedom of choice to decide whether and when they will have children and how many children they will have. In many cases, couples plan to have children in advance of their conception and birth (Figure 5–1). Couples often discuss how many children they want and prepare for the entry of children into their family system. In this section we explore some of the factors that influence how people reach the decision to become parents in contemporary times.

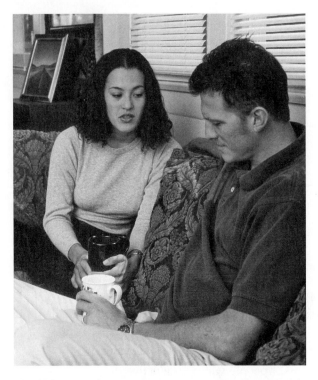

FIGURE 5–1 Many contemporary couples discuss and make plans before beginning a pregnancy.

The decision to become parents is a serious one that usually involves discussions between a couple. Complex issues are considered in this decision (see Figure 5–2). Today, economic considerations play a central role (Lino, 2006). Children are no longer considered an economic asset as they were in the past. To a contemporary American family, children can be an economic liability, and for this reason many people delay childbearing until they have established a sound financial base to support the many expenses involved. Others delay having children until decisions have been made about their desired lifestyle and whether children will play a part. In addition, a variety of social pressures influence one's decision to become a parent. For these reasons, the desire to become a parent has a strong psychological and emotional basis. Potential parents must examine the notion that children can fulfill different needs, values, and functions within a particular family system. These and other related factors are discussed in more detail in the following sections.

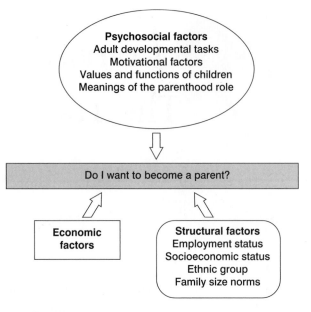

FIGURE 5–2 The decision about whether to become a parent is influenced by a complex of interrelated factors.

Parenting Reflection 5–1

How does our society view someone who does not want to be a parent? What factors may motivate someone to remain childless? Can someone who does not want children be considered to be emotionally and/or socially healthy?

Economic Factors

People apparently consider the economic costs of having children today more carefully than they did in the past. Economic factors also relate to a couple's desired lifestyle. These issues contribute to the delayed ages at which many couples have their first child (see Figure 5–3). Although accurate costs of childbearing and child rearing are difficult to obtain, it has been estimated that about one-fourth of the total lifetime income of a typical middle-class family in the United States is devoted to meeting the costs of having and raising a child from birth through age 18 (Lino, 2006). Another way to look at the financial outlay is the estimated total costs required for child rearing. For a child born in 2005, this may require $250,530 to age 18. This immense figure relates to

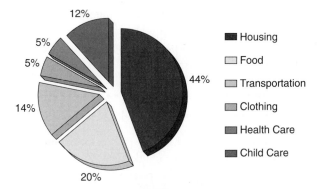

FIGURE 5–3   Percentages of income spent by a typical family middle-income family during the first 2 years of a child's life.

Source: Lino, M. (2006). *Expenditures on children by families, 2005. Miscellaneous Publication No. 1528-2005*. Washington, DC: U.S. Department of Agriculture, Center for Nutrition Policy and Promotion.

family expenses for providing a single family home, food, health care, and child care, for example (Lino).

Family expenditures to provide housing, child care, transportation, and food consume the majority of a family's income. These costs account for about half of the total outlay necessary in raising children to maturity (Lino, 2006) (see Figure 5–3). Another cost of child rearing not often considered by those contemplating parenthood is the potential loss of family income due to the mother not being employed. Many women choose not to enter the workforce or leave upon having a child and do not return to work until the child enters kindergarten. The loss of income due to the desire that children receive full-time parental supervision is an important issue to potential parents.

Structural Factors

Several structural factors that relate to and influence economic considerations enter into the decision to become a parent. First, the employment status of the mother is frequently an important consideration (Federal Interagency Forum on Child and Family Statistics, 2007). A related factor is the necessity of planning for child care should the mother return to the labor force. Finding a source of reliable, economical child care, especially for an infant, calls for careful consideration. Many families in the United States rely on relatives or in-home (family) day care of children when mothers are employed outside the home. Others rely on agencies, nonprofit organizations, or proprietary services for substitute child care. Use of these services is often seen as less desirable than parental care, although research strongly suggests that children are not harmed by nonparental care during the early years of their lives (National Institute for Child Health and Human Development, 1999, 2003). The relative advantages and disadvantages of nonparental child care are discussed in later chapters.

The socioeconomic status and ethnic group membership of a family also influence the decision to pursue parenthood. These factors are associated with the values and functions adults apply to having children and the number of children a couple desire.

A group's *fertility rate*—the actual number of children to whom a woman gives birth—reflects these factors as well (see Figure 5–4). Hispanics are currently the fastest-growing minority group in the United States due in part to a fertility rate that is considerably higher than other ethnic groups (Population Reference Bureau,

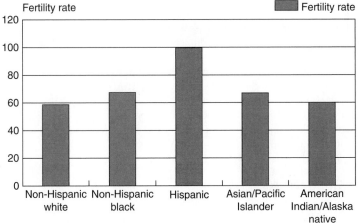

FIGURE 5–4   Fertility rates per 1,000 women by race and ethnicity, 2005.

Source: Hamilton, B. E., Martin, J. A., & Ventura, S. J. (2006). Births: Preliminary data for 2005. *National Vital Statistics Report, 55*. Hyattsville, MD: National Center for Health Statistics.

2003a). In addition, middle-class women tend to have fewer children than those of blue collar status (U.S. Bureau of the Census, 2006). This may be due in part to the higher level of education generally received by middle-class women, which is related to more prevalent use of birth control methods, differences in rate and type of employment, and a tendency to limit family size to maintain a certain lifestyle.

Due to our culture's strong **pronatalist** bias, adults who are married experience great social pressures to become parents (May, 1997). Perhaps the greatest pressure comes from a couple's parents in their desire to become grandparents. At the same time, there is considerable pressure on couples to limit the number of children they produce, which arises from societal concerns about overpopulation and from economic pressures.

Psychosocial Factors

A complex of psychosocial factors contribute significantly to people's decision to become parents. The reasons for having children have shifted from a strong economic base in the past to one that is psychological and social in nature today. An equally strong emotional component

is tied in with parenthood and parenting. This psychosocial complex is well illustrated in a series of questions that may be considered prior to beginning a pregnancy (see Parenting FAQs 5–1).

Parenting Reflection 5–2

What happens when one person in a committed relationship wants to have children but the other does not? How might this conflict be solved so that both persons can be satisfied to some degree?

Parenting Reflection 5–3

What are some advantages and disadvantages of having children in contemporary society? What are some ways that society's expectations of parents can be made more realistic in today's world?

Parenting FAQs 5–1

I've been married for more than 5 years now and have a wonderful relationship. There are no children and probably won't be any in the future. However, there are times when I'm uncertain that this is what I want. Can you offer some guidance on what to consider about making this decision about having kids?

A: It's good that you are making a conscious effort to make the decision about parenthood. Many people don't do this or don't have the opportunity for a number of reasons. Here are some points that you might include on your list of issues to examine:

- What do you want out of life for yourself? What do you think is important?
- How would a child interfere with your growth and development as an individual? How would a child enhance this process?
- Do you like doing things with children? Do you enjoy activities that children can do?
- Do you want a boy or a girl child? What if you don't get the one you want?
- Would you try to pass on to your child your ideas and values?
- What if your child's ideas and values turn out to be very different from yours?
- Does your partner want to have a child? Have the two of you discussed your reasons for wanting a child? Suppose one of you wants a child and the other doesn't? Who decides?
- Are you financially prepared for caring for a child?

Source: Adapted from Baker, C. (1977). *Am I parent material?* Washington, DC: National Alliance for Optional Parenthood.

FIGURE 5–5 There are a variety of reasons for wanting to become a parent. Children represent many things to parents, and the parenthood role holds different meanings for adults.

Motivations (Reasons) for Becoming a Parent. Many different personal reasons enter into a person's debate about assuming parenthood, and most people genuinely appear to want children (Figure 5–5). These reasons may have their basis in the beliefs of one's family of origin, social class, or ethnic group. Motivations for becoming a parent may be present long before an individual has children and are seen as antecedents of the varying attitudes people have toward this role in adulthood. When and if children are produced, adults' underlying reasons for becoming parents may be played out in a child-rearing script they follow without questioning. In many ways, the reasons for wanting to be a parent may be associated closely with the experience a

---

Focus On 5–1   **Reasons for Having Children**

These are the top 10 reasons both men and women gave for having children (not in ranked order):

- A new person is created with someone you love.
- Children make life richer.
- Children are an important part of being married.
- Someone to share things with.
- I enjoy being with children.
- The experience of raising children.
- Parenthood is one of life's greatest accomplishments.
- Feelings about continuation of life.
- It is part of being a real woman or man.
- Someone who loves you.

Source: Adapted from Burnell, G. M., & Norfleet, M. A. (1986). Psychosocial factors influencing American men and women in their decision for sterilization. *Journal of Psychology, 120,* 113–119.

person expects to have interacting with a child. Although these reasons are highly personal and unique to each individual, a strong psychosocial theme reflects pleasure in child rearing, feelings of love and affection, and attitudes of generativity (see Focus On 5–1).

There is a fatalistic component to some individuals' desire to be a parent. Some people may be strongly motivated to become a parent because they believe that procreation is the primary reason for their existence. People with such beliefs believe that contraception is immoral because it interferes with God's will. These beliefs are grounded strongly in many individuals' religious orientations.

A different aspect of a fatalistic reason to have children is to ensure continuation of one's family name. In some ethnic subcultures and family systems, males continue to be highly valued because family names are perpetuated through them.

The primary motivations for having children and becoming a parent can be altruistic in nature. These reasons include an unselfish desire to express affection and concern for children. The ability to express one's sense of generativity may be provided through parenting experiences.

Parenthood provides an outlet for the fulfillment of one's psychological need to be needed, according to Erikson's concept of generativity. This aspect can also be considered a narcissistic motivation to become a parent. Narcissism in this context refers to the expectation that having children will reflect on the goodness of a person and serve as a concrete, visible statement of maturity and adequacy as a sexually mature and active adult. It is also related to the need to achieve similarity with peers.

Another narcissistic aspect is the notion that children will provide their parents with emotional security and love. There is no guarantee, unfortunately, that children will reciprocate a parent's love.

Other reasons for assuming parenthood are instrumental in nature. For example, many parents may wish children to achieve specific goals for them. Their expectation, for example, is that children will reach levels of achievement that they have not been able to achieve, such as getting a college education, learning a particular skill, or being successful in a certain career. In essence, such individuals view the parenting experience as a second chance at life. Some parents may unconsciously believe that they can relive their own childhood through their children. Similarly, many are motivated by the

hope and determination that their children will not repeat their mistakes. Interestingly, some men may desire to become fathers because they missed having a close relationship with their own fathers and hope to relive this in a potential parenting relationship (Gerson, 1993).

Another instrumental reason for assuming parenthood is to secure an intimate relationship. Some people mistakenly believe that having children will rescue a troubled marriage, when the presence of children does not appear to help or hinder marriage satisfaction. Unfortunately, the increased strain on adults caused by managing multiple roles is likely to contribute to difficulties in a marriage. Studies that compare marriages with and without children find that marital satisfaction is greatest among couples who do not have children (Schulz, Cowan, & Cowan, 2006).

Yet another instrumental reason for assuming parenthood is having a child to please one's own parents. It is not unusual for older parents to place pressure—subtly or not so subtly—on their adult children to become parents. The desire to be a grandparent may be the paramount explanation. Middle-aged parents may wish to conform with their peers who are grandparents. Adult children may give in to these pressures to reduce the guilt that arises from being childless.

Parenting Reflection 5–4

Is it possible for some people to adapt unsuccessfully to becoming a parent? What happens when someone has a surprise pregnancy that was not planned, does not want to have an abortion, and does not believe that it is appropriate or moral to give a child up for adoption?

Meanings of the Parenthood Role. The last of the psychosocial factors we examine are the cultural meanings associated with the parental role (Figure 5–6). In most cultures, individuals have ideas about the characteristics and functions that are ideal in the social roles they have found to be necessary in that culture. These ideas are often exaggerated notions that shape an individual's thoughts, reactions, and behaviors. Many times, individuals accept these ideal notions as valid and do not question them.

The social meanings of parenthood and nonparenthood existing in our culture are described by psychologist J. E. Veevers (1973). These interpretations of

FIGURE 5–6   Children represent a number of values to adults. For example, children may provide their parents with many pleasurable experiences.

parenthood come from behavioral and social science research. It is important to understand the influence of these social meanings on individuals' behavior. Belief in the social meanings of parenthood may place social pressure on people and motivate them to become parents rather than remain childless.

Veevers uses six main themes to classify the social meanings of parenthood: morality, responsibility, naturalness, sex, marriage, and normality and mental health.

1. *Parenthood Is a Moral Obligation.* Many individuals may interpret parenthood as a moral obligation associated with adulthood. According to Veevers, the Judeo-Christian traditions that influence our culture arise from the Old Testament directive to be fruitful and multiply. These traditions support the pronatalist position of our culture that adults are obligated to reproduce and replenish society with new members. Procreation becomes a moral obligation for those who devoutly practice the teachings of religious groups that favor this position.

2. *Parenthood Is a Civic Responsibility.* Parenthood may be interpreted as a civic obligation in that the continuation of a culture depends on the reproduction of children. Veevers identifies a cultural belief that the alarmingly high costs of child rearing are

not disadvantages or acceptable excuses for not having children. Individuals who have the financial and social resources to be competent parents and yet choose to remain childless are traditionally considered by society to be selfish and irresponsible. It is partially for this reason that homosexuality traditionally is not valued by society, because most individuals of this orientation do not reproduce and have children.

3. *Parenthood Is Natural for Adults.* Traditional belief holds that parenting is an expected and natural behavior of adulthood. According to Veevers, this attitude refers to the belief that conception is a natural consequence of sexual intercourse between opposite-sex adults. This idea of parenthood is carried over from the period before the introduction and acceptance of reliable contraceptives. People have assumed that a childless individual had some type of physical problem that prevented procreation and, therefore, that the individual was an unnatural or abnormal person who had little value to society. Veevers states that this assumption is erroneous. According to her logic, if humans had an instinctual drive to reproduce and provide for children's care, then the method of socializing children and performing caregiving would be common to every culture

of the world. In fact, anthropologists have shown that there is much cultural variation in parenting styles, and hence human behavior is not governed by instinct.

4. *Parenthood Is a Statement of Human Sexuality.* Parenthood has sexual meanings and implies that an individual adult is capable of reproduction. Since parenthood validates, communicates, and confirms heterosexuality, it may be considered an aspect of a person's sexual identity. This view calls into question the psychological and physical condition of childless adults.

5. *Parenthood Is a Confirmation of Marriage.* Closely associated with the sexual meanings implied in parenthood is the notion that parenthood gives true meaning to a committed relationship between adults. Traditionally, children are believed to round out a marriage, improve the relationship between a couple, help a troubled or stagnant relationship, and prevent divorce.

6. *Parenthood Is Normal Adult Behavior.* The final idea discussed by Veevers is the normality of individuals who have children. Traditionally, childbearing is thought to fulfill a personal destiny for women more than for men. From this view, a woman who is childless is seen as unnatural, abnormal, and lacking in normal mental health. Implicit is the assumption that parents are socially mature people. Having a child is considered to be a means of achieving adult social status and being recognized for it. Parenthood implies caring for dependent children and being concerned for their welfare; conversely, nonparenthood implies caring more for one's own well-being than for that of others.

It is difficult to determine exactly the extent to which these beliefs continue to be held in the general population. As Veevers notes, several organizations have been formed in reaction to these pronatalist attitudes, such as the National Alliance for Optional Parenthood. Certainly, the impact of the Women's Movement also has contributed to reducing the prevalence of these beliefs. A growing segment of the adult population of the United States appears to be choosing not to become parents. Forty-five percent of all women of childbearing ages in the United States, that is, between 15 and 44 years, were childless in 2004 (Dye, 2005). The number of childless women is highest between 15 and 29 years

and declines thereafter. Furthermore, traditional attitudes about the social meanings of parenthood seem to be more prevalent among older people than among younger individuals. Young adult women, for example, tend to describe a childless adult as happy, normal, natural, sensitive, and emotionally stable, while middle-aged adult women describe this individual as maladjusted, inappropriate, unloving, and sexually inadequate. Young women today apparently hold more positive attitudes about nonparenthood due to exposure to alternatives to parenthood as acceptable options of adult life (Coll, 1991).

Another way to study the meaning of parenthood is to examine the concept of *responsible fathering* (Doherty, Kouneski, & Erickson, 1998; 2000; Levine & Pitt, 1998). This concept implies a set of social and ethical notions that constitute what this role means within families and within society. It also reflects a desire to include nurturance within a traditional male sex- and gender-role ideology that is in balance with the instrumental functions of enforcing limits on children's behavior. Furthermore, it emphasizes the moral duties of men to children once they have taken the reproductive responsibility of helping to create a human life. A responsible father, then, is one who (Levine & Pitt)

■ waits to make a baby until he is prepared emotionally and financially to support his child,
■ establishes his legal paternity if and when he does make a baby,
■ actively shares with the child's mother in the continuing emotional and physical care of their child, from pregnancy onward, and
■ shares with the child's mother in the continuing financial support of their child, from pregnancy onward.

These ideas about how to configure someone's role as a father can serve as a template for future behavior and a means for evaluating one's behavior and conduct in this role.

These notions are confirmed when examining the transition to fatherhood and the addition of subsequent children to a family in working to transform the lives of new fathers (Knoester & Eggebeen, 2006). Becoming a father encourages men to become more involved as a coparent of their children, increase their intergenerational and extended family interactions, their involvement in service-oriented activities, and work longer hours at their jobs and occupations.

Focus Point.   Several factors operate to influence the decision of many adults to become parents or to remain childless. These include: (1) economic considerations that relate to the costs of childbearing and child rearing and affect other factors such as employment of both adults in a family, the kind of lifestyle desired, and number of children produced; (2) structural variables such as the employment status of the adults, socioeconomic and ethnic group backgrounds of the family members, and desired family size; and (3) psychosocial factors such as parenting as an expected developmental task of adulthood, personal reasons or motivations to become a parent, the values and functions that children may serve for adults, and meanings ascribed to the role of parent. Making a decision about prospective parenthood is a critical issue for many couples in their marriage relationship.

TRANSITION TO PARENTHOOD

The birth of a first child transforms individuals into parents. Assuming this new family role in addition to others already held is both challenging and rewarding. People evolve gradually into parenthood roles as they assume increasing responsibilities in raising and caring for a child. The transition is usually initiated when a couple learns that a pregnancy is in progress (Figure 5–7).

Expectant Parents' Reactions to Pregnancy

When a couple learns of a pregnancy, especially their first, they can expect several reactions. Many of the direct experiences of pregnancy apply mainly to a mother, of course. However, a pregnancy also affects the mother and her partner in several ways, although the experience is unique to each.

Pregnancy has been found to be the 12th most stressful life event that adults experience (Holmes & Rahe, 1967). An expectant mother undergoes a variety of changes that can cause her stress. These include adjusting to a changing body image as the pregnancy progresses, challenges to physical and psychological well-being, feelings about what it is like to be pregnant (especially for the first time), dealing with fears of the unknown, and shifting mood states that may be related to fluctuations in hormone levels (Schneider, Roughton, Koehler, & Lubach, 1999). Emotional reactions in pregnancy are important as

FIGURE 5–7   The initiation of a pregnancy signals many changes for a couple in their family and work roles, daily routines, resources of time and money, self-image, and committed relationship.

well because high levels of anxiety in mothers have been associated with increased fetal activity, which may contribute partially to lower birth weights in these infants. High-activity levels continue to be observed in these babies following birth (Monk et al., 2000).

For the most part, most women and their partners react favorably and with great anticipation to the news that a pregnancy has begun. This appears to be especially the case when the pregnancy is the first one and when the pregnancy is desired.

Like parenthood, pregnancy has different connotations and meanings for different individuals. For some, pregnancy validates one's sexuality and verifies one's femininity or masculinity in serving as proof that one is capable of conceiving or impregnating. For many individuals, the initiation of a pregnancy revives memories of childhood and brings anticipation of the parenthood role.

Not everyone who learns of the beginning of a pregnancy reacts with joy, pleasure, or anticipation, however. Emotional reactions that are less than positive are attributed to (1) feelings of ambivalence about the possibility of becoming a parent, (2) marital difficulties, (3) lack of a suitable social network to provide emotional support during the pregnancy, or (4) lack of desire for the pregnancy (Fleming, Ruble, Flett, & Shaul, 1988).

These negative attitudes also have a bearing on the manner in which labor and delivery are experienced. It is important to note also that whether a woman has optimistic or negative expectations about parenthood prior to a child's birth influences the quality of her experiences as parent following birth (Harwood, McLean, & Durkin, 2007). However, one study reports that higher levels of relationship functioning occur more frequently among those who have unplanned than planned pregnancies (Bouchard, Boudreau, & Hébert, 2006). This may be due to the pregnancy acting as a heavy stressor to cause a couple to work harder in resolving conflicts together.

When a pregnancy is confirmed, a couple must often focus on new issues they have not yet considered in their relationship. For example, many begin to ponder what it will be like to have a child and to be a parent, what kind of parent they will be, in what kinds of activities they will participate, and what kind of person the child will be and become. Expectations of what parenthood involves and how each partner will contribute to this effort also have important bearings on what happens after a child is born (McHale & Rotman, 2007). Perhaps one of the benefits of the 9 months of pregnancy is that it allows such mental preparations to take place before one actually has to perform as a parent. Expectant parents have time to begin thinking of themselves as a family in the traditional sense rather than as a couple. By attending childbirth education classes, reading books and articles about child rearing and child development, and arranging and participating in prenatal medical care, couples begin preparations for this change in their family system. They equip a nursery, receive baby showers, and shop for the things they will need in caring for an infant. This change is to be a significant one, and it will prompt related changes in the family system as the couple moves from being newlyweds to being a couple in the process of producing children. These changes are discussed in more detail in the next chapter.

· ·

Focus Point. The potential of new parenthood causes changes for both the woman who is pregnant and her partner. Women who anticipate motherhood positively adjust better to being pregnant and to experiencing labor and delivery. Pregnancy signals impending changes in personal and marital identities for a couple. It prepares them to make adjustments in moving to the next stage of their family life career.

· ·

Adjusting to First-Time Parenthood

When adults become parents for the first time, profound changes may be expected to take place in every aspect of their family life and relationship (S. M. Cox et al., 2001; LaRossa & Sinha, 2006; von Klitzing, 2006). The absence of children typically during the first few years following marriage or commitment allows a couple to focus on each other's needs and on their own. They evolve routines, rules, policies, and roles that establish boundaries and expectations for behavior as a married couple. These serve as the foundation for the myriad adjustments and transitions they will experience over the career of their family system.

Most people do not make rapid adaptations and changes at the beginning of a new stage of development. Rather, a series of events and happenings signal that changes must be made in order for the family system to maintain its balance and ability to function effectively. The events surrounding the pregnancy and delivery of the first child signal that a couple must now begin to shift their thinking and identities to accommodate their new role as parents. As individuals move into this new developmental stage of family life, they are also moving into a new stage of their own psychosocial development, which Erikson calls the sense of generativity.

The presence of the new baby produces many profound changes in both the individuals and the family. The relationship of the parents as marriage partners becomes transformed into a more complicated interactional network (Figure 5–8). In accordance with the principles of wholeness and interrelatedness in family systems theory, a new baby's presence affects the entire family system in some manner and causes realignments to occur in response to this new situation. The adjustments required of a couple in order to incorporate a new baby into the family system appear to be facilitated when they have established a highly competent marriage relationship and functional patterns to regulate behavior prior to the child's birth (Rholes, Simpson, Camptell, & Grich, 2001).

Many adults may find this period of new parenthood to be especially disconcerting. Some new parents feel that they have had inadequate or insufficient preparation for the adjustments they must make in their marriage and their personal lives, and they are unsure of their ability to nurture a small infant. Alice Rossi (1968)

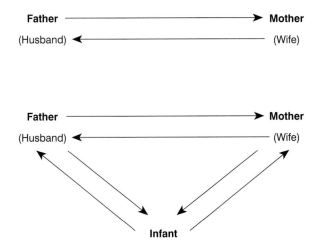

FIGURE 5–8   The addition of a baby into a family system changes the interaction patterns already established between the mother and father. The interactional bonds increase from two to six, creating a more complex social environment and affecting the family ecology.

FIGURE 5–9   First-time parenthood is no longer considered to be a crisis event but rather a transition in one's personal development in adulthood and in a couple's committed relationship.

describes several factors that contribute to difficulty in adjusting to first-time parenthood:

■ Few specific educational experiences that prepare people for parenthood are not readily available in our society.
■ The experience of pregnancy involves only a limited degree of preparation for parenthood.
■ Our society provides little guidance on how to ensure successful parenting behavior and experiences.
■ The transition into the new role of parenthood is abrupt and disruptive.

The "Parenthood as Crisis" Studies

A number of early research studies on new parenthood are considered to be the classic forerunners to the contemporary view of first-time parenthood. These early studies laid the foundation for contemporary studies that focus on the problems, challenges, and adjustments individuals face as they make the transition into parenting roles for the first time. When this topic was first being investigated, the early research viewed new parenthood as a crisis event in a couple's marriage career. Through greater understanding of the issues involved in new parenthood, it is now seen as a transition experience

rather than as a negative, crisis-producing event in the career of a family system (Figure 5–9).

The abruptness of change into new parenting roles served as the basis for family sociologist E. E. Le-Masters' (1957, 1977) proposal that the birth of the first child is a crisis event in a couple's marriage relationship.

LeMasters proposed that our society supports a romantic complex about parenthood. Extensive folklore about the joys of parenthood creates unrealistic impressions and expectations about what is involved in child rearing and what it is like to be a parent. LeMasters reported data suggesting that people become disenchanted with their marriage after having their first child. He interviewed 46 middle-class couples who had had their first child 5 years prior to the interview, and 83% reported an extensive or severe crisis in adjusting to the baby's presence and subsequent influence on their relationship. Mothers reported experiences or feelings such as losing sleep, worrying about their appearance and housekeeping standards, being chronically tired, and giving up social contacts and the income from employment outside the home. Fathers reported similar reactions and also mentioned dissatisfaction with a decline in the sexual responsiveness of their wives.

Although the LeMasters study brought attention to the effects of the first child on the parents' marriage relationship, other researchers questioned the validity of these findings. Everett Dyer (1963) performed a subsequent investigation in an attempt to replicate the results of the LeMasters study. Dyer's results confirmed the prediction that the severity of the crisis was dependent on (1) the degree of cohesiveness of the marital and family organization at the time of the baby's birth; (2) the couple's degree of preparation for parenthood and marriage; (3) the degree of adjustment required in the marital relationship after the birth; and (4) other variables such as the number of years the couple had been married before the child's birth. Most couples in Dyer's study who reported a severe crisis in reaction to the first birth were able to recover and reorganize their relationship within several months following the birth.

Family sociologist Dan Hobbs (1965) performed additional research that focused on the reports of a more representative group of new parents than those interviewed by LeMasters and Dyer. In his study, Hobbs found that 86% of the couples reported having only slight crisis reactions, a finding that was diametrically opposed to that of LeMasters and Dyer.

Later studies have confirmed Hobbs's initial findings (Hobbs & Wimbish, 1977; Russell, 1974). This research prompted a reevaluation of the challenges of a first birth and brought about a revised viewpoint labeling the change in a family system a *transition* rather than a crisis. More recent research has addressed other factors that influence adjustment to the new parenthood role for first-time parents. These are discussed in the following paragraphs.

Timing of First Birth

Researchers generally report that the timing of the transition to new parenthood in a person's life and marriage career is determined by rather complex social factors (Chakraborty, 2002). There is a trend in the United States to delay first marriage and childbearing to later ages in adulthood than was customary in the past (Fields, 2003). Children are typically produced by most couples within 2 years following their first marriage. However, many couples delay having their first child for a variety of reasons. The postponement of parenthood to later ages is attributed to unfavorable economic conditions and the pressures of career and educational goals. Many of these economic and structural factors influence a married couple's decision to enter into parenthood. Later ages at which marriages occur today are also associated with fewer numbers of children being produced. However, the reduction in numbers of births is not due solely to age at first marriage, but to complex social structural variables such as those just described (Morgan, Botey, Chen, & Huang, 1999).

The age of parents at the birth of their first child is associated with other effects observed in various areas of their lives. A particular dilemma is when a person's becoming a parent is off-time developmentally according to what is normative for peers and agemates, such as the case of teenage pregnancies. When people have their first child at a young age, their ability to pursue educational goals is hampered. Similarly, the more education people have, the older they tend to be when having their first child (Hofferth, Reid, & Mott, 2001).

How Does Parenthood Affect a Couple's Committed Relationship?

The committed relationship of a couple acts as a foundation for their family system. Forming such a relationship requires time, effort, and commitment to resolving conflicts, developing patterns, and achieving a level of healthy functioning. The focus of the first years following marriage and commitment are devoted to achieving these ends.

Our culture supports romantic notions about parenthood and child rearing that may deceive adults about what these roles involve and require. Folklore implies that parenthood improves a couple's marriage relationship and that a truly successful marriage is one in which happiness predominates all the time.

However, these notions are usually cast aside in light of the reality of everyday life as a couple. Becoming a parent causes a restructuring and reorganization of a couple's committed relationship. A new baby, especially the first produced by a couple, produces obvious effects that are both positive and challenging. Researchers who study the effects of parenthood on marital satisfaction have consistently reported that, rather than improving a couple's relationship, the presence of children is associated with decreasing martial satisfaction (Bradbury, Fincham,

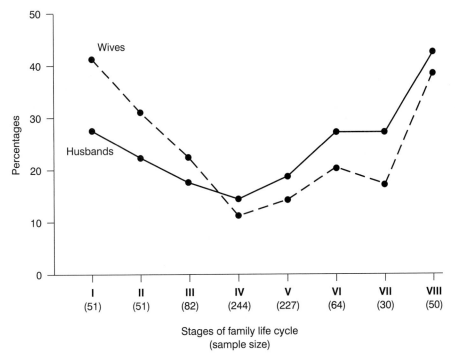

FIGURE 5–10   The percentage of individuals at different stages of family development who reported that their marriage was going well "all the time."

Source: Rollins, B., & Feldman, H. (1970). Marital satisfaction over the family life cycle. *Journal of Marriage and the Family, 32*, 25. Copyrighted 1970 by the National Council on Family Relations, 3989 Central Avenue, NE, Suite 550, Minneapolis, MN. Reprinted by permission.

& Beach, 2000) (see Figure 5–10). The quality of marital satisfaction begins to decline following the birth of the first child (Lawrence, Nylen, & Cobb, 2007). It continues to do so in association with increasing age of children, culminating at its lowest point when children reach middle childhood and then increasing as children grow through adolescence and into early adulthood. This phenomenon is more marked among wives than among husbands (Glenn, 1990).

At first examination of this information, it may appear that children are detrimental to a couple's marital happiness. However, researchers who study the topic believe that the increasing amount of **role strain** during the initial years of child rearing causes the decline in marriage satisfaction rather than the mere presence of children. Role strain occurs when adults attempt to fulfill several competing social roles simultaneously and to a high degree of performance and efficiency. In most family systems today, this means that both adults attempt to cope with the multiple roles of worker, parent, and marriage partner. When individuals try to perform all these roles at a very high level of proficiency, the

effect is that performance in all roles suffers to some degree. Since most individuals understand that children's needs often must take priority over personal needs, their roles as marriage partners are allowed to take less precedence and priority in terms of expending energy and resources. Essentially, while coparenting arrangements become an aspect of a couple's committed relationship, this is likely to be maintained at the expense of other aspects involved in the couple's relationship (Van Egeren, 2004). For example, new parents may experience a decline in sexual relations or in social activities during their transition to parenthood since infant care demands a greater proportion of their energies, time, and resources (Condon, Boyce, & Corkindale, 2004; Pacey, 2004).

This information strongly suggests that it is important for couples to develop a strong committed relationship prior to the production of children, since the relationship usually does not receive considerable attention while they are actively involved in child rearing. Most couples have some idea that their lives will change when they become parents. However, most are unaware that their marriage relationship will be challenged to some degree. Many more are equally surprised to discover that the introduction of children tends to reorganize the marriage into a traditional sex-role orientation. In many cases, women assume traditional mothering and housekeeping roles while men gravitate more toward their careers and their role as provider. This tends to occur even among couples who have agreed to promote an egalitarian philosophy about roles within the home and family (Bird, 1997; Coltrane, 1990). Several explanations have been suggested for this phenomenon:

- Women, because of their biology (e.g., the ability to breast-feed), may have a different reaction to child-bearing than men, one that causes a greater motivation and interest in parenting (Rossi, 1977).
- Social scripting acquired in early childhood about parenthood becomes activated when individuals assume this role in adulthood (F. D. Cox, 2001).
- Economic considerations may dictate who performs what jobs and responsibilities in the family. For example, because men are typically paid more for their work than women, many women assume parenting and home responsibilities while men assume the role of family provider (Cox, 2001).

It is important to be cognizant that becoming a parent for the first time involves certain costs as well as benefits to a couple's committed relationship. One of the costs that is newly investigated is the influence of co-habitation versus marriage on the transition to parenthood. Apparently, cohabiting women experience greater declines in social and psychological well-being upon becoming a first-time mother (Woo & Raley, 2005). However, if couples become aware that problems can be anticipated in their committed relationship following the birth of the first child, especially, then they are likely to have an increased awareness of the need to maintain their relationship (Curran et al., 2006). In addition, a new mother's perceptions of emotional support from her partner appears to positively impact her marital quality during this challenging period of adjustment (Palmer, 2004).

The arrival of a child is not likely to destroy a couple's relationship, but it is not likely to salvage one that is troubled. Although both partners may expect to observe decreases in opportunities for shared leisure activities, there are more opportunities to enjoy activities involving both adults.

●●

Parenting Reflection 5–5

How can couples prepare and cope successfully with the projected decline in their marital satisfaction if they know in advance of having children that this is likely to occur?

●●

●●

Focus Point.   New parents experience a period of adjustment to their new roles following the birth of their first child. Although early researchers viewed this as a crisis event in the family career, a more contemporary view is one of transition. The transition to new parenthood is influenced by several factors, such as the timing of the first child's birth in the adults' lives and the sex of the adult. One of the major adjustments that occurs is the shift in the priorities of the marriage relationship toward the individuals' new roles as parents. Researchers report that satisfaction with marriage often declines because of the stress adults experience in managing their new roles.

●●

NEW AVENUES TO PARENTHOOD: ASSISTED REPRODUCTIVE TECHNOLOGY

Many people wish to become parents but are unable to do so in the usual fashion. The reasons preventing their ability to reproduce are often medically related, such as when a man has an abnormally low sperm count. In other instances, the reasons are more social in nature, as when a woman decides that she wants to become a mother but is not cohabitating or is not married.

Medical technology has advanced to levels that were unimaginable in the past, which allows people to have children under some of the most incapacitating reproductive situations (Figure 5–11). These services first became available in 1981 and have become more sophisticated in recent years. Although the success rates of these methods are fairly low (12 to 20%) and they may cost thousands of dollars that may or may not be covered by insurance plans, many people are willing to endure such hardships to achieve biological parenthood. Other individuals who have fertility problems adopt children or become foster parents as a means for achieving parenthood.

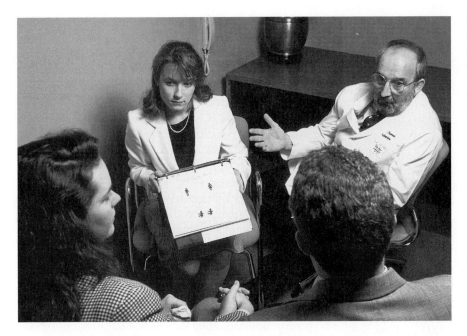

FIGURE 5–11 Couples experiencing difficulties in conceiving or who have a history of genetic disease have a number of medically assisted options available to help in becoming parents.

About 12% of the women of childbearing age in the United States have received an infertility service (National Center for Chronic Disease Control and Prevention, 2006). The procedures known as Assisted Reproductive Technology (ART) focus principally on methods that artificially fertilize ova and successfully transfer them to a uterus for further development to birth. Most attempts involve the harvesting and use of fresh, as opposed to frozen, ova or embryos. Because ART involves a process that takes about 2 weeks, the methods are referred to as cycles rather than as a particular procedure. Figure 5–12 shows the outcome of cycles in 2004 using this technology.

Artificial Insemination

One of the oldest assisted technologies available involves injecting sperm into a woman's cervix. Several routes may be taken with this method. For example, when a man has a low sperm count, the sperm from several of his ejaculations are combined into one injection. If the man is infertile or a woman has no male partner available, it is likely that artificial insemination by donor (AID) will be used. In these situations, the donor is matched according to characteristics desired such as physical appearance. When AID is used, the donor's identity is often anonymous.

Fertility Drugs

A cycle of ART typically begins with the use of drugs that stimulate ovulation. These drugs often cause the release of multiple ova rather than just one, which increases the chances of fertilizing many of these. When this occurs, decisions are necessary to determine how many fertilized eggs will be harvested for in vitro fertilization and

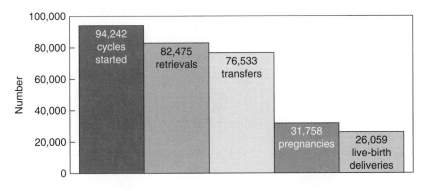

FIGURE 5–12 Outcome of assisted reproductives technology cycles using fresh, nondonor eggs or embroys by stage: 2004.

Source: National Center for Chronic Disease Prevention. (2006). Assisted reproductive techology success rates. 2004. Atlanta, GA: Centers for Disease Control and Prevention.

how many embryos will be transferred to a uterus or frozen as reserves.

In Vitro Fertilization (IVF)

This method is being used by an increasing number of couples who have difficulty conceiving a child. It is the most promising avenue for parenthood among those women whose infertility results from blockage of the fallopian tubes. In the course of this treatment, fertility drugs are administered to the woman to facilitate overproduction of ova. At the time of ovulation, a mature egg is removed surgically, fertilized by sperm from her partner or from a donor in a laboratory dish, and then implanted into the mother's uterus. It is customary for several ova to be fertilized in this manner since the rate is fairly low for the successful implantation and survival of the zygote. As a result, this method frequently results in multiple births.

Two newer methods have higher success rates. These include: (1) *gamete intrafallopian transfer* (GIFT) and (2) *zygote intrafallopian transfer* (ZIFT). Both these techniques involve implanting an egg or sperm or a fertilized egg (zygote) into a woman's fallopian tube.

In vitro fertilization methods may be combined with another procedure termed **intracytoplasmic sperm injection** (ICSI). This is often used when a man's sperm count is abnormally low. It involves the direct introduction of sperm into an egg in a laboratory. Success rates are slightly higher when IVF methods are combined with ICSI (about 33%).

Ovum Transfer

This procedure is used when a woman produces poor-quality ova or has had her ovaries removed. This method is the female counterpart of AID in which an egg is provided by a donor female (usually anonymous) that becomes fertilized in the laboratory using the sperm of the woman's partner or by an anonymous male donor. Sometimes, the donor egg is fertilized inside the donor by artificial insemination. The donor's uterus is flushed out several days following the insemination, and the zygote is retrieved and implanted in the woman's uterus. One of the advantages of this procedure is that it can be used with postmenopausal women.

Surrogate Motherhood

Sometimes a couple who experiences fertility difficulties will contract with a fertile woman to conceive a child by artificial insemination, often by the sperm from the man. The surrogate mother is paid a fee for performing this service in addition to expenses covering prenatal care and delivery. According to the usual contractual terms, the surrogate mother agrees to relinquish all parental rights to the father and his partner when the baby is born.

This method of assisted conception is fraught with legal problems and, according to some, ethical issues. The legal problems are traced to the groundbreaking case of Baby M in 1988. A surrogate mother changed her mind about relinquishing custody of the child at birth. The court decided that she was not allowed to have custody but did grant her visitation rights. Some states have laws prohibiting surrogate parenthood or have limited the terms of the contracts that are written for this purpose. While many states prohibit payment for adoption, surrogate parenthood is not adoption since the legal parent is the father. Some ethicists worry that to allow surrogate parenthood would encourage the practice among poor or disadvantaged women as a means for livelihood in providing a questionable service for more advantaged individuals and families. Other questions that this practice raise include the right of access by others such as singles or cohabitating couples and how to resolve the problems that would arise if a contracting couple divorced or separated prior to the birth of a child carried by a surrogate mother. Other issues that are likely to arise following the child's birth include the child's right to information about the surrogate mother's medical history.

Issues Related to ART

A number of ethical, legal, and sociopsychological issues are involved in ART, and some of these are related to cultural issues associated with parenting in particular contexts (Ehrensaft, 2005). For example, some societies do not permit the use of ART for individuals who are not married, are single, or are homosexual. Difficult decisions often must be made regarding which embryos are selected for implantation and what must be done with those that are not chosen. Should the children who are conceived with this technology be told of their origins? When a surrogate parent is involved, the legal issues, especially, multiply. Many find that payment for accepting donor eggs or for carrying a pregnancy to term involves moral issues as well.

Some concerns also exist about the quality of parenting among those who have used medically assisted conception procedures. Basically, these relate to the role of biological parenthood in influencing the strength of psychological attachment between children and parents that is assumed to be diminished in these cases. One study suggests that this factor is not as important as it might appear since the quality of parenting was judged to be better among those using these techniques for conception when compared with parents who conceived children naturally (Golombok, Cook, Bish, & Murray, 1995; Golombok, Murray, Brinsden, & Abdalla, 2003). In fact, adoptive and medically assisted parents scored similarly in this regard. Apparently, the great desire and the lengths to which couples with fertility difficulties and those who otherwise seek ART in becoming parents, go to attain parenthood act as significant motivations to perform well in parenting roles (Mitchell & Green, 2008). Children conceived via various assisted reproductive technologies are reported to be no different from children conceived naturally (Blasco & Verney, 2003; MacCallum, Golombok, & Brinsden, 2007; Tully, Moffitt, & Caspi, 2003).

• •

Parenting Reflection 5–6

Is it likely that one day in the future all pregnancies will be managed by in vitro methods? What would be the circumstances involved that lead to and result in this situation?

• •

• •

Focus Point. Assisted reproductive technology is now available for helping many individuals experiencing fertility difficulties to become parents. While these methods are costly and not widely available, they include a variety of approaches that attempt to circumvent various problems of reproduction that a man or a woman or both have in causing a conception to take place.

• •

ADOPTION ISSUES

Adoption is the oldest solution to adult infertility and a way of caring for children whose biological parents are unable to do so (Ostrea, 2003). The decision to adopt often takes place after a number of fertility treatments are unsuccessful (Bausch, 2006; Daniluk & Hurtig-Mitchell, 2003). The process experienced by infertile couples in their quest for parenthood is termed *mazing*

(Sandelowski, Harris, & Holditch-Davis, 1989). This refers to the routes taken in seeking parenthood that begin with failure to reproduce naturally, followed by myriad fertility treatment experiences that are unsuccessful, and proceeding to exploring the options available to become parents via the adoption process.

Adoption involves the legal, social, and psychological processes of including a younger person into a family system and coming to accept this person as one's relative (Schwartz, 2000). Because our culture's legal and social heritage comes from England, American attitudes and laws tend to stigmatize adoption (Pavao, 2004). When adoption laws were originally written in the United States, custom placed a significant emphasis on the importance of blood ties among family members. This was particularly important because of the way family property was inherited. In more recent times, however, laws in this country have been revised to make adoption easier and more accessible to more diverse individuals and couples. Before the 1970s, agencies largely restricted adoption to middle-class, white, affluent families. Today, it is possible for single people (both heterosexual and homosexual), older people, dual-career families, and others to adopt children of different racial and ethnic backgrounds (DeBlander & DeBlander, 2004; Erich, Leung, & Kindle, 2005; Mallon, 2004; Pavao, 2004; Ryan, 2008; Ryan, Bedard, & Gertz, 2007; Varon, 2003).

The status of adoptive parents continues to be marginalized by society (Schwartz, 2000), and a variety of cultural beliefs surround adoptive families and their children. Adoptive parents tend to believe that, regardless of their degree of emotional stability or maturity, regardless of how much they try, it is impossible in the long run for them to replace or compensate for a child's loss of biological parents (Adesman & Adesmec, 2004). It is likely that this perception is also present in society as a whole. Involuntarily childless women tend to believe that society promotes the notion that the biological tie between natural parents and children is important for psychological bonding and love (Eshleman, 2004). When it occurs between adoptive parents and children, the love and bonding in this relationship is perceived as second rate at best. Society may consider adoptive children to be second rate because of their unknown genetic past and may not consider adoptive parents to be bona fide. Some people also believe that the attachment between adoptive children and their parents is problematic, especially when children are adopted at older ages when the critical period for establishing emotional attachment or bonding in infancy has passed.

These perceptions of societal beliefs may influence the success or failure of the adoption process for the families involved (Wegar, 2000). In effect, the degree to which individuals accept and internalize such beliefs may influence their ability to learn to be parents. Adoption agencies may need to consider ways to assist new adoptive parents in learning parenting skills that will counteract negative views of adoption, adoptive parents, and the reasons for adoption (Caldwell, 2004; Pavao, 2004).

There is a heavily heterosexist, pronatal cultural belief in the United States about marriage and family life. According to this belief, reproduction and childbearing are glorified and romanticized, and childlessness is devalued as a viable option for married individuals. As more people begin to devalue the presence of children in their lives and make the conscious decision not to reproduce, there may be a greater acceptance of this status among adults. In addition, as foster parenting, stepparenting, and other types of family forms become more common, society may begin to accept the greater diversity of family forms (see Chapter 2). Furthermore, advances in reproductive technology that were unheard of 20 years ago have allowed more infertile couples to become biological parents. These methods tend to devalue the importance of biological ties and encourage the consideration of alternative family forms as viable means of creating family systems.

Several additional factors are associated with the decision to adopt a child (Bitler & Zavodny, 2002; Children's Bureau, 2006; Keck & Kupecky, 2004; Ostrea, 2003; Pavao, 2004; U.S. Department of Health and Human Services, 2004):

■ The reduced population of adoptees and the downward trend in adoption continues to occur but seems to have slowed in recent years and may be due to the increased number of illegitimate births and the decreased number of unmarried mothers who retain custody of their children.

■ Adopting a child is primarily a function of childlessness, infertility, and age.

■ Adopted children are as economically advantaged as children raised by never-married, single-parent mothers.

■ More white women with out-of-wedlock children seek to place children for adoption than do black women of similar status.

■ Children of either sex are acceptable to those adopting, while minority children and those with disabilities are preferred less. There is a greater preference for children under 13 years of age and the preference increases as the age of children decreases.

■ In 2005 (the most current complete data available), about 51,000 children were adopted. The majority of children adopted today involve public agencies and international adoptions.

The process by which most adoptions take place can be lengthy, expensive, and frustrating. Not every application for adoption is approved by a particular agency, and not all result in a completed adoption. Typically, potential adoptive parents can expect these steps to take place as they attempt to achieve parenthood (Adoption Media, 2007; Crea, Barth, & Chintapalli, 2007; Dickerson & Allen, 2006): (1) finding and contacting an agency that will facilitate locating a group of acceptable infants and/or children eligible for adoption; (2) participating in a home study to determine the goodness of fit between the parents and potential adoptive infants and/or children; (3) searching for an appropriate child for adoption; (4) arranging for trial visits with a potential child for adoption; and (5) seeking a court decree declaring the adoption to be legal and finalized.

Types of Adoptions

Today a variety of adoption options are available to potential parents and to those placing children for adoption (Caldwell, 2004). No local, state, or federal registries maintain a central database for matching potential parents with adoptive children. This is partially due to differences in laws governing adoption from state to state and from nation to nation. However, the presence of laws that govern adoption, the age and developmental status of an available child, and the potential compatibility between the parents and an available child also may play a role in the type of adoption a couple might pursue.

Public Adoption. Public adoption typically takes place through an agency licensed for placing children for adoption (Neil, 2002; U.S. Department of Health and Human Services, 2004). These agencies may be nonprofit and sponsored by charities or religious organizations. Potential parents often locate the agencies through word of mouth, ads in local newspapers or Yellow Pages, Web searches, or referrals from lawyers, social workers, or medical sources. The agencies typically offer counseling and education for potential parents regarding the adoption process and what to expect following adoption. Often there is a waiting period of 5 years or longer as the potential parents experience screening procedures and the search is made for an appropriate child for placement. Potential parents can expect to pay an application fee (often quite high), the legal fees involved in formalizing the adoption, and even the medical costs incurred by the birth mother.

Private Adoption.   Private adoptions do not involve an agency but occur by the involvement of a third party, often an attorney, who arranges the adoption between the potential parents and the birth mother (Varon, 2003). These adoptions offer greater control to the potential parents but may be significantly more expensive than public adoption. However, it is not unusual for this to be a more risky adoption in that the birth mother has greater latitude in changing her mind, even after the potential parents have paid her medical expenses.

Closed, Open, or Semiopen Adoption.   Whether public or private, an adoption may be closed, open, or semiopen. Until recently, all adoptions were **closed** in that the identities of both the adoptive and biological parents were unknown to each party and no communication took place between these families. It was thought that this was the best way to handle identity and attachment issues in the adoptive family for both parents and children. An increasing number of adoptions in the last few years are **open,** meaning that it is possible to determine identities of biological parents. Adoptees and their adoptive parents have access to information records. A **semiopen adoption** permits access to information for all parties but no contact.

However, open adoption arrangements are controversial (Sobol, Daly, & Kelloway, 2000). Adoptive parents may find open records relating to their adopted child's biological parents and birth circumstances to be ominous (Grace, 2003; Rushton, 2003; Townsend, 2003). Biological parents may wish for their anonymity to be intact regardless of the desires of a biological child to know his or her identity. On the other hand, adoptees

often cite the need to know the medical history of biological parents and family for a variety of reasons. Because many states have laws allowing an adoptee access to records of their adoption, reunions with birth parents, most frequently the mother, are occurring more frequently (Pavao, 2004). These have unpredictable outcomes that may be very positive, very negative, or a mix.

Transracial Adoption.   The problems encountered among adoptive families sometimes are heightened when the race of the child is different from that of the parents and other family members. Several issues have been identified as critical adjustment challenges for multiracial adoptive families (Kennedy, 2004). (1) When adoptive parents see themselves as "rescuing" a child from a potentially disadvantaged life, they tend to cast the child into a victim role and expect the child to be grateful for their generosity. (2) Some extended family members are not likely to accept a child who is of a different racial group; this child will feel discrimination. (3) The insidious influence of racial stereotyping may affect adopted families; for example, an Asian child may be expected to excel in academics or an African American child, in athletics. (4) A racially different adopted child may experience prejudicial treatment by peers at school because of his or her adoptive status in a racially mixed family. Despite these challenges, research has demonstrated repeatedly that transracially adopted children are not harmed by their experiences, although there are reports of identity issues (Figure 5–13). In fact, children may benefit from such placement (Swize, 2002).

The issues involved in transracial adoption are especially accentuated for African American and Native American children. This may especially be the case when transracial adoptions also are international (Ishizawa, Kenny, Kubo, & Stevens, 2006). These groups of children are overrepresented in the foster care population when compared to the representation of children in the general population (Perez, O'Neil, & Gesiriech, 2004). Interracial adoptions are viewed skeptically today because of objections raised by professional groups based on questions about children's identity issues and assertions of cultural genocide (Swize, 2002). As a consequence, interracial adoptions declined to about 8% of all adoptions in the late 1980s. The position disfavoring interracial adoption is accentuated by the passage of the Indian Child

FIGURE 5–13 Families formed by transracial adoption have unique needs and challenges; however, research shows that children are not harmed by such experiences.

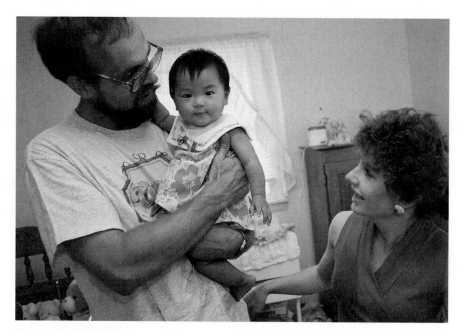

Welfare Act of 1978, which requires placement of adoptive children into the child's extended family, other members of their tribe, or other Native American families. Congress has acted to support this type of adoption, perhaps in contradiction of earlier legislation. The Multi-Ethnic Placement Act of 1994 and the Adoption and Safe Families Act of 1997 prohibit the delay or denial of placement of children based on race, color, or national origin of the parents. The difficulty in enforcement of these laws may explain why transracial adoptions continue to occur (Barth, Webster, & Lee, 2002).

● ●

Parenting Reflection 5–7

You are the parent of a transracial adopted child. You've been asked to address a group of potential adoptive parents who are likely to pursue this option for creating an adoptive family. What advice would you provide for these adults about what to expect, what to avoid, and ways to react to others who would make negative judgments about this decision?

● ●

International Adoption. Some potential parents tire of the bureaucratic procedures and lengthy wait period often involved in domestic adoption and turn to agencies that assist in placing children for adoption from foreign countries. As such, these adoptions often are the last resort for potential adoptive parents (Robi & Shaw, 2006). The numbers of these adoptions have increased in recent years. Americans have adopted orphans from all over the world with the majority coming from Asian countries (Office of Immigration Statistics, 2007). The majority of these children were infants at the time of adoption, lessening the problems encountered with older adopted children involving cultural issues. One benefit that has aided adopting families was enactment of the Child Citizenship Act of 2001, which confers U.S. citizenship to foreign-born children when adoption is finalized.

International adoptions, however, are noted for their high risk of many kinds of difficulties (Bowie, 2004; Gunnar & van Dulmen, 2007; Layne, 2004; Murphy & Knoll, 2003). Prospective parents must arrange for large payments such as all agency and in-country expenses, medical checkups, documents, visa and travel expenses, meals, and lodging. They may not be able to choose a desired child. In addition, they may experience obstacles in gathering a health history about the child and frustrations with agencies and government restrictions. On the other hand, international adoption is more likely to occur successfully for single, gay or lesbian, or older adults seeking to become parents (Humphries & Parks, 2006). Regardless, as a result of this option in adoption, more American families are multicultural as part of their nature. Multicultural adoptive families also have more resources to call upon today than in the past (Chasmoff, Schwartz, Pratt, & Neuberger, 2006). Numerous Web sites, for example, offer information, links for support, and opportunities and guidance in the adoption process involving nonnative-born children (e.g., Adoption Media, http://international.adoption.com/; Families Through International Adoption, http://www.ftia.org/). In the end, however, the success of an international adoption may depend on the ability of children to function at high levels of overall competence (McGuinness & Pallansch, 2000).

Parenting in Adoptive Family Systems

What is the nature of parent-child relations in family systems that only have adopted children as compared with those who have children born as well as adopted into the family? Relatively little is known about parenting and the result of parenting experiences among adoptive families (Brodzinsky & Pinderhughes, 2002; Chiang & Finley, 2001; Lal, 2002; Noy-Sharav, 2002; Pavao, 2004; Schwartz, 2000; Solomon & Poirier, 2007). For the most part in families where there are only adopted children, researchers report few differences from families with only natural children.

Adoptive parents are challenged in their ability to adjust to their new status (Brodzinsky & Pinderhughes, 2002). The transition to parenthood is abrupt for adoptive parents as compared with the opportunity natural parents are afforded by a 9-month pregnancy and the physical experiences that accompany a pregnancy. In some respects, the situation is likened to becoming a family instantly (Baldo & Baldo, 2003).

The rapid transition into parenthood by adoptive parents is often accomplished by what is termed *leapfrogging* (Weir, 2003). This refers to the swift trans-

formations that occur in identity development, self-perception, and other adjustments that are made to see oneself and one's partner as parents because of the adoption process. Childless couples frequently report feeling left out in comparison with their peer couples who are parents. By leapfrogging into new parenthood, newly adoptive parents feel that they become a part of their social network.

In addition, adoptive parents often do not receive the social support that natural parents are afforded by being given baby showers, for example. This adjustment challenge is especially heightened when an older child is adopted as compared to an infant.

● ●

Parenting Reflection 5–8

You are the Adoptive Parent Trainer for an adoption placement service. What would you include as important topics to cover in preparing new adoptive parents of infants for what to expect from this "instant family" experience that lacks the benefit of preparation provided by a pregnancy?

● ●

Disclosing Adoption In the distant past, adoptive parents were advised to keep the true status of their adoptive child a secret. More recently, however, adoptive parents are urged to tell children about their adoptive status but to provide few details about their known origins. This is a topic of considerable controversy (Perry, 2004). The general consensus is that a dialogue must be established about a child's adoptive status. The age at which it should occur is highly debatable. Parenting FAQs 5–2 illustrates the major issues relating to disclosure for adoptive parents.

Adopted children can be expected to experience a range of reactions to this disclosure (Penny, Borders, & Portnoy, 2007) that includes no awareness to anger, resentment, or sadness to a sense of peace and acceptance. Adopted children may need professional assistance in adjusting to this disclosure, as this often has long-range implications in their life (Ryan & Walker, 2007).

**Parenting
FAQs 5–2**

We are the adoptive parents of a beautiful baby boy. He's a preschooler now, and I think it's time to begin telling him about his adoption. My wife disagrees with me. She says we should wait until he's older, like in elementary school or junior high school. What would you advise us to do about this disagreement?

A: I think it's important that adoptive children know of their situation. Experts advise parents to begin a dialogue during an adoptive child's preschool years regarding his or her adoptive status. This dialogue is a continual one, stretching throughout the child's growing years in the family and even extending into adulthood. Parents should consider the following guidelines when they inform children of their adoption:

- Tailor the details of the child's adoption to his or her age and/or developmental abilities.
- Do not necessarily wait for the child to bring up the issue. Adoptees may be reluctant to bring up the topic because they do not want to seem disloyal. However, too much discussion about the topic can indicate that parents have not resolved the issue of their infertility or are not yet comfortable with the topic.
- Start the story of the adoption at the child's beginning. For example, talk about where the child lived before the adoption.
- Refer to the biological parents as real people who exist somewhere.
- When discussing the biological parents' decision to place the child for adoption, try to show empathy for the difficulty of their position. This is best accomplished by telling the child that the biological parents made a difficult decision that was in the best interests of the baby. Do not say, however, that the biological parents gave the child for adoption because he or she was loved so very much. This serves to confuse rather than elucidate the child's questions.
- Inform the child that there are many other children like him or her. Explain that adoption is no cause for shame.
- Help the child understand that even though he or she has two sets of parents, the adoptive arrangement is permanent and the adoptive parents are responsible for his or her well-being and rearing.

Source: Adapted from Melina, L. R. (1986). *Raising adopted children: A manual for adoptive parents.* New York: Harper & Row.

Focus Point. Some adults who wish to be parents adopt children. Potential parents may choose to pursue one of several types of adoption. Multiracial adoptive families and those involving international adoption have unique challenges. Many factors influence the decision to adopt a child. The process of adoption often follows a predictable path that may be long and costly. A key issue among adoptive parents is telling children that they are adopted. Later, many adult adoptees often seek to reunite with birth parents for a variety of reasons.

FOSTER CARE

Some parents are separated from their children and may be denied visitation or even parental rights because of their abusive and neglectful behavior. Accompanying a dramatic increase in the number of families who experience poverty and related challenges is an equally dramatic increase in the number of children experiencing out-of-home placements. When a community or state agency has determined that children are not safe in their parents' home or that it is not in their best interest to be exposed to an unhealthy parent-child environment, children can be legally removed from their parents.

Foster Children

The most common placement is into **foster care** or **family foster care**. In this setting, children are cared for by trained and licensed adults who provide substitute parental care. Some of these homes are especially intended for children with special needs. Another kind of foster care is provided by a child's relatives. This arrangement is often referred to as *kinship care*. In each of these settings, the foster parents are compensated for the service they provide, although costs often exceed the amount that is provided by the supervising agency.

Demographic Data on Foster Care in the United States

The federal government collects information relating to foster care and publishes this information annually (Children's Bureau, 2006). The most current data from 2005 are summarized here.

■ The number of children in foster care was 513,000, a decline of about 10% from 2000. The average age was 10 years. The largest numbers were infants aged 1 year and adolescents aged 16 years.

■ The average length of stay in foster care for all children was 2 years, 5 months.

■ About 73% of all children in foster care were white or African American. Black children are overrepresented in the foster care population, however, as compared to those in the general population.

■ The large majority of foster children are cared for by a nonrelative.

■ The majority of children in foster care are boys.

■ Most children in foster care wish to be reunited with their parents or to be adopted. These goals are most often attained when foster care is terminated.

■ More children enter the foster care system than exit. The majority of those who exited were reunited with their parents.

■ Those children who were waiting to be adopted spent about 3 1/2 years in the system. The majority of these children were between 12 and 16 years of age.

■ The parents of about 21% of all children in foster care had their parental rights terminated.

Parental abuse and neglect account for the most common reasons for placement into foster care. As many as 80% of all families involved in child protective services are affected by alcohol or drug problems (Children's Defense Fund, 2004).

● ●

Parenting Reflection 5–9

Suppose you are a caseworker for a child protective service. How would you explain what was happening and why to a child who is being placed into foster care because her parents had been charged with running a methamphetamine operation in the family home? How would you respond to this child's assertion that this was happening because her parents didn't love her?

● ●

Foster Parents

Foster parents may be married or single, heterosexual or homosexual. They come from all social backgrounds and may or may not be fully employed outside their homes (Lindon, 2004). Every state has its own criteria for accepting individuals as foster parents. Some commonalities in these criteria are that individuals must (1) be 21 years of age minimum; (2) lack a criminal record or history of child abuse or neglect; (3) have a regular source of income; (4) successfully complete training in foster care; (4) be Red Cross certified in first aid; and (5) be approved with an inspection of their home.

Adults who become foster parents often are motivated by their own childhood experiences in foster care or by altruistic interests in meeting the needs of children who come from difficult family circumstances (J. G. Barber & Delfabbro, 2004). Many of the children arrive with emotional and behavioral problems and may have been placed repeatedly since being removed from their parents' care (M. F. Cox, Orme, & Rhoades, 2003).

Foster parents are uniquely challenged by dealing with a variety of issues not experienced typically by other adults who care for children (Orme & Buehler, 2001; Pew Charitable Trusts, 2007). These issues include: (1) connecting with and supervising a child who often has been abused, may be rejected or unloved by his or her parents, and thus has innumerable trust issues; (2) being paid little for demanding work; (3) dealing with a variety of agencies, bureaucracies, social workers, and even angry, defensive biological parents; (4) having little community support or respect for being a foster parent. These issues frequently account for the high rate of burnout observed among many foster parents.

• •

Parenting Reflection 5–10

You are in charge of developing a training program for potential foster parents. What would be the major topics you would include in the 16 hours of training taking place in 2-hour sessions for 2 months? What outside speakers would you invite to address the trainees?

• •

Despite the odds, many foster parents and the children they care for have good outcomes (Ellerman, 2007; Golding, 2003; Kufeldt, Simard, & Vachon, 2003; Wilson & Fyson, 2007). Certainly, those foster parents who have the greatest degrees of support from their child welfare system are the most likely to have good outcomes: children successfully completing their education, having satisfying relationships with peers and in intimate relationships, and avoiding conflicts with law enforcement. Such support frequently is the form of therapeutic participation, appropriate supervision and involvement from social work agencies, and adequate economic support from the child welfare system. Many foster children come to prefer living with their foster parents than with their biological parents. Many hope for and gain adoption by foster parents, who may have pursued this course as a means of testing out a situation with a child prior to adoption.

On the other hand, the outcome of foster care can be disappointing for both adults and children when children remain too long in this type of care, have histories of traumatic maltreatment by biological parents and other adults, and have had many different placements, for example (Holland & Gorey, 2004; C. D. Lee, 2004). Some 40% of adult welfare recipients or prisoners were in foster care as children (Dumaret, Coppel-Batsch, & Couraud, 1997). Other research findings report that adult outcomes of placement in foster care as a child can range from higher incidence of emotional depression, greater likelihood of marital unhappiness and social isolation, increased likelihood of homeless-

ness, and criminal involvement to early parenthood (Harden, 2004).

Several ways that involvement in this system exacts certain costs for both foster children and parents may include (Pew Charitable Trusts, 2004a, 2007)

1. the difficulties for foster children to overcome feelings of insecurity and to develop and maintain important relationships with adults,

2. the price of frustration, exasperation, and confusion exacted from poor communications between social agencies and judicial systems and the foster children and parents they supervise,

3. the failure of the foster care system to respond sensitively to the individual needs and differences of participants,

4. the cost that results from not receiving timely help for all parties, foster children, foster parents, and biological parents,

5. burnout by foster parents and those who provide supervision, caused by shortcomings in the system (e.g., inadequate training, lack of adequate staffing, etc.), and

6. the stigma associated with the concept of foster care and associated involvement with this system as a child or as a parent.

Numerous governmental, charitable, and social agencies have studied a variety of options to improve the foster care system in the United States. A central goal is to move children out of this system and into adoptive homes as quickly as possible. Since its inception, foster care has had the goal of providing only temporary, short-term care for children when parental rights have been terminated or questioned. Currently, many children may remain in foster care longer than is healthy. The obvious solution is to shorten their stay and attempt to provide adoption as an exit from foster care as quickly as possible (The Pew Charitable Trusts, 2004b, 2007). Two options that have been studied as viable solutions include (1) improving federal financing mechanisms that will facilitate faster exit of children from foster care and into adoption with the eventual goal of eliminating the need for foster care, and (2) improving the ability of the judicial system to make better decisions more quickly that are in the child's best interest for personal safety and welfare.

Focus Point.   When children are removed from their parents' care, they are placed into foster care or family foster care. This frequently occurs due to parental abuse and neglect and is intended as a temporary solution in providing care for children. Data collected by the federal government indicate that the length of stay in the foster care system is far from temporary for most children. In addition, certain demographic variables are characteristic of children in foster care.

Foster parents usually are not related to foster children, although some children are cared for by relatives. Foster parents resemble other adults in most communities and must meet criteria established by state social agencies to be licensed. In addition, they must complete approved training to be foster parents. These parents face challenges unique to their situation of caring for unwanted or neglected children. The majority of children placed in foster care grow to achieve acceptable outcomes as adults. Some of the greatest problems arising within the foster care system may be alleviated by shortening the time children spend in this system and moving them into adoptive homes.

FACILITATING THE TRANSITION TO PARENTHOOD

The discussion thus far has identified adjustments and some difficulties in becoming a parent, especially for the first time. There is considerable agreement about what produces these problems for individuals and couples. How can those considering parenthood or those who are expectant or new parents prepare for what awaits them? What kinds of support can assist these individuals and couples in their transition to parenthood?

First, support groups may offer a means for people to gain information and education about parenthood (Doherty, Erickson, & LaRossa, 2006). These groups assist individuals and couples in several ways. (1) Men are included and welcomed, giving the message that they are essential participants in the parenting process. (2) People gain reassurance that others share similar fears, misgivings, and stressfulness about becoming parents or on becoming parents. (3) Expectations about parenthood and childrearing can be examined in a safe environment. (4) Such experiences help couples to network with one another and to form social supports that often take the place of family support that may not be available. Research indicates that such interventions can also help couples strengthen their relationship during the challenging time of the transition to new parenthood (Schulz, Cowan, & Cowan, 2006).

Second, parenting classes may be particularly helpful to new parents, especially in the first few weeks and months following a child's birth (Kelley, Schwerin, Farrar, & Lane, 2007). These classes may be structured according to topics (e.g., infant nutrition, physical care) and meet for several weeks. The classes may be informal and combine educational as well as supportive experiences. For example, an emerging parenting education experience in many large cities is known by various names, such as Boot Camp for Dads (Bishop & Ault, 2002; A. Murphy, 2003). The daylong session is offered on a weekend, and new fathers are asked to bring their children to the session with them. They are assigned to an experienced father who has previously graduated from the Boot Camp experience and whose children are older. This exposes new fathers to a mentor to whom they can relate more effectively. The fathers gain insights about what it means to be a new father, what infants are like and what kind of care they need, what to expect from themselves and their partners, and so on. Such educational experiences help new parents to learn about resources, equipment, and methods of child care.

The transition to new parenthood can be facilitated when couples are able to successfully negotiate coparenting roles, changes in the division of labor in performing household tasks, and renegotiating these issues when conflicts arise (Cowan, Cowan, & Pruett, 2007; A. E. Goldberg & Perry-Jenkins, 2004; Moura, 2004). Families continue to provide support for new parents but usually for a limited period following the child's birth. Grandparents are often called upon to provide assistance with older children, help with household chores, provide information about child care, and generally be supportive.

Another aspect of support for new parents is family leave time from employment. The Family and Medical Leave Act of 1993, a federal law, requires qualified employers to grant up to 12 workweeks in unpaid leave during any 12-month period to employees for the birth and care of a newborn child with continued benefits in effect during this time. Jobs are also protected during this period and are reinstated upon completion of the leave. Leaves that are shorter than 12 weeks frequently result in poorer adjustment to work, relationship, and parenting responsibilities by both new mothers and fathers after returning (Feldman, Sussman, & Zigler, 2004).

POINTS TO CONSIDER

- The decision to become a parent is often based on a conscious decision-making process by many adult individuals. The decision to become a parent can be influenced by complex issues, such as (1) economic considerations relating to the costs of childbearing and child rearing; (2) structural factors such as employment status of the adults, values and beliefs, and the desired family size; and (3) psychosocial factors such as parenthood as an expected developmental task of adulthood, personal reasons or motivations, the values and functions that children may serve for adults, and meanings ascribed to parenting roles.

- The birth of a couple's first child prompts a transition of a family system into the childbearing family stage of the family life career. The adjustments that adults make initially focus on realignment of patterns set up early in a marriage.

- The difficulties some couples experience at the birth of their first child relate to inadequate preparation for parenthood and the abruptness with which these changes take place. Several factors mediate these adjustments: (1) the timing of the birth in the adult's personal developmental path, (2) the level of personal self-esteem, (3) the employment status of the mother, (4) the quality of patterns established in the family system prior to the first child's birth, (5) the degree of commitment to being a parent, (6) the good health of the mother and child, and (7) the expectations (either positive or negative) of what it will be like to be a parent.

- The economic, social, and psychological costs of childbearing are considered when individuals decide whether to become parents. Parenthood affects a couple's committed relationship in that satisfaction usually declines during those years that a family is involved in child rearing. This is believed to be due to role strain of the adults rather than to the presence of children within the family system.

- New medical technologies are available for assisting individuals and/or couples who have fertility difficulties to conceive and become parents. These technologies are expensive and not widely available. They include (1) artificial insemination, (2) in vitro fertilization, (3) ovum transfer, and (4) surrogate motherhood. Some of these involve ethical and legal issues.

- Adoption involves challenges for both adults and children. Adopted children usually have greater chances of an improved life situation, although society tends to stigmatize adoptive families.

- There are a number of reasons why people choose to become adoptive parents.

- Prospective parents may choose to pursue different options for adoption, each with its own advantages and disadvantages.

- Adults are encouraged to discuss openly the circumstances surrounding a child's adoption.

- Children are separated from parents and parental rights terminated when children are abused or live in an unsafe home environment. When this occurs, they are usually placed into the foster care system to be cared for, most frequently by a nonrelative.

- Most of the children in the foster care system are white or African American. The average length of stay in the system is slightly more than 3 1/2 years. Most children wish to remain with their foster families or to be adopted.

- Adults who become foster parents must meet criteria established by the state in which they reside and become certified by attending a training course. They assume this role for a variety of reasons, often because they wish to have a trial period of observing a potentially adoptive child.

- Foster parenting is a challenge often because children have been abused, are suspicious of adults, and have emotional or behavior problems. Foster parents must deal with different agencies and officials. The pay they receive for housing and caring for a child is quite low, and most payments are intended to cover the cost of caring for a foster child. A high degree of burnout is observed among many foster parents.

- Outcomes for foster children can be devastating or positive. The majority fare well as adults.

- Many observers note that the foster care system in the United States is in serious difficulty in that certain costs are observed among foster children, foster parents, and the foster care system that provides supervision. The best recommendation for improving the system is to speed up the time to move children from the system into adoptive homes.

- New parents may need assistance as they become adjusted to their new family role. Sources of assistance include support groups for new mothers, new fathers, or both; parenting classes; and assistance from family members.

CHAPTER 6

Pregnancy and Childbirth

Focus Questions
■ ■ ■ ■ ■ ■ ■ ■ ■ ■ ■

1. What critical factors influence the course of pregnancy?
2. What are current trends in providing prenatal care?
3. What are the different types of delivery?
4. What are current trends in childbirth management?

■ ■ ■ ■ ■ ■ ■ ■ ■ ■

The birth of a baby is a significant event in the lives of parents and for the family system into which it arrives. The baby's arrival is anticipated with an array of feelings ranging from great excitement to high anxiety. This may be particularly so when a couple is having their first child, whose conception was desired and planned (see Chapter 5).

This chapter discusses the experiences that arise from a pregnancy and the options associated with childbirth. Many Americans today carefully plan and time the conception of their children. The high cost of bearing and rearing children is one important reason this occurs. Pregnancy provides the first opportunity for parents-to-be to offer nurturing caregiving to their unborn child. It is a highly critical period in the life of the unborn child. The environment the mother provides for the child she carries can have long-term consequences for the baby, its parents, and the entire family system. Pregnancy and childbirth are important aspects of parenting (Figure 6–1).

PREGNANCY CONSIDERATIONS

The period in the uterus before birth is one of the most crucial stages in an individual's life span. During the average 280-day period, biological foundations are established that will influence much of the person's developmental potential over his or her lifetime.

In earlier times, development before birth was surrounded by mystery. Because much of what occurs during this period is hidden from direct observation, the beginnings of life were largely misunderstood and explained through superstition and speculation. Folklore about pregnancy encouraged the notion that almost everything a pregnant

FIGURE 6–1. The birth of a baby is a significant event and initiates numerous changes for a family system.

woman experienced would ultimately affect the developing child. Physical defects in a baby were believed to be caused by maternal experiences. For example, birthmarks were thought to result from the mother's having spilled wine or eaten too many strawberries during pregnancy, and a harelip was thought to result from the mother's having seen a rabbit. Similarly, it was believed that if a pregnant woman listened to classical music or read classical literature, the child would have strong musical or literary tendencies.

Such folklore has been discarded as scientists have gained information on how life begins, how the genetic code is transmitted, and how the internal and external maternal environments actually influence fetal development. Dramatic advances have been made in knowledge about caring for babies prior to their birth, especially for premature neonates and those of low birth weight. Genetic science has progressed to where it is now possible to clone or make an identical genetic copy of many species, including human beings. Cloning human embryos, however, has been banned in the United States (Itzkoff, 2003).

Characteristics of Prenatal Development

The time before the birth of an individual is significant and unique in many ways. Many experts consider this time in the life span to be the most important because of its crucial effects on later stages. It can be characterized briefly in the following three ways.

1. *It is the shortest stage of the life span.* The average length of pregnancy is 280 days, although the period does vary somewhat for every pregnancy. Remarkably, during this relatively short time the individual develops from a one-celled organism at conception to having more than 200 billion cells at birth.

2. *It is the period of most rapid growth and development in the human life span.* The first trimester (90 days) of pregnancy is the *embryonic stage*, or the formative phase of an individual's growth and development. During this stage the fertilized egg differentiates into specialized cells that make up the body and organ systems. By the end of this embryonic stage, the body has a distinctly recognizable human form and contains all the organs essential for functioning after birth. The second and third trimesters are the *fetal period* of the pregnancy. During this time, the body experiences refinements and the most rapid increase in weight and length. At the beginning of this period, the fetus weighs approximately 1 ounce and is about 1½ inches long. At birth, the infant weights about 7½ pounds and is about 21 inches long.

3.   *It is a highly critical period in human development.*   The embryo is vulnerable to many factors that can enhance or hinder its development. Environmental and genetic factors can have permanent effects, adversely or positively, on the embryo. These factors can result in congenital birth defects, miscarriage, prematurity, low birth weight, and tendencies toward certain behavioral traits.

••

Focus Point.   The period of prenatal development is one of the most crucial stages in the life cycle. During this short period of rapid growth, myriad factors can affect the individual's future development.

••

CRITICAL FACTORS OF PREGNANCY

During pregnancy the developing baby is exposed to a number of environmental influences that can have both short- and long-term effects on the baby's development (Evans & Aaronson, 2005). Environmental influences that can be harmful to an unborn child, such as smoking or drinking alcohol, should be avoided during pregnancy. Appropriate parenting before a child's birth involves being mindful of these factors and how they can impact a child's development over his or her life span.

Age of the Mother

The age of the mother is one factor that contributes to the probability of having a baby with low birth weight (Harms, Johnson, & Murry, 2004). Babies who weigh 5½ pounds or less at birth are considered to be of low birth weight (Federal Interagency Forum on Child and Family Statistics, 2007). Low birth weight is often associated with death, brain and central nervous system damage, and mental retardation (Newburn-Cook et al., 2002). For these reasons, low birth weight is considered to be a congenital birth defect that has implications for the health and well-being of the infant, not only at birth but later in life. For example, learning difficulties and cognitive problems among school-age children are highly associated with low birth weight (Lawrence & Blair, 2003).

Women under 20 and over 40 years of age have a higher probability of delivering babies of low birth weight, especially if they are African American (Federal Interagency Forum on Child and Family Statistics, 2007; see Figure 6–2). These women generally experience what is termed a high-risk pregnancy, due both to their age and to related social factors. For example, there is a greater frequency of high-risk pregnancies in certain ethnic groups, although this factor alone does not fully account for the phenomenon. In addition to low birth weight, other complications arising from high-risk pregnancies include circulatory and respiratory difficulties, brain damage, and physical and mental handicaps.

Older women experience higher rates of miscarriage and giving birth to children who have some type of genetic disorder. For example, the incidence of Down syndrome, a type of genetic disorder that causes mental retardation and certain physical abnormalities, increases significantly among women who bear children after 40 years of age (Vontver, 2003). This is thought to result from chromosomal disturbances in the ova older women

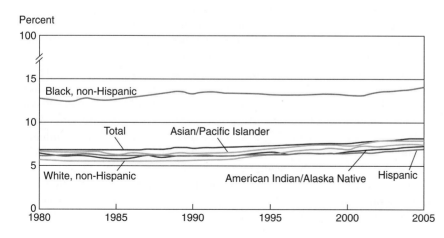

FIGURE 6–2.   Percentage of infants of low birth weight by mother's race and Hispanic origin, 1980 to 2005.

Source: Federal Interagency Forum on Child and Family Statistics. (2007). *America's children: Key national indicators of well-being, 2007.* Washington, DC: U.S. Government Printing Office.

produce and hormonal changes that take place with aging. On the other hand, adolescent girls who become pregnant deliver babies with problems that are more likely due to attitudinal and behavioral causes rather than physical problems. For example, improper nutrition and lack of adequate prenatal care and supervision contribute to the high incidence of birth complications among teenage mothers. A more detailed discussion of adolescent childbearing is found in Chapter 12.

Other factors contributing to rates of low birth weight in the United States include (1) the increasing numbers of large multiple births resulting from fertility treatments; (2) increases in the use of assisted reproductive technologies (ART); (3) changes in the obstetrical management of pregnancy, which include increases in Caesarean and induced deliveries; and (4) the general trend in delaying childbirth to later years in adulthood (Federal Interagency Forum on Child and Family Statistics, 2007).

What are the ideal ages for women to bear healthy children? Apparently, because of both physical and social factors, many women experience healthy pregnancies with positive outcomes between the ages of 24 and 35 years of age (Vontver, 2003).

Nutrition During Pregnancy

The nutrition and health of a pregnant woman are important related factors that influence the quality of development of the growing child (Anderson, 2003). These factors have a strong impact on the well-being of both the fetus and the mother, and they can influence the course of subsequent pregnancies. One of the most significant aspects of nutrition during pregnancy is the association between adequate weight gain by the mother and an increase in the infant's birth weight.

The United States has one of the highest rates of newborn death among the developed nations of the world (Federal Interagency Forum on Child and Family Statistics, 2007). This has been attributed to restrictions on weight gain in pregnant women on the advice of health care workers. Weight gain is a normal result of pregnancy and is important in its influence on neonatal birth weight and on the mother's ability to produce breast milk following the baby's birth. Until recently, weight gain was restricted to about 21 pounds, on the assumption that a relatively low-weight infant would be quicker and easier for the mother to deliver. Today, the recommended weight gain is between 25 and 35 pounds for most pregnant women who are of normal body weight and mass (J. A. Martin et al., 2006). It is anticipated that this change will result in a lowered infant mortality rate, decreases in numbers of infants of low birth weight, and better health overall for babies. However, many women are overweight at the time of conception and should gain only about 15 to 25 pounds. These weight gains should be steady over the course of the pregnancy rather than occurring rapidly. It should be stressed, also, that a pregnant woman should not diet to lose weight during this time.

Maternal nutrition during pregnancy is critically important because the quality of the mother's diet will be reflected in the health and well-being of her baby. A woman generally does not need to increase her caloric intake considerably during pregnancy to have a nutritionally balanced diet. It is more important that she eat a well-rounded diet consisting of a variety of foods (Riley, 2006), including dairy products, fruits and vegetables, and grains. Following prescribed guidelines, dietary intake during pregnancy should be increased by about 300 to 500 calories and include an extra serving of protein. Sodium intake may need to be monitored and the diet adapted if indicated as a means of managing certain metabolic conditions that can develop in pregnancy, such as toxemia. If weight gain occurs according to these guidelines and nutrition is adequate, the possibility of miscarriage or of having a stillborn or infant with low birth weight is significantly reduced (Federal Interagency Forum on Child and Family Statistics, 2007).

Some nutrients may play a critical role in influencing the quality and nature of a baby's development before birth. For example, a lack of adequate amounts of folic acid (a type of B vitamin) in a pregnant woman's diet is associated with high risk of spinal cord defects in a developing baby. In the United States, grain products are supplemented with this nutrient (Honein, Paulozzi, Matthews, Erickson, and Wong, 2001). It is also available in prenatal vitamin/mineral supplements and is available naturally in fresh fruits and vegetables.

An expectant mother's nutritional and health status can be adversely affected by her emotional state (D. B. Nelson, Grisso, Joffe, Brensinger, Shaw, & Datner,

2003). High levels of anxiety and depression during pregnancy can interfere with the mother's appetite and interest in eating a nutritionally sound diet and, therefore, adversely affect the health and well-being of the baby (Dipietro, Millet, Cosstigan, Gurewitxch, & Caulfield, 2003).

Exercise

Expectant mothers need to prepare their bodies for pregnancy and childbirth by participating in moderate levels of physical exercise. Examples of these activities include jogging, swimming, walking, cycling, and tennis. Women generally are the best judges of this level of exertion, but they should avoid pushing themselves above their reasonable limits of physical endurance in these kinds of activities (Committee on Obstetric Practice, 2002). Regular exercise provides many health benefits to an expectant mother, such as maintaining regularity and improving respiration, circulation, and muscle tone. Regular exercise also is associated with an elevated mood.

Prenatal Medical Supervision

Part of good prenatal parenting is providing the mother with medical supervision. Mothers who have at least five or more prenatal visits with a health care professional that begin during the first trimester increase the chances of having a healthy, full-term baby (Gabbe, Niebyl, & Simpson, 2003). Medical supervision for expectant mothers includes obtaining a health history, appropriate medical examinations and tests, and counseling about a variety of concerns and issues, such as method of childbirth, appropriate nutrition, supervision of any drugs and prescriptions, and preparation for childbirth. Most importantly, these visits with health care professionals can help expectant mothers manage weight gains appropriately and provide screening for a number of conditions affecting the health of both the mother and her unborn child.

Drugs and Chemical Agents

Physicians generally urge their pregnant patients not to take *any* type of drug—prescription, nonprescription, or recreational—without medical advice (American Academy of Pediatrics Committee on Drugs, 1994). Although a developing baby is well protected within the uterus, many substances pass across the placenta to the baby via the mother's blood. Certain drug and chemical agents can cause malformations and other problems. The developing embryo is most sensitive to interference from these agents, because it is during the embryonic period (first 90 days of gestation) when organ systems are being formed (see Figure 6–3). Effects of drug use or exposure during pregnancy can be manifested following a child's birth as well. For example, mercury is present in many fish species today, and pregnant women are warned to be cautious about consuming these (Centers for Disease Control and Prevention, 2004). High levels of mercury in such foods are associated with a number of neurological disorders.

A number of drugs and other kinds of chemical agents are known to have *teratogenic* effects—that is, they cause the abnormal development of an embryo. Among the most widely publicized is thalidomide, a drug used in the early 1960s to control the nausea or morning sickness that pregnant women sometimes experience. Thalidomide was later found to cause birth defects, such as absent or deformed limbs and organ translocations and malfunctions. Other drugs that may be prescribed in clinical-level dosages that are teratogenic include the antibiotic tetracycline, certain psychotropic medications, and certain anticancer drugs.

Other drugs can cause developmental problems. Thyroid drugs taken by the mother can produce congenital goiter in the developing baby. Conflicting views exist about whether ingesting LSD and marijuana in pregnancy correlates with birth defects in babies. Even aspirin has deleterious effects if taken frequently in late pregnancy, in that it can cause problems in blood clotting for the baby and delay the normal beginning of labor. Exposure of the baby to female sex hormones through the mother's ingestion of contraception pills during the very early stages of pregnancy can cause defects in the baby's heart, reproductive system, anus, and central nervous system.

Other drug substances must be carefully avoided during pregnancy. These include

Alcohol.   Attention has been directed recently to alcohol consumption during pregnancy and its association with birth defects in babies (Lumeng, Cabral, & Gannon, 2007). Moderate consumption of two or more ounces of alcohol daily by a pregnant woman increases

FIGURE 6–3. Critical periods occur in embryonic and fetal development in which the developing baby is sensitive and vulnerable to the influence of teratogens (substances known to cause developmental malformations) it experiences as part of the maternal environment. Major organ system deformities, as indicated by the black lines, occur when growth is occurring most rapidly. Minor physiological and structure damage is indicated by the white lines.

Source: Moore, K. L. (1974). *Before we are born.* Philadelphia, PA: Saunders.

the risk of having a child with **fetal alcohol syndrome (FAS).** It is estimated that about 0.2 to 1.5 per 1000 births in the United States involve some type of defect related to FAS (Centers for Disease Control and Prevention, 2004). This is comparable to the number of infants born with Down syndrome or spina bifida. The FAS-related defects can range from a combination of several conditions, such as slowed growth both pre- and postnatally, brain and central nervous system disturbances, mild mental retardation, organ malformations, and malformed facial features. Many of the immediate and short-term disturbances affecting children with this syndrome eventually disappear a short time after birth.

However, several serious, long-term effects can cause problems for many years, such as learning disabilities and hyperactivity, that affect school performance (Coggins, Timler, & Olswang, 2007; Sokol, Delaney-Black, & Nordstrom, 2003).

Even moderate drinking, one or two drinks daily, appears to cause harm to a developing baby (Sood et al., 2001). Because the risks for damage to the baby are so high, physicians urge women to avoid alcohol completely from the time they begin thinking about becoming pregnant to the time when they wean their child from breast-feeding (American Academy of Pediatrics Committee on Substance Abuse, 1993, 2001.)

● ●
Parenting Reflection 6–1

Should a mother who has a substance addiction be allowed to have custody of a new baby? Would the decision to allow custody have conditions such as the mother participating in a treatment program? Do medical personnel have an obligation to report such mothers to child protection agencies?

● ●

Cigarettes (Nicotine). When an expectant mother smokes, nicotine and other chemical agents found in cigarettes can have an adverse effect on the developing child (Bourgeois, 2004). One of these includes an increased risk of miscarriage. Another is a higher risk of respiratory disease following the baby's birth (Jedrychowski et al., 2007). The general finding is that mothers who are chronic heavy smokers (more than one pack a day) are more likely to have babies of low birth weight and to be at greater risk of miscarriage and stillbirth, as well as other complications (J. A. Martin et al., 2006). Pregnant women who smoke are also more likely to experience bleeding. Substances in cigarette smoke may elevate the heart rate and blood pressure of a fetus, causing it to increase its movements within the uterus and depriving it of adequate nutrients by reducing the mother's appetite. This reduction of essential nutrients contributes to low birth weight for these babies. Long-range effects in children of mothers who smoke during their prenatal development include poorer school performance, hyperactivity, perceptual-motor difficulties, and learning disabilities (Gabbe et al., 2003; Marlow, Wolke, Bracewell, & Samara, 2005). In this regard, the effects of nicotine resemble the effects of alcohol on prenatal development.

Caffeine. It appears that caffeine found in coffee, tea, chocolate, or soft drinks does not harm a developing baby prior to birth (Bech, Obel, Henricksen, & Olsen, 2007; Leviton & Cowan, 2002). This is relative to the expectant mother drinking small to moderate amounts of any of these substances. However, drinking large amounts (four or more cups of coffee daily) appears to be associated with a significantly higher risk of sudden infant death syndrome occurring following birth (Studd, 2004).

Recreational Drugs. The high use of recreational drugs, such as marijuana, heroin, ecstasy, and cocaine, in the United States is of great concern due to the effects observed in infants whose mothers used these substances during pregnancy. However, some research is unclear about the effects of certain substances (Schutter & Brinker, 1992).

Cocaine (including crack cocaine, which is smoked rather than inhaled as a powder) is a particularly addictive substance. Infants born to women who are addicted to cocaine are also addicted and must receive special medical care following birth. The short- and long-term effects of this substance in infants are especially troublesome (Macmillan et al., 2001). Typically, these infants are of low birth weight and often are not carried to term before birth. They tend to be undersized in general and have smaller heads than average. Babies exposed to cocaine before birth often have urinary tract defects and are apathetic, fretful, and less alert (Scher, Richardson, & Day, 2000).

Some states have enacted legislation or social policy regarding the welfare of so-called "crack babies" born to addicted mothers. While the U.S. Supreme Court overturned these laws in 2001, many people hold the perception that these infants have been abused by their mothers' addictive behavior. To the contrary, research has confirmed that the infants of addicted mothers studied were no worse off in a variety of developmental domains than children of mothers who smoked tobacco or marijuana, consumed alcohol, or provided a poor home environment (Beeghly, Frank, Rose-Jacobs, Cabral, & Tronick, 2003; Frank, Augustyn, Knight, Pell, & Zuckerman, 2001; Rose-Jacobs, Cabral, Posner, Epstein, & Frank, 2002). However, crack babies are more likely to be of low birth weight, to experience a number of physical problems related to in utero exposure to cocaine, and to experience withdrawal symptoms (American College of Obstetricians and Gynecologists, 2005; Bauer et al., 2005).

Heroin is an especially problematic illicit drug that has extremely deleterious effects for both a mother and her developing fetus. This substance causes a number of serious problems for a newborn, such as low birth weight, increased chances of a variety of birth defects, a number of behavioral disturbances such as excessive trembling, poor sucking ability, poor sleeping patterns, poor cognitive functioning, and increased chances of sudden infant death syndrome (Briggs, Freeman, & Yaffe, 2005; Steinhausen, Blattman, & Pfund, 2007).

Although evidence is not conclusive, findings from research suggest that heavy marijuana use by pregnant women is associated with developmental problems in their offspring. These include information-processing problems, low birth weight, attachment problems, and higher risk of using drugs later in life (Anand, 2003; Mereu et al., 2003; Reichman & Teitler, 2003). These findings and others indicate that it is not wise for a woman to risk such conditions in her children by heavy use of marijuana during pregnancy.

Other illicit drugs may also contribute to problems for a developing fetus that continue following birth. There is very little human research on in utero exposure to ecstasy. Results are inconclusive in the few studies that have been performed (Van Tonningen-van Driel, Garbis-Berkvens, & Reuvers-Lodewijks, 1999). Methamphetamine use is highly addictive for adult users and also causes a number of problems for a developing fetus and following birth (L. M. Smith et al., 2006). For example, exposure to this illicit drug before birth is associated not only with poor growth rates in utero as well as low birth weight. In addition, such exposure also appears to increase the likelihood of a variety of birth defects (Forrester & Mertz, 2007).

••

Focus Point. Use of illicit drugs by a pregnant woman has many deleterious effects on a developing fetus; these effects are likely to continue to manifest in a variety of ways following birth.

••

Infectious Diseases

Several types of infectious diseases can be transmitted from mother to child, both before birth through the placental membrane and during birth from contact with the mother's vaginal tract. The severity of these infections depends on when the disease is contracted by the mother during the course of her pregnancy.

German measles (rubella) is one of the best-known examples of disease agents that can harm a developing embryo. Infection of the developing baby with this viral agent can result in deafness, blindness, heart defects, central nervous system damage, mild mental retardation, or a combination of these conditions, depending on when the pregnant woman contracted the disease. The greatest potential for harm to the developing baby exists during the embryonic stage of development.

Unfortunately, because the symptoms of this disease in the mother closely resemble those of the common cold or an upper respiratory infection, detection of the disease is difficult. Fortunately, most women in the United States have been vaccinated against this disease (Plotkin, 2001).

Other diseases are known to damage the baby's central nervous system during the fetal stage of development. For example, conditions caused by the *cytomegalovirus* and the disease *toxoplasmosis* can contribute to brain damage, learning disabilities, sensory problems, and even death (March of Dimes Foundation, 2002).

The cytomegalovirus appears to be associated with improper or poor hygiene. It enters the nasal and throat passages of a fetus during birth and quickly makes its way into the central nervous system. It can be easily contracted among older children in day-care centers if proper personal hygiene is not practiced with great care. Toxoplasmosis is an infection caused by a parasitic agent that normally is found in farm animals, pets, and poultry. Because it completes its life cycle only in cats, infection can occur from inhaling the dust created when cleaning a litter box. It can infect humans, especially when immune responses are not fully functional, as is normally the situation with young infants and newborns or in individuals who are infected with the HIV virus that causes AIDS. Toxoplasmosis results in various disorders in infants, such as encephalitis, which causes brain damage, central nervous system dysfunctions, and digestive disorders (Kravetz & Federman, 2002). If a pregnant woman transmits the disease to her fetus, the newborn may suffer blindness or mental retardation. Pregnant cat owners are well advised to relegate litter box cleaning to someone else.

Sexually transmitted diseases such as syphilis, gonorrhea, and HIV (Human Immunodeficiency Virus), which causes AIDS (Acquired Immune Deficiency Syndrome), can also be transmitted by a pregnant woman to her developing baby (Williams, Norris, & Bedor, 2003). AIDS is an especially dangerous disease for all concerned. The HIV agent disables the fetal immune system, often resulting in the child's death within a short period of time following birth. Mothers who are infected with this virus become exposed in several ways, such as having unprotected sexual intercourse or sharing contaminated needles with an individual who is infected or from contact with infected blood. They may not develop AIDS symptoms themselves until a later time. Congenital

HIV infection is believed to take place in late pregnancy and is affecting an increasing number of babies born to infected mothers worldwide (Kourtis, Bulterys, Nesheim,& Lee, 2001). The AIDS virus can also be transmitted via a mother's breast milk to her infant.

In the United States, the incidence of AIDS among women is increasing dramatically, and 75% of women with AIDS are of childbearing age (Bulterys, 2001). Currently, it is estimated that more than 80% of children with AIDS in the United States contracted this disease from their mothers during pregnancy. Pregnant women who are infected with HIV can be treated with AZT, a drug commonly prescribed for those with AIDS or HIV infection. This treatment can substantially reduce the likelihood that an infant will be born with this virus, especially if mothers avoid breast-feeding following birth.

Venereal diseases contracted by a woman in pregnancy also have a negative influence on developing babies. Syphilis germs transmitted from mother to baby across the placenta affect the child's bones and body organs. Women with gonorrhea pass the disease agents to their child during birth, often leading to blindness in the neonate if not treated properly. Genital herpes is caused by a virus that also may be passed to an infant during birth (Sullivan-Bolyai, Hull, Wilson, & Corey, 1983) and is believed to be responsible for about one-third of all deaths in newborns. If the mother is known to be infected, the risk of transmission can be minimized by a cesarean (surgical) rather than vaginal delivery.

Chlamydia is a type of bacteria that is the cause of the most frequently experienced sexually transmitted infection in the United States (Centers for Disease Control and Prevention, 2006). It can affect both women and men. In women, the disease can have serious effects on the reproductive system, resulting in infertility. While the initial symptoms are often mild in nature, these become more severe as the disease progresses. Like many other sexually transmitted diseases, having this infection dramatically increases the chances for HIV infection. When a pregnant woman has this infection, she is at much greater risk of having a premature delivery and infecting her child at the time of birth. Infants born to mothers with this disease, if untreated, are at risk for eye and lung disorders.

Human papillomavirus (HPV) is another common sexually transmitted disease that can initially cause genital warts in both men and women that can later become cancerous (Centers for Disease Control and Prevention, 2006). Pregnant women are advised not to use creams often prescribed otherwise to treat the disease as birth defects may occur in a developing fetus. There is a vaccine now available to prevent certain strains of this virus. Many states are considering requiring all prepubertal girls to be vaccinated in order to enroll in school.

Metabolic Disorders

Women who are diabetic and become pregnant have a significantly high incidence of miscarriages, stillbirths, and infants born with multiple defects. Diabetes is not ordinarily transmitted to the child but does have an important influence on the child's development. This disorder is an inability of the mother's pancreas to produce a proper amount of insulin, the hormone that metabolizes sugar. As a result, an excessive amount of sugar exists in the mother's blood and urine. To compensate, the pancreas of her fetus enlarges and produces greater than usual amounts of insulin. Babies who manage to survive in this environment are usually overweight and have a bloated appearance at birth. In addition, their adjustment following birth is more difficult (Studd, 2004).

Another metabolic disorder is *phenylketonuria* (PKU), which is an inability to metabolize protein. Mothers with PKU and certain thyroid disorders face a greater risk of having a child who is mentally retarded (van Spronsen, Molendijk, Erwich, and Smit, 2003).

Paternal Risk Factors in Prenatal Development

Mothers are not solely responsible for conditions that place a developing baby at risk for harm. While the evidence points largely to what the maternal environment presents for better or for worse to a developing baby, certain conditions from fathers can cause problems for the baby as well. For example, abnormal sperm development can be attributed to a man's exposure to lead, recreational drugs like marijuana and cocaine, cigarettes, alcohol, radiation, and environmental chemicals such as pesticides (Westheimer & Lopater, 2004). As with women, the reproductive cells (sperm) of men are likely to experience genetic mutations as age increases. These changes occur more frequently in the sperm cells of aging men than in the ova of women as age increases and may be a significant cause of birth defects in the children fathered by older men.

• •

Parenting Reflection 6–2

What can government agencies do to help disadvantaged mothers-to-be to have healthier pregnancies?

• •

• •

Focus Point. The quality of an individual's development before birth may be influenced positively or adversely by a number of factors, including age of the mother; the quality of her diet; the quality of medical care during pregnancy; her exposure to certain drugs, chemicals, or disease agents; and the presence of certain metabolic conditions such as diabetes. Certain risk factors are also related to fathers.

• •

CURRENT TRENDS IN PRENATAL CARE

Every individual's right to be normal is encouraged and assisted by adequate care prior to birth. The field of **perinatology** is one area of medical science that has emerged in recent years to address this important need. Perinatology is concerned with the detection and treatment of illness in developing individuals during the prenatal stage. This new field of medical care has brought about advancements in knowledge and techniques for diagnosing the health status of individuals while they are still in the uterine environment (Sinclair, 2003).

Adequate prenatal supervision may be an important factor in reducing the incidence of low birth weight and prematurity in infants (Lawrence & Blair, 2003), a condition that has long-range implications for parents as well as children. However, the quality of prenatal care women receive varies according to their social, ethnic, and demographic backgrounds. Black and Native American mothers are generally reported to receive little care or to start their care late in the course of their pregnancy (Federal Interagency Forum on Child and Family Statistics, 2007; Martin et al., 2006). Adolescents and women over age 45 are likely to receive the least amount of prenatal care of the age groups usually surveyed. Amount of education is an important factor affecting whether women seek prenatal care. Mothers who do not complete high school are more likely to begin care late in pregnancy or receive no care.

Medical genetic counseling is an example of new advances in prenatal medical care. Until recently, physicians could provide only a minimal amount of information to parents who already had a child with birth defects about why the defects occurred and how to prevent them in future pregnancies. Expectant parents could be given only general advice about the probability that their child would be defective in some way at birth. Intensive research efforts to learn more about hereditary influences on birth defects have led to the development of remarkable new diagnostic tools and methods. Parents and potential parents can be given accurate information to assist them in making decisions about beginning a pregnancy or about the progress of a particular pregnancy. A genetic counselor investigates parents' medical backgrounds by obtaining their family history. Blood and other tissue samples are obtained to perform a chromosome analysis in order to identify genetic abnormalities. If a pregnancy is already in progress, various types of prenatal diagnostic tools are available to determine the status of the baby's health.

• •

Parenting Reflection 6–3

Is it a good idea to require couples, as part of the process of obtaining a marriage license, to submit blood samples for screening for potential problems with pregnancies?

• •

Prenatal Diagnostic Methods and Equipment

Ultrasound allows the creation of a **sonogram** (see Figure 6–4). This is much like an X-ray picture without the hazards of radiation. This method may be used to measure the growth of a fetus, to assess gestational age and structural abnormalities in the fetal body, to allow early detection of multiple pregnancies, and as a guide in other procedures such as amniocentesis.

Sonoembriology is a more recently developed advancement in ultrasound technology. High-frequency transvaginal probes are analyzed with digital image processing, which makes early detection of abnormalities in

FIGURE 6–4. A sonogram of a fetus can assist in determining important information such as fetal age, sex, and the presence of certain abnormalities.

the embryonic part of prenatal development (Kurjak, Kupesic, Matijevic, Kos, & Marton, 1999).

Amniocentesis is one of the better-known and widely used prenatal diagnostic tools (see Figure 6–5). This procedure, usually performed at about the 16th week of gestation, allows a physician to determine early in pregnancy whether a child has a hereditary disorder. Amniocentesis involves withdrawing a sample of the amniotic fluid that surrounds the fetus and examining a variety of cells shed from its skin. First, fetal position in the uterus is located by means of ultrasound scanning. Next, the physician inserts a long needle into the mother's abdomen and through the uterine wall, avoiding both the placenta and the fetus, and withdraws a small amount of amniotic fluid for testing.

The fluid sample is placed into a centrifuge and spun rapidly to separate the cells from the fluid. The liquid portion then can be analyzed for a variety of biochemical abnormalities caused by genetic disturbances, such as Tay-Sachs disease, a crippling central nervous system disorder that leads to early death. The remaining cells from the fluid are cultured for a short period and examined under the microscope for any abnormal genetic patterns. This examination assists in diagnosing abnormalities caused by missing, broken, or additional chromosomal matter. The sex of the developing fetus can also be determined by this method, which allows for diagnosis of sex-linked genetic diseases such as hemophilia. Many genetic diseases can be detected early through amniocentesis. A new type of ultrasound test measures the nose bone of a fetus, allowing for early detection of Down syndrome (a type of mental retardation; Cicero, Curcio, Papageorghiou, Sonek, & Nicholaides, 2001). This test is used in place of amniocentesis, especially when miscarriage is a risk for the expectant mother.

Alpha-fetoprotein (AFP) screening (Hui, et al., 2003) may be performed as early as 16 weeks following conception. This test, or series of blood tests, may be used to detect the presence of spinal cord defects such as spina bifida (a condition where the spinal cord is exposed, leading to paralysis and other central nervous system disorders) and anencephaly (the absence of

FIGURE 6–5. The procedure for performing amniocentesis and analysis of amniotic fluid.
Source: Friedman, T. (1971). Prenatal diagnosis of genetic disease. © Scientific American, Inc. All rights reserved.

FIGURE 6–6. In chorionic villi sampling, a biopsy is made of the tissue forming the early placenta structure by entering the uterus via the vagina and cervix. The tissue can be examined microscopically for disorders, and chromosome analysis can be performed to detect genetic disorders.

Source: Turner, J. S., & Rubinson, L. (1993). *Contemporary human sexuality.* Upper Saddle River, NJ: Prentice Hall.

normal brain formation). Because this test can produce false positive results, other diagnostic methods, such as amniocentesis or sonography, are used to confirm the results.

Another newly developed procedure available to health care professionals is **chorionic villi sampling** or biopsy (Studd, 2004; see Figure 6–6). Chorionic villi are small, hairlike structures that precede the developmental structure of the placenta. These are derived from tissue of the early embryo following implantation into the uterine wall. Ultrasound is used to locate the embryonic tissue mass in a woman's uterus, and a small catheter is inserted through the vaginal opening into the cervix. A very small section of the villi tissue is then removed from the uterine wall. An analysis similar to that performed with amniotic fluid can then be carried out on the villi tissue. This procedure, performed between the 8th and 11th week of pregnancy, allows for an even earlier diagnosis of genetic disorders than is provided through amniocentesis. This information is especially important for women who conceive when they are over age 40, because the probability of genetic abnormalities in infants increases significantly as women approach this age. A major disadvantage of this procedure is the risk of spontaneous abortion (Bourgeois, 2004).

A procedure known as **umbilical cord sampling** allows tests to be performed for infections, anemia, certain kinds of metabolic disorders, and other medical conditions (Chinnaiya et al., 1998). Using ultrasound for guidance, a sample of the developing baby's blood can be withdrawn from its umbilical cord for these tests. While these tests provide essential information for medical intervention, the procedure carries risks, such as miscarriage and hemorrhage.

When medically assisted technology, such as in vitro fertilization, is being used for conception, **preimplantation genetic diagnosis** can be made for identifying genetic defects before a zygote is implanted into a woman's uterus (Damewood, 2001). While this procedure can prevent the progression of a pregnancy producing a baby with genetic disease, other ethical issues can be raised if the procedure is not used judiciously.

Maternal blood sampling allows detection of fetal blood cells that can be examined for certain genetic conditions in the developing fetus, such as Down syndrome.

Embryoscopy is a technique in which a small viewing instrument is inserted into an expectant woman's abdomen to allow visual examination of an embryo as early as 6 weeks after conception. This permits early diagnosis and possible treatment of structural abnormalities (Studd, 2004).

Physicians may also use an instrument called an **endoscope** for direct examination of a developing fetus (Studd, 2004). The endoscope is especially useful for investigating defects not detectable through amniocentesis. The procedure is similar to amniocentesis in that a hollow needle is inserted into the uterus. The endoscope needle, however, contains a fiber optic device that allows the physician to visually inspect the fetus to detect structural defects. An additional needle also may be used to withdraw a small blood sample from the fetus; the blood can be analyzed to diagnose a number of genetic problems, such as sickle-cell anemia.

An electronic **fetal monitor** is also a useful instrument in providing prenatal care (Bourgeois, 2004). This instrument amplifies the heartbeat of a fetus and can be used as early as 5 months after conception. The device permits health care professionals to study the fetal heart rate for significant variances from normal patterns. The instrument is also useful in following the progress of labor and its effect on the fetus. Any significant change in heart rate is a signal of distress in the baby during labor and signals the need for immediate care.

Fetoscopy allows a fetus to be examined while inside the uterus via fiber optics (Cox, Werner, Gilstrap, & Cunningham, 2001). In addition to allowing direct observation, a sample of the fetal blood can be removed for testing, especially for genetic disease. This permits early treatment, via surgery or with drugs, prior to birth for a variety of conditions.

••

Focus Point.   The medical field of perinatology is a new source of prenatal care and supervision. Other advancements include medical genetic counseling, new methods of diagnosing fetal health conditions, and equipment for monitoring prenatal development.

••

ADJUSTING TO PREGNANCY

The birth of a child transforms individuals into parents. Assuming this new family role in addition to others already held is both challenging and rewarding. People evolve gradually into parenthood roles as they assume increasing responsibilities in raising and caring for a child. The transition is usually initiated when a couple learns that a pregnancy is in progress.

Expectant Parents' Reactions to Pregnancy

When a couple learns of a pregnancy, especially their first, they might expect several reactions. Many of the direct experiences of pregnancy apply mainly to a mother, of course. However, a pregnancy also affects the mother and her partner in several ways, although the experience is unique to each.

Pregnancy has been found to be the 12th most stressful life event that adults experience (Holmes & Rahe, 1967). An expectant mother undergoes a variety of changes that can cause her stress. These include adjusting to a changing body image as the pregnancy progresses, challenges to physical and psychological well-being, feelings about what it is like to be pregnant (especially for the first time), dealing with fears of the unknown, and shifting mood states that may be related to fluctuations in hormone levels (Schneider et al., 1999). Emotional reactions in pregnancy are important as well because high levels of anxiety in mothers have been associated with increased fetal activity, which may contribute partially to lower birth weights in these infants. High activity levels continue to be observed in these babies following birth (Monk et al., 2000).

For the most part, most women and their partners react favorably and with great anticipation to the news that a pregnancy has begun. This appears to be especially the case when the pregnancy is the first one and when the pregnancy is desired.

Like parenthood, pregnancy has different connotations and meanings for different individuals. For some, pregnancy validates one's sexuality and verifies one's femininity or masculinity in serving as proof that one is capable of conceiving or impregnating. For many individuals, the initiation of a pregnancy revives memories of childhood and brings anticipation of the parenthood role.

Not everyone who learns of the beginning of a pregnancy reacts with joy, pleasure, or anticipation, however. Emotional reactions that are less than positive are attributed to (1) feelings of ambivalence about the possibility of becoming a parent, (2) marital difficulties, (3) lack of a suitable social network to provide emotional support during the pregnancy, or (4) lack of desire for the pregnancy (Fleming et al., 1988). These negative attitudes also have a bearing on the manner in which labor and delivery are experienced.

When a pregnancy is confirmed, a couple must often focus on new issues they have not yet considered in their relationship. For example, many begin to ponder what it will be like to have a child and to be a parent, what kind of parent they will be, in what kinds of activities they will participate, and what kind of person the child will be and become. Perhaps one of the benefits of the 9 months of pregnancy is that it allows such mental preparations to take place before one actually has to perform as a parent. Expectant parents have time to begin thinking of themselves as a family in the traditional sense rather than as a couple. By attending childbirth education classes, reading books and articles about child rearing and child development, and arranging and participating in prenatal medical care, couples begin preparations for this change in their family system. They equip a nursery, receive baby showers, and shop for the things they will need in caring for an infant. This change is to be a significant one, and it will prompt related changes in the family system as the couple moves from being newlyweds to being a couple in the process of producing children. These changes are discussed in more detail in the next chapter.

● ●

Focus Point. The potential of new parenthood causes changes for both the woman who is pregnant and her partner. Women who anticipate motherhood positively adjust better to being pregnant and to experiencing labor and delivery. Pregnancy signals impending changes in personal and marital identities for a couple. It prepares them to make adjustments in moving to the next stage of their family life career.

● ●

EFFECTS OF THE BIRTH EXPERIENCE FOR ADULTS

A variety of outcomes can be anticipated in association with the type of delivery a couple experiences. Today, childbirth is recognized as being a psychological as well as a physical event that has implications beyond the immediate (Ratcliffe, 2007). Reactions to childbirth can be experienced as feelings of ecstasy and intense spirituality or as one of the more singularly negative experiences of one's lifetime (Kendall-Tackett, 2001). One of the most significant aspects of this event is the importance and role of the birth experience in promoting bonding, or attachment, between parents and the child (Figure 6–7). Some research suggests that the first few minutes following birth are crucial in this respect and constitute a critical period for the parent-child relationship (Waldenstroem, 1999a). Skin-to-skin contact between each parent and the newborn, as well as expressing

FIGURE 6–7. Emotional bonding between parents and a newborn begins following birth.

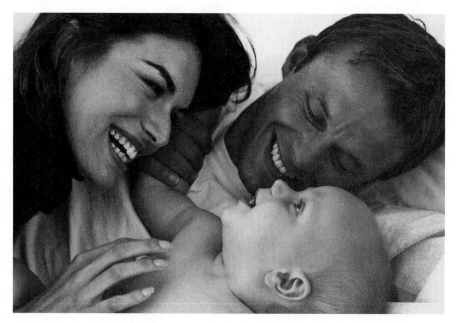

physical affection and maintaining eye contact, are believed to facilitate emotional bonding. Family-centered childbirth methods may also enhance the process. It has been speculated that a birth experience that promotes bonding between parent and infant prevents later parenting difficulties that have been associated with prolonged separation of the adult and child at birth.

The active involvement of the father or partner in childbirth may serve to make this experience more positive and thus more meaningful (Price, Noseworthy, & Thornton, 2007). Research generally indicates that preparation during pregnancy by both partners, but especially by the adult male, assists the woman in coping more positively with the experiences of pregnancy and delivery and leads to greater satisfaction. In addition, the father's participation in childbirth appears to stimulate his interest in the child, in child-rearing experiences, and in his role as a parent.

Immediate access to the newborn by the mother and father that is accomplished by rooming-in experiences, for example, may act to increase the confidence of the parents in performing competent child care under supervised conditions. This may also lead to fewer incidences of future parenting inadequacy. However, there do not appear to be any long-term deficits in the mother-child relationship when these early contacts do not occur (Eyer, 1992).

Adults experience stress reactions to delivery in different ways (Haig, 1995). The level of stress experienced may be higher among those who are first-time parents. This relates more directly to the transition first-time parents are experiencing into their new role and the varied related changes occurring in conjunction with this transition. These are discussed in more detail later in this chapter. For parents who are having their second or third child, there continues to be some stress associated with childbirth. This may relate, in part, to memories of past experiences of being a new parent of a newborn. These stimulate a more realistic appraisal of the impact that a newborn child has on changing family life, routines, and resources. In addition, a mother's satisfaction with the birth experience is related in part to the frequency of obstetrical interventions (surgical procedures, fetal monitors, episiotomies, enemas, etc.).

Many women will experience an emotional letdown following birth as an expected outcome of the delivery process. However, a small percentage of women experience a condition known as **postpartum depression (PPD).** This condition is different from the so-called maternity blues that can be experienced by both new mothers as well as fathers. Postpartum depression is a type of clinical depression that includes feelings of not wanting to provide child care, severe mood swings, continual fatigue, lack of joy in life, and/or withdrawal from relationships (Mays & Lechman, 2007). It is treatable, often with antidepressant medications in combination with psychotherapy. This condition has implications for the quality of the relationship between the affected mother and child. Of particular concern is the interference that can occur in the attachment process between mother and infant.

Postpartum psychosis differs from PPD in that it is a serious psychiatric condition. Women experiencing this condition often have delusions (e.g., that their child is satanic) as well as hallucinations that accompany the symptoms of PPD. Some women with this condition have gained notoriety for their psychotic episodes in which they actually killed their children (see http://www.npr.org/programs/morning/features/2002/feb/postpartum/020218.postpartum.html). This condition is also treatable with medication and psychotherapy.

● ●

Parenting Reflection 6–4

What parting advice would you offer to new parents who are taking their new baby home about what to expect in the months to come in their marriage, home routines, and social life?

● ●

● ●

Focus Point.   Adults can expect to experience several different types of outcomes in association with childbirth. The type of delivery may influence the adults' reaction, especially affecting the quality of emotional bonding that occurs between parents and the newborn. The active involvement of the newborn's father in the birth experience may facilitate his involvement in child-rearing experiences. Contemporary trends in childbirth such as rooming-in may facilitate emotional bonding of parents and child as well as bolster the confidence of parents in their ability to provide competent care for their infant.

● ●

THE BIRTH EXPERIENCE

The birth of a baby is a momentous event for a family system. It is a particularly memorable occasion for couples who are experiencing it for the first time. Until recently,

Western culture has approached birth as a medical event rather than as a family affair (Molter, 2003). However, today adults can choose from a variety of options for childbirth. Perhaps one of the advantages of these options is the return of childbirth to a family-centered experience and the recognition by medical personnel that the birth of a child is more than a matter of medical concern.

Types of Delivery

In the past, the majority of women in the United States delivered their babies by one standard, traditional method, which involved the use of medications that rendered the woman unconscious during the birth of the child. Physicians and women came to disapprove of this method for several reasons. Birth had become a highly managed medical affair rather than a family-centered experience. In addition, the anesthetics used for delivery eliminated the woman's participation in the event and had undesirable effects on the baby during labor. The period of recovery from the birth experience lengthened for both mother and child.

Medications used in delivery have been regarded negatively in recent years. Nevertheless, their use is warranted in certain instances. Physicians and certified midwives today know how to administer and monitor the effects of such drugs more carefully. At the same time, alternatives to medications have been developed that tend to enhance the birth experience and offer many benefits both to parents and the infant.

The various options to traditional childbirth are discussed in the following paragraphs.

Medicated Deliveries. Numerous drug agents are used in labor and delivery to minimize discomfort to the mother. Such drugs include **analgesics,** which primarily relieve pain and produce a semiconscious state; **amnestics,** which are used in combination with analgesics to produce "twilight sleep" and depress memory formation; **sedatives,** which produce a calming effect; and **tranquilizers,** which have a stronger, more soothing effect than sedatives (Studd, 2004).

All medications used in labor and delivery affect the fetus as well as the mother. Although these drugs enhance some body mechanisms, they usually work to depress most bodily functions, such as respiration, heart rate, blood pressure, and kidney function.

Use of regional anesthetics is also appropriate in some situations (Bourgeois, 2004). These agents, such as novocaine, block sensations in the mother's uterus, pelvic area, and vaginal region, preventing her from feeling pain during delivery. Such drugs allow a woman to be conscious during the birth process but limit her participation. In some instances, the drug can pass across the placental barrier and affect the fetus to some degree as well. The methods using local anesthetics include the **spinal,** or **saddle block,** in which analgesic drugs deaden the nerves leading from one specific area of the spinal cord, such as that affecting the uterus and pelvic areas; the **pudendal nerve block,** which deadens the nerves functioning in the vaginal area; and the **paracervical nerve block,** which deadens the nerves supplying the uterus, cervix, vagina, bladder, and rectum.

All medications used during labor and delivery today are administered with great care, with special attention given to their effects on the well-being of the fetus. Some evidence suggests medications used during delivery have long-range effects on the child (Studd, 2004), such as delays in developmental progress (e.g., sitting, walking, talking). Hence, decisions about whether to use these drugs in delivery and to what degree warrant serious consideration.

Cesarean Deliveries. In some situations it is not possible or desirable for a woman to experience a vaginal delivery. In such cases, a **cesarean section delivery** is performed to protect the health and well-being of both fetus and mother. Conditions indicating cesarean delivery include diabetes in the mother; an extremely large fetus; genital herpes in the mother, which can be transmitted to the infant during a vaginal delivery; an insufficiently dilated cervix; the possibility of severe hemorrhaging by the mother; multiple births; or breech presentation of the fetus (Ratcliffe, 2007).

The cesarean section is a surgical procedure named after Julius Caesar, the ancient Roman emperor who, according to legend, was born in this manner. The procedure is performed by making an incision through the woman's abdominal wall and into the uterus. The fetus and placenta are removed through this small opening. To prevent discomfort to the mother, a local anesthetic is usually administered in the form of a saddle or spinal block. It is not unusual today for some women to undergo more than one cesarean section.

There are different reactions to having a cesarean rather than a vaginal delivery for the mother and infant (Ratcliffe, 2007). There appears to be a greater risk for the infant's survival following birth by this procedure in comparison to a vaginal delivery. However, few long-range effects have been conclusively identified. Mothers who have experienced abdominal delivery appear to be at higher risk of mild depressive reactions following delivery as compared to other procedures. This especially may be the case when a vaginal delivery has been anticipated but prevented by circumstances warranting the abdominal procedure. Some women report having great feelings of loss of control due to their inability to participate in their delivery when this procedure is used. Another compounding factor is the lengthy convalescent period and use of highly technical equipment in the delivery and aftercare, which tend to create a more impersonal birth experience for both mother and newborn.

Parents appear to react differently to children born through the abdominal procedure. They are reported to be more involved with children's activities, to see their children in more positive tones, and to value their children more when compared to parents who have experienced the vaginal delivery of children. This may be attributed to the greater risks taken in giving birth through this procedure as compared with other approaches (Fenwick, Gamble, & Mawson, 2003).

Hypnosis.　Hypnosis is sometimes used as an additional means of reducing the use of drugs and anesthesia during delivery. The method has a limited use, however, because not everyone can be trained to enter a hypnotic state, and because special training is required for the physician or health care professional and the patient.

Prepared Childbirth.　Various methods used today emphasize the parents' preparation for childbirth, such as training for the delivery through educational experiences and learning specific techniques of pain control, encouraging the conscious participation of the mother by minimizing the use of drugs during labor and delivery, and encouraging the participation of the mother's partner in labor and delivery. Such approaches stress that, even though women have been socialized to expect discomfort and pain during labor and delivery, prepared childbirth techniques can help them relax and redirect their conscious attention away from those discomforts.

● ●

Parenting Reflection 6–4

What are some advantages and disadvantages of allowing older children, relatives, and friends to observe and participate in a couple's birth experience?

● ●

One of the more popular approaches to prepared childbirth is known as the **psychoprophylactic method,** or **natural childbirth** (Goldberg, Brinkley, & Kukar, 2005). This technique was originally developed in the former Soviet Union based on Pavlovian concepts of classical conditioning. Its aim is to substitute a neutral response for the conditioned response of fear and tension. The neutral response is an acquired breathing pattern that is learned and performed in association with a uterine contraction. Fernand Lamaze (1958), a French physician, studied this method while visiting the Soviet Union and introduced it to the Western world. He refined the technique, emphasizing the increased participation of the mother during delivery (Figure 6–8).

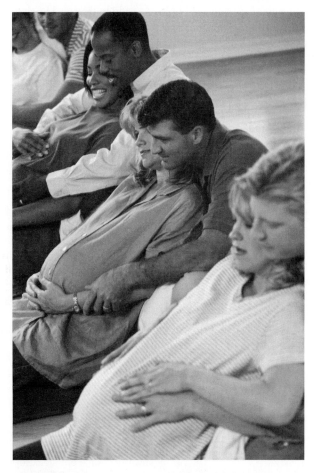

FIGURE 6–8.　In many communities, prospective parents may take classes that prepare them for childbirth. Many are based on the Lamaze method and include a coach (usually the mother's partner) who assists during labor and delivery.

These methods have great appeal to both physicians and couples for many reasons. The minimized use of drugs in labor and delivery enhances the well-being of both mother and child. Babies born through such deliveries typically have significantly higher-rated health status. The mother's recovery is speedier, and there are usually fewer complications from the delivery. Furthermore, delivery of the baby becomes a family matter in that it involves the active participation of both the mother and her partner. The mother's partner often acts as a coach in assisting her to perform the breathing patterns properly and offers encouragement and support. Their relationship may become more enriched as a result of the months of training and preparation for the birth (Vontver, 2003). The information gained from these experiences also helps to reduce fear and anxiety surrounding labor and delivery.

Contemporary Childbirth Trends

Many hospitals and birthing facilities offer a homelike atmosphere for the labor and delivery experience (Bourgeois, 2004). More couples are coming to view the birth of a child as a family experience and not as an illness requiring strict hospital care routines.

Birthing rooms are more comfortable and relaxed than traditional labor rooms, which are usually sparse and functional in design. Birthing rooms are furnished much like a bedroom in a home, with a large bed, decorated walls, plants, and draped windows. Children, other relatives, and friends are welcome in this room. Should complications occur, medical equipment is nearby. The birth of a baby in this environment occurs much like the home deliveries that were common earlier in the last century.

Another innovation in the birth experience is called **rooming-in,** in which the baby is placed in a bassinet near the mother's bed and the mother takes the major responsibility for caring for the baby after delivery. This is thought to enhance opportunities for families to share in the birth experience and to develop stronger and more meaningful emotional bonds earlier in the baby's life (Cox et al., 2001).

Birthing centers and home deliveries are an option for low-risk deliveries (Cox et al., 2001). Birthing centers provide facilities similar to those found in hospital settings that are hotel-like while providing easy access to medical equipment and staff. Home birth entails giving birth in one's home environment with the attendance of

Parenting FAQs 6–1

My wife wants me to help her when it's time for her to give birth to our child. This is our first. I want to be supportive of her, but I'm just not sure if this is such a great idea. It seems to me I'd be out of place at the time. I always thought the father wasn't welcome during childbirth. None of my friends have done this so I don't know who to ask about it. What are the benefits and disadvantages of having me there during childbirth?

A:. It's good that you want to be supportive of your wife because being a part of the childbirth experience can be a good way to show your support at a time when she really needs you. Things have changed considerably about childbirth since your father and mother gave birth to you. Today, most young couples like yourself make childbirth a team effort by using prepared childbirthing methods that weren't so popular when you were born. The idea many women have today about the issue is that if their partner was interested in being present at conception, he can certainly be there at the time of birth as well. The benefits of your presence and involvement are many and some may be long term in nature. For example, being involved in childbirth helps you to see how you played a role in the conception of your child. It helps you to bond with your child and to take ownership in the child's presence in your life and that of your wife. Your presence makes childbirth a family experience rather than one that is strictly a medical situation. Sorry, but I can't think of any significant disadvantages of you being involved. Some men fear, for example, that they will lose interest sexually in their wives by witnessing them giving birth. On the contrary, many men find that their participation has stimulated their interest in their wives and helped to develop a greater respect for them.

a nurse-midwife or physician. This setting is not often used due to difficulties in having access to emergency medical equipment and the high cost of malpractice insurance for health care professionals.

Although most deliveries in the world are by midwives (Daly, 2003), in the United States the use of midwives had become rare until recent years. Today, many women are choosing to use the services of a midwife rather than a physician to provide prenatal care and delivery of their baby. There are two classes of midwives in the United States: the **direct-entry midwife,** who is not a certified health care professional but has learned midwifery skills and is allowed to deliver babies in some states, and the **nurse-midwife,** who is a certified health care professional with advanced training in obstetrics, maternal nutrition, family planning, and related topics. The involvement of midwives in prenatal care and obstetrics is a controversial issue, especially within the medical community.

A **doula** is someone who cares for a new mother when she is in labor and sometimes for a period following delivery (M. T. Stein, Kennell, & Fulcher, 2004). Doulas are like midwives in having been present in numerous cultures worldwide for centuries. These individuals provide important and useful social, emotional, and physical support for new mothers and have a positive impact on the mother's experiences in the days following birth. Women who have the support of a doula are reported to have shorter labor, cope more effectively with the responsibilities of being a new mother, and have fewer labor and delivery problems (Campbell, Lake, Falk, & Backsstrand, 2006; Gordon, 2000).

Many women today wish to use alternative birthing centers rather than the impersonal labor and delivery suites found in a typical hospital environment. Some even go so far as to ensure the type of delivery they desire by arranging for home births to be supervised by a midwife. Where the delivery takes place is often influenced by factors considered important by the parents. For example, those who choose home delivery typically do so to avoid separation from the newly born infant, whereas those choosing hospital delivery do so to ensure safety for the mother and infant.

Health care professionals working with pregnancy and delivery are becoming more concerned about the birth experience of the fetus as well as of the mother. The impression thus far about the birth experience is that it is a stressful event for all, but perhaps more for the fetus because of its less-advanced state of development than the adults involved in the process. In response to this impression, an alternative approach to traditional delivery methods has been proposed by Frederick Leboyer (1976), another French physician. Leboyer's method seeks to minimize the adverse effects of the birth experience for the fetus. Birth occurs in a quiet, softly lighted room, and immediately after birth the baby is placed on the mother's abdomen to be stroked and handled nurturantly. After the umbilical cord is cut and tied, the baby is bathed in warm water. This is believed to soothe the baby while the vernix is being cleaned from the skin. This approach is in stark contrast to the usual, traditional environment and approach used in most delivery suites. These rooms typically are brilliantly lit, and the baby is handled vigorously following birth to help it begin breathing. Leboyer views his method as a gentler and more humane way to introduce a baby to life outside the mother's uterus. Leboyer's approach is controversial, however.

In addition to these differences in procedure promoted by LeBoyer, delivery tables are giving way to the use of *birthing chairs*. Delivery tables, which place the mother-to-be on her back with her legs raised and feet anchored in stirrups, were originally designed for the convenience of physicians delivering the baby. The birthing chair is believed to be more helpful to the mother and does not hamper the ability of the person assisting in the delivery (M. D. Barber, Lambers, Visco, & Bump, 2000). It typically resembles a captain's chair design but may have a portion of the seat cut away in a semicircle to allow access to the woman's vaginal area. Because the delivering mother is placed in a comfortable semisquatting position, she is able to make use of gravity and her anatomy to push when necessary during the delivery.

• •

Parenting Reflection 6–5

If you had a choice between using a medical doctor or a midwife for your delivery, which would you choose and why? Should states allow greater use of midwives as a means for helping more women have greater access to health care prior to and during childbirth?

• •

••

Focus Point. Childbirth has become, once again, a family event rather than one closely managed in hospitals under strict medical supervision. New methods of childbirth promote the involvement of both partners in this event, and some institutions provide facilities that allow participation of others in the experience, such as relatives, older children, and friends. This greater involvement of the family in childbirth is thought to promote emotional bonding of these individuals with the baby following birth, thereby producing beneficial effects for all. Some families choose to use the services of a midwife to conduct prenatal and childbirth care. Leboyer suggests alternative ways for conducting childbirth that are believed to minimize the stress of birth for the baby.

••

POINTS TO CONSIDER

■ Development before birth has unique characteristics in that it is (1) the shortest stage of the human life span; (2) the stage during which growth occurs most rapidly; and (3) a highly critical period of human development due to the extreme vulnerability of the embryo to a variety of factors.

■ Factors that can positively or adversely influence the developmental progress of a fetus include (1) environmental factors; (2) age of the mother; (3) maternal nutrition and exercise; (4) exposure to drug and chemical agents in the mother's bloodstream; (5) exposure to infectious disease agents contracted by the mother; (6) mother's prenatal medical care.

■ A variety of procedures are also available that provide diagnostic information about the health and well-being of an embryo or fetus prior to birth such as sonography, amniocentesis, chorionic villi sampling, umbilical cord sampling, endoscopic examination, and use of a fetal monitor.

■ Most expectant parents welcome a pregnancy, especially if it has been planned and desired. The birth experience can be either a highly significant event in one's life or a highly stressful, negative experience. Most experience the birth a child with positive reactions, while for some women, birth can produce severe, emotional reactions that are difficult to cope with and may be serious in their psychiatric implications.

■ A variety of childbirth approaches are available to families today. The contemporary trend is toward the increased use of family-centered methods that feature (1) a more relaxed, homelike atmosphere; (2) more active involvement of the mother's partner; (3) less frequent use of drugs during labor and delivery unless warranted; (4) more active involvement and participation of both the mother and her partner in preparing for childbirth; and (5) active caretaking of the newborn by the parents before discharge from the health care facility.

CHAPTER 7

Parenting Infants and Toddlers

Focus Questions

■ ■ ■ ■ ■ ■ ■ ■ ■ ■

1. What are the principal developmental landmarks of infancy that parents should know?
2. What is the nature of parent-infant relations?
3. What kinds of community supports do families with infants need?
4. What stressors and coping mechanisms are revealed by a systemic family development snapshot of families with infants and toddlers?

■ ■ ■ ■ ■ ■ ■ ■ ■ ■

Infancy is the period of the life span that extends between birth and 3 years following birth. Most individuals perceive a baby as being passive and dependent on others. However, findings from new studies about the nature of infant development depict an infant as showing highly competent behaviors and being actively involved in learning to master his or her interactions with the environment (L. G. Miller & Albrecht, 2004).

Most people are aware that infants require much attention, supervision, and care to grow and develop properly. Theorists and researchers also acknowledge infancy as a landmark stage in the human life span (see Figure 7–1).

● ●

Parenting Reflection 7–1

What are some sources of contemporary ideas about the nature of infants? Are these depictions realistic?

● ●

DEVELOPMENTAL LANDMARKS OF INFANCY

As with other stages of the life span, infancy has its own unique developmental tasks and landmarks that lay the foundation for current and future developmental progress. Many complex developmental changes and events are singular to this time of life. Many

FIGURE 7–1. Infancy is a time of life when children experience many new things for the first time as they discover their world.

developmental events that occur in infancy are the product of maturational changes, such as changes in size, weight, and body proportions; changes in physiological structures and functions; and the development of particular physical skills, including walking and speaking. Other significant developmental events that occur in infancy are more psychological in nature and are more sensitive to environmental influences. These are important as well in influencing how the relationship between parents and children takes shape and becomes configured in particular ways unique to the individuals and their family system.

Healthy adjustment in infancy focuses on accomplishing the challenges of the developmental tasks and landmarks appropriate to this time of life. These are outlined in Focus On 7–1. Traditionally, these lead from complete dependence and helplessness at birth to the ability to function independently of adults to a certain degree. For this development to take place, infants necessarily need to acquire a trusting attitude about their caregivers and their environment and establish initial personal boundaries that permit self-individuation.

Knowledge of developmental events that occur at each stage of a child's life span is important to parents and other caregivers. All humans are born with a ca-

pacity for experiencing certain events that have been programmed to occur and for experiencing other events subject to modification by the environment in their impact. Infants are active participants in influencing their social environment and the responses of those who provide their care. As a result, parents and caregivers need to be aware of certain cues that a baby will provide to assist caregivers in their behavior. These cues are often a part of the developmental process, and to recognize them, caregivers need to observe a baby's behavior and know what occurs appropriately at different times.

PARENTING INFANTS AND TODDLERS

Meeting the Needs of Infants and Toddlers

Most adults are cognizant of the extreme degree of dependency of an infant on its parents or caregivers. The need for dependence on adults is necessary for survival and for enhancing a child's developmental progress. The nature and degree of dependency in infancy and childhood among humans differs from that observed among the young of other species. Anthropologists

Focus On 7–1   **Major Developmental Landmarks in Infancy**

The Newborn (birth to 2 weeks)

- Establishing respiration within normal limits
- Establishing circulation to the lungs and away from the umbilical cord
- Establishing body temperature regulation
- Establishing digestion and elimination processes
- Exercising neonatal reflexes
- Adjusting to light and sound
- Establishing sleep pattern

The Infant (3 weeks to 18 months)

- Acquiring self-regulated skills of locomotion (walking), manipulation (hand skills), and self-feeding with solid food
- Maintaining a sleep-wake cycle
- Exploring sound production in preparation for speech
- Establishing initial sensorimotor schemes and mastering object permanence
- Establishing an emotional attachment to parents or primary caregivers
- Experiencing basic emotional states germane to infancy (e.g., social smiling and crying) as a means for communication
- Establishing an attitude of basic trust versus mistrust

The Toddler (18 months to 3 years)

- Refining self-regulated skills
- Establishing early speech patterns
- Refining and modifying basic sensorimotor schemes and establishing elementary logic and reasoning
- Learning to control the elimination of body wastes
- Establishing an attitude of autonomy versus shame and doubt
- Establishing self-differentiation and exploring personal boundaries
- Developing initial conscience

have attributed this to the larger brain of humans that allows for higher-order mental processes not found in other species (Morris, 1986, 1996). It takes much more developmental time for a human's brain to be wired in establishing the myriad neural circuits that allow mature functioning. For example, the brain at birth weighs only 25% of its total adult weight, but by age 3, the brain has attained about 90% of its adult weight. However, there is more to attaining maturity than achieving an adult brain weight. Socialization and edu-

cation continue for many years beyond age 3. For most of the developmental periods between infancy and early childhood, parents provide caregiving that is largely physical and emotionally nurturing in nature. As children grow older past these years, physical caregiving diminishes relatively while psychological caregiving increases.

Feeding.   The sucking reflex is one of the earliest reflexes to appear during prenatal development and is exceptionally well developed at birth in full-term new-borns. This necessary reflex, which is easily elicited by almost any stimulation to the lips, cheeks, or mouth area, ensures that an infant can obtain nourishment before teeth emerge for chewing.

One of the initial decisions in providing care at this time is whether to breast- or bottle-feed an infant. This is a choice that affects all family members and should be fully discussed before implementing a final decision, ideally before a baby is born. There are as many advantages or benefits as there are costs or disadvantages of both these methods. Each family needs to determine its priorities and how each method would or would not work best for their circumstances. With many women reentering the work force after a short period following birth, it is not unusual for a new mother to utilize a breast pump to extract her milk, which is provided via a bottle by the baby's caregiver while she is working.

There are important reasons why a couple should discuss this decision prior to a child's birth. Several research articles have addressed the problems some men experience when their wives breast-feed a newborn baby (Spock, 2004). While most men are supportive and encourage their wives' breast-feeding, some men experience stress and generally troublesome negative reactions to this feeding practice. The most common negative reaction is jealousy or feelings of being displaced by the infant as the primary focus of the wife's affection. Suggested ways to prevent or alleviate such negative reactions include: (1) improving the birth experience for the husband by involving him in the process, (2) promoting early physical and social contact between the father and the infant, (3) improving communications between the husband and wife during the postpartum period, and (4) encouraging the father to become more actively involved in routine caregiving activities of an infant following birth.

Most normal infants require a feeding once every 3 or 4 hours during the first few months after birth. After adding solid foods to a baby's diet, usually during the fourth to sixth months, the number of feedings is reduced throughout the day and continues to decline as the baby grows older. Babies can generally feed themselves after they have developed the motor skills and coordination necessary to hold a cup and drink from it and to bring food to their mouths and chew it properly. These events are a result of maturational processes and cultural expectations or experiences. Developmental norms have been established that show the times at which these events can be expected to occur.

● ●

■ Parenting Reflection 7–2

Why should a father be involved in the decision to breast-feed a new baby? Should all decisions relating to infant care be jointly made by a child's parents?

● ●

Weaning and Introducing Solid Foods. The shift from liquid to solid foods involves the process of **weaning.** Although extended breast-feeding may continue through the second and third year following birth, most infants are weaned when they indicate a readiness to begin taking solid foods. Such indications include drinking from a cup, grasping a spoon easily, drinking more than a quart of formula daily, and enjoying playing with food (Figure 7–2).

A major concern in the weaning process is providing an adequate amount of protein and iron to meet the infants' growth requirements. Lack of adequate sources of these nutrients can lead to malnutrition and eventually to permanent damage, especially to the brain and central nervous system (Spock, 2004).

There is much disagreement about when to introduce solid foods into an infant's diet. Some infant specialists recommend that solid foods can be safely started between 3 and 4 months after birth, while others suggest waiting until 6 to 8 months after birth (American Academy of Pediatrics, 1999).

Health and Medical Care. If a woman experienced relatively good health during her pregnancy, then it is likely that the baby will also enter the world in a healthy state. However, certain physical conditions that appear to be of concern are relatively normal for infants. These are briefly outlined here:

■ Spitting up or vomiting is common; caregivers learn to be prepared for the inevitable in this regard.
■ Wheezing, sneezing, and hiccupping are to be expected, especially in the first few months following birth.

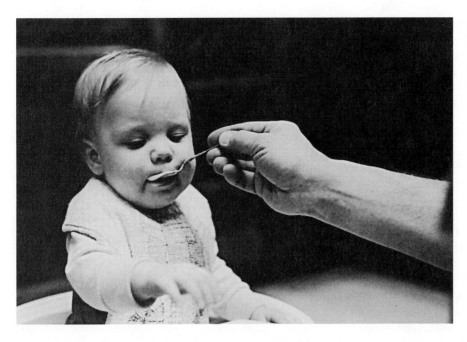

FIGURE 7–2. Solid foods are introduced sparingly to infants. There is much disagreement about when to begin this process.

- Constipation is more common among babies who are bottle- rather than breast-fed. Diarrhea also can be expected frequently because of an immature digestive system.
- Rashes occur commonly, especially in the diaper area, because of sensitive skin and exposure to acidic urine. Other kinds of rashes are attributed to yeast and bacterial infection.
- Other skin conditions may be observed, such as cradle cap (seborrhea) caused by an overly oily scalp; prickly heat rash, which occurs in hot weather; and impetigo, a highly contagious skin infection.
- Thrush is a yeast infection in the mouth due to an immature immune system.
- Obstructed tear ducts sometimes develop due to an infection and are not considered serious but are something that needs medical attention.

It is important to provide well-baby medical care that will allow health care professionals to examine the baby regularly. Many physical disorders can be detected early if babies are receiving this care. Immunizations also must be received in infancy to provide protection from communicable diseases such as measles, diphtheria, mumps, and polio. While most families can provide this care and have medical insurance coverage, families living in poverty or who have employment difficulties often forego this treatment due to financial constraints. Fortunately, most states provide treatment for those who are medically indigent.

Sleep-Wake Cycle.   A popular belief about infants is that they sleep a great deal of the time. This may be the situation in the early months of this life stage, but individual sleeping patterns are subject to wide variations (Spock, 2004). Some infants require long periods of sleep, while others sleep for only short, restless periods. Sleep during the first several months after birth is interrupted only long enough for the baby to feed. This round-the-clock pattern of alternating periods of sleep with feeding extends to longer intervals of wakefulness after the third month. During the remainder of the time until the baby approaches age 2, sleep needs decrease to 10 to 14 hours daily. Most toddlers need a morning and afternoon nap through the preschool years, which is definitely welcomed by most parents as a means of obtaining uninterrupted work time.

As most infants approach their second birthday, a pattern of **negativism** often appears in their willingness either to take a nap or go to bed at night. A child's resistance to bedtime may be a means of expressing a growing sense of autonomy or may arise from a fear of the dark or of being left alone. Children may express their difficulty in developing self-regulated sleeping patterns by resisting the establishment of bedtime routines. Parents may respond to these behavioral cues by staying with the child to provide reassurance and by not asking the child if she or he is ready to go to bed, since the response will most likely be negative. American society is perhaps the only major Western culture that expects its children to develop this self-regulated pattern early in life, with little guidance from adults. American parents simply place an infant into a crib and close the bedroom door, while parents in many other cultures typically sing a short, soft lullaby or rock an infant to sleep.

Providing Structure and Nurturance for Infants. The psychosocial focus of an infant is on learning to trust the integrity of caregivers and the environment in providing and meeting the infant's needs. At some level of consciousness, infants are likely to make decisions about themselves, others, and things in their world that relate to trust (J. I. Clarke & Dawson, 1998). Interactions with people, with the environment, and with things in the environment lead the infant to conclusions and expectations about how his or her needs will be met.

Interactions between parent and infant experiences are congruent at this time. Adults are experiencing interactions with infants that assist in establishing their sense of generativity. While adults are learning "to make be and to take care of," the infant is learning "to get and to give in return." The reciprocal nature of this interaction helps to ensure that each participant experiences opportunities to fulfill his or her particular psychosocial need.

Listed in Table 7–1 are the behaviors of parents that meet their infant's needs for structure and nurturance. Behaviors that can be detrimental to infants by not meeting their needs appropriately are also listed. Understandably, most of the parenting behaviors that are observed in providing care for infants between birth and 6 months of age are nurturant in nature, whereas those that are observed in providing care between 18 months and 3 years include increasing elements of structure.

Parents of toddlers are especially concerned about beginning efforts to control their child's behavior and to elicit the child's compliance with their requests and demands. One study provides insightful information on how parenting style influences how parental demands are shaped and their influence on children's compliance (Kuczynski & Kochanska, 1995). The researchers observed a group of 70 mothers and their toddlers in a naturalistic setting. Three types of maternal demands were observed: (1) *caretaking demands* that were related to

---

Parenting FAQs 7–1

We have a toddler who just doesn't want to stay in her bed once she's put down at night. She'll get up five or six times before going to sleep. It's exhausting for us to go through this every night. What can we do?

A:. Children this age often experience separation anxiety in relation to bedtime. Some children, however, perform this kind of routine as a matter of gaining parental attention. Try to analyze why this may be going on with your child. If your child is being cared for by someone else during the day, it might be helpful to sit with her with the understanding that it will only be for a short period during which she is to go to sleep. This can get out of control, however, because she can routinely expect one of you to stay with her.

Remember that you are helping your child to develop a bedtime routine at this time in her life. To develop one that is healthy for all concerned, consistently but firmly lead her back to bed over and over again each time she reappears after being put down for sleep. Don't be tempted to lock the child's bedroom door. This can generate fears that are difficult for her to control and create another problem. You might install a radio or tape player to provide soothing music at bedtime as well. Developing a bedtime routine of reading calm, peaceful stories also helps children to settle down; a pleasant bath time is also helpful for many children. It is important, however, to continue to enforce the ultimate rule of bedtime: Once you are put to bed, it's time to go to sleep.

TABLE 7–1.   Parenting Behaviors for Infants

Age	Behaviors Providing Structure/Nurturance	Behaviors Not Providing Structure/Nurturance
Birth to 6 Months	• Affirming infant's attempts to meet developmental tasks. • Giving loving, consistent care. • Responding appropriately to infant's behavioral cues. • Thinking on behalf of infant; anticipating needs. • Holding infant lovingly and maintaining eye contact during feeding. • Providing nurturance by touching, looking, talking, and singing to infant. • Seeking help and information when uncertain about what to do. • Acting in reliable and trustworthy ways toward infant.	• Not responding to infant's behavioral cues. • Failing to hold and touch infant sufficiently. • Responding rigidly, angrily, and agitatedly to infant. • Providing food before infant has given cues of hunger • Punishing infant for his or her behavior. • Failing to provide a healthy physical environment. • Failing to protect infant from harm and danger. • Criticizing infant for anything he or she does. • Acting in ways that discount an infant's existence, i.e., acting irresponsibly in ways that fail to meet the needs of an infant.
6 to 18 Months	• Continuing to affirm infant's attempts to meet developmental tasks. • Continuing to offer love, safety, and protection. • Providing a safe, childproofed environment. • Protecting infant from harm and danger. • Continuing to provide food, nurturing touch, and encouragement. • Saying "yes" twice as often as "no" to infant. • Providing a variety of experiences for infant. • Providing feedback about infant's behavior to him or her. • Refraining from interrupting infant's speech or behavior. • Responding to infant's invitations to play.	• Continuing to fail to protect infant from harm and danger. • Restricting infant's freedom of movement. • Criticizing, punishing, or shaming infant for attempts to establish personal autonomy or to explore the environment. • Expecting infant not to want to touch things. • Expecting infant to become instantly toilet trained. • Acting in ways that discount infant, i.e., acting in ways that prevent the infant from accomplishing basic developmental tasks and needs.
18 Months to 3 Years	• Affirming toddler's attempts to meet developmental tasks. • Continuing to offer love, cuddling, safety, and protection. • Encouraging toddler's ability to think. • Encouraging child to reach conclusions based on information. • Explaining rules, reasons, how tos, do nots, and other information to toddler.	• Communicating too many "don'ts" about toddler's behavior. • Getting involved in power struggles with toddler. • Trying to create a compliant child in order to maintain image of self as a "good" parent. • Referring to toddler as a "terrible two" both to the child and to others. • Refusing to set limits consistently or provide expectations for toddler's behavior.

(continued)

TABLE 7–1. Parenting Behaviors for Infants *(continued)*

Age	Behaviors Providing Structure/Nurturance	Behaviors Not Providing Structure/Nurturance
18 Months to 3 Years	• Accepting toddlers' expressions of positive and negative emotions. • Teaching toddler about options for expressing negative feelings. • Setting and enforcing reasonable limits that have been discussed with partner in advance, if possible. • Remaining calm in times of toddler's emotional outbursts, neither giving in nor overpowering the child. • Giving simple and clear directions to toddler; encouraging and praising accomplishments. • Expecting toddler to begin thinking about own feelings and those of others. • Reframing attitude about toddler as a "terrific two."	• Setting expectations for toddler's behavior that are appropriate for an older child. • Expecting toddler to play well with other children. • Failing to teach toddler about how to make simple choices in behaviors. • Shaming toddler for anything. • Acting in ways that discount toddler.

Source: Adapted from Clarke, J. I., & Dawson, C. (1989). *Growing up again: Parenting ourselves, parenting our children.* Minneapolis, MN: Hazelden.

providing physical care and supervision (e.g., "Wash your hands," "Watch out for the stairs"), (2) *demands for appropriate behavior* that involved teaching and reinforcing rules for acceptable behavior (e.g., "Don't do that"), and (3) *demands for competent action* that would help the child or others (e.g., "Please share your toy"). Younger toddlers received more of the first type from mothers, while older toddlers received more of the third type.

The parenting style was found to be associated in this study with the type of demand that a mother used with her toddler. Those who were using an authoritarian style peppered their demands with prohibitions for the toddler's behavior, while those using an authoritative style couched their demands in terms that promoted the child's competencies within a rationale of guidance. Interestingly, the researchers found that those mothers using an authoritative style were more likely to gain compliance from their toddler than mothers using an authoritarian style. When the children and their mothers were again observed by the researchers after the children had reached 5 years of age, fewer behavior problems were observed among the children of the authoritative-style mothers.

Promoting Brain Development. Parents play an important role in promoting an infant's brain development. This influence begins with the environment provided by the mother during pregnancy (see Chapter 6) and continues following birth with the provision of adequate nutrition, health care, stimulation, nurturance, and interaction.

An infant's brain experiences rapid growth during the first 2 years following birth. At birth, the brain is functionally operational but lacks the ability to perform critical thinking skills and use of language. The neonatal reflexes that are present at birth such as sucking and grasping are formed at the subcortical level. This part of the brain contains those mechanisms that regulate heart rate, respiration, sleeping patterns, and so on. These reflexes are important in that they serve as the first avenues for allowing the infant to interact with its environment. These reflexes lay the foundation for all mental functioning that will follow in this stage and in that of those that follow.

At birth, there are immense numbers of neurons in the brain that are unconnected. The infant's brain is basically in an unsculpted state at birth regarding these neural connections that allow for the myriad physical, motor, and cognitive tasks and skills to develop (Stiles, 2008). Meeting an infant's nutritional needs is critical at this time in life in order for these brain changes to take place that allow this organ to function more efficiently. In addition, stimulating sensory experiences are also critical in this regard (Bangalore, 2007).

Parents play a particularly important role in this manner of providing stimulating experiences and interactions that promote brain development. The quality of parental caretaking, especially in the manner by which nurturance is expressed to an infant, plays a critical role in this regard (Kim & Swain, 2006). When a parent holds an infant in a nurturing manner while it is fed (loving touch), looks into its eyes (visual stimulation), and talks soothingly to it (auditory stimulation), then several sensory modalities are stimulated simultaneously. Later, as the baby grows older, the brain appears to be constantly fine-tuning the neural connections in the brain as well as continuing to develop new ones. This is dependent, in part, upon parents and family members continuing to provide nurturance and interactions that help infants learn to be curious, to want to explore, to touch, to taste, and thoroughly experience their world through their senses. In this manner, social as well as physical stimulation are important and a necessary component of providing appropriate care for an infant. Later, culture becomes transmitted via language, observation of family and community members, and by socialization experiences provided by parents.

We will discuss this important function of parenting infants in other sections of this chapter on attachment and cognitive skills.

Facilitating Attachment.   **Attachment** is an attraction to someone that is based on psychological bonding. Attachment is also described as a strong affectional tie between an infant and his or her primary caregivers (Ainsworth, 1973) (Figure 7–3). As such, attachment is a process that affects both parents and infant. It is one of the few developmental phenomena that appear to be found universally in all humans and in all cultural settings. It is essential for an infant's survival and well-being. When an infant fails to attach properly to caregivers, the consequences are damaging to his or her emotional, physical, social, and psychological well-being.

Attachment is constructed through interactions of an infant with primary caregivers. An infant who is experiencing normal developmental progress behaves in ways that signal a desire to be near caregivers, and the behav-

FIGURE 7–3.   Attachment in infancy is a strong emotional tie to a primary caregiver. It is critical to and affects later development.

iors usually serve to attract caregivers' attention. Infant behaviors that stimulate attachment to caregivers include crying, smiling, clutching, and touching. Such infant behaviors elicit responses from caregivers that facilitate the attachment process—smiling at, gently handling, stroking, feeding, and talking to the infant, for example.

Attachment between infant and caregiver is believed to occur in four phases (Bowlby, 1982):

1. *Undiscriminating social responsiveness* is observed at about 2 to 3 months of age. This stage is characterized by an infant's orientation to all humans, seen in the baby's visual tracking, visual exploration, listening and becoming quiet when being addressed by someone, and becoming relaxed when held. Opportunities to examine the faces of caregivers appear to facilitate this phase of attachment (Trevathan, 1983).

2. *Discrimination in social responsiveness* is observed at about 4 to 5 months of age. This phase is

characterized by an infant's recognition of familiar persons, by smiling in response, and by restless behavior when the person leaves its field of vision. Also indicative of this stage is anxiety expressed in reaction to encountering unfamiliar people.

3. *Seeking physical proximity and contact with familiar people* occurs at about 7 months of age. At this stage, an infant clings to, crawls toward, and actively seeks to touch and have contact with a familiar person.

4. *Goal-corrected partnership* occurs at about age 3 years and completes the attachment process. The child has now learned to predict the behavior of caregivers and to adjust his or her own behavior to maintain some degree of physical closeness to them.

Attachment is important in establishing an infant's sense of basic trust in people and the environment and in helping the infant feel secure in exploring the environment (Ainsworth, 1977). Children who successfully attach to caregivers learn to express curiosity in their world, which helps promote mental and social growth throughout their life span. Children who have successfully attached in infancy appear to have a greater capacity to deal with novel situations, to cope with failure, to exert greater perseverance in problem solving, to participate in loving relationships with others, and to maintain healthy self-esteem.

Social referencing appears to be related to attachment. This behavior is observed when infants look to their parents' faces as a means of obtaining informational cues (Baldwin & Moses, 1996). Facial cues guide infants' decisions about how to act and how to react to situations. Apparently, cues and emotional information from parents program many reactions that become automatic and habitual responses to similar situations that arise later in life.

Attachment is not a one-sided affair that affects the infant. While this is critical for a baby's survival and well-being, parents also must also experience a positive, secure attachment to an infant in order to fully provide for its care. The elementary basis of this interactional pattern that helps both infants and parents to bond was explored first through studies of what occurs in infant development when there is deprivation of adequate parental stimulation and interaction.

A controversial issue about contemporary family life relates to attachment during infancy. In about 97 % of all married-couple families in the United States, both adults are employed outside the home (U.S. Bureau of the Census, 2007a, 2007 b). Most single parents are employed as well. The daily separations that result raise concerns about the ability of infants to form attachments with caregivers and the quality of those attachments. The issue of whether such repeated separations are harmful cannot be settled as yet. Some studies find significant differences in the attachments between infants of employed mothers versus infants of unemployed mothers, while others do not. A mother's attitude about her employment may play a role in the nature and quality of her infant's attachment. For example, infants of employed mothers who were highly anxious about not being able to care for them around the clock tended to develop avoidant attachments rather than secure attachments (Stifter, Coulehan, & Fish, 1993). This issue relates to the importance of an infant developing a secure attachment to parents and other caregivers.

Initial attempts to study the effects of early nurturing experiences for infants began when investigators examined institutionalized infants and children in the 1940s and 1950s. At that time, infants and children who were abandoned or orphaned were placed into large group homes, where they received minimal care and attention from only a few adults. Researchers found that these children exhibited delayed development in many areas, which was attributed to inconsistent mothering and lack of nurturance (Bowlby, 1952; Goldfarb, 1945; Ribble, 1943; Spitz, 1945). Typically, children raised in institutions were described as suffering from a condition known as **marasmus**. This is characterized by poor muscle tone, developmental retardation, apathy, sleep problems, and emotional depression. Symptoms of physical and mental illness in many of these individuals were attributed to the lack of appropriate mothering experiences.

Behavioral scientists realized that it would be unethical and immoral to deprive a human infant of mothering experiences and chose instead to study the short- and long-term results of the lack of adequate, appropriate mothering in animals. A well-known series of studies by Harry Harlow and his associates (Harlow, 1958; Harlow, Harlow, & Hansen, 1963) examined the effects of depriving infant monkeys of significant mothering experiences. Harlow discovered that separating infant monkeys from their mothers following birth resulted in severe emotional trauma in the mothers. The infant monkeys' lack of direct physical contact with their mothers was identified as contributing to the disturbed behavior patterns when they grew to maturity. Among these behaviors were staring into space, stereotyped rocking movements, inability to mate, poor social interactions with other monkeys, and hyperaggressiveness.

In another study, two groups of infant monkeys were separated from their natural mothers and place with two artificially constructed surrogate mothers. One of the surrogates was built of bare wire mesh. The other was built of wood and covered with soft terry cloth (see Figure 7–4). The infant monkeys received nourishment only from the wire-mesh surrogate yet preferred the soft-textured surrogate. This result stressed what Harlow referred to as **contact comfort,** or an infant's need for soft, comforting, nurturance sensations provided by its caregiver.

The results of Harlow's study showed that neither group of monkeys spent more time clinging to the terry-cloth surrogate. However, infants reared with the

FIGURE 7–4. Wire-mesh and terry-cloth surrogate mothers used in Harlow's research on the nature of love. Photo courtesy of the University of Wisconsin Primate Laboratory and Harry F. Harlow.

terry-cloth surrogate were found to be more curious, more interested in exploring the environment, and better adjusted socially than those who were reared by the wire-mesh surrogate. Nevertheless, both groups developed in unhealthy ways into their adulthood. Neither group acquired normal monkey social skills; they were overly aggressive, preferred isolation to intimacy with other monkeys, and had poor mating abilities.

The important element of nurturing behavior from caregivers apparently is sensory stimulation that acts to communicate love and nurturance to an infant. Touching, handling, fondling, and stroking express affectionate attention and care. From the earliest beginnings of life outside the uterus, it is believed that individuals learn to experience love and to express it to others through these sensory means. In infancy, this is thought to occur in relation to the development of an attachment between parents and infants. Early experiences in relation to the type of care given to an infant are thought to play an influential role in determining later behavior and development.

All this attention to the process of attachment helps to explain why the relationship established between an infant and its caregivers is very important. This has been studied extensively by a number of behavioral scientists, who have advanced what is known about the importance of attachment. For example, one of the classical methods for studying attachment in contemporary studies is the use of the "Strange Situation" test (Ainsworth, 1983; Ainsworth & Wittig, 1969). In this setting, a mother and infant enter a laboratory playroom that is equipped with interesting, appealing toys as well as an adult stranger. Shortly after entering, the mother then leaves the baby with the toys and the stranger while observers record the baby's interactions with both. Later, the mother returns, and observers again record the infant's reactions. This is repeated eight times with variations.

The reunion with the mother allows the researchers to determine different types of attachment of the infant: (1) *Securely attached* infants are not overly animated with the mother's return and used her as a base for exploring the room and as a source of comfort upon being reunited; (2) *insecure/avoidant* infants either ignore or avoid the mother upon her return, do not appear to be distressed when the mother releases them, and react to the stranger in a similar manner as to the mother; and (3) *insecure/resistant* infants are reluctant to explore the playroom, cling to the mother, and attempt to hide from the stranger. These infants initially seek contact with the mother upon her return but then show signs of rejecting her. These children have been found to display more maladaptive behaviors and appear to be angrier children (Ainsworth, 1993).

Some researchers have wondered if the Strange Situation test is valid (Crittenden, Claussen, & Kozlowska, 2007). One of the main objections to this method of assessing attachment is that it may not be effective in other cultural settings. For example, Japanese infants tested with this method are typically found to display high degrees of insecure/resistant attachment, perhaps because they spend more time with mothers than infants in the United States (Miyake, Chen, & Campos, 1985). This has led other ways to assess this phenomenon, such as in-home observation by objective researchers. This does not mean that the Strange Situation method cannot be used in this research but that researchers need to be mindful of the cultural context of families and the broad range of behaviors that indicate certain types of attachment in children.

The point here is that successful, secure attachment between infant and parents affects all participants and influences later behavior of the baby. There is some connection, for example, between attachment and a child's cognitive development. In addition, attachment continues to play an important role in a child's social relationships, not only in childhood and adolescence but especially in adulthood, when it becomes manifested in a revised manner in intimate relationships.

Focus Point. Attachment is a process in which both parents and infants participate. Secure attachment of an infant ensures its survival and impacts its development in other areas. For parents, attachment to their infant facilitates their nurturant caregiving behaviors, which, in turn, support the attachment process of their infant.

Toilet Training. While much parental attention and behavior is directed in ways that communicate nurturance to infants and toddlers, a shift occurs when most children reach 18 months of age toward providing elementary measures of structure. This shift in parental behavior usually comes in response to a change in a toddler's behavior that indicates a drive towards establishing a sense of autonomy (from Erikson's psychosocial theory). This drive is to establish one's independence from parents as a separate entity and to dismantle the strong emotional ties promoted during attachment experiences with parents. Essentially, from a family systems theory point of view, toddlers discover their ability to set personal boundaries between themselves and others as they discover that they are distinct individuals and not an extension of their parents. A toddler's attempts at self-differentiation are healthy for everyone but also may produce conflicts and power struggles. Strives toward autonomy occur when a toddler learns to be

---

Parenting FAQs 7–2

Do you have any suggestions for how to handle a toddler's temper tantrums? These seem to happen everywhere, at home and in public.

A: Reacting to temper tantrums is an exercise in parental control. However, it is helpful to understand that these are not a personal attack on you but what happens when toddlers' or preschoolers' emotions become uncontrollable. Even adults can have temper tantrums, better known as *outbursts*. Children can learn to control these with a fair degree of success if taught by patient parents.

With toddlers, you can begin the learning process by remembering to stay calm yourself. Try to analyze why the tantrum is happening: Is it because the child is tired and needs to nap or be fed, for example? If this is the case, just holding the child firmly and rocking gently will often help to calm things down. Going to a quiet place, if in public, may also contribute to calming the child. Some children kick and/or bite when upset emotionally in this manner, so restrain the child carefully to avoid injury to yourself. If you can reframe the temper tantrum experience your child is having as being similar to an electrical power outage, it can help you to stay calm. We don't plan an outage; it just happens, and often we just need to be patient and stay calm until the power returns.

self-assertive in a variety of ways. Using the word "NO!" to show noncooperation with parental demands and requests, trying to dress oneself without supervision, testing limits parents have placed on what can be played with, and toilet training are good examples of how personal autonomy is tested by toddlers. We will focus next on toilet training as one of the most important skills that all toddlers are expected to master in our society that help to establish personal autonomy and self-differentiation.

Training for society's standards for handling bodily eliminations usually begins when infants are between 24 and 30 months of age and typically is completed by 36 months. The process of learning to control the release of urine from the bladder and feces from the bowels is usually accomplished easily by most individuals. In some situations, however, difficulties occur. Many adults are unfamiliar with ways and methods for toilet training that are successful and unstressful for both the infant and themselves. Opinions and directions can be found in most child-care books, from pediatricians and family physicians, or from relatives and friends who have accomplished this with other children. The use of positive rewards and reinforcement in appropriate ways is often the most successful route for teaching toilet training.

Some parents believe that shaming an infant for accidents or mistakes in toilet training will motivate him or her to achieve this developmental task successfully and speedily. Instead, toilet training is likely to become a power struggle between parent and child. The unhealthy attitude of shame and doubt that results can cause the child to question his or her ability to be autonomous.

Fortunately, most children who experience problems with toilet training eventually are able to accomplish the task (Figure 7–5). For example, being exposed to children in day-care programs who are toilet trained can help them to adopt the appropriate behavior cue due to a desire to conform to other children.

Parenting Reflection 7–3

What would be the long-term effects of the development of basic trust and of the development of mistrust during infancy?

FIGURE 7–5.   A sense of autonomy is established when toddlers accomplish self-differentiation in new ways, such as setting personal boundaries via temper tantrums or mastering toilet training, for example.

Providing Appropriate Toys and Play Equipment.   Infants need appropriate play equipment and materials to stimulate cognitive development and social interaction skills (Focus On 7–2). Simple toys are often all that is necessary in this regard. This is especially reassuring for parents who lack financial resources to provide what they see in stores and being used by other families. Infants can develop adequate cognitive skills by parents providing toys and play equipment that encourage visual and tactile exploration. Materials that encourage these behaviors also promote the development of curiosity in the world, which will have long-range effects.

One of the most important factors parents should consider in choosing infant toys is safety. While most large manufacturers are mindful of this in developing

---

Focus On 7–2   **Age-Appropriate Play Equipment for Infants**

Birth to One Year	*One to Two Years*	*Two to Three Years*
Rattles	Bath toys	Tricycle
Crib mobiles	Simple puzzles	Outdoor swings
Teething rings	Musical instruments	Picture books
Texture balls/boxes	Toy phone	Scene toys
Crib gyms	Simple picture books	Crayons
Stuffed toys	Interlocking blocks	Puzzles
Push-pull toys	Ride toys	Wooden blocks
Shape sorters	Wheel toys	
Squeak toys	Musical toys	
Nesting/stacking toys	Wagon	
Cloth/hard cardboard books		

---

and making infant toys, parents need to keep these points in mind when selecting toys for infants and older children: (1) no sharp edges, (2) no small parts that can be swallowed or inhaled, (3) no cords or strings, and (4) no loud noises (Consumer Product Safety Commission, 2004).

Parents can choose appropriate toys and play equipment by considering the chronological age of their baby. Focus On 7–2 shows a listing of examples of age-appropriate play equipment.

Promoting Cognitive Development.   Infancy encompasses the first stage of cognitive development according to Jean Piaget (1967). He termed this stage the ***sensorimotor period***. The label refers to the major developmental task infants must accomplish in which they coordinate motor acts with sensory data or perceptions of their environment. For example, they learn that the sources of sounds are combined with walking toward them, touching them, and/or exploring them with their eyes. They become more adept at reaching for objects that they see and guiding their hands to grasp these and bring them to their mouths.

Another developmental task to be accomplished is an understanding of permanence in their physical and social environments. This is known as ***object permanence***. For example, for about the first six months after birth, an infant becomes upset when its parent leaves its field of vision as it is thought that they believe the parent has permanently disappeared; that is, what cannot

be seen doesn't exist. As development takes place and interactions continue to take place, an infant will look for an object that's been covered up with a cloth by searching for it. The time-honored game of peek-a-boo is a classic exercise in helping infants to learn object permanence. In other words, the understanding develops with experience in knowing that an object or person continues to exist even though it cannot be seen.

Infants also are unable to form mental images of things and people in their worlds. Their understanding is limited to what they know of things and people from their perceptions and from the actions the things perform. For example, if it were possible to ask an infant to describe a ball, it would likely be as something that you play with, that rolls away, that bounces, and that is colored, for example.

Parents and other caregivers play an important role in facilitating cognitive development during this period by their interactions with infants and the experiences they provide. This is the basis of what Vygotsky termed the *zone of proximal development* (see Chapter 3). Parents can provide many activities and interactions with infants that they could not achieve on their own. Parents guide an infant to learn about cues for appropriate behavior, to understand that it is appropriate to experience their world via their senses, and to be curious about exploring their environment. Essentially, when playing with their baby, parents begin to socialize her or him into their family values system, their cultural system, and the importance of social interactions.

The role of language emerges also during this period as the basis for learning and development in later stages of cognitive development. While an entire chapter could be devoted to this topic, suffice it to say that it is once again the parents who perform a significant role here in helping infants to begin to learn to speak and to communicate with words. While behavioral scientists postulate that there is a basic brain pattern and anatomy to support language development at birth (Chomsky, 1968, 1975), this is shaped and influenced by parents when they talk and interact with their baby, regardless of the particular language spoken in the home.

Research also points to the ability of parents to stimulate their baby's brain development through what are termed *enrichment activities*. These include interactions that emphasize providing a variety of play equipment, of sensory experiences, use of language, and social interactions, for example (Fowler, Ogston, Roberts, & Swensen, 2006). The role of rewarding or praising the baby when he or she is responsive to such activities is also important. In addition, when infants are securely attached to parents, their cognitive and brain development are enhanced as well.

Communication.   An infant's first attempts at communication with its world comes in the form of crying. Parents soon learn that they must try to decipher the meaning behind a particular kind of crying in order to meet an infant's needs. This is best accomplished by spending time with the baby and learning to associate a particular cry with a particular need, such as for changing a diaper, providing food, checking for illness, and so on. Many infants also will use crying to indicate their desire to be held, nurtured, and comforted. Others respond to being walked or rocked as well. Parents will need to rely on an infant's cries, then, as a means of communicating until the basics of language have been acquired and begin to be manifested sometime around the second birthday.

Safety Concerns.   When infants become capable of walking, they experience a change in their perspective of their world. A toddler moves about with increasing speed and can more freely explore the physical world. Infants at this age have a natural curiosity about their surroundings. As Piaget (1967) notes, children are the world's most natural scientists in exercising their curiosity by discovering and experimenting with things that surround them. Toddlers need the experiences of ex-

ploring their environment to recognize that they are distinct individuals, separate from other people and things but also a part of their surroundings. Infants act on their environment and in the process discover how their environment acts. Adults have forgotten the joys of these small but important discoveries. Infants learn that balls make intriguing movements when they are kicked, bounced, or thrown; that pots and lids make fantastic sounds when hit on the floor; that water is very attractive and makes fascinating sounds and movements, as when the toilet is flushed . . . and flushed . . . and flushed again!

This propensity to become involved with the environment is responsible for some of the conflict between parents and children at this stage of life. Most parents can tolerate just so much noise and mess from children. Children's safety also becomes a preoccupation of parents; parents learn that an infant's or toddler's movements can lead to dangerous involvements, and they react to these behaviors by childproofing the home to ensure that children can explore and experience objects within a safe environment (Table 7-2). Cleaning solutions are placed out of children's reach, ashtrays and breakables are moved from tables, gates are placed across stairways and doors, electrical outlets are capped, and so on. Homes where a toddler resides are easily recognized by the protective measures taken by parents to ensure the child's safety. Parents may provide a selection of toys that stimulate toddlers' curiosity and exploratory behavior, but household objects such as pots often prove just as fascinating to a child this age. Thus, the lifestyle of family responds and is modified by a child's behavior and stage of development. This responsiveness demonstrates the ability of a family system to adapt to the changing developmental abilities of its members. In these ways, parents also provide structure for children's developmental progress in infancy.

Focus Point.   Development in infancy is characterized by developmental tasks that are unique to this time of the life span. The infant achieves a variety of physical, social, and psychological abilities, such as walking, acquiring healthy attitudes of basic trust and personal autonomy, learning basic sensorimotor and communication skills, and becoming attached emotionally to parents. Parents are mindful of meeting other needs of infants, such as providing proper nutrition and health care, sleeping patterns, and addressing safety issues.

TABLE 7–2. Methods of Childproofing A Home

Area	Hazard	Methods
Furniture	Drawers dump on child	Place safety catches
	Soiled upholstery	Use slipcovers or fabric protection
	Broken valuables	Pack away for now
Toys	Sharp edges/corners	Choose other toys
	Harmful toxins	Choose others toys
	Swallowing small parts	Choose those larger than a plum
Stairs, Windows	Falling	Place gates; lock windows; supervise child
Kitchen	Burning	Turn pot handles away; supervise child
	Poisoning	Move cleaning solutions

Source: Adapted from Duvall, E. M., & Miller, B. (1985). *Marriage and family development* (6th ed.). New York: Harper & Row.

EVOLVING PERSONAL CONCEPTS OF PARENTHOOD

As discussed in Chapter 5, becoming a parent for the first time is a critical adjustment for the adults in a family. The first child has a major role in shaping the emergence of parenting skills for the new mother and father. While an infant is experiencing the psychosocial stages of establishing the senses of basic trust and autonomy, parents are usually experiencing a new challenge in their own personal development in acquiring a sense of generativity. For many adults, the parenthood role adds a new, different, and perhaps more meaningful experience in acquiring their attitude of generativity. When children are being produced, the adults now turn their psychosocial focus more directly on the dimension of parenthood. They develop initial ideas about what it means to be a parent, what they understand to be the needs of children, what goals they have in child rearing, and what kind of parenting style they find appropriate and comfortable.

People may not think much about parenting or how to behave in this role until the need arises. However, when children are being produced, adults discover ample opportunities to examine their existing beliefs, attitudes, and behavior as parents. This seems to be the time when adults consider and develop the self-regulating patterns for parenting behavior and parent-child interactions. These self-regulating patterns form the basis for guiding how each adult should act as a parent, what rules the adults wish to have in regulating and evaluating children's behavior as well as their own, and what goals or outcomes they wish to accomplish with their children. (Review the discussion in Chapter 5 pertaining to the transition to parenthood and that in Chapter 3 relating to patterns that guide the operation of a family system.)

It is crucial to discuss and agree on these issues. Even more pressing are the day-to-day concerns about how to act as a parent in providing care and nurturance for an infant whose daily needs are rapidly changing. Initially, the tasks that parents perform involve providing safety and care for the infant. Later, as the infant grows and changes, parents need to provide psychological and social stimulation. Later still, especially following the second birthday, parents must use different parenting skills to support the child's socialization tasks related to gaining personal autonomy. For example, parents must deal with the expressions of anger and negativism a child exhibits at this stage of development. New parents need to examine just how they wish to respond to these outbursts of emotion from their child. Parents must find ways to allow independence to be expressed without damaging the child's belief about his or her inner nature or self. During this stage of a family's development, parents learn an important lesson about working with children: One's behavior as a parent must change in tandem with the changing behavior and needs of children. Children have an important influence on one's conduct as a parent.

●●●●●●●●●●●●●●●●●●●●●●●●●●●●●●●●●●●●

Parenting Reflection 7–4

Should new parents be given a parenting kit to take home following delivery? What are some things that such a kit might contain that would be helpful, especially to first-time parents of an infant?

●●●●●●●●●●●●●●●●●●●●●●●●●●●●●●●●●●●●

Androgynous Parenting Roles

Many men and women who become parents today are likely to hold attitudes different from those of their parents about how parental responsibilities are to be conducted. Many adults today may espouse egalitarian concepts about parenthood roles. Researchers label these as *androgynous* in that parenting roles may be shared rather than being distinct or based on gender. Although both partners tend to say they want to share parenting responsibilities equally, women continue to perform more of these tasks than men (Bianchi et al., 2000). Today, many men fully expect that they will be actively involved in providing care and support for their infants (Fox, Bruce, & Combs-Orme, 2000). Although the involvement may be configured to the role of "father as a helper to mother" in providing child care, the expectation is for full fatherly involvement nevertheless. Adults can experience some difficulties in sharing child-care responsibilities. The most difficult area reported is employers' rigidity about the time frame for performing work responsibilities.

Goodness of Fit

Another factor that can influence the nature and quality of care that parents provide to a baby is the notion of **goodness of fit**. This refers to the congruence or match between the temperament of a baby and that of its parents and family system (Thomas & Chess, 1987). Babies manifest their own particular, individual temperaments or sensitivity, even before birth. Some infants appear to be highly sensitive, which is observed by reactions to environmental stimuli by withdrawal, avoidance, and severe emotionality. Others appear to need more than ordinary levels of stimulation, such as banging the floor with objects far longer than what would appear to be appropriate. These types of sensitivities may not match well with the temperament of the parents or family (Ayers, 1972). For example, some infants seek to be held and cuddled and appear to thrive on such treatment. Others find this to be uncomfortable rather than satisfying. When a parent is so inclined to want to hold his or her baby and cuddle it while the baby finds this to be undesirable, then the quality of parent-child relations is likely to be adversely affected. Thus, the stage is set in infancy for the dance that occurs between parent and child. Parents of several children soon learn, for example, that they must take each as an individual and as one who has its own unique, particular style and personality. To attempt to apply the same child-rearing methods and approaches to each child without taking such individual differences into consideration is not wise.

●●●●●●●●●●●●●●●●●●●●●●●●●●●●●●●●●●●●

Focus Point. Few significant differences are found in the overall performance of men and women in providing care for infants. Some differences are noted in interaction styles that relate more to the enactment of psychological scripts of appropriate parenting. Many middle-class men and women attempt to develop androgynous parenting roles rather than those based on traditional sex-role stereotypes of fathers and mothers. Such parents share in performing parenting roles. The goodness of fit between the temperaments of an infant and that of its parents is critical in influencing how parenting may proceed to unfold.

●●●●●●●●●●●●●●●●●●●●●●●●●●●●●●●●●●●●

SUPPORTS FOR PARENTS OF INFANTS AND TODDLERS

The issue of child care has received a great deal of attention in recent years. Consider the following statistics relating to the use of nonparental child care by families of infants and young children in the United

States (Federal Interagency Forum on Child and Family Statistics, 2007; U.S. Bureau of the Census, 2007a, 2007b):

■ The changing structure of American families has resulted in dramatic increases in the number of single-parent families in which the mother is the primary economic provider and in the numbers of dual-earner families in which both adults are gainfully employed.

■ About 62% of all married women over 18 years of age were employed outside the home in 2006.

■ In 2005, about 89% of all children in the United States living with two parents had at least one parent who worked year-round. That same year, this percentage decreased in homes headed by a single-parent father or mother by about 10 points.

■ In 2005, about 61% of all children in the United States 5 years of age and under had been in some type of child-care arrangement since they were born.

■ Even if a mother is unemployed, many families use day care and nonparental child care as enrichment experiences for children and to provide time for mothers' personal enrichment. In 2005, about half of these children of unemployed mothers were being cared for by a relative.

Given this information, questions may arise about who is raising America's children and the quality of care being given. Use of nonparental child care has not had a good reputation in the past in the United States, especially when infants are involved. Traditionally, the preferred mode of child care in our culture has been for parents, typically the mother, to provide care. Many families today obviously are finding this type of child-care arrangement impossible and perhaps, in some respects, even undesirable. An increasing number of families use nonparental child care conducted by a relative, often the father (Federal Interagency Forum on Child and Family Statistics, 2007; Manlove & Vernon-Feagans, 2002). Apparently, major cost savings result when this arrangement is used. Fathers may not necessarily provide a great deal of the infant care nor help to make child-care arrangements easier or more satisfactory, but the incentive provided by using them results in halving child-care costs. This may be a primary motivation for many young families.

Concerns about the effects of day care or large-group care on children, and especially on infants, have been expressed for many years (Azar, 1997; Lamb &

Ahnert, 2006). Debate has continued about providing care for infants by someone other than the mother in someplace other than the home. Maternal deprivation was found to have serious deleterious effects on infant growth and development and was interpreted as strong evidence that infants should be cared for by their own mothers.

Opinion continued in this vein until the 1960s, when increasing numbers of women began to return to the workforce. Use of nonparental child care increased accordingly. Researchers reversed the attitude that such care produced harmful effects on infants and children when it became apparent that attachment to parents was not adversely affected. However, a national study found that about 46% of infant care programs were considered to be of high quality. One particular study (Lamb & Ahnert, 2006; National Institute of Child Health and Human Development, 2006) and others suggest the following interpretations:

■ Nonparental care of infants can offer an enriching experience that enhances and stimulates their developmental progress.

■ Quality care for infants had the greatest impact on infants from disadvantaged families.

■ Some less-desirable behavioral traits, such as boisterousness, heightened physical and verbal aggressiveness, and lack of cooperation with adults, could be observed at later ages in children who had been in infant group-care settings.

Controversy has surfaced among developmental researchers who have studied the effects of group care on infant and child development and reported disturbing results (Belsky, 1990; Belsky & Rovine, 1988). Belsky, for example, reversed his earlier beliefs and concluded in a 1988 study that infants spending more than 20 hours a week in nonparental care are at risk of developing an insecure attachment. Other researchers question this contention (National Institute of Child Health and Human Development, 1999). At issue are differences of opinion and interpretations of research findings by the investigators. Most of the studies have found beneficial effects of nonparental infant care.

The main source of nonparental care of infants today is by a nonrelative in a private home, or by what is known as *family day care* (Federal Interagency Forum on Child and Family Statistics, 2007). The employment status of mothers contributes significantly to choosing a day-care provider who is a relative. Fifty-three percent of employed mothers tend to have a relative rather than a nonrelative provide care for their babies. In fact, the majority of mothers in one study preferred the father to provide this care (Riley & Glass, 2002).

The stability or consistent use of a nonparental care provider of infants is a major concern for both parents and researchers. Changes in the nonparental care provider occur less frequently for infants than for older children. In all, only about one-fourth of the families change nonparental care providers within a year. Changes occur more commonly when the provider is not a relative.

It may not be possible to conclude at the present time what long-term effects may occur as a result of nonparental group care for infants. What may be interpreted from research findings is that infant care apparently is not harmful (National Institute of Child Health and Human Development, 2003a, 2003b). However, the problem of how to provide care adequately for individuals at this vulnerable time in their lives has not been completely resolved.

Focus Point. Due to the large number of women who are employed outside the home, an increasing number of families use nonparental care of infants. Concerns have been expressed about whether such experiences harm the adequate attachment of infants to parents. This is a controversial issue for which there are no clearly definite answers today. Some researchers report that nonparental care causes no harm to infants while others suggest it does. The stability of care and quality of experiences may be crucial factors in determining the effects of nonparental care on infant and child development.

Parenting Reflection 7–5

What are some pros and cons of using nonparental child care for an infant when both parents must work outside the home?

SYSTEMIC FAMILY DEVELOPMENT SNAPSHOT

(Before reading this section, it may be helpful to review the systemic family development model and the metaphor used to illustrate its concepts from Chapter 3.)

We will use the metaphor of a round layer cake and a slice taken from the cake to discuss a point in developmental time in a hypothetical family system in the chapters dealing with parenting infants and toddlers through parenting adolescents and young adults. The slice will reveal the stressors being experienced by each generation so that we may gain a better understanding of what is affecting the entire family system at this point. We will also identify and discuss the means for coping with the stressors and observe hypothetically how various family roles, patterns, and boundaries might be reestablished to regain a degree of homeostasis previously experienced by the family. To illustrate the discussion, we will use a hypothetical family system, three generations of the Curtis family.

Examples of Stressors Affecting Each Curtis Family Generation

First Generation (Grandparents)

■ Adjusting to the aging process experienced in middle age
■ Adjusting to the midlife transition experiences
■ Assisting adult children in completing their individuation process
■ Adjusting to the death of parents, relatives, and colleagues
■ Beginning preparations for retirement
■ Establishing grandparent and in-law roles

Second Generation (Young Adult Parents)

■ Establishing work roles and objectives
■ Balancing work and family roles
■ Maintaining a household that meets the needs of infants and toddlers; providing finances for this household
■ Deciding on family size
■ Adjusting to pregnancy, childbirth, and infants
■ Adjusting to changes in their committed relationship related to additional family roles (e.g., parenthood, in-laws)
■ Learning to parent infants and toddlers

Third Generation (Infants and Toddlers)

■ Establishing an attachment with parents
■ Establishing the attitudes of trust and autonomy
■ Mastering cognitive tasks of infancy
■ Mastering toilet training

Typically, families that are in the process of producing children remain focused on this family task for 3 to 5 years. This phase in family life is preceded by the adjustment period following a formal marriage or upon an agreement to become committed as a couple. The median age at first marriage in the United States was about 28 years for men and about 25 years for women in 2000. We would estimate the ages of both sets of the hypothetical couple's parents at the time of their marriage as (1) groom's father to be 52; (2) groom's mother to be 50; (3) bride's father to be 49; and (4) bride's mother to be 47.

The young couple in the hypothetical family, Butch and Lisa Curtis, have produced two children; their first, Mary, was born 2 years after they married, and Joey was born 2 years later. The stressors and means for coping that affect each generation will be discussed separately.

At the time we are taking a slice of developmental time, Mary is 2½ and her brother, Joey, is 6 months old. This places the ages of the various adults as follows: (1) groom's father, George Curtis, is 56; (2) the groom's mother, Joan Curtis, is 54; (3) the bride's father, Harry Scott, is 53; (4) the bride's mother, Susan Scott, is 51; (5) Butch Curtis is 32; and (6) Lisa Curtis is 29. These ages are important in that they provide clues as to where all family members are in developmental time.

First Generation (Grandparents)

We will address the older generation first in examining our slice of developmental time. All the older adults compose the first generation in this particular family system. All have entered middle age in their adult development and are experiencing a typical progression through this developmental stage. The oldest of the four generation members, George Curtis, is beginning to look forward to retirement. He has worked as a post office employee for almost 30 years. His father recently died from Alzheimer's disease, and George is having a difficult time acknowledging his father's death. His mother passed away several years ago, and George doesn't understand why he seems to be paying little attention to this recent significant family event. Joan Curtis is also stymied by his reaction but is attempting to persuade George to enter into therapy as a way of discovering his feelings about his father's death. For now, George is resisting this suggestion. Joan has had her own challenges recently with a new supervisor who is much younger than she and, in her opinion, much less experienced. Her work is enjoyable, but she is starting to question whether to seek other employment or stay put because of seniority status.

The Scotts are dealing with a particularly difficult situation in that Susan was diagnosed with breast cancer 6 months ago and has been undergoing chemotherapy treatments. It has been especially challenging for Harry because he feels there is little he can do to protect his wife from the dreadful side effects of the treatments and even less from the distinct possibility she may die soon. Luckily, their medical insurance provides for most of the cost, and they can attend support group meetings as well as couple's therapy to deal with stresses from this situation. However, Harry has turned to alcohol as a way of handling his uncertainties, which Susan finds to be another source of stress. She has found solace in her spiritual life, and for now this is what sustains her.

All this has also affected their daughter and son-in-law. Lisa Curtis is fearful both for her mother and for herself as she can envision developing this same condition at some point in her future. To make matters even more confusing for this family, no one talks about the situation, the feelings associated with their fears, or what the future could hold.

Second Generation (Adult Parents)

Butch Curtis has recently changed jobs after experiencing a long period of unemployment that was difficult on everyone in his immediate family. Financially, things look better than they have in a long time. Lisa carried a heavy burden in being the sole provider for her family while Butch was unemployed, a position she was thankful for but also found to be uncomfortable in some respects. Now that Butch is working again, they are faced with finding child care for both their children. Lisa is not especially satisfied with group care and wants to find someone to care for the children in their home. Calling on her parents or in-laws is not feasible because of their own situations. Butch has also brought up another issue that they had talked about off and on for several months now. This is whether to have another child. Lisa is unclear on her feelings about this and has discussed the issue with several friends to learn about the pros and cons of having three versus two children.

Both Butch and Lisa have managed to adjust to being parents for the first time and find that taking care of a new baby is more manageable than what they experienced after bringing Mary home. However, both have expressed discontent about not having much of a social life or getting private time. They feel fortunate to have Butch's parents nearby, and George and Joan have been generous in offering to take the children overnight occasionally.

Third Generation (Children)

The children of this family are highly dependent on the adults for their care. Luckily, they have had good health and are growing as expected. The only major difficulty at this time is with Mary's toilet training. She appeared to have accomplished this about the time her brother was born. The change in things at home with the new baby resulted in her loss of control, and she is having accidents more than usual. Lisa anticipates that this will not improve with Butch going back to work and other changes in the home routine. At times, Lisa feels that she is neglecting the children because she can't be a full-time mom. However, she is working through these feelings when she sees how well the children's needs are being met and with the equipment, food, medical care, and clothes they can provide for the children.

Joey is having some problems with separating from his mom and dad when taken to the sitter's home, and Lisa experiences the most difficulties when this happens. Perhaps more than her husband, Lisa feels torn between the difficulties her parents are having, her own situation, and the developmental changes her children are undergoing. This is a stressful time for the first and second generations of this family system.

• •

Parenting Reflection 7–6

Can you identify the ways that this Snapshot reveals how the concept of interrelatedness (from family systems theory) can be observed in this family system at this particular point in developmental time? What were some ways that the family system used to adapt or cope with the effects of the various stressors being experienced?

• •

POINTS TO CONSIDER

■ Basic developmental tasks of infancy focus on achievement of significant physical milestones, mastery of basic motor competencies, and emerging social and mental competencies.

■ Parenting infants and toddlers focuses on meeting a variety of needs of children at these ages: (1) promoting brain development; (2) providing food and helping establish self-feeding; (3) attending to health and medical needs; (4) observing an infant's sleep-wake cycle and encouraging good sleeping habits; (5) providing structure and nurturance; (6) facilitating the attachment between parents and an infant; (7) facilitating the child's development of a sense of autonomy versus shame and doubt via toilet training; (8) providing appropriate toys and equipment; and (9) promoting cognitive development.

■ Becoming a parent, especially for the first time, is a significant event that requires a critical adjustment for the adults of a family system. New parents evolve concepts of parenting from many sources, including social scripts developed from their families of origin, exposure to society's expectations of appropriate parenting behavior, and personal interpretations of what constitutes appropriate parenting behavior. New parents evolve ideas that serve as self-regulating patterns for how they fulfill this role within their family system. It is helpful if new parents develop a vision of how their parenting experiences should take place.

■ First-time parents may take advantage of educational programs to help learn how to parent infants effectively. Participation in these programs may increase satisfaction with parenting and boost confidence.

■ New parents often make a commitment to develop androgynous roles as caregivers of their children where gender does not factor in to assignment of role responsibilities.

■ Many families with infants use the services of nonparental child care, especially when both parents work outside the home. In many situations, nonparental care by a relative is the major source of supplemental child care. Controversy exists as to the effects of nonparental child care on infants.

■ A systemic family development snapshot reveals the stressors that may affect different generations of a family system and the ways members cope with these stressors in healthy and unhealthy ways.

CHAPTER 8

Parenting Preschoolers

Focus Questions

1. What are the principal developmental landmarks of early childhood that parents should know?
2. What is the nature of parent-preschooler relations?
3. What are some positive methods of guidance that work well with young children?
4. What are some common behavior problems observed among young children?
5. What kinds of community supports do families with preschoolers need?
6. What stressors and coping mechanisms are revealed by a systemic family development snapshot of families with preschool-age children?

Early childhood is the period in a person's life between the ages of 3 and 6. Children of these ages are also known as *preschoolers*. The interactions within a family system change to reflect an increasing involvement of young children as participating members of the family. A major challenge to parents at this time is to adjust to a developing child whose behavior and personality traits are emerging rapidly. Preschoolers are adventuresome creatures who are curious about their world and quickly learn many things (Figure 8-1). Parents and others typically find much pleasure and enjoyment from their preschool-age child but also begin to experience conflicts as the child tests limits and boundaries adults have set for them. The rate of developmental change is slower during these years relative to what was observed in infancy and prenatal development.

DEVELOPMENTAL LANDMARKS OF EARLY CHILDHOOD

There is much for a preschooler to learn and accomplish during the years before entering formal schooling. The basic skills of locomotion, communication, and interaction are acquired by most individuals in infancy. In early childhood, expansion in the size of a child's vocabulary and in other elements of language development allow him or her to perform unlimited tasks. It is a time to begin learning in earnest the basic social skills necessary for effective interactions with others. Language becomes the tool

FIGURE 8–1. Early childhood is the life stage between age 3 and 6. This period is viewed as a special time during childhood.

of socialization and personal expression. Young children learn through modeling and observation of others and come to comprehend their parents' expectations and instructions by these means. As young children acquire a number of physical and social skills, they become more other-oriented rather than largely self-oriented. This important change in perspective enables a developing child to capitalize on a wide range of experiences as she or he learns to cope with and master the environment.

As with all other life stages, several unique developmental tasks and landmarks are associated with the early childhood stage. These are listed in Focus On 8–1.

••

Focus Point. Early childhood is characterized by unique developmental tasks and specific landmarks. The period is notable as the time when young children actively acquire knowledge and basic skills that are both physical and social in nature.

••

PARENTING YOUNG CHILDREN
Meeting the Needs of Preschoolers

Parenting behavior will undergo modification as children grow from infancy into the years of early childhood. These changes occur in response to the changing developmental needs and abilities of preschoolers. From the perspective of family systems theory, parenting changes or adapts in response to meeting new and different needs presented by preschoolers. The children present different challenges to parents in attempting to master the developmental tasks presented at this stage.

The behavior of preschoolers is enhanced by parents who are responsive to changes in their children's needs (Table 8–1). At the same time, parents find that their need to be needed by their children changes accordingly. Children, in effect, assist in shaping and modifying the parenting behavior of adults. Parents learn that their growing preschooler also recognizes the changes in his or her maturity and will resist being treated as a younger child might be. Older preschoolers are particularly sensitive to adults who attempt to interact with them in a patronizing manner that fails to recognize their perceived status as big kids. From ages 3 to 6, the child's increasing attempts to express initiative act as a psychological flag to parents that they can no longer take their child's behavior for granted. Throughout the years of early childhood, a child tries to prove to parents that "I can! Let me show you that I can!"

As children become more capable of verbal communications with others, parents react by shifting from physical methods of child rearing to those that are more verbal and psychological in nature. Parents who believe in permissive and authoritative methods of child rearing may begin to use an increasing amount of reasoning and verbal directions in interacting with preschoolers. These reactions to children's changing nature assist and guide the autonomous behavior that prepares children for their next stage of development.

Meeting Nutritional Needs. Preschool children typically have a small appetite, which results in consumption of small amounts of food. Young children now eat meals with their families and are taught to use utensils rather than hands. Table manners also may be taught at this time. Preschoolers are eating the same types of food as other family members and usually don't require special dietary foods. Because they require fewer calories,

---

Focus On 8–1   **Major Developmental Tasks and Landmarks in Early Childhood**

Physical

- Slower rate of growth in weight and height
- Small appetite; may be a picky eater
- Uses a preferred hand
- All primary teeth erupt
- Major gross motor skills mastered (e.g., running, climbing); fine motor skills emerging (e.g., artwork)
- Prevalent upper respiratory diseases
- High energy level

Psychosocial

- Expanding awareness of self, others, and things
- Gaining independence and some self-control
- Mastering a sense of initiative versus guilt
- High curiosity level
- Beginning socialization experiences (e.g., appropriate social and sex-role behaviors)
- Learns by doing and from mistakes
- Play that is more social and creative in nature

Cognitive

- Thought that is both preoperational and intuitive, related dynamically to perception, and largely pre-logical in nature
- Building a database of information about the world
- Preoccupation with classification and grouping things
- Expanding vocabulary
- Memory improving
- Flaws in thinking, including egocentrism, animism, jumping to conclusions, and centering

---

parents begin to learn what they will eat at meals, often in smaller portions than other family members. Most parents understand that children require good nutrition to grow properly and that they need adequate amounts of protein, calcium and other minerals, and vitamins from a variety of food sources and supplements. Most parents also are aware that preschoolers can develop preferences for foods that are not healthy, such as those containing large amounts of refined sugar or those considered to be empty-calorie foods, such as potato chips. Eating problems can develop in early childhood that can lead to obesity in later years. Parents may unwittingly contribute to these by requiring children to eat all food that they are served (Rolls, Engell, & Birch, 2000). These problems are discussed in greater detail in the Dealing with Behavior Problems section of this chapter.

Focus Point. Preschoolers can be expected to have small appetites. They need to be encouraged to try different foods and food preparations. Parents may unwittingly encourage the later development of eating problems by enforcing strict eating requirements.

Health and Safety Issues. Young children do not yet have a fully mature immune system, nor have they developed antibodies to combat many illnesses. The wide availability of immunizations against a large number of formerly debilitating and fatal diseases has helped to extend life expectancies of people in many countries around the world. It is important, then, for preschoolers to have adequate health care that includes immunization.

TABLE 8–1. Behaviors of Parents of Preschool-Age Children

Behaviors Providing Structure and Nurturance	Behaviors Not Providing Structure and Nurturance
• Affirming child's accomplishment of developmental tasks	• Teasing child
• Continuing to provide for safety, protection, and love needs	• Behaving inconsistently
• Supporting exploration of the environments of people and things	• Not allowing child to learn to think and make independent choices
• Encouraging acceptance of gender identity; teaching acceptance of both sexes	• Not providing information or direct answers to questions
• Encouraging expression of feelings and associating feelings with actions	• Responding with sarcasm and ridicule
• Providing information that is as accurate as possible; correcting misinformation	• Using messages with mixed meanings
• Providing appropriate positive and negative consequences to behavior	• Discounting child
• Giving clear, concise directions	
• Encouraging the separation of fantasy from reality	

Source: Adapted from Clarke, J. I., & Dawson, C. (1989). *Growing up again: Parenting ourselves, parenting our children.* Minneapolis: Hazelden.

Most deaths today among young children are caused by injury in or near the home rather than illness (Federal Interagency Forum on Child and Family Statistics, 2007). Accidental injury is the leading cause of death in childhood and adolescence in the United States (U.S. Bureau of the Census, 2006). In early childhood, this often occurs in relation to car accidents as a pedestrian, a passenger, or on tricycles. Use of appropriately designed children's car seats is required now in all states for both infants and young children.

Many accidental deaths and injuries to young children occur in or near their home. Many of these involve a child's ingestion of poisonous or toxic substances, such as fertilizer, gasoline, or cleaning products. While parents are urged to store these safely, it is also wise to have the telephone number of a local poison control center, emergency facility, or physician handy in case it is needed quickly. In addition, it is important for parents to insist on childproof caps for medication bottles. Other safety measures include the use of helmets for skiing and tricycle riding. Parents need to teach their children rules of safety when walking or playing outside the home. Some children are more impulsive than others and can experience greater numbers of injuries and close calls (Schwebel & Plumert, 1999). These children require an extra-strict parental eye and perhaps more intensive safety instruction than other children. Perhaps just as important is making sure that play equipment both indoors and outdoors is safe and can be used safely by young children.

••

Focus Point. Preschoolers generally have good health but may experience a number of illnesses. Accidental injury is the leading cause of death of preschoolers, with the majority of these occurring within or near the home.

••

Providing Structure and Nurturance for Young Children. During the early childhood period, child rearing increasingly includes greater attention to teaching children about structure as it is interpreted by the particular family system. Structure comes in several forms, such as the rules promoted by the family, the roles taught to children by precept and by example, and the ways family members communicate with one another. In family systems theory, these are referred to as *family patterns.*

Nurturance is provided when parents consistently attempt to meet the particular needs of young children and act in ways that are supportive of their psychosocial growth (see Table 8–1). There is a greater emphasis on providing assertive care rather than supportive care because preschoolers are not yet able to take greater control over their actions.

At this time in a child's life, several types of parental behaviors can promote feelings of guilt that may inhibit developmental progress and lead to unhealthy self-esteem. Most of these behaviors are considered to be variations of acts that serve to discount or belittle a child's character (J. I. Clarke & Dawson, 1998).

Using Rules in Teaching Structure.   The discussion in Chapter 3 indicated that rules are used in family systems as a primary means for maintaining the group's efficient functioning. Rules are one means by which parents teach structure to children and help children to internalize controls that guide their behavior (J. I. Clarke & Dawson, 1998). When a family system evolves and formulates rules that promote healthy parent and child behavior, some are negotiable and others are nonnegotiable. **Nonnegotiable rules** cannot be debated or changed, while **negotiable rules** are subject to discussion and alteration. In healthy families, a mixture of such rules guides the behavior of family members. In these families, nonnegotiable rules generally relate to safeguarding children's well-being in reasonable ways. These are not arbitrarily derived by the parents, nor are they abusive or rigid in nature. Instead, the purpose of such rules is to teach responsible behavior, good citizenship, and effective interpersonal skills. Nonnegotiable rules may define limits as well as appropriate behaviors with which children are expected to comply for their own well-being. For example, the rule "Play in the back yard, not in the street" informs a preschooler that a parent cares about the child's well-being and is willing to define the places where the child can play safely. Other nonnegotiable rules might include: "You must go to bed at eight o'clock;" or "You must eat some breakfast every day."

Negotiable rules can be questioned by children and discussed with parents. Young children quickly learn which rules are negotiable and which are not. For example, the implicit rule in some families is that children are to eat whatever is served to them for meals, but children may learn that they can question what they are expected to eat. Perhaps children may resist eating spinach because of its odious taste, smell, or appearance. They may bargain with their parents for what they will eat at the meal and what they will not until some agreement is reached between them. In essence, negotiable rules help to teach children how to think and use discussion as a means of conflict resolution (see Figure 8–2).

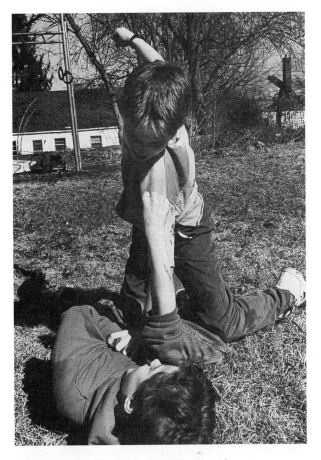

FIGURE 8–2.   Family systems evolve rules as a means of providing structure to children. Some rules are negotiable and others are not. Rules are used as a means of socializing children into appropriate behavior patterns. Consequences help to enforce rules. Children learn that some behaviors are acceptable but others, such as expressions of physical aggression, are not.

Parenting Reflection 8–1

Can a family system have too few or too many rules that govern the behavior of family members? What effect would each of these situations have on young children, and what would be the implications of each on children's future development?

Enforcing rules and consequences of rules can be a problem for parents, especially those who are first-time parents of young children. It is often just as difficult for parents to remember to use positive reinforcement to help teach structure as it is to enforce the consequences of transgressions to rules. Such structure is most effective when administered with nurturance and love by parents.

•••

Focus Point. Young children need to learn about structure from their parents. This is typically taught via rules that are both negotiable and nonnegotiable in nature. Consequences of rules help preschoolers begin to learn self-control of their actions.

•••

•• •

Parenting Reflection 8–2

How would you, as a parent of a preschooler, use rules to manage their behavior to encourage a sense of initiative rather than a sense of guilt?

• •

Beginning Socialization. Socialization refers to the processes by which children are taught to conform to social rules, to acquire personal values, and to develop attitudes and behaviors typical or representative of their cultural environment. The socialization process begins in earnest during early childhood, when parents and other caregivers begin to take an active role in teaching a young child these lessons. The lessons are not always given by formal instruction. Some are learned by observing the behavior of others, particularly adults.

Young children are expected to learn the patterns by which their family system functions and operates and to adopt the rules, behavioral expectations, and limits or boundaries their family system establishes for them. Some psychologists call this helping a child to internalize behavioral standards promoted by parents and other caregivers. This is what is referred to in this text as providing experiences that teach *structure* to children. A child who has learned structure has the information about which to judge any action as appropriate and acceptable or inappropriate and unacceptable. At the level of preschool children, such lessons are introductions to family functioning. Implicit is the understanding that transgressions and mistakes are to be expected from young children as they learn.

Depending on the nature of a particular family system, certain standards may be promoted more than others. Despite the diversity of families today, almost all teach certain kinds of behaviors and values to children. For example, nearly all families attempt to teach children to acquire prosocial behaviors such as learning to be empathic, controlling impulsiveness, gaining self-control, and limiting aggression. These are briefly discussed in the following paragraphs.

Prosocial Behaviors. Most young children are taught to show some degree of social interest in others. **Prosocial behaviors** promote helpfulness and concern for others. These altruistic behaviors show an awareness of other people's feelings and appropriate ways of reacting to those feelings. This calls for knowledge in using a social skill known as **empathy,** which is the ability to accurately comprehend the thoughts, feelings, and actions of others. Empathy differs from sympathy, which is the ability to feel the same way that others do. Learning to be sympathetic, however, is the first step toward becoming empathetic.

The origins of sympathetic behaviors can be found in infancy when children are observed to comfort another child's distress (Radke-Yarrow, Zahn-Waxler, & Chapman, 1983). In early childhood, empathic responsiveness is observed when children share belongings and comfort or help others who are distressed. However, these behaviors are not performed as spontaneously or as frequently as parents and others would prefer.

It is unclear at this time how an adult model facilitates empathic behaviors in young children. It appears that when children have opportunities to observe such behaviors, they tend to behave more frequently in empathic ways toward others (Rock, 2002). Researchers note, however, that these behaviors are observed throughout infancy and childhood regardless of the degree of parental influence or instruction.

Aggression. Psychologists define **aggression** as any hostile action that causes fear and leads to forceful contact with another (Parens, 1995). Aggressive actions directed at people or things can be verbal, physical, or both, and they can be either positive or negative.

Our culture values nonviolent social aggressiveness. An example is a steady, determined, and controlled effort in reaching solutions to problems and exploring learning experiences. In effect, this cultural concept of aggressiveness is synonymous with, and a logical extension of, the idea of initiative. Concern arises, however, when aggression is expressed as hostile or violent behavior that harms others or excludes children from social interactions with others.

Some researchers believe that aggressive expressions in childhood follow a normal developmental progression. Aggressive expressions steadily increase from late infancy into the years of early childhood (Parens, 1995), then peak in early childhood and decline thereafter. Thus, aggression in preschoolers is part of their normal growth and development. It may serve healthy functions such as helping them discover personal boundaries and communicate or enforce these with others.

Some researchers suggest a genetic tendency toward aggressive behavior (Parens, 1995). Other researchers believe that the family environment promotes such behavior. The premise for this observation is that children who are treated in harsh, aggressive ways by parents also act aggressively toward others. Another possibility is that children adopt the model of aggressive behaviors they observe on television and in the movies. Despite the variety of explanations, young children clearly act aggressively at times for various reasons, and parents and other caregivers frequently are challenged to teach young children how to control aggressive impulses. Children are given a confusing message when they are spanked by adults for hitting others. Research points to the role of reinforcement as a powerful means for helping children learn to act in nonaggressive ways. When adults positively reinforce prosocial behaviors that are incompatible with aggressiveness, children learn that there are more beneficial ways to express themselves. One popular method is to isolate children from others briefly. Social learning theory suggests other alternatives, such as modeling for children appropriate ways of handling the feelings that motivate aggression.

Delaying Gratification.

Adults often ask preschoolers to delay getting what they want to have immediately. This is a difficult task for a young child to master. The expectation for this behavior from young children is especially characteristic among middle-class families. Children are expected to defer having a smaller need satisfied immediately in exchange for receiving a greater benefit later. This is an important lesson in self-control. It helps to bring impulsiveness under willful restraint.

Individuals can cope with difficult situations in later life more successfully if lessons about delaying immediate gratification are introduced in early childhood (Schwarzchild, 2000). Teaching young children to think "It is good if I wait" can also help them in controlling impulsiveness.

Encouraging Positive Sex-Role Development.

An important aspect of an individual's self-concept is **gender identity,** the knowledge that humans are either male or female. An individual's biological sex immediately predicts a variety of reactions from others at birth. Children first learn gender or sex roles according to parents' interpretations of masculinity or femininity. In early childhood, parents and other caregivers use reinforcement to shape gender identity. These become modified and refined in middle childhood and adolescence. The result of such socialization experiences is that individuals make personal interpretations of masculinity and femininity at later ages. Sex-role development, then, has both cognitive and behavioral aspects. It is not clear whether gender-related differences in behavior are due to cultural factors or to biological factors (Bornstein & Masling, 2002). However, gender roles appear to vary from one culture to another in some respects. For example, the practice in some cultures that women and girls are allowed to eat only after the males in the family have eaten is obviously a cultural factor. On the other hand, the fact that males tend to exhibit more aggressive behaviors than females regardless of culture would appear to point to a biological factor.

Young children appear to acquire rigid stereotypes of what it means to be male or female (Dresner, 2000). This rigidity is largely due to the inflexible thought processes typical of young children. It is only to be expected that young children understand whatever they see as something that is factual. For example, preschoolers typically use visible physical cues, such as clothing and hairstyle, to recognize someone as either male or female (Bem, 1989). It is not unusual for many young children to believe that long hair always indicates that a person is female, even when other features indicate the person is a male. The notion that gender conforms to external genitalia is not mastered until age 6.

A child's sex-role development begins at birth, when parents are told, "It's a boy!" or "It's a girl!" This immediate classification is made more permanent and public by naming the child, usually with a name that conforms to the child's sex (although androgynous names are becoming more common). From this point forward, children are channeled into one sex role or another by being dressed and given hairstyles that identify them as a male or female and cause others to treat them accordingly (Lester, 2003).

A preschool-age child's knowledge of sex-appropriate role behaviors comes from several sources. These behaviors are reinforced and modeled to children by adults and others in the family system (Maccoby & Jacklin, 1974). In addition, reinforcement from other same-sex children helps to promote sex-appropriate behaviors, especially among boys.

Teaching young children about androgynous sex roles is difficult but not impossible. The challenge lies in encouraging preschoolers to avoid stereotypes about sex roles. One method is to promote their involvement in activities and with toys traditionally associated with both genders. For example, boys can be encouraged to take on feminine play roles such as playing house, and girls can be encouraged to play with building blocks and trucks. In addition, observing adult behavior in nontraditional roles can affect children's ideas about sex roles. Children form a more balanced impression, for example, when they see Dad doing the laundry and Mom mowing the lawn.

It may be helpful to recognize that preschoolers' rigid interpretations of sex-role orientations and behaviors help them to understand these social roles and organize their behavior accordingly. However, encouraging children to maintain inflexible beliefs indefinitely may limit their full potential as human beings. Traditional sex-role orientations are problematic in that they tend to be rigid and restrictive. Higher levels of self-esteem and social competence are found among adults who adopt more androgynous sex-role orientations (Woodhill & Samuels, 2003).

Teaching Young Children About Sexuality. It is commonly believed that children are not interested in or aware of their sexuality until puberty. This is a misconception, as many parents soon discover when their children reach preschool age. Rather than relating just to physiological functioning and behavior, *sexuality* refers to the broad aspects of sexual interests, attitudes, and activities that are an expression of a person's total being. Sexuality plays a significant psychological role throughout an individual's life span, not just following puberty. Although it is difficult for behavioral scientists to study the

sexual interests and activities of children, childhood sexuality has been investigated for many years. It has had an important impact on the psychoanalytical theory of personality development proposed by Sigmund Freud.

Young children commonly ask many questions as a means of gaining information about their world, and questions relating to sexual issues and bodily functions are an expression of this interest. A typical question that can be expected from most 4-year-olds is: "Where do babies come from?" It is also common for sexual themes to emerge in dramatic play activities such as when young children play house or the proverbial scenario of playing doctor (see Parenting FAQs 8–1).

Parents are the primary source of sexual socialization and information for young children (Westheimer & Lopater, 2004). Most parents are aware of their responsibilities in this regard, although some are anxious about answering a child's sexually oriented questions or feel incapable of providing accurate information due to their own ignorance about such matters. Although the accuracy of information parents provide in addressing young children's sexuality and sexual interests is important, perhaps of greater importance are the emotional tones and affect that parents communicate when discussing these issues. For example, although young children are unable to comprehend the mechanics involved in human reproduction due to their level of cognitive development, they easily absorb any feelings of embarrassment that accompany a parent's answers to sexual questions.

Parents may read an abundance of excellent printed material about what kinds of sexually related questions to expect from young children. It may be helpful for parents to rehearse the answers they might provide to their preschoolers. Parents should understand that the messages they convey about sexuality, both verbal and nonverbal, will affect children's attitudes and values when they have reached maturity.

Teaching Young Children About Dying and Death. Until recently, sexuality was a stringently taboo topic in parent-child relations. Today, parents are encouraged to take an active role in shaping children's values and attitudes about their sexuality. However, teaching children about the realities of dying and death remains a topic of socialization that many parents find especially difficult (Cook & Oltjenbruns, 1998).

As unpleasant and difficult as discussion of this topic may be, parents should attempt to teach young children

Parenting FAQs 8–1

Our 4-year-old, who is just full of all kinds of questions, just asked me what was wrong with a woman who is obviously pregnant. I had been expecting the usual "Where do babies come from?" question rather than this. I've delayed giving a complete answer until I could ask around how other parents have approached the facts of life with their preschooler. Can you give me some pointers as well?

A: Although it's always good to answer questions as completely as possible at the time they are asked by children, you can't always respond like this. However, I hope you said something like, "There's nothing wrong with the woman who has the big belly. I'll talk with you more about this later when I can explain this to you." Preschoolers sometimes have a knack for asking the toughest questions at the more inopportune times. It's good you are checking with other parents who have been challenged by this perennial question from children. Here are my suggestions to add to your list:

1. Keep your explanations about the facts of life as simple as possible.
2. Don't make up stories; stick to the facts and the truth; for example, "The woman's belly is big because there's a special place inside where a baby is growing. It's called the uterus."
3. Don't immediately assume that your child is ready for the complete facts of life discussion when asking this question. Remember that she or he is now probably wondering after hearing your explanation just how can a baby really be growing in there? How does it eat? Did it get there because the mother ate it? If you don't get additional questions after explaining about the woman's belly, you can either let the discussion end or perhaps think about prompting your child's understanding about the situation by asking him or her other questions relating to sex education.
4. However, it's perhaps not best at this time in your child's level of cognitive development to go into significant detail about conception and pregnancy. What is being demonstrated here is a lesson about parents as resources of information on many topics of interest to children. You will want to encourage your child to develop this attitude that you can help to interpret the world and act as a reliable source of information on many topics. If you don't know something, admit it and include a statement about this being something you can both learn about, and then research the topic.
5. Understand that children will ask many questions about sex and sexual matters. Don't believe that a one-time explanation will be sufficient for all time. Perhaps the best advice here is to learn to overcome any embarrassment you might feel about discussing such matters with your child and that their curiosity is appropriate. Children will be asking the same question again or in different forms at later ages as they mature in their cognitive abilities. Details can be added as they grow older.

about the reality of mortality (Cook & Oltjenbruns, 1998). Parents need to remember that very young children cannot understand the finality of death. For example, when preschoolers play cops and robbers, they are able to resume normal functioning after playing dead. When they watch cartoon characters experience serious injury, they see them spontaneously recover. Another difficulty in this regard is the inability of preschool-age children to comprehend the full meaning of "forever" as relating to the finality of death. Many young children also reach the conclusion that death happens only to those who are old, sick, or fatally injured. This belief

leads to questions when a parent or sibling becomes ill, for example, that relate to whether the person will die. As with socialization experiences that teach young children about sexuality, there is no specific design for how parents can teach young children about dying and death.

Focus Point.   Parents of preschoolers begin instructing their preschooler about appropriate behaviors that are expected of them by their family and by society. Instruction also is directed at helping children understand gender or sex roles, sexuality, dying, and death.

Attachment Revisited. The quality of attachment that a child develops in infancy has long-term consequences, some of which begin to appear not only in late infancy, but also in later stages of the life span. While this is not the only factor to influence other areas of a child's development, it contributes partly in significant ways.

Perhaps the most obvious way that the quality of attachment established in infancy becomes manifested in later life stages is seen in relationships that a child develops with others besides their parents (Ainsworth, 1989). For example, children who have established secure attachments in infancy appear to gain more satisfaction from relations with peers in early childhood (Schneider, Atkinson, & Tardif, 2001). In addition, researchers have even identified the quality of attachment spilling over to affect preschool children's mathematical skills (Dobbs, Doctoroff, Fisher, & Arnold, 2006) and their adjustment to nonparental child care (Ahnert, Gunnar, Lamb, & Barthel, 2004).

In general, there are many benefits to a child's acquiring a secure attachment in infancy that are observed in early childhood and also include: higher levels of social competence and self-esteem, ability to function independently, empathy, leadership skills, and problem-solving abilities in novel situations (James, 2006). Children coming from disadvantaged family systems are at higher risk for developing insecure attachments and, thus, having the likelihood of more serious problems in these same areas. Programs aimed at assisting these children and their families, such as Project Head Start, can help alleviate or reduce these problems by intervention experiences during the infancy and preschool years prior to entrance into the formal school system. We examine the influence of quality of nonparental child care on these kinds of developmental outcomes in the last section of this chapter.

Parents of preschoolers also reflect their own attachment issues. Those parents who developed a secure attachment while in their own infancy have been found to be more responsive to their own children's signs of distress and to respond appropriately (Edelstein et al., 2004; George & Solomon, 1999). In addition, other methods of intervention for those at-risk parents who developed an insecure attachment in childhood may be applied, such as home visitation from a social worker or child development specialist and participation in a community-based parent education intervention program (Gowen & Nebrig, 2002).

Facilitating Cognitive Development. Children shift to a new type of thought process typically around age 3. Piaget (1967) calls this a change to the **preoperational** mode of thinking. Parents and other caregivers readily recognize that a preschooler, unlike an infant, thinks. Thinking becomes more noticeable as young children solve problems in their play and daily activities. They now have an active memory and information-processing skills. They also show indications of the ability to use elementary logic (Flavell, Miller, & Miller, 2001).

Thought during this new period of mental changes focuses on internalizing the environment. Children accomplish this by an increasing use of symbolic thought and mental imagery (Beilin, 1992). They come to rely on representational thought more frequently as they progress through the stage of early childhood.

Parents may need to be informed that preschool-age children do not understand the world as an adult or even as an older child does. Piaget described the nature of preschool-age thought as intuitive in nature, meaning that these children often jump to conclusions, make decisions, and interpret the world based on insufficient facts. They are increasingly occupied with classifying things in their world according to likeness or similarity. This stage reflects the beginnings of more-ordered logical processing of information.

Preschoolers make judgments and reach conclusions based on their limited understanding of operations and rules. They use a minimal amount of cues and information in doing so, since they cannot completely absorb and use extensive amounts of information to reach conclusions. This stage of cognitive development is a time when young children are acquiring knowledge about things, people, and their environment. Later cognitive developmental functioning allows them to make use of this information.

Mental changes are facilitated by new language skills and perceptual abilities as well as the changes in brain functioning that occur in early childhood. The preoperational label implies that a child's thought processes are prelogical in nature. These prelogical skills lay the foundation for many other, more complex mental changes emerging in subsequent stages of the life span.

Preoperational thought among preschoolers is relatively inflexible in nature. This means that once young children adopt a particular point of view, they have difficulty understanding another competing one. It also means that young children's thought is dynamically tied to their perception. Preschoolers, like infants, use sensory information extensively but in an entirely different manner. The maxim "What you see is what you get" is a good way to remember how preschoolers form their ideas of their world. An object's appearance is often the only means preschoolers use for making judgments or evaluations about that object.

Piaget (1967) used several concepts to describe the relative rigidity of preschoolers' thoughts: equating appearance with reality, egocentrism, centering, irreversibility, inability to solve problems involving conservation, preoccupation with classification, animism, and precausal thinking. These eight concepts are briefly outlined here and the implications of parenting a preschooler to facilitate cognitive development follow.

1. *Appearance and reality.* Young children define reality almost exclusively as what they see, hear, and otherwise experience via their senses. They have almost no ability to generalize beyond the obvious or the information at hand (Flavell, 1986). It is generally recognized that preschoolers' thought is bound by their perceptions. Judgments, decisions, and conclusions are based on what is seen in their world.

   Keeping this in mind, parents of a preschooler need to have realistic expectations about their child's inability to make reasonable judgments and conclusions. This is the basis for using supportive care at this time of a child's life. Parents will need to make many decisions on behalf of their child to protect them from harm and injury, for example. Keeping an ever-watchful eye is imperative since children this age are not and cannot be made completely aware of the consequences of their actions.

2. *Egocentrism.* Piaget (1967) believed that the preoperational thought of young children is limited partly because of a cognitive trait known as **egocentrism**. Piaget did not use this word in our usual sense of meaning "selfish" or "conceited." Rather, he used it to describe how young children focus on their own viewpoint of the world and are unable to consider other alternatives. From their perspective, their own vantage point is all that is possible in understanding what they see in the world.

   Young children typically believe that they are the center of their universes, that things function and happen for their sole benefit. Appearances fuel this conclusion. For example, a young child on a walk at night might be asked what the moon is doing while she is moving. The child will likely explain that the moon follows her everywhere (after all, that is what it appears to be doing).

   Egocentrism is both a joy and a source of frustration to many parents of preschoolers. The joy comes from the opportunity to hear their charming perspectives on their world. The parental frustration connected with egocentrism may be associated with misunderstanding a child's prelogical reasoning where egocentrism is at the heart. Some parents become very upset when they hear their preschooler make what they interpret as "tall tales" to explain their actions and punish the child for lying. For example, when a parent might confront a preschooler about some kind of misbehavior, the child is likely to create a story about how he or she was manipulated into doing so by a monster who has now escaped into the wilds. Such logic is frustrating as many parents view this as undesirable and unacceptable. It might help to stimulate creativity and curiosity in the preschooler if the parent would continue with the story just to see where it would end. Parents need to understand that they would not be promoting a habit of lying as children outgrow this kind of thinking as they grow older.

3. *Centering.* Piaget called another aspect of preoperational thought centering (Piaget & Inhelder, 1969). Young children concentrate on only one aspect of an object they see or an activity they do. They have difficulty in perceiving other aspects or elements simultaneously. When young children are attracted to the color of something, for example, they usually can't consider its size or shape at the same time. They can separate all the yellow buttons from a large pile of assorted buttons, but the task of separating all the yellow, wooden, round ones is too difficult for them. The ability to make fine discriminations such as this occur at later stages in the life span.

   This is important for parents to remember when giving directions for young children to follow. They can follow only one concise, simple command at a time rather than a complicated series of actions to perform at once. One method used by the Montessori approach to educating children is to break down complex tasks into simple, easy-to-follow steps. By remembering this characteristic of early childhood, parents can avoid much conflict and frustration with their children in requesting them to follow certain directions such as how to go about picking up their toys following play.

4. *Irreversibility.* Young children typically cannot understand that some operations or processes can be reversed. To a young child, things operate in only one way and that way is irreversible (Piaget, 1967). For example, when asked if he has a sister, a preschool-aged boy can be expected to reply, "Yes, her name is Julie." However, when asked if his sister has a brother, the boy can be expected to reply, "No." Young children appear to be incapable of retracing the logic of their thinking.

The trait of irreversibility implies that parents, again, need to be mindful of expectations of preschool-age children. We cannot expect them to have long memories and adequate information input and storage to retrieve information and trace events from a beginning point to an ending point and then backward.

5. *Conservation problems.* Young children cannot understand that something retains the same properties when it is rearranged or reshaped. This mental skill comes in the next stage of cognitive development. Again, their comprehension of size, volume, and shape is influenced by what they see rather than understanding how these can be changed without disturbing the content or context of an object.

Parents may be stymied when trying to explain complex notions such as the value of coins to their preschooler. In this case, young children often will believe that a nickel is worth more than a dime because it is larger in size. Trying to convince a child who is trapped in their perceptions about a concept can be frustrating to parents. Understanding with this notion of coins and what they will purchase comes with time, experience, and additional instructions from parents.

6. *Classification.* The mastery of **classification** skills is a challenge that is accomplished by age 6. Centering an egocentrism account for the inflexibility of thinking that prevents younger children from being able to group things according to shared likeness.

It is not easy for a young child to master this skill, but parents can help to facilitate a variety of learning experiences that foster classification skill development. Teaching a child about different animals is one example here. At around 3 years of age, all animals

are alike to a young child. Every animal seen is called a "dog," for example. Parents usually attempt to correct the child by pointing out that they are seeing a cat, perhaps. Now, this is confusing to a preschooler since both animals have four legs, a tail, and fur. Parents usually discover that it is the vocalizations made by animals and their size that help the child to understand that while they are very much alike in many respects, they can be identified correctly by their call.

Parents may facilitate classification skill development by providing sorting tasks taking centering of the preschooler's thought processes into consideration. Classification skill development can also be facilitated when showing an older child an array of objects and asking them to identify the one that is not like the others. Parents may be expected to repeat these kinds of activities many times with young children to help them master this skill.

7. *Animism.* Young children believe that all things, including inanimate objects, are alive (Bullock, 1985). This **animism** is a charming aspect of preschool-age thinking. It is often observed when young children are involved in solitary play and talk to their toys using private speech. In many respects, it is an extension of egocentrism and prelogical thinking. Young children may use animistic thoughts to develop hypotheses about a complicated world.

Appropriate parenting in this case calls for accepting this type of thinking as part of the nature of a young child. To scorn the child and discount their beliefs about inanimate objects is inappropriate. This is, again, a cognitive trait that will disappear as children gain experiences and grow through the next stages of cognitive development.

8. *Precausal thinking.* Preschoolers often jump to conclusions. They base their decisions on a limited amount of information or knowledge of circumstances or on how close one event follows another. They simply do not have the ability to use deductive reasoning to reach conclusions.

Parenting in this regard calls for gently correcting children when they have come to erroneous conclusions with the expectation that children this age will dispute their word.

The author was an assistant working in a university preschool program as a graduate student. A memorable episode involving precausal thinking, egocentrism, and other cognitive flaws with preschoolers took place one afternoon when I was supervising my group of 4-year-olds playing dodgeball. The children tired of playing this on a level space of ground and moved to play the game on a slight hill nearby. One ball thrower stood at the top of the incline and another at the bottom with the other children playing the game in between the two. The little boy at the bottom of the hill stopped the game after a few minutes. He said he had observed that ball *always rolled back down the hill after stopping . . . why was this so?* Because this was a group of intellectually gifted children, I had been instructed to explain such questions in detail using accurate information. In this regard, I had the opportunity to talk to the group about gravity, shape of the ball, inertia, and so on. While they were fascinated with these ideas, the small questioner looked me squarely in the eye and said, "I don't believe all that is correct!" In reply, I asked how so? His answer: "The ball always rolls down the hill because it knows I'm at the bottom." I realized that point could not be argued at that time with him but with repeated lessons about the force of gravity in other contexts over the rest of the school year.

Piaget (1967) also noted that a wide variety of experiences allow children to be exposed to the infinite elements of their world and stimulate cognitive as well as language development during these years. Parents play an important role in supervising preschoolers' experiences and providing a number of these for their children. Shopping at the supermarket, taking a walk, going on a trike-hike, or just reading to children are examples of ways parents can take advantage of stimulating their child's mind. Parents also become recognized by their preschooler as a resource of information about the world. This is particularly appealing to a 4-year-old who poses an endless stream of questions to parents. While this constant bombardment of questions may become irritating at times, parents need to understand that they play a significant role in their child's life by acting as an interpreter and helping to give meaning to children's understandings of their world. It is also in this manner of interacting with preschoolers that parents may begin to share their family values, beliefs, and worldviews to children.

Focus Point.   Cognitive development in early childhood focuses on children acquiring a database of information about their world. Language skills facilitate this process. In addition, parents facilitate appropriate cognitive development by providing a variety of experiences and equipment for preschoolers.

Providing Appropriate Toys and Play Equipment. Toys and play equipment help preschool-age children to develop a number of different skills and abilities. Play is how young children begin to gain an understanding of the world in which they live socially, physically, and mentally.

Preschool-age children progress through various types of play as they gain in social and mental skills. Three-year-olds may prefer and enjoy solitary play activities where they have no competition in exploring objects and things. Children this age do not share possessions easily with others and will often do well simply by playing alone or with the same kinds of play equipment being used by another child. Four-year-olds are becoming more creative in using their imaginations and are learning how to share and play with other children. A number of different kinds of toys and play equipment appeal to children this age as they master gross motor skills and begin to explore fine motor skills. Five-year-olds can play fairly well in a small group of other children and participate in more complex types of play and equipment such as building blocks, pretend play, art activities, and science activities (see Focus On 8–2). Many young children today are fairly computer literate in that they have been exposed to games using their family's home computer equipment. Many of these are educational as well as recreational.

Parents should always keep safety factors in mind when choosing toys and play equipment for preschoolers. In addition, affordability may be an issue when selecting toys. Some community agencies have toy-lending libraries, which are especially helpful to budget-minded families or those wishing children to be exposed to a wide variety of toys without making a large financial layout.

Focus Point.   Preschoolers need appropriate toys and play equipment that encourage the appropriate physical, psychosocial, and mental skills germane to this stage of development.

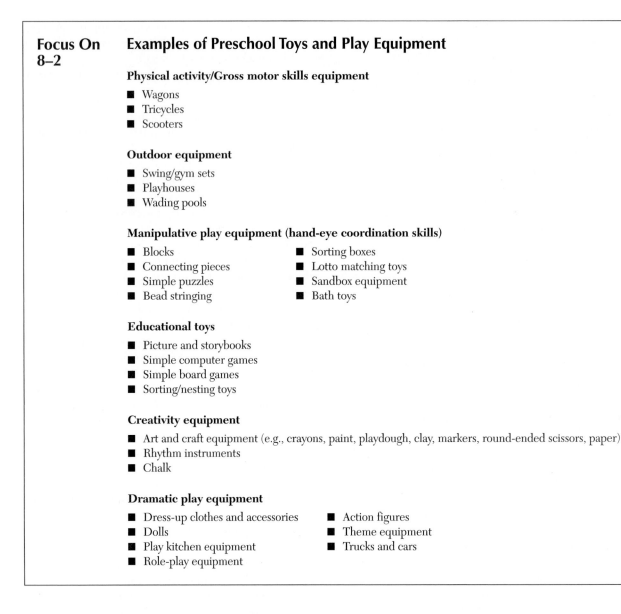

Focus On 8–2

Examples of Preschool Toys and Play Equipment

Physical activity/Gross motor skills equipment

- Wagons
- Tricycles
- Scooters

Outdoor equipment

- Swing/gym sets
- Playhouses
- Wading pools

Manipulative play equipment (hand-eye coordination skills)

- Blocks
- Connecting pieces
- Simple puzzles
- Bead stringing
- Sorting boxes
- Lotto matching toys
- Sandbox equipment
- Bath toys

Educational toys

- Picture and storybooks
- Simple computer games
- Simple board games
- Sorting/nesting toys

Creativity equipment

- Art and craft equipment (e.g., crayons, paint, playdough, clay, markers, round-ended scissors, paper)
- Rhythm instruments
- Chalk

Dramatic play equipment

- Dress-up clothes and accessories
- Dolls
- Play kitchen equipment
- Role-play equipment
- Action figures
- Theme equipment
- Trucks and cars

POSITIVE GUIDANCE METHODS WITH YOUNG CHILDREN

When a child enters the preschool years, parents can expect to alter or adapt their parenting style to include an increasing number of behaviors that are considered to be supportive care. These are blended with other behaviors that involve structure. To be effective now, parenting must be customized not only to meet the needs of young children but also to include the values that a family wishes a young child to begin learning and ways that will accomplish immediate goals, such as a child's compliance with parental wishes. In essence, parenting young children is geared to what works best with a particular child who is at a particular level of development.

One of the biggest challenges facing parents of young children is communication since language becomes the vehicle for beginning socializing experiences.

However, effective communication between parent and child is tested by the vocabulary and cognitive limitations of preschoolers. One of the time-tested approaches to help parents work with children under these circumstances focuses on teaching preschoolers to learn to listen and, in turn, how to gain a child's full attention when communicating (Ginott, 1965). Ginott advocates methods that were developed in progressive nursery schools during the 1940s and 1950s. These are summarized here:

1. *Communications with children are based on respect and skill.* Parents are advised not to attack or criticize a child's personality or character but to focus on the offensive behavior, that is, separate the misbehavior from the child who does it. For example, Ginott suggests that parents not say, "You're a rotten kid when you do that." Instead, he recommends parents say something like, "I'm very angry and irritated at what you've done, not at you." By making the distinction between the act and the child making the act, parents help a child avoid fusing the two, which can be damaging to a young child's healthy self-esteem and fuel feelings of guilt. Guilty feelings are not healthy, positive ways for a child to learn to avoid poor behavioral choices as these tend to freeze higher thought processes and prevent critical thinking. When guilt is being experienced, that is almost all that can be experienced at the time rather than learning to think critically about how to act differently in the future in similar situations.

2. *Praise and positive reinforcement should not be overused by parents.* When these are used, they should be directed to reinforcing a child's realistic attempts and accomplishments rather than to communicating how good he or she is in the parent's eyes.

3. *In dealing with conflicts or stress in interactions with children,* Ginott advises that parents accept the fact that children's behavior is bound to cause tension at times. He suggests one way to gain children's attention so that they can hear and begin to understand what parents are saying when giving guidance. This involves using words that are likely to be new to a child such as, "I don't like it when you act so *obnoxious* to your sister." This also helps to boost a child's vocabulary construction.

4. *A number of adult patterns are considered to be self-defeating.* Threats are invitations for misbehavior to occur because children can view these as a dare to do something forbidden. Sarcastic comments serve only to make children feel bad about themselves, and children soon learn not to listen to parents who moralize and preach about their faults and shortcomings.

5. *Communication becomes more effective when physical differences are minimized between parents and children.* One way to achieve this is by getting on eye level with children. One can accomplish this by squatting by them, sitting down with them, or holding them on the lap.

6. *Children need to learn to take increasing responsibility for their behavior as they grow older.* Children can be helped to learn this point when parents offer choices in acceptable alternatives in their behavior. Instead of asking yes-no questions or fill-in-the-blank questions such as, "What do you want to wear this morning?" Ginott suggests that parents say, "Do you want to wear your blue pants or the green ones?"

7. *Discipline and responsibility are learned by children through parents' setting reasonable limits that they can understand.* Comments such as, "Stop doing that!" identify unacceptable acts but fail to guide children into acceptable behaviors. Alternatives should be given: "If you need to hit something, Tommy, use the sofa cushion; not your sister;" or "Tell your sister how angry you are; don't use your fists to communicate."

While seemingly out of date because of when these were first promulgated, Ginott's suggestions continue to be fully in line with positive principles of child guidance. His recommendations are a consistent recognition of a humanistic approach to parent-child relations that recognize a child's contributions to interactions with parents in influencing their behavior toward him or her. These approaches promote effective communications as well as mental health of both parents and children.

Other methods of positive guidance that have been found useful with preschool children extend what was discussed more broadly in Chapter 4. These include:

■ Try to find the reason/s underlying a child's misbehavior (as a means for helping to understand the child's actions.

■ Don't expect a preschooler to behave like an older child.

■ Accept mistakes as a part of human nature and view them as tools for learning how to act appropriately.

- Use encouragement along with reinforcement, for example, "I can see how hard you tried not to goof up; I hope you can try just as hard next time this happens; I'm proud of you for trying."
- Clearly identify what is appropriate and what is not.
- Use time-outs instead of spanking. Sit the child in a corner for a short while.
- Talk out a problem rather than solving the problem for the child.
- Take away a privilege.
- Explain that there are alternative ways to act and help the child identify these.
- Don't use shame or guilt as a means to motivate a child to behave appropriately.

DEALING WITH BEHAVIOR PROBLEMS OF YOUNG CHILDREN

Many young children will experience to varying degrees any one of a score of possible problems as a normal part of their developmental progress. Although these problems are not necessarily detrimental to their progress, they are troublesome, especially from the parents' point of view (Parenting FAQs 8–2).

Most of the behavior problems young children experience are temporary in nature. As such, these behaviors present challenges for young children in their interactions with others, especially within their family system. Most problems are stage specific. In other words, certain problems observed among preschoolers

are unique to their stage of the life span, whereas others occur more commonly among older children.

Parents are often disturbed by the appearance and continued presence of certain kinds of behavior problems among preschoolers. An immediate response is to attempt every possible means to eliminate the troublesome behavior from the child's repertoire on the notion that once ingrained, such behaviors become permanent and habitual. Some parents turn to professionals, such as pediatricians, family physicians, child psychologists, and early childhood education specialists, for guidance in dealing with these problems. Others seek information from articles and books that address specific problems of young children such as toilet training, bed-wetting, or eating difficulties. The more problematic cases may require professional consultation and custom-designed treatment approaches. Those that occur more commonly among preschoolers are briefly discussed in the following paragraphs.

Bedtime and Sleeping Problems

The most common bedtime problems among young children include crying, resisting going to bed, repeatedly getting out of bed, and getting into bed with parents (Spock, 2004).

Resistance to going to sleep is especially troublesome, since a young child who gets too little sleep is irritable the next day (Tobin, 2002). Several issues may account for resistance to sleeping. First, parents may have trained their child improperly from the time of early infancy. Infants normally whimper when they are going to

---

Parenting FAQs 8–2

My 4-year-old has an imaginary playmate, who has the form of another child. She talks with the playmate, pretends she is playing with it, and insists that I also acknowledge its presence. I'm beginning to wonder if this is normal or not. What should we do about this situation?

A: It's understandable you might question the normality of what your preschooler is up to by having an imaginary playmate. Such behavior in older people is usually associated with mental illness. However, in the case of preschoolers, the presence of an imaginary playmate is indicative of several things: (1) Your child is, most likely, very lonely; (2) she has invented a playmate to solve this problem; and (3) by having done so in this manner, she is demonstrating a high level of intelligence. It is likely that your child is an only child or one who is isolated from other children her age. One solution to dismissing the imaginary playmate is to enroll her in a preschool or day-care program where she can have the company of other children regularly. Most imaginary playmates become replaced by real ones in this manner.

sleep. Parents who interpret this as cries of distress and rush in to pick up the infant train him or her to expect such attention at bedtime. Eventually, a young child may not be able to go to sleep without being held and rocked by a parent or other caregiver. Second, a young child may not be allowed time to relax and wind down prior to bedtime. In some homes, parents are not aware that it is important to promote what experts call *sleep hygiene routines* beginning in early childhood. In some homes, the period shortly before bedtime is used as playtime, especially with a father who may encourage active, rough-and-tumble play that can excite rather than relax the child.

Parents can help preschoolers develop good sleep hygiene habits that promote relaxation and preparation for sleep. Restful activities such as baths, reading stories, or quiet play serve as signals to preschoolers that bedtime is approaching. One of the more successful approaches is to use "planned" ignorance (Spock, 2004), whereby parents provide their full attention to a preschooler during the quieting-down period prior to bedtime but do not reenter the child's bedroom after the child is in bed. This policy of "Once in bed, you stay in bed" is established with the child's full knowledge and expected compliance. Usually, preschoolers will go to sleep within about 20 minutes after being put to bed.

Bad Dreams and Nightmares.   Fears are common among young children and can take on additional dimensions in the fantasy world of dreams and nightmares. Although a nightmare may last only a few minutes, a young child can recall it in intricate detail. Bad dreams or night terrors can last much longer, and a child is usually unable to recall specific details that were frightening. These are commonly observed among children who are experiencing extreme stress in their lives, as when parents are divorcing, for example (Spock, 2004).

Talking with young children about their fears is often an appropriate approach for helping them to understand how fears can be manifested in frightening dreams. It may be helpful to hold the preschooler nurturantly and rock him or her for a short time. Comments that inform the child that such frightening experiences are not real but are created by the imagination help in reassuring a preschooler. Parents also might examine the preschooler's bedtime and sleep hygiene routines and eliminate activities such as watching television shows that stimulate harmful fantasizing.

Problems of Elimination

Preschoolers can occasionally experience problems with bodily elimination functions. Typically, these include regression. Loss of elimination control (e.g., bed-wetting) is not considered problematic until a child reaches the school-age years.

Regression in toilet training might happen (1) as a reaction to the birth of a new baby into the family system; (2) as a reaction to extreme fatigue, excitement, or illness; (3) as an expression of anxiety; or (4) as a result of forgetfulness during periods of intense concentration during play activities or television viewing.

Commonsense measures help young children overcome these periods of regression in their elimination training. Reminding a child to use the bathroom may be all that is required to resolve the problem. In addition, protecting a child from situations that are overstimulating or frightening may be an easy solution.

● ●

Parenting Reflection 8–3

How would you advise a parent of a young child that a behavior problem might be serious enough to warrant professional consultation but is not indicative of abnormal developmental progress?

● ●

Eating Problems

Young children are included in eating meals with other family members and sharing the family diet. Most parents understand that young children may eat the same foods as other family members, but in smaller portions. They are aware that the particular nutritional needs of young children include adequate amounts of protein, calcium, and vitamins from a variety of food sources. Many parents also know the unhealthy aspects of allowing young children to eat a lot of "empty-calorie" foods in their diet, such as snacks with high amounts of sugar and/or fat.

Young children may gravitate toward acquiring problems with eating such as (1) resistance to eating, (2) dawdling over food served at meals, and (3) developing peculiar desires for nonfood items, known as a *pica* (Tobin, 2002).

Because some parents are knowledgeable about what constitutes an adequate diet, they become conscientious about what foods are served to young children. However, overzealousness can cause young children to become resistant to eating. When children feel pressured to conform to parental desires and eating policies, they tend to resist eating certain foods. For example, if parents firmly believe that vegetables must be consumed when served at meals, some young children resent the pressure to comply with parents' expectations and stop eating vegetables altogether. Parents may react by becoming greatly concerned about the child's nutrition and fret about the short- and long-term effects on the child's health and well-being. At times, some parents pressure children to eat "something" at meals, which may exacerbate the problem even more.

● ●

Focus Point.　Many parents observe certain kinds of behavior problems among preschool-age children as a normal part of development. Many of these are related to conflicts between parents and children and with other family members. A variety of sources can help parents work with children in such situations.

● ●

SUPPORTS FOR PARENTS OF PRESCHOOLERS

Community services that provide alternative forms of nonparental caregiving are more numerous and accessible to families with preschool-age children than to families with infants. About 61% of all children younger

than 5 years who were not in kindergarten in the United States were in some type of nonparental child care program in 2005. The type of supplemental care provided for children varies according to their age and the type of child care parents desire (Federal Interagency Forum on Child and Family Statistics, 2007). While infants are more typically placed in home-based care by either a relative or nonrelative, preschoolers who are not yet enrolled in a kindergarten program are more likely to be cared for by a relative or placed in a group center-based program (Overturf-Johnson, 2005).

The most common type of supplemental care for those who are not enrolled in kindergarten is a preschool-type, day-care program. This is unlike day-care situations for infants, who most frequently are cared for by a nonrelative. Families today use such services for a number of reasons. Many mothers of young children are employed outside the home, for example, and this type of care is necessary to help the family provide for children's needs. Other families wish young children to have enriching experiences that are not usually available in the home. Others wish their child to experience educational opportunities in preparation for public school. Most programs today provide educational stimulation for young children in addition to custodial care.

Relatives provide more than half of the child care for families of preschool-age children (Federal Interagency Forum on Child and Family Statistics, 2007; Overturf-Johnson, 2005; Figure 8–3). Of those who are relatives providing care, fathers, grandparents, and siblings

FIGURE 8–3.　Percentage of children from birth to age 6 not yet attending kindergarten, by type of child-care arrangement in 2005.

Source: Federal Interagency Forum on Child and Family Statistics (2007). *America's Children: Key national indicators of well-being: 2007.* Washington, DC: Author.

provide the greatest amount of child care for preschool-age children when mothers are employed outside the home. Among providers of child care who are not relatives, slightly more than half of preschool-age children are cared for by day-care centers and by nonrelatives in their homes.

There continues to be much discussion about the advantages and disadvantages of nonparental child care for preschoolers. A variety of concerns have been raised about the short- and long-term effects of such care on children's developmental progress. Researchers have examined issues such as attachment, the quality of parent-child interaction, the degree of children's compliance, and other behavioral effects in children who have experienced nonparental care. In reviewing the research on such issues, Belsky (1990) cites several important factors. When nonparental care is sensitive and responsive to children's needs, for example, young children are observed to be compliant, cooperative, and achievement oriented. In many respects, nonparental child care is like that which is provided by parents: The relationship that nonparental adults promote with children has a greater impact than the methods used in working with children. This parallel implies consequences based on the quality of nonparental care. Negative emotional attitudes of nonparental caregivers and their failure to respond to

children's needs are thought to result in problem behavior. Generally speaking, the intellectual gains offered by preschool programs are greatest for low-income children rather than middle-class children, due to the differences in home environments (Erel, Oberman, & Yimiya, 2000).

The features of each type of supplemental child-care program are discussed here briefly.

Child-Care Centers

These programs are used more commonly when young children are not enrolled in kindergarten (Figure 8–4). Child-care or day-care centers typically offer care of children for varying lengths of time. The kinds of programs used most commonly by families with preschoolers involve groups of children. Some programs are nonprofit and are sponsored by companies, community agencies, or educational institutions. Others operate as a business venture for profit.

Day care in the United States has not had a respectable reputation until recently. In the past, most day-care programs provided nothing more than custodial care. Today, this is changing as more staff members are trained in early childhood education. In many respects, there are few differences between preschool and day-care programs today.

FIGURE 8–4. Many families with preschool-age children rely on nonparental child care. A variety of programs and services are available to assist families with child care.

●●●●●●●●●●●●●●●●●●●●●●●●●●●●●●●●●●●

Parenting Reflection 8–4

Should early childhood educational experiences be required prior to a child's enrollment in first grade? Why or why not?

●●●●●●●●●●●●●●●●●●●●●●●●●●●●●●●●●●●

Is Day Care Harmful to Young Children? Researchers continue to investigate this question and have learned that it involves complex issues (Belsky, 1990; National Institute for Child Health and Human Development, 1999, 2003). The context in which young children receive care may be associated with different child outcomes. It is important to take both the quality of child care and the characteristics of a family into consideration when examining long-term influences on children's development. For example, young children show the least competence in peer relation skills when they acquire insecure attachments to both parents and nonparental caregivers. This does not occur when they have a secure attachment to their day-care provider but not to their mother. Apparently, incompetent peer relationship skills are counterbalanced by the context of the nonparental caregiver-child relationship as compared with the parent-child relationship.

For the present, it may be safe to say that there appears to be little difference in the effects of parental and nonparental care on young children. There is one caveat to this statement: The quality of nonparental care must be high (National Institute for Child Health and Human Development, 1999, 2003). Child development experts describe factors indicative of a high-quality nonparental care program as: (1) clean, (2) safe, (3) adequately staffed, (4) providing opportunities for comfortable play with other children, and (5) showing respect for children's individual needs. Not all day-care programs are rated high in these factors. Until researchers examine the complete array of circumstances that affect children's development, this question will remain unanswered.

In 2002, a new federal initiative was introduced that is part of the *No Child Left Behind* legislation. This program attempts to strengthen the Early Head Start and Head Start programs by providing additional funding and training for staff members, create a stronger state-federal partnership in the delivery of early childhood programs, and fund research projects that will develop curricula for stimulating reading and language skills for children. This legislation may assist these programs even more in building quality child-care programming, especially for those that serve disadvantaged families and children.

●●●●●●●●●●●●●●●●●●●●●●●●●●●●●●●●●●●

Parenting Reflection 8–5

Would you be more likely to work for an employer who provided day care for children of employees as an employment benefit over an employer who did not? Why or why not?

●●●●●●●●●●●●●●●●●●●●●●●●●●●●●●●●●●●

Preschool Programs

Preschool programs are more educational than custodial in nature. Many young children have some type of preschool experience rather than day care. Most communities have several types of programs available for families with young children. Preschool programs are typically short-term in duration, with sessions for 2 to 3 hours in the morning or afternoon. Children can attend for varying numbers of days throughout a week. The more common types of programs are outlined briefly in the following paragraphs.

Specialized Curriculum Programs. Some preschool programs offer a particular curricular focus, such as one based on Piagetian cognitive theory, the Montessori method, or an open classroom model. The theoretical philosophy of a particular program is emphasized over other factors. The materials used in a Montessori program foster sequential thinking skills. Young children are taught to proceed sequentially to reach goals or solutions to problems. A cognitive-based curriculum may provide opportunities for young children to classify objects as one of many activities.

Special-Needs Programs. Some families have a child with atypical needs. These children can benefit from preschool programs designed to meet their needs. Such programs typically involve children with special physical or mental handicaps. There is a trend, however, to incorporate children with special needs into other preschool programs, due to a belief that all children will benefit by gaining greater empathy for one another.

Compensatory Programs.　Compensatory preschool programs are specially designed to provide a variety of experiences for children from disadvantaged families. Head Start is an example of such a program. Activities promote a preschooler's acquisition of language, social, and cognitive skills to enhance the child's self-concept and a sense of initiative. Nutritional and health needs are addressed as well. Unique to these programs is parental and family involvement, which serves to strengthen family functioning.

Excellent long-range benefits result from participation in these programs (National Institute for Child Health and Human Development, 1999, 2003). Children who have attended Head Start programs score higher on achievement tests and have higher grades in elementary school. These children are also less likely to be placed into special education classes or to repeat a grade. Their preschool experience in compensatory programs makes them similar to other children in this regard.

· ·

Focus Point.　Many parents seek assistance in providing child care by using services from sources outside their family systems. These are frequently provided by agencies and institutions that provide child care or by services offered by individuals in their homes. Generally, these are stimulating experiences for preschoolers if an educational component exists in the services provided. Parents are concerned about the quality of these services and the effects on children's developmental progress. A variety of types of programs serve different needs and purposes in supplementing parental care for preschoolers.

· ·

SYSTEMIC FAMILY DEVELOPMENT SNAPSHOT

(Before reading this section, it may be helpful to review the systemic family development model and the metaphor used to illustrate its concepts from Chapter 3.)

Our slice of developmental time is taken at the midpoint of the early childhood stage of the oldest child in the Curtis family. Mary Curtis is now 4 years old. This slice is taken about a year and a half after the first we made in the previous chapter when Mary was a toddler. We begin examining the snapshot with a brief review of the stressors that can be affecting a family system at this time. The second generation in this family is experiencing an increasing level of stress due to **role strain** affecting the young adult parents. Role strain refers to the pressures experienced when several competing roles must be managed simultaneously. When this occurs, role performance typically declines in at least one or two of the roles while another is given priority attention. The role given priority shifts and changes even during the course of a day. In the case of the second-generation Curtis family, the roles that must be juggled by both young adults are work, parenting, and marital relationships. Typically, this challenge is first encountered by families that have at least one preschool-age child. The relationship most often selected to receive the least amount of attention and maintenance is the marriage relationship. Because of this, people notice they are experiencing a decline in marriage satisfaction, which can be confusing and upsetting (Talmadge & Talmadge, 2003). Women typically experience this role strain to a greater degree than men, perhaps because they often bear the greater involvement and responsibilities in parenting and household maintenance (Bianchi, Milkie, Sayer, & Robinson, 2000). Couples cope with this initial awareness of dissatisfaction in a variety of ways that can be healthy or unhealthy in nature.

Examples of Stressors Affecting Each Curtis Family Generation: 1½ Years Later

First Generation (Grandparents)
■ Continuing adjustments to the aging process experienced in middle age

- Continuing assistance to adult children in completing their individuation process
- Continuing adjustment to the death of parents, relatives, and colleagues
- Continuing preparations for retirement

Second Generation (Young Adult Parents)
- More challenges in balancing work and family roles
- Maintaining a household that meets the needs of preschoolers and toddlers; providing finances for this household
- Refining parenting behaviors and styles
- Meeting personal adult needs while performing family and work responsibilities
- Maintaining a healthy committed relationship while coping with marital dissatisfaction
- Cultivating relationships with other friends and families

Third Generation (Preschooler and Toddler)
- Completing developmental tasks and milestones of infancy and early childhood

At the time of this slice of developmental time, here are the ages of all members of this family system: (1) groom's father (George Curtis) is now almost 58; (2) the groom's mother (Joan Curtis) is now 56; (3) the bride's father (Harry Scott) is now 55; (4) the bride's mother (Susan Scott) is now 53; (5) Butch Curtis is now almost 34, and (6) Lisa Curtis is now 31. The first child, Mary, is 4, and her brother, Joey, is 2 years old.

The Third Generation (Children)

The children have changed the most rapidly of all family members in the short period of time since the last snapshot. Mary Curtis is very much an inquisitive preschooler who attends a full-time day-care program provided at her mom's place of employment. Mary had some problems initially being away from her mom and dad for the entire day but has since learned to look forward to her "school." Sometimes she gets to spend the day with one set of grandparents or the other. This usually happens if she is sick and can't go to the day-care center. Her parents have some concerns about some problem behaviors she now manifests when she is angry or upset. Apparently, she has learned these from other children or from not being watched closely enough by the center staff. She now bites and pulls others' hair when she wants her own way. Her mom has arranged a meeting with her child's teacher to discuss this undesirable

new behavior. Lisa also wants to discuss what she perceives as Mary's poor eating habits and interests with the teacher. This concerns her considerably.

Mary's younger sibling Joey is attempting to master toilet training, which is a strain on his parents. They feel they aren't able to give him the attention he needs to master this task and may have to delay this for awhile. Joey also attends a half-day care program and is picked up for the rest of the day by one of his grandparents. Lisa and Butch feel fortunate to have parents who are willing to help out with this child-care arrangement.

For the most part, the children seem to have normal developmental progress relative to that of their friends' children these ages. Mary and Joey seem to have frequent upper respiratory illnesses, and Joey picked up a case of impetigo not long ago. Apparently, being in day care with many other children exposes them to a greater-than-average number of microbes. When Lisa asked the children's doctor about this, she was told that this is normal and helps children to develop a strong immune system.

The Second Generation (Adult Parents)

This generation is experiencing the greatest amount of stress. Lisa and Butch now must juggle work and family responsibilities that are even greater than the last time we saw the family development snapshot. Butch now is working longer hours and has taken on more work responsibilities to help meet their financial needs. This means he is often and unpredictably late for evening meals. Lisa, who also works, is taking on more overtime work to help with expenses. They have recently experienced increases in several critical areas of their budget, including mortgage, medical insurance, and food costs. They want to replace some furniture from days before they were married and would like to have a short vacation away from the children in the summer. Both have recently remarked that they miss seeing each other and find they have increasingly less time for social and romantic time together.

Butch and Lisa are finding that they appear to have splintered aspects of their life as a family and as adults. On the one hand, they acknowledge the necessity of working and working hard to get ahead. They also understand that to get the material possessions and to maintain a household requires that both of them work. However, trying to do this while meeting the needs of their preschooler and toddler is becoming a real challenge. This is especially the case when one of the children becomes ill while at day care and needs medical attention. Day-to-day parenting obligations require both of them to switch quickly between attending to the entirely different needs of a preschooler and a toddler. By the end of the day, they are exhausted and have little energy to give to one another. They occasionally leave the children with a sitter or with a set of grandparents so that they can have some quality alone time together. But those times are becoming less frequent as the children grow older. Lisa is more unhappy with what seems to be a more stressful marriage arrangement than she ever expected. Sometimes they argue more than usual, and the arguments sometimes don't get resolved, possibly because they are tired. They have discussed the possibility of seeing a marriage therapist and may do so at some point in the future to work on improving their relationship.

The relationship between both parents and Mary is good. They enjoy playing with her and watching her grow and develop. They are discovering the need, however, to begin discussing what rules they will have for regulating Mary's misbehavior and the consequences of these rules. Fortunately, Lisa and Butch come from similar family backgrounds, where both sets of parents raised them in similar ways with similar rules. They have managed to agree on most of the rules they have formulated for Mary and how they will enforce them. Lisa has taken a child development course and a parenting course at a local college, so she knows some of the basic ways of working with children these ages. Butch is allowing Lisa to take the lead as he learns how to talk with Mary instead of talking "down" to her as a parent. They both enforce time-outs as a way for helping Mary become composed after an emotional outburst. They both learned a great deal about parenting from their earlier experiences with Mary and find that this helps tremendously in working with Joey. Apparently, Lisa and Butch are evolving an authoritative parenting style that they will use with both children for a number of years to come.

The First Generation (Grandparents)

The grandparents continue to deal with stressors that were observed in the previous developmental snapshot. All are becoming more involved as grandparents as they actively assist with child care. Lisa's parents appear to be more comfortable with this greater involvement than Butch's parents. These roles seem to be evolving as each set of grandparents works to define what they want their role to mean and become.

Susan Scott (Lisa's mother) has had a good response in treatment of her cancer, and the disease is now in remission. The experience has made her take stock of what is truly important in life; one of her conclusions is that the people in her life are treasures, and she takes nothing for granted about time and how she uses it. The cancer episode took a toll as well on Harry, her husband.

He is deeply thankful that they have a new lease on life with time that he also sees as a precious commodity. They have truly fallen in love all over again as they experience a depth in their relationship that was not there before the disease struck. This illness has affected other family members as well. Lisa has seen what her mother has had to endure and wonders if she also will develop this disease later on in her life. It is frightening for her to think about, and she has come to value her mother's presence more deeply. Butch's parents also have reacted in similar ways as they have observed what the Scotts have experienced. Joan Curtis sees Susan Scott as a role model of courage and bravery as she has dealt with the serious aspects of the disease. Now that Joan has had the opportunity to see how someone else copes with the challenges posed by cancer, she feels as if she, too, will know how to face similar challenges in her future.

George Curtis now sees retirement on the horizon. While viewing this as a great escape from the stressfulness of his work, he also now is beginning to have some twinges of uncertainty about his future. He's never felt like this before about anything and is attributing his mixed feelings to simply growing older. Joan, his wife, occasionally becomes frustrated with George as he ruminates about what retirement may hold for him. And she also wonders how he will fare in a new life where his identity will not be rooted in being an employee.

Parenting Reflection 8–6

If changes occuring in one generation affect the other generations to some degree, how are stressors occurring in the third generation affecting the first generation? Is Butch and Lisa's marriage at risk for divorce because of the increasing levels of role strain being experienced? How does this role strain of the parents affect the children?

POINTS TO CONSIDER

■ The time of a child's life between ages 3 and 6 years constitutes the stage of early childhood. During this time, a child's developmental tasks and milestones focus on continued physical changes, new psychosocial skills and abilities, and changes in mental development that allow for greater use of language skills and information processing. Preschoolers are characterized as (1) being highly curious in learning about their environments, (2) discovering emerging personal competencies and gaining in self-awareness, (3) beginning to learn family and cultural expectations for appropriate behavior, and (4) discovering social roles and family interaction patterns.

■ Parenting behavior changes in response to the particular needs of preschoolers. Parents continue to provide nurturance in the form of greater degrees of assertive rather than supportive care. Structure is introduced for the first time, often through the use and enforcement of rules to control children's behavior and to help them begin to learn self-control. Parents begin to expose their preschooler to socialization practices for the first time. Young children begin to learn family as well as cultural expectations of appropriate behavior. Typically, these may involve certain behaviors that a family values as well as behaviors that are necessary for functioning in social interactions (e.g., prosocial behaviors). Parents also teach preschoolers about their gender- or sex-role as a part of the socialization process. Socialization of children this age also typically includes some instruction about sexuality and about dying and death.

■ The general decline in the rate of physical growth during these years prompts parents to hold different expectations regarding how to provide appropriate nutrition for young children.

■ While the health of preschoolers is good generally, parents provide assertive care in protecting them from ac-cidents and injuries, which largely occur within or near the home.

■ The quality of a child's attachment in infancy is manifested in various outcomes that continue to appear in early childhood.

■ Cognitive development in early childhood is termed preoperational thought and is characterized in unique ways compared with sensorimotor development in infancy. Various limitations exist, however, that prevent the development of mature rational thought processes at this time.

■ Because young children have limited cognitive and language skills, parents must customize their methods of guidance taking these factors into consideration. A number of different methods can be used, however, to promote positive interactions of guiding young children.

■ Behavior problems considered to be normal can be expected among many young children. These are due largely to problems children experience in learning appropriate behaviors, problems parents experience in teaching children what is expected of them, or daily adjustment difficulties.

■ Supports for caregiving in early childhood include the use of alternative types of nonparental child care that include child-care centers, home-based care by relatives and others, and other substitute caregivers. Child-care programs vary according to philosophy and objectives in assisting families with young children. A variety of outcomes, mostly positive and beneficial, can be anticipated from a child's participation in such programs.

■ A systemic family development snapshot reveals examples of the stressors that may affect the different generations of a family system in healthy as well as unhealthy ways.

CHAPTER 9

Parenting School-Age Children

Focus Questions
■ ■ ■ ■ ■ ■ ■ ■ ■ ■

1. What are the principal developmental landmarks of middle childhood that parents should know?

2. What is the nature of parent/school-age-child relations?

3. What are some common behavior problems observed among school-age children? How do these differ from what was observed among young children?

4. What challenges affect the ability of parents of children with special needs to raise their children effectively? What kinds of assistance are available for these families?

5. What are the effects of maternal employment on both parents and children?

6. What stressors and coping mechanisms are revealed by a systemic family development snapshot of families with school-age children?

■ ■ ■ ■ ■ ■ ■ ■ ■ ■

The period of the life span termed **middle childhood** begins when a child enters school at about 6 years of age and extends to puberty, which can be expected to begin near the end of the 12th year. The developmental events and changes that occur during this time lead to increased maturity and responsibilities. Middle childhood is characterized by a more advanced level of developmental abilities that is accompanied by greater expectations for behavior by parents and others.

Parents and others now hold higher expectations for school-age children than they did for preschoolers. They take a more serious approach to supervising and providing care for children of these ages. Parents and children now must work with the school system to ensure a successful academic experience and mastery of basic academic skills. Children now begin to detach from their dependency needs for parents as they separate from their families for longer periods during the day. There is an increasing orientation to peers rather than to parents and family members. School-age children are also faced with the central psychosocial task of developing a healthy sense of industry as opposed to a sense of inferiority. Although this focus constitutes the major concern of children at this time, many supplementary developmental tasks arise during this period as well. These tasks complement a child's emerging sense of self, and achieving these skills assists a child in developing healthy self-esteem that extends to many different, but related, aspects of his or her life.

Parents continue to experience the challenges of interacting with a child whose emerging self-concept is sensitive to psychological bruises inflicted by increasingly complex interactions with others outside the family system. Parenting style and behaviors in caring for growing children become modified during this period. The changing nature of school-age children requires major modifications in the style and nature of parental interactions. The methods and techniques of parenting or guiding children that were successful during a child's earlier years no longer are as efficient or effective. Essentially, parents must become psychological rather than physical helpers of a school-age child. The change in the nature of caregiving often comes about rather subtly as a child progresses through the years of elementary school.

DEVELOPMENTAL LANDMARKS OF MIDDLE CHILDHOOD

During the years of middle childhood, children are challenged by developmental events and changes that lead to increased maturity and responsibilities. They are faced with the central task of acquiring a sense of industry as opposed to a sense of inferiority, according to Erikson (1950, 1964). Although this challenge becomes the primary psychosocial focus of children in middle childhood, they are also expected to achieve many additional developmental

tasks during this period. These tasks complement a child's emerging sense of self, and achievement of these skills helps children acquire healthy self-esteem during their school-age years (Figure 9–1; see Focus On 9–1).

The events of early childhood lay the foundation for the developmental tasks and milestones addressed during middle childhood. The higher expectations held for children during these years are reflected in a significant change. Both parents and school systems expect children to acquire an attitude or feeling of duty and accomplishment (industry) as a result of the experiences they have in middle childhood. This attitude may be described in several ways: (1) a positive attitude toward work assignments and routine jobs leading to the development of a positive work ethic; (2) mastering tools or mental and social skills our culture expects children this age to master over time (i.e., academic skills such as reading, writing, and calculation and learning group politics through group and individual activities with peers); and (3) acquiring an ability to take responsibility for personal actions and behavior.

The development of a healthy attitude toward work and duty in performing one's responsibilities means that school-age children are expected now to begin an assignment or task and complete it satisfactorily without having to be continually reminded to do so. The nature of the task may not be as important as the process of beginning the job and performing it to acceptable standards outlined by those in authority. The overall feeling or reaction that should emerge during this life stage is pride in

FIGURE 9–1. School-age children are expected to begin mastering basic skills required for effective functioning in society, such as reading, writing, and calculation.

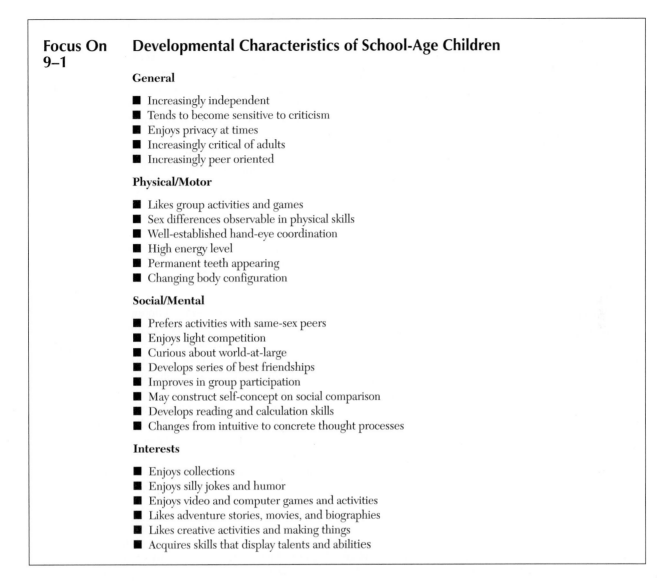

Focus On 9–1   **Developmental Characteristics of School-Age Children**

General

- Increasingly independent
- Tends to become sensitive to criticism
- Enjoys privacy at times
- Increasingly critical of adults
- Increasingly peer oriented

Physical/Motor

- Likes group activities and games
- Sex differences observable in physical skills
- Well-established hand-eye coordination
- High energy level
- Permanent teeth appearing
- Changing body configuration

Social/Mental

- Prefers activities with same-sex peers
- Enjoys light competition
- Curious about world-at-large
- Develops series of best friendships
- Improves in group participation
- May construct self-concept on social comparison
- Develops reading and calculation skills
- Changes from intuitive to concrete thought processes

Interests

- Enjoys collections
- Enjoys silly jokes and humor
- Enjoys video and computer games and activities
- Likes adventure stories, movies, and biographies
- Likes creative activities and making things
- Acquires skills that display talents and abilities

accomplishing a variety of skills and in demonstrating one's dependability in performing assigned tasks. Learning a basic American work ethic is accomplished in this manner as children learn that they are rewarded accordingly if assignments and tasks are performed satisfactorily in the eyes of parents, teachers, and other authority figures.

Entrance into the school environment signals changes and adjustments for the child, the parents, and the family system. An additional social group now takes on increasing importance in children's lives. This group is composed of other children, approximately the same age and with similar abilities, who become a child's peers. As a child progresses through this stage and through adolescence, the peer group assumes an increasingly significant role in facilitating a child's socialization process.

Throughout these years, the cultural expectations of parents and other adults in authority concerning how children should behave and what they should be learning combine with the maturation process to include new developmental objectives for school-age children. These objectives, which are largely social and mental, are communicated to children through their parents, the school environment, peer groups, and social programs in which they participate.

PARENTING SCHOOL-AGE CHILDREN

How Does Parenting Change?

The nature and style of parenting change when children reach the school-age years. The major source that motivates these changes is the different nature of a school-age child. The developmental tasks and milestones school-age children experience are entirely different from those experienced by preschoolers. They are more complex than those of infancy and early childhood and are more social and psychological than physical in nature. However, physical skills acquired in this period play a significant role in shaping children's self-concepts.

Parenting children in middle childhood, as in earlier stages, focuses on helping them accomplish their essential developmental tasks and milestones. Parents learn that they must respond to, or interact with, a school-age child differently than they did when the child was younger. Methods and parenting styles that were effective with preschoolers lose their high degree of effectiveness with school-age children. Children have new accomplishments and emerging abilities during middle childhood, and they may not permit parents to continue a response style or interaction pattern that was appropriate when they were younger. Parents essentially learn that they must now become psychological rather than physical helpers for their school-age children.

Parents begin training children for increased self-control in early childhood. This previous training results in a greater sharing of social power between parents and children during their school-age years. This sharing results in **coregulation** as a predominant parenting style. Parents of school-age children exercise general supervision while children gain in moment-to-moment self-regulation (Maccoby, 1984), and parents tend to exercise their power more typically when children misbehave in their presence.

Parents increasingly use psychological methods as a means of helping children achieve a higher level of self-control. These methods often consist of reassuring children, helping them to recover from social blunders, and giving positive reinforcement for efforts to learn new skills. The ratio or balance of assertive versus supportive care shifts during this time as parents expect these children to take more responsibility for their actions and decisions. School-age children continue to need their parents but in ways that are very different from preschoolers.

The expectations parents hold for school-age children change, which also reflects the shift to coregulation. For example, parents of school-age children expect them to: (1) gain more refined social skills that reflect an increasing ability to cooperate with adults and other children; (2) show more sophisticated information processing skills that are reflected in schoolwork; and (3) be able to begin assignments and tasks without being directed by an adult and complete them to a level of competence and satisfaction determined by an adult (Parenting FAQs 9–1).

Parenting FAQs 9–1

I need some help with a perennial issue I constantly hear from my 8-year-old. Every time he wants something new like a computer game or whatever, he backs up his reason with, "Everybody I know has it." I'm running out of patience with this. Any suggestions about I can help him to stop using this kind of reasoning?

A: When children this age are told that they can't have something that they want, this is usually the comment they will use to try to manipulate you into giving in. Children can learn to use guilt with parents just as they might have observed their parents doing so to get what they want from children. So, perhaps the first place for you to begin is for you to examine if this is a pattern you employ to manipulate your child, and, if so, begin using different ways to obtain their compliance. Next, no one likes to be denied something they desire, especially children. You can learn to disregard the additional comment that is manipulative. These situations are good opportunities to teach children about handling money and how to manage it. You can begin to give an allowance based on a child's contributions to household management tasks. Then, the next time he brings up wanting something, you can point out that this is what his allowance is for. You can also compromise by offering to share the expense with him. You can teach your child (and yourself) to avoid power struggles and manipulation to learn skills that will be useful in his adulthood.

Focus Point.   The nature of interaction changes between parents and children during this stage of the family life career. Essentially, parents adopt different and more specific interaction styles based on the authoritarian, permissive, and authoritative models. Parents also change from being primarily physical to being psychological helpers of school-age children. These changes are initiated in response to the developmental needs and nature of school-age children, which differ from those of preschool-age children.

Meeting the Needs of School-Age Children

Promoting Good Health Habits.   We are more aware today than in the past that the typical American diet is based on large amounts of saturated animal fat, high calories, and use of refined ingredients such as sugar and flour. This dietary lifestyle is associated with the high levels of coronary heart disease, hypertension and strokes, diabetes, and some cancers found in adulthood. Some evidence points to the beginnings of these conditions in middle childhood when children eat this type of diet (Center for Health and Health Care in Schools, 2005). Of major concern is the increasingly high incidence of type 2 diabetes among school-age children, obesity, and even undernutrition. Several factors complicate this situation: (1) Many school-age children do not have adequate physical activity and exercise daily; (2) many eat unhealthy diets; (3) many eat snacks that consist of "empty" calories; and (4) many arrive at school without having eaten breakfast.

Child obesity becomes more observable during this stage. There has been a steady increase in the number of school-age children and adolescents who are overweight for the past 30 years (Federal Interagency Forum on Child and Family Statistics, 2007). About 16% of school-age children were considered overweight in 2004 (Center for Health and Health Care in Schools, 2005). Boys and girls are similar in these rates of obesity. Ethnic group plays a role in this situation in that Hispanic boys and African American girls are at highest risk of being overweight.

Helping school-age children develop healthy eating habits and food preferences can be challenging for parents and other adults. Perhaps the best approach is to have healthy foods in the family's diet and adults modeling good eating habits for children. School-age children may not be immediately attracted to or satisfied by eating the proper kinds of vegetables and fruits without adult supervision and encouragement. By simply preparing meals at home that include these kinds of foods, parents help children learn these habits without being admonished that healthy foods are "good for you." Adults often mistakenly indicate that such foods aren't tasty, but "you have to eat them anyway." Or they attempt to develop good eating habits by bribing children (e.g., "Eat your spinach so you can have dessert"). When parents stock up on and serve healthy foods, they help children avoid empty calories. Many parents may need to resist pressure from children to purchase soda pop, potato chips, and sugary breakfast cereals.

School breakfast and lunch programs also can promote healthy nutrition and eating habits among children this age by offering healthy food choices through a la carte items and limiting availability of junk foods in vending machines (Center for Health and Health Care in Schools, 2005).

Recess time offers many opportunities for physical activity that can contribute to good health. In addition, physical education is required in almost all states at the elementary school level (Centers for Disease Control and Prevention, 2003). However, fewer than 40% of elementary-school-age children participated in organized physical activities, e.g., soccer, in 2002. Hispanic and African American children were significantly less likely to participate in such activities but were more likely to participate in free-time physical activities.

Health and Safety Concerns.   In addition to promoting good health via healthy eating habits and nutrition as well as physical activity, parents have other health and safety concerns for school-age children. Children entering this stage should have received the basic series of immunizations and vaccinations to prevent many infectious diseases. Many school districts in the United States require these in order for children to be enrolled in preschool programs and day-care facilities. They are also often required for enrollment in public school kindergarten programs.

Because permanent teeth now appear at the beginning of this period, dental care is important. Many children are first introduced to a dentist in early childhood, but this becomes more important in middle childhood. Dental professionals can assist parents in helping children learn the fundamentals of dental hygiene and how to prevent cavities.

Some illnesses are common to this period. Because many children are in close contact, it is likely that infectious diseases and other conditions are spread easily. Common colds and upper-respiratory diseases are frequently experienced (Bundy et al., 2006). Classic childhood infections that are to be expected include chickenpox, rubella, mumps, and conjunctivitis ("pink eye"). Other disorders may be experienced, such as "growing pains" caused by rapid growth spurts, causing painful joints and aching muscles, allergies, pinworms, head and body lice, and ringworm (fungus infections).

Accidents and injuries also become more common and affect different areas of a child's body than what was observed in early childhood. Because school-age children are more active physically and have a wider physical environment in which they play and participate, injuries commonly involve the head and the limbs (Tinsworth & McDonald, 2001). Accidental injury involving vehicles, falls, and bicycles are the leading cause of death among children this age (Miniño, Heron, Murphy, & Kochankek, 2007). Parents need to exercise considerable assertive care to prevent these kinds of accidents and injuries from occurring if possible. Proper supervision during play, use of passenger seatbeats, wearing helmets while biking, limiting boundaries where play is to take place, and teaching personal safety on the street and in the home, for example, are just a few ways that child safety can be promoted.

Providing Structure and Nurturance. Parents and other adults who work with school-age children recognize the value of children's experiences in earlier stages, which assist them in learning about structure. During middle childhood, adult caregivers are interested in helping children acquire even more refined abilities, as children are expected to become more skilled at internalizing their own structure. An appreciation for rules is a basic part of experiences that help school-age children internalize, or become more self-directed.

A focus on **nurturance** helps parents guard against the negative aspects of an exclusive emphasis on rules in experiences that teach structure. The nurturance of school-age children requires that parents and other caregivers be sensitive to children's developmental needs and emerging abilities at this time (J. I. Clarke & Dawson, 1998). Adapting parenting styles is a major challenge for many parents; they must shift to more responsive methods

than those established in a child's preschool years. This shift moves away from focusing attention, energy, and resources on providing physical care to providing psychological care that is supportive of school-age children. Table 9-1 outlines a guide to parental caregiving behaviors that may either facilitate or hinder effective experiences in providing structure and nurturance to school-age children.

Parenting school-age children focuses on reinforcing their efforts to attain appropriate developmental tasks. Parents often accomplish that goal when they shift their styles and interactions to psychological assistance and guidance of children. For example, psychological controls such as reasoning are more effective with 9-year-olds than with 3-year-olds. Taking privileges away is another method that some parents find useful, as compared with a less-useful method such as spanking.

Psychological guidance primarily consists of reassuring children, helping them to bounce back from social blunders with friends, and providing positive reinforcement for their efforts in acquiring new skills (Figure 9–2). The competitive nature of school-age children and the high degree to which they expect immediate results and success in almost every endeavor compels their need for secure and stable adults. These adults appear, from the child's perspective, to weather every imaginable adversity or difficulty.

Parenting Reflection 9–1

What are some examples of family rules that promote structure for school-age children? What are both positive and negative consequences of such rules?

Responding to a child's changing developmental demands in middle childhood means learning to lessen the more stringent controls imposed during early childhood. It means allowing the child to gain freedom to practice making decisions within safe limitations. In other words, parents learn that children desire and require increasing degrees of freedom during this time in their lives. The psychosocial focus of school-age children is facilitated when parents and other adults reinforce the greater desire for independence and provide opportunities for learning a sense of industry.

The increased involvement of children with peers, school activities, and activities outside the family system

TABLE 9–1   Behaviors of Parents of School-Age Children

Behaviors Providing Structure and Nurturance	Behaviors Not Providing Structure and Nurturance
• Showing approval for child's efforts to achieve developmental tasks • Showing approval for child's establishment of personal learning style • Providing generous amounts of positive reinforcement for acquiring learning skills • Acting as a reliable resource for child's questions about others, the world, and sexual matters • Helping child consider choices and options in his or her behavior; promoting cause-and-effect reasoning • Establishing and enforcing negotiable as well as nonnegotiable rules • Reminding child that he or she is loved and cared for even when child disagrees with parent • Taking responsibility for personal actions and encouraging child to do the same • Encouraging child to develop personal interests by providing instructional experiences from trained individuals who act as models and examples	• Enforcing rules inconsistently • Insisting on perfection from child in every respect • Expecting child to learn everything without proper instruction or assistance • Failing to provide child with adequate amounts of unstructured time to explore personal interests and learn the relevance of rules • Failing to allow child to experience periods of moodiness • Maintaining rules that are rigid and inflexible or failing to provide and enforce rules that govern behavior • Maintaining many nonnegotiable rules; failing to examine personal values; expecting child to provide for his or her own supervision • Discounting child

Source: Adapted from Clarke, J. I., & Dawson, C. (1989). *Growing up again: Parenting ourselves, parenting our children.* Minneapolis: Hazelden.

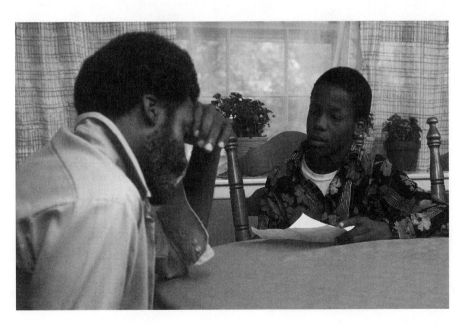

FIGURE 9–2. Parental nurturance involves increasing degrees of supportive care for school-age children while decreasing degrees of assertive care.

means more frequent periods of absence from the home. Parents may find it difficult to keep a stable and predictable schedule of routines in the home. Keeping children's schedules from becoming chaotic and allowing periods of unstructured personal time can be challenging for many parents.

Letting go of school-age children also means that parents need to accept the reality that they increasingly value peers and best friends as significant others in their lives. Letting go of children involves allowing them to take overnight trips to a friend's home and, in the later years of middle childhood, to go to overnight slumber parties or on camping trips with youth groups. Many children experience their first extended absence from their family system during summer camp sessions and visits with relatives.

Parenting Reflection 9–2

When parents want to promote a sense of industry for school-age children, is it more helpful to purchase kits that children can use for some specific arts-and-crafts activity or to supply children with a variety of materials and let them decide what they might wish to create with them?

Promoting Peer Relations.   Our culture is a composite of different subcultures, such as familiar racial, ethnic, and age groupings. Individuals have experiences with a number of subcultures throughout their life spans. During the middle years of childhood, children experience one of the first and most important subcultures: the childhood **peer group** (see Figure 9–3).

Peer groups are formed both spontaneously, as in a neighborhood playgroup, or when children are grouped by age when placed into elementary-school grades. In the early part of middle childhood, peer group functioning is less structured and group adherence is loose as compared with the latter part of this period. Children learn a number of social lessons from the group politics that take place within these groupings (Pellegrini, Kato, Blatchford, & Baines, 2002). Like other social systems, peer groups have their own rules, communication styles, and boundaries and show other functions found in systems theory (see Chapter 3). The social skills promoted and learned with peer groups include: (1) companionship, especially for play activities; (2) creating a testing ground for behavior, acceptable and otherwise; (3) transmitting information, accurate or inaccurate; (4) teaching rules and logical consequences, (5) promoting gender role development; and (6) influencing children's self-concepts.

FIGURE 9–3. Peer groups become an important social force that serves a number of functions among school-age children.

There are many sources that influence a child's self-concept development, which include past experiences, hypotheses a person generates about himself or herself, family members' input, and that of teachers as well. The feedback provided by a peer group, however, is seen by many school-age children to have the greatest degree of truth about themselves as compared to these other sources. This feedback can be largely negative at times due to the all-or-nothing thinking style of school-age children, but it does not reflect the true inner character of a child. The characteristic thinking style of middle childhood (discussed in the next section) can confound an accurate notion of the self. As school-age children grow older, they shift away from using absolutes to determine levels of accomplishment and rely more on **social comparison** processes based on how they fare in relation to other children their age. Often, the children that serve as comparison targets are considered to be less competent or successful, thereby protecting the self-image.

A healthy sense of self is promoted when children are helped to understand the extent of their personality traits, their collective strengths, and their weaknesses. A habit may be formed at this time in life when the feedback, especially the negative sort, may be overwhelming. By not knowing any different, it is only natural for school-age children to agree with the criticisms and negative input about themselves they hear from others their age. Some children this age can be very cruel in their comments and actions toward others they wish to discount. For some children, crafting a positive personal self-concept occurs when others are discounted and ridiculed (see Focus On 9–2). When this is discovered by parents and teachers, it is possible for the adults to help these children construct a realistic sense of self. Parents and teachers are important as interpreters of reality for children. A parent or teacher who can provide accurate interpretations of others' behavior and unkind words can counterbalance the negative impressions that children this age can draw about the accuracy of negative peer feedback. This healthy sense of self acknowledges strengths and weaknesses of one's character. School-age children learn that everyone is a mixture of these elements and that other people have feelings and emotions just as they do. They can be helped to understand that the negatives and weaknesses sometimes attributed to them by peers do not cancel out the positive aspects and strengths of their characters.

Focus On 9–2   What About Kids Who Are Bullies?

The recent incidences of school violence and killings in the United States have prompted parents, teachers, school systems, and communities to examine the issues that have contributed to these tragedies. Issues that have repeatedly emerged are the tendency of some children to become schoolyard bullies, the role of the school in preventing this type of maltreatment from occurring, and the long-term consequences of this kind of continued maltreatment.

Almost all children experience some form of bullying and teasing by another child during the elementary and junior high school years (Nation, 2007; Turkel, 2007). While there are some personal characteristics of victims that may invite bullying, for example, being passive, a loner, or crying easily, children without such characteristics can be mistreated by a bully.

Those children who bully others tend to be abused by parents, watch more television featuring violence, and generally misbehave both at home and school (Olweus, 1995). They feel little remorse for their abusive actions and frequently lie to get around punishment.

Bullying, then, is a very real problem of everyday life for many school-age children and perhaps has long-term consequences (Roberge, 2007). This problem behavior will not go away on its own, however. Schools can become bully-proofed, wherein children who are victimized can be taught how to defend themselves, for example, learning how to defuse situations that could lead to victimization, to leave situations where bullying can occur, and increasing their tolerance levels to taunts (Nation, 2007). In addition, schools can implement zero-tolerance policies that make bullying behavior intolerable. Schools may be held accountable increasingly for failing to help curb this type of abusiveness of children by other children.

Parents and teachers are aware that some children will not fit easily or readily into peer groups and can sometimes be rejected by other children. When this occurs, adults often seek an explanation about why other children view the rejected child in negative terms (Rys & Bear, 1997). For example, children who are seen as unpopular by other children may be viewed as hostile and overly aggressive, immature, impulsive, different in appearances, or insensitive to others (P/K/Smith, Smees, Pellegrini, & Menesini, 2002). Adults should be concerned when children have experiences with rejection since these may contribute significantly to a negative self-image, conflicts with other children, and impaired social development at later stages in the life span. Adults can arrange occasions for supervised play with other children so that children can learn social skills that lead to more positive peer experiences.

● ●

Parenting Reflection 9–3

What are some things you could do as a parent or teacher to bully-proof a child who is being picked on constantly by another child? What would you do to help the child who is the bully?

● ●

Promoting Cognitive Skills. Psychologist Jean Piaget (1967) referred to cognitive development during middle childhood as the period of **concrete operations**. By the time children reach their school-age years, they can understand and use certain principles or relationships between events and things. In using and comprehending these relationships, children operate with objects, symbols, and concepts. They are increasingly able to internalize the environment by using symbolic thought. They learn to add and subtract, classify and order, apply elementary rules of logic to reach conclusions, and apply rules in governing their behavioral choices. They begin to understand the functioning of systems in which they participate by learning that certain operations produce certain results. They are now able to use imagery to perform certain actions mentally that had to be performed physically in the past. Declining egocentrism helps to promote these changes in mental processing.

Certain characteristics are typical of concrete operational thought:

■ *Classification* improves as children become increasingly adept at employing a mental skill known as *decentering*. This means that school-age children can attend to several attributes or details of a task simultaneously. This may explain why children this age are attracted to forming collections of objects and things such as dolls, race cars, model airplanes, buttons, and so on.

■ Grasping the concept of *reversibility* allows a child to understand operations such as addition and subtraction. School-age children learn that subtraction is the reverse operation of addition. Science lessons also incorporate this concept as when sunlight is split into its color components by use of a prism and then reversed back into sunlight again.

■ *Conservation* problems become better understood during this period. Their solution of these problems is not confounded by their perceptions, as is the case with preschool-age children. While they may be able to master conservation of volume problems, this ability does not easily transfer to solution of other kinds of conservation problems such as those involving weight or number. Additional experience with use of mental imagery helps children to grow in this respect.

■ *Seriation* is an extension of classification problems where school-age children become able to scale objects according to the concepts of greater than ($>$) and less than ($<$) Doll B, which is taller than ($>$) Doll C.

■ *Understanding time* is important in our culture and has bearing on much daily behavior. School-age children become capable of telling time by reading a clock piece, knowing the days of the week as well as the month and the year. They become more knowledgeable of what constitutes the past as well as the future. An increased ability to understand cause-and-effect relationships helps these children to be able to predict what day will occur 3 days from now, for example.

Certain limitations occur, however, in the logical processes involved in this period. Just as thinking in early childhood is limited by egocentrism, thinking in middle childhood is limited by cognitive distortions in reasoning. One major limitation is known as all-or-nothing or black-and-white thinking or **cognitive conceit** (Elkind, 1976). In such problems with reasoning, a school-age child may reach a conclusion that there is one and only one right answer to a problem or situation. For example, school-age children eventually observe a teacher making a mistake. Because of cognitive conceit, they incorrectly conclude that the teacher cannot be trusted to provide correct information because of this one mistake. If a teacher is not always right, they reason, she must be frequently wrong. Similarly, if a child reasons that since she can consistently give correct answers on several issues or topics, she is, therefore, an authority on all. This is a type of cognitive distortion that may continue throughout someone's life span, or it may become resolved at a later stage in life (Burns, 1999).

School-age children increasingly use mental skills as part of their daily lives, much of which involves school activities. Parents and other adults play an important role in facilitating a school-age child's cognitive development in several ways. For example, children at this time are making use of a large database of information they acquired earlier in the preschool years. They are attempting to expand this database and make greater sense of their world. Adults hold more challenging expectations of them than of preschoolers. As a result, it is often easy to expect things of school-age children that are beyond their capabilities at this time. By understanding that school-age children still are not able to think logically all the time and are learning the basics of such thinking, parents can customize the

ways they provide structure and nurturance at an appropriate developmental level. By understanding that school-age children see the world differently than adults, parents will not expect understanding beyond their child's ability.

Helping Children Adjust to School.   Entrance into the school system is a significant event that influences a number of social and cognitive changes in middle childhood. For example, in this setting a school-age child is introduced to peers, often for the first time. The child is also exposed to other adults in authority, such as teachers and youth-group leaders, who assist in the child's growth process. New expectations for behavior change yearly as children progress through the school system (Figure 9–4).

Although the education of children was once the responsibility of a family system, it is now institutionalized in other agencies in the United States. The school system has gained in significance as our culture has become more technologically oriented. Children in middle childhood are expected to become proficient in basic skills, such as reading, writing, and calculation. They are also expected to learn many facts and information about the world. Parents expect that children will succeed in their learning experiences if they are assigned to properly trained teachers. Teachers are also expected to

FIGURE 9–4.   The school environment acts as an important source of socialization for school-age children.

conduct effective educational programs that equip children with basic skills.

Some parents assume that once children become a part of their school environment, they need to relinquish more responsibility to teachers to help children achieve academic success. However, many teachers feel that they cannot be expected to assume the degree of responsibility that supports children's academic success. Perhaps the best arrangement in this regard is teaming the efforts of both parents and teachers to help children to be academically successful (Bickart & Jablon, 2004). When researchers study how to motivate parental involvement in children's homework, they have found that parents are more involved when they are prompted both by children and the school to provide assistance with assignments. However, parental involvement has little effect in improving children's academic performance. The researchers point out, though, that other positive outcomes could result from greater parental involvement in children's homework, such as being more aware of what was going on with their children at school.

Parents can do more to assist a child's educational achievement in addition to being involved with their school (Hill & Taylor, 2004). For example, it is important to provide the structure necessary to give order to a child's day by observing schedules for going to bed on time in order to be rested for school, limiting television or computer game time, and providing regular mealtimes. Giving a child his or her own space for quiet study and schoolwork is also important. Talking with a child about his or her school and after-school activities, what kind of play takes place with friends, and what projects he or she is working on also provides support.

The type of parenting style employed with children this age, in general, also contributes to school success (Ginsburg & Bronstein, 1993). Children who show academic achievement and success are more likely to have parents who use an authoritative approach. These children are likely to be independently motivated to learn and perform well in school. Children who show underachievement and difficulty with success in school are likely to have parents who use either an authoritarian or permissive approach to child rearing. Children in authoritarian homes are likely to depend on extrinsic motivation (from parents) to perform academically while parents in permissive homes do not appear to care how children fared in school.

Parenting Reflection 9–4

Beyond the basics, what are some topics that elementary schools should and should not teach children?

Focus Point. School-age children are challenged by a variety of developmental tasks that focus on complex social, mental, and physical skills that lead to increased maturity. Social development in middle childhood relates to adjusting to the school environment, establishing relations with peers, and experiencing refinements in self-concept. New mental skills reflect refinements in cognition, allowing a child to learn reading, writing, and calculation. Parents play an important role in promoting children's academic performance and success.

Teaching About Sexuality. Children's education about sexuality continues to take place during middle childhood. Schools now play an important role in working with parents to help children grow up with healthy attitudes about sex and sexual matters. Many school systems in the United States provide units on sex education, beginning in kindergarten and continuing throughout the elementary grades. Often these units are presented in conjunction with input provided by parents who serve on school district advisory committees. Most parents apparently wish to have some assistance in helping children learn about sexuality and welcome the professional abilities of trained teachers to introduce the topic to school-age children.

School-age children continue to ask occasional questions about their bodies and sexual matters that deserve honest answers from parents. In this situation, parents may act as interpreters and narrators of family values for their children. Some parents fear that school systems replace them in this role by providing children with formal educational experiences about sexuality. However, most teachers prefer that parents take an even more active role in teaching children about such matters (McElderry & Omar, 2003).

Parents have an important responsibility in preparing older school-age children for the approaching physical and psychological changes related to puberty. Beginning when children are about age 9, most parents can initiate discussions about this approaching developmental event. Opportunities for discussion are important because preteens are more likely to listen to parents' views on topics relating to sexuality than are children who have already entered adolescence. For example, it is important that girls be prepared for menstruation and that boys understand about nocturnal emissions. Both boys and girls are also interested in their anatomy and desire more detailed information about the functioning of the reproductive system than do preschool-age children. Many excellent resources are available to assist parents in becoming more knowledgeable about sexual issues and preparing children for puberty.

Computers and the Internet. It's an inescapable reality that children today need to become computer literate to prepare for their future. The Information Age that was predicted in the 1970s has definitely arrived. The use of computers has become commonplace in homes, schools, and workplaces and the vastness of the Internet has grown beyond all expectations. It is likely that computers will have an even larger place in our society in the future.

The use of the Internet and home computers can augment what children are learning in school and how the school is using these as instructional tools. School-age children should be able to use computer software for writing reports, researching topics, and playing educational games. Some children may even desire to learn how to write software and develop the skills necessary for developing Web sites.

Most adults are aware now that children need supervision when using computers to cruise the Internet. Parents need to learn about software filters that protect children from sites containing pornography and chat rooms that can draw people who want to exploit children. Forbidding access to computers and the Internet because of inherent risks is not in the best interests of children. Rather, parents need to understand that children should learn to negotiate this arena safely. To be computer illiterate can place children at a distinct disadvantage in their present and future.

Parents should develop rules and regulations that outline how much time a child is allowed to use the computer and the Internet and that specify behavior while using the Internet. For example, children should be taught never to give out personal information to anyone or any Web site. They should know how to deal with accidental viewing of unacceptable material and how to observe rules of Netiquette and controlled supervised use of instant messaging services. If rules are not observed, parents may need to investigate installing hardware and software that limit time use by children. A contract is available for parents to use with children in regulating Internet and computer use (e.g., see http://www.komando.com). Some children can be determined to work around rules, regulations, and limitations that parents have placed to prevent them from being exposed to the Internet's more unsavory elements. In this event, parents might wish to consult Web sites for helpful assistance in fine-tuning methods to protect children.

NORMAL BEHAVIOR PROBLEMS OF MIDDLE CHILDHOOD

The types of behavior problems observed in school-age children reflect the difficulties they experience in adjusting to the challenges of developmental tasks; therefore, these problems are considered to be age specific. Some, but not all, involve conflicts between parents and children regarding expectations the adults hold about appropriate standards of behavior. Others may be negative, attention-getting behaviors. Some problems, such as learning disorders, are diverse in their origins and can involve inherent developmental difficulties. Several types of commonly observed behavior problems are discussed here briefly. They include noncompliance, antisocial behaviors, and learning disorders.

Noncompliance

One of the most common complaints of parents is that school-age children fail to comply and cooperate with parent requests and disobey rules established by the family system. This issue, which begins to appear when children are preschool age, can escalate during middle childhood into a full-blown power struggle between adults and children.

Children at this age tend to test the limits of adults' patience, particularly if they are asked to do something they do not want to do. Standard replies to parental requests include, "In a minute, Mom," or "Just let me finish what I'm doing, OK, Dad?" Parents are adapting their expectations for children; instead of asking a child simply to get involved in an activity or chore, they insist that tasks be completed satisfactorily. Some adults may believe that a child needs only one prompting to perform the task before the consequences of the family task completion rule are enforced. But initially, most parents are patient, understanding that children must adjust as they learn the mechanics and limits of family expectations.

There comes a time, however, when parents know that their school-age child should be complying with rules and policies without great resistance or hesitation. Some of the most frequently prescribed methods of prompting children's compliance involve the use of behavior modification techniques. One technique teaches parents how to phrase their requests in ways that communicate exactly what is expected of children in keeping with family rules and policies. Essentially, parents are taught how to give clear, concise directions so that school-age children can understand parental expectations. Parents are told to give a child at least 5 seconds to comply and to provide positive consequences or rewards for their appropriate, cooperative behavior.

Another method stresses the use of positive social reinforcement by using what is called *time-out*, or separating a child from an activity to be alone for a specified period of time. Although rewards, such as hugging, tend to promote the appearance of compliant behavior, the use of time-out becomes associated in the child's mind with being noncompliant.

Antisocial Behaviors

Antisocial behaviors promote ill will between others, interfere with effective communications and interactions, constitute negative ways of getting attention, and serve as a means of expressing anger and hostility or of coping with frustration and anxiety (Paul, 2000). Although some of these behaviors begin appearing in the latter part of early childhood, a number are observed more typically during middle childhood. They reflect problems in adjusting to the demands of developmental tasks during these years and can act as a challenge to effective, healthy functioning. Several are observed more commonly than others during middle childhood, and they cause particular concern among adult caregivers. These behaviors include lying and stealing.

Lying. Lying refers to the deliberate falsification of information with the specific intent to deceive the listener (American Psychiatric Association, 2000). Although young children are often unable to separate fantasy from reality, the ability to understand what is true and what is not follows a child's level of moral and cognitive development. Typically, most children come to understand the importance of truthfulness in their interactions with others at about age 6 or 7.

Parents can assist children with problem lying in several ways. First, it is helpful for a parent to evaluate his or her own behavior and actions so that children do not learn from the model the parent presents. For example, parental honesty helps children learn how to be trusting and how to generate others' trust in their own integrity. Second, when parents observe children lying, they should tell the children that lying is unacceptable behavior and will jeopardize their effective interactions with others. School-age children can be helped to understand how the consequences of such behavior relate to the nature and degree of their personal integrity. In such instances, reading the Aesop's children fable "The Boy Who Cried Wolf" may be an effective instructional method for helping them understand the importance of truthfulness. Third, quizzing children about their misbehavior often promotes defensive lying. Parents can avoid this approach by informing a child that they are aware of his or her misbehavior. Discussions can proceed from this point in a straightforward manner to resolve the problem behavior. Fourth, parents should try to determine the causes that underlie a child's lying behavior (Spock, 2004).

Stealing. Stealing occurs more commonly among school-age children than most people imagine. Although many parents feel that stealing is an innocuous behavior in early childhood, it becomes a matter of concern among parents of school-age children and adolescents.

Children steal for a variety of reasons: (1) They may lack training in a sense of personal property rights; (2) they may be trying to bribe friends, perhaps to avoid being teased or to gain their approval; (3) stealing may occur as a means of coping with feelings of inferiority or of being different from others in some manner; (4) they may steal simply because they cannot resist the temptation to have something they want very much; and (5) they may steal to express revenge against parents or as a means of gaining their attention.

The problem of stealing is handled first by informing children of the unacceptability of this behavior. Parents and other adults should deal fairly and honestly with instances of stealing. They may review their own behavior and reveal instances in which they have modeled dishonesty to children. Then parents can consciously work to avoid having their own actions contribute to the problem behavior of their child. Scrupulous attention to the details of property rights is important as well; parents should explain the difference between a child's property and that of others. It may be helpful to give children allowances if they are not receiving them. Allowances can help them learn the work ethic of their family system, which may be associated with financial rewards. Removing temptation from children or reducing it by keeping money put away or protected may also be helpful.

Learning Disorders

Learning disorders that affect poor school achievement are frequently observed in association with other types of behavior problems in middle childhood (American Psychiatric Association, 2000). Children with behavior problems also tend to demonstrate other types of maladaptive patterns during this period.

Five basic conditions are classified as learning disorders (American Psychiatric Association, 2000); several are discussed here. They interfere with an ability to process information correctly to facilitate learning and formal instruction. Researchers generally understand that learning disorders involve a complex variety of different but related conditions and factors that hamper the ability of a child to learn and progress in school. The complexity of the situation becomes compounded by the effects observed in other types of troublesome behaviors that relate to a child's inability to learn and perform adequately in the school environment. (1) *Ability deficits* may account for many of the problems school-age children experience with school performance. (2) Many professionals attribute learning problems to children's *emotional disorders*, such as anxiety, depression, and unhealthy self-esteem. (3) *Biological factors* can account for learning problems that stem from prenatal or postnatal exposure to harmful substances, such as maternal intake of alcohol or cocaine, deprivation of oxygen, accidents involving the central nervous system, infections, and inadequate protein intake. (4) *Ecological factors* contribute to learning disorders when, for example, labeling a child as troublesome or as a slow learner negatively influences his or her behavior and learning skills. (5) Children may lack *adequate knowledge* of how to learn, which may also contribute to such problems.

Attention Deficit Disorder (ADD). Attention Deficit Disorder (ADD) has recently received a significant amount of study by behavioral and medical researchers. This condition is the most commonly diagnosed behavior disorder in childhood and is believed to have strong neurobiological and genetic bases (Satyen, 2003). Some studies identify biological factors that influence its occurrence, such as the use of alcohol during pregnancy, while others identify tendencies that are due in part to genetic disturbances transmitted in some families.

Children who are diagnosed with this learning disorder have been found to be at high risk of failure in their educational experiences (American Psychiatric Association, 2000). They are unable to concentrate for long periods of time, are often hyperactive, and have difficulty processing information. The disruptive effects of these children within classrooms also interfere with the ability of other children to participate in learning experiences. Children with this disorder are found to have average or higher-than-average intelligence.

Families, especially the parents of children with ADD, are challenged with dealing with the extreme exasperation and frustrations of the condition and how it affects everyone. Children with ADD can be in constant motion from the time they awake in the morning until the time they finally go to sleep at night. They have difficulty following directions, appear to constantly forget rules and parental admonitions, and generally are a handful for parents and teachers. It is not unusual for many parents to blame themselves for how their children with ADD behave, because the children essentially appear to be out of control. The fact is that children with ADD cannot control their actions, but parents are not responsible for their children's behavior. Most adults respond to the diagnosis of ADD with relief that the problem finally has a label and that they are not at fault.

Although the ramifications of this disorder are discouraging for children and parents, the condition is responsive to a variety of treatments (Paul, 2000). For example, drugs such as Ritalin may produce a calming effect on a child's behavior. Behavior modification techniques may be used in training children to increase their attention when performing tasks. Family therapy may be helpful in assisting a family system to deal with the crises associated with a child whose behavior has an extremely disruptive effect on family functioning. When parents and children consult with therapists who are trained in working with children with this disorder and their families, significant progress can often be expected in helping everyone involved cope with the great stress associated with ADD (Weingartner, 1999). Parents can also obtain information and support from the National Resource Center on ADHD (http://www.help4adhd.org/). Many other Web sites also provide information.

Specific Reading Disability. Reading difficulties can be associated with a number of causes, but **dyslexia** is a primary culprit in causing many reading problems. This condition ranges from mild to severe in its effects on reading and information processing. It is most frequently associated with perceptual problems in dealing with word comprehension and in processing information into forms the brain recognizes. Specifically, dyslexia is associated with the following difficulties or combinations of these problems: (1) an inability to perceive the significance of the relation of one written symbol to another, (2) failure to correlate written and spoken words and to synthesize them into meaningful words, and (3) difficulties in perceiving the meaning of words or groups of words.

Some children tend to reverse the order of letters in certain words; they perceive *was* as *saw* and *dog* as *god*. Other children confuse a letter with its mirror image: *p* as *d* or *b* as *d*. Typically, children who have reading problems are thought to have average or higher-than-average intelligence before entering school. They fail to learn to read during their first 2 years of school, and the problem may become compounded but undetected for the next several years of elementary school. This is because children learn to memorize and develop other schemes that mask their inability to read adequately. Children who experience dyslexia or another reading disability recognize that their inability to read adequately places them at a disadvantage in comparison with peers who do not have this problem (Kim, 2004). As a result, they experience feelings of deep shame and guilt about something over which they have little control. Their self-concept and self-esteem are harmed by such feelings. Parents and teachers may not recognize the problem until a child is well into the intermediate levels of elementary education.

In the primary grades of elementary school, children with reading problems usually make their best grades in mathematics. In the intermediate elementary and later grades of junior high school, however, they begin having trouble calculating figures (Kim, 2004).

Intervention strategies are frequently tailored to the specific needs of a child with a learning disorder. Once a trained specialist has diagnosed the problem, treatment can begin in the form of specialized educational experiences or placement into a special educational environment. Current awareness of learning problems is particularly acute among most well-trained educators. Children who have such problems are usually identified and assisted early so that more serious problems may be prevented from interfering with later experiences in school (Hallahan & Kauffman, 2004).

Parents may find a number of resources useful in learning about these disorders and appropriate treatment. Local libraries and bookstores usually hold a variety of text titles on this topic. In addition, Web sites are also useful in beginning the search for information (e.g., Learning Disabilities Association of America, http://www.ldaamerica.org/). Ultimately, however, children will need professional screening to determine the type, nature, and extent of a learning problem before any particular method of treatment can be considered. Medical and educational specialists can provide referrals to appropriate professionals for treatment.

••

Focus Point. Many problems of school-age children's behavior relate to difficulties in achieving the developmental tasks of this period. Others relate more specifically to interaction difficulties with parents and peers. Some are more specific to learning disorders that are discovered through experiences in the classroom. A variety of methods may be helpful in dealing with these problems.

••

PARENTING CHILDREN WITH SPECIAL NEEDS

Our society has only recently begun to understand and recognize that some children, often because of circumstances beyond their control, have unique needs. These needs relate to a group of disabilities that involve problems in seeing, hearing, walking, talking, climbing, or lifting or in providing self-care tasks known as **activities of daily living (ADLs)** (Hildebrand et al., 2008). These needs create unusual demands on family systems and parents. In some situations, children have unique developmental difficulties and problems that label them as **exceptional**. In this regard, the term refers to individuals who are different in some manner from the large majority of others their age. Other children have special needs because of chronic, life-threatening illnesses, such as AIDS, diabetes, or cancer.

In the past, little support was available in most communities for assisting these individuals and their families in meeting their special needs. For some children, negative community attitudes and labels served as forms of discrimination that prevented access to the life experiences and community services available to those with normal developmental abilities. In many respects, early efforts to provide services for individuals and families with special needs could be called *segregated services*, since these were provided under separate support when children were isolated from others (Hildebrand et al., 2008). Negative social stigma is still evident in many cases, particularly for those individuals with chronic illnesses, such as AIDS.

Community-based programs for assisting these individuals and their families have been developed only recently. Generally, the field of special education, which serves those individuals who need such services in their hometowns, has emerged only within the last 30 years. Certainly, a variety of legislative acts at state and federal levels have assisted in bringing about the widespread availability of such services at the community level.

Characteristics of Children with Special Needs

The definition of exceptional children, or those with special needs, was formerly restricted to those with emotional, developmental, or mental difficulties that placed them at a disadvantage in comparison with others or that incapacitated them in their ability to function within the larger society. More recently, however, the meaning of exceptionality has broadened to include those groups of individuals with learning disabilities and other handicaps, as well as those with chronic and terminal illness (Rigazio-DiGilio & Cramer-Benjamin, 2000). Children with special needs in the student population of the United States are generally about 13% of the population. In general, males outnumber females who have special needs. For example, Attention Deficit Hyperactivity Disorder (ADHD), formerly included as a learning disability, stands on its own as a separate and distinct condition requiring special needs attention. The

classification scheme is so broad that intellectually gifted children also have been termed exceptional because these individuals and their needs are often misunderstood by others in their community. The process of including a child in any of these categories often involves extensive, comprehensive evaluations by a variety of medical, psychological, and educational professionals.

Family Reactions

Unless there has been some indication prior to birth that a child is likely to have a developmental disorder, parents and other family members usually have little preparation for accommodating a child with special needs. Parents experience a limitless variety of reactions to having a child who has special needs. These reactions may vary according to the nature of the exceptionality, the degree of impairment, the socioeconomic status of the family system, the availability of professional assistance, the financial resources available to supply the assistance, and the presence of unimpaired children in the family (Leyden, 2002). Parents can be expected to experience a grief and mourning process in reaction to the confirmation of a child's disability. The discovery that a child has special needs essentially represents a loss for most parents, in particular, the loss of a future of normal developmental progress for the affected child (Osborn, 2004).

In many respects, the news serves as a crisis or as a stressor event for a family system, and additional reactions follow for most families. The family as a system must adjust to this newly recognized status of the affected child and begin to search for the numerous ways and means to meet the child's particular needs and those of family members. This process can take months, even years, as the family strives to accept and reconcile their unique situation in comparison with other families. Ways must be found to include the child into the family's routines and patterns. Parents, especially, must learn ways to strengthen their committed relationship and find ways to meet the needs of other children in the family. Those family systems that use the crisis and stresses of this situation to their advantage are likely to become stronger by developing healthy coping strategies that may also be applied in other future family crises. On the other hand, those families that acquire unhealthy coping strategies experience even higher levels of stressfulness and greater levels of family disorganization. Ultimately, some will dissolve as the result of the chronic strains experienced under such circumstances.

Generally, many parents experience a process in adjusting to having a child with special needs by which they attain acceptance of the situation although others may experience ambivalence and even rejection of the child. For many, it is difficult to overcome the tendency to personalize this unfortunate circumstance. In some respects, mothers may react differently from fathers when it becomes known that their child is exceptionally different from others.

Parental attitudes about an exceptional child and the circumstances involved in having this child as a family member influence the nature and quality of caregiving (Ripley, 2003). Mothers tend to become the family member assuming the greatest amount of caretaking and nurturing for a child with special needs. However, because fathers and other male family members are expected to be more actively involved in child care today, it is not unusual to see levels of family stress diminish and come more under control when this occurs.

The siblings of a child with special needs are also affected by the child's presence (Meyer, 2003). It is possible to observe the interrelatedness concept found in family systems theory. Having a sibling with special needs brings some benefits to other children, such as learning empathic skills, gaining in tolerance and compassion for those who are seriously different from others, and developing a greater appreciation of personal health status. On the other hand, siblings often report negative effects such as feelings of jealousy because of lack of parental attention, resenting the affected sibling's presence in the family, or shamefulness and guilt about the affected sibling. Parents should be mindful of the possibilities of these negative reactions. In addition, girls often complain that brothers aren't expected to assume surrogate parent or caregiver roles to a similar extent. By equalizing these responsibilities between male and female siblings, the psychological risks—to girls, especially—may be minimized.

Cultural backgrounds of families also influence their reactions to an exceptional child. Cultural beliefs color differences in what it means to have a child with special needs as a family member. For example, in an Anglo-European family, a child's disabilities are described and understood in medical and scientific terms; in Native American families, the child's disability is placed on spiritual intrusion or the breaking of cultural taboos. Other cultures may attribute the situation to bad luck, an evil influence on a family, or punishment for ancestral sins (Rigazio-DiGilio & Cramer-Benjamin, 2000).

Chronic stress is one of the most frequently observed family reactions to having a child with special needs (Krauss, 2000). Family members can learn healthy coping strategies such as attending support groups, journaling, participating in individual and family therapy, tapping into spiritual resources, and sharing caretaking responsibilities, for example. Networking with other families experiencing similar circumstances is also a helpful source of coping with stress. Unhealthy coping also may manifest in some families when the child with exceptional needs is scapegoated, abused, and emotionally mistreated.

Supports for Families with Exceptional Children

Families with a child with special needs tend to be smaller than average in size and to have lower incomes than the general population (U.S. Bureau of the Census, 2006). Because of their unique circumstances, these families typically make use of more community services and resources in gaining assistance for their child. Several sources provide infrastructural support for these families.

Federal Legislation. Federal legislation has helped to address the needs of exceptional children and their families. Public Law 94–142, first enacted in 1975, is based on two assumptions: (1) that all children with special needs have a rightful and appropriate place in the public school system, and (2) that all parents have an important role in the education of their children with special needs. Essentially, the law gives parents the right to monitor and judge the appropriateness of the educational experiences their children with special needs receive. The law provides for appointing a surrogate parent for children who are without parents and for funding for special education programs. The law requires that each child with special needs enrolled in public school systems be provided with an individualized educational program (IEP) developed by an education specialist working in conjunction with the child's parent(s). An IEP must be written, tailored to meet the child's specific needs, and signed by the child's parent(s). It must include a statement of present level of educational performance at the time of initial implementation, a list of goals and objectives, and specific educational services and support to be provided. It must also include plans for the child's participation in the classroom, length of institutionalization (if applicable), and the way goals and objectives will be evaluated at the completion of the plan. Although IEPs are controversial, their value may be shown by the attention now given to meeting the needs of children and their parents along with the more intense involvement of parents in children's educational experiences.

Public Law 99–457, enacted in 1986, has also influenced the assistance provided to families with exceptional children. It requires states to establish comprehensive multidisciplinary approaches to provide early intervention to infants and toddlers with special needs. It extends the ages of children being served from birth through age 25, emphasizing a focus for services during the prekindergarten years. This law requires that individualized family service plans (IFSP) be provided to children with special needs. An IFSP is written for each child between birth and age 3 by a multidisciplinary group of professionals and the parents. It includes the following: (1) an assessment of the child's present level of functioning and developmental status; (2) a statement of the family's strengths and needs in facilitating the child's developmental progress; (3) a list of goals and objectives for the child's progress; (4) the means by which the child is expected to achieve these goals and objectives or the experiences that will promote their accomplishment; (5) the means by which the child will be transitioned from early intervention experiences into a preschool program; (6) the time frame during which these will be provided; and (7) the name of the child's case manager.

In 1991, another federal law, Public Law 102–52, provided states with an additional 2 years to develop systems to serve eligible children with special needs. Public Law 102–119, also enacted in 1991, reaffirmed the early-intervention approach to the 1975 Education of the Handicapped Act and strengthened the involvement of families in the educational process of children with special needs.

Taken together, all these laws comprise the Individuals with Disabilities Education Act (IDEA; Turnbull & Cilley, 1999). In complying with this legislation, states have established an Interagency Coordinating Council that oversees the delivery of early intervention services to families and children with special needs. Families are protected from having to advocate individually for their children with special needs, as each state is required to provide a state education representative. This person has sufficient authority to actively provide policy planning and implementation for children with special needs and their families.

The IDEA has not sailed through Congress without hitches. There have been disagreements about providing for the costs of these services to individuals and families and resistance to policies relating to disciplining children with special needs at school. President Clinton was finally able to sign the legislation authorizing the IDEA in 1997. In its finalized form, this legislation: (1) reduces incentives to segregate students with special needs, (2) increases federal funding for services, (3) increases the involvement of teachers and parents in developing IEPs for children, (4) generally increases the flexibility of states to provide services, (5) affirms the importance of classroom discipline for all students, and (6) enhances the provision of services to infants and toddlers.

The Elementary and Secondary Education Act of 2001 (also known as the No Child Left Behind Act) contains provisions that address the needs of exceptional children in supplementing other legislation. This legislation, considered controversial by some observers (see http://www.nea.org/esea/), allows school districts to provide programming that may increase parental involvement, reallocate financial resources to provide research-based curricula, and heighten accountability of instruction. This law also permits children with disabilities to become classified as having cognitive disabilities, which qualifies special education classrooms and programs for financial assistance.

Community Services. The kinds of services needed to assist exceptional children and their families often depend on the age and specific problems of the child. Some problems become evident long before a child enters the public school system. In some instances, these problems are noticed at birth or when expected developmental progress fails to occur within the months or years after birth. It is also not unusual for problems to be discovered through special screening activities that regularly occur in many communities. When infants and young children are seen on a regular basis by a physician or health care professional, the doctor or nurse may discover and evaluate the child's current or future developmental problems. Early detection is crucial because treatment and therapy can often alleviate many potential difficulties if begun soon in a child's development. Available community services for parents of infants and young children with special needs include day-care centers, hospital programs, public school programs, Head Start programs, and programs offered through colleges and universities.

Respite care is a community service for families and disabled individuals. This service provides temporary relief for developmentally disabled individuals who live at home and also acts as an important element in preventing their institutionalization. This supervisory service assists families in coping with emergency situations that require the absence of primary caregivers and also provides relief from the daily stresses involved in caring for a disabled family member.

Educational Programs. School-age exceptional children are included to the maximum extent possible in existing public school programs, a practice known as **mainstreaming,** or, more recently, **inclusion** (Leyden, 2002). These programs are supplemented by special education classes. Because all children do not profit from this educational arrangement, some may be placed exclusively in special education classes. School districts offer a variety of programs and services for exceptional children, which often change as the needs of the children change (Ripley, 2003). These services may include the following:

- *Regular classroom experiences,* in which the child receives special attention and an individualized program
- *Resource room experiences,* in which the child is enrolled in a regular classroom but goes to a specially equipped room to receive part of the daily instruction
- *Consulting teacher experiences,* in which the child's instruction by a regular teacher is supplemented by a special education teacher
- *Day school,* in which special educational programs are conducted in a separate room or building (for cases in which the child's needs cannot be met by including him or her in a regular classroom program)
- *Residential schools,* which provide education and other treatment experiences that cannot be provided through any other means (usually reserved for those children who are visually or hearing impaired, severely mentally retarded, emotionally disturbed, or severely physically handicapped)
- *Hospital or homebound programs,* which serve the needs of a child who must be confined to bed or experience a lengthy convalescent period as the result of some type of disability

Parents and family systems are especially concerned that children with special needs be provided with appropriate environments (Rigazio-DiGilio & Cramer-Benjamin, 2000). However, they typically experience mixed feelings about this issue. For example, children with special needs are protected and supported when they are placed in special education environments but miss out on important stimulation and interaction experiences because they are segregated from other students. When inclusion all but eliminates the unique attention these children require, they tend to suffer from not receiving such specialized services. The decisions about where and how to provide services for children involve complex issues. Complicating these decisions is the lack of training and experience that creates antipathy among mainstreaming teachers toward students with special needs (Ripley, 2003).

Other Services. In addition to involving parents in the educational experiences of exceptional children, some kinds of support help the adults and other children in the family system. These families often need professional counseling, and several helpful strategies have been developed for these family members. Three methods are usually applied in these situations (Rigazio-DiGilio & Cramer-Benjamin, 2000):

1. *Informational counseling* occurs when children are first diagnosed and parents are informed of test results, prognosis, and treatment approaches.
2. *Psychotherapeutic methods,* most prominently behavior modification and reflective counseling, are taught to parents and siblings, who use the methods in working with the exceptional child or sibling. Pediatric psychotherapy is offered to the affected child in dealing with emotional and behavioral problems.
3. *Group therapy approaches* place a number of parents or siblings into a support network in which individuals share feelings, reactions, and experiences to help each other cope with the stresses in their family systems.

* * *

Focus Point. Parents of children with special needs deal with issues in child rearing not usually confronted by other parents. Child rearing in these circumstances can be difficult but can have particular rewards as well. Members of such family systems experience numerous reactions and effects, which invariably influence the quality and nature of parent-child relations. These families need and receive a variety of community resources that assist them in dealing with their particular challenges. Federal legislation efforts continue to provide needed support.

HOW DOES A WOMAN'S EMPLOYMENT AFFECT HER FAMILY SYSTEM?

Many women become employed outside the home at this stage of the family life career. The entrance or return of a woman into the workforce becomes a potential stressor event for a family system. This change in a woman's employment status affects adaptations in boundaries, rules, and patterns that were formed earlier. Any significant change is disruptive to the efficient, smooth functioning of a family system. When one aspect of a system is altered, other aspects cease to function effectively until adjustments are made to restore homeostasis. Family systems strive to maintain equilibrium and balance. This change in a woman's role pattern produces a variety of ripple effects in the behavior and functioning of other family members.

Adjusting to these changes effectively constitutes a crisis event for many family systems. Job-related stress, especially affecting at least one adult in dual-earner families, can have negative implications on parent-child relationships (Haddock, 2002).

Effects on Adults

Women in contemporary American society now include provider as part of their role pattern within family systems. Today, most women balance work outside the home with more traditional domestic responsibilities (U.S. Bureau of the Census, 2006). In 1970, about 90% of married couples in the United States had conventional earnings arrangements where the husband was the sole provider (Raley, Mattingly, & Bianchi, 2006) while wives contributed equally with husband's earnings in 9% of couples. By 2001, husbands were the sole provider in 24% of married couples and wives now contributed equally with husbands in 24% of couples.

The entrance of the oldest child into the school system initiates employment for a significant number of women. Many families need the additional income provided by the woman's employment, but many women also find that full-time domestic roles have failed to provide sufficient personal fulfillment. Many also have college degrees and wish to make use of their educational training. There are positive as well as negative effects of employment for women and their families. For example, when employed, married women tend to increase their positive self-esteem, personal competence, and economic security (Elgar & Chester, 2007; Hoffman, 1986), but the entire family must make adjustments to accommodate this return to the labor force.

Researchers have examined the effects of women's employment on family systems, and they have noted the following: (1) Changes occur in family functioning that require adjustments in the roles of other family members. These adaptations relate to household chores, leisure time, recreation, and interpersonal interaction. (2) Conflicting evidence is found regarding the effects of women's employment on marriage adjustment for a couple.

Parenting FAQs 9–2

I returned to work when our youngest of three children turned 5 years old. My husband agreed that he would help more with what needs to be done around the house and with the kids when I went back to work. However, it's not working out. I'm still doing about as much as I did before I went back to work and, frankly, I'm getting exhausted. I can't do it all myself. What can you suggest to help me gain more cooperation from my husband in sharing the workload around here?

A: Obviously, it's time for a discussion with your partner. Take more of a direct approach in the discussion by making a list beforehand of all the chores and tasks that must be done to run your household and work life efficiently for everyone. Discuss what you are willing to do and what he is willing to do, making sure that no one is doing excessively more than the other. You may have to let go of your need to have certain tasks performed in certain ways in order for him to cooperate. After all, he probably has his styles of performing certain tasks that are different from yours. The compromise may be that at least he is doing these chores even though possibly not completely to your satisfaction.

The greatest degree of adjustment in family systems to a woman's employment, perhaps, occurs in relation to role responsibilities for almost everyone. Changes usually occur in who does what and when. Many studies report that men become more involved in household chores, parenting responsibilities, and home life after the woman is employed (Bouchard & Lee, 2000). However, men's involvement overall may not have altered considerably in this regard.

Research suggests that employed mothers experience role overload. They continue to bear the principal household maintenance responsibilities in addition to holding a job outside the home (Crouter & Manke, 1997; Menaghan & Parcel, 1990). This evidence suggests several points:

■ The division of family work is inequitable because male partners fail to contribute more time to housework or child care when women are employed.

■ Traditional sex-role orientation and philosophy continue to be maintained in determining what work is done by whom, even after women become employed.

■ Most women desire their partners to become more involved in household responsibilities and child care.

■ Role overload has negative implications for women's health and well-being.

■ Men continue to be more psychologically identified with their work roles than family roles when wives are employed. It should be noted, however, that women's social power within a family system increases significantly after employment. As a woman's level of education also increases, there is a greater likelihood of shared household responsibilities with a partner.

Adults in a dual-earner family system, then, are challenged in numerous ways to balance work demands with family responsibilities. This is a continual, daily challenge for many adults that can produce stress that is felt throughout the entire family system. Both men and women, however, apparently are able to achieve this balance successfully but with some differences (J. O. Berry & Rao, 1997; Milkie & Peltola, 1999). Men appear to be more challenged when they experience longer work hours, perceive unfairness in sharing housework, experience marital unhappiness, have wives who work fewer hours than they do, and are unhappy with the trade-offs they make at work for their families and vice versa. Women appear to be more challenged in achieving a balance when they are employed full-time and have young children.

Effects on Children

Many concerns are expressed about how employment of mothers affects children. Generally, the belief is that children are affected adversely rather than beneficially when mothers are employed. They are thought to receive less supervision, less interaction time, and less discipline than do children of full-time mothers. This issue has been discussed in previous chapters regarding fears about infants and preschoolers being harmed by the experiences of nonparental caregiving.

As with any other complex issue, researchers report a number of mixed findings on how this situation affects school-age children. Generally, they find no significant adverse effects on children (Barling, 1990; DeCaro & Worthman, 2007; Hangal & Aminabhavi, 2007; Menaghan & Parcel, 1990). Some problems are reported, however, that relate more to a child's gender and the social class of the family system when mothers are employed.

School-age boys and girls can benefit from their mother's employment, but girls may be especially influenced in positive ways. For example, girls of employed mothers tend to have higher levels of emotional maturity and achievement, due perhaps to the model they observe in their mothers. Both boys and girls tend to have less rigid sex stereotypes about women in general when their mothers are employed.

On the less positive side of this issue, boys who are poorly supervised in addition to having employed mothers are reported to have the poorest conduct (Crouter, MacDermid, McHale, & Perry-Jenkins, 1990). Both boys and girls of employed mothers seem to be more self-sufficient than other children, and they tend to be given more responsibilities by parents as well. Although they also tend to be less compliant and cooperative with adult directions, these differences are generally small and minor. Other research indicates that those employed mothers who feel the greatest levels of harassment and role strain are the most likely to have children who display maladjustment and behavior problems (Budig & England, 2001). It is reasonable to assume that those parents who have heavy work schedules or have more than one job are less likely to devote attention to children and parenting roles and responsibilities.

Focus Point. The entrance or return of a mother into the work force constitutes a crisis for a family system, just as any other change would. Many adjustments occur in other aspects of the system to bring it back into equilibrium and homeostasis. Adults are affected by changes in their family role patterns and use of time.

Many employed mothers experience role overload as they continue to perform family roles in addition to work roles. Employment of mothers does not appear to cause detrimental problems for school-age children. Many may benefit in various ways from their mothers' employment status.

SYSTEMIC FAMILY DEVELOPMENT SNAPSHOT

(Before reading this section, it may be helpful to review the systemic family development model and the metaphor used to illustrate its concepts from Chapter 3.)

Our slice of developmental time is taken at the midpoint of the middle childhood stage of the oldest child in the Curtis family. Mary Curtis is now 9 years old. This slice is taken about 5 years after the snapshot we examined in the previous chapter when Mary was a preschooler. We begin examining the snapshot with a brief review of the stressors that affect a family system at this time. The second generation in this family continues to experience even greater levels of stress due to role strain affecting the young adult parents. However, the first generation now faces a critical adjustment following the death of Lisa's mother, Susan Scott, from complications relating to breast cancer. The third generation of the children also has had to deal with adjustments of their own, although children are often more resilient than adults in accepting the necessity of making changes.

Examples of Stressors Affecting Each Curtis Family Generation: 5 Years Later

First Generation (Grandparents)

- Adjusting to the aging process that continues in the latter part of middle age
- Adjusting to increasing frequency of deaths among spouses, colleagues, coworkers, and friends
- Making final preparations for retirement

Second Generation (Young Adult Parents)

- Continuing adjustments in balancing work and family roles
- Adding new roles to existing array
- Adjusting household and work routines to meet the needs of school-age children
- Adapting parenting behaviors and styles to meet the needs of school-age children
- Avoiding divorce and coping in healthy ways with the lowest level of marital satisfaction that will be experienced
- Attempting to meet personal adult needs

Third Generation (School-Age Children)

- Mastering developmental tasks and milestones of middle childhood

At the time of this slice of developmental time, here are the ages of all members of this family system: (1) the paternal grandfather (George Curtis) is now 63; (2) the paternal grandmother (Joan Curtis) is 61; (3) the maternal grandfather (Harry Scott) is 60; (4) the maternal grandmother (Susan Scott) is deceased; (5) Butch Curtis is 39; and (6) Lisa Curtis is 36. The first child, Mary, is 9 years old and the second child, Joey, is 7 years old.

The Third Generation (Children)

The children are in elementary school now; Mary is in fourth grade and her brother, Joey, is in second grade. Mary's parents perhaps had the greater adjustment to make when Mary first entered first grade since she was their first child to embark on this major change. Joey's entrance into first grade in the last year was not quite so earthshaking for the parents. Mary has become a typical trail-blazing, first-born child who coaches her little brother about the ins and outs of what he will encounter in each new school grade. She has enjoyed this advantage and likes helping her little brother with learning to read, write, and make calculations. Now that she is 9 years old, she is allowed to participate in the local Girl Scout program and is excelling with these activities. This coming summer, she will get to go to camp for one week as a reward for her sales in the annual cookie drive. Joey also belongs to a youth program called the Tiger Cubs, a program especially geared to boys in the first and second elementary grades. Both children are involved in other activities that take place throughout the week. Both children are on separate soccer teams, and Mary has gymnastics class twice weekly and dance classes on Saturdays.

Both children are doing relatively well with their schoolwork. Mary loves to read and has a current interest in biographies of famous people from the past such as Eleanor Roosevelt. She is particularly fond of the computer games available at school and at home. Right now, she is learning how to use the instant messaging feature so that she can visit with friends at night; sometimes they participate in online games together. Mary's mom has placed some restrictions on just what she can and cannot do on the Internet, and Mary is closely supervised with time limits as well. Joey seems to enjoy math more than reading and plays with educational games when he has his share of computer time at home.

Mary feels the importance of the trust her parents have placed in supervising herself and her little brother when they can't be home some days after school is out. She has learned to act responsibly in these situations and observes the rules her parents have established about what can and cannot be done when they aren't around. She knows, for example, how to answer the phone if someone calls for one of her parents, how to prepare snacks without using the stove, and what to play with Joey when both have finished homework assignments.

Both children experienced stress during this past year when their maternal grandmother died from cancer. This is their first encounter with this life event, and they don't completely understand why their grandmother died. All both children know and remember most vividly was that everyone in their family was very upset and cried a great deal. They were allowed to attend the funeral but didn't understand very much about

what was going on. They miss their grandmother and wish that their grandfather would not be so unhappy. They have been with their parents to visit the cemetery on Memorial Day when they were given flowers to place on the grave site. Joey brought along one of the toys that his grandmother had given him for his last birthday and left that as well. Lisa and Butch have been very open with the children in answering their questions about dying and death. Although this has been difficult at times to discuss, they know it is important for their children to learn about this part of life and not to be confused about the issues.

The Second Generation (Adult Parents)

Lisa and Butch have experienced some difficulties over the past several years. Butch was promoted in his work position and now works longer hours that also take him away from the family for short periods of time as he travels. This situation is very different from the family's experience when Butch was unemployed about 7 years ago. Lisa finds this change more challenging than she anticipated since she has the primary responsibilities of managing her own work role in relation to what the children require from her. Because of the children's different, hectic, and often conflicting schedules, she has found it necessary to call on her father and her in-laws to lend their time and help when Butch is unavailable. At times Lisa feels like she's living in a three-ring circus instead of a normal family because of all the running around that must be done. Her day often begins at 5 A.M. to get her part of the housework done and get everyone in the family off to begin their day. Sometimes, she feels exhausted by 9 A.M. The day often is not over until 11 P.M. By then the children have taken care of their homework and gone to bed while Lisa has finished other housework chores and has finally had time to watch a bit of TV. There seems to be little time for family fun and interaction.

Butch and Lisa have noticed that they have more conflicts with each other now than ever before. The arguments lately have centered on Butch's lack of involvement with the family and with his household responsibilities. Lisa is beginning to feel that she can't take on anything more than what she is doing right now. She feels an increasing resentment about Butch giving greater priority to his work over his family and household responsibilities. He maintains that if they are to have a future with some financial safety, then they must accept this current situation. Their personal time together has dwindled almost to nothing, and Lisa sometimes thinks that when they do have time together, it becomes focused on settling arguments rather than expressing affection. She fears that her marriage may be threatened by the possibility of a divorce if things don't improve soon. Both of these young adults are tired, more emotionally distanced than ever before, and uncertain of how things are headed in their future.

Both Lisa and Butch are aware that their conflicts are affecting their children, and they are working to reduce and restrict their heated discussions to protect the children's anxieties. Not long ago, Lisa heard Mary weeping while in her room. When she came to Mary's bedroom, she quickly asked her to explain what was bothering her. At first, Mary didn't want to discuss anything with her mom. but with Lisa's gentle encouragement, she found the words to tell her mother she was afraid she was going to become like many others in her class. She told her mother that about half of her classmates had parents who were either divorced or divorcing. When Lisa asked Mary why she thought this was happening to her parents, Mary responded that she had heard many arguments late at night between her mom and dad. Rather than discounting or diminishing Mary's fears, Lisa was truthful in admitting that she and Butch "had issues right now," but she went on to assure Mary that she and Butch were committed to each other, to their relationship, and to their children and family members. In doing so, she was trying to show Mary that while children can't be involved in adult matters, she and her brother had parents who were working on their problems together and expected to ride out the difficult times by learning now to work together more closely.

Complicating an already stressful situation was the death of Lisa's mother about 6 months ago. They had anticipated that this would happen one day but remained hopeful and optimistic as Susan Scott managed her illness and treatments with a good attitude. However, Susan experienced a turn for the worse as the cancer was detected in her pancreas and lungs. In less than 6 weeks, she died. Lisa and Butch were with the other family members (except the children) when she died. She and her mother had the opportunity to bring some closure before she died and Lisa was thankful for this. They were able to make peace with one another and settle some old issues that had not been completely addressed. Butch was supportive to Lisa during this time, and she sees this commitment as evidence that he still loves her very much. Perhaps this event was what both needed to help bring them closer after feeling some estrangement.

They have recently discussed entering therapy to work on their current problems. In talking with friends who have weathered similar problems, Lisa has gained some pointers and has discussed with Butch some ways that they might improve their marriage and home life. Butch has agreed, for example, to take complete charge of the children on the weekends so Lisa can have some personal time to use as she wishes.

The First Generation (Grandparents)

The first generation has been affected more so by Susan Scott's death than they expected. Losing parents was difficult, but Harry Scott never thought he would survive his wife. Now, being alone after so many years of marriage, he feels lost and uncomfortable. It is hard at times to fight the feelings of depression and loss. He has not slept well in the months following Susan's death and has avoided dealing with some issues he knows he will have to attend to eventually. Lisa is attentive to her father as he struggles with a new identity of being a widower. She also is attentive because she has heard from friends that when older men reach this new status, they often become emotionally depressed to the point of committing suicide. She is in daily contact with her father to monitor him as closely as she can. Harry has recently joined a support group for cancer survivors and their partners. He finds it difficult to talk about his feelings but has learned a great deal just from listening to others. The group is helping him to learn about these feelings and how to deal with a new lifestyle. Harry also finds that helping to care for his grandchildren is a much-needed and welcomed distraction from his own problems. He enjoys spending time in play with both grandchildren. He also understands how helpful this is for his daughter and son-in-law and that he is playing a useful role in his family.

Butch's parents, Joan and George Curtis, also have been affected by Susan's death. They have become closer as a result and value their time together more deeply now than ever before. As such, their marriage has been strengthened. As they observed Harry and Susan deal with their own issues, they have learned how to lean more upon each other for support and nurturance. George now is looking forward to his retirement because this will allow him to have more time with Joan and do some things they have had to put off until now, such as travel. Both have taken a greater interest in their health since this may be an important key to having time together following retirement.

The three surviving older adults have noticed how their adult children are struggling with issues in their work and family life. They know they can't intrude by offering unsolicited opinions and suggestions about what they think Butch and Lisa need to do, but they have indicated they are willing to listen and discuss anything if their children so desire. In some ways, they don't understand the issues because these are different from what they encountered at a similar point in their own development as a family.

Parenting Reflectzion 9–5

Can you determine how each generation in the snapshot uses boundaries? Is this family system one that is open or closed? Does morphogenesis or morphostasis appear to be functioning in this family system when this snapshot took place?

POINTS TO CONSIDER

- The time between 6 and 12 years is called *middle childhood.* During this period, children master several developmental tasks and milestones, including (1) achieving a sense of industry vs. inferiority; (2) developing a new individuality; (3) establishing relationships with peers; and (4) refining existing skills and acquiring new physical, social, and mental skills.

- Parenting increasingly shifts to psychological assistance and guidance when children are of school age. Parenting styles change and become adapted in relation to the new developmental needs of children. Coregulation becomes a predominant approach by most parents of school-age children. Children take on greater responsibility to police their own actions. Children are also allowed greater latitude in their activities and behavior because of their more advanced abilities. Parents increasingly provide more advanced levels of structure, best conveyed in nurturant terms. Many parents also incorporate new models of parenting styles in providing structure and nurturance to children at this age.

- Socialization experiences continue to occupy the efforts and energy of most parents of school-age children, especially focusing now on facilitating children's moral development. Parents serve an important function in providing interpretations and acting as narrators. This role assists children in learning how to reason morally, consider options and choices for their behavior, and gain knowledge about family values and a sesnse of what is right and wrong. The school may assist parents in helping school-age children learn in greater detail about their sexuality. It is important for parents to prepare preteenage children for their approaching puberty. Parents also play an important role in helping their school-age children to become computer literate and in protecting them from unsavory, inappropriate Web content and online predators.

- Certain behavior problems can be expected in some school-age children that are specific to diffculties in adjusting to the developmental tasks of this life stage. They may involve (1) problems in cooperating with adults' expectations of appropriate behavior, (2) difficulties in attending school and in mastering the skills essential to successful functioning in an academic environment, and (3) problems in adjusting to interpersonal skills and achieving appropriate standards of behavior expected by those in authority.

- Families of children with special needs have particular problems not usually shared by other families. Parents and family members experience a variety of reactions to having a child with special needs present; this child has a number of influences on the family system as a whole. The ability of families to cope with the stresses and demands of having a child with special needs often depends on the availability and nature of a variety of sources of assistance. Community programs and federal legislation work to address the needs of exceptional children and their parents.

- Many married mothers become employed or reenter the workforce when their children become school-age. This change in a woman's employment status affects adaptations in boundaries, rules, and patterns that were formed earlier in their families. Both adults and children are affected by this change, and the family system reacts by making major adjustments in roles, rules, and other patterns to maintain homeostasis.

- A systemic family development snapshot reveals examples of the stressors that may affect the different generations of a family system as well as the ways that members cope with these in healthy as well as unhealthy ways.

CHAPTER 10

Parenting Adolescents and Young Adults

Focus Questions

Parenting Adolescents

1. What are the principal developmental milestones of adolescence that parents should know?

2. How is parenting conducted with teenagers and young adults? How is this different from when children were younger?

3. How do parents meet the particular needs of adolescent children?

4. What stressors and coping mechanisms are revealed by a systemic family development snapshot of families with adolescent children?

Parenting Young Adults

1. What are the unique challenges of parenting young adults?

2. What is the nature of grandparenting in contemporary families? What styles may be observed? What are some unique challenges in grandparenting roles today?

Adolescence is the stage of the life span that represents a transition period between childhood and adulthood. Chronologically, it begins at age 13 and extends through age 18. The developmental event of puberty, which usually occurs at the beginning of adolescence, signals the end of childhood. At this time, individuals become sexually mature and capable of reproduction. The stage of adolescence is technically divided into two periods: (1) *early adolescence,* which begins at puberty (about age 13), ends at age 16, and involves a variety of physical changes associated with the achievement of sexual maturation; and (2) *late adolescence,* which begins at age 16, continues until age 18, and involves many psychosocial changes (Steinberg, 2004).

Parents may anticipate the adolescent stage of their children's life span with mixed feelings. Traditionally, the period is described as one of storm and stress, not only for the teens who experience it but also for their parents and family systems. Parents may fear that their worst nightmares about their children will come true. A more contemporary view of adolescence describes this stage as one of increasing autonomy as children gain increasing degrees of personal responsibility and a time of significant transitions (Steinberg, 2004). Parents may view these gains in more realistic terms colored by trepidation and apprehension about the many hazards that can threaten the health and well-being of adolescent children. As with other stages of the life span, adolescence presents both children and their parents with unique challenges for growth and adaptation. Those challenges are briefly outlined as characteristics of this life stage.

DEVELOPMENTAL LANDMARKS OF ADOLESCENCE

Three features distinguish a child's development during adolescence from previous stages. The first is characterized by *rapid physical and psychological change*. Adolescence is a period of metamorphosis in an individual's life involving dramatic changes in body proportions and physical size, sexual maturation, and personality shifts. The second change involves *individual emancipation*. Western culture emphasizes the teenage years as the appropriate time for establishing one's independence as a mature person and assuming full responsibility for oneself (Figure 10-1). The third relates to behaviors as well as attitudes that involve experimentation, idealism, and uncertainty that often bring teens into conflict with adults, especially parents. Adolescence is a transition period between childhood and adulthood that has few guidelines for how to behave, what to expect, and feeling secure about what the future holds. Adolescents are known for unrealistic expectations and aspirations. These attitudes are expressed in relationships with peers and family members. High hopes for the future lead teenagers to create dreams and idealistic notions about their own abilities and skills in coping with the world. The tendency to experiment is found in myriad ways from new uses of language, exploration of self-expression via clothing, musical tastes, and friendships, as well as with sexual awakening. The specific developmental tasks and milestones that individuals encounter in adolescence focus on acquiring and refining more advanced skills, abilities, and attitudes that lead toward preparation for adulthood. These are outlined in Focus On 10–1.

FIGURE 10-1. Adolescence is a time of rapid changes as individuals seek to establish a personal identity and embark on individuating from their family of origin.

PARENTING ADOLESCENTS

Many parents anticipate that when a child reaches adolescence, it is like going to war since this stage of the life span is associated with rebellion, tension, conflict, and emotional turmoil. In reality, this depiction is not far from the truth for some since adolescence is a difficult time both for children and parents. While some teenagers reach the outer limits in their behavior and attitude, however, most adolescents do not act out, and the stereotypes described here do not normally apply.

Parenting styles and behaviors must adapt once again to meet the needs of a different child. And once again, the adaptation often is not initiated by the parents but rather by the adolescent, who may demand to be treated differently now that he or she is older. Meeting

Focus On 10–1 **Developmental Characteristics of Adolescence**

- Establishing a sense of personal identity as opposed to role confusion
- Establishing new and more mature relationships with peers of both sexes
- Accepting the physical changes that accompany puberty
- Determining one's sexual orientation and accepting one's sexuality
- Initiating the process of individuation
- Initiating financial independence
- Selecting and initiating preparations for an occupation or higher education
- Initiating the learning of skills involved in participating in healthy intimate relationships
- Manifesting socially responsible behaviors
- Determining a set of values and an ethical system that will guide behavior

the developmental needs of a child who is attempting to become autonomous and eventually to individuate from the family system presents challenges not found in previous periods of parenting children. Most parents understand that adolescents continue to need guidance, rules, and support in this process of growing toward maturity.

Family professionals stress that one of the more difficult challenges of parenting adolescents is the fine line parents walk between being supportive of a teen's efforts to individuate and maintaining certain limits and boundaries for appropriate behavior (Gnaulati & Heine, 2001). Adolescents need experience in making personal decisions, but sometimes these decisions can have traumatic consequences. Family systems become unhealthy when there is a demand for complete uniformity and conformity among all members, when everyone is expected to adhere to the same beliefs, values, and behaviors. Although parents and adolescents must agree on rules and other family patterns, this agreement occurs ideally through negotiation and input from all concerned. When no latitude is permitted for individual expression and differences are not tolerated, a family system becomes endangered in its ability to function in healthy ways. This approach may have been appropriate at earlier stages of the family life career as a reflection of the developmental limits and inabilities of children to participate fully in family life and decisions; however, it becomes less appropriate as children reach the adolescent years.

Revised Parenting Styles

A common misconception of many parents is that a particular style of child rearing does not change once it is established; they assume they will use the same style throughout the years of child rearing. In reality, children's changing developmental progress affects changes in parenting styles throughout childhood and adolescence. Most parents make adaptations in child-rearing strategies, methods, and interaction styles to meet the particular needs of adolescents. Because of the different developmental status of adolescents, parents must shift to accommodate these needs by altering their parenting style to become more authoritative, less authoritarian, and, eventually, more permissive in nature.

Parenting during this stage is particularly challenging for a variety of reasons (Santrock, 2007). Adults must discover ways to help teens learn to make decisions that minimize potential harm to themselves and others. Communication between parents and teens requires patience and effort to achieve effective functioning of this family system microenvironment. A unique challenge is adjusting the relationship to allow an adolescent to individuate from the family system. By doing so, adults must gradually relinquish control and place increasing amounts of personal responsibility on teens to become self-regulated.

Glen Elder (1962) conducted the classic study that describes styles commonly used in parenting adolescents. The study included 7,400 adolescents from homes that had two parents, and it classified parenting styles on a continuum that differed in the degree of control exercised by adults. According to the study, at least seven styles could be observed:

- *Autocratic.* Teens were allowed no freedom to express their opinions or to make any decision affecting how they conducted their lives.

- *Authoritarian.* Teens were allowed to express their opinions, but parents continued to make decisions affecting their lives.
- *Democratic.* Teens and parents shared power between parents and adolescents, but parents had veto power over decisions made by teens.
- *Permissive.* Teens took an increasing degree of responsibility for their own decisions and actions but with the understanding that parents continued to have input into the decision-making process.
- *Equalitarian.* Teens and parents had equal power and status, and they made decisions by joint effort.
- *Laissez-faire.* Teens took complete control and responsibility for making decisions about their lives and conduct. Parents understood that they could contribute information and opinions that teens could freely disregard.
- *Ignoring.* Parents took no part or had no interest in an adolescent's behavior.

Most of the parents in this study used democratic or equalitarian styles, although fathers tended to be stricter than mothers. The stricter styles generally were more prevalent in larger family systems, those with low incomes, and those with younger adolescents. Four general reasons may explain these differences. First, fathers may rely on the stricter approaches because they generally use power assertion in their interaction styles, as they have been socialized to do. This tendency is especially evident when they settle conflicts that typically occur with younger adolescents. Mothers, perhaps also because of their socialization experiences, tend to use love-oriented instead of power-assertion methods to control children's behavior. These methods are largely psychological and focus on using praise and positive reinforcement. They also tend to promote a strong sense of responsibility among children for regulating their own behavior.

Second, stricter parenting styles may be used more commonly in family systems where there are larger numbers of children because adults often have greater time- and resource-management pressures. Contemporary family life is hectic and often chaotic at the stage when adolescents are present in the system.

Conflicting schedules of all family members contribute to this situation. Stricter methods among larger groups may facilitate family functioning to a certain degree. It may occur, however, at the price of an adolescent's achievement of high-level individuation. Use of stricter parenting styles with adolescents is even more probable among single-parent family systems, especially in those headed by mothers (Wordlaw-Stinson, 2003). This is apparently due to the unique parenting responsibilities in these family systems. The situation is exacerbated among those having young adolescents.

Third, social class differences in family systems are apparent in parenting styles with adolescents (Hoffman & Youngblade, 1998). Middle-class families tend to use methods based on persuasion and negotiation. They include the democratic, equalitarian, and authoritative styles. Lower-class family systems generally rely on stricter approaches with children and adolescents. Cultural influences emphasize the responsibility of parents to control the behavior of children, especially by forceful, power-assertive methods. Financial independence, however, may be the exception in this regard. Blue-collar families may expect and demand that their adolescent children become financially independent at earlier ages than adolescents in middle-class families. This expectation may be due to the decreasing level of family income at this stage of the family life career as compared with that of middle-class families, who can afford to defer the financial independence of adolescent children.

Fourth, conflicts occur more frequently between parents and young adolescents (Steinberg & Silk, 2002). These clashes may occur because of the intense focus of young adolescents on identity formation. Predictably, parents initially react to these efforts by using styles that are strict and controlling.

Research consistently shows that adolescent-parent relations are best when decisions are perceived by both as being consistent and collaborative, the needs of all family members are respected, and decisions are seen as fair and reasonable as opposed to arbitrary (Steinberg & Silk, 2002). As in previous stages of parenting children, the authoritative parenting style continues to be associated with positive adolescent outcomes.

••

Focus Point. One of the challenges to the relationship between parents and teens relates to how parents must adapt in providing structure and nurturance. A significant task involves the ability of parents and teens to communicate effectively. Adults who use democratic styles in parenting adolescents usually have improved interactions. Those using stricter styles have more conflicts, which are frequently related to adolescent attempts at individuation.

••

Meeting the Needs of Adolescents

Meeting Nutritional Needs.   Appetites of both teen girls and boys increase dramatically during adolescence. The proverbial teenage boy is depicted as a having a cavernous, almost insatiable appetite that allows him to consume enormous amounts of foods having enormous calorie counts. In addition, the stereotypical adolescent doesn't eat an especially healthy diet but one that is constituted of many empty-calorie foods that fail to qualify as being adequately nutritious.

Because adolescents are very peer oriented, it may be difficult for parents to encourage or even insist on appropriate nutritional foods for their teens. Most adolescents want to be like their friends in many respects, including the foods that they consume.

Adolescent diets typically are not especially health oriented but may appear similar to the array of foods found on many fast-food menus. Even if parents have diligently supplied food that is healthy and nutritious, teenagers may adopt an approach to diet that runs counter to what parents have taught and presented in the home. Not wanting to be different from others their age in just about every aspect, foods consumed by teens may or may not follow what they've eaten at home, especially when away from parental presence.

Conflicts can take place when teens do not appear to be following family practice in this regard. Such conflicts can often make the matter worse because of the tendency for teens to rebel in such confrontations. Parental concerns here focus on the knowledge that teens need good, healthy food in order to complete their growth processes. Parents also may fear that their teen may be headed in the direction of acquiring an eating disorder (this is discussed in a later section of this chapter). Adolescent concerns revolve around becoming an individual and asserting their personal tastes, not eating different foods from their friends, and knowing that some other parents of friends may not be so concerned as theirs about good nutrition. Nevertheless, rather than inviting stubborn refusal to cooperate with parental desires, it is often advised that parents make no issue of the situation unless teens are intentionally attempting to consume foods that are patently harmful to their health (Nissenberg & Pearl, 2002). Instead, teens are likely to continue an already established family eating pattern even though there may be relapses into the temptations of fast-foods.

Health and Safety Issues.   Adolescence and young adulthood are perhaps the times in one's life when health and well-being are at their peak. However, health and safety issues occurring during these times often have a significant impact in the present as well as in the future.

Adolescents should begin having an annual visit with a health care professional for screening for a variety of health issues. These visits also allow for confidential discussions of issues of a personal nature that a health care professional can address. Health care professionals can also bring other issues up for discussion with the teenager relating to health, exercise, and sexual matters. Other situations involving the health and well-being of teens call for monitoring by parents and other family members.

Substance Abuse.   Parents and other members of society are extremely concerned about adolescent use of drugs and chemical substances. Estimates vary considerably about the extensiveness of drug use among teenagers. Indications are that adolescent drug abuse remains stable in comparison with past years in which information has been gathered (Federal Interagency Forum on Child and Family Statistics, 2007).

Despite the influences of the media and peers, adolescents who have been reared by parents who rely on an authoritative style appear to have stronger internalized standards that help to insulate them from pressures to abuse substances (W. A. Collins, Maccoby, Steinberg, Hetherington, & Bornstein, 2000). Teens who apparently care what parents think about such matters (e.g., parents who disapprove of smoking and/or drinking) are less likely to drink alcohol, smoke cigarettes, or use other drugs (Figure 10-2).

Closely related to substance abuse by adolescents is the increased likelihood of injury and death from accidents involving alcohol and/or drug use and automobiles (U.S. Bureau of the Census, 2007a, 2007b). This is the leading cause of death among teenagers today in the United States and leads to much sadness, grief, and loss when friends end their lives in this manner. The shock often is lifelong for many teens and their families. In addition to accidents and fatal injuries in automobiles caused by drug and alcohol use is the increasing problem of teen text messaging while driving. This misuse of modern communications technology increases the chances of problems while driving and has resulted in some states enacting legislation prohibiting this practice, especially by adolescents.

FIGURE 10-2. Substance abuse is a serious problem of adolescence that can continue into later years of life.

Suicide. Suicide is the second leading cause of death, following fatal accidental injuries and death from firearms, among individuals between 15 and 17 years old (Centers for Disease Control and Prevention, 2007). It is the third leading cause of death among children between 10 and 14 years of age (Federal Interagency Forum on Child and Family Statistics, 2007). Contemporary teenagers increasingly complete suicide successfully; the rate has more than tripled within the last 30 years. While suicide occurs more commonly among white youth, no ethnic group is spared this phenomenon among adolescents. Most adolescents attempting suicide are female, although males are more likely to succeed in completing the act.

It is not completely clear why some adolescents want to commit suicide, particularly at a time when, for many people, their lives are just beginning. Suicide may be related to a variety of issues (Groleger, Tomori, & Kocmur, 2003). Many teenagers who contemplate suicide and attempt to end their lives are emotionally depressed. Depression distorts a person's ability to reason logically and clearly to reach solutions to personal problems. Living situations frequently seem hopeless to people who are emotionally depressed, and suicide appears to be the only solution to their life situations. Suicide among adolescents is also related to substance abuse, which is frequently accompanied by depression (Tubman, Wagner, & Langer, 2003).

Many teenagers who attempt and succeed in committing suicide may also be emotionally depressed about their sexual orientation (Savin-Williams & Ream, 2003). Gay and lesbian youth are about six times more likely than nongay youth to attempt suicide; they account for about 30 percent of those who complete suicide successfully. These individuals apparently experience much anguish and inner turmoil because of the social stigmas associated with homosexuality. They choose to commit suicide rather than suffer rejection, disapproval, and shame, reactions they anticipate from family and friends.

Teen Pregnancy and STDs. There has been a decline in the number of teen pregnancies in recent years (J. A. Martin et al., 2006), but the decline has not eliminated this problem. Teen pregnancy continues to be a matter of concern for society, schools, and the adolescents and families who are affected. Teen parents, their children, and their families face many serious short- and long-term consequences. This problem is discussed in greater detail in Chapter 14.

Sexually transmitted diseases (STDs) are a new health concern occurring for the first time in adolescence.

Chapter 10 Parenting Adolescents and Young Adults ■ 225

These may be transmitted via heterosexual or homosexual acts. The most common types in our society are syphilis, gonorrhea, chlamydia, herpes simplex, venereal warts, and HIV infection, and Acquired Immune Deficiency Syndrome (AIDS). The high frequency of unprotected sexual behavior and multiple sex partners results in an equally high rate of STDs among adolescents. This group represents about 25 percent of all sexually active individuals, and almost one-half of all new STDs reported are contracted among those between 15 and 24 years of age (Centers for Disease Control and Prevention, 2006).

Even more alarming is the recent finding that one in four teen girls between 15 and 19 years has at least one STD (Centers For Disease Control and Prevention, 2008). This extremely high rate of contracting these diseases is thought to be a combination of the failure of abstinence-only sex education programs that attempt to discourage sexual activity among teens and those cognitive and social factors that inhibit teenage boys and girls from using contraception.

Eating Disorders. Adolescents generally have problems with nutrition and proper eating habits. Many are concerned with what they perceive as deficiencies in their features and appearance as contrasted with their desired body image. Improper nutrition can lead to both underweight and overweight conditions that indicate malnutrition. Some adolescents, however, believe that they are obese when they are not and experience other distortions in body image (Lewis, 2002). Many experience low self-esteem related to weight concerns that may make them vulnerable to eating disorders.

Anorexia nervosa and ***bulimia*** are serious eating disorders that affect the health, well-being, and even the lives of teenagers. Both conditions affect teenage girls more than boys and are commonly observed among contemporary adolescents. The conditions have serious consequences that can disturb normal adolescent behavior and development and also result in death.

Anorexia is characterized by an abnormal fear of obesity. It involves distortions of body image and "the relentless pursuit of thinness" (American Psychiatric Association, 2000). An anorexic girl is commonly between 12 and 20 years old. She usually comes from a seemingly stable, well-educated, and socially competent family; she is bright, well-behaved, and physically attractive (Mizes & Miller, 2000).

Anorexic teenage girls appear to be obsessed with their body weight. They are preoccupied with achieving a weight that matches the body image they perceive in a distorted way. The condition begins with dieting to achieve a particular weight level; however, the girls don't include a maintenance schedule. They continue to diet to a point that threatens their health and well-being because they are unable to perceive their body image in realistic terms. Controlling their weight and what they eat becomes their central life focus.

The causes of this condition are not completely clear. Several explanations have been proposed, which include these three factors (Haas & Clompton, 2001):

1. Heavy cultural conditioning emphasizes slim figures among young women in order for them to be attractive to males.

2. Girls may develop the condition to avoid and delay dealing with the many changes associated with puberty.

3. They may develop the condition to rebel in a passive-aggressive way against strict, overprotective parents, the lack of adequate personal boundaries, or their inability to individuate or attain personal autonomy from parents.

Anorexia is one of the few psychological disorders that can have fatal consequences if left untreated (Lewis, 2002). Therapy can involve hospitalization to treat malnutrition and individual psychotherapy to help a young woman to become more autonomous in less damaging ways. Family therapy is helpful in resolving enmeshment between family members, improving communication, and helping the family system acquire healthy ways of resolving conflicts.

Bulimia involves consuming huge amounts of food that are then purged from the body by vomiting or using excessive amounts of laxatives (Lewis, 2002). Consumption occurs in periodic binges, and it appears to occur in stressful situations as a means of coping with some difficulty. Unlike anorexics, bulimics know that their behavior is not appropriate. They binge and purge in secret to avoid discovery and suffer from feelings of shame and guilt. The condition is similar to anorexia because it, too, revolves around the need to control one's eating and is motivated by distortions of body image.

Unlike anorexia, bulimia itself is not life threatening. Unfortunately, it is a common method of weight control used by many adolescent females, and bulimic-related death can occur as a result of suicide, a correlate of depression. Many bulimics are emotionally depressed and have personality dispositions toward perfectionism. They are described as having an obsessive desire to control and manage themselves as well as others in their lives. They are considered to be heavily dependent on others' approval as a basis of their self-worth.

This condition, like anorexia, responds to treatment through means such as group psychotherapy and is also responsive to antidepressant medications. These methods are useful in helping bulimics to achieve a better understanding of femininity and healthful ways of dealing with stressful situations (Mizes & Miller, 2000).

Researchers have known for some time that cultural and family values influence the development of eating disorders, especially among female children. These two factors can combine in a family ecology to produce such a behavioral problem in adolescence. It appears that having a critical family environment, coercive parental controls, and a dominating discourse about body weight within the household work together to increase the likelihood of an adolescent developing an eating disorder (Haas & Clompton, 2001). However, other research points to biological influences that may cause a genetic predisposition to eating disorders (Vink, et al., 2001). With proper medical and psychotherapeutic treatment, both of these disorders can be brought under control and individuals have a good prognosis for treatment.

∙∙

Focus Point. A variety of issues involve the health and safety of adolescents. These ordinarily do not affect all teenagers, but a significant number are sidetracked into avenues that have short- and long-term adverse effects on their development.

∙∙

Providing Structure and Nurturance for Adolescents. A recurrent theme stressed in this text is that the nature of the relationship between parents and children is renegotiated and redefined as parents respond to the changing developmental needs and demands of developing children.

Much parental reluctance to accept any changes in their children is related to the functioning of the family system. The cohesion of a family system is threatened when any change takes place that affects the system's functioning. Systems have a strong tendency to seek to maintain the status quo because change in any aspect threatens the system's integrity. Family systems, in particular, face challenges that call for changes. When a child becomes an adolescent, his or her desire for individuation poses a serious threat to the family's functioning and its ability to maintain cohesion as a system. The family reacts in ways typical to other stressful situations it confronts.

Parents may seem particularly reluctant to release a teen from the controls, limits, and boundaries that were established in earlier developmental stages. Although many parents realize that this change must take place eventually, the equalization and transfer of power toward greater self-regulation occurs more slowly than most teens prefer.

Nevertheless, researchers have consistently validated the benefits of authoritative parenting styles in mediating positive developmental outcomes for children (Gray & Steinberg, 1999). The benefits for adolescents from this parenting style continue to remain in effect while parents make alterations in response to the individuation process of their teenagers. For example, behavior problems of adolescents appear to be diminished while academic competence can be enhanced when parents maintain what can be termed **detached involvement** or supervision. This variation on the authoritative parenting scheme relates to the perception adolescents hold of their parents as being involved in their lives while allowing them enough slack from parental supervision to feel autonomous. Parents, in this vein, are still providing structure for adolescents, but the structure is perceived as being fairly administered, yet firm and warm in its tone.

∙∙

Parenting Reflection 10–1

Is there such a thing as a **generation gap** or is this a media fabrication? How would this influence interactions, communications, and mutual understanding between generation members in families with adolescents?

∙∙

TABLE 10-1   Behaviors of Parents of Adolescents

Behaviors Providing Structure and Nurturance	Behaviors Not Providing Structure and Nurturance
• Showing approval for teen's efforts to achieve developmental tasks • Continuing to offer love, safety, and protection • Accepting teen's feelings and sharing own past feelings about puberty to build empathy with teen • Not discounting teen's behavior, feelings, and attitudes • Understanding teen's need for individuation and supporting efforts to establish it • Celebrating the teen's growing independence and gains toward attaining adult status • Encouraging, supporting, and accepting teen's emerging personal identity; accepting that it may be different from what you desired or hoped for the teen	• Responding to teen in uncaring ways • Withholding love, especially nurturing touch • Responding inappropriately to teen's developing sexuality • Using rigid rules, having no rules, or enforcing rules inconsistently; refusing to negotiate rules • Failing to expect teen to think and reason about solutions to problems • Engaging in negative teasing about teen's emerging sexuality, interests, dress styles, friends, or idealisms • Failing to confront teen's self-destructive behaviors, such as substance abuse • Thwarting and sabotaging teen's efforts to individuate from the family • Refusing to accept teen's wide range of emotional expressions and feelings • Discounting teen's behavior, feelings, and attitudes

Source: Adapted from Clarke, J. I., & Dawson, C. (1989). *Growing up again: Parenting ourselves, parenting our children.* Minneapolis: Hazelden.

Table 10-1 outlines some ways in which parents of teens can be responsive and supportive or unhelpful in providing structure and nurturance.

Parenting Reflection 10–2

Is it a good idea for parents to forbid their teenagers from activities and people of which they disapprove? If not, what can parents do when their teen makes what seems to be unwise decisions?

Focus Point.   One of the challenges to the relationship between parents and teens relates to how parents must adapt in providing structure and nurturance.

Peer Group Influences.   The peer group plays a special role in the process of personal identity formation among adolescents (see Parenting FAQs 10–1). Adolescence resembles a tribal experience with others of similar ages. The interactions with peer groups in adolescence are similar in purpose to those that occurred during middle childhood, but the peer group takes on additional functions for teens. As do school-age children, teenagers use their peers as a device for making self-evaluations. In adolescence, however, this group becomes a new source for redefining the teen's personal identity. In many respects, teens view their peers as an extension and reflection of their own self-images or of what they may wish their self-images to become. There is an enmeshment of personal identity of the self with others.

The push for autonomy from parental influence and control reaches its peak in adolescence. This change gives a teenager freedom to test limits, discover areas of ability and weakness, and make mistakes while learning many skills and problem-solving strategies. Boundaries between the self and parents become more distinct at the same time that boundaries between the individual and the peer group first begin to blur in early adolescence. Allegiance and loyalties once attributed to parents now

Parenting FAQs 10–1

My 15-year-old has been hanging around with some kids I don't like. I think they are beginning to have a negative influence because he's dressing and talking now in ways I don't approve of. What should I do?

A: This is a tough one for any parent. Let me assure you first that there are many factors that influence your child's social development. His peers are one of these and may seem to be the overriding influence socially, especially during adolescence. However, you and your family have a history with this child that is not usually discarded by your teen upon coming into contact with his peers. It may seem that way at times, but remember that this is a time of experimentation for your teen. Adolescents are trying many different things now and observing the results. I would not suggest forbidding your teen to socialize with those you find offensive or troublesome. Try first to analyze what it is that troubles you about these kids. Is it really how they dress, or are you bothered by their gain in being a part of your child's life while you take an increasingly lesser role as your teen grows older? Sometimes it's easy to blame a child's friends as being the catalyst for changes in your parenting relationship. By forbidding your teen to see the others, you are inviting rebelliousness. and your child will find ways to deceive you in order to be with friends. If indeed you suspect that your child is becoming involved in dangerous activities with these other teens, you can gain some control and influence by not enabling the relationships your teen has with those you find to be troublesome. This can be accomplished by limiting your teen to socialize with the others only in situations and places where you can make closer observations, such as in your own home.

shift to peers. This change creates tensions between an adolescent and the family system. Peer pressures to conform to established or imagined standards are high during this time. Acceptance and validation from others help to bolster self-confidence, while rejection works against positive self-esteem because the adolescent experiences strong feelings of alienation.

By late adolescence, changes occur in cognitive abilities. Experiences with peers have provided lessons in beliefs, attitudes, and notions about the various aspects of the self. These lessons result in crystallization of personal identity as boundaries are drawn between the self and the social group. Experiences within the family, school, and social systems now bring the adolescent into his or her own as an individual. The teenager makes connections that provide him or her with initial answers to the questions posed throughout this period: "Who am I? Who do I belong with? Where will I go with my life?"

The sense of identity that is forged in adolescence is not an achievement of a final destiny or a static goal in the search for who one is and where one can go in life. This sense of identity that emerges from adolescent experiences is a foundation attitude that retains certain constants throughout the life span. The person later acquires, develops, and refines other roles and understandings about the self, which become integrated into this basic personal identity during the years of adulthood.

Promoting the Individuation Process.   The experiences of adolescence are a struggle toward the eventual emancipation of a teenager from the family system in which he or she has been raised. The process leading to emancipation, or **individuation,** is part of the identity formation that is central to adolescent development. Although this process begins in adolescence, it may not be completed until years later in adulthood. Some individuals, however, never completely achieve the degree of emancipation or individuation they truly desire or that is expected by society as an appropriate developmental task. It involves becoming a true individual in that one develops a personal belief system to guide decisions and behaviors, acquires financial independence, and assumes emotional self-care. The process requires questioning and challenging and may account for some of the tension experienced between parents and adolescents.

Often a teen's advancement toward emancipation includes working at full- or part-time jobs (Figure 10-3). Making social decisions (such as choosing friends, dating, or becoming sexually active) also helps a teenager

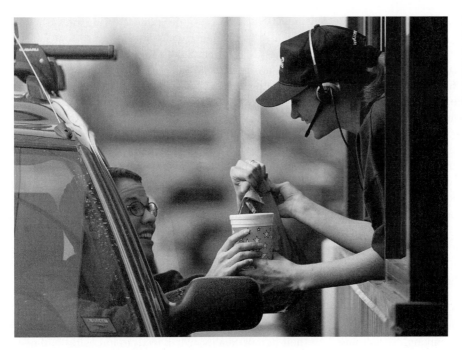

FIGURE 10-3. Employment helps adolescents learn work skills that can be applied to future occupations and helps them individuate from their families of origin.

take greater developmental steps toward maturity and personal autonomy.

Supporting Cognitive Changes. During adolescence, important changes take place in an individual's cognitive abilities. Thinking and comprehension during early and middle childhood are governed by perceptions. Children use their perceptions of the environment to develop hypotheses about their worlds that they believe are borne out by factual experiences. In adolescence, an individual's understanding of people, events, and circumstances becomes more flexible and abstract reasoning becomes possible.

Piaget (1967, 1972) labeled thought during adolescence as a period of formal operations. Thinking during this time of life becomes increasingly characterized by scientific reasoning. This is the emergence of true deductive reasoning ability as a teen learns to generate hypotheses about something and logically work through the alternatives and options as implied outcomes for an acceptable conclusion. Experimentation often helps adolescents rehearse this type of thinking. Scientific reasoning also gives rise to a increasing flexibility in thought that is seen in the game of thinking. This requires divorcing oneself from reality and playfully considering the various hypothetical possibilities

in certain situations. For example, it is common for an adolescent to play the role of devil's advocate in discussions on moral issues. Teens who are developing formal operations cognitive skills apply these to a variety of different types of problems—moral decisions, understanding the actions and words of others, and developing a basic belief or value system to guide their own behavior.

The continual weakening of the role of egocentrism during middle childhood and adolescence allows the emergence of these kinds of advanced, flexible thinking styles. However, as in middle childhood, cognitive egocentrism acts as a distortion that can hinder the achievement of fully mature thinking. In adolescence, egocentrism manifests itself in these ways:

■ *Pseudostupidity* is the tendency to interpret something in more complex ways than is necessary or intended; it is the "making mountains out of molehills" that can continue to persist as a habitual way of reacting to others' behavior and to problems. This tends to produce indecisiveness in some circumstances.
■ Young adolescents typically believe that they are the center of everyone's attention or that every move and action they undertake is under the scrutiny of an *imaginary audience*. This can make some overly

self-conscious about their appearance, what they say, and whom they are seen with.

■ Adolescents typically fall under the spell of their belief in their *personal invincibility* (Elkind, 1974). This is the belief that bad things happen only to other people and that they are protected or exempt from harm or injury when taking chances with risky behaviors. This cognitive flaw perhaps explains why some adolescents undertake risky experimentation with drugs, sexual activity, and driving behaviors.

■ Teenagers show a certain degree of *apparent hypocrisy*, meaning that there is considerable incongruence between what they say they believe and how they act. This may be observed in stubborn arguments with adults, especially parents. For example, teens can be very critical of parental insensitivity to their needs yet feel that they don't have to be sensitive to their parents' needs.

These cognitive flaws can be diminished by examining and questioning one's style of thinking. By learning to depend on logical reasoning and gathering information based on facts, it becomes possible to achieve higher levels of formal operational thought.

Helping Teens Handle Puberty. Puberty is perhaps the central developmental milestone of adolescence. It involves both physical and psychological aspects as part of the identity formation process. In this developmental event a child becomes a sexually mature individual. However, because adolescents are not yet mature emotionally, the feelings that accompany the physical changes of puberty can be confusing, conflicting, and difficult to understand. Many parents are also unsure about how to help their adolescent child handle the various aspects related to puberty. Perhaps the greatest part that a parent can have is maintaining open lines of communication with their maturing child so that issues can be discussed openly and honestly.

Sexual Orientation Issues. During adolescence, many individuals discover their sexual orientation, which serves as the foundation of sexual identity. **Sexual orientation** is the self-awareness and knowledge that one is sexually attracted to and directs emotional affection toward people of the same or opposite sex. Those who orient to others of the same sex are known as *homosexuals*. Those who orient to others of the opposite sex are known as *heterosexuals*.

There is no clear, definitive explanation of how a person's sexual orientation is determined (Strong, 2004). Apparently, the foundations for someone's sexual orientation are influenced by genetic and biological factors interacting with environmental factors that occur beginning prior to birth. The large majority of adolescents are heterosexual. Estimates vary about those having a homosexual orientation. Adolescents who are gay or lesbian commonly experience great difficulty in accepting their homosexuality. Adolescents are sensitive to any behavior or social position in which they might be seen as different from others. Young adolescents are especially fearful of rejection by peers because they interpret such reactions from others as an invalidation of self. Given the deeply ingrained negative societal opinion about homosexuals, most teenagers who discover their homosexual orientation are reluctant to acknowledge it publicly, afraid of risking even further rejection. This reluctance is especially common among boys who are gay.

Many gay and lesbian adolescents react by hiding their homosexuality, which leads to unhealthy and negative outcomes (Hatheway, 2003). Role confusion, rather than a fully integrated personal identity, may begin for these individuals if they fail to incorporate this aspect into their personal identity. Those having difficulty accepting their homosexual orientation typically make strong efforts at denial, trying to pass as heterosexual to avoid social stigmatization and isolation. Unhealthy self-esteem, alienation from others, fear of intimacy, social isolation, and stifled emotional expression are frequently observed during this denial. Gay and lesbian teens usually are not afforded the equivalent types of dating experiences available to nongay teens, which may contribute to those feelings.

Dating and Sexual Activity. Dating is the first interpersonal social experience that many teens have with heterosexuality. The way in which teens date has changed over the last 30 years. In the past, a boy traditionally approached a girl with a proposal for socializing at his expense. Their behavior was ritualized because both knew what was and was not expected to occur during the date.

Today, heterosexual teens are much more informal in the way they socialize together. Much of this socialization is part of peer group activities rather than between individuals. Interaction is more casual and informal than in the past. For example, teens enjoy hanging out at shopping malls or having small parties where everyone comes together to enjoy the company, meet new people, and have fun. The age at which adolescents begin to date is a significant predictor of the age at which sexual activity also begins (Steinberg, 2004). Both activities are initiated earlier today than they were in the past. The age at which sexual activity begins also varies according to a teen's ethnic background. For example, black teens tend to experience intercourse for the first time at earlier ages than white teens do (about age 15 to 16 for blacks versus age 18 to 19 for whites). Other predictors of early sexual involvement include opportunity (being in a steady relationship), sexually permissive attitudes, association with delinquent peers, and alcohol use.

While it is unlikely that completely accurate statistics can ever be obtained about the ages at which adolescents first become sexually active, it does appear that this occurs earlier among more adolescents than previously (Bernstein, 2004). However, use of condoms and other birth control methods is more prevalent than in the past, resulting in fewer teen pregnancies.

Sexual activity places teens at risk for pregnancy as well as exposure to sexually transmitted diseases. Use of contraceptives, especially condoms, is known to reduce this risk considerably. Sex-education programs that promote abstinence from sexual activity apparently do not succeed in accomplishing this goal since there is a high rate of sexually transmitted diseases among teen girls, especially aged 15–19 years (Centers for Disease Control and Prevention, 2008). The increased use of condoms may reflect the influence of more effective sex-education programs that provide factual information, especially regarding the transmission of AIDS.

Supporting Sex Education for Teens.   Exploration and experimentation are necessary behavioral components that motivate the identity formation process in adolescence. Many adults are uncomfortable acknowledging that adolescents are curious about their sexuality, particularly because puberty has made them capable of reproduction; it is no longer an abstraction (Steinberg, 2004). Some adults object to school courses that provide teenagers with explicit sexual information. They may object for several reasons: (1) fear that sexual information will stimulate experimentation with sexual activities, (2) concern about moral issues, (3) fear that teens will be taught values that differ from those of their family system, (4) lack of parental control over what is taught,

or (5) fear that schools will undermine parental authority. Most adults favor sex education in schools, however, and only a few appear to prohibit their teenage children from participation (Bellows, 2004).

Compounding the issue of the need for sex education is the fact that teens do not think logically about hypothetical issues in general (Flavell et al., 2001). Sexual decision making involves some of the many different kinds of skills that teens must acquire in their identity formation process. They may obtain much information in sex-education courses; however, it is unclear how teens use this information in making sexual decisions that affect their behavior. Some adults fear that if teens are given information about sexual behavior or methods of birth control, they will become more curious, which may lead to sexual activity. But this response does not appear to be the case. Exposure to sexual information may have the effect of delaying the age at which adolescents begin to experiment sexually rather than stimulating it (McKay, Fisher, Maticka-Tyndale, & Barrett, 2001).

One of the most important contributions parents can make to their teen's exposure to sexual information is providing them with the skills to make healthy sexual decisions. For some parents, this means helping their teen to understand the desire for sexual abstinence. For others, it means being sure that their adolescent understands the principles but most especially the importance of safer sex practices. Each family system will need to determine how it will approach and deal with this aspect of an adolescent child's identity development and act accordingly. Many will want to take advantage of the opportunities provided by most school systems today for professionally guided educational experiences for their teens, while others will seek strict control over the information that is presented and in a particular context.

Equally important is the balancing of information that is strictly factual with that which addresses the emotional aspects of sexuality. Teens need support as they explore their first romantic encounters and preparation for all that this entails as best as is possible. For many parents, this experience is a reminder of what they encountered as adolescents. However, when most contemporary parents were teenagers, sexually transmitted diseases were not fatal and teen pregnancy was less acceptable than today. In this regard, many parents of contemporary adolescents need updating on sexual information to discuss these issues with their adolescent children.

• •

Parenting Reflection 10–3

The AIDS epidemic has changed a long-running debate on what public schools should and should not teach in sex-education courses. What should adolescents learn in these courses and when should this be taught?

Some high schools have clinics where teens may obtain condoms and other methods of birth control. Do you think this practice encourages sexual activity or serves as a means of realistically assisting adolescents in making healthy sexual decisions?

• •

SYSTEMIC FAMILY DEVELOPMENT SNAPSHOT

(Before reading this section, it may be helpful to review the systemic family development model and the metaphor used to illustrate its concepts from Chapter 3.)

Our slice of developmental time is taken at the midpoint of the adolescence stage of the oldest child in the Curtis family. Mary Curtis is now 15 years old. This slice is taken about 6 years after the snapshot we examined in the previous chapter when Mary was a school-age child. We begin examining the snapshot with a brief review of the stressors that can affect a family system at this time. Perhaps the greatest levels of stress are being experienced now by both the third generation (the adolescent children) and their parents. However, the first generation is experiencing major life changes. Altogether, this is a time of challenges for the entire family system as homeostasis has been disrupted at all levels.

At the time of this slice of developmental time, here are the ages of all members of the family system: (1) the paternal grandfather (George Curtis) is now 69; (2) the paternal grandmother (Joan Curtis) is 67; (3) the maternal grandfather (Harry Scott) is now 66; (4) there is now a maternal stepgrandmother (Kim Scott) due to Harry's remarriage—she is 63; (5) Butch Curtis is now 45; and (6) Lisa Curtis is now 42. The first child, Mary, is 15 and the second child, Joey, is 13 years old.

Examples of Stressors Affecting Each Curtis Family Generation: 6 Years Later

First Generation (Grandparents)

■ Adjusting to the aging process that continues in the latter part of middle age and in the first years of late adulthood

■ Adjusting to increasing frequency of deaths among spouses, colleagues, coworkers, and friends
■ Adjusting to declines in personal health and that of one's partner
■ Making final preparations for retirement and adjusting to the life changes precipitated by retirement
■ Beginning life reviews
■ Adjusting to widowhood and to remarriage in late life
■ Preparing for one's death and that of one's partner

Second Generation (Adult Parents of Adolescents)

■ Providing for widely different needs of all family members
■ Experiencing recovery of marital satisfaction
■ Bridging communication issues between adults and adolescent children
■ Supporting the individuation process of adolescent children
■ Reworking and adapting family roles and rules
■ Adapting parenting styles to meet the needs of adolescents
■ Managing provider and family roles effectively

Third Generation (Adolescent Children)

■ Mastering developmental tasks and milestones of adolescence (see Focus On 10–1)

The Third Generation (Adolescents)

We begin our examination of the Curtis family snapshot with the third generation, the adolescent children. Mary Curtis is now a freshman in high school at age 15. She is both excited and nervous about beginning high school. Junior high was lots of fun, and she excelled in her schoolwork. Now, she knows things will change in many respects on entering high school. Academics are more difficult, but the payoff is new friends, old friends, and, of course, boys! She has her parents' permission to begin dating if she desires and if the boy meets a few standards set by her parents. There are many new freedoms now, but these are controlled by the rules her parents set with Mary's agreement. She has already been on several double dates with friends and has gone to a few parties. Her first big school dance is coming up in a few weeks, and Mary has been asked out by three boys for the occasion. Luckily, Mike, the boy she likes the most, asked her first. She definitely has feelings about him as they have spent more time together. These feelings are confusing in some ways because she doesn't always understand what they mean. The feelings seem to peak when they are alone and making out. Some of her girlfriends have already "gone all the way" with their boyfriends and talk about their experiences quite a bit. Mary isn't sure what to do about all this but thinks she should try to talk things over with her mom before proceeding as her friends have done. She feels she could trust her mother's thoughts and believes she is lucky to have a mom who is open-minded. Most of her friends keep secrets like this from their parents.

While Mary likes school, she is almost bored with some of her subjects and finds that her mind turns to daydreaming when she is uninterested in something during class. The daydreams focus on a variety of themes and ideas, such as what kind of work she will do when she grows up, if she will ever be married and have children, and if she will have a handsome husband someday with an important job and live in a trendy home. But reality soon returns as she knows she must do well in school now to be accepted to a good university.

She often thinks about new clothes and makeup, but her parents keep her on a small allowance in return for housework she does while her mother and father work. This isn't enough to cover the costs of what she really wants, so she had been investigating the possibility of a job at one of the local fast-food restaurants. She has even filled out an application but has not yet handed it in because she needs to discuss this with her parents. She has been exploring some what-if scenarios with her mother about working part-time, and her mom seems to think she could try this out as an experiment to see what would happen with her schoolwork. She needs the permission of both parents to get a job permit, however, so her mother has agreed to discuss this first with her dad to

work out any objections he might have. Mary also is looking forward to getting her driver's license in a few months. Her parents have agreed she could do this if she has proven that she can be trustworthy and responsible this year. She has agreed to show this by observing curfew rules, keeping at least a B average in all her subjects, and being responsible about her household chores. Her parents recently added one other stipulation to this list—not getting into any trouble that involves her friends.

One of the biggest problems Mary faces now is what to do about hanging out with friends. Some are drinking alcohol and trying drugs like Ecstasy, especially the boys. Some have been smoking cigarettes now for more than a year, and some have tried pot. Some of them have pressured Mary to try these things, but she has managed so far to try pot only once. She didn't like the way it made her feel, and she got ill from the experience. This was yet another thing to talk over with her mom since she wasn't exactly sure what to do to keep her friends while saying no to drugs and other wild behaviors.

Mary's brother, Joey, is now 13 and in seventh grade. Mary is surprised at how much he has changed in the last year. He is taller but very skinny. His braces are the most prominent part of his facial expressions. And he is always doing dorky things either by himself or with his friends. Mary thinks they all need to be hung out to dry for another year. Not that high school boys are totally cool, but these kids are in a totally different class!

Joey always seems to be hungry. No matter how much he eats at a meal, he has hunger pangs 30 minutes later. His allowance goes quickly for junk food from vending machines near home and school. And he is always outgrowing his clothes, it seems, within weeks after his mom has replaced them. He sleeps a lot more than he used to, and it's not unusual for him to crawl out of bed about noon on weekends. His body confuses him in some ways; at times he seems uncoordinated and unsure of where his arms or legs are in space. He can just as easily fall or trip going upstairs as he can do fancy tricks on his skateboard. And he doesn't understand the changes he sees in his genitals. He listens with keen interest when his friends talk about such matters and it makes him feel better to know he isn't some kind of a freak. The exercise sport classes he takes now require that all the boys take showers, and this is a convenient place to make comparisons between himself and the other guys.

Joey looks at girls differently now; in fact, it seems that he has just discovered that girls share the planet. However, he feels shy and awkward when one looks at him and smiles, and he hasn't had the courage yet to even hang out with a girl. He has gone to only one dance at school so far, but only a few couples actually danced together; everyone else got into bunches with their friends and just jumped around.

His passion is playing video and computer games with his buddies and going to the skateboard park after school and on weekends. These are places and times when they can get away from disapproving adults and older sisters and do their thing without interference. Joey has gotten into lots of arguments with his parents lately; it seems that is all they do at meals and other times. He thinks his father is especially bossy and has been driving hard rules that are difficult and unreasonable, like having to tell them everywhere he goes, whom he is going with, and being back home at a set time. Joey's parents insist on meeting his friends before they allow him to go to their houses for a weekend overnight; that is truly unreasonable, he thinks. And they always give him a once-over after he comes back the next day. They seem suspicious of things like smoking, drinking, and who knows what else. He tried to dress like some of his buddies in that way-cool Goth style, but his parents put that off-limits the minute they saw him come home wearing black fingernail polish.

The Second Generation (Adult Parents)

Lisa and Butch feel that they have learned many lessons about parenting adolescents from working with Mary, but lately parenting Joey has called their skills and patience into doubt. Boys must be more of a challenge and a handful as teenagers than girls, but then again girls present their own unique challenges for parents. All the questioning of just about everything, the defiance, the testing of rules and boundaries, the conflicts, and the rebellious experimentation that they had seen in varying degrees with both of their teens has had a definite impact on them as individuals, as parents, and as a couple.

Many conflicts have arisen between themselves and Mary about certain issues, such as her need to demonstrate responsible behaviors for them to trust her when she is away from home with friends. Now innumerable tugs-of-war occur with Joey about most everything. His negative attitude permeates their home life and shows

up in a poor attitude about schoolwork, disagreements about dress style and hygiene, intolerance and insensitivity about his family members, his apparent lack of respect for people in authority, constant nagging to get him to perform tasks around the house, forgetting to keep commitments until the last minute, and the constant fear that he is getting in with the wrong crowd of kids. They had seen Mary grow away from these kinds of problems and knew that they have to hang in with Joey in trusting that this too would pass away some time in the future. They love their son very much and hate to see how difficult it is for him to be dealing with all these boundary issues.

Butch and Lisa have talked with friends who weathered the adolescence of their children about the situation with Joey and have gathered many opinions and ideas. Lisa even attended a parenting class offered through Joey's school by the PTA about "Surviving the Storm and Stress of Adolescence." What seems to work the best for now when they need to be strict about something is denying privileges and working out bargains with Joey. For example, they have learned that he responds well to arrangements where he is offered a reward such as staying out an hour later than normally past curfew in return for keeping to school assignment deadlines and doing his work as directed.

Lisa and Butch are not aware that they are going through what is known as the *midlife transition experience*. Perhaps there is some connection between the turmoil that their teenagers are experiencing in confronting their new selves and the many issues and decisions that must be made. Butch began to express this uneasiness before Lisa had as he tried to talk about his confusion about some things and the feelings of uncertainty that have come into his consciousness. He wonders about what it will take to make him feel really happy. He hasn't found it in his work, volunteer activities, or some aspects of his family life, especially in dealing with a young adolescent boy. And he has not yet mentioned unhappiness with their marriage. In fact, things between Butch and Lisa have improved considerably just within the last year or so. They have found more time to spend together just talking when the kids are out for the evening. They are doing more things together again, like shopping and working in the yard. They have even had some rare private time for several weekends when the kids were out of the home for visits with friends. They had almost forgotten what it was like to be able to go to a movie as a couple or just rent a video and have pizza and wine like they did before their kids arrived. Both these adults have discovered that what makes the difference in their lives are the relationships with family and friends.

The First Generation (Grandparents)

The first generation of this family system is confronting the full reality of what it means to grow old and become senior citizens. All four of these individuals have reached retirement status and have learned how to adjust to living on a fixed income while having the opportunity to enjoy the luxury of leisure time. There had been many adjustments to a new lifestyle produced by this new social status. At first, George Curtis felt wonderful about being released from the daily grind of having to go to work. However, the availability of too much time caused confusion, restlessness, and a sense of loss. Joan, his wife of almost 45 years, also struggled with the changes in the household routine in having her husband home all the time.

As he struggled to find a new direction in his life, George sometimes seemed like a child who was underfoot and in the way. Joan had heard from other wives in similar situations that this was a good time to offer options and choices for how George could find new meaning in his life. Some men developed hobbies (that could be expensive), others were content to plan and go on trips, and others resolved this issue in creative ways. As they explored what both of them could do with their newfound time and opportunities, George and Joan finally found an outlet that afforded good use of their time and was helpful to others. They now volunteer at a shelter for homeless people. Joan puts her wonderful interpersonal skills to good use in working with the literacy program that helps people of all ages learn or improve their reading skills. George found his place in working with the life skills program, where he could share his vast experience in financial management by just helping people learn about budgets, credit management, and even balancing a checking account.

Harry Scott, Lisa's father, had taken longer to recover from the grief of his first wife's death than he had anticipated. It seemed that he had become stuck in his grieving process. Lisa became concerned that her father was emotionally depressed to the point of watching him closely for signs of suicidal ideations. Fortunately, after much discussion and persuasion, Harry agreed to enter

therapy to work on the issues related to his grief. At the same time, he also sought help in dealing with his heavy involvement with drinking that had occurred in conjunction with Susan's death. After much hard work, he recovered from both problems and was able to pick up and go on with his life.

In an odd twist, Harry met the woman who became his second wife at a support group for widows. Kim Scott was widowed a short time before Harry's wife died. Coincidentally, both of the deceased spouses had died of cancer. As Harry and Kim participated in the group sessions, they listened to others' descriptions of problems similar to their own and the various ways that people managed their emotions and reactions. They became friends through informally continuing those discussions over coffee following the group sessions. The time spent talking for hours helped to lay the foundation for a strong intimate relationship based on sharing, authenticity, and mutual care and respect.

The remarriage came as a surprise to some members of the family but not to others. Lisa was overjoyed that her father had found love again and that the person was someone who truly cared for her father. She missed the close relationship with her mother but knew she could not impose the same expectations on this new relationship with her stepmother. On the good advice of a friend, she has learned to allow this to develop and grow in its own way.

The grandchildren have had different reactions to their grandfather's remarriage. Joey resents having to spend time with his maternal grandparents and flatly refuses to be seen in public with them. Mary, on the other hand, finds her new stepgrandmother to be a great ally, someone she can approach to talk about things she wants to run by her parents after rehearsing with Kim.

Death seems to be a more common denominator in the lives of all four members of the first generation. Not only had they experienced the deaths of spouses, but now there are more and more memorial services to attend for friends, colleagues, and coworkers who are dying in greater numbers as they grow older. Each is also experiencing health problems that range from arthritis to hypertension to cataracts to dry-eye syndrome. Conversations often focus on these health issues and related economic problems such as medical insurance coverage, social security payments, Medicare management, and the increasing cost of long-term care insurance. Prescription costs are becoming unbearable, and much discussion centers on how the government needs to do something about this problem. Such conversation topics are a sore point with Butch at times and with the teenagers most of the time because they find these topics boring and mundane.

Harry and George have found a common ground of interest: genealogy. Both are learning how to trace their family's backgrounds and have shared much information with each other as they learn to navigate the Internet as a research tool. All this interest in the past has sparked an interest for Kim Scott to begin assembling the infor-

mation she needs to write her memoirs. Joan is also caught up in the enthusiasm of the others by learning how to quilt so that she could pass heirloom-quality hand-me-downs to her son's family.

This generation is relatively content in their old age, fortunately. And they are well insulated from the pressures their children and grandchildren are experiencing as they navigate the troubled waters of the "adolescent experience," as Joan calls it. They are there for support if their family needs them but are enjoying the fruits of their earlier labors in raising children into adulthood.

PARENT–YOUNG ADULT CHILD RELATIONS

By the time someone's child has reached the years we designate as early adulthood (18 to 45 years), the general perception is that one's work and involvement as a parent ceases. The child is no longer considered to be an immature person but someone who is responsible for their own welfare, capable of making their own decisions, and owning the consequences of their behavior and actions. The parenting relationship continues but in an altered form. The transformation of the relationship between parent and child has actually been taking place all along in keeping pace with the developmental changes occurring in the child over time (Figure 10-4). The child has long depended on the parent for protection, nurturance, and training. Now, the relationship as well as the child matures into a new form.

Upon the child's attaining adulthood, the overall goal of parenting should have been accomplished: helping a child to become a fully functioning, effective person in adulthood. However, this transformation is not simply accomplished when the child becomes legally mature at age 18. Dependencies continue in some modified form between the adult child and the parent. But the dependencies are not like those observed among infants and older children. Rather, these share similarities to the dependencies found to some degree in all intimate relationships among adults found in families. The transformation is to a relationship originally based on power and responsibility of the older person in guiding and directing the development of the younger person to one in which the participants share a more balanced field of interaction. The relationship between parents

and adult children ideally becomes one that is more distinctly adult in nature.

Parenthood does not come to a complete halt, then, when children reach their 18th birthday or even later; however, the relationship between parents and young adults is modified once again in response to the new developmental needs of adult children. Most young adult

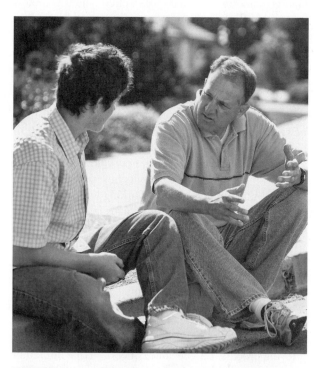

FIGURE 10-4. The relationship between parents and a young adult child must be transformed into an adult-adult relationship in order to be successful.

children experience these first years of adulthood as a transition period while they complete the final aspects of individuation from their family systems. For example, many are not yet completely financially independent while they complete their college educations or even for some time afterwards. Others, although involved in a marriage relationship, have not been employed long enough to equip their homes, build a sound financial base that provides for their own children's needs, or establish themselves in occupations to ensure a sound financial future. Parents continue to provide support, often in the form of financial assistance, to young adult children during this period. In addition, they may provide other aspects of support when young adult children temporarily return to live in the family home and the structure is shifted to a renested family system.

Relations between parents and children during this stage can be strained and confusing (Parenting FAQs 10–2). Parents sometimes are unsure of how to relate and communicate with children who are quickly becoming independent adults but who are still dependent

in some respects. They continue to feel responsible for giving advice to their children but may feel unprepared and ill-equipped to do so in ways that are truly helpful. Adult children probably feel as many conflicting emotions as their parents do in this regard. On the one hand, they may desire to confide in parents, but on the other, they may feel resentful of the intrusive and judgmental nature of parental advice.

Prolonged Dependencies Between Parents and Young Adults

Prolonged dependency can take place in a relationship between parents and children that is unhealthy when children become young adults. Parents can maintain this state when adult children are supported financially and emotionally far beyond the time when such ties are normally severed and adult children fully individuate. Sometimes situations beyond the control of the family system maintain these ties. For example, higher education is extremely costly today, and young adults frequently

---

Parenting FAQs 10–2

I recently moved back into my parents' home because I've just completed my undergraduate education and am in the process of looking for employment. I've been back home now for almost a year. I'm having a hard time with my parents, who increasingly are treating me like an errant teenager who's out of control . . . which I'm not. I just haven't found the right job yet. They're trying to enforce rules on my behavior and lifestyle that were in place when I was a teen. . . I don't think this is appropriate at all but don't know how to go about trying to negotiate a more mature, adult relationship with my folks. Can you suggest some ways to attempt this?

A: It's frequently difficult to raise parents, don't you think? (LOL!) You will need to work hard on maintaining your temper and your patience as you work with your folks to help them realize you aren't a teenager anymore. Persevere in being willing to work on this new relationship as everyone involved must learn to forge new roles, new rules, and new boundaries. Here are some additional thoughts to consider:

- Be willing to contribute to the work of the household in as many ways as possible, especially if you can't contribute financially.
- Talk rationally and keep a level head when you are discussing how you want to see this new relationship to be transformed.
- Be willing to listen and try out what your folks suggest what you need to do to contribute to the new relationship.
- Be willing to negotiate new rules and boundaries for your behavior that are acceptable to everyone involved in the new relationship.
- Suggest experimental periods to be implemented in testing new rules and boundaries; be willing to renegotiate rules and boundaries that don't appear to be working out to everyone's satisfaction.

seek assistance from parents to meet financial obligations. But other situations can also cause prolonged dependency, such as overparenting or prolonged investment in the aspects of parenting that promote children's dependencies.

Some parents foster extended dependency of adult children, for example, when they have intensely continued to be overinvolved in their children's lives. They may have given children too many material possessions and not enough limits. They may not have fostered analytical and decision-making skills or used a parenting style that encouraged and facilitated individuation during adolescence and early adulthood (Gordon, 2004). As a result, the adult child fails to individuate successfully from the family system, largely because dependency prolongs and even thwarts the normal individuation process. The usual, anticipated outcome of individuation is a redefined relationship between parents and adult children that is more adult in nature.

How Do Parents Promote Prolonged Dependency of Adult Children?
Most parents want their children to grow up and achieve an independent existence. Essentially, most healthy parents want their child-rearing responsibilities to end at some point. Then why do some parents continue to create situations where they remain heavily and actively involved in a caregiving role? The explanations are complex, just as the individuals involved are complex. However, several factors emerge as possible answers (Arnett, 2003; Ifejika, 2003).

Parents ideally shift away from authoritarian styles to those that are more democratic and equalitarian as children grow older. This shift occurs in response to the changing developmental nature of children as they grow and mature. Equalitarian parenting styles support a child's individuation process by shifting the source of social power to a more balanced position between parent and child. They recognize a child's more mature status and his or her ability to solve personal problems, learn from mistakes, and make his or her own way in the world. By reacting in ways that are authoritarian, overprotective, or disinterested, parents promote prolonged dependency in their adult children.

How Do Adult Children Promote Their Prolonged Dependency on Parents?
Prolonged dependency is not created and maintained by parents alone. A child also plays a part by maintaining a dependency role

longer than is developmentally appropriate. Contributions stemming from the adult child that can promote abnormally prolonged dependence on parental involvement include factors such as: (1) an abnormal fear of assuming responsibility for one's own life and decisions, (2) addictions and substance abuse, (3) an abnormal fear of failure in the adult world, or (4) lack of motivation to leave the comforts of the parental home (Arnett, 2003; Ifejika, 2003; van Poppel, Oris, & Lee, 2004).

Parenting Reflection 10–4
What happens when a family system does not accept or support the efforts of young adults to individuate completely from the system? What are short- and long-term effects of such prolonged dependence between family members?

What Can Be Done to Normalize Parent–Adult Child Relations?
Parents often realize that they are partially responsible for creating the dependency of adult children. Some understand what has happened when children do not progress in mastering appropriate developmental tasks for their age. Others become aware when adult children return home and do not move on with their lives after an extended period of time. Therapists suggest a number of ways that parents can help to remedy their role configuration in fostering this unhealthy situation so that all family members can move forward developmentally. For example, an obvious solution is to stop playing the role of a caretaker parent in enabling an adult child's lack of developmental progress. Parents can let go of the ways in which they have usually responded to children's dependency needs. For example, boundaries are adapted within the relationship to reflect less involvement in the affairs of adult children. Another solution is to make a conscious and demonstrable change toward a more equalitarian stance in relating to adult children. When prolonged dependencies occur as part of improper or poor parenting skills, parents can change the relationship with their adult children by changing themselves (J. Adams, 2004). Another solution is to set deadlines for certain tasks to be accomplished, such as finding a job, moving into different quarters, and so on.

However, parents sometimes wish to continue promoting their child's dependency, while an adult child wishes to individuate more fully. Often changes are initiated in the parent-child relationship when children become aware that they are, indeed, *adult children* of dysfunctional families (Ramey, 2004). This term comes from contemporary psychotherapy; it describes individuals who have experienced a stifling of their healthy emotional developmental progress at some point in their developmental past. This stifling occurs when children grow up in family systems where they are affected by physical, emotional, or sexual abuse; parental alcoholism or drug abuse; and/or ineffective and unhealthy parenting styles. Many people discover that they are adult children when they try to recover from various addictions manifested in early adulthood. These range from addictions to substances, such as food or drugs, to addictions to people or relationships.

When young adults struggle for individuation from dysfunctional parents and family systems, they can find assistance in psychotherapy, support groups, and 12-step programs. In this case, the adult child, not the parent, struggles to let go of dependencies and inappropriate patterns of interactions, but the struggle can be immensely difficult for everyone concerned.

Adult children make aggressive attempts to individuate from unhealthy parents as a means of resuming healthy developmental progress. The parents, however, often resist this significant change in their relationship. At this point, it is often best to have the assistance of a competent therapist. When one person in an unhealthy family system attempts to produce change, the system often reacts to the loss of equilibrium by experiencing even more chaos.

While the adult child who is attempting to change the nature of the relationship with their parent knows that freedom comes only from acting differently, the unhealthy family system abhors change. Parents who have a toxic relationship with their adult children can be expected to resist the children's attempts to individuate. However, many individuals recovering as adult children are parents themselves, and they do not wish to perpetuate unhealthy parenting patterns with their own children. By fully individuating from an unhealthy family system, these courageous individuals pursue a healthy developmental path toward their own full potential as human beings and the potential of their children (Clarke & Dawson, 1998).

∙∙

Focus Point.   The relationship between parents and young adult children can sometimes stagnate and fail to

mature and become transformed. Sometimes parents are responsible while adult children are sometimes responsible. Various ways can normalize this stagnated relationship configuration.

∙∙

ATTACHMENT REVISED

By establishing a basic idea of who one is and where one is going in life in adolescence, an individual is prepared to move on to their next stage of psychosocial development. Erikson (1950, 1964, 1982, 1986) believed that establishing a sense of intimacy is the primary developmental task of early adulthood. To achieve intimacy, people must learn how to lower the personal boundaries they have constructed to protect their innermost, authentic selves from others. This requires trusting that one will not be harmed psychologically and emotionally by another in this intimate setting. Essentially, the lessons learned first in infancy about trusting a parental caretaker lay the foundation for learning how to trust another in an intimate adult relationship. The attachment that was developed with parents serves as a template for this type of trust that is an important component of an adult love relationship (Figure 10-5).

When a young adult begins to pursue the development of an intimate relationship, it takes much practice

FIGURE 10-5.   The development of attachment to parents in infancy lays the foundation for a mature love attachment in adulthood.

and many opportunities to discover what is involved, what is required, what one wants, and with whom. While there have been many attempts by behavioral scientists to quantify and identify how this takes place, perhaps one of the better explanations and blueprints about what adult love involves has been described in Sternberg's (1986) triangular theory of love. He believes that love is composed of three parts: (1) *passion,* or the physical and/or sexual attraction to someone; (2) *intimacy,* or the emotional connection with another that involves authentic self-disclosure which leads to trust, closeness, and warmth; and (3) *commitment,* or the decision to love someone and remain with them over an extended period and "for better or worse." When all three of these are experienced in an intimate relationship, then Steinberg believes that one is experiencing consummate love.

The nature of love that is felt in infancy is thought to be self-directed, and for good reason. Apparently, there is a significant need for an individual to learn (in this context of nurturant parenting) that he or she is the object of someone's intense love. It is believed that unless people learn self-love (that they are of importance and worth because of loving parental treatment and to love themselves accordingly) in infancy, they are unable to love others later in life (Fromm, 1970). In the sequence of development, an infant who has been loved by nurturant parents learns such self-love. The self-love or positive regard for oneself is generated to the self, back to the parents, then to other family members, and later to possessions. As children grow older and make accompanying shifts toward independence, they learn the need for interdependence. This characteristic assists them in developing healthy intimate relationships in adulthood in which they depend on another as well as on themselves. A person progresses, then, from infantile love ("I love you because I need you") to mature love ("I need you because I love you"; Fromm, 1970).

FUNCTIONING AS A RENESTED FAMILY SYSTEM

Families in which children have become adults are characterized by the changes in status and roles of all family members. Those produced by the emancipation of the children can cause conflicts, adjustment problems, and even emotional crises for family systems. Launching their children into the adult world essentially may complete the parents' development of a sense of generativity.

However, because of various social and economic circumstances today, some parents find that it takes many years to launch children successfully and completely into adult independence and autonomy.

Transitions of adult children into their own lifestyles do not happen as smoothly as research or textbooks describe (Secunda, 2004). Many young adult children, mostly males, return to their parents' homes to live temporarily. Usually this is a limited arrangement because the adult children become unemployed, seek retraining, change career objectives, or divorce.

The kind of family structure experienced during childhood and adolescence may have a bearing on when adolescents and young adults launch themselves away from their families of origin (Goldschneider & Goldschneider, 1998). The family structure factor can also influence their return into the family of origin at later times. Growing up in nontraditional family settings, such as stepfamilies, decreases the likelihood of an adolescent's enrollment into a program of higher education, for example, and increases the likelihood of leaving the family of origin early to become married or to attain full individuation. Under such circumstances, researchers find that there is also a lessened likelihood of returning to the family of origin after becoming individuated.

Undoubtedly, everyone involved in this type of family structure is likely to have mixed feelings about the situation (Secunda, 2004). On the one hand, parents understand the need to be supportive of their adult child and wish to be as helpful as possible. On the other hand, parents may be understandably resentful of the new demands on resources, time, and energy required in having an additional person or persons in their daily lives. The adult child may also harbor mixed feelings. He or she may appreciate what the parents are providing in a time of need and at the same time resent conflicts that can arise in the resumption of old interaction patterns between parent and child.

Both children and parents resent the dependency on parents and view this period as developmentally off-time. Many problems result from parents who continue to act intrusively in the lives of children who are used to independent functioning. For example, families describe conflicts about the hours adult children keep, the way they maintain their personal space, and lifestyle choices such as sexual behavior.

Researchers have not studied problems in these families adequately enough to know exactly how these conflicts are resolved. Most likely, they are not resolved unless the adult children can resist falling into old dependency patterns and parents can resist acting as caregivers. During renesting, both parents and adult children may need to renegotiate the rules and patterns that govern their relationship.

Another trend has recently become observable to researchers who study financial security among Americans and other domestic issues (American Savings Education Council and American Association of Retired Persons, 2008). This trend is the continuing reliance of many young adults on financial assistance from parents and friends into the upper years of early adulthood, that is, those more than 39 years of age. This trend is related to a downward national economy in which recessionary trends have influenced high rates of unemployment, increased rates of job loss, significantly higher prices in certain commodities such as gasoline and wheat, and an unprecedented number of mortgage foreclosures. This trend of continued financial reliance on families of origin is likely to extend the issues faced by renested families into many more years than the lower end of early adulthood of adult children.

● ●

Parenting Reflection 10–5

Are teenagers and young adults different today than they were 20 or 30 years ago? What has changed and what has remained fairly constant about the nature of young people over the years?

● ●

GRANDPARENTING

At some point in time, it is likely that many parents will become grandparents when their children have become adults. As such, grandparenting comes, for most, at the end of their parenting careers. The stereotypical image of grandparents is that of a kindly middle-aged or elderly person in a rocking chair dispensing advice and wisdom to one and all. Today, it is not unusual for someone in their late 30s or early 40s to be a grandparent. According to one study, the average age at which participants became grandparents was 48 years (Davies & Williams, 2002). Rather than taking a sedentary approach to life, today's grandparent most likely is physically active, still

employed, and at times providing full-time care for grandchildren (Kornhaber, 2002).

Today's grandparents and their activities as a grandparent are different from that of previous generations. First, more people are grandparents, and it is estimated that more than 90 percent of older people are great-grandparents (Kornhaber, 2002). When considering the greater length of life expectancy, it is more likely that children today will have the opportunity to know and have a relationship with both sets of grandparents. Since about 90 percent of Americans who are 65 years of age or older are great-grandparents, it is also more likely that today's children will have experiences involving this grandparent than previous generations. The most frequent activities grandparents report having with grandchildren include sharing dinner, watching television, playing games and sports, reading together, and going shopping (Davies & Williams, 2002). A majority of those studied see a grandchild at least once a week, but many live long distances away, which prevents regular visits. The shift away from parenting responsibilities often is replaced by grandparenting assuming a major role in the lives of many middle-aged people.

Second, the high divorce rate in contemporary society has changed the nature of grandparents' relationships with grandchildren from what perhaps was observed in the past. The legal status of grandparents is a nebulous issue, and few states have enacted statutes that outline grandparental rights with regard to visitation with grandchildren (Taylor, 2001).

Third, many grandparents take an active role in raising and providing care for grandchildren. A substantial increase has occurred in the numbers of households headed by grandparents who provide the primary caregiving for grandchildren whether the children's parents are present or absent. When grandparents have compared parenting their grandchildren with parenting their children, they report themselves as more relaxed, more involved, and wiser (Dolbin-MacNab, 2006). They reported challenges as well. This type of family was discussed in greater detail in Chapter 2.

Although some grandparents are not especially involved with grandchildren and their role is downplayed in family life, other grandparents make important contributions to family life and have significant influence on family systems. These include (1) accepting behaviors and traits of grandchildren that adult parents are not able to tolerate; (2) providing nurturance for grandchildren that adult parents may not be able to provide; (3) providing instruction for grandchildren in values, ethics, and morals; (4) providing backup support for parents in raising grandchildren; (5) providing parents with options for solving interaction problems and conflicts with grandchildren; and (6) acting as an equalizer to provide balance within a family system (Kornhaber, 2003; Kropf & Burnette, 2003; Mueller & Elder, 2003).

The Grandparent Role

While greater numbers of grandparents may be found in families today, the role continues to lack clear definitions and boundaries for outlining how someone is to act in this capacity. Grandparents do not readily know what is expected of them nor how they are to interact with grandchildren, and adult children and grandchildren are often equally unsure about these interactions.

It is more appropriate, perhaps, to view a person's grandparent role as having a variety of aspects, often based on the nature of the relationship with each particular grandchild (Mueller & Elder, 2003; Reynolds, Wright, & Beale, 2003). When viewed from this perspective, a grandparent role does not have a monolithic definition but one that is composed of different aspects

(Figure 10-6). The relationships between grandparents and grandchildren vary in many respects. For example, one grandchild may be perceived as being special to the grandparent in certain ways while another may be viewed as an irritant and vexsome. Undoubtedly, the nature and quality of the relationship as well as how the grandparent conducts his or her interactions with a grandchild is mediated on such perceptions.

It is not clear how people make the transition into this role (Kornhaber, 2003). For many, the transition begins when they learn of the pregnancy of the adult child carrying the potential first grandchild. The older adult parents fantasize about what they will experience as grandparents. Because this is a first-time experience, the first grandchild often takes a special place in the lives of grandparents. The transition experience appears to vary from person to person, however. Some find this difficult, especially if becoming a grandparent is perceived as being developmentally off-time rather than on-time (Kopera-Frye, Wiscott, & Begovic, 2003).

Childhood experiences with grandparents appear to influence the current involvement of men and women with their own grandchildren (Hayslip, 2003). Apparently, people pattern their grandparenting role and behavior based on the models they observed as children.

FIGURE 10-6. Grandparenting can involve a variety of aspects ranging from full-time care of grandchildren to seeing grandchildren only on holidays or birthdays.

Although there is general ambiguity about the grandparent role, it appears that several prominent aspects or components can be found in this role: (1) Grandparents may act as the family "watchdog" in providing support to adult children and grandchildren when needed and in ameliorating the negative impacts of serious family problems of adult children, such as drug abuse, divorce, or chronic emotional or physical illness. (2) Grandparents may provide nurturance to all family members, especially unconditional love, which may not be available from other adults in a family. (3) Grandparents serve as the family historians in acting as the bridge between the past and the present that aids in developing a sense of family and family identity. (4) Grandparents may provide companionship for grandchildren in shared social activities that promote close emotional attachment.

There appear to be at least four to five distinct grandparenting styles that typically change as grandchildren grow older. This evolution or modification of grandparenting styles that change in tandem with grandchildren's development reflects similar changes in parenting styles that occur as children experience developmental changes. These styles are outlined in Focus On 10–2.

Grandparenting styles may be mediated by a variety of factors (Cherlin & Furstenberg, 1986; Kornhaber, 2003). First, gender may temper how someone approaches his or her grandparenting role. Women may be more actively involved with grandchildren than men because of their socialization and past experiences in parenting children. Grandfathers, for example, may emphasize interactions relating to tasks outside the family with grandchildren, while grandmothers may emphasize issues relating to interpersonal dynamics within the family.

Second, physical proximity is an important factor that mediates how the grandparent-grandchild relationship will be shaped and how it will unfold. The magnitude of physical distance between grandparents and grandchildren will frequently determine how involved the older adult is with grandchildren and how interactions will occur. Third, ethnic group influences grandparenting style. For example, a large majority of older Latinos report the desire to live in the same neighborhoods with adult children and grandchildren. In addition, grandparents who are heads of households where they raise grandchildren are likely to be members of ethnic minorities (Federal Interagency Forum on Child and Family Statistics, 2007).

Grandparents have had few rights to visit with or be a part of grandchildren's lives following divorce of their adult children. Unless states have enacted legislation outlining such rights, grandparents may not be allowed to see their grandchildren if the custodial parents disapproves. Some instances involve grandparents petitioning a court to receive visitation rights over the objections of the custodial parent (Stein, 2007). If granted, the court

Focus On 10–2	**Grandparenting Styles**	
	Style	*Traits*
	Surrogate Parent	Primary caregiving; active involvement in child rearing
	Remote	Infrequent contact with grandchildren; makes appearances on special holidays and events
	Fun Seeker	Maintains recreational relationship focusing on leisure activities with grandchildren
	Reservoir of Family Wisdom	Maintains strict boundaries based on patriarchal authority; passes on family legends, folklore, and information
	Formal	Maintains stereotypical grandparent role; promotes distinct boundary between parental and grandparent role

Source: Adapted from Cherlin, A. J., & Furstenberg, F. F. (1986). *The new American grandparent.* New York: Basic Books; McCready, W. (1985). Styles of grandparenting among white ethnics. In V. Bengston & J. Robertson (Eds), *Grandparenthood* (pp. 49–60). Beverly Hills, CA: Sage.

allows such visitation according to what is perceived to be the best interests of the child to continue the relationship with their grandparents.

Stepgrandparenting

Finally, divorce of adult children as well as that of grandparents themselves can temper how the grandparent-grandchild relationship will be conducted (Taylor, 2001). When the grandparents themselves divorce after years of marriage, some may diminish their involvement with grandchildren because of the circumstances surrounding their divorce. When adult children divorce, a different situation is created that leaves many grandparents uncertain as to their rights for access to grandchildren. Since mothers typically are awarded custody of children following divorce, the relationship between paternal grandparents and grandchildren is often weakened more in comparison with that between maternal grandparents and grandchildren (Ahrons, 2007).

Divorce of adult children can sometimes strengthen the relationship and involvement of grandparents and grandchildren. In this regard, grandparents assume the major caretaking responsibilities for raising grandchildren, often in the absence of the children's parents. These circumstances present unique challenges for both grandparents and grandchildren (Kopera-Frye et al., 2003; Reynolds et al., 2003). For example, grandparents may not be aware of how to promote the educational progress of grandchildren in their school performance nor what is important for children to accomplish.

Grandchildren may be uncertain of the role of their parent in their lives when their grandparent has assumed the major responsibilities for providing nurturance and structure. These arrangements typically occur when some type of serious family problem affects the adult child. Quality of life issues become prominent due to the financial problems that typically affect older adults who may be on fixed incomes or dependent on public assistance for their support.

• •

Parenting Reflection 10–6

What kinds of support can be provided to assist coresident grandparents to provide appropriate and effective caregiving for their grandchildren?

• •

Stepgrandparenting issues have received very little attention from researchers. If grandparent roles are nebulous in many respects, this is particularly the case for stepgrandparents. Because stepgrandchildren are usually older when remarriages of adult child parents occur, there may be little opportunity for the stepgrandparent-stepgrandchild relationship to develop. However, because both parties may have had experiences with this relationship prior to parental divorce, it is likely that both wish to take advantage of opportunities for the new relationship to develop.

CARING FOR AGING PARENTS

It is highly likely that at some point in the lives of adult children that they will be called upon to provide care for an elderly parent. The American population is increasingly larger in the numbers of elderly individuals as well as in the longer life expectancies that most can experience (U.S. Bureau of the Census, 2006). Not all families desire nor can they afford to purchase caregiving services for elderly members as this is frequently seen as a responsibility of children to provide for aging parents (Connor, 2000).

Researchers who have studied parent-child relationships between adult children caregivers and elderly parents have found these observations:

- Because more generations of families live longer than ever before, family relationships are more numerous and complex as younger members maintain ties with elderly parents, grandparents, great-grandparents, and even older relatives (Crimmins, 2001).
- A serious consequence of increased life expectancy is that more people live longer with more serious health problems (Crimmins, 2001).
- More adult children provide care for elderly parents from ethnic minority than white families (Mezey, Berkman, Callahan, & Mitty, 2004).
- The vast majority of adult children caregivers are women (Cancian & Oliker, 2000).
- While many adult child caregivers are young, most are likely to be middle-aged, married, parents themselves, and working full-time (Himes, 2001).

Because there is the expectation that elderly parents will be cared for by children or even grandchildren, professionals refer to this provision of emotional support, services, and financial assistance as *eldercare*

(Ingersoll-Dayton, Neal, & Hammer, 2001). There is a wide range of activities covered by this type of family work such as making phone calls, assisting with personal hygiene, chauffering for errands and appointments, housekeeping tasks, meal preparation and purchasing food, and paying bills. As such, adult child caregivers can expect to perform informal caregiving for an estimated 18 hours weekly or more depending on the needs of the elderly parent (K. A. Connor, 2000). When this type of caregiving is not feasible, adult children often resort to arranging for paid service providers to meet the needs of their parent.

Many adult child caregivers rely on siblings to help with the responsibilities they are faced with in caring for their aging parent. However, this is not always possible, nor are some siblings reliable in providing assistance, making the care burden especially heavy for the principal adult child provider.

Elderly parent–adult child provider relations often follow a caregiving trajectory (Cancian & Oliker, 2000; Cicirelli, 2000). This begins with concern for the welfare of an elderly parent and expressing this to siblings and others. This progresses to giving advice to the elderly parent on conducting their affairs, for example, "Be sure to remember to take your medicine." Then, the adult child caregiver assumes greater responsibilities by providing services needed by the elderly parent while often consulting with family members and professionals in making decisions.

It is at this point, if they have not already occurred, that conflicts surface between the elderly parent and adult child provider. The elderly parent may become resentful of lost power and control over their life and activities and feel threatened by loss of independence. They may also resist deferring to the adult child provider's decisions, causing increasing stress and tension within the relationship.

Fueling the problems within the already strained parent-child relationship is the significant role reversal that takes place as the adult child provider assumes greater responsibilities out of necessity in caring for an elderly parent who is likely to have one or more chronic illnesses or disabilities. When these points are reached, the adult child caregiver progresses more swiftly toward **burnout,** resulting in poor quality of caregiving. This is especially the case when the adult child provider works full-time, tries to maintain a marriage relationship, seeks to conduct his or her own parent-child relationships and grandparent-grandchild relationships, and has little assistance from

siblings or spouse. It is not unusual that caregiver stress of this magnitude can lead to elder abuse that is emotional, physical, and/or verbal in nature (Connor, 2000).

Several possibilities may help to alleviate situations that can prevent or minimize caregiver burnout. These might include (1) encouraging men to become as responsible as women in providing eldercare, (2) involving wider community supports such as eldercare and respite programs, (3) more government funding support for programs that educate as well as provide services about eldercare, and (4) making this type of family work more financially rewarding through tax credits and other incentives (Cancian & Oliker, 2000).

....

Focus Point.   Family systems enter a new stage when the oldest child enters early adulthood. Parenting focuses on assisting adult children to individuate fully and to maintain a home base while this process is taking place. Parents in healthy family systems shift to a more equalitarian interaction style with adult children, which supports the efforts of adult children to emancipate completely into adult lifestyles.

Grandparenting roles are unclear for the most part although researchers have identified distinct aspects that make up the role. Grandparenting styles also have been identified and appear to be modified by several different factors, such as gender, ethnic identity, and geographic closeness. Divorce of grandparents or of adult children can also significantly alter the nature and conduct of this relationship.

Many adult children can expect to provide care for an aging parent, especially those having chronic illnesses or disabilities. A variety of characteristics define the nature of parent-child relations under these circumstances. The relationship can become strained and contribute to caregiver burnout.
....

POINTS TO CONSIDER

Parenting Adolescents

■ Parenting adolescents presents new and different challenges that have not been encountered previously in childrearing. Stereotypes of teenagers are misleading in what most parents can expect during this period of a child's life. One of the more difficult challenges of parenting adolescents is the fine line parents walk between being supportive of a teen's efforts to individuate while maintaining certain limits and boundaries for appropriate behavior.

■ Parenting styles and behaviors must adapt once again to meet the needs of a different child. And once again, the adaptation often is not initiated by the parents but rather by adolescent children who may demand to be treated differently now that they are older.

■ The personal developmental tasks of adolescents initiate a rewriting of the rules and patterns that govern the conduct of parent-child relations. The relationship between parents and adolescents has two central objectives: to promote greater individuation and achievement of adolescent self-regulation and to develop an equalization of power within this subsystem in a family system. If successful, such redefinition can preserve the effective functioning of a family system. Essentially, the challenge facing most parents of adolescents is learning that they must relinquish control over their child for development to take place appropriately.

■ Parents as well as peers provide assistance in a teen's development of a personal identity. This basic self-identity involves recognition that the self-concept is composed of many different but related aspects that make up the total personality.

■ Teenagers are concerned about individuating, or establishing independence from the controls and influence of parents and other adults. Individuation is a healthy aspect of personal identity development at this time of the life span. Adolescents' emancipation is established in a variety of ways that can be both positive and negative. Positive demonstrations include working in part-time jobs, choosing their own friends, and showing responsibility in a number of ways. Less positive demonstrations include various acting-out behaviors such as substance abuse.

■ Adjusting to the physical changes associated with puberty is a major developmental task of adolescence. Teens need assistance in understanding the physical, social, and psychological changes that take place. They may need particular assistance with sexual orientation issues. Parents also usually recognize the importance of education about sexual issues at this time of life. Teenagers especially need parental guidance in learning sexual decision-making skills considered appropriate by their family.

■ A variety of issues relate to health and safety during adolescence. Some are associated with negative acting-out behaviors such as substance abuse, while others such as eating disorders often reflect significant problems taking place in the family system. Many teens are at risk of committing suicide, particularly if there are sexual-orientation issues in question. Adolescents also are at greater risk to be the victims of serious violent crimes and of contracting sexually transmitted diseases.

■ A systemic family development snapshot reveals examples of the stressors that may affect the different generations of a family system as well as the ways that members cope with these in healthy as well as unhealthy ways.

Parent–Young Adult Relations

■ The relationship between parents and adult children is different than those experienced previously. The relationship is more mature in nature, reflecting the new developmental status of the young adult. The individuation process usually is completed at some point in early adulthood, and parents support this process in a number of ways. Difficulties sometimes occur when either parents, adult children, or both experience problems in releasing their dependencies on one another.

■ Changes also can take place in the family form as the renested family structure may emerge periodically to meet the needs of adult children. Renesting often takes place during times of personal crisis for the young adult child that relates to finances or changes in marital status.

■ Many parents assume a grandparenting role during this time when their adult children become parents themselves. Grandparents typically evolve and custom-design the style they wish to conduct in this role.

■ Adult children often provide care for elderly parents. These parent-child relationships have certain characteristics, such as more caregivers being from ethnic minority than white families and more being middle-aged women. The type of care provided is referred to as eldercare and is largely informal in nature but highly demanding of the caregiver's time and energies. While many providers rely on siblings and spouses for assistance, this may not always be available. The relationship between adult child providers and parents usually becomes strained over time. As stresses increase for the provider, the likelikhood of burnout increases, which can lead to elder abuse. Suggestions have been made for ways to help alleviate or prevent caregiver burnout.

PART III

Challenges for Contemporary Parents and Children

A commonly held belief is that the majority of families in the United States today meet the traditional notions of family form and composition. In this framework, the ideal family is depicted as having two opposite-sex adults, in which the man is the major provider and the woman is the housewife-mother, and their children. This belief in the prevalence of such a family form is misleading; in reality, fewer than 21% of all families in the United States today fit this form (U.S. Bureau of the Census, 2007a, 2007b). As noted in Chapter 2, diversity in form and structure is the norm among contemporary American families.

Today, the pluralistic context in which people define their families unseats the concept of a typical family. Over the past 50 years significant changes in many aspects of American society have influenced the kinds of families that have become more commonplace. These changes include the products of a high divorce rate, resulting in increasing numbers of binuclear families. A related change has been the increasing numbers of remarriages, resulting in parallel increases in stepfamilies with their own unique challenges and issues. Adolescent pregnancies that are carried to term continue to take place in spite of declines in the numbers of teen pregnancies. Many adolescent girls and their families have chosen to retain custody of these children, creating unique parent-child relationship issues. Likewise, gay and lesbian couples and families are becoming more visible throughout American society. These families are currently in the spotlight politically and socially as our society debates the pros and cons of same-gender marriage.

Another common misconception about American families implies that people (and families) that differ from the perceived norm are unhealthy and dysfunctional. This myth holds that these differences are responsible for producing an environment in which children grow up to be unhealthy in their emotional, social, and psychological development. These notions are examined in the chapters of Part III as we discuss those family situations that appear to create differences among family systems in comparison with those that are more traditional in nature.

Many families in the United States, however, experience problems and situations that affect their ability to function in healthy ways. Effective parenting may be difficult to achieve due to a number of factors operating against this optimal goal. Some parents do not perform well in this capacity and may abuse their children. In extreme circumstances, parental rights may be temporarily or permanently suspended and children removed from their parental homes. When this occurs, the state assumes legal guardianship and children are placed into the foster care system, where they may become adopted by another family. In the final chapter of the text, we examine those situations in which parents abuse their children physically, sexually, and/or emotionally and where effective parenting is seriously impaired by an adult parent's addiction. These serious parental behaviors harm all family members.

CHAPTER 11

Parenting in Single-Parent Family Systems

Focus Questions

■ ■ ■ ■ ■ ■ ■ ■ ■ ■

1. What major factors are responsible for creating single-parent family systems?
2. How does divorce affect parents as individuals and as caregivers?
3. How are children affected by parental divorce?
4. What important issues relate to child custody decisions?
5. What are the characteristics of a single-parent family headed by a woman and that headed by a man? How is parenting conducted in each of these family systems?
6. What major adjustment issues are encountered in single-parent families? What kinds of support are available to these families?
7. What stressors and coping mechanisms are revealed by a systemic family development snapshot of a single-parent family?

■ ■ ■ ■ ■ ■ ■ ■ ■ ■

Many people believe that the ideal family form in the United States today consists of an adult man who acts as the main provider, a woman who ideally is only a housewife and mother, and their several children. This kind of family is commonly depicted as the best and most acceptable type and is, therefore, frequently modeled on television programs and in other media. Over the years, people with traditional views of family life have promoted the belief that this ideal family is the only kind that is healthy and strong and least dysfunctional. It is touted as the best milieu in which to raise children.

Families that represent the traditional image have increasingly become a minority in the United States within the past 30 to 40 years (Figure 11–1). Today, these families constitute a distinct minority, accounting for only 12% of all families in the United States in 2006 (U.S. Bureau of the Census, 2007a). Some observers of American family life attribute this decline to the demise of family values in society, values that are believed to promote the maintenance of the traditional type of family system. The increasing rate of divorce over the years parallels the increasing number of *binuclear* (a term seldom used by family sociologists) or single-parent families that are created when this alleged shift in values occurs (U.S. Bureau of the Census, 2006). However, divorce alone does

FIGURE 11–1. Single-parent family systems have become a more common family form in the United States. Most of these are headed by women rather than men because women usually are awarded custody of children.

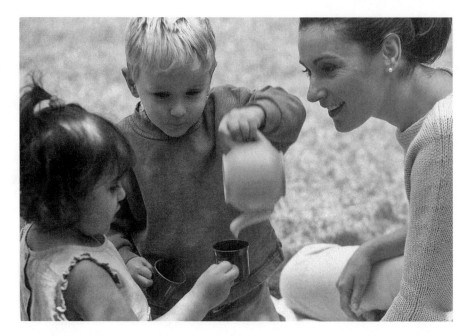

not exclusively account for the diversity that is a global characteristic—the norm—of family systems in contemporary American society. Many adults who divorce also remarry, which creates, in turn, a new family system that resembles other families but is unique in its functioning and structure. These families are called *blended families*, or stepfamilies. Other family systems are also formed in different ways and have different structures.

Divorce is the most frequent reason that creates single-parent families. Being a single parent is not necessarily devastating for either adults or children. However, divorce is a stressful experience that can be uncomfortable for the family system because old familiar patterns are dismantled by the separation of the adults. Family systems theory describes divorce as an event that produces disruption in a family system. In place of the chaos that emerges when a marriage is dissolved, a new family form evolves, known as a **single-parent family,** which is based on the former family system but has significant modifications. Essentially, the new family form reflects the children's membership in two separate and distinct households or families known as a binuclear family—one headed by the father and the other by the mother. Basically, these are separate one-parent households. Increasingly today, both parents hold joint custody of the children. One usually is designated as the physical custodian, meaning that the children reside the majority of time in this parent's household.

Researchers continue to explore issues that relate to the adjustment of individuals in the new single-parent family system following divorce (Knox & Schacht, 2008). New patterns, rules, roles, and modifications to the parent-child subsystem restore equilibrium and balance and allow the system to function. Researchers find that several factors influence healthy adjustment and that unhealthy dysfunction can also take place in certain circumstances. It is important to note, here, that while divorce is the major factor in creating single-parent families, there is a significant trend in the increase of single, unmarried women who bear children (Federal Interagency Forum on Child and Family Statistics, 2007).

This next section examines the myriad effects of family life on single-parent family systems, including a number of adjustments by both adults and children in adopting a new lifestyle and interaction patterns. For many individuals, these adjustments may be relatively temporary since the majority of divorced adults eventually remarry.

DIVORCE, SINGLE-PARENT FAMILIES, AND PARENT-CHILD RELATIONS

Single-parent family systems are one of the more common types of families in the United States today. These are composed of an adult male or female parent and one

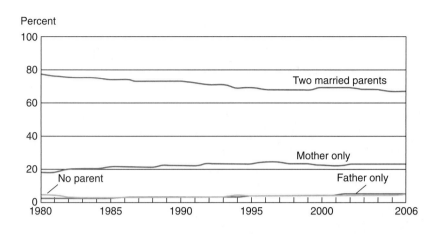

FIGURE 11–2. Percentage of children ages 0–17 years by presence of married parents in the household, 1980 to 2006.

Source: Federal Interagency Forum on Child and Family Statistics. (2007). *America's children: Key national indicators of well-being, 2007.* Washington, DC: U.S. Government Printing Office.

or more children under 18 years of age who reside in separate households following divorce. This family type is increasing at the fastest rate of all family forms (see Figure 11–2). In 1970, approximately 3.8 million families were headed by a single parent. By 2005, this number had increased to almost 13 million (U.S. Bureau of the Census, 2007a). One-parent families in the United States accounted for about 32% of all family types with children. Although almost three-fourths of all single parents are white, this type of family occurs more prevalently among African Americans as a group (U.S. Bureau of the Census, 2007a). One-parent families accounted for about 62% of all African American families as compared with 28% of all white families. Among Hispanics, single-parent families accounted for about 36% of all family types, while 16% were among all family types among Asians.

A single-parent family system can be created in several ways: (1) divorce, desertion, or separation of the adults; (2) death of an adult; or (3) giving birth to a child out of wedlock. Of these reasons, divorce is the most common (Figure 11–3). The federal agency charged with collecting data on divorce ceased doing so in 1996, but it is still possible to gauge the prevalence of divorce

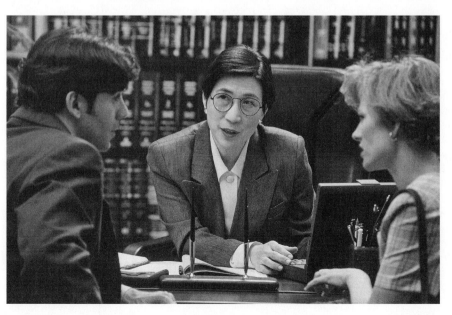

FIGURE 11–3. Divorce is the leading factor in creating one-parent family systems in the United States.

by the living arrangements reported for children living in the United States. In 2006, for example, about 67% of all children in the United States lived with both biological parents as compared to 23% who lived with either a single-parent mother and 5% who lived with a single-parent father (Federal Interagency Forum on Child and Family Statistics, 2007). The majority of single-parent families are those in which women have sole custody or are the physical custodian of children, although there are significant increases in the numbers of such families where men are the head of households. Many of these families include an unmarried adult partner of the parent where both adults cohabitate. Exceptions to this are those women who are financially independent who become single parents by choice (Segal-Engelchin, Erera, & Cwikel, 2005).

Because our society has promoted the belief that parenting is conducted best by families with two adults, much concern has been expressed about the effects of divorce and the experiences of growing up as a child in a single-parent family system. Family and child development researchers have been aware that differences may exist in families with one adult as compared to those with two adults. These differences are observed in a number of areas, such as interaction patterns, communication styles, parenting styles, and behavior problems among children (Knox & Schacht, 2008). As may be

expected, the principal difficulties in single-parent family systems are traced in part to the lack of sufficient people to adequately perform the roles needed in an efficient family life.

This factor, however, does not disrupt family system functioning in dysfunctional ways. Furthermore, most research findings suggest that while similarities exist in single-parent families headed by women and those headed by men, the sex of the parent is an important factor in determining the type of family life experience in each family system.

Each family system that experiences the loss of one adult's presence through divorce adapts in distinct ways in responding to this stressful change. Divorce, in particular, forces such responses in the new single-parent family system. Because this is the primary cause of its creation, the divorce process involves various aspects of adaptation. Divorce is one of the most difficult processes a family system can experience (Clarke-Stewart & Brentano, 2007). It has short- and long-term effects on both the original first-marriage family system and on others that follow, such as the single-parent family and the stepfamily created upon remarriage. In keeping with the prediction from family systems theory, everyone in a family system, adults and children, is affected to some degree and in various ways by the divorce.

Parenting FAQs 11–1

I have some questions about divorce. What if my partner doesn't agree to this? How is child support determined? What happens if my partner doesn't comply with the terms of our divorce agreement?

A: These are good questions that most people don't know to think about before divorcing. First, in most states that have no-fault divorce laws, all it takes is for one person to declare legally that the marriage is irretrievably broken and the divorce proceedings may begin. You will need to consult a lawyer for legal advice on how to begin this process. Second, many states now have a formula by which child support is determined. Usually, a couple's gross annual income is the basis of the formula used to determine how much each adult will contribute to child support. In some states, this formula may include how health insurance, child-care, and/or educational expenses are shared by each adult, for example. Third, let's suppose your divorce agreement includes stipulations about child support and visitation. The agreement is that children are picked up at a designated time on Friday and returned by a designated time on Sunday. However, if your ex-partner habitually disregards those scheduled times or is not paying the amount of child support ordered by the court and is habitually late, you have recourse to these actions. You can return to court for legal redress of your complaints of the violations to the divorce agreement, and/or you can call upon the county sheriff's office for assistance in having the terms of your agreement enforced. Sometimes, mediation is helpful in such situations as well.

In the case of the formation of two single-parent family systems following divorce, each family must reconstruct new boundaries and patterns (rules, communication styles, and roles) by adapting to the crisis of divorce. All in the family are affected to some degree but in different ways by the myriad changes resulting from parental divorce. But each family, to survive and adapt successfully to these changes, does so to maintain homeostasis and to avoid further confusion, disorganization, and chaos.

Parenting Reflection 11–1

Are there any advantages or benefits in single parenthood as compared with married partnership?

Parental Adaptations

Family systems theory predicts that all members of a family system are affected when some type of change takes place in just one person. Divorce dissolves the effective functioning of the committed relationship between the adult partners. In turn, it disrupts the functioning of the parent-child relationships as well as the functioning of the entire family system (Benedek & Brown, 2004). Divorce has a number of effects on both the adults and children in a family system. Adults experience a variety of reactions when divorce is pursued as a solution to marital difficulties (Knox & Schacht, 2008). These effects include emotional reactions such as depression, weight loss, sleep disturbances, and an increase in the likelihood of substance abuse. Anger and hostility often color any attempts at interactions between the divorcing adults. These kinds of reactions often take lengthy amounts of time to decrease in intensity. Changes in lifestyle often accompany divorce due to significant changes in financial status of both adults. Other changes and adaptations may be implemented to restore homeostasis to a single-parent family system as an evolved family form (Clarke-Stewart & Brentano, 2007).

Because divorce affects all family members, it is important for adults to interpret what is happening to children so that they can understand the changes taking place in their family of origin, which include the following four areas:

1. *Family metacognition.* The system acknowledges that divorce is imminent and that adults no longer share similar feelings of love and attachment. It also acknowledges other feelings of adults and children, such as sadness and even hate.

2. *Physical separation.* Separation of the adults has highly disruptive effects on the family system by dismantling the boundaries, rules, behavior patterns, and roles that have made the system operate effectively. Removing the father's presence from the family system (which commonly occurs) can leave children with feelings of abandonment. In general, divorced fathers are more emotionally depressed than divorced mothers (Knox & Schacht, 2008).

3. *Family system reorganization.* Divorced adults forge a new relationship with different rules, roles, and interaction patterns. Their ability to resolve issues in healthy ways determines if the new single-parent family system will be reorganized in a functional or dysfunctional manner. The new single-parent family system also adapts by evolving new rules, roles, and interaction patterns that respond to new living conditions.

4. *Family redefinitions.* As the new single-parent family system takes form and assumes higher degrees of effective functioning, the system is perceived differently by the members and by the noncustodial parent. The noncustodial parent also reorganizes interaction patterns, boundaries, and rules that govern how he or she relates to the single-parent family system and its members. Therefore, children often learn two sets of patterns because they are now members of two single-parent family systems composed of the custodial parent system and the noncustodial parent system.

Parenting Reflection 11–2

Has the increased acceptability of divorce led to the breakdown of healthy family values in the United States, as certain organizations maintain?

A major challenge for many parents who divorce is their ability to acknowledge that they continue to share parenting responsibilities and relationships with their children, even though their marriage relationship has been dismantled (Knox & Schacht, 2008). Many people divorce with the expectation that their contact and involvement with the former spouse has been completely terminated. However, the relationship becomes transformed in several ways:

■ Visitation rights of the noncustodial parent forces some type of contact with the former spouse.

■ Children may perpetuate the remnants of the relationship by sharing information about one parent with the other and discussing life and events in their new family systems.

■ If joint custody has been arranged, spouses are committed to making major decisions together that affect children's welfare.

■ While parents attend to their own particular reactions and adjustments to the divorce, they are often mindful of their children's reactions. That topic is explored in the next section.

• •

Focus Point. Divorce has a variety of effects on adults. Most involve dealing with emotional adjustments as individuals make the transition from being a couple to being single people. Even though adults make different adjustments to the divorce, they continue to share a connection by being their children's parents. It seems that a person is never completely divorced when children are involved.

• •

Children's Adaptations

About one-fifth (23%) of American children lived only with their mothers, 5% lived with only their fathers, and 5% lived with neither of their parents in 2006 (Federal Interagency Forum on Child and Family Statistics, 2007). The number of single-parent families has increased considerably in the United States since 1960. This type of family system now constitutes a sizable proportion of the population (U.S. Bureau of the Census, 2007b). The marital status of parents influences where children will live and with whom, as well as the quality of life they will experience. In line with the increase in single-parent families, there has been a concomitant decrease in the number of children living with two parents. In 2006, for example, about 67% of all children in the United States were living with two parents as compared with 77% in 1980 (Federal Interagency Forum on Child and Family Statistics, 2007).

Researchers have learned that children's reactions to parental divorce involve a process of adjusting to

change rather than a single, simple reaction (Clarke-Stewart & Brentano, 2007; Knox & Schacht, 2008). This process is tempered by other factors, such as the child's age, sex, and past experiences. For many children, the parental divorce involves significant losses, and children can experience a variety of grief reactions. Children appear to undergo this process in three distinct stages:

1. The *initial stage* occurs after parents inform children of their decision to separate. It is marked by high levels of stress, during which aggressive conflicts markedly increase. A mood of unhappiness pervades.

2. The *transition stage* commences about 1 year after the parents' separation and lasts for up to 3 years. At this stage, high levels of emotionalism have diminished; it is characterized instead by the restructuring process of evolving new family system patterns, changing the quality of life, and establishing visitation routines with the noncustodial parent.

3. The *restabilization stage* occurs about 5 years after the separation when the new single-parent family system or stepfamily has been completely instituted.

Divorce may be one of the few major family crisis events in which adults become more focused on their needs than on those of their children (Benokraitis, 2004). In many respects, the functioning of the parent-child relationship is disrupted because of this change in focus. The effects of divorce on children may be due to this change rather than to the divorce *per se*. Researchers report different findings about the specific effects observed in children of divorcing parents (Clarke-Stewart & Brentano, 2007; Knox & Schacht, 2008). Several factors have been identified in recent years that appear to influence the nature and course of children's adjustment to this family crisis:

■ Age and sex of children when parental divorce occurs
■ Adults' use of available social support networks to help children adjust to the process
■ Attitudes of the culture toward divorce and single-parent families

The effects of parental divorce on children may be either short- or long-term and positive or detrimental. Short-term effects, for example, include behavior difficulties at home and at school that occur in association with the initial reactions to parental separation.

Long-term effects may not appear until adolescence or adulthood when individuals become involved in intimate relationships and experience difficulties in establishing them (Amato, 2006; E. Price, 2004). Other long-term effects appear in the course of development as children experience the adjustments required at later phases in the process of reacting to parental divorce. For example, low quality of the parents' marriage is reflected in troubled parent-child relationships as long as 8 to 12 years prior to divorce. Sex of a child can also mediate such reactions. For example, boys have more adverse reactions to parental divorce than girls do, but girls react more adversely to parental remarriage.

The age of children at the time of parental divorce seems to be one of the driving factors in influencing how a child reacts and how he or she adjusts after the divorce. Researchers have identified certain kinds of reactions that vary according to the children's age when parental divorce occurs.

Regressive behaviors such as temporary loss of toilet training as well as increased aggressiveness, fretfulness, and negative attention-getting behaviors such as whining or destroying toys may be observed among preschoolers whose parents are divorcing or have divorced. School-age children may manifest feelings of being abandoned or rejected by their absent parent, a drop in school performance, adverse interactions with peers, or boundary shifts with their mother during or following parental divorce. Adolescents also may manifest similar feelings of abandonment or rejection, delinquency and negative acting-out behaviors, heightened conflicts with their parent, decline in school performance, and emotional depression (E. Price, 2004; Weight, 2004).

The first year after parental divorce may be the most difficult and stressful for both children and parents (Pryor & Rodgers, 2001). However, the disruptive effects young children experience often continue beyond this first year. Boys generally continue to experience greater degrees of disruptiveness than girls do, especially it parents continue to experience high levels of discord and conflict. Figure 11–4 illustrates an 8-year-old's representation of her family following her parents' divorce.

Divorce is perhaps more problematic when children are adolescents (Hetherington, 2006). The context of the

FIGURE 11–4.   In this drawing an 8-year-old girl represents her family. Her mother and father have divorced, yet she is aware that she is a member of two distinct family systems. The line attempts to show how her father is a part of one family but not of the other. (Drawing by Brianne Pfaffly.)

parent-child relationships is altered when adolescents experience the divorce of their parents. Girls may experience more serious difficulties than boys do. Some research suggests that teenage girls may project anger about their noncustodial fathers onto their custodial mothers. These girls may also experience role reversal and blurring of boundaries between themselves and their mothers, a situation also occurring among school-age girls. Adolescent girls may resent this change in their relationship with their mothers. It is also not unusual for some adolescents to have divided allegiances to both parents. This division relates to high levels of conflict and hostility and a low degree of cooperation between parents. As a result, many teenagers feel caught between loyalties to individual parents, and researchers have noted that poor levels of adjustment are related to the disruptive changes associated with parental divorce.

The disruptive effects of parental divorce on children and adolescents may last a long time (Amato, 2006; Amato & Afifi, 2006; Conway, Christensen, & Herlihy, 2003; Pryor & Rodgers, 2001; Wallerstein & Blakeslee, 2003; Wallerstein, Lewis, & Blakeslee, 2001). Many adolescents make adequate adjustments in the years following the divorce and arrive at adulthood as competent individuals. However, one-half of those studied in a comprehensive longitudinal investigation were found to enter adulthood as unhappy, angry, underachieving, self-deprecating, and fretful individuals. Researchers believe that those unhealthy reactions were artifacts of the parental divorce that took place many years earlier. One study suggests that adjustment of adolescents in homes where parents are in high conflict but do not divorce experience lower feelings of well-being and poorer quality in parent-child relationships than those whose parents divorced (Amato; Amato & Afifi).

While some researchers believe divorce leaves children and adolescents emotionally scarred and handicapped in future intimate relationships, the issue remains essentially unresolved until more extensive research is conducted (Amato, 2003).

Parenting Reflection 11–3

Can growing up or living in a single-parent family be a healthy experience for children? What benefits might they gain from this experience?

The numerous research findings about the effects of divorce on children present a highly negative, dour, and depressing picture. They may also be helpful. Parents who are considering divorce may be more aware of what can occur in single-parent family systems as a result. Thus, they can better prepare by making arrangements that assist children and themselves when they cope with this stressful event. Some generalizations about the research include the following:

■ Children experience the effects of parental divorce in ways that are more disruptive and stressful than those experienced by parents.
■ Divorce is a process rather than an event, and it is experienced by the whole family system rather than by adults alone.

Parenting FAQs 11–2

My brother is getting divorced, and things seem to be pretty nasty. He just told me that the court has appointed an attorney to be a Guardian Ad Litem for the children. This seems unusual and something I've never heard of before with other couples I've known who have divorced. I don't understand this. Can you please explain?

A: It is not unusual for a court to appoint an attorney or another qualified professional to represent the interests of the children of divorcing parents. This person is called the Guardian Ad Litem (GAL), as you note, and serves as an agent of the court acting in the best interests of the children. This person acts as an advocate for the children in the divorce proceedings and will sometimes recommend actions that go against the parents' wishes. This is because of the unique representation of the GAL for the children instead of the parents. The appointment of a GAL usually happens when at least one parent requests it or because the court has reservations about the ability of either or both parents to act in the best interests of the children in the divorce proceedings.

- Divorce has both immediate and long-term effects on children, which vary with their age and sex at the time the divorce takes place.
- Children whose parents divorce during their developing years almost always see it as a milestone event in their lives that may shape many developmental aspects in their adulthood.

It is important to reiterate that the effects of divorce on children and adolescents are not clear-cut. Many conflicting, complicated, and complex findings are reported in the research literature. Some critics of these findings point to the samples of children studied, noting the small sample sizes and the fact that the children were often under the care of mental health professionals because of problems experienced in relation to parental divorce. It is safe to state that not all children whose parents divorce react in the exact manner described in these studies. However, it is equally safe to conclude that no child of divorced parents completely escapes the impact of disruption on a family system during divorce (Amato & Sobolewski, 2004).

• •

Focus Point.   Researchers have observed a number of effects on children when their parents divorce. They note that children's age at the time of divorce is an important factor in determining their reactions to this event. Many parents fear that their children will experience serious and harmful effects as a result of divorce. Researchers generally find that divorce produces disruptive effects but that most children successfully adapt and adjust within several years. However, observers note some residual effects that last for many years after the divorce.

• •

Custody Arrangements

Parents must confront a major decision when they divorce: Who will have custody of children, and how will the noncustodial parent and children have access to each other for visitation? The Family Law Section of the American Bar Association lists several standards that court officials may apply in determining the custody arrangements of children following the divorce of their

parents (American Bar Association, 1996, 2001). The section includes the following five standards:

1. Custody should be awarded to either or both parents according to the best interests of the child.
2. Custody may be awarded to persons other than the father or mother whenever such award serves the best interests of the child.
3. If a child is old enough and able enough to reason and form an intelligent preference, his or her wishes about custody should be considered and given due weight by the court.
4. Any custody award should be subject to modification or change whenever the best interests of the child require or justify such modification or change.
5. Reasonable visitation rights should be awarded to parents and to any person interested in the welfare of the child, at the discretion of the court, unless such rights of visitation are detrimental to the best interests of the child.

Before the 1920s such decisions about child custody were not an issue in divorces because custody was automatically assigned to the father; women had no legal rights in this regard. They lacked the right to vote and to sign contracts. In subsequent years, however, women have gained legal status in the United States and the child-custody issue has changed. In almost 90% of cases, child custody is awarded to mothers rather than to fathers.

• •

Parenting Reflection 11–4

What can divorced parents do to prevent their child from feeling like a football that is continually being tossed from one parent to the other in order to meet the requirements of joint custody or noncustodial visitation?

• •

Even though mothers stand a good chance of being awarded legal custody of children, divorcing couples still must negotiate to reach a decision about which parent should have full custody, or if both will share custody (Figure 11–5). They must reach visitation and support decisions and consider other important details relating to the best interests of children. These details might include, for example, how each parent will contribute to the children's medical and dental expenses, clothing costs, and

FIGURE 11–5. A critical element of divorce is negotiating terms that are agreeable to both parties.

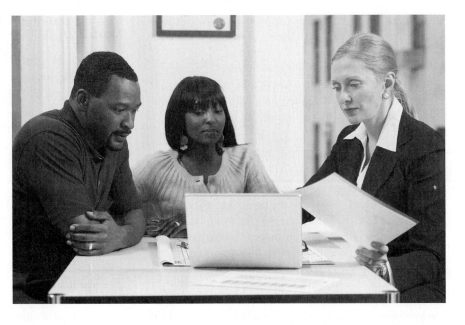

college education and in what percentage. It is not easy for many couples to reach these decisions in an objective, fair manner without involving some type of legal mediation or the intervention of a court's judicial decision.

When divorcing parents consider custody issues, five factors frequently favor one parent over the other (American Bar Association, 1996):

1. The wishes and preferences of children
2. Whether or not a parent wants custody
3. The perceived need to place a child with a same-sex parent
4. The perceived need to keep a child with the mother because people believe she is the socially appropriate person for custody
5. A parent's ability to provide stable, continuing involvement in the same residence or geographical area

Courts apparently use certain specific variables relating to the quality of children's adjustment after parental divorce when they make decisions about custody, rather than relying on the general rule of assigning it to only one parent (American Bar Association, 2001). For example, according to such guidelines, a child is likely to be placed with a same-sex parent because he or she generally has better prospects of healthy social adjustment.

A single parent's sole custody of children can create problems that, at times, appear to outweigh the situation's advantages. The experiences of single-parent families, described later in this chapter, give the impression that they can be problem-ridden, stressful, and unpleasant for many individuals, especially women. Many of the problems associated with sole custody reflect the noncustodial father's resentment, anger, and frustration in dealing with what is perceived to be a no-win situation. Many men feel they are systematically disenfranchised from having input into important decisions about their children's lives and from having access to quality interaction time with their children. As a result, postdivorce conflict with the ex-spouse continues or escalates, which, in turn, affects the manner and context of children's interactions with their fathers. Noncustodial fathers typically disengage from the parenting relationship because their ability to function adequately in this role is greatly diminished by their withdrawal from the former family system (Amato & Sobolewski, 2004).

Compounding the situation is the dismal record of consistent child-support payments by many noncustodial fathers (Grall, 2006). Many fathers feel they are cut out of their children's lives and, therefore, they should not have to maintain financial support. They often use this claim when they live far away from their children, particularly when they live out of state.

Most divorcing couples must arrive at some decision regarding custody and visitation, which typically

Parenting FAQs 11–3

My husband's attorney has requested an evaluation for child custody since we can't agree on these arrangements. Just exactly what is involved in such an evaluation? Who should pay for it? How can I be assured that whoever does the evaluation isn't biased in favor of my husband? Why is this necessary anyway?

A: Having an evaluation performed by a qualified professional may be the best way to resolve the impasse between you and your husband regarding custody arrangements. Usually, attorneys representing you and your husband agree on a particular mental health professional who is highly regarded in your community for conducting fair, accurate, and appropriate evaluations of how custody arrangements best meet the interests of the children involved, not necessarily those of the parents. Sometimes the court will appoint the person to conduct the evaluation if the attorneys can't agree on someone. You will need to trust the recommendation of your attorney or the court that the evaluator has the reputation for being fair and unbiased.

Evaluations can be expensive, sometimes ranging between as much as $3,000 and $10,000 or more, depending on where you live. Costs typically are shared by both parents. An evaluation is conducted when both parents insist that they know what is best for their children even though the conditions of what each considers to be appropriate for the children differ. An evaluation helps the court to decide what is in the best interests of the children. It is not unusual, however, for the court to disregard what the evaluator recommends and determine its own orders concerning child custody. So, there is some risk that this expensive exercise will not result in what the evaluator recommends.

involves lengthy discussions and compromises. They may arrive at this decision with the help of lawyers, divorce-mediation professionals, or therapists. But even with this help, some divorcing couples have a hard time reaching decisions of any sort.

Joint Custody.   A recent trend in custody decisions involves **joint custody,** or awarding the responsibility for child care and supervision to both parents. In many cases, joint custody, rather than single-parent custody, may be a viable solution that is in the best interests of the children (Knox & Schacht, 2008). This alternative has both advantages and disadvantages to those involved and in its implementation and execution. However, many feel that the advantages outweigh the problems if parents can work together in the mutual interest of their children.

Researchers find that joint custody has several positive effects (Everett & Everett, 2000; Kaslow, 2000; Lowenstein, 2002; Weinraub, Horvath, & Gringlass, 2002):

■ More contact between ex-spouses
■ Fewer problems in securing father's cooperation in consistently meeting financial-support agreements

■ Fewer feelings of being overwhelmed by child-care responsibilities
■ More access to beneficial interactions between children and fathers (typically not the case when mothers have sole custody)

Parenting Reflection 11–5

Should joint custody become the norm among divorced parents with children? Why or why not?

Fathers who share joint custody with mothers are also more involved with parenting responsibilities, have more contact with their children, and use parenting resources more extensively than noncustodial fathers do (Knox & Schacht, 2008). They tend to be more satisfied with joint rather than sole custody arrangements, but mothers appear to prefer sole custody. When fathers hold joint custody with mothers for children, the mother is also more likely to receive support payments from the father, helping to prevent the children from experiencing a poverty-level existence (Grall, 2006).

Parenting Reflection 11–6

Is it right to force men to pay child support when they fall behind or to garnish wages to do so? Should a noncustodial mother pay child support to a custodial father even though she earns less than he does? Would noncustodial fathers be more willing to pay for child support if the federal government made this a line-item credit on annual tax returns?

Although joint custody seems to sidestep problems associated with sole custody of children, it does create other problems (Everett & Everett, 2000; Knox & Schacht, 2008):

■ It is more expensive to maintain because each parent must supply housing, equipment, toys, food, and often clothing for children.

■ It requires a degree of connection with ex-spouses that many people are not prepared for and may not desire.

■ It will not work properly if the adults are not committed to maintaining civil discussions that remain on topic about child-rearing issues.

■ Constraints on relocation to another community or residence can impair decision making.

■ Children may feel confused and overburdened because they have commitments to two family systems instead of one.

■ Children may have problems adjusting to the transition from one family system to another.

■ The possibility of disturbances in the relationship between siblings may occur due to split living arrangements with parents.

Managing Coparenting Arrangements. It is imperative that divorcing parents establish new rules and boundaries regarding their coparenting relationship with children that emerges when separation and divorce are taking place and following this event. The temptation for many is to involve children in the adult business of the divorce, and the children can become pawns in the matter. This is unhealthy for children and parents as well. Many children also feel forced or obligated to take sides with one parent or another to the detriment of all parties involved.

Parenting Reflection 11–7

Are two parents really better for children than just one? Why or why not?

When parents are separating in preparation for divorce, it is important that they maintain lines of communication between each other to resolve their differences. Children are inevitably a part of the matters to be discussed. However, to avoid the feelings of anger, frustration, and guilt that can accompany the discussions involving children's affairs, divorcing parents might limit the topics to the health needs, educational concerns, and time sharing of children (Judges of the 29th Judicial District of Kansas, 1985). When these new rules and boundaries involving discussions of children are followed, additional rules, patterns, and boundaries can be shaped to redefine the relationship between each individual parent and the children. This should allow for the development of the new family system that the children will experience, known as the single-parent family.

Sometimes divorcing parents are tempted to express their hurtful feelings about their divorce and the divorcing partner by playing "pain games" that can interfere with effective parenting (Judges, 1985). Basically, three types of games may serve as unhealthy ways to express unpleasant feelings associated with divorce:

1. *Cut Down.* This is any type of discounting of the other parent to a child, such as making negative comments or using derogatory labels. When children hear such statements, they may feel that these also apply to them because they are half of each parent.

2. *Messenger.* In this game, one parent solicits a child to be a messenger as a means of communicating with the other parent. Children can sometimes distort even innocent, simple messages they might be asked to give to the other parent. It is not healthy for children to play the go-between role in the altered relationship between divorcing parents.

3. *I Spy.* Divorcing parents may be tempted to use a child as a source of information about the other parent. This is a ploy to find out what the other parent is doing, whom he or she might be seeing socially, what purchases he or she might have made, and so

on. Asking children to provide information about the other parent places them in a position where they can violate a sense of trust between themselves and the other parent, which is not healthy.

Single-Parent Families Headed by Mothers

The majority of single-parent families in the United States are headed by women who have either never married or have divorced (U.S. Bureau of the Census, 2007a, 2007b). Among these families, quality of life is a major concern (Holyfield, 2003). Women appear to face more difficulties resulting from divorce than men. These difficulties are attributed to economic conditions related to employment and the support of children. Family income is lowest among single-parent families headed by women (DeNavas-Walt, Proctor, & Smith, 2007). In 2001 the median income for families of married couples was estimated at $69,716. This figure contrasts sharply with the estimated median income of $31,818 for single-parent families headed by women. The estimated median income of single-parent families headed by men, by comparison, was $47,078. Because of the low level of income among these mothers, many of these family systems can expect to experience poverty-level existences that seriously affect the quality of life, especially for children (see Figure 11–6; Mather, Rivers, & Jacobsen, 2005). In addition, the majority of these families are found in white communities; however, a substantial proportion of all children are born to black and Hispanic single-parent mothers (Grall, 2006).

Financial Difficulties.   Single-parent families headed by mothers can expect to experience financial difficulties. A father's child support and maintenance payments are important sources of income for such families; they help provide an adequate quality of life. They do not, however, adequately reflect typical expenditures on children by mothers who are physical custodians (Peterson, Song, & Jones-DeWeever, 2003). Because of this dependence on typically inadequate support payments and other factors, such as less education or fewer years in the labor force, most single-parent families headed by women have lower annual incomes than those headed by men. To make matters worse, women do not always successfully obtain support payments from the absent father (Grall, 2006). In 2003, about 86% of single-parent

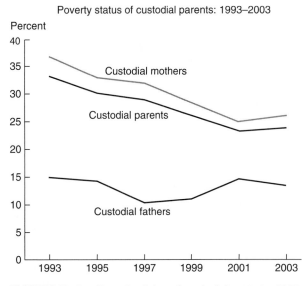

Poverty status of custodial parents: 1993–2003

FIGURE 11–6.   Poverty status of custodial parents, 1993 to 2003.

Source: Grall, T. S. (2006). Custodial mothers and fathers and their child support: 2003. *Current Population Reports, Series P60–225.* Washington, DC: U.S. Bureau of the Census.

mothers were awarded some amount of child support. However, only about 45% of those received the full amount that had been awarded. This factor, in addition to differences in education, job experience, and training, creates the likelihood that more custodial mothers than fathers are poor.

State laws differ in the manner for determining how much someone must pay in providing child support. Most commonly, many have requirements that 17% of a nonresident, noncustodial parent's gross income should go toward child support. This figure increases as the number of children involved increases, and it can rise as high as 31% when four or more children must be supported. While these fathers most likely could afford to pay more in child support, many have established new families and must also contribute to the support of new biologically produced children as well as to those they have previously fathered. The conflict between honoring the responsibilities owed to children from former marriages and those produced in new relationships often creates a dilemma for all the affected individuals.

Child support is determined at the time a divorce becomes finalized by court decree. The divorcing individuals often make arrangements finalized in a contractual agreement that the court legalizes. Both parties may make decisions that have adverse financial consequences due to the emotional coerciveness present in negotiations leading to such agreements (Schmitz & Tebb, 2003). It may be helpful, therefore, to include a therapist or a divorce mediation professional in the negotiations as a means of achieving objective decisions regarding child support. That person may assist both divorcing adults in securing arrangements that help to ensure children receive adequate financial support in accordance with other related variables affecting the agreement.

The most common reason for failure to pay support regularly and in its full amount is attributed to financial problems by the noncustodial parent (Weinraub et al., 2002). However, some parents fail to honor their child support agreement for other reasons, including: (1) withholding payment as a means of expressing anger toward the custodial ex-spouse; (2) feelings of discrimination about the amount awarded by a court; or (3) unemployment or underemployment. In other instances, many noncustodial parents provide support in forms other than money such as gifts, paying for medical and dental expenses, or clothing (Grall, 2006).

Becoming divorced means that most women with children will become employed to provide support for their families. Typically, they earn wages and salaries at levels lower than men, often because of different levels of education, training, and work experience. Economic conditions are a primary source of stress among single-parent families headed by women (Mather et al., 2005). One in 3 single-parent families headed by women exists below the poverty level, as compared with 1 in 10 two-parent families. This factor may significantly contribute to changing the quality of life, social functioning, context of the parent-child relationship, and various related effects in these family systems (Grall, 2006).

The implications of economic conditions in these families, then, have both short- and long-term consequences. Children who are not supported as they are entitled perhaps experience these consequences to a more serious extent than their mothers, although quality of life affects everyone in these families. Essentially, numerous ripple effects stem from such dire financial conditions in single-parent families headed by mothers.

Role Strain. Single-parent mothers experience additional role strain within their new binuclear family system. Divorced women experience different degrees of role strain than divorced men. Because most women are granted full custody of children, they must now function as the sole full-time parent in their new family system. What was stressful in managing competing roles in a two-parent family system is even more stressful after divorce. The time demands in such systems are particularly stressful (Federal Interagency Forum on Child and Family Statistics, 2007). There is less time for most activities, and employment responsibilities receive the highest priority. Child care and personal needs receive the least time; however, quality of attention to children does not appear to decline.

As with role strain in intact families with children, performance in all the competing roles falls as the number of roles and levels of stress increase concomitantly (Goode, 1993). Combined with other factors that produce stress such as financial problems, this factor may account for other changes taking place in this new single-parent family, one of which is discussed in the following section.

Changes in the Parent-Child Relationship. Many single-parent mothers experience changes in their relationship with their children. The parent-child subsystem changes as all participants redefine the parameters of the relationship in this new family form. In many respects, two distinct parent-child subsystems emerge. In general, there may be few differences in the relationship between mothers and daughters and mothers and sons in single-parent family systems when children are young. However, children in family systems headed by single-parent mothers continue to experience adjustment difficulties 4 to 6 years following parental divorce, as compared with children whose mothers have remarried (Clarke-Stewart & Bretano, 2007).

One effect of role strain on other factors operating in single-parent families headed by mothers is their increased reliance on more authoritarian patterns of interacting with children (Clarke-Stewart & Bretano, 2007). The functioning of the parent-child subsystem is generally disrupted following divorce, and this disruption is especially accentuated in the relationship of mothers and sons. It is less likely to affect mothers and their preadolescent daughters, who often forge a relationship that is more emotionally intimate and close. As the new family system evolves new patterns and establishes some degree of stability, many single-parent mothers generally shift to patterns of child rearing that are more authoritative. This tends to promote healthier, more positive adjustment among children.

After divorce, it is not unusual for single-parent mothers to institute changes in the boundaries, patterns, and rules that define the usual adult and child role behaviors (Everett & Everett, 2000). A mother may transform the definition of her role, particularly in relation to the oldest child, to that of a peer/partner. She may expect that child to be more mature than he or she is developmentally ready to be. As the mother transforms the nature of the relationship with this child, she significantly increases her shared personal feelings and opinions about a variety of topics. Accordingly, the child's role becomes transformed; he or she is now the mother's *confidante*. The mother increasingly relies on this child for emotional support and assigns him or her much of the missing adult partner's responsibilities. As a result, the child may be forced into interaction patterns calling for developmental maturity that he or she does not have or is not prepared to provide for the mother.

The pressures children experience in these situations come from not having their emotional needs met by their mothers, who are usually unaware of this problem. When a mother transforms the child's role to one similar to the absent adult partner's, a conflict can emerge that imitates the marital conflicts with the former spouse. The child discovers that he or she is in a no-win situation, pressured to assume the missing partner's role but punished for behaving like the former spouse. Some researchers also report a particular interaction between mothers and daughters. At times, they may experience competition, jealousy, and conflict that are not found between single-parent mothers and sons (Everett & Everett, 2000). When children find themselves in these situations, some may not feel comfortable expressing their feelings of frustration and confusion. More likely, they respond with psychosomatic reactions and acting-out behaviors that serve as symptoms of their concerns and fears. Not surprisingly, when mothers disclose intimate details about personal problems, such as financial matters or negative feelings about ex-husbands, daughters report strong feelings of emotional distress (Koerner, Jacobs, & Raymond, 2000).

Therapists and researchers working with single-parent families note that parents may encounter certain pitfalls that can develop into clinical issues, including responding to children as a reminder of the former spouse, developing overdependence on children, seeing children as a burden, and focusing on surviving rather than on parenting children and attempting to meet their developmental needs (Kaslow, 2000). One study, however, questions the pathological implications of most studies of single mothers for leaning on children for emotional support and advice (Arditti, 1999). This study reports that adult children instead viewed this as contributing to a sense of equality, closeness, and promotion of friendship with their mother. Rather than constituting boundary violations, these interactions may help, from this researcher's point of view, to build strength in single-parent families headed by women. However, more work will need to be done to fully substantiate this view.

Focus Point.   Most single-parent families are headed by mothers who have been divorced. These families can expect to experience financial problems due to several factors. Researchers commonly observe role strain among these parents, who must adjust to holding several competing roles simultaneously. The relationship between mothers and children also changes as the boundaries previously established between adult and child roles become blurred. Many women find their status as single mothers to be stressful but manage to adjust in a variety of ways.

Single-Parent Families Headed by Fathers   Single-parent families headed by fathers constitute the minority of these family systems in the United States, although the percentage of families headed by men has increased steadily over the past 40 years (Figure 11–7). In comparison with single-parent mothers, fathers heading this type of family system earn considerably higher incomes, which promotes a different quality of family life. In addition, they are reported to have fewer adjustment issues than custodial single-parent mothers (Hilton & Kopera-Frye, 2004).

Boys are more likely than girls to live with a custodial father. Some researchers attribute this tendency to the belief that boys in such situations benefit from being raised by fathers, while girls benefit from being raised by mothers (Jordan, 2003). This is often contrary to the bias of court officials, who may believe that it is in the best interests of all children to be raised by a single-parent mother than by a father as a single parent.

FIGURE 11–7. An increasing number of single-parent family systems in the United States are headed by men.

Parenting Reflection 11–8

Why is sole custody of children granted to fewer divorced fathers? Why are women reluctant to relinquish full custody to the father?

Men assume the custodial parenting role following divorce for a variety of reasons. However, it continues to be customary in our culture for women to assume this role, although in the past a man commonly accepted single parenthood after the death of his spouse. The idea that men can conduct their parenting activities as capably as women and that children are not harmed by single-parent fathering experiences is a relatively new concept. Its increasing acceptance is reflected in the corresponding increase in the number of men who are awarded custody of children following divorce.

Unlike single-parent mothers, single-parent fathers gain custody of their children through two likely avenues:

1. Men may assert their right to gain custody of children because they feel capable and motivated to parent their children effectively, although the mother may contest their ability.

2. Men may consent to assume custody when mothers show no desire to continue their parental rights or are unable to do so because of emotional or physical problems.

Men make more positive adjustments to being a custodial single father when they have a strong desire to perform well in this capacity. Many men wish to continue positive parenting activities that may have been established when the children were born.

Greater Financial Freedom. Single-parent fathers typically earn higher incomes than single-parent mothers. Fathers achieve greater economic security due in part to a higher level of educational attainment and more years of employment. Those advantages enable them to hold jobs that earn higher levels of income and put them in a more favorable employment and financial situation after they become single parents (Grall, 2006; Kaslow, 2000).

Discrepancies in income between single mothers and fathers account for many of the differences in the quality of life in these family systems. As stated earlier, incomes of single-parent families headed by men are typically higher than of those headed by women. Single-parent families headed by men also tend to have fewer people who must be supported by the father's income, as opposed to those families headed by women. These differences contribute to the higher quality of life in single-parent families headed by men: Financial resources are more abundant.

Role Strain.   A single-parent father experiences role strain differently than a single-parent mother. Like the single-parent mother, he must adjust to the additional responsibilities of child rearing in addition to providing the family income. The challenges facing most fathers differ from those of mothers, however, in a variety of ways.

Many single-parent fathers were not involved in managing household tasks before the divorce, but they have little difficulty when they assume responsibility for home management (Everett & Everett, 2000). However, they report that meal preparation and food shopping can be major problem areas because many lack these skills. Single-parent fathers tend to share household management tasks with children rather than secure help from outside resources. Single-parent mothers, by comparison, tend to perform these tasks themselves rather than expect children to cooperate, which promotes greater levels of role strain. Single-parent fathers with daughters tend to expect them, more than their sons, to assist with household management tasks, possibly due to differences in the socialization of children. When the families of single-parent fathers are compared with two-parent families, however, children in the single-parent systems do not perform as many household management tasks. This difference may be due to several factors:

■ Single-parent fathers may intentionally not involve their children in tasks in an effort to prove their own competence as household managers.
■ These fathers may attempt to ease the transition and tensions that children experience when they shift to new family patterns after the divorce.
■ Children have difficulty becoming familiar with the routines and patterns of two different households.

Some single-parent fathers may have difficulty synchronizing child care, household duties, and wage-earning responsibilities into a workable and manageable routine. Arranging child care may be a major problem for many fathers, particularly those with young children. Rather than hiring housekeepers or sitters, single fathers generally rely on the same child-care resources as do other parents. Many custodial fathers are likely to work longer

hours while holding a full-time job, which can contribute to role strain (Lin & Chen, 2006).

Structuring older children's activities is also a common problem among many single-parent fathers. Single fathers of older children typically rely on after-school activities, such as dance instruction or athletics, to help them adequately supervise children. Most fathers also adapt their work hours to increase their availability.

Changes in the Parent-Child Relationship.   Single-parent fathers can perform child-care responsibilities effectively (Kaslow, 2000). One concern of the authorities who make custody evaluations and recommendations often centers on a father's ability to perform effectively as a single parent. Today researchers generally recognize that most men can conduct caregiving responsibilities in a competent manner that is healthy and beneficial to children (Cabrera, 2003). Fathers are particularly competent when they have been actively involved in providing care since a child's infancy and when they willingly accept child custody after divorce. Because individuals in our society have moved increasingly toward the creation and enactment of androgynous parenting roles, many men have learned how to provide for children's needs and to express nurturance in caregiving.

Single-parent fathers tend to promote different expectations for their children than single-parent mothers (Knox & Schacht, 2008). For example, single fathers appear to demand more independence from children. As many gain experience in child-rearing activities, they shift away from authoritarian methods to those that are authoritative in nature. They become less traditional, less discipline-oriented, more concerned about the quality of care they provide and the experiences children have with nonparental caregivers, more interested in children's educational experiences, and more protective about dangerous situations to which children might be exposed.

Many single-parent fathers also express concerns about raising a daughter in a family system that lacks the sex-role model provided by an adult woman. They wonder how they can provide socialization experiences for girls that will help them learn appropriate sex-role behaviors.

Single-parent fathers tend to seek support and assistance from others outside their family system when they need help as caregivers. These sources include relatives, such as their own parents, professionals, religious leaders, physicians, and teachers. Many discover that these sources are helpful in providing information and guidance about child care that improves the fathers' abilities to parent children effectively.

• •

Focus Point. Single-parent fathers experience situations that are similar to those of single-parent mothers, but researchers also observe differences. Family systems headed by custodial fathers constitute a minority of single-parent families. Single-parent fathers are typically better educated than single-parent mothers and earn significantly higher incomes. They often have custody of sons rather than of daughters. Men may gain custody of children after a divorce because they actively seek it or because the mother has defaulted on her parenting rights. Like single-parent mothers, fathers experience role strain as they add increased involvement with child rearing to their other responsibilities. These men usually perform adequately as caregivers, but researchers notice certain differences in interaction patterns with children when these single families are compared with two-adult families.

• •

The Dilemma of Nonresident, Noncustodial Fathers

Many individuals, both within and outside of family systems, may wonder if nonresident fathers are of any worth or value, other than paying child support, to their children. Even these fathers may ponder this issue. Until recently, researchers who have studied these fathers have presented information and data that would tend to answer this negatively. Being a nonresident, noncustodial father, for example, increases men's risks of injuries, addictions, and premature death (Weitoff, Burström, & Rosén, 2004). These may be due to the feelings of loss and grief experienced by these fathers (Spillman, Deschamps, & Crews, 2004). The consensus of research, until recently, has given little strength to the notion that children's contact with their nonresident father has significant benefits for them (Wilcoxon, 2002) or for these fathers. Evidence has been strong, on the other hand, in showing that nonresidential fathers' payment of child support as well as involvement with their children are positively associated with measures of children's well-

being (Harper & Fine, 2006; Mandel, 2006) and that they desire to continue to be involved with their children for the long term (Laasko & Adams, 2006).

Some aspects of the research regarding the relevance of nonresidential fathers in their children's lives may be problematic (Amato & Gilbreth, 1999; Amato & Sobolewski, 2004). Two important dimensions influence the role of nonresidential fathers in their children's well-being. First is the degree to which children feel close to their nonresidential father and desire contact with him. The second hinges on whether the nonresidential father uses an authoritative parenting style when interacting with his children. Taking these dimensions together with regular payment of child support, a marked association appears with children's academic success and the tendency of children to deal with problems in healthy ways.

It is not uncommon for nonresidential fathers to want to make the little time they have with children during visitation to be the most positive experiences possible. Guilt over not being able to be a full-time parent may also contribute to the desire to minimize children's problematic behavior in this time with the father. Additionally, it is not uncommon for nonresidential fathers to approach parenting not from an authoritative but from an adult-companion position. When nonresidential fathers avoid this latter approach with children and act in authoritative ways, such as praising children, disciplining their misbehavior, setting and enforcing limits, assisting with schoolwork, and talking about problems, positive effects are observed in children's well-being as measured by postdivorce adjustment and academic performance, for example (Amato & Gilbreth, 1999; Amato & Sobolewski, 2004).

Results of an ongoing study of single-parent families (Ahrons & Tanner, 2003) report some long-term effects of relationship changes for adult children and their noncustodial fathers 20 years following the parental divorce. Most participants felt that the relationship had improved over time or remained stable. However, relationships worsened over time when conflicts between the biological parents increased, the father remarried early in the postdivorce years, and the father generally had low involvement with children in the early postdivorce years. Participants describing their father-child relationships as poor also reported having poor relationships with other family members involving biological relatives and steprelatives.

Focus Point.   Child custody is a central issue for most divorcing parents. Legal decisions are made with the best interests of children in mind. Sole custody is customarily awarded to the mother rather than to the father. Decisions about sole custody are sometimes difficult to make and can involve lengthy, expensive legal assistance. Joint custody continues to gain favor as a means of overcoming the disadvantages of sole custody, although it has unique problems.

Strengths of Single-Parent Families

The problems and challenges faced by single-parent families often overshadow their strengths (C. Anderson, 2003). As noted earlier, the challenges experienced by these family systems tend to provide the opportunities for people to grow and develop in ways they might not imagine otherwise. Women, for example, generally say, in afterthought, that their single-parenting experience helped to build personal strengths and confidence. In addition, these family strengths also have been identified (Benedek & Brown, 2004; Jordan, 2003; Weight, 2004): (1) the ability to incorporate parenting skills traditionally found in two-parent families; (2) a positive attitude about the changes in family life; (3) effective communications between all family members; (4) family management skills; and (5) the ability to become financially independent.

It is also important to note that there are few differences between children raised by single-parent mothers and fathers (Everett & Everett, 2000; Kaslow, 2000). Children are often placed for custody with same-sex parents based on the notion that it is in their best interest for this type of arrangement. Conversely, it is believed that children raised by single-parent mothers or fathers are disadvantaged because they lack exposure to the opposite-sex parent. This finding of no significant differences in children regardless of this type of family structure may result from adults becoming more androgynous in their behavior. Modeling androgynous gender roles to children may offer many benefits that promote their well-being far beyond the years of childhood and adolescence into adulthood (Bem, 1975). In addition, children are likely to learn resilience from their experiences in growing up in single-parent families, a life skill that will serve them in good stead in adulthood to face many life challenges (Helton & Smith, 2004).

SYSTEMIC FAMILY DEVELOPMENT SNAPSHOT

(Before reading this section, it may be helpful to review the systemic family development model and the metaphor used to illustrate its concepts from Chapter 3.)

One of the strengths of the systemic family development model is its ability to be applied to all types of family forms and structures. For this reason, it is possible to examine what is taking place in single-parent family systems that are headed by mothers or by fathers. These families typically have experienced divorce, one of the most stressful life events producing numerous changes and challenges for individuals and their family systems. We will briefly examine an example of one single-parent family in which the divorced parents hold joint custody of children and in which the mother is the physical custodian.

When the snapshot is taken, the two children in this family are 10 and 7; their father is 38 and their mother is 35; and the only grandparent living is their maternal grandmother, who is 61. The parents were divorced about 1 year ago. The mother retained the family home, and the father moved into an apartment nearby. The children are members of a binuclear family system.

Single-Parent Family Headed by a Mother

Ashley Miller was exhausted by the end of the day. She felt like this just about every day now. Ashley found it difficult to see happiness in anything any more.

Ashley had not worked full-time outside the home while she was married, but she was forced to take a job 12 months ago when her divorce from John Miller became final. She had reluctantly started work as a grocery store clerk because jobs were so scarce in their small community. Her job was demanding and her feet hurt from standing on a concrete floor every day. Sometimes customers were irritable and difficult; this was especially challenging on those days when she herself was not up to par emotionally. The hours were long and the pay was just enough to meet most of the expenses each month.

John had agreed to provide child support since he had a much larger salary than she did in his job at a local factory. Without his financial help, she knew that she would have to apply for food stamps. He had mostly been regular with the checks, but a few had come late and not in the complete amount. When she discussed this with him, he always explained that he had financial problems as well and would make up the missing amount in later checks. For the time being, she simply let this all go in hopes that she could trust his word as she could in the past. Still, when this happened, it forced her to cut corners, and she and the children often had to do without some things they would normally have.

The divorce had been a difficult experience. Things had progressively become more difficult and strained between Ashley and John over the years. They had married 2 years before their first child was born and appeared to be an ideal couple. But as the second child arrived, John increased his work hours and Ashley had taken a part-time job to help make ends meet. As the children grew older, John spent less time being a parent and more time working harder as a provider in order to gain a promotion that would bring in more money. And he helped less around the house as well. Many times, arguments focused on what Ashley regarded as his reneging on a commitment made earlier to share equally in parenting and housework responsibilities. He contended, in defense, that if she wanted the kind of home and furnishings she desired, then this was the price both of them had to pay. In the end, the price became their marriage. They had tried to work out things in therapy but this went nowhere because John maintained that he

had become burned out on the marriage itself. He wasn't sure he wanted to be married anymore and only saw a great deal more unhappiness for everyone if they continued to be together.

One thing John and Ashley shared was a concern about how the split would affect their children. Now, in therapy, the direction turned to how to prepare the children for the imminent change in their family life. They were able to work out many details relating to their divorce with the therapist rather than with lawyers: how they would arrange joint custody, designating Ashley as the physical custodian; how often John would have visitation with the children; how medical and dental expenses would be handled under whose insurance; and what would happen to their house. The therapist helped them to understand how their children might react so they could be prepared as parents. They rehearsed telling the children about the divorce and why it was happening and other related issues.

The couple wanted to keep changes to a minimum. Toward this end, Ashley gained title to the house, keeping a change in residence at bay for a while and allowing the children to continue to go to their current school. Fortunately, their school counselor had recently organized a support group for children whose parents were divorcing and for those whose parents had divorced. The therapist strongly recommended this program to Ashley and John as a way of supporting their children in handling the stressfulness of their parents' divorce.

One other detail needed attention in this first year following divorce: how to arrange for her mother to have visitation with the children. John and his mother-in-law had not always gotten along, and following the divorce he had mixed feelings about his former mother-in-law having much involvement with her grandchildren. The children had complained several times about wanting to see their grandmother, but this had been delayed because of John's misgivings. When they had each worked with their own lawyers in finalizing the divorce agreement, John's had informed him that grandparents had no legal rights to visitation in their state. John informed Ashley about this information and had wanted to place a clause in the contract specifically stating that Ashley had to gain his consent before letting the children have visitation with their grandmother. He feared that the hard feelings between them would be expressed by his ex-mother-in-law to the children. Ashley would not agree to this, and the point had delayed signing the contract for several months. They finally reached a verbal agreement by working with their therapist that they would discuss grandparent visitation before arranging it and that John would have veto power if he ever felt uncomfortable.

Lately, Ashley had discovered through the children that John had been entertaining lady friends during the time when the children were at his apartment. She was unsure how to handle this. She felt insecure and jealous, but she was disturbed more about the appropriateness of this arrangement and how the children could be affected. She had made an appointment with the therapist to discuss this to learn of her options and how to handle her feelings about John's social life.

The school counselor had called her at work to discuss something that her daughter, Brittany, had shared with the support group. Brittany, age 10, had mentioned that her mother was sharing personal problems with her and that she felt helpless and unsure of what to say in response. The counselor had gently suggested that Ashley should rethink these interactions with Brittany. He told Ashley that sometimes this effort to involve a child in an adult's world was not in the child's best interest. He explained that this often forced children to attempt to

become mature long before they were emotionally capable. Ashley, of course, was not aware these discussions could be harmful and quickly had discontinued them.

Being a divorced, single mother was not what Ashley had ever imagined would happen to her. She sometimes found herself daydreaming about what it would be like if she ever remarried. She had heard other coworkers who were in a similar position remark that they would live with someone instead of getting married again because of trust issues. She wondered if this would be a possible option for her if she ever fell in love again.

Parenting Reflection 11–9

Does this binuclear family system have open or closed boundaries? How did boundaries change following the divorce of the parents between themselves and the children? How did this family system use resources to help cope with the crisis event of divorce?

POINTS TO CONSIDER

- There are a variety of family forms in the United States. Differences in family composition and structure most likely result in differences in the ways in which adults conduct parenting functions.
- The single-parent family is one of the most visible types of family systems in the United States today. Most are headed by a woman who becomes the head of the household through divorce, separation, the death of her spouse, or birth out of wedlock.
- Divorce is the most common avenue through which single-parent family systems are created.
- While many mothers continue to be granted child custody, the trend is toward granting joint custody to both parents. This arrangement has many advantages if parents can work cooperatively and communicate with one another about parental role responsibilities. But joint custody also creates problems that must be addressed by everyone involved. When couples cannot reach agreements about custody, they may need to engage a mediator who can help bring closure to their divorce and custody proceedings.

- Women have different experiences as single parents than men do. Single-parent family systems headed by women are characterized by (1) financial difficulties, (2) additional role strains for the mother, and (3) changes in the parent-child relationship.
- An increasing number of men are gaining custody of their children. Single-parent family systems headed by men are characterized by (1) greater financial freedom in comparison with the families of single mothers, (2) additional role strain for the fathers, and (3) a less disrupted lifestyle than that experienced by single mothers.
- Divorce has several effects on adults: (1) rediscovering feelings of self-worth, (2) experiencing a sense of failure about the former marriage relationship, (3) developing a fear of intimate relationships, (4) experiencing depression and alienation, and (5) experiencing changes in lifestyle. The continuing relationship between adults, despite the divorce, presents challenges to adjustment.
- Parental divorce has several effects on children. The timing of divorce in a child's life results in different

levels and types of adjustment. Generally, preschoolers exhibit regressive behaviors and a variety of other types of behavior problems, particularly during the first year after the divorce. School-age children react to their parents' divorce by feeling angry with their parents, experiencing pervasive fears, feeling helpless about the situation, and perhaps feeling rejected by the absent parent. These children become more involved in household responsibilities and experience changes in interactions with both parents. Adolescents often experience problems with personal identity; fears of being abandoned, rejected, and unloved; fears about the failure of their own marriages in the future; and delinquent behaviors. The effects of parental divorce on children are both short- and long-term. Researchers currently believe that some of these effects can be observed for many years after the parents' divorce.

■ Single-parent families have strengths that derive from the experiences of these families in adapting to the crisis of divorce and the resulting challenges for all members of both binuclear systems. These strengths provide opportunities for personal growth that might not occur in other types of family systems.

CHAPTER 12

Parenting in Stepfamily Systems

Focus Questions

■ ■ ■ ■ ■ ■ ■ ■ ■ ■

1. How are stepfamilies created, and what are their distinguishing characteristics?

2. What are similarities and differences in stepmother and stepfather roles?

3. Are developmental changes observed in stepfamily systems?

4. What are the strengths of stepfamilies? What are major adjustment issues and how are these resolved?

5. What stressors and coping mechanisms are revealed by a systemic family development snapshot of a stepfamily?

■ ■ ■ ■ ■ ■ ■ ■ ■ ■

One trend noted by demographers over the past 40 years in American family life is the increasing tendency of adults to divorce and remarry, often several times (Bramlett & Mosher, 2002; U.S. Bureau of the Census, 2007a, 2007b). This pattern has been labeled serial monogamy, sequential polygamy, or conjugal succession (Pasley & Ihinger-Tallman, 1987).

A new type of family system is formed when a single parent remarries. Some researchers refer to it as a *reconstituted* or *blended family system*, but **stepfamily** is the more common label (Ihinger-Tallman & Pasley, 1997). Regardless of the name applied, remarriage of adults restores the adult family role that was vacant in a single-parent family system. Because the vast majority of single-parent families in the United States are headed by women, the person usually filling the vacant adult role is a man who may or may not have been previously married himself. Occasionally, two single parents and their families are merged by the remarriage of the adults (Figure 12–1).

The problems and challenges facing stepfamilies are different from those of other family systems. The adults face the usual tasks of establishing an intimate relationship as a newly married couple. However, this process becomes more complicated because children are not introduced gradually into the family structure. The ability of the new stepfamily system to survive and cope with these challenges occupies much of the time, attention, and resources of the system, especially in the early years following remarriage.

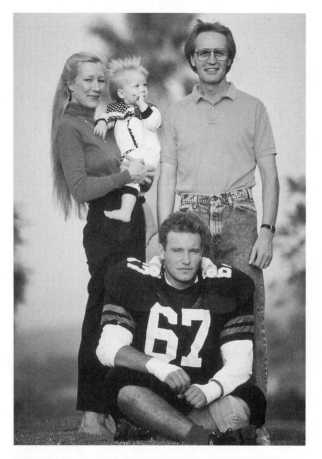

FIGURE 12–1. Stepfamilies are often formed by the remarriage of at least one adult. Researchers have observed wide age differences in children of these families.

INCIDENCE AND CHARACTERISTICS OF STEPFAMILY SYSTEMS

Remarriages are not a new phenomenon of family life (Berger, 2000). In the past, many married adults became single and remarried after the death of a spouse. Divorce has only recently become the leading cause of single status after a first marriage.

Demographers have studied a number of factors and patterns in the occurrence of remarriage in the United States (Bramlett & Mosher, 2002; Clarke-Stewart & Bretano, 2007). Remarriage is more likely to occur if an adult has been divorced rather than widowed.

The probability of remarriage is highest among white divorced women and least likely among black divorced women. Women who were under age 25 at divorce are more likely to remarry than women ages 25 and over at divorce. Remarriage is more likely if divorced women live in communities with lower rates of male unemployment, poverty, and receipt of welfare. And interestingly, women living in nonurban areas are more likely to remarry than those living in cities. These patterns may be explained in part by the age of individuals when they become single. People who are widowed are usually in their late adulthood years and are less likely to remarry because of their advanced age. Divorced individuals tend to be much younger by comparison. Remarriages are considered to be high-risk relationships in that there is an even greater chance of another divorce taking place (McCarthy & Ginsberg, 2007). Unfortunately, little is known currently about the causes and factors involved that lead to redivorce (Ganong, Coleman, & Hans, 2006). However, those couples who have stable, functional remarriages report having higher satisfaction and greater pride in their new relationship than first-marriage couples.

Almost two-thirds of the people who divorce each year in the United States eventually remarry (Bramlett & Mosher, 2002; Figure 12–2). In the typical divorcing couple, the man is about 37 years old, the woman is about 33, and typically they are parents of at least one child (Federal Interagency Forum on Child and Family Statistics, 2007). This suggests that many men and women remarry when they are about 10 years older than they were at their first marriage. Generally, however, remarriage is more likely to occur among younger, rather than older, individuals (Bramlett & Mosher). The median interval between divorce and remarriage is about 3 years for women, with about half remarrying within 5 years of their divorce. Ethnic group identity also influences remarriage rates; for example, more whites tend to remarry than blacks or Hispanics.

Cohabitation occurs more commonly for many divorced adults, which is another distinction from that of first marriages (Fields, 2003). This may reflect the desire to test a relationship before making the commitment involved in marriage. Cohabitation prior to remarriage appears to have little effect on a couple's relationship (Stanley et al., 2006). Another distinction of courtship prior to remarriage is the influence of the children's presence. Not only do single parents, especially those who hold custody of children, have a

FIGURE 12–2. Remarriages often involve older adults with at least one being a parent of an older child.

more challenging time in locating prospective partners, they have other considerations as well. For example, single parents must figure out how to handle the presence of a potential partner spending the night when children are present or how to help children understand when a relationship with a potential partner has broken up. This may be especially challenging when children have developed an attachment to the potential partner.

Remarriages are also characterized by the difference in developmental levels of the adults at the time of remarriage as compared with those at first marriage. Because of what they have experienced in their first marriage and because of developmental changes, divorced people tend to have different expectations of a remarriage and of themselves (Gerlach, 2003). For example, many women with children who remarry have career goals and plans that may be stronger and more definite than those at first marriage. Many know that they can survive a divorce and are more committed to making another marriage work successfully, or their ideas of what a marriage requires are clearer as compared with the first marriage. Remarriages do not differ significantly from first marriages in terms of marital happiness or in the degree of partners' well-being (Ihinger-Tallman & Pasley, 1997). This lack of difference may be attributed to the issues just discussed.

● ●

Parenting Reflection 12–1

Is it possible to distinguish a stepfamily from a first-marriage biological family?

● ●

Like other contemporary family structures, stepfamilies are characterized by their diverse nature (Berger, 2000). For example, some stepfamilies involve only one adult who has been married previously; in others, both adults may have been previously married only once; and both adults may have been previously married more than once. Some involve a remarriage when children were infants and thus perceive themselves as an ordinary family.

Because remarriage most frequently involves individuals who have been previously divorced, it is likely that children of one adult or both will be included as part of the new family system. Researchers describe seven characteristics of stepfamilies that distinguish them from first-marriage families (Berger, 2000):

1. *When children are involved, a new family system is created instantaneously without the benefit of gradually adding new members.* In the family life career of first marriages, adults can gradually develop new patterns (rules, boundaries, and roles) for their

family system that affect effective functioning. Stepfamilies are challenged by the immediacy of developing patterns without gradually adding children to the system. In many instances, the patterns formed for one adult's single-parent family system after divorce are the template for those initially used in the new stepfamily system.

2. *The remarriage of adults may occur at a time when the necessities and tasks of the stepfamily life career are incompatible with the developmental needs and tasks of the adults.* In some situations, there is a conflict between what is required for healthy, individual adult development and what is required to establish a new marriage relationship and new stepfamily system patterns.

3. *Ex-spouses and ex-grandparents can continue to have input into and influence on the new stepfamily system.* Unlike the family systems based on first marriages, stepfamily functioning is complicated and seriously challenged by the influence of past relationships from former family systems. For example, the adults may continue to be influenced by their former spouses because they are still the biological parents of children who are part of the new stepfamily system.

4. *Wishes and expectations of adult marriage partners may not be fulfilled by the new marriage relationship in the stepfamily system.* When adults remarry, they tend to anticipate that the new relationship will overcome or compensate for problems or deficiencies in the previous marriage. However, this expectation places an extra burden on the new marriage to fulfill needs that may be unrealistic.

5. *Both children and adults may have mixed feelings of allegiance and guilt that interfere with effective stepfamily system formation.* Children in stepfamilies can become confused about where their loyalties to others should lie because they are members now of two separate and distinct family systems. For example, it is not unusual for stepchildren to feel as if they are being pulled in several directions at once, which tests the strength of their personal boundaries. Adults also carry mixed feelings about their past and its influence on their present functioning into the new family system. It is not uncommon, for example, for remarried men to feel torn between the need to provide for their biological children from their previous marriage and to meet the needs of the family system to which

they now belong. In addition, whereas many men are relieved that their former relationship has ended, some continue to resent the continuing degree of involvement with that severed relationship through children and financial responsibilities.

6. *Children may not be willing participants in the new stepfamily system.* Although adults may consult children about the new marriage relationship, they often do not seek a child's approval before deciding to remarry. Typically, children are not supportive or accepting of the new marriage, but are often expected to cope with a situation they would rather avoid or ignore. Many children of divorced parents fantasize that their biological parents will somehow be reunited and that their family life will return to its former state. Many continue to hold resentments about the divorce, which tends to make life unpleasant and difficult in the new stepfamily system as children resist the efforts of the remarried adults to forge new family system patterns.

7. *All stepfamily members experience role confusion.* A major task of the system is to establish new patterns that regulate the functioning and behavior of all members. This task is common to all family systems, but it is especially difficult among stepfamilies because of the past histories of the adults and children involved. The role of stepmother or stepfather is not clear, and systems must develop patterns and concepts to define this role, often by trial and error. New rules must be established that all members can agree with for the system to function in a healthy way. Boundaries are a special challenge to effective stepfamily functioning (Stewart, 2005). For example, they may relate to personal property, psychological intimacy, and family routines or traditions. Clear communication, commitment to the new family system, and willingness to discuss issues and reach agreeable solutions are necessary for these new patterns to become established and adapted.

••

Focus Point. Stepfamilies are created by the remarriage of at least one adult. Many people who have been divorced remarry within a relatively short period of time. Children are frequently part of the new family system. Researchers note that these families can be distinguished from those based on first marriages in a variety of ways.

••

STEPFAMILY FORMATION

The problems that challenge stepfamily systems are unique, and these systems may experience a greater level of stress than that usually encountered by family systems based on first marriages (Figure 12–3). Generally, problems may occur from the following sources (Hildebrand et al., 2008; Lee-Baggley, Preece, & De-Longis, 2005; Pasley & Ihinger-Tallman, 1987):

■ Merging different family cultures and identities as the new system establishes roles and patterns
■ Developing new modes of distributing time, energy, material goods, finances, and affection
■ Establishing new bonds of loyalty to the stepfamily system while learning to manage loyalty bonds to former family systems
■ Dealing with marital conflict and children's misbehavior

Stepfamily system formation involves different structures than does first-marriage formation (Papernow, 1984, 1993). First-marriage families differ in having a history of time to allow the adults to develop an intimate relationship and areas of shared interests, values, and habitual patterns that guide interactions and conflict resolution. The gradual addition of children to a biological family allows the adults to develop and adapt parenting roles and patterns, learn to resolve their differences, and create a shared value system as needs arise.

When a first-marriage couple divorces, they create a single-parent family system that most prominently affects the children, who become members of two distinct binuclear systems. A major consequence of change in the parent-child relationships is the dismantling of the usual generational boundaries between adults and children. Adults often look to children for the support and nurturance formerly provided by the spouse.

At the beginning of a stepfamily's life, the stepparent at first seems to be an outsider to the existing alliance between the biological parent and his or her children. This alliance is based on the patterns established in the former single-parent family system and has its own history, methods of problem solving, rules, boundaries, patterns, and operational styles firmly in place. The greatest challenge to the survival and effective, healthy functioning of a stepfamily system may be overcoming the obstacles and resistance encountered in adapting previously established patterns and styles to accommodate the needs of the new stepfamily system.

Patricia Papernow (1984, 1993) developed a model that describes stepfamily formation. She depicts three major stages that involve substages (see Focus On 12–1). It takes a relatively long period of time for a stepfamily to find itself and its identity. Many difficulties can challenge effective family formation and functioning. For example, one of the disadvantages that challenges effective stepfamily formation is that the children involved frequently are adolescents (Leake, 2007). Because of their developmental focus on individuation from their families, struggles can be expected when the adults involved demand their teenager's participation in activities that are aimed to develop a family identity.

••

Focus Point.   The structure of stepfamilies is different from that of biological families. Single-parent families are created when adults divorce from their first marriage, which changes the relationship between the biological parents and children. When a biological parent's marriage to a new partner forms a stepfamily, other changes emerge in the parent-child subsystem, such as the alliance between the biological parent and children adapting to include the stepparent. A stepfamily life career progresses through distinct stages that may occur over a long period of time.

••

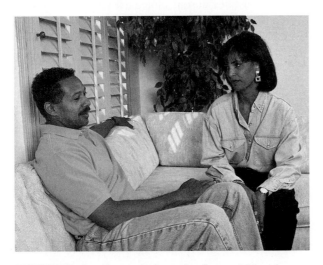

FIGURE 12–3.   Remarried couples face additional challenges in establishing new relationship bonds. The success of a new stepfamily often depends on the health of the new marriage relationship.

Focus On 12–1

Stages in Stepfamily Formation

Early Stages: Getting Started and Avoiding Pitfalls

Stage 1: Fantasy

Everyone involved commonly holds unrealistic expectations that they hope will be fulfilled in the new family system:

■ Children will be rescued from problems associated with the divorce of their biological parents.
■ Children will be able to get their biological parents reunited by sabotaging the biological parent's new relationship.
■ The biological family will be healed by introducing a new adult into the vacated role.
■ Stepparents will be adored by stepchildren and welcomed enthusiastically by the biological family.
■ The biological parent will finally have unmet needs satisfied by the new partner.
■ The biological parent will be able to share parenting responsibilities again with another adult.

Stage 2: Assimilating the New Adult

The biological parent attempts to merge the stepparent into the biological family but usually cannot accomplish this goal successfully at this time. The stepparent notices by now that he or she is an outsider and discovers feelings of jealousy, resentment, and inadequacy.

■ Both stepparent and stepchildren experience problems in establishing and working on a relationship.
■ Problems are perceived differently by everyone involved. The stepparent expresses frustration in dealing with what is seen as an impenetrable biological family solidarity. The biological parent doesn't understand the frustrations of the stepparent. The stepchildren may begin to experience loyalty conflicts toward their absent biological parent and the stepparent.
■ The biological parent feels caught in the middle between wanting a good adult relationship and the problems experienced by children in dealing with a new adult in their family.

Stage 3: Awareness

Many stepfamilies stagnate in their development at this stage due to difficulties in communication between all parties. To avoid this, all family members need to:

■ apply labels to feelings being experienced,
■ understand why the feelings are being experienced,
■ state personal needs more articulately,
■ listen to what the stepparent describes as perceived rules and boundaries in the biological family that have failed to include the stepparent.

Middle Stages: Remodeling the Family

Stage 4: Mobilization

The stepparent's role to initiate changes intensifies at this point. A showdown becomes inevitable; if the changes and compromises cannot be made, there is considerable risk that the stepfamily will dissolve via divorce of the adults.

Focus On 12–1

- Some changes and demands may appear to be trivial, but these represent the need for further weakening of the biological family's alliances to accommodate the stepparent into a new family structure.
- The biological parent may feel pulled in two directions: meeting the perceived needs of children and giving more allegiance to the new relationship.
- If the changes and adaptations are successfully implemented (e.g., having more private time for the adult couple), the new stepfamily now can truly be formed.

Stage 5: Action

This is when the changes and adaptations may be implemented on a larger scale to form the new stepfamily.

- New family rituals and traditions are helpful to facilitate a sense of family.
- Boundaries and rules are tested out to more clearly define the adults' committed relationship and the stepparent-stepchild relationship (e.g., restricting discipline of children solely to the biological parent and removing the stepparent from this responsibility).
- The stepparent now plays an even larger role in the new family.
- The adult couple work together more closely as a team in a variety of matters.

Later Stages: Putting It All Together

Stage 6: Contact

This stage serves to solidify the actions taken to forge a new stepfamily.

- Children have been reassigned out of the primary relationship with the biological parent as it was modified in the single-parent family experience and maintained in earlier stages of stepfamily formation.
- A workable relationship has been negotiated for the stepparent and stepchildren without involvement of the biological parent.
- Each member's family role becomes validated and authentic.

Stage 7: Resolution

The new stepfamily achieves a new identity.

- The stepparent becomes accepted by the stepchildren as an "intimate outsider." A true friendship emerges between them.
- The family gestalt differs completely from earlier; instead of uncertainty and stress, the feeling is one of confidence and comfort in relationships.
- The family learns to let go of dependencies that helped in forming the new family structure.

Source: Adapted from Papernow, P. L. (1984). The stepfamily cycle: An experimental model of stepfamily development. *Family Relations, 33,* 355–363; Papernow, P. L. (1993). *Becoming a stepfamily.* San Francisco: Jossey-Bass.

STEPFAMILY ROLES AND RELATIONSHIPS

A stepparent's role is distinct from that of a biological parent (Parenting FAQs 12–1). It differs in having a high degree of role ambiguity (Berger, 2000; Papernow, 1993). Our culture promotes many stereotypical images of stepparents that are largely negative in nature (Leon, 2005). These images can be found, for example, in stories and fairy tales told to children. Stepparents, particularly stepmothers, are depicted as evil, uncaring, self-centered

Parenting FAQs 12–1

I'm seriously considering marriage to a wonderful woman I've been dating for almost 2 years. There are school-age children involved. I've never been married before. I have no clue what it's like to be a father, much less what is involved in being a stepfather. Can you tell me what to expect if I become a stepfather?

A: You are in a unique position that may be to your advantage. Since you don't bring any preconceptions about fathering to this situation, you may not already have certain ingrained ideas about what you should be doing as a parent. However, this is an instant family situation. You are the newcomer in an already established and long-term relationship between the children and their mother. It might help you to understand what you are confronting to consider these factors about the role of a stepfather:

- **Uncertainty about the degree of authority in the stepfather role.** The challenge is accomplishing the transition from being a friend to stepchildren before remarriage to establishing a parenting relationship after remarriage.
- **Uncertainty about the amount of affection to show to stepchildren.** Some stepfathers feel uncomfortable kissing and hugging stepchildren and do not always enjoy play activities with them.
- **Uncertainty about disciplining stepchildren and enforcing rules.** A major source of conflict between stepfathers and biological parents involves agreeing on what needs enforcing and what is unimportant. It is difficult for many biological mothers, even if they have given prior approval, to deal with stepfathers' attempts to discipline their children.
- **Uncertainty about how to deal with financial conflicts.** Many stepfathers feel sandwiched financially between two different families. Members of the new stepfamily often see the financial contributions of the stepfather as a measure of love and devotion to the new family system.
- **Uncertainty about dealing with guilt regarding perceived abandonment of one's own biological children.** This feeling frequently interferes with establishing good relationships with stepchildren because a sense of allegiance remains strong toward the biological children.
- **Uncertainty in dealing with loyalty conflicts.** Problems emerge regarding the time children spend with biological parents versus stepfathers.
- **Uncertainty in dealing with sexual conflicts.** The incest taboo in families is weakened in stepfamily systems. Adults and children in these families can be sexually attracted to and involved with one another. This is unhealthy, illegal, and inappropriate abusive activity, especially for children.
- **Uncertainty in dealing with conflicts about surnames.** Some stepfamilies have problems with the differences in last names of the adults and children.

Sources: Adapted from Robinson, B. F. (1984). The contemporary American stepfather. *Family Relations, 33,* 381–388; Coleman. M., & Ganong, L. H. (1991). Remarriage and stepfamily research in the 1980s: Increased interest in an old form. In A. Booth (Ed.), *Contemporary families: Looking forward, looking back.* Minneapolis, MN: National Council on Family Relations.

individuals who mistreat and abuse stepchildren. To a certain degree, popular television shows and movies reflect the lack of clarity in the stepparent role.

Belief in these negative stereotypes varies according to someone's current family situation. Perceptions of stepparents, and particularly those of stepmothers, are generally negative when compared with perceptions of biological parents. However, individuals currently living in single-parent family systems and stepfamilies tend to hold less-negative opinions than those living in first-

marriage families. Negative perceptions about stepparents seem to decrease as people become more sensitive, familiar, and appreciative of the problems and challenges that face stepfamilies (Bloomfield, 2004).

Expectations about how someone should perform a social role frequently influence actual behavior. Although research does not specifically detail exactly what may be expected of people in stepparent roles, studies find that stepparents are expected to share equally in the parental status of the new family system. However, the stepparent is expected to be involved to a lesser degree than the biological parent (Berger, 2000). Additionally, social disapproval is considerably less if a stepparent refuses to become involved with stepchildren than if a biological parent refuses to become involved with offspring.

Special parenting problems may arise for a person who occupies the vacant role in a former single-parent family system. Both men and women who become stepparents may approach their new role with some trepidation or fear of the unknown. These individuals come into a family situation in which they are often considered an outsider. The entire family interaction pattern must change to include the new person's cognitive style and personality pattern. For example, a single-parent mother who marries or remarries is confronted with relinquishing her sole authority in managing family affairs, and she must now share decision-making responsibilities with her new partner. Although many women welcome this change, others state that they must work hard to realign their role with that of the new partner (Pasley & Ihinger-Tallman, 1987). And, as we have seen in other situations, family systems tend to resist any change that displaces any current homeostasis or functioning, whether this may be healthy or unhealthy in nature.

Although some remarriages are generally reported to be happier and more successful than first marriages, most of the problems associated with stepfamily functioning are related to parenting children from the former marriages (Berger, 2000; Bloomfield, 2004). The difficulties of a stepparent may be enhanced when stepchildren live with the remarried couple rather than elsewhere, particularly if they live with a stepmother.

● ●

Parenting Reflection 12–2

Why are clearly defined role functions and behaviors for stepparents lacking in our society?

● ●

Stepmothers

The uncertainty associated with stepparent role expectations causes many problems for individuals who assume these roles (Berger, 2000). The stepmother role is made even more difficult by two basic myths: (1) A stepmother is bad; and (2) she requires instant love from the stepchildren. To counter these impressions, the step-

mother who believes in these myths may overcompensate by contributing too much to the relationship between herself and her stepchildren. The situation becomes impossible, however, because the stepmother eventually realizes she cannot possibly please everyone involved, including herself. Her own children may complicate the situation by feeling that they are left out, ignored, or receiving less attention than their stepsiblings. As a result, it appears that successful stepmothers experience a process in establishing an identity as such (Bradley, 2006). This process involves working through the stresses and ambiguities associated with their stepmother role by developing new perspectives and an empathic understanding of what the role involves. Other stepmothers have been found to deconstruct the myth of the evil stepmother by depicting the biological mother as the one who is "evil" while portraying herself as "good" (Christian, 2005).

● ●

Parenting Reflection 12–3

How do stereotypes about stepmothers depict these individuals? Are there similar ones about stepfathers? Do these truly influence the behavior of individuals in these roles? Could these become self-fulfilling prophecies about stepparents?

● ●

Families in which the mother role is filled by a stepmother are found to have more problems than those with a stepfather. This may be due to differences in the ways in which stepfamilies are formed. Fathers who gain custody of children after remarriage often do so because the mother has difficulty handling the child or because the child has experienced problems following the parental divorce. Another difficult situation among families with stepmothers involves a woman who has never had children of her own but who quickly assumes a parenting role after her first marriage or remarriage.

Relationships with stepchildren may vary depending on their sex. Stepmothers and stepdaughters are found to have the least favorable relationship of all steprelationships studied. The girls in these relationships who do not feel loved report more feelings of hostility and lowered self-esteem. A factor that may contribute to a poor stepmother-stepdaughter relationship is the child's regular contact with her biological mother. This seems to create tensions within the stepfamily because children may find it more problematic to replace mothers than fathers in their lives.

Age of stepchildren is also a factor in influencing the nature of the relationship with their stepmother, especially among those who have live-in stepmothers. Preschool-age children have the least problems in interactions with stepmothers, while school-age and adolescent children have poorer relationships with their stepmothers by comparison. The stepmothers of these older children have more disagreements with their spouses, more conflicts over ways of disciplining children, and less satisfaction with their marriages than do stepmothers of younger children.

Despite these challenges, there are successful stepmothers who turn out well in their new role and make significant contributions to their new family (Whiting, Smith, Barnett, & Grafsky, 2007). The methods most often used by these mothers to cope with their challenges include using supports from outside as well as inside their family system, positive attitudes, use of positive communication styles, and working to maintain a quality marital relationship.

Stepfathers

Stepfathers encounter similar kinds of problems in developing and performing their family role (Berger, 2000; Marsiglio, 2004). The stepfather-stepchild relationship may be at risk, however, for as long as 2 years following the remarriage. Unlike the stepmother, he may not be as handicapped with myths and stereotypes about his new role. One study reports that multiple stereotypes may be applied to this family role, many of which can be positive rather than negative in nature (Claxton-Oldfield, O'Neill, Thomson, & Gallant, 2005). The less-structured nature of his role has both advantages and disadvantages. On the positive side, he can forge a new identity and impression when establishing a relationship with his spouse's children. Some research suggests that stepfathers are less likely to be authoritative in parenting style than are biological fathers. Problems abound, however, in several areas. For example, establishing disciplinary patterns and using controls related to stepchildren's behavior are often prime problem areas for stepfathers. Disagreements often result with the spouse over how the stepfather conducts his disciplinary actions with stepchildren.

Stepfathers also experience problems in relation to their financial affairs. Many must make some kind of child support payments to their biological children from a former marriage. This money may be very much needed by the new stepfamily, which can produce feelings of resentment about the former marriage experience. Guilt feelings may derive from the sense that biological children have been abandoned after the formation of the new stepfamily system. Some men feel, however, that when another man becomes involved as a stepfather to their biological children, then this man should help to bear the financial costs of raising and caring for these children. Research suggests that biological fathers reduce their social and economic investments in children with whom they no longer live when they remarry and become involved in a stepfamily. One study reports that biological fathers in new stepfamilies are likely to adjust child support payments to nonresidential children to accommodate the financial needs for supporting the new biological children (Manning & Smock, 2000).

A man's satisfaction with being a stepfather is associated with several factors. First, being a biological father appears to work against a man's development of a positive relationship with stepchildren. Men who do not have children of their own and who become stepfathers appear to develop more positive relationships with stepchildren. Second, positive relationships between stepfathers and stepchildren are enhanced by the amount of communication that occurs between them. Third, when stepfathers feel that they have the biological mother's support to become involved in disciplining children, they report greater levels of satisfaction. This factor may also be due to the eagerness of younger children in accepting a new father into their lives. Older children and adolescents are less willing to make adjustments and to be tolerant and accepting of a new individual in their family life. Finally, a critical event takes place in stepfamily formation when the stepfather accepts the stepchildren as his own and makes the transition from being an outsider to being a paternal figure (Marsiglio, 2004). This is all dependent, of course, on the contingencies of stepchildren making a similar transition in accepting the stepfather into the family circle.

Stepgrandparents

If we acknowledge that the family role of grandparents in contemporary times is ambiguous, consider the even more unique status of the stepgrandparent role. The legal status of stepgrandparents is even less clear. The little research available about this family role indicates that stepgrandparents are more likely to view stepgrandchildren like biological grandchildren if they are young when an adult child remarries. When stepgrandchildren live with the grandparent's adult children, the likelihood for a relationship developing between stepgrandparent and stepgrandchildren increases considerably. However, stepgrandparents appear to be generally overall less satisfied with relationships with stepgrandchildren than biological grandparents (Christensen & Smith, 2002). One study (Haberstroh, Hayslip, & Wohl, 2001) reported on the perceptions of adult grandchildren of their stepgrandparents. The researchers suggested that stepgrandparents can improve the relationship with their grandchildren by behaving in a more actively grandparental manner, establishing a closer relationship with their adult child, and increasing their visits with the stepgrandchild at family gatherings and holidays, for example. The quality of the stepgrandchild-stepgrandparent relationship appears to be influenced to a greater extent by the adult children than by the factors exclusive to the stepgrandparent-stepgrandchild relationship. Stepgrandchildren perceived the quality of the relationship with their biological grandparent to be stronger than their stepgrandparent relationship.

Stepchildren/Stepsiblings

Usually, the quality of life for children is thought to be enhanced when their biological mother remarries. As discussed earlier in this chapter, single-parent families headed by a woman typically experience either a poverty-level existence or a borderline standard of living. When children live in these conditions, they fare less well than children living in more affluent families in terms of quality of life, medical care, nutrition, education, and economic security (Federal Interagency Forum on Child and Family Statistics, 2007).

Researchers, however, report that children from stepfamilies fare no better nor no worse than children from single-parent families in terms of ratings of well-being (Berger, 2000). When compared with children from intact, first-marriage families, children from both stepfamilies and single-parent families are rated as less well adjusted. It should be stressed, however, that most children in these family forms are not found to demonstrate serious problems.

The research literature is also ambiguous regarding whether children of different ages and gender adjust differently to the arrival of a new stepparent (Berger, 2000). Children are expected to make a series of adjustments when biological parents divorce and later remarry. These adjustments typically focus on making a transition in family structure and functioning. These adjustments are stressful and have manifestations in school performance, behavior, and other socioemotional factors. Obviously, children living in intact, first-marriage families do not experience anything comparable that can affect their development, providing one major explanation of why researchers report such disparate findings.

Two findings remain consistent among the majority of studies about children growing up in stepfamilies (Berger, 2000; Bray & Hetherington, 1993): These children, especially girls, can be expected to reject their stepfather and to leave their stepfamilies at an earlier age than those growing up in single-parent or two-parent households. Their reason for leaving is to establish their own homes and lifestyles prior to marriage or to become married. One explanation for these early departures is the tensions that exist between themselves and their parents and stepparents. Apparently, exiting the stepfamily is seen as a more viable way to resolve these tensions. Some researchers suggest that the friction that exists in stepfamilies involving female children is due to the disruption of the mother-daughter relationship by the mother's male sexual partner who has an ambiguous relationship with the daughter.

Sibling relationships become complex when stepfamilies are formed that involve children of both adult partners (Berger, 2000). Forging stepsibling relationships presents other challenges for stepfamilies to accomplish. The usual problems often observed in biological sibling relationships, such as rivalry and jealousy, can become even more intense when stepsiblings are involved. It is not unusual for coalitions to develop between siblings of each adult that create a "my children are being mistreated by your children" scenario. Furthermore, sexual tensions can exist when stepsiblings are pubertal or adolescent, although this topic has not been given credible attention by researchers. On a more positive note, stepsiblings can also develop strong relationships where mutual support can be found and friendships flourish (E. R. Anderson, Greene, Hetherington, & Clingempeel, 1999).

Ex-Spouses and Ex-In-Laws

Relationships are not severed but become altered for people in stepfamilies with ex-spouses and ex-in-laws. It is typical for these individuals to feel displaced and alienated when divorce transforms their relationship (Berger, 2000). Although the rights and boundaries that define the altered relationship between ex-spouses begin with the divorce agreement, few legal rights or clear distinctions inform ex-in-laws about their altered relationship with one another.

It is not uncommon for ex-spouses to experience feelings of jealousy, anger, and competition with their former partners (Berger, 2000). Likewise, ex-in-laws may also harbor similar feelings of resentment about one another. However, in other situations, ex-spouses and ex-in-laws work to make the situations more tolerable and amicable.

••

Focus Point. Stepfamilies involve challenging and complex relationships. The stepparent role differs from that of a biological parent. It is characterized by certain definitions for both men and women, although many negative images and stereotypes are associated with the role. The expectations of a stepparent are ambiguous, and remarriages generally are happier than first ones. Most of the problems of stepfamilies relate to a stepparent's child-rearing function. The stepmother may encounter more difficulties than the stepfather does, and her relationships can be influenced by the age and sex of children. Stepfathers encounter many similar problems, but their role is less restricted by structure and expectations, which allows for greater freedom in creating a unique role identity. Several factors affect a man's satisfaction with being a stepfather. Stepchildren and stepsiblings also experience challenging situations as new relationships are defined and developed. Ex-spouses and ex-in-laws, as well as stepgrandparents, experience unique situations as their roles and relationships become defined in a new family structure.

••

ISSUES AND STRATEGIES OF ADJUSTMENT IN STEPFAMILIES

The ability of stepfamilies to adjust to their new status, roles, and patterns depends on three central issues (Hildebrand et al., 2008; Pasley & Ihinger-Tallman, 1987):

1. Giving up the dream, or discarding unrealistic fantasies and expectations of the new family system and its members

2. Clarifying the feelings and needs of each family member

3. Making a commitment to create and adapt new rules, roles, boundaries, and family routines suitable to the new family system

Stepfamily systems must successfully accomplish several tasks to make the transition from early disillusionment to total commitment to the new family system (Bloomfield, 2004; Glenn, Erwin, & Nelen, 2000). A variety of strategies are useful in reaching this final point.

First, the biological parent and the stepparent need to determine long-range goals for the organization of the new family system. This vision is determined by thinking about the needs of all family members. One helpful way to initiate the process of planning is to have the remarried couple conduct a guided fantasy exercise. This allows them to visualize how they want things to be at some future time in their family life. Discussion about the stepparent's role function is especially important at this time. The couple can use input from the stepchildren, relatives, or a trained therapist in setting long-term goals.

Second, it is helpful if the remarried couple agrees that the biological parent is in charge of setting and enforcing limits for his or her biological children. It is recommended that when enforcing limits, the stepparent should learn to say, "Your parent says that you should." When the biological parent is away and has left the stepparent in charge, it is helpful to instruct children to obey the stepparent in much the same way that they are expected to obey a sitter. The biological parent gives instructions to children that they are expected to follow under the stepparent's supervision. When both adults have biological children, it is helpful for them to understand that it is OK to have different rules for the different children. There is a tendency for stepfamilies to try to follow the old first-marriage family system's model of developing and imposing the same rules for all children rather than understanding that the new family system is nothing at all like the previous one. Conflicts will probably occur between the biological parent and the stepparent, and couples may need assistance in learning how to negotiate compromises.

Third, stepparent-stepchild bonding often needs assistance. This occurs much in the same manner as it does between biological parents and their children during infancy. The process is characterized by nurturing without setting limits on children's behavior. When the stepparent insists that the biological parent should take over the limit-setting functions, bonding can occur between the stepparent and stepchildren. This process may take a year or longer, depending on the age, personality, sex, and other factors of the children. The stepparent must also learn about individual differences that characterize each stepchild.

Fourth, adjustment to becoming a new family system is facilitated when the stepfamily develops its own rules, boundaries, and traditions. This step may be as mundane, but important, as determining who performs what household chores. Negotiation is the usual method for developing rules and traditions, and it is helpful if the stepparent and stepchildren engage in their own discussions in this regard. However, if the biological parent and stepparent cannot reach agreement on a particular rule, it is important for the stepparent to concede to the biological parent because children usually will not obey any rule that their biological parent does not support. Children confirm their awareness of the biological parent's lack of agreement when they tell the stepparent, "You can't make me do that because you aren't my real parent."

Part of the negotiation strategy for the adults regards the biological parent's motivation to make compromises with the stepparent's point of view. This depends on the biological parent's perception of the stepparent's positive contributions to the children's lives. If the biological parent refuses to negotiate, the stepparent has the option of withdrawing this support to gain cooperation in discussion with the biological parent. Sometimes professional help is needed to assist the remarried couple in reaching a settlement on these issues (Figure 12–4).

Fifth, stepfamilies need to develop ways for interacting with the households of their ex-spouses. This is facilitated when the stepparent encourages the children's relationship with the same-sex parent in the other household and by avoiding competition with him or her. It is important for the stepfamily to differentiate itself from the other family by establishing recognizable boundaries. One way to accomplish this is to encourage the understanding that each family system has its own rules and that this difference is acceptable. Couples' groups also help in coping with conflicts between households. In these groups, the remarried couple learns new ways of dealing with these stresses and comes to understand that the situation is not unique.

FIGURE 12–4. Family therapy can help stepfamilies learn new ways to resolve conflicts and problems.

Parenting Reflection 12–4

What are some indicators that a stepfamily needs to seek assistance in resolving issues that fail to support family cohesion?

Other sources of support for stepfamilies come from support groups, self-help publications, educational experiences, and therapeutic intervention (Carlson & Trapani, 2006; Michaels, 2006; Ziegahn, 2002). A variety of self-help books are available on the topic of stepfamilies. They primarily focus on the problems these family systems face and offer a number of strategies for dealing with these issues in healthy ways.

Educational strategies can include lectures, workshops, and seminars on the topics of stepfamilies and remarriage. These programs assist individuals in developing more realistic expectations of stepfamily life that facilitate the creation of long-term goals. Marriage and family enrichment programs are also offered by churches and other organizations, and they are intended to assist stepfamily development (Hawkins, 2003).

Therapy is often the last resort when communication has failed and remarried couples seek assistance in resolving their conflicts (Berger, 2000). A variety of mental health professional assistance is available in communities to provide help to stepfamilies, including psychologists, marriage and family therapists, psychiatrists, counselors, social workers, and members of the clergy. Stepchildren should be included in the therapeutic program or may need other special attention. Therapeutic groups led by mental health professionals also offer educational and supportive means for promoting emotional closeness or family cohesion among stepfamily members. Children often call on teachers for help. When this occurs, teachers can play an important role in helping children understand that the problems unique to stepfamily life can be resolved. Teachers may work with parents or refer the family to professional assistance.

It is important to stress here that because stepchildren may complain about problems in their new family, it may appear that the stepfamily home life is deleterious to their development. Adjustment problems are more prevalent among children in stepfamilies, and they can cause a higher level of stress than that experienced by children in first-marriage families. Even though this stress can affect school performance and other aspects of their lives, the children are not necessarily harmed by having a stepfamily experience.

Support groups are another source of therapeutic assistance for stepfamilies. They allow a remarried couple to discuss and hear matters of mutual interest that relate to their problems. It is also helpful to hear how others in similar circumstances cope with problems and reach creative solutions (Smith, 2002).

Parenting Reflection 12–5

Can stepfamilies have strengths not possessed by first-marriage families?

Focus Point.   The success of a stepfamily may depend on its ability to overcome obstacles that challenge the development of the new family system. The stepfamily may use several strategies to reach this objective as well as a variety of sources for support, such as therapy and support groups.

SYSTEMIC FAMILY DEVELOPMENT SNAPSHOT

(Before reading this section, it may be helpful to review the systemic family development model and the metaphor used to illustrate its concepts from Chapter 3.)

We will examine the functioning of a stepfamily by taking a slice in developmental time from the new family formed by the remarriage of Ashley Miller, the mother of the single-parent family described in the Chapter 11 snapshot. This snapshot is taken six years after Ashley's divorce was final. She is now 41 years old; her daughter, Brittany, is now 16; her son, Michael, is now 13. The only living grandparent is Ashley's mother, who is now 67. Ashley's new husband is Tim Matthews, age 47, a di-

vorced father of three children living with their mother as physical custodian. Tim holds joint custody of his biological children with his ex-wife. Legally, he has no parental rights with Ashley's children unless he decides to adopt them. Tim moved into Ashley's home, to which she gained title following her divorce, following a brief courtship of slightly less than 6 months.

A New Stepfamily

Ashley Matthews ... she was just now getting used to having this new name. It still sounded somewhat unfamiliar to her, especially when someone called it out, but she knew that would pass. She had had the new name now for about 3 years. The first year after marrying Tim Matthews was like a long, extended honeymoon. Things had gone relatively smoothly when Tim moved into her home. They had dated for about 6 months prior to remarriage; she had had some reservations about getting remarried but felt that she knew Tim well enough to make a commitment. The children had seemed at the time to like Tim and thought he was relatively "cool" for someone his age. Now, almost 3 years into the new stepfamily, she was starting to have some doubts if this had been the good decision it seemed at first.

Ashley's misgivings related to feeling pulled in two directions in her new family. On the one hand, Tim had been complaining enough now that it required serious attention. His most common observation was that he felt like an outsider. This had come as a shock to Ashley because she had believed that Tim fitted in relatively well and easily into their routine. As it turns out, he had not felt a part of the group almost from the time he had moved in. On the other hand, her children also had their own complaints about Tim. They had loudly resisted any of his attempts to discipline them when he believed they were acting unruly. Their disputes were loud and sobering in how vociferously they had communicated that he was NOT their father and NEVER would be. In the end, these disputes had not been resolved to the satisfaction of anyone. Ashley often felt that if she didn't back up her children, she would lose their love and loyalty. Conversely, if she didn't back up her husband, she was afraid he would question her loyalty to him and to their relationship. It seemed to be a no-win situation, so she had kept her silence until now.

The tension in the home had become so heavy within the last several months that there were sometimes long periods when the children tried to avoid any communication, even during meals, or Tim would withdraw from interacting with any of them. Ashley had finally persuaded everyone that they needed to get professional help. In essence, she made an ultimatum for the entire family, including herself, that they must work out their differences. She would not allow anyone not to participate. She had practically begged, pleaded, and did whatever it had taken to get Brittany to agree. The children were told that if they had been determined to destroy their mother's remarriage, they had another thought coming because she and Tim had no intention of splitting up. This may have been what the children

had needed to hear in order to understand why they needed to participate in the recovery process.

After several months in family therapy, Tim finally let out the long list of ways he felt he had been treated as an outsider. He was responding to the therapist's request for everyone to discuss at least two things they found uncomfortable in the new family. As it turned out, he had felt that Ashley was part of the problem, not just the children. Tim described many times over a meal when someone would mention what essentially was an "inside joke." Since he didn't understand it, he couldn't join in with the laughter that ensued. He hated the way certain meals were prepared but hadn't said anything because he felt this was imposing himself. In reality, he was also hurt that no one had asked what his favorite dishes were and how he liked certain dishes prepared. Everything had been business as usual just as they had established their routines as a family before he had arrived. He felt like a guest, even an unwelcome one at times.

The children then mentioned a laundry list of complaints. They felt that Tim was intrusive and had butted in to their family's way of doing things by wanting to impose his way of working with issues with no discussion. Other complaints were mostly the standard teenage fare of resenting the constant demands to do things together as a family and to have family vacations together.

Ashley was finally able in this session to voice her feelings of being pulled in two different directions by her loyalty and love. Tim was surprised to hear this, and the children reacted by being astounded that their mother would even consider putting Tim above their own interests. The therapist intervened at this point by stating that the children needed to understand the importance of the adults' marriage to the well-being of the new family. She explained that their mother needed to be supportive of her new husband, and vice versa, for the marriage to work. She also pointed out that preserving the integrity of the marriage was not any indication of lack of support, love, or loyalty to the children. These were two different relationships that worked independently as well as integratively within the entire family relationship.

At the end of the session, the therapist gave assignments to the different relationships in this stepfamily. The adults were to have discussions to work out discipline matters for the children. Ashley would be in charge of enforcing the rules, and Tim would back her up but not impose any rules of his own that had not been worked out with Ashley beforehand. In addition, they were to have "date nights" away from the home and from the children where they would have time to develop a closer, more intimate committed relationship. The therapist also assigned the children and Tim specific projects. She hoped that these exercises would allow Tim and the children to form a relationship that was not grounded in power assertion on anyone's part. By reconfiguring these relationships, they could form friendships. This might take a while to accomplish, but she had seen it happen with others when they shared a commitment to keep working on the matter.

Ashley and Tim knew their new family was at a crossroads, but by working with the therapist and allowing the teens in their family greater freedom to express feelings appropriately, taking these new roads would bring them into a different family configuration.

POINTS TO CONSIDER

■ Remarriage in the United States involves several factors and patterns. It is more likely to occur among individuals who have divorced, and individuals who remarry generally are young adults. The median interval between divorce and remarriage is about 3 years. Ethnic background influences remarriage; for example, whites are more likely than blacks to remarry.

■ Stepfamilies are distinguished from those formed by first marriages in a variety of ways. When children are involved, a family system is transformed and re-created instantly without the benefit of gradually adding new members. One remarried adult may be facing the developmental tasks of the stepfamily life career at a time when those tasks are incompatible with the other person. Ex-spouses and ex-grandparents can continue to make their influence known in the new stepfamily system. Spouses' wishes and expectations may not be fulfilled in the new marriage. Both children and adults may have mixed allegiances and feelings of guilt. Children may not want to be part of the new family system. All members of the new family system experience role confusion until patterns can be established through experience and negotiation.

■ Stepfamilies encounter a series of developmental tasks similar to those of single-parent family systems.

They also experience a sequence of stages in their life career: (1) fantasy, which represents the time when all members hold unrealistic expectations for the new family system; (2) assimilation, in which attempts are made to include the new family member in the existing biological family network; (3) awareness, when members of the stepfamily can recognize and give labels to their confused feelings; (4) mobilization, or the time when the stepparent acts to initiate changes in the biological family network to promote assimilation; (5) action, or the time when new boundaries are formed and erected, differences are negotiated, and new patterns of interaction are established; (6) contact, or the time that is characterized by developing and increasing the authenticity of interactions within the stepfamily system; and (7) resolution, or the period when strength is built into the relationships of the stepfamily system.

■ The stepparent role is distinct from that of a biological parent because it has a high degree of role ambiguity. This is especially the case for stepmothers. Typically, the role is characterized as one that includes many interaction problems with other family members, especially children.

■ Families in which the mother role is filled by a stepmother may have more problems than those with a stepfather. This difference may be due to the ways in which these new family systems begin their family life careers. The quality of relationships with children appears to depend on a child's sex and age.

■ Stepfathers have similar difficulties but are not hampered by stereotypes and myths about their role. They encounter problems in disciplining stepchildren and in dealing with complex financial arrangements involving two separate family systems. Sex and age of stepchildren are factors influencing the quality of the relationship with a stepfather.

■ Adjustment in stepfamilies hinges on resolving three basic issues: (1) giving up the dream, or discarding unrealistic fantasies and expectations of the new family system and its members; (2) clarifying the feelings and needs of each family member; and (3) making a commitment to creating new rules, roles, boundaries, and routines for the new family system.

■ A variety of strategies assist stepfamily members in adjusting to this new status. (1) Adults decide on long-term goals for organizing the new family system. (2) They agree that the biological parent is in charge of enforcing limits for his or her children. (3) They facilitate the bonding process between the stepparent and stepchildren. (4) They develop patterns involving rules, boundaries, and traditions for the new family system. (5) They develop ways of interacting with the households of ex-spouses. (6) They seek assistance from self-help literature, educational strategies, psychotherapy, and participation in support-group activities.

■ Stepfamilies have particular strengths that include: (1) opportunities for stepchildren to learn problem-solving, negotiation, and coping skills, as well as the ability to be more flexible and adaptable; (2) the presence of more adults for support; (3) exposure to a wide variety of people and experiences; (4) exposure to a good model of marital interaction; and (5) the possibility of a better experience than that offered by the single-parent family.

CHAPTER 13

Homosexuality and Parent-Child Relations

Focus Questions
....

1. What challenges confront parents and family members who learn that a child is gay or lesbian?

2. Why are some gay men and lesbian women parents?

3. Does sexual orientation affect one's ability to parent children effectively?

4. Are children harmed by being raised by gay or lesbian parents?

....

Homosexuality has always been recognized as an aspect of human nature and sexuality (Bozett & Sussman, 1989). However, in cultures with a strong Judeo-Christian heritage, homosexuality is labeled most negatively, and **homophobia,** the irrational fear, dislike, or disgust of homosexuality and homosexuals, and **heterosexism,** the belief that heterosexuality is superior and preferable to homosexuality, occur most strongly (Herek, 1984, 1993). Because of these beliefs, many people do not understand the nature of homosexuality and express hostility, fearfulness, intolerance, and unacceptance toward homosexuals.

A family is traditionally considered to be the one place where people are nurtured emotionally, loved unconditionally, and accepted for who and what they are. This may be an unrealistic expectation for many individuals, but for gays and lesbians it is especially so. Serious and painful problems are involved in being a homosexual member of a family composed largely of heterosexuals in which heterosexuality is promoted as socially conventional and totally acceptable. It is especially difficult for many gay and lesbian children to develop a healthy, positive self-esteem growing up in a heterosexual family because they fear rejection if they disclose their true sexual orientation (Connolly, 2005). Most homosexuals feel caught in a no-win situation. They risk rejection if they disclose their orientation; however, if they keep it secret, they deny their basic core identity, which also promotes poor self-esteem and other interpersonal disturbances as well.

Gays' and lesbians' fears of rejection are well founded on their personal perceptions as well as their observations of the actions and beliefs of others (D'Augelli, 2005). There is little social affirmation for homosexuality in our society. Gays and lesbians can be terminated from their employment or housing because of their sexual orientation. Laws do not sanction homosexuals' committed relationships. Many states have enacted legislation limiting marriage only to opposite-sex individuals and/or banning recognition of domestic partner relationships. A movement is under way to amend the U.S. Constitution to ban same-gender marriage. Only in 2003 did the U.S. Supreme Court finally extend the right of privacy to homosexual activity in states that had enacted sodomy laws. Employment benefits are not universally accorded to partners of homosexual individuals in the United States. Homosexuals are officially barred from military service despite the new "don't ask, don't tell" policy, denied basic civil rights that are extended to other groups, and are unwelcome in many churches and religious groups. If they are parents, homosexuals may be denied parental rights and custody of their children. Many states prohibit gays and lesbians from adopting a child, and only the biological parent in a gay relationship has parental rights in most states.

Progress has been made, however, in more prevalent positive attitudes about homosexuality. For example, homosexuality is no longer considered to be a mental illness. In 1969, the American Psychiatric Association and the American Psychological Association declared that it was no longer considered a diagnostic classification. The conclusion still drawn by many gays and lesbians, however, is that they are not full members of society with the same constitutional rights and privileges that others have, despite the fact that they are taxed equally with heterosexuals.

DETERMINANTS OF SEXUAL ORIENTATION

Researchers have been unable to establish clearly the origins and causes of sexual orientation. The literature has a long history of holding various environmental influences as the determining factors in homosexual orientation, but that theory is considered questionable today (Dode, 2004). One psychoanalytical-based approach points to family influences in particular. It proposes that male homosexual orientation occurs because an individual has an extremely dominant mother and a relatively nondominant, emotionally distant father (Bieber, 1962). Other approaches propose that sexual orientation is a learned phenomenon among males and females, which suggests that individuals can willfully choose as well as change their sexual orientation. No convincing evidence resolutely proves any of these as fact (Harry, 1989; Milic &

Crowne, 1986; Whitam & Zent, 1984). Another hypothesis that has greater credibility is that high levels of stress during pregnancy influence the likelihood of homosexual orientation of a woman's child because the stress acts to produce particular hormones that affect brain formation leading to the development of this orientation (Money, 1987). More current thinking is that a variety of markers point to a biological basis of sexual orientation, straight as well as gay (Brookey, 2000; McKnight, 2000).

Considerable popular support persists for the view that environmental factors are the cause of homosexual orientation. For example, many heterosexuals believe that gay people willfully choose their sexual orientation. There is no conclusive scientific support for such an opinion. In fact, evidence continues to grow supporting the position that people are born with a particular sexual orientation, homosexual as well as heterosexual, that is manifested after reaching puberty (McKnight, 2000; Patterson, 1995; Strickland, 1995).

Although some people have long believed that genetics and biological factors play an important role in determining sexual orientation, little convincing evidence has been found until recently. Studies comparing the sexual orientation of identical twins suggest a strong familial and genetic basis for homosexuality. Research points to a biological basis for male sexual orientation due to differences in certain brain structures found in homosexual and heterosexual individuals (Oldham & Kasser, 1999). These structures are associated with areas of the brain that govern sexual orientation and behavior. According to this view, individuals cannot choose their sexual orientation, although it is unclear how environmental factors may interact with these biological predispositions to influence sexual orientation. Other research provides data linking genetic and prenatal influences to the development of sexual orientation. For example, one study reports that women who experienced prenatal exposure to maternal estrogens were more likely to be lesbian or bisexual in orientation (Meyer-Bahlburg et al., 1995).

Another investigation studied a group of preschool-aged girls and boys who had a condition known as congenital androgen hyperplasia (Berenbaum & Snyder, 1995). This exposure to high levels of androgen (a male sex hormone) during prenatal and early postnatal periods leads to the development of masculine characteristics. While the boys were not affected deleteriously by their condition, the researchers noted the girls preferred boys' toys and play activities over those usually associated with girls, which was believed to be a reliable predictor of homosexual orientation upon attaining puberty for these girls. Furthermore, research suggests that gay males have a greater than average number of older brothers and can be expected to be of later birth orders among their sibling constellations (Blanchard, Zuckey, Bradley, & Hume, 1995; Bogaert, 2003). This older-male-sibling effect is attributed to the mother developing sensitivities to androgen during the pregnancy of older male babies, which heightens the chances of an increased masculinization of later-born male children.

Various theories have tried to explain why this phenomenon is observed among gay males. The most plausible explanation may be that mothers of later-born gay men who have more brothers than average experienced something similar to an allergic reaction to the testosterone being produced by their male fetuses during pregnancy. In a manner similar to that found among pregnant women having a problem with the Rh blood factor, the degree of incomplete androgenization of the fetal brain increased with each pregnancy, culminating in a greater probability of the later children developing a homosexual orientation after puberty.

INCIDENCE

A large number of family systems in the United States today include a homosexual child. Studies estimate that individuals with exclusively homosexual orientation comprise from 7 to 12% of the male population and 5 to 7% of the female population (Bagley & Tremblay, 1998; Kinsey, Pomeroy, & Martin, 1948; Kinsey, Pomeroy, Martin, & Gebhard, 1953; Strong, 2004). According to recent Bureau of the Census figures, this estimate translates to about 23 million men and about 12 million women (U.S. Bureau of the Census, 2007a, 2007b). Assuming that these individuals come from an average-sized family of about four people, the potential number of people with a homosexual relative is more than 100 million, or nearly half the population of the United States. In addition, about 25% of the gay and lesbian population of the United States are biological parents of children from heterosexual relationships. There may be about 10 million children in the United States who have a gay or lesbian parent (Patterson, 1992).

There is no clear estimate of the number of families who know they have a homosexual member because not all homosexuals have disclosed their orientation to family members. This secrecy occurs for several reasons, many of which may relate to fear of rejection or a desire to avoid the unpleasant homophobic reactions of family members. Disclosing sexual orientation to parents and other family members is a critical experience for most gays and lesbians because of the risks involved. Nonetheless, those who make their orientation known affect change in the identity of their family of origin as family members adapt to the news.

FAMILY SYSTEMS WITH GAY OR LESBIAN CHILDREN

It is common for parents to develop and acquire a variety of expectations about themselves and their children. These expectations guide and shape parenting behavior and may serve as self-fulfilling prophesies for those involved in this family subsystem. Generally, these expectations are positive and reflect wishes, desires, hopes, and dreams for parents as well as children. Most parents do not include an expectation that any of their children will be gay or lesbian upon reaching puberty. When it is revealed by a child that he or she is, indeed, gay or lesbian, the revelation usually comes as a shock and creates a crisis experience for the entire family system (M. M. Lee & Lee, 2006).

One of the most difficult but health-promoting acts performed by a homosexual person is disclosing this information and identity to others, especially family members. This process is known as **coming out** (Figure 13–1). Many heterosexuals do not understand the importance of this act and do not welcome the news because they have already learned negative attitudes and concepts about homosexuals and homosexuality. For homosexuals, the significance of disclosure lies in presenting themselves to others as whole, authentic people unashamed of who they are. Homosexuals share this act of intimacy in the hope that the disclosure will not result in rejection but eventually lead to honest acceptance and unconditional love (Eichberg, 1990).

● ●

Parenting Reflection 13–1

What would you do and say if your best friend shared the news with you that one of his or her children is gay or lesbian?

● ●

FIGURE 13–1. Coming out or disclosure of one's sexual orientation is a stressful but critical experience for a family system.

Family systems theory predicts that when one family member experiences change in some manner, all other members of the system are also affected to some degree. A child's disclosure of his or her homosexual orientation is unlikely to be part of the vision that most parents hold for their child or for themselves as parents. The disclosure of homosexual orientation disrupts a family system largely because of the significantly negative social stigma that people commonly associate with homosexuality (Singer, 2001). Family disruption initially relates to members' difficulties in reconciling these negative attitudes, beliefs, and myths about homosexuality with what they know about the particular family member (D'Augelli, 2005). These beliefs and stereotypes usually govern the initial reactions of family members after the gay or lesbian child discloses his or her orientation, and they may override what the family members already believe they know about the child as an individual and as a family member.

Disclosure as a Family Crisis

A child's disclosure of his or her homosexual orientation acts as a stressor event for the family system, which most likely produces a crisis reaction. The child's revelation challenges the family's perceptions of him or her, and a conflict develops as members attempt to reconcile negative stereotypes and beliefs about homosexuality with what they know about the child as a person (Rust, 2003).

Family systems react in predictable ways to any significant change or crisis event that may be external to the system or internal among members (Savin-Williams, 2001; Savin-Williams & Dube, 1998). According to Hansen and Hill's (1964) ABC-X model of family crisis management, family systems demonstrate common modes of reaction when their functioning is challenged by a significant stressor event. As we have seen from family systems development theory, there are many stressor events that families confront throughout their life span, such as an adult's job loss, a chronic illness of one member, divorce, marriage, and even births. To briefly review, this model proposes that when A (a stressor event) interacts with B (the family's use of resources and abilities to cope, with the stressor) and with C (the family's definition of the stressor event), then X (a family crisis) will occur (see Figure 13–2). The family system's reaction to the stressor event is a response or process based on these complex interactions.

Family coping strategies (the B factor) differ in reaction to stressor events. These strategies include withdrawing from interactions with people outside the system, discussing the situation only among the adults, denying that there is a problem, using anger and other negative emotions, and seeking assistance from others outside the system. These coping strategies, however,

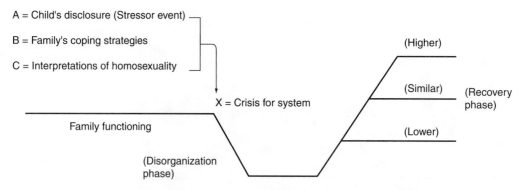

FIGURE 13–2. Patterns of family reactions to stress and crisis. This figure represents the process of the ABC-X model of family crisis management relating to a child's disclosure of homosexual orientation.

Source: Adapted from Hansen, D. A., & Hill, R. (1964). Families under stress. In H. Christensen (Ed.), *Handbook of marriage and the family*. Chicago: Rand-McNally.

may or may not be immediately set into motion after a homosexual child's disclosure. Factors that collectively represent the system's and its members' interpretations (the C factor) may temporarily override other means that the family eventually employs to resolve the crisis of disclosure.

According to the ABC-X model, a family system's interpretation of the stressor event influences the system's reactions. The model predicts that when members perceive they are the cause of the problem, the family system as a whole suffers. The group is hampered in its ability to function in healthy, effective ways.

Some families interpret the revelation of a child's homosexuality in terms that are far more serious than those of other families. For example, many parents typically assume personal guilt for their child's homosexuality, believing they have done something wrong in their child rearing. They mistakenly believe that they have somehow performed poorly as parents and are failures (Fairchild & Hayward, 1989). Parents also report feeling sad, fearful for their child, shocked, depressed, and hurt following their homosexual child's disclosure (LaSala, 2000a; Mosher, 2001). It is more typical of siblings, however, to react with anger and confusion rather than guilt. They often experience feelings of alienation toward the homosexual sibling, who now seems to be a stranger rather than someone well known (Merighi & Grimes, 2000). Interestingly, a homosexual child often comes out to family members incrementally, reflecting the degree of emotional closeness he or she feels toward specific family members. For example, the child may tell the mother first, then the siblings, and finally the father.

Observers also note other efforts as the system attempts to interpret the disclosure (Merighi & Grimes, 2000; Waldner & Magruder, 1999). These may occur in two particular patterns. First, heterosexual family members frequently attempt to understand the homosexual child in relation to their family values concerning homosexuality. In reacting to the child's disclosure, parents and other family members have been exposed to, and very possibly believe, the negative stereotypes and myths about homosexuals. Most individuals know few openly gay or lesbian people to provide evidence that disputes or challenges negative stigmas and stereotypes.

In addition, sexual orientation is a private part of a person's identity, and a homosexual identity or acknowledgment is achieved late in the developmental sequence, usually in adolescence and early adulthood. Family members have had many opportunities to come to know the person without the benefit of this private knowledge about homosexual orientation, which the person may choose to disclose or family members may discover accidentally. Even if parents have suspicions about a child's homosexual orientation, the revelation of homosexuality constitutes a crisis for most parents and family systems: They may have previously assumed that the person is heterosexual like themselves. Cognitive dissonance may become evident as heterosexual family members try to reconcile negative family values about homosexuality with positive family values about the family member. Generally, the more negative the family values about homosexuality, the more negative the interpretations of and reactions to the homosexual child, and vice versa. These negative reactions may range from physical, emotional, and verbal abuse and attack to abandoning the child.

A second pattern relates to the interpretation and definition a family system makes and ascribes to the homosexual child after disclosure. The members frequently negate the child's family role as brother, son, daughter, sister, or cousin (Strommen, 1989a, 1989b). The gestalt or integrated patterns are revised to state, "There is a stranger in our midst now." Essentially, the family recognizes that it does not seem to know this person after all. What was secret and hidden (the homosexual identity and orientation) is now public to the family. This recognition raises questions about intimacy and what else the family may not know about the child.

Several factors predict the nature and strength of a family's determination of a child's disclosure to be a crisis, which relate to the values that the system holds about homosexuality (Strommen, 1989a, 1989b). First, the more a family system subscribes to traditional, conservative religious teachings about homosexuality, the more negative the reactions to, and interpretations of, a child's disclosure. Second, if family members promote traditional, rigid conservative beliefs about gender roles, then these individuals generally react negatively to any homosexual, whether or not the person is external or internal to the family system (Savin-Williams, 2001). Third, rules that govern the functioning of a family system can influence the likelihood of negative reactions to disclosure (Green, 2002). For example, some family rules relate to maintaining an image or reputation in the community ("We maintain family respectability at all costs"; "As a family we solve our own problems"; or "We must be as our religion teaches us"). Fourth, age and gender of family members can influence reactions in positive or negative ways. Generally, the younger children and much older adults in a family system may be more accepting and react more favorably to the disclosure than others. However, members of the same sex as the homosexual child can be expected to react more negatively than members of the opposite sex. This is especially the case for males in the family system, although fathers, brothers, uncles, and grandfathers may be expected to react unfavorably regardless of the sex of the homosexual child.

In keeping with the prediction made by the ABC-X model, the degree to which a family system interprets a stressor as disruptive becomes a self-fulfilling prophecy. After taking stock of family values relating to homosexuality and combining them with interpretations and meanings given to the homosexual child's disclosure, the system often concludes that the family is experiencing a crisis (the X result in the ABC-X model) caused by the revelation. If people perceive a child's revelation as extremely severe, their adjustments to new perceptions of the child are much more difficult. This reaction is in accord with the devastating nature people ascribe to the news.

When a family system determines that the disclosure constitutes a family crisis, the system moves into a phase of disorganization in family functioning. Families typically resist the changes that accompany the stressor event they interpret as a crisis because the ultimate goal of the system is to maintain established *homeostasis*, or balance. A child's disclosure of homosexuality temporarily disrupts the patterns of interaction and communication and the roles of all family members. They often do not know how to act toward the homosexual child after the disclosure. They may pressure the child to change his or her sexual orientation and keep the disclosure a secret from others outside the immediate or extended family. Essentially, reactions of family members disrupt the stability of the family system and tend to enhance or minimize **entropy,** disorder or chaos in effective functioning that results from lack of input from outside a family system.

The disorganization phase begins to be resolved as a family system moves into a recovery phase. Members make efforts to reach solutions that are appropriate to their particular style of functioning. Depending on the particular family system, as members attempt to reestablish homeostasis, the resolutions reached in adjusting to a homosexual member may be healthy or unhealthy. A healthy family system may initiate processes that involve **negative entropy** (attempts of the system to move away from disorder and chaos by accepting and using information from external sources) and **morphogenesis** (responses by the family system to implement changes in its rules, interactions, communications, and roles). In this way, the family moves toward positive **adaptation** in response to the homosexual child's disclosure. This tends to promote and enhance effective functioning of the family system (Figure 13–3). Such a family often seeks assistance, information, and

FIGURE 13–3. Support groups for family members of gays and lesbians, such as Parents FLAG, provide education and understanding for those seeking greater insight about homosexuality and the ways family systems are affected by having a homosexual member.

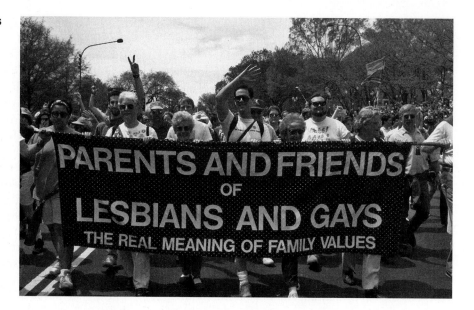

education from outside sources, such as therapists, books, or support groups, that result in growth, change, innovation, and adaptation in structure and patterns (M. M. Lee & Lee, 2006; Planck, 2006).

Family systems that seek to find healthy solutions to this particular crisis may come to recognize that family secrets are unhealthy and disruptive to the effective operation of the system. Members may realize that an individual's sexual orientation is not a matter of personal choice and that no one can willfully choose to be heterosexual or homosexual. They may accept that a person's only choice is to be honest and to act authentically about his or her sexual orientation. Many family members, in seeking to understand a gay or lesbian child, acquire accurate information by educating themselves about homosexuality in appropriate ways and from reliable sources (Green, 2002; Savin-Williams, 2001). For example, they may seek out the services of psychotherapists and counselors who have expertise in homosexuality and read a variety of books on the topic. They may attend support groups devoted to helping families understand homosexual members, such as Parents and Friends of Lesbians and Gays (Parents FLAG; see M. M. Lee & Lee, 2005; Figure 13–3). These efforts facilitate a family system's ability to change its negative values about homosexuality and to create a climate of acceptance and tolerance for the homosexual child. The system's health is promoted by its understanding that differences are appropriate among members.

Some family systems do not have healthy patterns for coping with crisis, or they may be heavily influenced by the negative factors previously discussed. These families may be expected to react in ways that promote the continued dysfunctionality of the system, which may lead to serious impairments. From the perspective of family systems theory, these systems move toward higher levels of entropy and try to maintain *morphostasis* (attempts to maintain previously established family system organization, structure, and patterns) as a means of reestablishing homeostasis.

Such attempts promote even greater disorganization in the system, which prevents effective functioning. For example, members may shun and reject the gay or lesbian child; refuse to discuss anything relating to the child's homosexuality, relationships, or lifestyle; or shame the child and act in ways that express intolerance, such as disinheriting or banishing the child from the family system. When parents and other family members choose rejection as a means of resolving this crisis, the choice reflects their need to respect social conventions about homosexuality rather than express unconditional love for the homosexual family member and respect for individual differences among members. Members may blame the child for causing the disruption to the family system and resent the child for his or her actions.

The alienation heterosexual members feel when they discover they do not really know the homosexual child highlights the ineffective coping solutions often enacted in unhealthy family systems. These solutions frequently include scapegoating the homosexual child, denying the child's news or refusing to discuss it, developing alliances with other heterosexual family members, or not including the child in family activities. These family systems often fail to move further toward resolving the crisis in ways that are healthy and promote effective family functioning. Instead, a hostile, ambivalent family atmosphere, especially as it relates to the homosexual child, becomes the normative family style to restore homeostasis to the system (LaSala, 2000b).

In keeping with the ABC-X model predictions regarding outcomes (see Figure 13–2), those systems that react to and resolve the crisis of a child's homosexual disclosure in unhealthy ways may reach levels of functioning similar to or lower than those before the crisis. In many instances, a homosexual child may withdraw his or her participation in the family system due to the negative, unaccepting reactions of members. This tends to weaken and alter the family's ability to function adequately and may be similar to losing a family member through death. In more extreme situations, a family system's unhealthy resolution may contribute to the homosexual child's likelihood of developing serious emotional depression. This depression can lead to suicide, which may account for the high suicide rate among adolescents who have difficulty accepting their homosexual orientation (Sullivan & Wodarski, 2002; van Wormer & McKinney, 2003).

Those systems that resolve the crisis in healthy ways may reach levels in recovery that are similar to or greater than what existed before the crisis. In these families, the pain that members initially experience after the child's disclosure becomes transformed into deeper degrees of personal growth and appreciation. Family members consider themselves to have become better people who are more open and less judgmental of others (Lewallen, 1992). Essentially, these families turn the crisis into learning experiences that can result in a better quality of life for everyone.

In reality, this description of a family system's experiences in reacting to a homosexual child's disclosure does not fully convey the deeply emotional aspects, the difficulties in reaching resolution, or the length of time each family takes to work through this process (Williamson, 1998). Parents, in their role as caregivers, must often struggle to resolve conflicts between their need to give unconditional love, nurturance, and visible support to a gay or lesbian child and their perceived responsibility to respect social norms that promote prejudicial and discriminatory views about homosexuality (Weinberg, 1972). If families are to respond to this crisis in healthy ways, they need to find a solution that allows their expression of unconditional love to take precedence over their need to respect socially conventional beliefs. However, to find this solution, parents most likely need to express their grief about the losses that relate to a child's homosexual orientation. These losses may include, for example, no longer being potential grandparents, no longer having a child who is conventionally similar to other children in the family, no longer anticipating marriages and relationships that are sanctioned and recognized by the community, and no longer being like other parents of heterosexual children. Parents must allow the grief and mourning process to proceed in order to heal these and many other losses. (One study, however, questions the existence of a sequential process that families experience upon receiving disclosure from a child about his or her sexual identity [Savin-Williams & Dube, 1998]). By doing so, they facilitate the healing of their family system and the reconstruction of a role definition for their homosexual child as an accepted family member. They also confront homophobic and heterosexist feelings and notions that prevent expressions of love and intimacy toward their child.

GAY AND LESBIAN FAMILIES

One common belief holds that gays and lesbians do not participate in family life and that the very nature of their lifestyle is antifamily and singles-oriented (Lev, 2004). This belief is a stereotype based on homophobic and heterosexist attitudes about gays and lesbians in American society. In reality, gays and lesbians participate in family forms that are not easily distinguished from others found in our society. It is not widely known in society at large, but a common denominator in homosexual culture is the lack of constraints that define the rigid following of norms, roles, and behaviors. As applied to family life, gays and lesbians have reinvented notions of what it means to be a family, how this family functions, and who participates in the membership (Benkov, 1994; Herek, 2006; Weston, 1997). These families are referred to as **families of choice.** Membership, roles, and rules governing this type of family structure are custom designed according to mutually agreed conditions. As such, families of choice are formed by conscious decisions about who constitutes the family, how it is defined, and what it means to each participant. Many gays and lesbians do not feel the need to conform to family structure based on consanguinity or legally sanctioned marriage, as is the norm in heterosexual culture to which these communities are denied. They focus instead on providing a social support network based on compatibility, love, intimacy, emotional warmth, interest, and a sense of community. According to societal norms, these elements compose the essence of family life. The primary reason gays and lesbians approach family life in this manner can be traced to the negative societal stigmas attached to homosexuality. These stigmas deny homosexuals the right to marry and can bring about estrangement with families of origin in many instances. When children are involved, it is difficult to distinguish gay and lesbian families from heterosexual stepfamilies, except in the same-sex composition of adults who act as parents (Herek; Patterson, 2006).

The beginning of gay and lesbian kinship formation takes place when an individual initiates what is known as the coming-out process. This multifaceted process occurs in stages and perhaps is never completed (Green, 2002). Gay and lesbian individuals develop a personal identity based on their sexual orientation, similar to that experienced by heterosexual individuals. Part of this identity is the desire to become emotionally close to another person just as heterosexuals do (Gottman et al., 2003). Gays and lesbians participate in loving, committed relationships that often endure for long periods of time and resemble those found among heterosexuals (Kurdek, 1995). Distinct differences are found, however, in gay and lesbian committed relationships. Primarily, their committed relationships strongly emphasize egalitarian functions since they are not forced to adopt and maintain traditional gender-role models typically found among heterosexuals that emphasize differences in social power in the relationship (Gottman et al.; Kurdek, 2003).

Like other families, those formed by gays and lesbians bring strengths as well as challenges to family members (Lev, 2004). While providing individuals with a sense of togetherness and support, the families of gays and lesbians experience the trials of prejudice and discrimination and lack wide acceptance within their larger communities. The omnipresence of AIDS and its multifaceted effects can permeate all aspects of family

life. These families must develop healthy ways of coping with continual stresses while maintaining the tasks of day-to-day living. By expanding the very idea of family that transcends traditional limitations, gay and lesbian families demonstrate how to deal with societal adversity in healthy ways.

Gay and Lesbian Parents

Many people are probably surprised that homosexual men and women form families that include children (Figure 13–4). This situation occurs more frequently than most people believe because such families often appear to be identical to those composed of heterosexuals with the exception of the gender of the adults involved.

Because our culture harbors beliefs and attitudes that are antagonistic toward homosexuality, many people have a difficult time reconciling the notion that it is appropriate for gay and lesbian adults to be parents

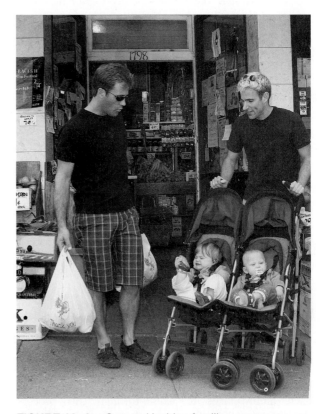

FIGURE 13–4. Gay and lesbian families are more visible in society today.

(V. Clarke, 2002; Tasker, 2002). It is doubtful that parenthood among gays and lesbians is a new phenomenon, but it may be more highly visible in today's society. The following discussion examines the issues relating to those gays and lesbians who have become parents and how their sexual orientation affects their children.

Gay Fathers.   The gay father is a newly emergent figure in homosexual culture, and researchers have relatively little information or knowledge about these individuals as compared with heterosexual fathers. Homosexual males who are fathers have a unique and more complex social-psychological environment than those of most homosexual or heterosexual men. Their challenges of adjustment relate to identity issues, acceptance of self, acceptance by other gay men, and matters relating more specifically to parenting and child custody issues (Bigner, 1996). Other concerns relate to the development of a long-term, committed relationship with another gay man who accepts and copes with children as a central issue of the relationship.

The man who is both a homosexual and a father is an enigma in our society. The term **gay father** even seems contradictory, although this contradiction is mostly a matter of semantics. *Gay* is associated with homosexuality, while *father* implies heterosexuality. The problem lies in determining how both terms may be applied simultaneously to a person with same-sex orientation who is also a parent. What complicates our understanding of this individual is that the idea of a gay father contradicts the stereotypical image of gay men, which emphasizes that gays have an antifamily lifestyle that values being single (Hain, 1999).

Researchers estimate that about 20 to 25% of self-identified gay men are also fathers (Bigner, 1999). This group clearly constitutes a minority within a minority in our culture. It is impossible to estimate accurately the number of gay men who are parents because many are married to women or remain *closeted*, undisclosed about their sexual orientation, for other reasons.

According to several researchers, the dilemma of the man who is both gay and a father involves the fact that he is a victim of divided personal identity (Bigner, 1996). More precisely, these men are described as socially marginal, challenged by having ties to the cultural worlds of both gays and nongays.

The process of identity development for a gay father requires a reconciliation of two polar extremes. Because each identity, homosexual and heterosexual, is essentially unaccepted by the other culture, the task for these men is to integrate both identities into a cognitive concept called *gay father*. This process is referred to as *integrative sanctioning* (Bozett, 1981a, 1981b, 1985, 1987; Bozett & Sussman, 1989). It involves the man's disclosure of his gay orientation and identity to nongays and his father identity to gays, thus forming close liaisons with people who tolerate and accept both identities simultaneously. It also involves distancing himself from others who are not tolerant and accepting. At the same time, he enhances his identity development by participating in the gay subculture.

Why Do Gay Men Become Fathers?   The reasons explaining why a gay man becomes a parent are not fully known because little factual information is available on gay fathers in general (Bigner, 1996, 2006; Patterson, 2000). We can speculate on one reason: A man might not be able to accept his homosexual orientation; therefore, he marries a woman and fathers children as a means of denying his true sexual orientation. Later, however, he divorces to pursue his identity as a gay man. However, an increasing number of gay men are choosing to become a parent because they, like their heterosexual counterparts, sincerely desire to have their own children for myriad reasons (see Chapter 2; Berkowitz, 2007). An openly gay man may willfully choose to become a father as part of a liaison established between himself and a lesbian woman because they both desire to become parents. Under these arrangements, a pregnancy is usually initiated via artificial insemination, although surrogacy is an option that is available as well in the path toward parenthood (Green & Mitchell, 2007). Some gay men enter into marriage with heterosexual women, with both partners knowing in advance the man's sexual orientation. Other marriages involve bisexual men, and many of these marriages continue intact for years.

Gay fathers' reasons for having children are generally similar to those of nongay fathers; however, some significant differences may exist between these groups (Bigner & Jacobsen, 1989b). Nongay fathers appear to want children for traditional reasons, such as continuing a family name or providing security for parents in their old age. Gay fathers appear to place greater emphasis on the fact that parenthood conveys adult status to people in the community.

The large majority of gay fathers, until recently, were involved in heterosexual relationships in which children were produced (Bigner, 2006). Having entered these relationships, often in denial about their actual sexual orientation or due to an especially strong sensitivity to society's general homophobic attitudes (Pearcey, 2005), many of these men eventually come to terms with their homosexual orientation and find it impossible to live a masqueraded heterosexual lifestyle that is inauthentic, unfulfilling, and dishonest (L. M. Peterson, Butts, & Deville, 2000). These men frequently gain the courage to disclose their homosexual orientation to their wives, perhaps in conjunction with the midlife transition that ordinarily prompts much personal self-evaluation and reorientation of life goals (G. Sullivan & Reynolds, 2003). Their wives usually experience upsetting, disruptive reactions to the disclosure (Buxton, 1994, 2004, 2005, 2006; Grever & Bowman, 2008). Few of these marriages remain intact following the man's disclosure. The men usually want to pursue the development of their homosexual identity, and the women do not wish to continue an involvement with a man who is not heterosexual and who they feel has deceived them. Some marriages survive this crisis because one or both partners feel a strong commitment to children or because a divorce would lower the standard of living for the individual and/or the family.

The adjustment of men who divorce and pursue a homosexual lifestyle is difficult and problematic as the man acquires the new identity of gay father (Benson, Silverstein, & Auerbach, 2005; Schacher, Auerbach, & Silverstein, 2005). These men enter the gay subculture at some disadvantage because they come out at later ages than other gay men. They usually seek to replicate the kind of relationships they experienced or desired in their heterosexual marriages. Because they are not like most other gay men, gay fathers often experience discrimination and rejection from other gays who are not fathers. Many gay fathers are successful in forging a partnership with another gay man that is based on long-term commitment, emotional and sexual exclusivity, and economic cooperation.

Little is known about the nature of these relationships or about the gay stepfamily system that may emerge from its formation (Lynch, 2000; Lynch & McMahon-Klosterman, 2006). However, it appears that satisfaction of all people involved in a gay stepfamily is improved when efforts are made to include the gay step-

father (Current-Juretschko & Bigner, 2005). This is similar to what is found in heterosexual stepfamilies as a means of improving the overall success of the family system (see Chapter 12).

Children of Gay Fathers. Several issues are unique to the parenting arrangements of gay fathers and their children (Lev, 2004; Patterson, 2006; Patterson & Redding, 1995; Tasker & Patterson, 2007). These issues are summarized in Focus On 13–1.

There is no hard empirical evidence proving that the homosexual orientation of fathers or other caregivers is detrimental to children's welfare (Bigner, 1996, 1999; Herek, 2006; Lev, 2004; C. Patterson, 2006; Patterson & Redding, 1995; Stacey & Biblarz, 2001; Tasker & Patterson, 2007). Furthermore, children of gay (and lesbian) parents do not differ significantly from children of heterosexual parents on key psychosocial developmental outcomes (Tasker, 2005; Tasker & Patterson). In fact, gay fathers are as effective as nongay fathers in their ability to parent children and provide for their care. Gay fathers are more nurturant with children and less traditional in perceiving the provider role as a prime aspect of their parenting role. They have positive relationships with children and try hard to create stable home lives for them.

These findings may be explained in the following ways. First, gay fathers may feel additional pressure to be proficient in their parenting roles because: (1) They may feel guilty about the difficulties that divorce and disclosure create for their children, and (2) they are sensitive to the fact that their parenting behavior is being scrutinized by ex-wives and others, and they may fear that custody or visitation rights will be challenged because of their sexual orientation. Second, gay fathers may be more androgynous than nongay fathers in their approach to parenting children. Their child-rearing styles may incorporate a greater degree of expressiveness and more nurturant behaviors than the child-rearing styles of nongay fathers do (Bigner, 1996; Bigner & Jacobsen, 1989a, 1989b). Heterosexual fathers may incorporate more elements of traditional male sex-role behavior, which is rigid and less nurturant, into their parenting behaviors.

A common fear and concern expressed in court proceedings by the judicial system, which determines the custody of children with a gay father, is that the children will also develop homosexual orientation. It should be noted that this fear masks a deeply homophobic and hostile reaction about homosexual parents rather than reflecting true concern for the best interests of children. The consensus of research is that the causes of sexual orientation are not known, but most researchers agree that sexual orientation does not seem to be transmitted from parents with a particular orientation to the children they raise (Strong, 2004). The parents of most homosexuals are heterosexual. If the sexual orientation of parents were transmissible to children, then heterosexual parents would only produce heterosexual children.

In reality, this is not the case. In addition, the pattern found in the general population of the incidence of homosexual orientation appears to be replicated among sons of gay fathers (J. M. Bailey, Willerman, & Parks, 1991). More than 90% of adult sons of gay fathers are reported to have heterosexual orientation. Apparently, these data strongly suggest that sons of gay fathers do not adopt their homosexual orientation by modeling that of their fathers, nor does living with a gay father appear to contribute in a substantial way to the sexual orientation developed by sons.

Focus On 13–1

Issues Relating to Children of Gay Fathers

The Father's Disclosure of Homosexual Orientation

- Gay fathers have a more difficult time acknowledging and disclosing their homosexual orientation to children than lesbian mothers do. This difficulty may be especially pronounced among black men.
- Gay fathers describe their children's reactions to disclosure as "none" or "tolerant and accepting."
- The age of children at the time of disclosure may affect their reaction. Those who have not experienced puberty may be more accepting than those who have.
- Children may have some difficulty relating to peers who are aware of the father's homosexual orientation, but the children apparently cope successfully with these problems, showing little harm to their self-esteem.

Parenting Skills and Effectiveness

- No empirical or descriptive evidence proves that having, being raised by, or living with a gay father is detrimental or harmful to the development of children.
- Most gay fathers have positive relationships with their children. Gay fathers make more serious attempts to create stable home lives and positive relationships with their children than are usually expected from traditional heterosexual parents.
- Gay fathers are similar to nongay fathers in their reasons for having children and do not differ from nongay fathers in their degree of involvement of intimacy with children.
- Gay fathers tend to be stricter, more nontraditional, and more responsive to children's needs and provide more explanations for rules than nongay fathers do.
- Sexual orientation is not a factor in determining the quality of parenting behavior and relationships.

Sources: Adapted from: Bigner, J. J. (2000). Gay and lesbian families. In W. C. Nichols, M. A. Pace-Nichols, D. S. Becvar, & Y. A. Napier (Eds.), *Handbook of family development and intervention* (pp. 279–298). New York, NY: Wiley; Committee on Psychosocial Aspects of Child and Family Health. (2002). Coparent or second-parent adoption by same-sex parents. *Pediatrics, 109,* 339–340; Patterson, C. J. (2000). Family relationships of lesbians and gay men. *Journal of Marriage & the Family, 62,* 1052–1069.

Perhaps one of the advantages that gay fathers offer to children of both sexes is the modeling of an androgynous sex role (Bigner, 1996, 1999, 2000) and their acceptance of gender nonconformity in children (Kane, 2006). Psychologists have identified androgyny as the ideal gender role (Bem, 1975). Individuals who have this gender-role identity and behavior manifest characteristics associated with both sexes regardless of their biological sex. Researchers have identified many advantages to having such a gender role and identity. Androgens are liked better than persons with a traditional masculine or feminine orientation (Hunter & Forden, 2002). Adult males who are androgens are described as having highly developed egos, showing greater flexibility in considering options to solving problems, and having a greater and deeper respect for individual differences in others. These individuals are also described as having an accepting attitude about sexual behavior, sexual relationships, and interpersonal relationships with others in general. In addition, androgens are reported to have higher self-esteem and feelings of self-worth.

Gay fathers can generally be expected to incorporate greater degrees of androgynous behavior and identification than heterosexual fathers (Bigner, 1996, 1999, 2000; Bigner & Jacobsen, 1989a, 1989b). This may be due to gay fathers feeling less of a need to depend upon traditional male sex-role behaviors and identity than heterosexual fathers appear to do. This does not imply that gay fathers are less masculine or that they are more feminine or effeminate as compared with heterosexual fathers, as depicted in the traditional cultural stereotype of gay men. Because gay fathers can combine both emotional expressiveness and goal instrumental behaviors in their behavioral repertoire, children can learn to adopt these androgynous behaviors as well. It is irrational to prevent a gay father from raising children based solely on his homosexual orientation, especially when the data strongly indicate that sexual orientation of children, and that of sons in particular, is not transmitted in this manner.

The benefits offered by gay fathers to their children relate to their ability to expand their interpretations of what it means to be a father beyond the limited traditional meanings of this family role (Bigner, 1999, 2000; Tasker & Patterson, 2007). The benefits to children are likely to become even more apparent upon reaching adulthood, when their relationships with others can be expected to be based on equality rather than on who holds the most social and physical power. Researchers have found that couples in which one person or both are androgens: (1) have higher levels of relationship satisfaction (Wharton, 2004), (2) divide decision making equally, (3) deemphasize the use of power by either partner in the relationship, and (4) have greater long-term life satisfaction that extends far into the years of late adulthood than couples with a traditional or undifferentiated gender-role orientation. This information provides even greater credibility to the consistent research findings that children experience no harmful influence on their developmental progress by being raised by, or living with, a gay father.

This is not to say that children of gay fathers (and lesbian mothers as well) do not have adjustment issues that relate to their parents' sexual orientation. Like children coming from other minority ethnic group families, these children face unique challenges. However, it must be emphasized that these challenges are tempered and adjustments are often facilitated by both parents (the gay father and nonlesbian mother) being committed to providing high quality parent-child relations and supervision (Gottlieb, 2003; Snow, 2004). For example, children of gay fathers (and lesbian mothers) may be at risk of homophobic bullying from peers should the sexual orientation of their parents be made public knowledge. This is similar to the experiences of children from ethnic minority families who must learn to deal with prejudice and bigotry in interactions with others. Just as these parents equip their children with the means to counter such negativity and maintain healthy self-esteem, children of gay and lesbian parents also are assisted by these adults to learn to cope positively with homophobic bullying from peers (V. Clarke, Kitzinger, & Potter, 2004; Peplau & Beals, 2004).

Lesbian Mothers. The parenting experiences and situations of lesbian mothers are generally similar to those of gay fathers; however, researchers observe differences in family dynamics (R. Brown & Perlesz, 2007; V. Clarke, 2007; Golombok, 1999; Lev, 2004; Mooney-Somers & Golombok, 2000; Nelson, 2007; Tasker, 1999; Figure 13–5). Lesbian women differ from gay men in the ways in which they become involved as parents. For example, although many women acknowledge their homosexual orientation after being married to a man and having children, many other lesbians use artificial insemination as a means of achieving parenthood (Green & Mitchell, 2007; Hermann-Green & Gehring, 2007;

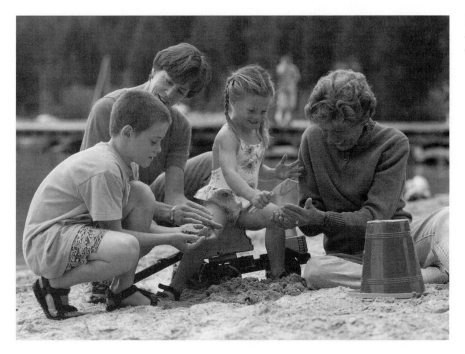

FIGURE 13–5. Lesbian families are similar to other families but experience unique challenges.

Stevens, Perry, Burston, Golombok, & Golding, 2003; Vanfraussen, Ponjaet-Kristoffersen, & Brewaeys, 2003). Adoption may also occur more frequently among lesbian women and couples than among gay men and couples (McClellan, 2001).

Lesbian couples face legal and social challenges when they form a committed relationship and use artificial insemination to conceive children (McClellan, 2001; Goldberg, 2006). From a legal standpoint, the use of artificial insemination has a number of uncertainties, particularly if a couple performs the process themselves instead of consulting a physician. The laws of most states commonly recognize the biological mother's legal custody of the child, which leaves the nonbiological or social mother with no legal parental rights unless she legally adopts the child conceived by insemination. However, many states do not permit the names of two women to appear on a child's birth certificate or allow adoption by a nonbiological mother. Furthermore, custody rights of fathers are relatively unclear in these situations as well, even if the identity of the father who has donated sperm is known. There continues to be legal testing of these rights in various court cases that will set precedents for the future in this matter. Generally speaking, if the father is known to the lesbian-led family,

it is possible to have legal documents written that spell out legal rights and responsibilities of fathers regarding custody and visitation, for example.

For many lesbian couples, parenthood via insemination is a well-planned, deliberate, major life decision often involving complex issues such as who will be the biological mother and how to choose a donor (known or anonymous), for example (Chabot & Ames, 2004; Goldberg, 2006; Green & Mitchell, 2007). As such, children are greatly valued, wanted, and desired; such motivation for parenthood may bode well in both short- and long-term consequences for both mothers and children.

Lesbian Family Dynamics.   Families formed by gay men or lesbian women share qualities in common with heterosexually formed stepfamilies (Erera & Fredriksen, 1999; Lynch, 2000; Lynch & McMahon-Klosterman, 2006). This is particularly the case with lesbian mothers, who more frequently have custody of children produced in a former heterosexual marriage (Hall & Kitson, 2000; Lorah, 2002). Other similarities may involve relationship issues in the new stepfamily. The partner of the lesbian biological mother (the children's stepparent or social parent) is rejected by the stepchildren, the stepchildren and stepparent compete for the attention and affection of the biological mother, and conflicts erupt over territoriality in the home.

Distinct differences within lesbian family systems distinguish them from other family forms, although it is important to remember that the families of gay men and lesbian women are not pathological (Lev, 2004; Tasker, 2002; Tasker & Patternson, 2007). Rather, these families experience challenges that other family systems do not face because of the larger society's negative attitudes and stereotypes about homosexuality. Four unique characteristics describe lesbian family systems due to the more active parental roles found in their structure as compared with those of gay men (Bennett, 2003; Ciano-Boyce & Shelley-Sireci, 2002; Dundas & Kaufman, 2000; S. M. Johnson & O'Connor, 2001; F. Nelson, 1999; J. M. Thompson, 2002). First, they experience a lack of legitimacy because they are not recognized as a family unit by their community; this lack of legitimacy presents unique problems, such as in family dealings with school systems. Second, these families must address issues unique to their status, such as more frequent confrontation with the stigmas associated with homosexuality. Gay fathers without full-time child custody do not usually experience these challenges. Parents often instruct children to keep the adults' sexual orientation a secret from others outside the family. Researchers observe a lack of community support for two lesbian women who are raising children as a family. For example, these individuals are sometimes evicted from rented residences or terminated from employment when their sexual orientation becomes public knowledge. As a result, lesbian parents may isolate themselves and their children from other families. The pressure of maintaining family secrets is unhealthy to the effective functioning of that family in relation to others and to the functioning of individuals within the system. These mothers may fear losing custody of children more intensely than gay fathers do, which makes this possibility a continual threat to the well-being of the lesbian family (Siegenthaler & Bigner, 2000). Children may not be allowed to invite friends home to play because the parents fear exposure, and the children may be shunned by others because they are seen as different.

Third, these families usually experience strained relationships with ex-spouses and other relatives. The negative feelings of ex-spouses may be compounded during postdivorce interactions due to the lesbian mothers' fears of losing custody of children. But despite all these problems, children of lesbian mothers are well adjusted, and families typically find creative and healthy ways for responding to the crises they experience.

Fourth, division of labor and parental roles take on unique assignments and situations. Each family must decide what each mother will be called, for example. Each family will need to determine if one mother or the other will be designated as the primary caregiver.

Both lesbians and gay men base the structure of their committed relationship on the androgynous principle of equality of partners (Gottman et al., 2003). This differs considerably from the structure typically found among heterosexual couples that uses gender to determine who does what in the relationship. Lesbian families with children typically report sharing household responsibilities, but the biological mothers can be expected to be more involved in child care while the nonbiological mothers report working longer hours in their employment. Children are found to be more well adjusted, however, when both mothers divide the child-care responsibilities equally (Bennett, 2003; Ciano-Boyce & Shelley-Sireci, 2002).

Children of Lesbian Mothers. The issues relating to children of lesbian mothers do not differ significantly from those relating to children of gay fathers (Tasker & Patterson, 2007). The main differences are that children of lesbians live in a different type of family system and have a different kind of parenting experience (Lev, 2004). However, no differences in general adjustment, gender-role identity, or cognitive or behavioral functioning are consistently reported in studies comparing children of lesbian and nonlesbian mothers (Bos, van Balen, & van den Boom, 2007; Golombok et al., 2003; C. Patterson, 2006; Tasker, 2002, 2005; Vanfraussen et al., 2003).

Four principal issues are relevant to children of lesbian mothers (Chrisp, 2001; S. M. Johnson & O'Connor, 2001; Kershaw, 2000; McClellan, 2001; Paechter, 2000; Stevens et al., 2003; Tasker & Patterson, 2007; Vanfraussen, Ponjaert-Kristoffersen, & Brewaeys, 2002, 2003): (1) dealing with the mother's disclosure of her sexual orientation, (2) dealing with the uniqueness of having a lesbian mother and its effect on the parent-child relationship, (3) coping with custody concerns, and (4) dealing with the homophobic and heterosexist reactions of others.

First, like the children of gay fathers, those growing up in lesbian family systems confront the dual challenge of coping both with their parents' divorce and with the fact that their mother is different from other mothers. While this difficulty is similar to what children of gay fathers experience, the differences are compounded by the fact that these children live with their mothers. Most gay fathers are largely absent from the daily lives of their children. In this respect, children of lesbian mothers share similarities with children of heterosexual mothers who become single parents after divorce.

Boys are more accepting of their mother's disclosure of homosexuality than girls. However, researchers generally find that the more accepting and relaxed the mother is about her sexuality, the more accepting the child is about having a lesbian mother. Another unique situation occurring in lesbian families is the matter of whether and how to inform children who are conceived by artificial insemination by donor (AID). Many children of lesbian mothers become aware of the uniqueness of their particular families in early childhood and begin to ask questions about their father. Typically, most children react positively to this news and are not harmed significantly if teased by peers in later years of childhood about their families and parentage.

Second, the context of the parent-child relationship changes after the mother discloses her sexual orientation. Girls develop more concerns about becoming homosexual than boys, perhaps due to their sex-role identification with the mother, although research does not bear out this fear becoming a reality (Stacey & Biblarz, 2001). Girls also tend to compete with their mother's partner for the mother's attention more than boys do. However, after the mother's disclosure, the family system appears to relax rigid definitions of family roles and allows greater flexibility in the parent-child relationship. The self-esteem of children of divorced lesbian mothers is no different from that of children of divorced heterosexual mothers. Children of both mothers experience problems that relate more directly to the effects of parental divorce than to the mother's sexual orientation.

Third, child custody can be a highly charged issue in lesbian families. It is a central concern of most lesbian mothers, particularly those who live in constant fear of losing their parental rights because of their sexual orientation. Most children of lesbian mothers wish to remain in their care and establish stable, significant relationships with a mother's female partner. Lesbian mothers, like gay fathers, are subject to a suspicious, homophobic legal system that assumes that children living in homosexual families will be sexually molested, become homosexuals themselves, and experience peer ostracism if the parents' sexual orientation becomes public knowledge. These issues directly relate to custody and parental rights that can threaten the continuation of a meaningful parent-child relationship in these family systems.

Finally, because these family systems exist in a hostile social environment that provides little support for their existence, many lesbian mothers turn to their children for implicit approval of their sexual orientation. At the same time, conflict may develop because mothers do not want their children to feel significantly different from other children. This is an especially troublesome problem for adolescents of lesbian mothers. When working through this concern in a therapeutic manner, children and lesbian parents learn that the child should not necessarily be expected to accept the parent's sexual orientation completely. However, it is important that the child come to respect the parents' lifestyle and the ways in which it is expressed. Some children also need assistance in working through the confusion between the love-hate feelings they have for their mother and the guilt that accompanies those feelings, which may relate to the mother's sexual orientation (Johnson & O'Connor, 2001).

● ●

Parenting Reflection 13–2

Suppose you are a lawyer representing a gay or lesbian parent in a custody hearing. What evidence would you present and what would you say to demonstrate to a judge that sexual orientation of a parent is irrelevant in determining the ability to parent children effectively and in healthy ways?

● ●

AN EMERGING FAMILY FORM

The discussion in Chapter 2 about the diversity in family forms becoming the norm in the United States is clearly reflected in a newly documented family form described by Segal-Engelchin et al. (2005). This new family configuration, termed the **heterogay family,** is headed by a heterosexual mother and a gay father, who conceive and raise children together but do not share a common physical residence. This new family type represents a variation of nonmarital families we have previously discussed as

FIGURE 13–6. A newly emergent family form is the heterogay family. This family cannot be easily distinguished from a heterosexual family.

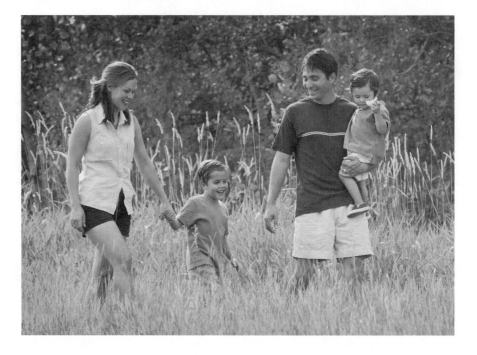

cohabitating couples who also coparent. It may be puzzling as to why this arrangement exists. The researchers find that it is a complex situation, but these mothers may highly value their independence and freedom but wish to have a partner who has no vested interest in a sexual or romantic relationship to be a coparent; hence, the choice of a gay man to be a father to their children. Because these families, to outsiders, appear to be like heterosexual families, they can capture the characteristics of both traditional and nontraditional families (Figure 13–6). Researchers also indicate that the children of these families appear to benefit from their family structure in having a stable and predictable family environment, in having a father who is involved in their upbringing and in sharing financial support, and in having generally positive psychosocial developmental functioning.

Focus Point. Some family systems include a homosexual member. A child's disclosure of his or her homosexual orientation frequently acts as a stressor event that disrupts family system functioning. Many parents and family members are influenced by the negative social stigma and images associated with homosexuality. The ABC-X model facilitates an understanding of a family system's reaction to the news of a child's homosexuality.

Family members frequently try first to understand the homosexual child in terms of these negative beliefs. They also may negate the child's family role as the system attempts to reconstruct a new role definition for the child that includes the notion of the child's sexual orientation. Healthy families resolve their conflicts about a child's homosexuality, for example, by educating themselves, participating in therapy, and participating in special support groups. By acting in these ways, family functioning resumes at the level prior to the child's disclosure or becomes even more efficient as a result. Unhealthy families fail to resolve these conflicts, which perpetuates the disruption in the family system for all members.

Not all parents are heterosexual; some are gay or lesbian. Their families, however, are not significantly different from other family systems, although unique challenges and problems are particular to their situations. Experiences of gay fathers are similar to those of lesbian mothers, but each type of family system faces unique challenges. Homosexuality per se does not prevent or hinder someone from being an effective parent. Research fails to support common assertions that these families create an unhealthy environment that harms children.

SYSTEMIC FAMILY DEVELOPMENT SNAPSHOT

(Before reading this section, it may be helpful to review the systemic family development model and the metaphor used to illustrate its concepts from Chapter 3.)

Our slice of developmental time is taken from a new family system that is about to experience a crisis due to the disclosure of a child's homosexual orientation. This family is composed of two generations rather than three. The first generation includes the adult parents, Todd (age 45) and Helen Jonas (age 42); the second generation includes their children: Donna, age 24; Ann, age 22; and Sam (age 18). This slice is taken at a time when the two older adults are focusing on two developmental stressors: (1) dealing with their own midlife transition experiences; and (2) the launching of their children into adulthood. The oldest daughter, Donna, has been grappling with her sexual orientation issues since junior high school and has just disclosed the news of her lesbianism to her parents after sharing this news with her younger sister. She lives near her family in the same town and is employed at a local software firm. The middle child, Ann, has recently completed her college education and is currently living at home with her parents temporarily until she finds employment. The youngest child, Sam, has just graduated from high school and will remain at home until he decides what direction he wants to take with his life.

The Second Generation (Adult Child, Partner, and Siblings)

Donna Jonas just made the most important decision in her life to date. She discovered, after years of wondering, worrying, and pondering, why she had been so very unhappy and even depressed when she was growing up. Ever since she was in junior high school, she had wondered why she didn't feel as if she was not a part of other girls' groups and why she seemed to be so unsure of herself around boys. There were only a few girls, in fact, she had ever felt comfortable with socially.

Now, it all made sense. After leaving home for college, she found that she could be more exploratory in trying to see how she fit into the world and could be freer to determine whom she was. College provided the environment and atmosphere to experiment with many ideas and learn about herself. She formed a number of friendships, some of which worked out well and others that fizzled. Some of her better friendships developed through the recreational activities she enjoyed, such as hiking and other sports. One of these relationships became very close as she felt she shared many things in common with another young woman, Jen, who was nearly her age. After spending a great deal of time together, Donna came to realize that she was in love with her best friend! And in thinking more about the situation, it became clear that she had never been happier in her life now that Jen was in her life and both had declared their affection for each other. She now knew that she was in a same-sex intimate relationship and all that this implied. Her unhappiness as a child was because she felt different and didn't know why until now. Everything fell into place.

Her relationship with Jen grew deeper and closer as time went on and both completed their degrees. Both young women knew that they needed to move in with each in order for their relationship to continue to develop. But, instead of presenting themselves as roommates, both understood the importance of revealing their relationship to their parents and family members. They had developed a network composed of other gay and lesbian people and even some heterosexual allies who supported them and helped them work through the doubts and misgivings about disclosing their sexual orientation to family members. They had even attended the local PFLAG chapter meetings to learn how to approach this difficult task with their families and to obtain resources that they could share with them.

Now the time had come to discuss this with their families. Donna had learned at PFLAG that it would take some time for all her family to absorb this news, and it might not be taken well or welcomed by anyone. But she was willing to take this risk because being true to herself was important, and she wished to portray herself authentically to those who had nurtured her as her family of origin. Since she felt closest to her sister, Ann, she decided to disclose to her first and then to her parents and brother.

Donna had rehearsed what she would say with Jen and a few other friends. She picked a time and place when she and Ann would feel relaxed and unpressured and asked her sister to have dinner with her. When the meal was completed, Donna said these words:

> *I have something very important to share with you, and I want you to know that this is difficult for me to say. I want you to know before I share this news with you that I am exactly the same person after saying this as I am now before doing so. The only thing that will be different after you hear what I have to say is that you'll know me more completely and better. Not too long ago, I realized I'm a lesbian. I'm certain I've been aware of this but didn't want to deal with it. It all became clear when I understood I had fallen in love with my best friend in college. We both feel the same about each other, and we've developed a very loving, secure, stable relationship. I've never been happier in my life. Now I know why I was so very unhappy before I went to college while growing up. Jen and I have been together now for about 4 years and want to take our relationship to the next level by moving in together. We may even want to start a family eventually. I know this is a lot of information for you to absorb right now but I do want to start talking about this with you and have you share in what's going on in our lives.*

At first, Ann was shocked—not by what Donna was saying but by the way she laid out everything on the table so straightforward and without shame or doubt. She had noticed how different her sister had become since something had happened, apparently, while at college. Now she knew! The only response she could think of to Donna's invitation to say something was: "Tell me something I don't already know about you." Ann had suspected something like this about her sister but wasn't completely sure until now. They were able from this point forward to share their thoughts and impressions about growing up together and the signs that Ann had observed that made her think that her sister was different somehow from herself and other girls but not knowing exactly how or why. As the evening progressed, they moved their conversation elsewhere and were able to plan how to share the news with their parents and brother. Donna felt reassured that she now had a new ally in her sister who would be as supportive as she could possibly be in helping her with some very difficult family business.

The First Generation (Adult Parents)

Todd and Helen Jonas thought they were fairly typical, fairly uninteresting people who had managed to brave a number of personal and family crises to reach this point in their lives. Their crowning achievement, they believed, was the successful rearing of three children into adulthood. Now that all of them had attained adulthood, they had begun to talk and look forward to what life would be like without children in their lives so centrally and hoped that their golden years of retirement would be almost storybook-like in nature. However, reality was that this part of their dream would have to be on hold for some time as their two youngest children needed to remain at home until both got their own directions in life. In some ways, their lives seemed to be on hold while their children became oriented.

Their oldest child, Donna, had seemed to be the least problematic of all in that she had been a quiet girl while growing up. Going away to college seemed to allow her to blossom into a bright, happy, young woman, and while there had been some probing as to what was responsible, they had always been given a general, vague answer as to what was responsible for Donna's happiness and bright new nature like, "Because I don't have to live with you guys anymore!" (laughingly).

They were made privy to the cause of her new self one day—very unexpectedly. Donna, with her sister at her side, broke the news of herself, her relationship with Jen, and her plans for her future, to both parents at the dinner table. Donna's disclosure to her parents followed the same general format as what she shared with her sister, since this seemed to work well. Predictably, both parents had nothing to say for the first few minutes after Donna had her say. Her mother was the first to speak:

> *I'm not sure what to say; this isn't something I was expecting to hear from you at all! I don't know what this all means . . . I'm going to have to think about all this . . . Are you sure? Are you really, REALLY, sure? I've got so many questions but I don't know how to ask them! What did your Dad and I do to make you this way? What are the neighbors going to say? What will my mother have to say? I'm sorry . . . I have to leave for a bit now.*

After her mother left, Todd Jonas just looked at Donna with tears running down his face.

> *I can't understand this either; it's a big pill to swallow all at once. You can't expect us to be jumping up and down with joy, although I have to admit I'm glad to see that you're happier than I've ever known you to be; I just didn't expect it to be because of this. What's this Jen like? And is this why you haven't introduced us to her? We've wondered how you've been spending all your time, but you've been so secretive. I think I really need you to know that your mother and I and everyone else in this family love you very much; I just don't know how to react to you right now and don't want to say something you might find hurtful. Give us some time to work on this, OK?"*

Two Years Later

Much had happened with the Jonas family and with Donna and Jen in the last 2 years. The two young women had found a nice apartment in a comfortable part of the city nearby, where they were in the midst of many other gay and lesbian couples living together. They affectionately called this part of town the Rainbow (GLBT) ghetto. The location provided them with many opportunities to form new friendships and attend activities that were part of their new community. They became part of a network of other lesbian couples, some of whom had become parents. They were interested in this aspect and option in their lives and were eagerly learning all the ins and outs of what parenthood involved for two women.

Donna was pleased with how her family had adjusted to her coming out experience. She, her sister, and her dad had talked with her brother when it was time to come out to him, and he took the news all in stride, just like Ann. To Sam, it was no big deal to have a lesbian sister. She had introduced her family to PFLAG, and both her parents had attended the support group now for these past two years. Her father, frankly, did remarkably well in reconciling his feelings about homosexuality and what he knew his daughter to be like. He had warmed well to a good relationship with Jen as both shared some common interests and could talk with ease with one another. Her mother, however, seemed to be neutral even after two years of seeing her daughter and Jen together as a couple. In talks together, Donna had learned that her mother felt great losses about her coming out. Helen revealed how hard it was to give up certain dreams she held for Donna, such as her falling in love with a nice young man, having a memorable wedding, and having as many grandchildren as possible. She shared that she didn't know whom to talk with in her own circle of women friends about Donna and her living arrangements. She didn't feel comfortable with having Jen and Donna attend church with them (to which Donna shared similar feelings about this kind of family activity). And when Donna and Jen came by for dinner or just to visit, Helen still found it difficult to interact comfortably with them. But she knew she must try because if she didn't, she was positive that she would lose her daughter from her life. So, in addition to attending PFLAG meetings (where she was learning to be comfortable around all these gay and lesbian people as well as other parents and family members), she had begun to work on her issues with a therapist who was experienced with these kinds of problems. All this wasn't lost to both Donna and Jen, as they knew how hard it must be for Helen; they wanted to support her as much as she would allow. And Donna was reassured to understand that her coming out, while affecting everyone in her family to some degree, was a continual, lifelong process that required patience, empathy, and understanding on everyone's part. She was thankful to have a family where she knew she was loved and accepted; some friends didn't have this luxury. She could look confidently to her future.

POINTS TO CONSIDER

■ Some family systems in the United States include a homosexual member. A child's disclosure of homosexuality to parents and family members frequently serves as a stressor event to the family system. The ABC-X model facilitates an understanding of family members' reactions to this crisis event. Most parents and family members are strongly influenced by negative images and beliefs about homosexuality and homosexuals that color their initial reactions to a child's disclosure. The sources that a family uses to cope with the disclosure may also be negatively biased.

■ Family systems may interpret the disclosure by reacting in ways that are healthy or unhealthy. At first, the system may seek to understand the homosexual child by applying learned negative beliefs and images to the child. Family values usually conflict with family members' positive knowledge of the child. The system may negate the homosexual child's role when dealing with this conflict. Healthy families resolve their conflicts about having a homosexual child by educating themselves about what competent, respectable researchers know about homosexuals and homosexuality. They may seek therapy for themselves, the child, and/or the family system to learn how to adjust to the crisis. And they may participate in support groups for relatives of gays and lesbians. In this way, families change their negative beliefs about homosexuals and learn to extend unconditional love and acceptance as a new family role is created for the homosexual child.

■ Gay men and lesbian women become parents for a variety of reasons. Research generally finds that these individuals act effectively as parents and that children are not harmed by living with, and being raised by, a homosexual parent. Many gay and lesbian families experience problems and circumstances that are similar to those encountered by heterosexual single-parent family and stepfamily systems.

■ A newly emergent family form is the heterogay family, which cannot be easily distinguished from a heterosexual family.

CHAPTER 14

Adolescent Parents

Focus Questions
■ ■ ■ ■ ■ ■ ■ ■ ■ ■

1. What are the principal reasons contributing to adolescent parenthood? How prevalent is this problem?
2. What are the implications for the adolescent girl and boy who initiate a pregnancy?
3. Are there short- and/or long-term consequences of a teen pregnancy?
4. What kinds of community support are available for teenagers who become parents?
5. What is being done to prevent or decrease teen pregnancies?

■ ■ ■ ■ ■ ■ ■ ■ ■ ■

Pregnancy among adolescents is not a new phenomenon in the United States. However, it has always been described as a problem that has both short- and long-term consequences for the adolescent parents, their child, and their families of origin (Figure 14–1).

The rate of adolescent pregnancies has been declining over the past 15 years and reached a point in 2004 not seen since the 1950s (Figure 14–2). This decline has been observed in every ethnic group surveyed in the United States while continuing to occur more frequently among minority ethnic groups except Asian/Pacific Islanders (Martin et al., 2006). The general decline in teenage pregnancies might be attributed to several factors, such as (1) a decrease in the number of sexually active teenage girls; (2) wider use of contraceptives among sexually active teens than in previous years; and (3) increased participation in school and church programs emphasizing more responsible sexual decision making. While the number of teenage marriages in the United States has declined in recent years, the overwhelming majority of adolescents who become pregnant carry the pregnancy to term and retain custody of the child.

However, more current data indicate that the teen birth rate rose in 2006 for the first time in 14 years (Figure 14–3). Between 2005 and 2006, this rate increased by 3%. The largest increase was reported among black teens, followed by Hispanic, white, and Native American teens (Hamilton, Martin, & Ventura, 2007). Researchers note that it is too early at the present time to know if this is the beginning of a new trend in the U.S. teen birth rate.

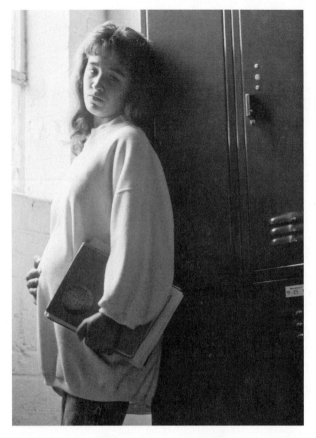

FIGURE 14–1. While teen pregnancy is physically possible, it is developmentally off-time for adolescents today.

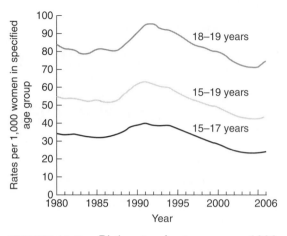

FIGURE 14–3. Birth rates for teenagers: 1990 to 2006.

Source: Martin, J. A., Hamilton, B. E., Sutton, P. D., Ventura, S. J. (2007). Births: Preliminary data for 2006. *National Vital Statistics Reports, 55*(7). Hyattsville, MD: National Center for Health Statistics.

Two groups of females are considered at risk when pregnant: those *under* age 19 and those *over* age 35 (Martin et al., 2006; U.S. Bureau of the Census, 2006). In relation to teenage pregnancy, the term **risk** refers to the dangers to health and well-being that a teenage girl and her baby may encounter when the girl experiences pregnancy during a period of her life that is developmentally off-time.

A teenage girl, the father of her baby, and the infant experience a variety of short- and long-term negative

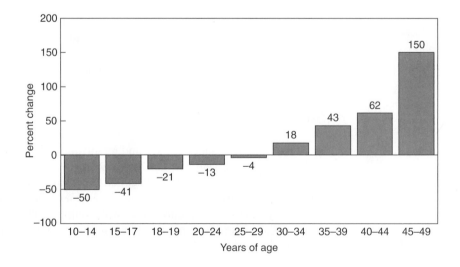

FIGURE 14–2. Percentage change in birth rates by age of mother: 1990 and 2004.

Source: Martin, J. A., Hamilton, B. E., Sutton, P. D., et al. (2006). *Births: Final data for 2004. National Vital Statistics Reports, 55*(1). Hyattsville, MD: National Center for Health Statistics.

consequences. These consequences and the associated complications of teenage parenthood are discussed in this section. The majority of research presented here focuses on the issues relating to teenage girls who become pregnant. Although an increasing number of investigations examine the effects of fatherhood for teenage boys, researchers continue to focus on teenage girls who conceive and experience pregnancy.

INCIDENCE, CAUSES, AND OUTCOMES OF TEENAGE PREGNANCY

Primary Factors

Slightly more than 800,000 adolescent girls became pregnant in 2004, continuing a decline in the birth rate among this age group that began about 10 years previously (Martin et al., 2006). This figure equates to about 1 in 8 girls between ages 13 and 19. Of those who become pregnant, about 10% experience miscarriage or have stillbirths; about 29% experience induced abortion, and about 61% carry the pregnancy to term and give birth. Eleven percent of all births, then, in the United States are to teen mothers. Less than half of these girls marry before giving birth; most are classified as unwed mothers. The large majority of the unwed girls who give birth choose to retain custody of their baby (Federal Interagency Forum on Child and Family Statistics, 2003). The vast majority of adolescents who give birth belong to black and Hispanic groups rather than whites.

Most adolescent girls do not become pregnant voluntarily (Wakschlag & Hans, 2000). The majority become pregnant because birth-control methods obviously are not used during sexual intercourse. For some, pregnancy occurs because of rape. The basic reasons that explain why teenagers become pregnant (see Focus On 14–1), however, are traced to the following four factors:

1. Increased frequency of sexual intercourse taking place at earlier ages than in the past

2. Social influences that deemphasize the negative stigma once associated with teen pregnancy

3. Lack of adequate contraceptive knowledge and use by sexually active teenage males and females

4. Personal attitudes about sexuality, pregnancy, and parenthood

Some believe that adolescent childbearing is an adaptive strategy for disadvantaged individuals because it occurs frequently among poverty-level and ethnic minorities (Kirby, 1999). From this standpoint, adolescent parenthood may be considered beneficial because there can be economic benefits to adolescent parents by becoming qualified for public assistance, for example. Others assert that adolescent parenthood is actually a cause for disadvantaged status. From this view, teen childbearing is thought to contribute heavily to keeping individuals in a position where they fail to complete their education, which, in turn, keeps them from obtaining jobs that pay well or that maintains their condition of receiving public assistance (Collins, 2000). The overwhelming evidence from research suggests that parenthood is largely undesirable among adolescents, regardless of the outcomes for the young parents or their children (Breedlove, Schorfheide, & Wieczorek, 2000).

More Teens Are Sexually Active.   Researchers believe that there has been a continued increase in the incidence of sexual intercourse among teenagers that was first observed almost 35 years ago (Alan Guttmacher Institute, 2006a). Some researchers estimate that about one-fourth of all teenage girls have participated in sexual intercourse by age 15 and that 4 out of 5 have had intercourse by age 19. This estimate contrasts with the figures for teenage boys. About 13% have had sexual intercourse by age 15, an estimate that increases to about 65% by age 19. Apparently, young adolescents rarely participate in sexual intercourse, but it becomes increasingly common as age increases during this period of life. As such, 7 in 10 teens are believed to have had sexual contact at least once by age 19 (Figure 14–4).

Research suggests that many teenagers are sexually active at younger ages than most adults imagine (Alan Guttmacher Institute, 2006a). For the most part, sexual activity among teenagers is believed to occur frequently and with a variety of partners. Instead of being promiscuous, however, adolescents often become intensely involved with one person over a period of time that involves sexual intimacy. Sexual activity increases the risks of negative consequences, including exposure to sexually transmitted diseases (e.g., AIDS), pregnancy, and a variety of deleterious psychosocial effects (Weinstock, Berman, & Cates, 2004).

Focus On 14–1   **Contributing Causes of Teenage Pregnancy**

■ Serious emotional problems, such as lack of adequate social adjustment, extreme feelings of isolation, loneliness, or a low level of self-esteem

■ Extreme embarrassment about sexual matters, causing gross lack of correct information about conception and contraception

■ Negative feelings about intercourse among girls, which can lead to rejecting the time and effort necessary to ensure safer sexual practices and experiences

■ Religious beliefs that may control or inhibit sexual activity but also compound guilt feelings that interfere with a sexually active teen's effective use of contraceptives and other safe-sex practices

■ Eagerness and impulsiveness to participate in sexual activity without taking the time and effort to ensure safe experiences

■ Desire to punish a parent toward whom angry feelings or resentments may be harbored

■ Guilty or negative self-image or self-esteem that prevents the teenager from feeling that he or she deserves to be protected from the consequences of sexual intercourse

■ A desire to prove and substantiate one's masculinity or femininity

■ A desire to be recognized as a person with adult social status

■ An attempt to create a captive love or trap a mate

■ A desire to receive unconditional love from another person (perceiving a baby as a substitute for parental or marital love)

■ A syndrome of behavior problems, including conduct disorders, involvement in criminal activity, teacher ratings of acting-out behavior, or participation in delinquent behaviors such as substance abuse

■ Certain family background markers, such as a single-parent versus a first-marriage family of origin, level of parents' educational achievement, a parent who was sexually active as a teenager, older siblings who are sexually active, experiencing a particular type of parental supervision in adolescence, parental involvement in elementary schooling, and racial or ethnic background

Sources: Breedlove, G. K., Schorfheide, A. M., & Wieczorek, R. R. (2000). *Adolescent pregnancy.* White Plains, NY: March of Dimes Birth Defects Foundation; Kirby, D. (1999). *Looking for reasons why: The antecedents of adolescent sexual risk-taking, pregnancy, and childbearing.* Washington, DC: National Campaign to Prevent Teen Pregnancy; Kirby, D. (2001). *Emerging answers: Research findings on programs to reduce teen pregnancy: Full report.* Washington, DC: National Campaign to Prevent Teen Pregnancy; Mersky, J. P., & Reynolds, A. J. (2007). Predictors of early childbearing: Evidence from the Chicago longitudinal study. *Children and Youth Services Review, 29*(1), 35–52.

Researchers are particularly concerned about the spread of the AIDS-causing HIV virus among teenagers, who have a high level of sexual activity that is largely unsafe and unprotected (Tinsley, Lees, & Sumartojo, 2004). Because the virus can also pass through the placenta during pregnancy and infect the developing fetus, many adolescent mothers and their children may experience this devastating disease in the coming years. Another serious health concern that arises in association with unprotected sexual contact is exposure to the human papillomavirus, which causes at least 70% of cervical cancer cases among women. A vaccine is now available to prevent this infection, and a number of states are considering legislation requiring girls to be vaccinated upon enrollment in certain upper-elementary and junior high school grades (Cohen, 2007). This legislation is controversial at the present time.

Several antecedent conditions contribute to the age at which teens become sexually active and to the

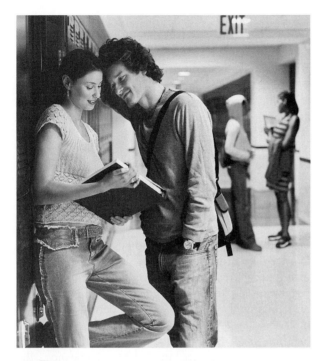

FIGURE 14–4.   Teenagers are more likely to experience sexual intimacy as age increases.

number of different partners (Alan Guttmacher Institute, 2006a; Baumer & South, 2001; Franke-Clark, 2003; Phillips, 2003; Raffaelli & Crockett, 2003; Susman, Dorn, & Schiefelbein, 2003):

■ The level of sex hormones associated with puberty may increase at earlier ages in children than in the past. These hormones establish the interest in and motivation for sexual activity.

■ Adolescents' cognitive and emotional development usually lags behind physical development; therefore, teenagers may not be completely aware of the risks involved in early, unprotected sexual activity. For example, cognitive distortions may give rise to their belief that others, not themselves, are vulnerable to these risks.

■ Factors derived from the family of origin can influence the sexual activity of teenagers. For example, teens may be influenced by the past sexual history of the mother during her adolescence, older siblings who are sexually active, living in a single-parent rather than a first-marriage family system, unhealthy levels of family cohesion and adaptability, highly involved mother-daughter and negative father-daughter relationships, and the quality of the parent-child relationship. All these factors may affect the degree to which a child subscribes to family values regarding sexual behavior. In addition, the degree of adolescent girls' permissiveness about sexual activity may be related to a large number of sexually active girlfriends or having sisters who are sexually active, especially if an adolescent sister has become a mother herself.

■ Peer influences may affect a teen's sexual involvement. Many feel a great deal of social pressure to become sexually active—especially girls, who may be particularly susceptible to coercion from a male to participate in sexual intercourse.

■ Sociocultural factors, such as religious participation, ethnic background, or the family of origin's socioeconomic status, may influence the probability of a teen's participation in sexual activity.

Changes have occurred in social attitudes about teenage sexual activity and those who become pregnant. In the past, pregnancy was a degrading, humiliating status that destroyed an adolescent girl's reputation and ability to fully participate in adolescent social development. Boys were taught that it was wrong to impregnate a girl outside of marriage. In the past, an adolescent girl who became pregnant had limited alternatives in dealing with her situation. She could try to arrange an illegal, dangerous abortion, or she could leave her community to bear her child in a facility for unwed mothers. These institutions were often managed and sponsored by charitable agencies or religious groups.

Today, such attitudes no longer influence the course and outcomes of teenage pregnancies. Abortion on demand is legal in the United States, although teenagers' access to such procedures is regulated to some degree. Fewer social stigmas are associated with teenage pregnancy, and families are more supportive of pregnant teenagers by providing various forms of emotional, financial, and physical assistance. A variety of community programs also assist both expectant teenagers and those who have become parents. For example, some programs offer teens the opportunity to continue their education with as few disruptions as possible. Most teenage girls who choose to continue their pregnancy retain custody of their babies. Many of these young mothers receive the assistance of family members, especially their own mothers and grandparents, in caring for the babies and raising them to maturity as fully integrated family members.

Most pregnancies among teenagers occur because of their failure to use contraception and safer sex practices. Few teenagers are reported to desire pregnancy when they participate in sexual activity, but it happens for a number of reasons (Alan Guttmacher Institute, 2006a). Many adults are puzzled about why sexually active teenagers fail to use protective measures that will prevent the possibility of pregnancy. The explanation relates to the meanings adolescents attach to contraceptive use. For example, to use contraception is an obvious admission of sexual activity (Kosunen, Kaltiala-Heino, Rimpela, & Laippala, 2003). Teenagers' use of contraception reflects their understanding that consequences, such as pregnancy and disease, can result from such activity and that they are negative outcomes. Seeking and obtaining contraceptive devices have certain social, economic, and psychological costs that teenagers must weigh against the risks and costs of pregnancy. It also must be negotiated with a sexual partner, which many teens find embarrassing and feel inept at discussing. Contraceptives must be used regularly because many birth control methods must be performed daily or with each sexual act.

• •

Parenting Reflection 14–1

What are the pros and cons about health clinics located in junior and senior high schools dispensing contraceptives to any student who requests them?

• •

The personal attitudes of adolescents play an important role in influencing their use or nonuse of contraceptives (Strong, 2004). The total life situation of adolescents from low-income family systems tends to promote feelings of fatalism, emotional depression, and apathy. These attitudes work against the effective use of contraception among those who are sexually active. Teenagers may be influenced in their sexual activity and use of contraception by a variety of cognitive distortions and beliefs about their ability to become pregnant. These distortions relate among some teenagers to a flaw in cognitive processing at this life stage called the *personal fable*. They may not use contraception because of the erroneous, irrational belief that other people become pregnant but not them.

What Influences Teenagers to Use Contraception? American adolescents, in comparison with those of other countries studied, use contraception less consistently and effectively (Alan Guttmacher Institute, 2006b; Hyde & DeLamater, 2000). As a result, we observe the high rates of adolescent pregnancy and parenthood here as compared with significantly lesser rates in other developed countries, such as England, Sweden, and Japan (Blum, 2001).

When preventative methods are used, however, researchers find that certain antecedent conditions are associated with the use of contraception and safer sex practices among teenagers (Kershaw, Niccolai, Ethier, Lewis, & Ickovics, 2003; Longmore, Manning, Giordano, & Rudolph, 2003; Stevens-Simon, Sheeder, & Harder, 2005; Topolak, Williams, & Wilson, 2001). Psychosocial factors, such as perceiving oneself as being sexually active, are crucial. Apparently, having the cognitive and psychological maturity to perceive oneself in this way without guilt is vital in influencing a teen's use of birth control. In addition, if teens are able to delay becoming sexually active until late adolescence, the chances improve for their use of contraception because they have developed the abilities that promote effective sexual decision-making skills.

As teenagers become more sexually experienced, they tend to use contraception more regularly and correctly and bypass feelings of embarrassment that prevent younger adolescents from obtaining and using contraception. Furthermore, if teenagers from disadvantaged backgrounds can be assisted in continuing their educational experiences, then their chances of using contraception improve accordingly.

Families can influence contraceptive use by providing or failing to provide information to teenagers about birth control. Parents who disapprove of and do not tolerate adolescent sexuality and sexual activity are more likely to have teens who become pregnant. Researchers generally find that, contrary to popular opinion, the parents' openness to communicate and support tends to increase adolescents' use of contraceptives (Figure 14–5).

When parents are not involved in communications with adolescents about sexual activity and pregnancy, peers become an important source of influence and information for teenagers (Zabin & Cardona, 2002). When peers approve of contraceptive use, teenagers whose parents do not approve or do not discuss it appear to be influenced in positive ways to also use

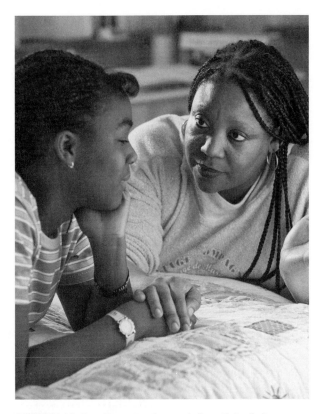

FIGURE 14–5.   Parents play an influential role in teenage children's likelihood to make wise sexual decisions when they are open to discussion and communication.

contraception. On the other hand, if the peer group is not using contraceptives, then the teenager will most likely follow suit.

When teenagers who are sexually active have access to family-planning services either in their schools or communities, there is a greater likelihood of preventing pregnancies (Topolak et al., 2001). School sex-education programs do not appear to have a significant effect on promoting teen sexual behavior or on increasing the likelihood of adolescent pregnancy in one way or another (Conner & Dewey, 2003).

Marriage as a Solution.   Teenagers typically do not choose marriage as a consequence of becoming pregnant (U.S. Bureau of the Census, 2006). Most frequently, the decision not to marry but to continue the pregnancy is influenced by a teenage girl's mother and the baby's father (Haveman, Wolfe, & Pence, 2001). Regardless of whether teens become married or not, however, the poorest socioeconomic outcomes occur when adolescents become parents, and marriage does not significantly improve their situation. Such marriages at this time and under these circumstances are also considered to be high risk and prone to early divorce (Parenting FAQs 14–1).

Another factor contributing to the decision about teen marriage relates to welfare benefits (Boonstra, 2000). Teenagers who are unmarried are more likely to

Parenting FAQs 14–1

Our 16-year-old daughter recently revealed that she is pregnant. We're past our shock and some of our anger about this situation now and are contemplating solutions to this dilemma. We are very fearful that she will not be able to continue her education and that she's ruined her life. We like the boy who's the father and are concerned about the baby's welfare now and in the future. We believe the best solution is for them to marry and live with one set of parents until they finish high school. Is this a good way to resolve this situation at least for now?

A: It's understandable you are concerned, worried, and fearful for your daughter in this situation. However, marriage may not necessarily be a good solution for this problem. Research generally reports that teen marriages don't last and can be very stressful for everyone associated with the situation. The teens' parents often have a difficult time staying out of their children's relationship. Grandparents in this situation often are called upon to assist with child rearing and child care, sometimes to everyone's detriment. The new parents need a tremendous amount of support in order to deal with this difficult situation, and marriage may only serve to complicate things in the long run.

receive welfare than are teens who are married. Racial background is also a contributing factor. Black adolescents who become pregnant are less likely to become married than white adolescents (Zabin & Cardona, 2002). This may be partly due to fewer numbers of employable, marriageable black males. The greater tendency among blacks to remain unmarried may also reflect differences in family system values; the families may be more tolerant of unmarried parenthood in general. The decision not to marry and to carry a pregnancy to term implies that teenagers must rely on their families of origin for support and assistance. In reality, unmarried teens receive less assistance from their families than do those who are married. In this manner, then, public assistance is a necessary and essential resource for many adolescent mothers.

Adoption as an Alternative. Adoption has been chosen less frequently as an option in adolescent pregnancy as more teenage girls choose to continue their pregnancies and retain custody of their babies (B. C. Miller & Coyl, 2000). This is especially the case among African American and Latino teens and among those from lower socioeconomic backgrounds. The adoption alternative is believed by some to be a better one for teen mothers, since it enables the girl to continue her education, attend to otherwise normal adolescent developmental tasks, and avoid experiencing a disadvantaged state of life. Others argue, however, that the decision to place a baby for adoption produces negative feelings of guilt, grief, and loss that can have long-term effects. These feelings can harm a girl's psychological well-being and adversely affect her future sexual and intimate relationships. These negative results of placement may be a long-term consequence rather than something that is observed in the time shortly following a child's adoption.

Placing a baby for adoption is a difficult decision for a teen mother to make and carry out. Although there is little research on how this process is experienced, it appears that those who choose to relinquish their baby have less influence from the child's father and more education. They often come from families with higher incomes, have high education and career aspirations, and are still in high school. Many adolescent girls who relinquish their babies for adoption may rationalize this decision by noting that they feel unready or unable to be a parent and to provide an adequate environment for their child.

Although most teenagers choose not to terminate their pregnancy by abortion or to place their baby for adoption, significant consequences result from the decision to retain custody of the child and to assume a parenthood role. As might be expected, teen mothers who choose to relinquish their child are reported to have more positive attitudes about adoption than those who choose to retain custody and assume parenthood status. The next section discusses these consequences for the adolescent mother and father, as well as for their child, when they decide to assume parenthood status.

••

Focus Point. A variety of factors explain or contribute to teenage pregnancy. The most obvious relate to the failure to use contraceptives among those who are sexually active. The majority of teens carry a pregnancy to term, although a substantial proportion choose to have an abortion. Most of the girls who give birth choose to retain custody of their baby, and most do not marry either during or following their pregnancy. Adoption has increasingly declined as a means for resolving teen pregnancy.
••

Adolescent Mothers

There are several short- and long-term consequences of parenthood for teenagers (Moore & Brooks-Gunn, 2002): (1) educational implications, (2) effects on marriage and family relations, (3) health considerations, (4) actual and potential labor-force participation, and (5) effects on the parent-child relationship. These consequences generally relate to the teenage mother rather than the father because research literature has focused almost exclusively on how pregnancy and parenthood affect adolescent girls (Figure 14–6).

Educational Implications. Pregnancy appears to be the most common reason for why an adolescent girl drops out of school and fails to complete her high school education (Alan Guttmacher Institute, 2006a, 2006b; Moore & Brooks-Gunn, 2002; Zachary, 2005). This is especially the case if the girl is African American. The younger the girl at the time of her conception, the less likely she is to return to school following the birth of her

FIGURE 14–6.   Teen pregnancy has both short- and long-term consequences for both the young mother and her child.

baby. It is possible, however, that teenage pregnancy rates might be higher when adolescent girls leave school early before finishing rather than vice versa (Fergusson & Woodward, 2000).

The most obvious, and perhaps most long-term, effect of a girl's educational disruption relates to economic consequences (Fergusson & Woodward, 2000). The lack of a high school diploma severely restricts the types of jobs available and the level of income earned. Typically, one can expect to have less prestigious jobs, less job satisfaction, and a less-satisfactory quality of life.

Some school systems today are aware that these dire consequences can affect adolescent girls for their lifetime. Special programs promote their continuation in school, teach parenting and family life skills, and assist in vocational development. These programs are discussed in greater detail later in this chapter. School retention can be enhanced when teen mothers reframe their anticipation of motherhood by reprioritizing their educational goals to remain in school and complete their education (SmithBattle, 2007). By doing so, they can be expected to desire improved grades, resolve to graduate, and show an interest in attending college. However, a number of competing demands such as conflicting

school policies, work demands, and parenting responsibilities can thwart these resolutions to do well in school.

Marriage and Family Relations.   Adolescent pregnancy is likely to hasten early marriage, but this option is not necessarily an appropriate solution. Teenage marriages are likely to be high risk, highly unstable, and prone to end shortly by divorce (Moore & Brooks-Gunn, 2002). About 60% of adolescents who marry divorce within 5 years, as compared with 20% of those who marry in their early adulthood years (Lichter & Graefe, 2001).

The classic study of adolescent marriage and parenthood (deLissovoy, 1973a, 1973b) points to the unhappy nature of teenage marriages. DeLissovoy studied the relationships of working-class, rural adolescents who were 17 years old and under. The adolescent husbands were generally more dissatisfied than the adolescent wives. For example, these young men felt that their wives did not participate enough in sexual activities, while the young women felt that husbands wanted too much sex. This dissatisfaction increased even more after 30 months of marriage. The young husbands were much more dissatisfied with the frequency of sexual activity, the degree of social activity, and opportunities to interact with mutual friends. For example, they wished to continue their buddy relationships and to participate in sports after school. The young wives felt left out and lonely because many had been dropped by former friends.

Most research suggests that the correlates of early childbearing and marriage produce much of the unhappiness rather than the pregnancy or the age of the couple (Barber, 2001; Haveman et al., 2001). The correlates include educational disruption, restricted job opportunities, and limited earning potential.

However, when the teen father is involved in the pregnancy and in active parenting following childbirth, then marriage is more likely to occur (Fagan, Schmitz, & Lloyd, 2007).

Health Implications.   Early studies of adolescent pregnancy reported many adverse physical complications for the young mother, including elevated death rates, increased prevalence of maternal toxemia, precipitate or prolonged delivery, anemia, postpartum infections, and hemorrhage (Children's Defense Fund, 1996, 2003). Other research, however, suggests that attributing these physical complications solely to the mother's age is questionable since other factors, such as quality-of-life conditions induced by poverty, can cloud this issue (Haveman et al., 2001). The health risks associated with adolescent pregnancy may be minimized if adolescent girls receive adequate and timely prenatal care and supervised nutrition (Borja & Adair, 2003). Obtaining adequate prenatal care, however, is more likely the exception rather than common practice among most adolescent girls who become pregnant. Inadequate nutrition also presents significant problems because teenagers are generally reputed to have deficient diets. Poor nutrition exacerbates problems associated with teen pregnancy by interfering with the normal growth patterns of the young mother. It also increases the likelihood that the baby will have a low birth weight, which jeopardizes survival and increases the chances of other birth complications (Stevens-Simon, Nelligan, & Kelly, 2001).

Mental health is also negatively affected by early childbearing (Turner, Sorensen, & Turner, 2000). Teen mothers have less social support and personal resources in coping with stress. In addition, the accumulation of major, potentially traumatic events they may experience as a single parent tend to greater mental health risks.

Labor Force Participation and Economic Consequences.   When teenage girls drop out of school because of pregnancy, their future is jeopardized because of the broad impact on their ability to provide adequate incomes for themselves and their children (Haveman et al., 2001). Most girls who fail to complete their high school education lack the entry-level skills that allow them to compete successfully in the job market. The income of adolescent mothers is about one-half that of mothers who have their first child in early adulthood (U.S. Bureau of the Census, 2006).

Because of the combined effects of the loss of educational opportunities, the lack of sufficient support networks, the unavailability of adequate child care, extensive medical expenses, and other related factors, teenage parents face major economic consequences during this time of their lives (Bissell, 2000). Both short- and long-term effects are evident when teenagers become parents. Their economic resources are often severely limited, and their parents are frequently unable to provide the type and level of financial support that will help to ensure adequate prenatal care, equipment,

and living conditions. Teen mothers usually lack the adequate resources to become effective parents, have fewer perceived alternatives to parenthood (such as completing their educations), and fail to see parenthood as being personally or socially restrictive (Jaffee, 2002).

Economic instability in the months following a marriage between teen parents who have both dropped out of school often causes separation within at least 2 years. In the long run, teenage parents can expect to hold low-paying, low-level jobs in which little satisfaction and economic gain are evident. Another economic consequence is that children born to teenage parents ultimately are more costly to a parent than those born to women who have their first birth in their 20s (Alan Guttmacher Institute, 2006a; Children's Defense Fund, 2003). This relates to the loss of potential income created by dropping out of school, the average national annual income and hourly wage among women according to their level of educational attainment, and the direct costs of having additional children. The lack of adequate job skills and educational qualifications also causes adolescent mothers to seek financial assistance from public welfare programs (M. E. Collins, 2000).

Parent-Child Relations.   Adolescents who become parents can expect to be single parents and to have large families, as compared to individuals who wait until their early adulthood years to have children (Wakschlag & Hans, 2000). Some investigations report that adolescent mothers are as competent as older mothers and that their interactions with infants and children are usually appropriate. However, other studies report that teenage parents have troublesome relationships with their children that may be abusive (Stevens-Simon et al., 2001).

While significant data point to problematic parent-child relationships among adolescents who are mothers, it does appear that there can be positive outcomes for children under certain circumstances (Luste, Bates, Fitzgerald, Vanderbelt, & Key, 2000). Children of adolescent mothers have been found to score high on certain measures that examine intellectual functioning when the mothers have more years of education, are employed, have fewer children on average than others in their position, live in more desirable neighborhoods, and are living with a male partner.

Several studies point to the risks of poor teen parenting, which are highlighted by the following characteristics (deLissovoy, 1973a, 1973b; Jaffee, 2002; Kimes,

2006; Moore & Brooks-Gunn, 2002; Stevens-Simon et al., 2001):

- Lack of knowledge about children's developmental needs
- Less sensitivity to behavior cues from infants
- Lack of interest in playing with children
- Less interaction time with children that is accentuated by ambivalent feelings about parenthood and a greater tendency to use physical punishment

The work by deLissovoy (1973a, 1973b) is particularly illuminating in this regard. Both adolescent mothers and fathers were questioned shortly after the birth of their baby regarding their knowledge of the developmental norms and events of infant growth and development. Teenagers are grossly ignorant about when to expect certain developmental events during infancy, which has broad implications regarding the ability of these young parents to provide quality, nurturant caregiving for infants and children. For example, teenage parents indicate that toilet training should begin at 24 weeks (6 months) of age and that beginning to teach infants about obedience to parental direction should begin at either 26 weeks or 36 weeks. How would parents and child react if this training actually did begin when the parents believed the infant's appropriate chronological age had been reached?

Adolescent parents typically demonstrate a range of nurturant caregiving behaviors toward children that include immature, egotistical styles as well as those in which attempts are made to recognize and meet the needs of both the parent and child (Moore & Brooks-Gunn, 2002). Other work suggests that rather than being at immediate risk of abuse and neglect due to parental ignorance, children of teenage parents may experience a delayed effect in this regard (Jaffee, Caspi, Moffitt, Belsky, & Silva, 2001). Adolescent mothers tend to have more births, lower incomes, fewer sources of social support, interrupted educational experiences, and lower quality of life that serve as sources of stress in mediating long-term child abuse and neglect (Borkowski et al., 2002).

When adolescent mothers are compared with older mothers, however, the teen mothers are found to have competent parenting skills in a number of aspects (Brophy-Herb & Honig, 1999; Hess, Pappas, & Black, 2002). Other factors rather than age alone may mediate the negative effects that children of teenage parents experience by virtue of their parenting. Social class back-

ground, for example, may produce differences in children's development manifested via maternal knowledge, attitudes, and behaviors that determine the quality of parenting experiences for children. These studies are unclear in their findings about the greater probability of abusiveness among teenage parents.

One researcher has described a culture of teen parenting (Higginson, 1998). This culture is depicted as emphasizing competition to be the best parent regardless of the area in question, such as in the ability to provide material possessions for children, the physical and cognitive development of children, and knowledge of parenting skills and abilities. This competition is observed between teen mothers and with older mothers. The competitiveness is believed, in part, to be driven by the teen mothers' overwhelming motivation to prove that they do not match, in any respect, the negative stigmas and stereotypes associated with adolescent parenthood. The consuming desire is to behave in ways as a parent that persuade and convince others that they are not abusive, welfare-dependent, or incompetent.

Despite their general ignorance about child development and caretaking, adolescent girls who are either pregnant or parents are found to be more realistic than their nonpregnant cohorts in their expectations about child development milestones (Stern & Alvarez, 1992). This level of knowledge might be attributed to the participation of pregnant and parental adolescents in special education programs that prepare them for parenthood. This finding, however, is diminished by the fact that pregnant adolescents showed significantly fewer positive attitudes about caretaking than those who were not pregnant. This information has important implications for later parenting behavior. It is not clear if adequate knowledge about children's developmental milestones can offset such negative attitudes about caring for them by their adolescent mothers. When teen mothers have the support and involvement of grandmothers in providing care for their infants, then their parenting competence appears to be considerably improved (Oberlander, Black, & Starr, 2007).

Adolescent mothers are reported to be more likely to feel emotionally depressed, nervous, tense, fretful, and ambivalent about their parenthood status (Schweingruber & Kalil, 2000). They are also less likely to feel positive about their child and about parenthood than older mothers are (Stevens-Simon et al., 2001). The less positive outlook is reflected in adolescent mothers' perceptions of infants as being more difficult in comparison with the view held by older mothers. The importance of this kind of perception among teen parents relates to the child's later development.

••

Focus Point.   Adolescent mothers generally have a difficult time acting in their parental capacity. A variety of short- and long-term consequences occur when adolescents assume this family role. Generally, adolescent parenthood is developmentally off-time in contemporary American society.

••

Adolescent Fathers

Adolescent fathers have not received the same degree of attention from researchers as young mothers (Figure 14–7); therefore, information about these young men continues to be scant in comparison (Gielen & Roopnarine, 2004). The dearth of research may be due to the attitude held by many in society that it is more important for adolescent fathers to be identified so that they may assume their legal responsibilities for their out-of-wedlock child. Those studies that have been performed examine personality characteristics, a father's involvement during a girl's pregnancy and after the child's birth, his role in pregnancy resolution decisions, his problems, and social outcomes associated with becoming an adolescent father (Florsheim & Smith, 2005; Thornberry, Smith, & Howard, 1997).

Because most adolescent girls who become mothers choose to retain custody of their baby and do not marry, an equal number of adolescent boys and young men are absent or nonresidential fathers. Although adolescent mothers do not seem to be labeled today by stereotypes, a stereotype of adolescent fathers depicts them as uncaring, uninvolved, and immature (Stainer-Person, 1998). This may be partly true for some adolescent fathers—those who do not acknowledge their role in impregnating an adolescent girl—but it is not true for all. Researchers describe these young fathers as frightened, withdrawn, confused, and guilty about what has happened (Heaven, 2001). Many feel overwhelmed by the girl's pregnancy and may use denial as a defense mechanism to avoid the anxiety associated with their responsibility. However, the quality of a teen father's relationship with the teen mother of their child prior to

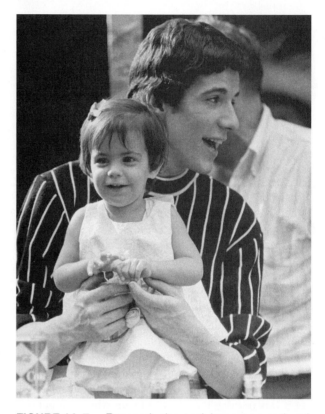

FIGURE 14–7.   Research about adolescent parenthood has focused almost exclusively on the teenage girls who become pregnant. Comparatively little is known about adolescent males who father children.

their child's birth appears to positively influence their involvement with coparenting following birth (Florsheim & Smith, 2005).

In many respects, adolescent fathers resemble those teenagers who are not fathers. However, a number of distinctive characteristics describe their particular situation (Fagot, Pears, Capaldi, Crosby, & Leve, 1998; Madden-Derdich, Herzog, & Leonard 2002; Saunders, 2002; Xie, Cairns, & Cairns, 2001). For example, more teen fathers are members of minority groups. Teen fathers typically have lower high school GPAs than nonfathers. Their relationship with the mother of their child is long term and stable. Most are nonresidential fathers but are involved with their child and the mother. They do not view teen parenthood as a negative life event because this is supported in their communities and families, and they feel that contraception is the responsibility of their female partner.

Adolescent fathers' lack of involvement in pregnancy resolution decisions may partly relate to the lack of clarity in their role as fathers. This confusion tends to shape their behavior as parents (Madden-Derdich, Herzog et al., 2002; Xie, Cairns et al., 2001). For example, some adolescent mothers rely on the men in their extended families and social networks to act as fathers for their children. Different men may enact the role at various times in a child's life: for example, the mother's current husband, the biological father, or the mother's biological father or stepfather. Once children are born, however, the majority of young fathers have contact with their child and the mother. In addition, the extent, nature, and context of the teen father's involvement with his child may be highly dependent on the mother's support and expectations. Furthermore, a teen father's levels of stress about parenting an infant appear to be positively mediated when both his parents and those of his child's mother are supportive (Fagan, Bernd, & Whiteman, 2007).

Many fathers of children born to adolescent girls are in their 20s, and the girls perceive them to be authority figures (Alan Guttmacher Institute, 2006a). Investigators commonly report that adolescent fathers have been involved in an intimate relationship with their child's mother for a long time and frequently continue to maintain this relationship after the child's birth. Although many young men state that they love the mother, the relationship is often characterized by a lack of commitment and little promise for continuation into the future. One study, however, notes that economic issues affect almost all of these young fathers (Rozie-Battle, 2003). For these young men, who are usually out of work, joblessness accounts for a diminished role as a father. In addition, it is possible to presume that a grandfather's presence could preclude the involvement of a teen father with his child, but this does not appear to be the case. The grandfather's support may increase the likelihood of a young teen father's involvement with his child (Madden-Derdich et al., 2002).

The problems that these young men experience by virtue of their socioeconomic status and their educational and lifestyle experiences are poignant. They are essentially no different from the difficulties of many adolescent mothers (Bunting & McAuley, 2004). For example, both teen mothers and fathers typically have problems with the adolescent girl's parents, experience situations that are developmentally off-time, and find

that they are ill prepared to be parents (Schweingruber & Kalil, 2000).

The fact that less research attention has been given to the adolescent father perhaps reflects both legal and social attitudes about these young men. It is difficult to prove the legal paternity of a child. Although sophisticated laboratory tests are available using DNA fingerprinting techniques, these methods are controversial and expensive. The laws governing the custody and legal rights of out-of-wedlock children traditionally have recognized the rights of the biological mother over those of the father. These laws, which have origins in old English common law, were adapted in the formative years of the United States. They have not been questioned until recently, when fathers became interested in establishing their rights and access to out-of-wedlock children. Recently, lawsuits argued in front of the Supreme Court have reversed the biological mothers' traditional rights, clearly outlining the legal rights of anyone who fathers a child out of wedlock. These rights range from custody and visitation to the child's rights to inheritance and support. They also guarantee a father's access to professional services when exercising his parental rights.

What factors would one assume to place teenage males at risk for becoming fathers? Researchers have identified these as not related or contributing to the likelihood of teen fatherhood (Anda, Chapman, & Felitti, 2001; Ornelas, 2007; Tan & Quinlivan, 2006; Thornberry et al., 1997):

- Coming from a home without a biological father or a home that offers less supervision
- Parental emotional depression
- Presence of family violence
- Commitment to school performance

However, these factors appear to predispose someone to become an adolescent father:

- Being a teen of color
- Being educationally disadvantaged
- Having parents who assumed this role early in life
- Having parents with little formal education
- Involvement with delinquent or deviant behavior (e.g., history of arrest, gang involvement, jail time, living in a juvenile home, drug use, early sexual activity)
- Experiencing adverse childhood conditions (e.g., household members who were substance abusers, mentally ill, or criminals)

More significantly, the cumulative, interactive effect of several of these domains places a young man at high risk for fatherhood during adolescence. While not all teen males experiencing these kinds of circumstances become fathers, the mechanisms that prevent this in some but not others are not clear at this time.

Some teen fathers make a "better-than-expected" adjustment to becoming a parent (Florsheim & Ngu, 2006). The young men in this study made a remarkable transformation to becoming committed to coparenting their child and developed an ability to empathize with their coparenting partner that has implications for programs serving these young men.

A variety of social and educational programs have been developed to help teenage fathers address the change in their lives when they become parents (Parra-Cardona, Wampler, & Sharp, 2006). These programs are discussed in the next section.

Parenting Reflection 14–2

Can parents of teenage expectant parents be held responsible in any way for this situation?

Focus Point. Researchers have studied adolescent mothers more than adolescent fathers. The adolescent father's parental role is less well defined than the adolescent mother's, although both parents share some of the same outcomes of pregnancy. Adolescent fathers have certain legal rights as parents. Most continue to maintain a relationship with the child's mother after the baby's birth.

CONSEQUENCES FOR THE CHILD OF AN ADOLESCENT PARENT

Although adolescent mothers may be competent in some aspects of parenting, the child born to an adolescent is at risk in numerous ways. These children are at greater biological, developmental, and psychological risk than those born to an older mother (Federal Interagency Forum on Child and Family Statistics, 2007). A high rate of infant prematurity and low birth weight are two consistent findings related to the outcome of adolescent pregnancy (see Figure 14–8). Generally, there is a higher mortality rate among infants born to adolescent mothers than to women who have their first child in early adulthood. The risk of low birth weight is inversely related to the mother's age at delivery. This statistic is particularly higher among black and poverty-level teenagers than among whites and those from middle-class backgrounds. The difference may lie in the accessibility to health care both before and following conception, nutrition, and quality of life issues.

Prematurity and low birth weight are associated with (1) lowered survival rates; (2) circulatory and respiratory difficulties; (3) higher incidence of brain damage, cerebral palsy, hypoxia, membrane disease, epilepsy, delayed developmental progress; and (4) prolonged hospitalization that has severe physical, psychological, social,

FIGURE 14–8. Percentage of infants with low birth weight by race and Hispanic origin in the United States, 1980 to 2005.

Source: Federal Interagency Forum on Child and Family Statistics. (2007). *America's children: Key national indicators of well-being, 2007.* Washington, DC: U. S. Government Printing Office.

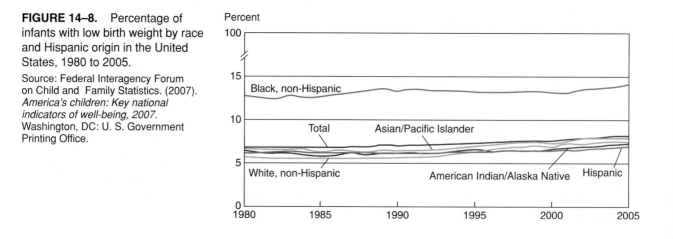

and economic implications (Levene, Tudehope, & Sinha, 2008). An infant is more likely to be born with physical, mental, and/or developmental defects if the mother is age 15 or younger. These defects include mental retardation, diabetes, physical handicaps, and various other associated congenital defects. The rate of infant birth defects increases as birth weight decreases. Girls age 15 or younger have the highest incidence of low-birth-weight babies, resulting in an infant mortality rate that is twice that of babies born to women between 20 and 40 (Martin et al., 2006). Several factors account for the high rate of health problems for infants born to teenage mothers: the developmental immaturity of the mothers, their lack of adequate knowledge about the importance of prenatal care, their tendency to seek prenatal care later in pregnancy, and their poor nutrition during pregnancy.

Researchers report other consequences for infants born to teenage mothers (Furstenberg, Levine, & Brooks-Gunn, 1990; Lefever, Nicholson, & Noria, 2007; Nicholson & Farris, 2007; Schatz & Lounds, 2007):

■ Significantly lower scores on intelligence tests and other measure of cognitive functioning
■ A tendency toward behavior problems, especially among boys
■ The likelihood of becoming teenage parents themselves, experiencing homelessness, incarceration, and/or juvenile delinquency
■ A tendency to repeat grades in school and to have some type of learning disability
■ A tendency to have slow developmental progress, especially among boys
■ The likelihood of experiencing disrupted marriages in adulthood
■ Early age of becoming sexually active and inconsistent use of contraceptives, increasing the chances of pregnancy
■ Greater likelihood of being abused, neglected, or abandoned

Researchers have also identified protective factors that can influence the adjustment of children born to teen parents that include developing resiliency in light of such stresses as just listed, having a father who is involved in their upbringing, having some type of religious affiliation, and having close ties to individuals in their communities (Howard, Carothers, Smith, & Akai, 2007).

....

Focus Point.   Children of adolescent parents also experience certain consequences, many of which are negative in nature.

....

SUPPORTS FOR ADOLESCENT PARENTS

A teenager who becomes a parent receives more support from his or her community today than in the past. Until about 20 years ago, the only type of assistance available was a residential service program where an adolescent could live while awaiting her baby's birth. Today, this type of service may continue to be helpful to some pregnant adolescents, especially those who have left their family or have dropped out of school. Services also target teens who are experiencing serious substance abuse, are abused by their family or boyfriend, or have run away from home. In many places, however, community services have been expanded to include a number of other social and human service programs that address the needs of pregnant teens and those who become parents. Some of these programs also assist in preventing repeat teen pregnancy and parenthood (Akinbami, Cheng, & Kornfeld, 2001; Sonenstein, Stewart, Lindberg, Pernas, & Williams, 1997).

The programs generally fall into one or more classifications, depending on whether they address educational needs, interpersonal skills, parenting skill development, or a combination. Regardless of the type of program, researchers identify those that are successful in their goals as (1) programs that provide individual attention to the participants, and (2) multicomponent, multiagency, community-wide programs involving, for example, parents, schools, and religious groups to reach those teens most in need of services (Nitz, 1999; Stevens-Simon, 2000; Urban Institute, 1999). Programs that attempt to facilitate change in the lives of families with teenage mothers are also effective in minimizing the deleterious effects of adolescent pregnancy on the quality of life (Figure 14–9). Essentially, these programs offer long-term benefits to their adolescent participants (Honig & Morin, 2001).

The federal government has provided funding for three model programs that address adolescent sexual activity, which often leads to pregnancy. These programs advocate restrictive abstinence or delayed sexual activity

FIGURE 14–9. Many American school systems provide educational programs to support teen parents. Most report successful results.

as a means of preventing pregnancy rather than focusing on contraceptive uses. These include (1) Section 510 of the Social Security Act, (2) the Adolescent Family Life Act's teen pregnancy prevention component, and (3) Community-Based Abstinence Education (CBAE). The total funding for these programs was $176 million for fiscal year 2006 (Alan Guttmacher Institute, 2006c). In addition, federal legislation has established a strict definition of abstinence-only sex education, requiring these programs to teach that sexual activity outside of marriage is wrong and harmful regardless of someone's age. These programs are prohibited by law from advocating the use of contraception or to discuss contraceptive methods except to emphasize their failure rates. These programs are intended to target young people between 12 and 29 years of age. Research, however, reports that these programs are not as successful in preventing teen pregnancy as hoped (Centers for Disease Control and Prevention, 2008).

Teens who are sexually abstinent report they have not had sex because they fear pregnancy or contracting diseases (Blinn-Pike, 1999). These programs are controversial, and little evaluative data substantiates the effectiveness of programs that promote delaying sexual activity or abstinence in lowering pregnancy rates (Centers for Disease Control and Prevention, 2008; Klein, 2006; Strasburger, 2006). Programs that provide counseling, peer education, or services to increase contraceptive use seem to be more effective in preventing adolescent pregnancy than these other approaches. Furthermore, those programs that inform teenagers that there is a high risk of contracting sexually transmitted diseases and that pregnancy can ruin their lives appear to be more effective (Alan Guttmacher Institute, 2006c). In addition, abstinence-only sex education programs appear to influence sexually active teens to delay or neglect use of contraceptives, which increases their risk of contracting STDs and initiating pregnancies (Bruckner & Bearman, 2005). In essence, then, sex-education programs that address both abstinence and contraceptive use comprehensively have been found to help teens delay becoming sexually active, reduce their numbers of sexual partners, and increase their use of contraception when they do become sexually active (Alan Guttmacher Institute, 2006c).

Some programs specifically target teenage fathers or boys who potentially could become teen fathers (Brindis, Barenbaum, Sanchez-Flores, McCarter, & Chand , 2005; Kandakai & Smith, 2007; Saleh, Buzi, Weinman, & Smith, 2005; Sonenstein et al., 1997). It is likely that programs targeting teenage girls specifically would be more effective if combined with these programs aimed at the young males. Such programs are based on: (1) changing males sexual habits to include greater use of condoms, not only to prevent the spread of STDs but also to reduce pregnancies; (2) requiring males to assume financial responsibility for their children as motivation to avoid future unintended pregnancies; (3) increased enforcement of statutory rape charges to reduce pregnancies and births; (4) strengthening the role of fathers in all families; and (5) teaching teen fathers how to become more involved with their children.

One study suggests that lack of adequate material resources contributes significantly to life outcomes for both teen mothers and fathers (Mollborn, 2007). Programs that promote the availability and use of resources such as housing, child care, and financial support appear to facilitate teen parents' educational experiences, especially for teen fathers.

Educational Programming

Many different types of programs have been developed to mainstream pregnant adolescents into public schools or to maintain the public school educational programs of those who are already parents (Hoyt & Broom, 2002). Some programs support the continuation of a teenager's education while providing child development and parenting information that promotes competent caregiving skills (McDonell, Limber, & Conner-Godbey, 2007). A main function of these programs is to lower the high dropout rate observed among teenage girls who become pregnant. Disruption of schooling has long-range, largely negative effects on teen parents and their children. Other programs offer child-care services as a means of promoting school attendance while providing other students with opportunities to observe infant and child behavior as part of child development and parenting courses (Akinbami et al., 2001).

Pregnant or married adolescents were formerly expelled from school or not allowed to participate in regular school programming or extracurricular activities. Recent government and judicial rulings have determined that school districts discriminate against these teenagers by establishing and enforcing policies that restrict their access to educational experiences. Many school districts in larger metropolitan areas have established special support programs especially for pregnant teenagers or those who are already parents. These programs address the impending birth and provide special instruction in parenting skills, maternal and child nutrition and health care, and prenatal care. They also teach required academic subjects.

Day-care services can provide practical experiences with infants and young children. One experimental program pairs adolescent mothers with older women who serve as mentors, role models, and friends (Waller, Brown, & Whittle, 1999). This apparently helps the young mothers learn parenting skills and acquire child development knowledge, motivates their participation in educational experiences, and results in fewer behavior problems. Other programs feature peer education approaches and base programmatic features on what teens themselves believe are the best ways to prevent pregnancies, such as being given more access to contraceptive information (Hacker, Amare, Strunk, & Horst, 2000; Philliber, 1999).

When teenagers participate in such programs, they enhance their rate of returning to or staying in school programs that lead to a high school diploma. Research reports that subsequent births among teen mothers are diminished when they remain in school, live at home with their parents, and are engaged in educational or work activities (Key, Barbosa, & Owens, 2001; Manlove, Mariner, & Papillo, 2000; Stevens-Simon, 2000).

Promoting Parenting Skills and Preventing Future Pregnancies

Participation in special programs can help teenagers who are pregnant or who already have children improve their parenting skills and prevent future unplanned, unwanted pregnancies (Ammen, 2000; Key et al., 2001). When teenagers have education and information about sexuality, child development, contraception, and parenting, that knowledge may result in certain outcomes: (1) increase in the number of teens using birth control, (2) reduction of repeat pregnancies, and (3) reduction of child-abuse cases. These programs are as effective with teen fathers as they are with teen mothers (Brown, Saunders, & Dick, 1999). However, more programs are aimed at meeting the needs of adolescent mothers. These programs may be especially helpful to ethnic minority teens who are at high risk of pregnancy and parenthood (Gilliam, 2007).

One way to assess the effectiveness of teen parenting programs is to measure child outcomes following parents' participation (Jaffee, Caspi, Moffitt, Belsky, & Silva, 2001). If a program is truly successful, it will help teen parents to do a competent job of parenting children that will be evident in a child's cognitive, emotional, intellectual, and physical development. This assessment does not exclude the importance of the maternal or paternal outcomes.

Many programs include information about child development norms and appropriate expectations for infant and child behavior. This information improves parenting skills and attempts to prevent abuse from teen parents with inappropriate expectations (Stevens-Simon et al., 2001). Programs give teen parents and expectant teens opportunities to observe infants and young children. They offer lectures about child development and use special learning tools to promote appropriate parental attitudes and expectations.

Some programs are developed specifically to prevent adolescent pregnancy, but the variety of approaches seems to have limited results in achieving this goal. For example, peer education involves students who train other students about the hazards and negative consequences of teen pregnancy (Akinbami et al., 2001; Philliber, 1999). Small adolescent support groups discuss sexuality and sexual issues to promote responsible sexual decision making. Some programs work specifically with minority groups that are especially at risk for adolescent pregnancy and for other behavior problems that interfere with attaining a high quality of life.

Some contend that the dilemma of adolescent parenthood can be most effectively addressed by implementing programs directed at the root of the issue: adequate sex education for teenagers that results in effective contraceptive practices (Urban Institute, 1999). This is a controversial problem. It is commonly asserted in many communities that sex-education programs only stimulate teens' interest in having early sexual experiences that lead to pregnancies. Research has not been able to provide a clear answer to the credibility of this assertion (Alan Guttmacher Institute, 1999). However, despite methodological problems in investigating this issue, some evidence suggests that contraceptive use and the ability to engage adolescents to effectively use contraception are associated with their participation in sex-education programs. Youths who participate in sex-education programs have been found to delay participating in sexual intercourse rather than initiating this early or experiencing increases in sexual activity.

Parenting Reflection 14–3

Why don't sex-education programs in junior and senior high schools have a greater effect on reducing the number of teenage girls who become pregnant each year? Why don't programs that stress abstinence or delayed sexual activity have a greater impact?

The federal government has been interested in developing programs that help prevent teen pregnancy. The Adolescent Family Life Act of 1981 was passed as an effort to achieve this goal but with the stipulation that demonstration programs it funded would advocate abstinence as the most effective means of eliminating teen pregnancy and that certain topics, such as abortion and contraceptive practices, would not be included in the curriculum. The effectiveness of such programs in preventing pregnancies by discouraging adolescent participation in intercourse does not appear to be valid (Centers for Disease Control and Prevention, 2008; Perrin & DeJoy, 2003).

One of the latest and perhaps most realistic strategies for helping teens avoid pregnancy makes use of a teaching device that looks, feels, and sounds like a real baby (C. Martin, 1996). This highly realistic tool is effective in helping young adolescent girls and boys have experiences similar to those that parents of a newborn often encounter. It is used in teen pregnancy–prevention programs offered by some middle and senior high schools in the United States.

There is limited research on the effectiveness of such simulation experiences in reducing or preventing teen pregnancies in the communities where programs use this approach as a teaching aid. However, it is likely that such experiences may be more effective than other approaches in building empathy with what it must be like to be a teen mother or father and the implications of early parenting on one's life plans (Barnett & Hurst, 2004; deAnda, 2006; Didion & Gatzke, 2004; Malinowski & Stamler, 2003; Mallery, 2002; Out & Lafreniere, 2001). One study, however, questions the effectiveness of this approach (Barnett, 2006).

Focus Point.   Programs that address the needs of adolescent parents are available in many communities in the United States. These programs offer a number of social and human services that assist adolescent parents and help to prevent future pregnancies. Public school systems provide special programs that help teen parents pursue their educational goals. They also offer psychological support and training in parenting skills.

POINTS TO CONSIDER

■ Teenagers continue to become parents today, although there has been a decline in recent years in the numbers who carry a pregnancy to term. Four basic factors influence teen pregnancy: (1) increased incidence of sexual activity among adolescents; (2) lack of adequate contraceptive knowledge and use; (3) social influences; and (4) personal, family, and community attitudes about teen pregnancy.

■ The majority of pregnant adolescents elect to keep their babies following birth. A minority place their infants for adoption. Some choose to get married; however, married adolescents are at high risk for divorce within a relatively short period of time.

■ Teen pregnancy has consequences for adolescent mothers and fathers, their child, their families of origin, and society. Most of these consequences are long term in nature and scope. Adolescent mothers may expect interruptions or disruptions in their education; less-than-positive implications regarding the health of the mother and child; the probability of lower economic status caused by low-paying, unsatisfying jobs; large families; and the likelihood of a troubled relationship with the child due to poor parenting skills.

■ Relatively little is known about adolescent fathers as compared with adolescent mothers because these young men usually play a less well-defined role in adolescent parenthood. A variety of characteristics distinguish these young men from those within their age range who are not fathers.

■ A variety of support programs and services may be available in many communities to assist adolescent parents. These are designed to help adolescent parents complete their education and learn adequate parenting skills. The programs also work to prevent pregnancies among adolescents and repeat pregnancies among those who are parents.

CHAPTER 15

Parent-Child Relations in High-Risk Families

Focus Questions
■ ■ ■ ■ ■ ■ ■ ■ ■ ■

Abusive Parents and Their Children

1. What are the major issues relating to parental abuse and neglect of children?

2. How are abusive parents and their children characterized? What are the major consequences of abuse for children?

3. What intervention strategies help parents to control their abusiveness and provide treatment for children?

Families Affected by Adult Dependency or Addiction

1. What effects can be observed in a family and its members when one or both adults are affected by a dependency or addiction to a substance, an experience, or some other agent?

2. What is codependency? What are the different kinds of codependent patterns? What kinds of roles are ascribed to children in codependent families? What is an adult child?

■ ■ ■ ■ ■ ■ ■ ■ ■ ■

Many families in the United States experience problems and situations that can affect their ability to function in healthy ways. Effective parenting in these families is difficult to achieve due to several factors that operate against this optimal goal. Families can be considered at high risk due to economic, health, psychological, or social factors that challenge effective functioning. Many families find they can successfully cope with such challenges by seeking help from professionals, social networks, relatives, and other sources. They learn to use healthy means for dealing with difficult circumstances. Other families, who perhaps are not especially healthy in general, often fail to respond to such challenges in healthy ways, and their status becomes even more endangered as a result. While every family can expect to experience crises at some time and frequently for a long period of time, each reacts in different ways to address and resolve critical situations and events.

This chapter discusses situations that have not yet been addressed in the text. These challenges are significant and represent issues that are specific to some families in the United States today. No family system is perfect or without problems that can threaten its ability to function effectively and in healthy ways. However, this chapter describes drastic situations. First, those families in which one or both parents abuse their children physically, sexually, and/or emotionally are examined. Abusive parents present a clear risk to their children, and the effects of such treatment can have lasting detrimental, even life-threatening, effects for children. When abuse occurs in families, such behavior of one or both parents creates an unhealthy family environment that damages all members. It frequently leads to dissolution of a family via divorce, and parental rights may be terminated. Second, we discuss the effects of addiction or dependency on an adult parent and how this affects the parent-child relationship. This condition has both short- and long-range effects on the entire family system.

ABUSIVE PARENTS AND THEIR CHILDREN

The media and other sources of cultural conditioning have led us to believe that most families are happy groups of people committed to nurturing, sustaining, and supporting each other. This is a highly romanticized notion of family life that ignores important and unpleasant realities of daily family interaction. Only within the intimacy of family systems do some people feel permitted to harm one another in physical, sexual, or emotional ways. For some, the family system is a battleground where atrocities to others occur with all-too-frequent regularity (Brandt, 2002; Gelles, Loseke, & Cavanaugh, 2004; see Focus On 15–1).

Early explanations of family functioning recognized conflict as inevitable in human relations. This was thought to occur because both individuals and social agencies tended to promote personal interests and needs over the welfare of the group. One of the primary tenets of the Freudian theory of personality development stresses the dual nature of human relations in which opposite emotions, such as love and hate, can be held simultaneously in relation to a love object. Recent research on family violence illustrates a returning interest in learning more about this unpleasant aspect of family life (Wallace, 2007; Winkler, 2004).

Definitions and Prevalence of Family Violence

Family researchers have only recently begun to study the issue of violence in families. Since the late 1960s and early 1970s, several cultural and social factors have promoted this interest (Gelles et al., 2004). First, there has been increased public sensitivity to the violence connected with the military hostilities in many regions of the world, such as the Middle East, Ireland, and the former USSR; the assassinations of public officials and celebrities; large-scale demonstrations of civil disobedience; widespread acts of terrorism; and the high homicide rates in large cities. Second, the Women's Movement has played a major role in focusing public attention on the issue of violence toward women and children, especially wife battering, marital rape, and incest. Third, researchers have been able to demonstrate that valid research can be conducted on this sensitive issue, although it poses many methodological problems (Miller-Perrin, Perrin, & Barnett, 2004; J. Miller & Knudsen, 2006).

There continues to be some confusion among researchers and the general public over what constitutes abuse, violence, and neglect within a family system. **Abuse** and **neglect** are sometimes interchangeable terms; they often refer to acts of physical aggression that result in injury and to nonphysical acts of maltreatment that are thought to cause harm to a person (Gelles et al., 2004). In some instances, abuse includes problems resulting from physical assault that have medical diagnoses and symptoms, and neglect refers to acts of parental negligence, such as failing to supervise children or properly provide for their nutritional needs. While this is a basic notion of abuse, **maltreatment** of children and adolescents is the term increasingly used. This term includes those acts that define abuse and neglect as well as radical parental acts, such as excessive punishment, child abandonment, infanticide, murder of children, and abandonment of a child's corpse. **Violence** is a rather broad concept that includes what many consider to be legitimate acts of force against family members, which often fall under the guise of discipline and parental control of children. The term also relates to illegitimate acts of violence, including those occurring as part of family conflict. Hitting is acceptable behavior in many families because many parents consider spanking a child to be necessary and normal parental behavior.

**Focus On
15–1**

Facts About Child Abuse and Neglect: 2005

- An estimated 899,000 children were victims of child abuse or neglect.
- 62.8% of child victims experienced neglect. Almost 17% were physically abused; fewer than 10% were sexually abused; and 7.1% were emotionally maltreated.
- Children ages birth to 3 years had the highest rates of victimization at 16.5 per 1,000 children. Girls were slightly more likely to be victims than boys.
- About 1 in 50 infants in the United States have been neglected or abused; nearly one-third of these were 1 week old or younger.
- African American and American Indian or Alaska Native children had the highest rates of victimization when compared to the national population.
- Child fatalities are the most tragic consequence of maltreatment. In 2002, an estimated 1,400 children died due to abuse or neglect.
- Three-quarters (76.6%) of children who were killed from abusiveness were younger than 4 years old
- Infant boys (younger than 1 year old) had the highest rate of fatalities.
- 42.2% of child fatalities were attributed to neglect. Physical abuse and sexual abuse also were major contributors to fatalities.
- 79.4% of perpetrators were biological parents. Female perpetrators, who were mostly mothers, outnumbered men.
- Of all parents who were perpetrators, fewer than 8% were associated with sexual abuse.
- More than one-half of all reports of child abuse and neglect were made by professionals such as medical personnel, teachers, police and lawyers, or social services staff. The remainder were made by neighbors, friends, or relatives.

Source: Centers for Disease Control. (2008). Nonfatal maltreatment of infants—United States, October 2005–September 2006. *Morbidity and Mortality Weekly Report, April 4, 57*(13), 336–339; Children's Bureau. (2007). *Child maltreatment 2005.* Washington, DC: Author; U.S. Department of Health and Human Services, Administration on Children, Youth and Families. (2008). *Child maltreatment 2006.* Washington, DC: Author

A generally accepted definition of family violence is described as "an act carried out with the intention or perceived intention of causing physical pain or injury to another person" (Gelles & Cornell, 1997). Examples of such acts range from spanking, shoving, hitting, slapping, pinching, shooting, cutting, or pulling to those acts that cause psychological harm or injury.

Violence in families can be directed at both children and adults and perpetrated by one against the other. Child abuse and neglect have received a great deal of attention from both researchers and the media. Even though there is a wide variety of types of abuse (see Figure 15–1) and researchers may differ in their definitions

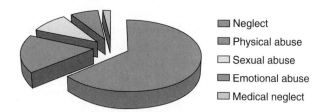

FIGURE 15–1. Percentage of children experiencing different types of abuse and neglect in the United States, 2005.

Source: U.S. Department of Health and Human Services, Administration on Children, Youth, and Families. (2007). *Child maltreatment 2005.* Washington, DC: U.S. Government Printing Office.

Focus On 15–2

Classifications of Child Abuse and Neglect

- *Physical abuse:* Infliction of any type of injury on a child, such as burns, bites, cuts, and welts
- *Sexual abuse:* Forcing, tricking, or coercing sexual behavior between a young person and an older person, with an age difference of at least 5 years between the perpetrator and the victim; includes fondling body parts, penetration of the child's body by nonsexual objects or the offender's sexual organs, and noncontact behaviors, such as voyeurism or pornography
- *Physical neglect:* Failure to provide a child with an adequate and nurturing home environment that provides the basic necessities of food, clothing, shelter, and supervision
- *Medical neglect:* Failure to provide a child with medical treatment when physical conditions necessitate such care (except in instances prohibited by religious beliefs)
- *Emotional abuse:* Speech, actions, and interactions that tend to destroy emotional well-being and a sense of self-worth and those that hamper healthy personal and social development
- *Emotional neglect:* Failure to show concern for a child and his or her activities
- *Abandonment:* Failure to make provisions for the continual supervision of a child
- *Multiple maltreatment:* A combination of several types of abuse or neglect

Sources: Gelles, R. J., & Cornell, C. P. (1997). *Intimate violence in families* (3rd ed.). Thousand Oaks, CA: Sage Publications; Gelles, R. J., Loseke, D. R., & Cavanaugh, M. M. (2004). *Current controversies on family violence.* Thousand Oaks, CA: Sage Publications; Straus, M. A., & Gelles, R. J. (2006). *Behind closed doors: Violence in the American family.* Piscataway, NJ: Transaction Publishers; Wallace, W. (2007). *Family violence: Legal, medical and social perspective* (5th ed.). Boston: Allyn & Bacon.

and understandings of the types of violence in families, a general categorization of physical and psychological abuse has emerged. This is especially the case for those acts that constitute child abuse and maltreatment (see Focus On 15–2).

Models of Family Violence

Seven basic models or theoretical explanations focus on why parents and children act violently against one another (Garbarino, Hammond, Mercy, & Ying, 2004; Gelles & Cornell, 1997; Gelles et al., 2004; Straus & Gelles, 2006; Wallace, 2007):

1. The **psychiatric model** assumes that abusive individuals in a family system are deviant or mentally and/or emotionally ill. This model isolates the personality characteristics of the offender as the primary cause of the abusive behavior. It attempts to link personality patterns or traits with the tendency to perform abusive acts and with other behavior patterns, such as borderline personality organization, alcoholism, substance abuse, and mental illness.

2. The **ecological model** examines the child and the family from a systems theory perspective. It explores the child's development within the family system and the functioning of the family system within its community. For example, when the community supports parental use of physical force against children but does not provide support for families in stress, the likelihood of family violence increases. From this viewpoint, abusiveness is a family problem that affects everyone, and the entire family must receive treatment to become healthy.

3. The **sociological model** stresses that social values and attitudes about violence shape violent behavior in family systems. From a cultural point of view, the use of physical force, particularly against children, is a sanctioned aspect of parenting behavior. Violence is a means of settling disputes and conflicts with others. The model also emphasizes that adults' violent behavior toward children is a reaction to stress and frustration. The strengths of these stimuli are closely related to the social status of the family system. People from lower social classes are thought

to experience greater environmental stress and to express their reactions through violent behavior that is often directed at children and other family members. Another tenet of this approach emphasizes that family structure and organization lend their influence to violent behavior. Crowded living conditions, high levels of unemployment, strained financial resources, and social isolation from other families place additional stress on the parent-child microenvironment, which can result in abusive behavior. Additionally, being an adolescent parent or living in a stepfamily situation may also increase the possibility of this behavior due to stressful living conditions.

4. The **social psychological model** covers a variety of approaches that explain violence among family members. Interaction patterns, the transmission of violent behavior from one generation to the next, and environmental stress are cited as prime motivators of violent behavior in families. According to this model, violence is learned by modeling and serves as a coping mechanism in response to stress. In addition, child abuse is considered a product of inconsistent punishment used by many parents. Violence may also be learned within the sibling microenvironment as a means of solving problems.

5. The **patriarchy model** emphasizes that violence occurs in families due to the traditional social dominance of adult males, which places women in a subordinate position and condones the use of violence to support male dominance.

6. The **exchange/social control model** suggests that violence occurs in families when the costs of being violent do not outweigh its rewards. For example, the rewards of violent behavior might be getting one's own way, assuming superiority over others, gaining revenge, or expressing anger and frustration. The costs might include receiving violent behavior in retaliation, being arrested and jailed, or becoming divorced. These costs also act as social controls to prevent and limit the possibility of violent behavior, but three factors tend to limit the strength of such costs in controlling violence: (1) inequality of the sexes, (2) the privacy of the family, and (3) subscription to cultural beliefs in machismo, or ultramasculinity that is expressed in aggressive, hostile, and violent ways.

7. The **information-processing approach** proposes that neglectful parents fail to process information appropriately about children's need for care because of four possibilities: (1) They do not perceive behavioral cues given by children, (2) they interpret such signals from children as not requiring a parental caregiving response, (3) they are aware that a parental response is required but fail to have one available, or (4) they choose a response that is either inappropriate or never implemented.

Factors Associated with Family Violence

Researchers describe several social-psychological variables related to the incidence and variety of violent behaviors expressed in families (Gallimore, 2002; Garbarino, 2001; Garabarino, Hammond, Mercy, & Young, 2004; Gelles & Cornell, 1997; Straus & Gelles, 2006). First, a **cycle of violence** appears to be manifested in two basic ways:

1. Individuals who had violent and abusive childhoods tend to become abusers of their own children.

2. A three-phase sequence in the expression of violent behavior begins with increasing tension, a loss of control manifested by violent behavior, and a reconciliation period characterized by the offender's contriteness and the victim's forgiveness.

Second, *socioeconomic status* of a family system is associated with expressions of violence, particularly in families from lower socioeconomic groups where the quality of life, environmental stresses, and cultural conditioning or standards may be felt more keenly and intensely than they are in other social groups.

Third, *stress* is closely related to domestic violence. Acts of violence or abuse form part of a person's coping mechanisms for stress. Sources of stress may include poverty, unemployment or part-time employment, financial problems, pregnancy and childbirth, or single parenthood.

Fourth, *social isolation* from other families increases the risk of abusive behavior directed toward children or a spouse. This may be a contributing factor to the likelihood of abuse occurring in single-parent families. The social networks provided by interactions with other families tend to act as a control mechanism to reduce the risk of such behavior.

In addition to these four variables, several other conditions can be linked to family violence. There is an association between **substance abuse** by parents and physical abuse and neglect of children. Substance abuse or chemical dependency, especially involving alcohol, may play a role in 50% to 90% of cases of physical abuse of children by parents. Intoxication and chemical dependency impair judgment, increase irritability, and enhance emotionally depressive reactions, thus increasing the likelihood of mistreating children.

Another factor associated with child abuse and neglect is *family form*. A majority of reported cases of child abuse occur in single-parent families. Rather than being a function primarily of single-parent household status, abuse of children may be more likely to occur in these homes because of the diverse effects of poverty on single-parent family functioning. Additionally, family form plays a role in that stepfathers appear to be more likely to abuse children rather than biological fathers.

There is strong evidence of intergenerational transmission of abusive behavior (Straus & Gelles, 2006). From this perspective, a child learns such behavior by being abused by one or more of their parents whose maltreatment serves as a model. This abusive behavior is replicated upon the child's attainment of adulthood and the assumption of parenthood with their own children. Thus, abusiveness is passed from one generation to another.

● ●

Parenting Reflection 15–1

You are grocery shopping and have just witnessed a parent viciously slapping and shaking her preschool-age boy. The child is screaming and crying loudly and the parent is continuing to yell at the child, calling him names and shaming him for what he has done. What do you do?

● ●

Characteristics of Abusive Parents

Because it is unlike other family problems, parental abuse of children requires different approaches in understanding the causes and motivations of such behaviors (Wallace, 2007). In these instances the parent generally has an extremely difficult time dealing with a

child's behavior and handling a problem of which he or she may or may not be consciously aware. No one characteristic is common to all abusive parents, although statistics point to the mother rather than father as being more likely to be the abusive parent (Children's Bureau, 2007). Researchers observe several attributes in various combinations in those adults who are prone to be abusive to their children. These characteristics are outlined in Focus On 15–3.

The child-rearing patterns of these individuals typically reflect a rigid, harsh authoritarian approach. For example, abusive mothers characteristically express inconsistency, hostility, and protectiveness (paradoxically) toward their children, often almost simultaneously. They seek to gain control over their children's behavior through methods based on producing a child's anxiety and guilt as well as through physical punishment (Timmer, Borrego, & Urquiza, 2002).

Although these characteristics of abusive and neglectful parents are general and broad in nature, it is important to distinguish between the characteristics of parents who behave in different ways that result in child maltreatment. These different types of abusive and neglectful parents are briefly outlined here.

Parents Who Physically Neglect Children.   Physical neglect of children constitutes the most frequently reported type of maltreatment of children by parents. This accounts for more than 60% of all reported child abuse in the United States (Children's Bureau, 2007). Parents who neglect their children physically fail to provide for basic needs, such as sufficient food for nutritional requirements, supervision, or medical care. Such inadequate care for children results in fatalities with about the same frequency as that occurring with physical abuse.

Parents who are reported for child neglect the first time are found to have recently experienced a family crisis due to illness or other health problem, divorce, or desertion (Institute of Medicine Staff Board, 2002). As might be expected, parents who chronically are physically neglectful of their children typically have poor parenting skills and abilities.

Such parents often live in poverty and experience high levels of stress that are accompanied by emotional depression and anxiety due to unemployment, inadequate nutrition, high levels of substance abuse, and low incomes. These are multiproblem families with a chaotic home environment and low personal functioning. The

Focus On 15–3

Characteristics of an Abusive Parent

- Had an unhappy childhood
- Was mistreated or abused as a child by parent(s)
- Had parents who failed to provide an adequate model of good parenting
- Is socially isolated from family, friends, or neighbors; has few outside contacts of an intimate nature
- Has low self-esteem; perceives self as inadequate, unlovable, incompetent, or worthless
- Is emotionally immature; may be considered an adult child emotionally; has a dependent personality
- Sees little joy or pleasure in life; may be clinically depressed
- Holds distorted perceptions and unrealistic expectations of children
- Is adverse to the idea of spoiling his or her child; strongly believes in physical punishment as a means of teaching children and helping them learn family patterns; practices an authoritarian child-rearing style; displays minimal nurturing behaviors to child; displays frequent outbursts of temper
- Has severely limited ability to empathize with others, particularly with his or her children; displays a general insensitivity to the needs of others

Sources: Children's Bureau. (2007). *Child maltreatment 2002: Summary of key findings.* Washington, DC: Author; Feindler, E. L., Rathus, J. H., & Silver, L. B. (2003). *Assessment of family violence: A handbook for researchers and practitioners.* Washington, DC: American Psychological Association; Flowers, R. B. (2000). *Domestic crimes, family violence, and child abuse: A study of contemporary American society.* Jefferson, NC: McFarland & Company; Heyman, R. E., & Slep, A. M. S. (2002). Do child abuse and interparental violence lead to adulthood family violence? *Journal of Marriage and the Family, 64,* 864–870; Institute of Medicine Staff Board. (2002). *Confronting chronic neglect: The education and training of health professionals on family violence.* Washington, DC: National Academy Press; Malley-Morrison, K., & Hines, D. (2003). *Family violence in a cultural perspective: Defining, understanding, and combating abuse.* Thousand Oaks, CA: Sage Publications; Stark, E. (2000). *Everything you need to know about family violence.* New York: Rosen Publishing Group.

families are socially isolated and maintain closed boundaries that do not allow access to support systems in their community. The closed nature of these families also makes them resistant to assistance and therapy to help them overcome or cope with their problems. Parental neglect of children can be damaging to children. Our society must take this problem seriously. Although this type of child maltreatment may be overshadowed by the more dramatic aspects of physical and sexual abuse of children, it is not simply a by-product of poverty that can be dismissed as inevitable.

Parents Who Physically Abuse Children. Many parents who physically abuse children are not aware that what they do is wrong and harmful (Flowers, 2000; Stark, 2000; Wallace, 2007). They perceive their parental responsibilities to be in authority over children. This approach is manifested in strong beliefs about the necessity of using physical punishment in teaching children how to behave, but even more significantly as a means of achieving control over children's misbehavior. They generally have low tolerance levels for children's behavior, being impatient and quick to anger. They may be described as having poor empathic abilities and as being insensitive to children's needs and natures. Some are belligerent, even paranoid, and as a result experience many negative interactions with other people, both within and outside of the family. Physical abuse of children usually occurs when these parents are responsible for young children in situations that they find highly stressful and are without sufficient support and resources to cope (Stark).

Other factors coincide to culminate in abusive actions of these parents toward their children. These adults are vulnerable to stress and typically cope poorly. They have been found to experience significantly more stressful and stress-producing events in their lives than parents who do not abuse their children physically (Runyon, Deblinger, Ryan, & Thakkar-Kilar, 2004).

Being abused as a child is an important predictor of whether someone will abuse his or her children physically as a parent. Substance abuse also plays a significant role in the behavior of abusive parents toward their children (Shultz, 2001). Alcohol abuse is especially associated with placing children at risk for physical abuse. The abusive behavior often occurs when parents are intoxicated and in even less control than usual of their actions. It is also likely that when substance abuse plays a role in the incidence of child abuse, the perpetrator grew up in a family where at least one parent was a substance abuser.

Parents Who Emotionally Abuse Children. Researchers have conducted fewer studies of emotionally abusive parents than other abusive types (Wark, Kruczek, & Boley, 2003). This may be due to the difficulty in identifying parental behaviors that fall into this category. It is also difficult to prove that emotional abuse has occurred between parents and children because the evidence is not as obvious when compared with other types of abuse. It also may be possible that emotional abuse of children is more widespread as acceptable parental behavior (Straus & Field, 2003; Straus & Gelles, 2006).

Parents who emotionally abuse children most likely experience low levels of self-esteem (Miller-Perrin et al., 2004). They are found to have poor coping skills and child management techniques. This deficiency may give rise to situations in which parents express their anger and impatience with children in ways that damage the children's self-esteem as well. As difficult as it may seem to understand, the attainment of adulthood does not automatically confer emotional maturity upon an individual. Some parents experienced difficult childhood and adolescent developmental paths that have impaired their ability to grow in healthy ways emotionally. Some are the products of homes in which their parents suffered addictions to drugs, work, gambling, or other substances. Such life experiences tend to result in creating a distorted emotional makeup known as an **adult child** (Ramey, 2004). Until adults who are disadvantaged by

stagnated emotional development can receive help in moving forward toward developmentally healthy emotional progress, it is highly likely their children will experience emotional abuse as well.

When parents become emotionally abusive, they express their impatience, frustration, rage, personal hurt, and disappointment with their children in various ways that damage the children's sense of trust and emotional well-being. Discounting a child's feelings and actions through name calling, putdowns, or sarcasm is considered emotional abuse. Telling children they will never amount to anything worthwhile is abusive. Other examples include shaming children when they make mistakes, handing down punishments that are humiliating, not allowing children to express feelings, or ostracizing children as punishment by not speaking to them, ignoring their presence, or destroying their favorite toys. When children are abused in these ways, it increases the likelihood they will become emotionally depressed (Doyle, 2001). This difficult mental state is observed to be four times as prevalent in children who have been abused than among children who have not been mistreated by parents. Because emotional depression is associated with suicidal ideation, these children are also at greater risk of suicide than others.

Parents Who Sexually Abuse Children. It is difficult for most people to imagine that adults are interested in engaging in sexual activity with children, especially if those involved are members of the same family. There is a strong taboo against incest in almost all human societies. **Incest** is sexual activity between members of the same family and is considered to be an aspect of sexual abuse involving children. Children cannot give consent to such activity. Especially in families where children are taught to obey their parents and other elders, children are incapable of declining and may not understand what they are consenting to do with an adult perpetrator (Witters-Green, 2003). Sexual abuse by parents is infrequent, occurring in an estimated 10% of cases reported (Children's Bureau, 2007). The majority of adults who sexually molest children are other relatives and nonrelatives with whom the child is familiar.

Until about 40 years ago, researchers thought that little sexual abuse or incestuous activity took place in American families. But when child-abuse legislation was instituted at this time, requiring such cases to be reported, researchers discovered that sexual abuse of children was more widespread than they had imagined. People have become more open in publicly disclosing their sexual abuse in childhood. Celebrities such as TV star Roseanne Barr and former Miss America Marilyn Van Debur have publicly acknowledged that they were sexually abused as children by family members. This has stimulated many people who experienced similar abuse as children to seek treatment and to help others acknowledge these experiences as part of their healing process. Although it may be impossible to gather exact figures showing the extent of sexual abuse of children, one national estimate is that almost 6 million children experienced abuse of some nature in 2006 (U.S. Department of Health and Human Services, Administration on Children, Youth, and Families, 2008). Of this number, an estimated 8.8% were sexually abused.

Sexual harassment is strongly similar to sexual abuse and involves inappropriate sexual touching and insinuations between parents and children. Children are abused sexually when parents engage in genital fondling, anal or vaginal intercourse, or oral-genital contact, for example. There are many risks involved with such activities for all concerned, but especially for the child.

Families in which sexual abuse of children has occurred are characterized as having poor boundary controls among members, especially between parents and children, poor quality of the adult marriage relationship, less harmony and stability in the family system as a whole, and a father who was probably physically abused as a child and acted violently within the family as an adult (Engel, 2000; Ferrara, 2001; Kinnear, 2007). Families in which sexual abuse of children has occurred are observed to have significantly greater difficulties in regulating anger and greater degrees of chaos or difficulties in managing roles (Howes, Cicchetti, Toth, & Rogosch, 2000). Some insights have emerged about the attitudes of men who have perpetrated sexual abuse that may serve to motivate such behavior. When compared to other men who have physically abused children, male incest offenders hold deviant attitudes that endorse male sexual entitlement in general and perceive children to be sexually attractive and sexually motivated. They minimize the harm caused to children by sexual activity with adults, especially family members. In addition, interviews with perpetrators reveal that these individuals, regardless of their gender, see their incestuous actions as fair and loving and a statement of their professed care for their child victims (Eldridge,

1997). Such views serve to minimize and discount any possible harm that they perceive children could experience from their behavior.

Treatment and Intervention for Abusive Parents

A wide variety of assistance is available to abusive parents (Feindler, Rathus, & Silver, 2003; Harway, 2000; Malley-Morrison & Hines, 2003; J. Miller & Knudsen, 2006). Usually, this assistance focuses on the individual adult but addresses the needs of the entire family. Services may include medical care, counseling, psychotherapy, marriage and family therapy, mediation, support groups, telephone crisis information, day care, parenting education, and temporary foster care for children. Some programs emphasize skill development that enhances parental prosocial attitudes and interpersonal relationships. Others address family support needs as a means for prevention and early intervention (Winkler, 2004). In instances that include legal involvement, courts may order the family to participate in therapeutic programs using parent education and psychotherapy (Wallace, 2004). In other instances, parents may seek out these services voluntarily.

It is unclear if these programs are completely effective in preventing future child abuse and neglect by parents (Garbarino et al., 2004). Using certain criteria to measure effectiveness, some critics observe that most treatment programs are not always successful for participants. Programs that emphasize parent education and early intervention with those prone to abuse may be more effective than others, especially in producing short-term effects for the parents (Dore & Lee, 1999). Programs may be most beneficial if abusive parents participate in support groups, such as Parents Anonymous or Parents in Distress, in addition to the parenting programs. These support groups are composed of self-referred individuals who are disturbed by their abusive behavior and fearful of the effects of continued abuse on their children and families. The groups are modeled after Alcoholics Anonymous. Group members meet weekly to discuss their problems and provide mutual support during and between meetings. Members are instructed to call another member when they feel most likely to commit an abusive act against someone in their family. Many communities also have safe houses that provide temporary shelter and initial assistance to women and their children who have been in abusive family situations (Correia & Rubin, 2002).

Family therapy using a systems theory approach may provide the most promise of effectiveness in helping both parents and children (Gelles et al., 2004). When families are treated by a competent therapist, all the elements related to the abuse are involved: the perpetrator, the victim, and the relationship.

••

Focus Point.   Violence in families is an unpleasant reality. Child abuse and neglect have received a great deal of attention in recent years. Seven basic theoretical approaches explain why abuse and neglect occur. Several psychological and social factors are associated with a variety of violent behaviors directed toward children and other family members. Parents who abuse and neglect children have particular characteristics. The types of abusiveness range from physical neglect and abuse to emotional and sexual abuse of children. Intervention and treatment programs have been developed, but results are generally unclear.

••

FAMILIES AFFECTED BY ADULT DEPENDENCY OR ADDICTION

Dependency on substances and addictions of various types have become a major concern of contemporary American society. Typically, alcoholism first comes to mind when thinking of substance abuse. There are many other drugs that produce dependencies besides alcohol, however, and people become addicted to things, events, and experiences as well as to substances. It is not possible to determine the exact number of adults in the United States who have a chemical dependency or addiction of some sort. However, it is estimated, for example, that about almost 4% of the U.S. population are dependent to some degree on alcohol (National Institute on Alcohol Abuse and Alcoholism, 2006).

There are a variety of costs suffered by a family when one person has developed a dependency or an addiction. The affected individual invariably experiences health problems that are related to this problem. When a serious addiction has developed, the economic costs can be enormous and adversely affect the family's quality of life, sometimes to the point of bankruptcy. The emotional costs can never be completely determined, because these can be long lasting and endure into a child's adulthood years. Chemical dependencies and other addictions have a cyclical effect and are frequently passed from one generation to the next. When a family member experiences such problems, children are placed at risk for developing similar addictions when they become adults, and the problem can be compounded with each successive generation.

Invariably, the abuse of substances and development of an addiction by a family member leads to a crisis, and many problems arise that chronically affect all family members. Among the most serious of these are the violence that can occur and the abuse that almost always accompanies these problems. Children are especially vulnerable to emotional damage from growing up in a family affected by parental chemical dependency or addiction. Although adolescents are vulnerable to developing dependencies and addictions, we will focus on those families in which one or both parents have developed this problem and examine the myriad effects on all family members.

UNDERSTANDING THE EFFECTS OF DEPENDENCY AND ADDICTION

The Affected Adult Family Member

When an adult family member develops a chemical dependency or another type of addiction, it is an understatement to say that the person is having some larger and deeper problem that is contributing to the dependency (Lindley, Giordano, & Hammer, 1999). The individual believes that the solution to the problem can be addressed by using a substance or something else to relieve negative self-feelings. There is some basis to the notion that the tendency to develop these obsessive, compulsive problems has a genetic base. However, some experts believe that an interaction between biological and environmental factors influences the likelihood that someone will develop such problems in adulthood (Fossum & Mason, 1986; Weinhold, 1991).

It is thought that the adult affected by chemical dependency or other addiction turns to the drug or substance for psychological relief from pain experienced because of low feelings of self-esteem (Wells, Glickauf-Hughes, & Bruss, 1998). The addictive substance somehow functions to medicate the user in the short term, allowing them to cope with whatever difficulty they may be experiencing (Covington & Beckett, 1988). However, it becomes so powerful with continued use that the user loses control over the ability to stop using it. According to Kellogg (1990), anything that removes or alters unwanted feelings that typically accompany deep-seated feelings of low self-esteem, such as anger, emotional pain, fear, anxiety, or depression, is addictive.

A **chemical dependency** or an **addiction** is defined in various ways by different experts. However, one of the better definitions of addiction is provided by Larsen (1987):

> *self-defeating learned behaviors, greatly exaggerated and complicated by a pathological relationship to a mood-altering substance, that diminish the capacity to initiate or participate in loving relationships*

In other words, the affected person develops an unhealthy intimate relationship with a substance or an experience that causes difficulties in having healthy intimate relationships with others, especially those in the person's family.

Today, it is understood that people can develop dependencies and addictions to things other than drugs. The compulsive use of events, people, experiences, and nonchemical substances such as food can qualify as dependencies and addictions. People become addicted to relationships, to the experience of falling in love, to gambling, to food, to their work, and a variety of other things as well as drugs such as alcohol, tobacco, caffeine, prescription medications, and so on. As long as the substance or the experience is capable of alleviating some kind of emotional pain, it serves as the basis for the problematic relationship the person develops with it.

Experts inform us that it is not necessarily the substance that causes the addiction but the relationship with the substance that becomes problematic (Kellogg, 1990; Springer, Britt, & Schlenker, 1998). According to this line of thought, the process of dependency and addiction is a result of one's decreasing ability to choose not to have the relationship with the addictive substance. The person's relationship with the substance or experience becomes dominant over all others.

Experts who study the problem of dependencies and addictions believe that the agent itself is not always addictive; this is particularly the case with nondrug agents such as experiences or food, for example. The problem develops when the relationship people establish in using the agent becomes skewed. This may explain why the same agent causes some people no problem but becomes the focal point of compulsive behaviors and addictions for others. Although there is a genetic basis for some portion of addiction, it is the interaction of this factor with environmental experiences that can ensure that addiction can occur at some point in life.

Apparently, the stage is set in childhood for later addictive behavior. Current thought about the origins of dependencies and addictions is that people develop behaviors labeled as codependent that have their roots in infancy and childhood. **Codependency** was first used to explain why an alcoholic usually was married to a person who enabled their addiction by needing to be with someone who had serious personality and behavioral problems. Today, the concept has been greatly broadened to describe how people develop problems with dependency on others (Granello & Beamish, 1998). Essentially, it is thought that people who are codependent failed to be parented properly in infancy and childhood. This ineffective parenting refers to the inadequate caregiving by adults who failed to meet their children's dependency needs.

All children are dependent on adults to have their needs met in appropriate ways. This situation lasts for some time into adolescence as human children look less to others to meet their needs for them as they grow older. The healthy developmental track is toward increasing independence, but in order for this to happen as intended, children need the assistance of healthy parents who assist them toward this goal. People who are codependent did not receive appropriate, adequate parenting experiences that allowed such developmental progress to occur. Rather, they experienced emotional and sometimes actual abandonment by their parents. Such abandonment takes many forms and, for all practical purposes, this kind of parental behavior is abusive. In many respects, parental abandonment reverses the order of family structure. Instead of having parents who take care of them, the child in such situations is forced to take care of parents, to conform to their demands, and behave in ways that meet their needs.

Larsen (1987) defines codependency as:

> *self-defeating learned behaviors, greatly exaggerated and complicated by a pathological relationship to a chemically dependent person or any person, that diminish our capacity to initiate or participate in loving relationships.*

Notice that this definition of codependency closely resembles the definition of chemical dependency described by Larsen earlier in this section. This is intentional because Larsen believes that any person who has a chemical dependency or any kind of addiction is a codependent with a substance-abuse problem. In this regard, an alcoholic is a codependent who drinks, for example.

It is thought that these obsessive, compulsive behavior problems occur because people experience some kind of deep emotional pain that responds to medication by using a particular substance or experience. The source of this deep emotional pain is thought to be shame felt about the self. In this regard, shame is deeply felt due to the inadequate parenting experiences in infancy and childhood. **Shame** is defined as an emotional wound (Bradshaw, 1988). It is a core belief that the person's character and self-esteem are inherently flawed because of who they are and what has happened to them. Shame differs from guilt. Guilt refers to what individuals feel when they have behaved in some unacceptable way or done something wrong. Shame is the belief that something is terribly wrong with them. When parents emotionally abandon children, children come to the conclusion that something must be inherently wrong with them; why else would their parents neglect them in such ways? Parents who behave in these ways with their children are emotionally damaged people who continue the abusive behavior with their children that they experienced at the hands of their parents. Unfortunately for a variety of reasons, the ability to parent children appropriately does not always occur. Some parents are not emotionally mature enough to provide adequate care because of their upbringing in families that were destructive in these same ways. Other parents are emotionally or mentally ill and do not always receive treatment for their problems. Some behave in this manner because of the stressful effects of poverty or the difficulties of being a single parent (Black & Krishnakumar, 1998).

Ineffective parenting also occurs when adults overprotect children, continually take care of everything for them, and allow little freedom for children to explore and discover themselves and their world (Melody, 1989). Unnurturing parents also are those who are overly strict and authoritarian in their approach to parenting. These parents overwhelm their children's ability to think critically, foster their dependence by having many nonnegotiable rules, and use physical punishment to enforce parental control over children (Bradshaw, 1988). At an extreme position of abusing children emotionally are those parents who ignore their children almost altogether.

When children have been emotionally abused by parents in these ways, they acquire painful emotional beliefs that affect their self-esteem adversely. Growing up with such feelings about oneself harms the ability to be intimate in relationships, which is also emotionally painful. Hence, these individuals discover substances and experiences at later times in life that at first alleviate this pain but later result only in even more shame and emotional pain because of the compulsive and self-destructive results of using the agent. In such ways, the intergenerational transmission of the tendency to develop dependencies and addictions partially takes place. When there also is a genetic basis for this tendency, the likelihood of transmission increases considerably.

••

Focus Point.   People can become dependent on or addicted to things, events, people, experiences, and substances. These usually occur because people seek relief from unwanted feelings that accompany their deep-seated feelings of inadequate self-esteem and shame. There is a progression through several stages of use of the agent in this manner that leads to dependency and addiction. People who have dependencies and addictions are said to be codependent. This condition refers to the long-term effects of experiencing inadequate parenting by adults who failed to meet their dependency needs as children.

••

Family systems theory predicts that when an adult is affected by some sort of dependency or addiction, everyone else in the family is also affected to some degree. The codependency literature first focused on the spouse of the person having the dependency or addiction. Much of the early work examined wives of alcoholics, and it was discerned that the women enabled much of their spouses' problem by denying or minimizing the addiction. For example, if an alcoholic husband had been drinking heavily and could not go to work the next day because of an excruciating hangover, the codependent wife would call in to his employer and make excuses for his absence from work to protect him. Such enabling was believed to facilitate the alcoholic husband's problem rather than confronting him with the dire consequences of how his drinking was affecting his work and jeopardizing the welfare of his family.

Therapists and others interested in this problem became increasingly aware in the 1980s that codependency involved much more than wives of alcoholics and other addicts. The definition of codependency became revised and broadened to describe what happens to children when their dependency needs are not met adequately by parents. The notion of codependency became something of a cultural phenomenon as public awareness increased about the prevalence and manifestations of codependency in adulthood. Now it is accepted among experts that codependency lies at the heart of the problem of the person who experiences substance dependency or addiction as well as of others in the family (Cullen & Carr, 1999).

Addicted adults and their codependent partners have developed over the years a variety of self-defeating behaviors that are practiced in their relationship (Larsen, 1987; Le Poire, Hallett, & Giles, 1998). These self-defeating behaviors emerged during their childhood and adolescent years as a means of coping with neglectful and abusive parents. The patterns also evolved as a means for gaining the approval, acceptance, and attention of parents who were failing to provide for their needs in appropriate ways. Now, in the person's adulthood, the patterns remain as a way of obtaining affection and love in an intimate relationship. However, the relationship goes even more awry because at least one partner's primary relationship is actually with a substance or experience that he or she has become dependent on or addicted to. The relative unhealthiness of this relationship, however, is a reflection of the dependencies and addictions of both people in the relationship. Each is practicing their addictions or dependencies in different ways. The partner of the chemically dependent or addicted person is also addicted, but most likely to the relationship itself.

The irony of what happens in adulthood to behavioral habits such as these is that they were once functional earlier in life but become self-destructive if allowed to continue in adulthood. These codependent patterns prevent the emergence of true intimacy and authenticity in loving relationships with others. Larsen (1987) and other writers (Kellogg, 1990; Melody, 1989; Norwood,

1985) outline six basic self-defeating behavior patterns observed in codependent adults:

1. *Caretaking* As a child, a future codependent person learned that his or her self-esteem could be generated by focusing on others' needs to the exclusion of personal ones. As a result, codependent people usually are neglectful of their own needs. People who develop this habit in relating to others (who often are very needy people) often become rescuers who bail them out, know how to get things fixed, and generally solve others' problems. Fueling such behavior of caretakers is a sense of grandiosity. Caretakers come to believe in their godlike abilities to know more and be better at almost everything than everyone else. Such a false sense of superiority actually masks deep-seated feelings of personal shame and self-deprecation. As children, this pattern might have evolved because of the need to take care of parents when they were intoxicated, for example. It is typical that in some types of parental abandonment, the usual roles become reversed between parents and children. Children who are assigned such responsibilities for their parents must grow up long before they are developmentally ready.

2. *People pleasing* As children, future codependent persons might have learned that their self-esteem is based on seeking others' approval, especially that of parents. There is a strong commitment to never rock the boat, never have others become angry at them, or bring what they consider to be undue attention to themselves. When people evolve this pattern, they quickly develop a false self and perform many actions that would be labeled as self-erasure. This pattern creates an inauthentic way of relating to others because these people pleasers are terrified that if their real self were known, people would not like them or want to be around them.

3. *Martyrdom* A person who develops a martyr pattern has learned to expect the worst in everything and everyone. Life is seen as a struggle and has meaning only if there is suffering to be borne. If things are going well for them, they often become anxious and can consciously or unconsciously sabotage events so that something becomes a disaster for them. It is not uncommon for martyrs to go from one seeming crisis to another. A core belief for

many of these codependent people is that they do not deserve anything good, decent, or worthwhile. As is often the case, this belief is a self-fulfilling prophecy, and matters typically turn out this way. Martyrs can be bitter, hostile people who usually project blame on others for their problems and difficulties rather than facing the pain of understanding that it is they who have the troubled outlook on life. As children, people with this codependent pattern were abused emotionally by parents who also might have modeled such behavior that was adopted by their children.

4. *Workaholism* As children, people who acquire this pattern learn to stay busy and active as a means of feeling good about themselves. This pattern may develop in people whose family lives as children were chaotic, unpredictable, and confusing. For some, parents valued productivity above all else from their children. This pattern may have become entwined with people pleasing as a way to gain the approval of others who are difficult to please. The goal of staying busy is a means of diverting their attention away from themselves and others and toward activity. It is difficult for workaholics to rest and relax, perhaps because this is an act of self-giving and they feel guilty for giving such attention to themselves. People who practice being workaholics communicate to their partner and family that work is more important than their family; this is a discounting act that is abusive to others. However, their work serves as a shield to protect them from the hurtfulness they learned as children from what happens in close relationships with others.

5. *Perfectionism* As children, people who practice perfectionism as adults learned that it was possible to avoid the pain of criticism and disapproval for making mistakes by trying one's absolute best to be perfect. These individuals became their family's "best little boy or girl" in the process, giving everyone the impression that they could do no wrong and in many instances coming very close to living up to that impression. There is a deep element of compulsion in this pattern that is painful, especially to those coming in contact with such an individual. Perfectionists see the world through lenses that carefully show in detail whatever is awry, in error, incorrect, or imperfect. These individuals have a

PhD in finding fault not only with things but also with people. It may be impossible for them to be satisfied or happy. They will never be completely happy perhaps until self-acceptance is mastered. This means coming to terms with one's humanity and that of others, understanding that humans should be imperfect and do things incorrectly at times. The practice of perfectionism as well as these other patterns is an attempt people learned as children to control their world and what happened to them in unhealthy families. Whereas learning perfectionism as children may have helped them to survive in a chaotic family, it will serve as a self-defeating pattern in adulthood to drive others away and maintain a false sense of security and control.

6. *Tap dancing* As children, people who learned a tap-dancing pattern most likely felt very insecure living in the midst of unpredictable parenting behavior. This pattern is a manifestation of mistrust for others in adulthood. Tap dancers find it practically impossible to make a commitment to another person because they believe it is safer to be free and on one's own. The label for this pattern describes the inability of the person to stay in one place emotionally with another person. People with this pattern can be confusing to others because they show mixed feelings about closeness. On the one hand, it is something they want very much and they perhaps try as best they can to accommodate such feelings. On the other, they become frightened when it appears necessary to show signs of commitment to another person. They are elusive in their relationships with others in adulthood. It often seems you can never pin them down on anything. There is much show in the beginning of a relationship of what appears to be closeness and intimacy, but this is practiced and not genuine. When the time comes to discuss making a commitment and defining the rules that outline an intimate relationship, the person is unwilling to discuss such plans and may sabotage the relationship by becoming involved with someone else. It is not unusual for tap dancers to have more than one relationship under way at the same time. Because people often become involved with those who complement their own patterns, tap dancers can be observed in relationships with caretakers and people pleasers. Caretakers can become

hooked on trying to fix and rescue a tap dancer, and people pleasers may be at the mercy of a tap dancer and constantly take personal blame for the other's inability to make a commitment; that is, "Something must be wrong with me because this person won't commit." The people pleaser can become addicted to figuring out how to do things right so the tap dancer will make a commitment.

• •

Parenting Reflection 15–2

After reading this section, do you think you may have developed one (or more) of these codependent patterns just discussed? If so, reflect on how this may affect your intimate relationship. If you are or if you became a parent, how would this affect your ability to parent children effectively?

• •

Children Affected by Dependent or Addicted Parents

Children may not be aware that one or both of their parents have a substance-abuse problem or other addiction because their parents use denial to avoid facing the problem. However, these children are affected by living in a home where this problem does exist for their parents, and the effects can last a lifetime. Not only are they likely to develop dependency problems similar to their parents' at some time in their lives, but they are likely to repeat the same kinds of unhealthy codependent patterns modeled by their parents when they assume this role after growing up. As we have seen in the previous section, they may choose partners in their intimate relationships who appeal to their ability to care for someone. Because they have failed to observe healthy behavior by their parents, it is likely that they have a poor notion about what the parameters of normal, healthy behavior are and become involved in marriages and relationships with people who behaviorally resemble one or both parents.

Experts consider the family atmosphere in homes where one or both parents have a substance dependency or addiction to be chaotic and abusive for children (Bradshaw, 1988; Melody, 1989; Wegscheider, 1989). Alcoholism in a family is associated with the increased

likelihood of physical and sexual abuse of children. Emotional damage also occurs to children living in these families. Dependent and addicted family systems have very rigid rules that enable the system to function in unhealthy ways. The problem is a family secret—one that eats away at the integrity of the system as a whole and the individuals who compose it (Imber-Black, 1993). Three basic rules are enforced strictly for children and all family members that are self-destructive for everyone: (1) Don't talk about the parents' problem of substance or experience dependency or addiction, (2) don't trust anyone outside of the family to understand the problem, and (3) don't feel anything because this will destroy the integrity of the family (M. L. Martin, 1993).

Children typically become assigned to a special role in many of these families that helps to maintain the system's unhealthy homeostasis and protect the family secret from becoming public. While these same roles can be observed in almost every kind of unhealthy family system, they are especially important in dependent and addicted families because they help children cope with the chaotic, unpredictable nature of family life. The following are four roles that children might assume:

1. *Best little boy or girl or family hero.* This child, frequently the oldest, often acquires caretaking as a codependent pattern since parents assign parenting duties and responsibilities for this child to perform. This child becomes a surrogate parent for other children by providing for their care when one or both parents are under the influence of the primary agent of their dependency or addiction. The codependent pattern of perfectionism can also be observed in this child. This may happen because the child learns that parental criticism can be minimized by avoiding mistakes at all costs. Because of this orientation, children assuming this role often become high achievers in school and extracurricular activities.

2. *Scapegoat.* Unhealthy family systems often create a role where one child is assigned the implicit position of problem child. He or she is expected to act out the family problems in various ways that are antisocial in nature. The purpose of this child's role is to behave so badly that the attention of parents and family is drawn away from the true cause of the family's problems. This is a sacrificial role that children usually are not aware they are

performing or why. As long as parents and the family can focus on fixing this child's misbehavior, they escape having to face the harsh reality of their own codependency problems.

3. *Mascot.* This child's role is similar in nature to that of the scapegoat but differs in how it is performed. Instead of being a problem child, some families expect a particular child to act out and distract them by being something like the class clown. This is the child who is carefree, jovial, and debonair. The purpose of this kind of behavioral orientation is to help the family minimize the actual problem so that the system can function to support the substance abuse or addiction of the adult(s).

4. *Lost child.* This child is expected to act as though he or she were invisible. This is the ultimate in self-erasure as this child learns to dull personal emotions, needs, and wants in order for parents to maintain their primary relationship to the dependency or addiction. This child can adopt a martyr pattern or even a tap-dancing pattern as a means of surviving the abusive treatment by parents who act as if he or she is a machine rather than a precious child. These children learn to stuff their emotions deeply inside and ignore feelings. As a result, they develop a high tolerance for physical as well as emotional pain.

Such roles as these facilitate the development of the habitual codependent patterns discussed in the previous section. Although these roles and the patterns of coping that emerge from them are functional in helping children survive their chaotic family life, they are handicapping conditions in adulthood that prevent them from functioning in healthy, intimate relationships. These children often personalize the problems that their families experience by feeling that they should be Superchildren. When parents are intoxicated or high, children frequently assume that they are the cause of such behavior, and that somehow, some way, they ought to be able to correct their parents' problem and make their family become healthy.

Because they have grown up in an unhealthy family system, children who have parents with a dependency or an addiction fail to develop in healthy ways emotionally. This is the case for all children who grow up in families where there is some type of serious problem affecting the ability of adults to function appropriately or in healthy ways due to physical or mental illness, poverty,

or other factors. Such an unhealthy upbringing usually results in stagnating children's normal developmental paths and they become what is called an **adult child** upon attaining maturity (Friel & Friel, 1988). Because these children have experienced chaotic, unpredictable parenting by adults who abandoned them emotionally, they were left without the usual assistance parents provide in nurturing children in healthy ways.

Adult children also can be characterized in other ways. Kritzberg (1985) lists a number of these by type. He notes that emotional characteristics include fear that is manifested in anger and resentfulness, distrust of others, sadness, loneliness, deep-seated shame and guilt, and numbness as a way of coping with painful emotional states. Mental characteristics are described as use of black-and-white thinking, lacking information about life, compulsive behavior and thinking, indecision, presence of learning disabilities, difficulty in thinking clearly, and hypervigilance. These emotional and mental attributes are associated with having grown up in an unhealthy family system where parental behavior created a chaotic and stressful environment (Fuller & Warner, 2000). Physical characteristics are stress related: tense shoulders, lower back pain, sexual problems, gastrointestinal disorders, lowered resistance to infections, and allergies. Behavioral characteristics of these individuals include crisis-oriented lifestyles, manipulative behavior with others, problems in intimate relationships, inability to experience enjoyment and pleasure, fearfulness of being noticed by others, and a tendency toward compulsive-addictive behavior.

Fortunately, help and support is available in most communities in the United States for families affected by addictions and dependencies. First, the medical community provides rehabilitation programs, many of which are covered by major medical insurance programs, for both the affected family member as well as for other family members. Many programs also are available that serve community members who are living in poverty status while experiencing these problems.

One of the most successful support programs that has a long history of effectiveness in helping people overcome addictions and dependencies is Alcoholics Anonymous. These programs exist in numerous communities in the United States and many are specifically focused at particular populations, for example, ethnic groups, GLBT individuals, or women. In addition, auxiliary programs are available for partners of addicted members as well as for children that help these individuals cope with this difficult family situation. In addition, there are numerous self-help books that are available via bookstores, the Internet, and in public libraries that focus on this family problem.

• •

Focus Point. Everyone in a family is affected in some way when an adult has developed a dependency or addiction. Their adult partner often becomes involved in their relationship because he or she developed a complementary codependent pattern that often enables their dependency or addiction. Children growing up in families affected by an adult's dependency or addiction problem also develop codependent patterns that help them to cope with their often chaotic and unpredictable family life and inadequate parenting. Children's emotional development typically becomes arrested and they develop into adult children. Codependent patterns that once were functional in childhood become a threat to the person's ability to function appropriately in intimate relationships in adulthood.

• •

POINTS TO CONSIDER

Abusive Parents

■ Violence in families occurs in a variety of ways and is frequently directed at children. Although it is difficult to obtain accurate information regarding the extent of such violence, child abuse appears to be the most prominent type of maltreatment among family members.

■ Seven basic models explain why violence takes place in families.

■ A number of social-psychological factors are associated with abusiveness, including a cycle of violence, a family's socioeconomic status, influence of stress, social isolation from other families, and family form.

■ Parents who abuse their children share a variety of characteristics that often reflect a poor parenting experience in their own childhoods. Children are not only neglected but abused physically, sexually, and emotionally.

■ A variety of approaches is available to assist and treat abusive parents.

Families Affected by Adult Dependency or Addiction

■ It is possible for someone to become dependent or addicted to substances such as food or drugs, as well as to experiences, people, relationships, or things. Such a problem affecting an adult in a family affects other members to some degree.

■ It is believed that the person developing a dependency or addiction uses the agent for psychological relief from the emotional pain experienced due to feelings of low self-esteem. A dependency or addiction represents a loss of choice over use of the agent. The person essentially develops an intimate relationship with the agent rather than with another person.

■ People can develop codependent patterns that influence their functioning in adulthood. The basis for the patterns are laid in childhood and are likely to be due to inadequate parenting that did not meet the child's dependency needs in appropriate ways; the person was emotionally abused by parents in this manner.

■ Children of a dependent or addicted parent are also likely to develop similar kinds of codependent patterns and be assigned to certain roles in the family (often of which they are unaware) that are unhealthy. One of the significant outcomes is that they fail to experience normal emotional development and become known as adult children when they are grown. These patterns can cause difficulty with their adult intimate relationships.

■ It is possible for people in families affected by dependencies and addictions to experience healthy recovery and treatment for their problems.

References

Abdul-Adil, J. K., & Farmer, A. D., Jr. (2006). Inner city African American parental involvement in elementary schools: Getting beyond the urban legends of apathy. *School Psychology Quarterly, 21*(1), 1–12.

Acs, G., & Nelson, S. (2002). The kids are alright? Children's well-being and the rise in cohabitation. Retrieved July 10, 2007, from http://www.urban.org/url.cfm?ID=310544.

Adams, B. N. (2004). Families and family study in international perspective. *Journal of Marriage and the Family, 66,* 1076–1088.

Adams, J. (2004). *When our grown kids disappoint us: Letting go of their problems, loving them anyway, and getting on with our lives.* New York, NY: Simon & Schuster.

Adesman, A., & Adesmec, C. A. (2004). *Parenting your adopted child: A positive approach to building a strong family.* New York: McGraw-Hill.

Adoption Media (2007). Considering adoption? Retrieved on August 14, 2007 from http://www.adoption.org.

Aggarwal, S., & Verma, T. (1987). Aggressiveness among children: A function of differential training by mothers. *Indian Psychological Review, 32,* 15–19.

Ahnert, L., Gunnar, M. R., Lamb, M. E., & Barthel, M. (2004). Transition to child care: Associations with infant-mother attachment, infant negative emotion, and cortisol elevations. *Child Development, 75*(3), 639–650.

Ahrons, C. R. (2007). Family ties after divorce: Long-term implications for children. *Family Process, 46*(1), 53–65.

Ahrons, C. R., & Tanner, J. L. (2003). Adult children and their fathers: Relationship changes 20 years after parental divorce. *Family Relations, 52,* 340–351.

Ainsworth, M. (1973). The development of infant-mother attachment. In B. Caldwell & H. Riciuti (Eds.), *Review of child development research* (Vol. 3). Chicago: University of Chicago Press.

Ainsworth, M. (1977). Attachment theory and its utility in cross-cultural research. In P. Leiderman, S. Tulkin, & A. Rosenfield (Eds.), *Culture and infancy: Variations in the human experience.* New York: Academic Press.

Ainsworth, M. (1989). Attachment beyond infancy. *American Psychologist, 44,* 709–716.

Akinbami, L. J., Cheng, T. L., & Kornfeld, D. (2002). A review of teen-tot programs: Comprehensive clinical care for young parents and their children. *Adolescence, 36,* 381–393.

Alan Guttmacher Institute. (1999). *Teen sex and pregnancy.* New York: Author.

Alan Guttmacher Institute. (2006a). Facts on American teens' sexual and reproductive health. Retrieved September 8, 2007, from http://www.guttmacher.org/pubs/fb_AT-SRH.html.

Alan Guttmacher Institute. (2006b). U.S. teen pregnancy rates are down primarily because teens are using contraceptives better. Retrieved September 9, 2007 from http://www.guttmacher.org/media/nr/2006/12/01/index.html.

Alan Guttmacher Institute. (2006c). Facts on sex education in the United States. Retrieved on September 9, 2007 from http://www.guttmacher.org/pubs/fb_sexEd2006.html.

Aldous, J. (1978). *Family careers: Developmental change in families.* New York: Wiley.

Allen, M., & Burrell, N. A. (2002). Sexual orientation of the parent: The impact on the child. In M. Allen & R. Preiss (Eds.), *Interpersonal communication research: Advances through meta-analysis* (pp. 125–143). Mahwah, NJ: Lawrence Erlbaum Associates.

Amato, P. R., & Afifi, T. D. (2006). Feeling caught between parents: Adult children's relations with parents and subjective well-being. *Journal of Marriage and Family, 68*(1), 222–235.

Amato, P. R., & Gilbreth, J. G. (1999). Nonresident fathers and children's well-being: A meta analysis. *Journal of Marriage and the Family, 61,* 557–573.

Amato, P. R., & Sobolewski, J. M. (2004). The effects of divorce on fathers and children: Nonresidential fathers and stepfathers. In M. E. Lamb (Ed.), *The role of the father in child development* (4th ed., pp. 341–367). Hoboken, NJ: Wiley.

Ambert, A. M. (1992). *The effect of children on parents.* New York: Haworth Press.

Ambert, A. M. (1994). An international perspective on parenting: Social change and social constructs. *Journal of Marriage and the Family, 56,* 529–543.

American Academy of Pediatrics Committee on Drugs. (1994). The transfer of drugs and other chemicals into human milk. *Pediatrics, 93,* 137–150.

American Academy of Pediatrics Committee on Substance Abuse. (1993). Fetal alcohol syndrome and fetal alcohol effects. *Pediatrics, 91,* 1004–1006.

American Academy of Pediatrics Committee on Substance Abuse. (2001). *Substance abuse: A guide for professionals* (2nd ed.). Washington, DC: Author.

American Bar Association. (1996). *The ABA guide to family law.* New York: Times Books/Random House.

American Bar Association. (2001). *A judge's guide: Making child-centered decisions in custody cases.* Chicago: Author.

American Civil Liberties Union. (2006). Domestic violence and homelessness. Retrieved July 8, 2007, from http://www.aclu.org/pdfs/dvhomelessness032106.pdf.

American College of Obstetricians and Gynecologists. (2005). *Your pregnancy and birth* (4th ed.). Washington, DC: Author.

American Psychiatric Association. (2000). *Diagnostic and statistical manual of mental disorders: Text revision.* Washington, DC: Author.

American Psychiatric Association. (2002). *Diagnostic and statistical manual of mental disorders: Text revision.* Washington, DC: Author.

American Savings Education Council and American Associated of Retired Persons. (2008). *Preparing for their future: A look at the financial state of Gen X and Gen Y.* Washington, DC: Authors.

Ammen, S. A. (2000). A play-based parenting program to facilitate parent-child attachment. In H. G. Kaduson & C. E. Schaefer (Eds.), *Short-term play therapy for children* (pp. 345–369). New York: Guilford Press.

Anand, K. J. (2003). Early exposure to marijuana and risk of later drug use. *Journal of the American Medical Association, 290,* 330–332.

Anda, R. F., Chapman, D. P., Felitti, V. J., Edwards, V., Williamson, D. F., Croft, J. B., et al. (2002). Adverse childhood experiences and risk of paternity in teen pregnancy. *Obstetrics and Gynecology, 100,* 37–45.

Anderson, A. S. (2003). Nutrition and pregnancy—motivations and interests. *Journal of Human Nutrition & Dietetics, 16,* 64–66.

Anderson, C. (2003). The diversity, strength, and challenges of single-parent households. In F. Walsh (Ed.), *Normal family processes: Growing diversity and complexity* (3rd ed., pp. 121-152). New York: Guilford Press.

Anderson, E. R. (1999). Sibling, half sibling, and stepsibling relationships in remarried families. *Monographs of the Society for Research in Child Development, 64*(4), 101–126.

Anderson, E. R., Greene, S, M, Hetherington, E. M., & Clingempeel, W. G. (1999). The dynamics of parental remarriage: Adolescent, parent, and sibling influences. In E. M. Hetherington (Ed.), *Coping with divorce, single parenting, and remarriage: A risk and resiliency perspective.* (pp. 295–319). Mahwah, NJ: Lawrence Erlbaum.

Arditti, J. A. (1999). Rethinking relationships between divorced mothers and their children: Capitalizing on family strengths. *Family Relations, 48,* 109–119.

Arnett, J. J. (2003). *Adolescence and emerging adulthood: A cultural approach.* Upper Saddle River, NJ: Prentice Hall.

Aroian, K. J. (2006). Children of foreign born parents. *Journal of Psychosocial Nursing & Mental Health Services, 44*(10), 1518.

Astington, J. W. (1993). *The child's discovery of the mind.* Cambridge, MA: Harvard University Press.

Ateah, C. A., & Durrant, J. E. (2005). Maternal use of physical punishment in response to child misbehavior: Implications for child abuse prevention. *Child Abuse & Neglect, 29*(2), 169–185.

Azar, B. (1997). It may cause anxiety, but day care can benefit kids. *APA Monitor, 28,* 13.

Bagley, C., & Tremblay, P. (1998). On the prevalence of homosexuality and bisexuality, in a random community survey of 750 men aged 18 to 27. *Journal of Homosexuality, 36,* 1–18.

Bailey, J. M., Willerman, L., & Parks, C. (1991). A test of the maternal stress theory of human male sexuality. *Archives of Sexual Behavior, 20,* 277–286.

Bailey, M. (2003). The corporal punishment debate in Canada. *Family Court Review, 41*(4), 508–516.

Baldo, A. J., & Baldo, T. D. (2003). A dual-career couple's experience with adoption: The dramatic impact of moving from couple to instant parenthood. *The Family Journal, 11*(4), 400–403.

Baldwin, D. A., & Moses, I. J. (1996). The ontogeny of social information gathering. *Child Development, 67,* 1915–1939.

Balkcom, C. T. (2002). African American parental involvement in education: A phenomenological study of the role of self-efficacy. *Dissertation Abstracts International, 63,* 495.

Bandura, A. (1977). *Social learning theory.* Englewood Cliffs, NJ: Prentice Hall.

Barber, J. G., & Delfabbro, P. H. (2004). *Children in foster care.* New York, NY: Routledge.

Barber, M. D., Lambers, A., Visco, A. G., & Bump, R. C. (2000). Effect of patient position on clinical evaluation of pelvic organ prolapse. *Obstetrics & Gynecology, 96,* 18–22.

Barber, N. (2001). On the relationship between marital opportunity and teen pregnancy: The sex ratio question. *Journal of Cross-Cultural Psychology, 32,* 259–267.

Barling, J. (1990). *Employment, stress, and family functioning.* Chichester, England: Wiley.

Barnett, J. E. (2006). Evaluating 'baby think it over' infant simulators: A comparison group study. *Adolescence, 41*(161), 103–110.

Barnett, J. E., & Hurst, C. S. (2004). Do adolescents take 'baby think it over' seriously? *Adolescence, 39*(153), 65–75.

Barry, J. (2007). *Environment and social theory.* New York: Routledge.

Barth, R. P., Webster, D. II, & Lee, S. (2002). Adoption of American Indian children: Implications for implementing the Indian Child Welfare and Adoption and Safe Families Acts. *Children and Youth Services Review, 24,* 139–158.

Bauer, C. R., Langer, J., Shankaran, S., Bada, H., Lester, B., Wright, L., Krause-Steinauf, H., et al. (2005). Acute neonatal effects of cocaine exposure during pregnancy. *Archives of Pediatric and Adolescent Medicine, 159,* 824–834.

Baumer, E. P., & South, S. J. (2001). Community effects on youth sexual activity. *Journal of Marriage & the Family, 63,* 540–554.

Baumrind, D. (1966). Effects of authoritative parental control on child behavior. *Child Development, 37,* 887–907.

Baumrind, D. (1991). The influence of parenting style on adolescent competence and substance abuse. *Journal of Early Adolescence, 11,* 56–95.

Baumrind, D. (1994). The social context of child maltreatment. *Family Relations, 43,* 360–368.

Baumrind, D. (1996). The discipline controversy revisited. *Family Relations, 45,* 405–414.

Baumrind, D., Larzelere, R. E., & Cowan, P. A. (2002). Ordinary physical punishment: Is it harmful? Comment on Gershoff (2002). *Psychological Bulletin, 128*(4), 580–589.

Bausch, R. S. (2006). Predicting willingness to adopt a child: A consideration of demographic and attitudinal factors. *Sociological Perspectives, 49*(1), 7–65.

Becerra, R. M. (1998). The Mexican-American family. In C. H. Mindel, R. W. Haberstein, & R. Wright, Jr. (Eds.), *Ethnic families in America: Patterns and variations* (pp. 153–171). Upper Saddle River, NJ: Prentice Hall.

Bech, B. H., Obel, C., Henricksen, T. B., & Olsen, J. (2007). Effect of reducing caffeine intake on birth weight and length of gestation: Randomised controlled trial. *British Medical Journal, 334*(7590), 334, 409.

Becnel, B. C. (1991). *The co-dependent parent: Free yourself by freeing your child.* San Francisco: HarperCollins.

Becvar, D. S., & Becvar, R. J. (1998). *Systems theory and family therapy: A primer* (2nd ed.). New York: University Press of America.

Beeghly, M., Frank, D. A., Rose-Jacobs, R., Cabral H., & Tronick, E. (2003). Level of prenatal cocaine exposure and infant-caregiver attachment behavior. *Neurotoxicology & Teratology, 25,* 23–38.

Beilin, H. (1992). Piaget's enduring contribution to developmental psychology. *Developmental Psychology, 28,* 545–552.

Bellows, B. B. (2004). *Sex education: Index and analysis of new information for parents, schools, churches, and counselors.* Washington, DC: A B B E Publishers Association.

Belsky, J. (1990). Child care and children's socioemotional development. *Journal of Marriage and the Family, 52,* 885–903.

Belsky, J., & Rovine, M. J. (1988). Nonmaternal care in the first year of life and the security of infant-parent attachment. *Child Development, 59,* 157–168.

Bem, S. (1975). Sex-role adaptability: One consequence of psychological androgeny. *Journal of Personality and Social Psychology, 31,* 634–643.

Bem, S. (1989). Genital knowledge and gender constancy in preschool children. *Child Development, 60,* 649–662.

Benedek, E. P., & Brown, C. F. (2004). *How to help your child overcome your divorce: A support guide for families.* New York: Newmarket Press.

Benkov, L. (1994). *Reinventing the family: The emerging story of lesbian and gay parents.* New York: Crown Publishers.

Bennett, S. (2003). Is there a primary mom? Parental perceptions of attachment bond hierarchies within lesbian adoptive families. *Child & Adolescent Social Work Journal, 20,* 159–173.

Benokraitis, N. V. (2004). *Marriages and families: Changes, choices, and constraints* (5th ed.). Upper Saddle River, NJ: Prentice Hall.

Bensley, L., Ruggles, D., Simmons, K. W., Harris, C., Williams, K., Putvin, T., et al. (2004). General population norms about child abuse and neglect and associations with childhood experiences. *Child Abuse & Neglect, 28*(12), 1321–1337.

Benson, A. L., Silverstein, L. B., & Auerbach, C. F. (2005). From the margins to the center: Gay fathers reconstruct the fathering role. *Journal of GLBT Family Studies, 1*(3), 1–30.

Berenbaum, S. A., & Snyder, E. (1995). Early hormonal influences on childhood sex-typed activity and playmate preference: Implications for the development of sexual orientation. *Developmental Psychology, 31,* 31–42.

Berger, R. (2000). Remarried families of 2000: Definitions, description, and interventions. In W. C. Nichols, M. A. Pace-Nichols, D. S. Becvar, & A. Y. Napier (Eds.), *Handbook of family development* (pp. 371–390). New York, NY: Wiley.

Berkowitz, D. (2007). A sociohistorical analysis of gay men's procreative consciousness. *Journal of GLBT Family Studies, 3*(2/3), 157–190.

Bernstein, N. (March 7, 2004). Behind fall in pregnancy, a new teenage culture of restraint. *New York Times* from http://www.nytimes.com/2004/03/07/nyregion/07TEEN.html#.

Berry, J. O., & Rao, J. M. (1997). Balancing employment and fatherhood: A systems perspective. *Journal of Family Issues, 18*(4), 386–402.

Berry, J. W. (1999). Emics and etics: A symbiotic relationship. *Culture and Psychology, 5,* 165–171.

Bianchi, S. M., Milkie, M., Sayer, L., & Robinson, J. (2000). Is anyone doing the housework? *Social Forces, 79,* 191–228.

Bickart, T. S., & Jablon, J. (2004). *What every parent needs to know about 1st, 2nd, and 3rd grades: An essential guide to your child's education.* Naperville, IL: Sourcebooks.

Bieber, I. (1962). *Homosexuality.* New York: Basic Books.

Bigner, J. J. (1996). Working with gay fathers: Developmental, post-divorce, and therapeutic issues. In R-J. Green & J. S. Laird (Eds.), *Lesbian and gay couple and family relationships: Therapeutic perspectives* (pp. 370–403). San Francisco: Jossey-Bass.

Bigner, J. J. (1999). Raising our sons: Gay men as fathers. *Journal of Gay and Lesbian Social Services, 10,* 61–77.

Bigner, J. J. (2000). Gay and lesbian families. In W. C. Nichols, M. A. Pace-Nichols, D. S. Becvar, & A. Y. Napier (Eds.), *Handbook of family development and intervention* (pp. 279–298). New York: Wiley.

Bigner, J. J. (2006). Disclosing gay or lesbian orientation within marriage: A systems perspective. In C. A. Everett & R. E. Lee (Eds.), *When marriages fail: Systemic family therapy intervention and issues.* Binghampton, NY: Haworth Press.

Bigner, J. J., & Jacobsen, R. B. (1989a). Parenting behaviors of homosexual and heterosexual fathers. *Journal of Homosexuality, 18,* 173–186.

Bigner, J. J., & Jacobsen, R. B. (1989b). The value of children for gay and heterosexual fathers. *Journal of Homosexuality, 18,* 163–172.

Bigner, J. J., & Yang, R. K. (1996). Parent education in popular literature: 1972–1990. *Family and Consumer Sciences Research Journal, 25,* 3–27.

Billingsley, A. (1993). *Climbing Jacob's ladder.* Upper Saddle River, NJ: Prentice Hall.

Bird, C. E. (1997). Gender differences in the social and economic burdens of parenting and psychological distress. *Journal of Marriage and the Family, 59,* 809–823.

Bissell, M. (2000). Socio-economic outcomes of teen pregnancy and parenthood: A review of the literature. *Canadian Journal of Human Sexuality, 9,* 191–204.

Bitler, M., & Zavodny, M. (2002). Did abortion legalization reduce the number of unwanted children? Evidence from adoptions. *Perspectives on Sexual and Reproductive Health, 34,* 25–33.

Black, M ., & Krishnajumar, A. (1998). Children in low-income, urban settings. *American Psychologist, 53,* 635–646.

Blanchard, R., Zuckey, K. J., Bradley, S. J., & Hume, C. S. (1995). Birth order and sibling sex ratio in homosexual male adolescents and probably prehomosexual feminine boys. *Developmental Psychology, 31,* 22–30.

Blinn-Pike, L. (1999). Why abstinent adolescents report they have not had sex: Understanding sexually resilient youth. *Family Relations, 48,* 295–301.

Bloch, J. S. (2003). The ultimate discipline guide. *Child, 18,* 88–89.

Bloomfield, H. H. (2004). *Making peace in your stepfamily: Surviving and thriving as parents and stepparents.* San Diego, CA: Peace Publishing.

Bluestone, C., & Tamis-LeMonda, C. S. (1999). Correlates of parenting styles in predominantly working- and middle-class African American mothers. *Journal of Marriage and the Family, 61,* 881–893.

Blum, R. W. (2001). Trends in adolescent health: Perspectives from the United States. *International Journal of Adolescent Medicine & Health, 13,* 287–295.

Bogaert, A. F. (2003). The interaction of fraternal birth order and body size in male sexual orientation. *Behavioral Neuroscience, 117,* 381–384.

Bold, M. (2001). *Boomerang kids.* Denton, TX: University of Northern Texas, Center for Parent Education.

Boonstra, H. (2000). Welfare law and the drive to reduce "illegitimacy." *The Guttmacher Report on Public Policy, 3,* 7–10.

Borja, J. B., & Adair, L. S. (2003). Assessing the net effect of young maternal age on birth weight. *American Journal of Human Biology, 15,* 733–740.

Borkowski, J. G., Bisconti, T., Weed, K., Willard, C., Keogh, D. A., & Whitman, T. L. (2002). The adolescent as parent: Influences on children's intellectual, academic, and socioemotional development. In J. G. Borkowski & S. L. Ramey (Eds.), *Parenting and the child's world: Influences* on academic, intellectual, and socialemotional development (pp. 161–184). Mahwah, NJ: Lawrence Erlbaum.

Bornstein, R. F., & Masling, J. M. (Eds.). (2002). *The psychodynamics of gender and gender role.* Washington, DC: American Psychological Association.

Bos, H. M. W., van Balen, F., & van den Boom, D. C. (2007). Child adjustment and parenting in planned lesbian-parent families. *American Journal of Orthopsychiatry,* 77(1), 38–48.

Boss, P. (1988). *Family stress management.* Beverly Hills, CA: Sage Publications.

Bossard, J. H. S., & Boll, E. S. (1966). *The sociology of child development.* New York: Harper & Row.

Bouchard, G., Boudreau, J., & Hébert, R. (2006). Transition to Parenthood and Conjugal Life: Comparisons between Planned and Unplanned Pregnancies. *Journal of Family Issues,* 27(11), 1512–1531.

Bouchard, G., & Lee, C. M. (2000). The marital context for father involvement with their preschool children: The role of partner support. *Journal of Prevention & Intervention in the Community,* 20(1–2), 37–53.

Bourgeois, F. J. (2004). *Obstetrics and gynecology.* Philadelphia: Lippincott, Williams, & Wilkins.

Bowen, M. (1978). *Family therapy in clinical practice.* New York: Aronson.

Bowie, F. (2004). *Cross-cultural approaches to adoption.* New York, NY: Routledge.

Bozett, F. W. (1981a). Gay father: Evolution of the gay father identity. *American Journal of Orthopsychiatry,* 51, 552–559.

Bozett, F. W. (1981b). Gay fathers: Identity conflict resolution through integrative sanctioning. *Alternative Lifestyles,* 4, 90–107.

Bozett, F. W. (1985). Gay men as fathers. In S. Hanson & F. W. Bozett (Eds.), *Gay and lesbian parents* (pp. 35–70). New York: Sage Publications.

Bozett, F. W. (1987). Gay fathers. In F. W. Bozett (Ed.), *Gay and lesbian parents* (pp. 3–22). New York: Praeger.

Bozett, F. W., & Sussman, M. B. (1989). Homosexuality and family relations: Views and research issues. In F. W. Bozett & M. B. Sussman (Eds.), *Homosexuality and family relations* (pp. 15–28). New York: Harrington Park Press.

Bradbury, T. N., Fincham, F. D., & Beach, S. R. H. (2000). Research on the nature and determinants of marital satisfaction: A decade review. *Journal of Marriage and the Family,* 62, 964–980.

Bradley, J. M. (2006). Finding their way: An exploration of stepmother role identity and discovery. *Dissertation Abstracts International: Section B: The Sciences and Engineering,* 66(9-B), 5120.

Bradshaw, J. (1988). *Bradshaw on: The family.* Deerfield Beach, FL: Health Communications.

Bramlett, M. D., & Mosher, W. D. (2002). Cohabitation, marriage, divorce, and remarriage in the United States. *Vital Health Statistics,* 23(22). Hyattsville, MD: National Center for Health Statistics.

Brandt, D. (2002). *Homes of fear: The curse of family violence.* Monrovia, CA: World Vision International.

Bray, J. H., & Hetherington, E. M. (1993). *Families in transition: Introduction and overview.* Journal of Family Psychology, 7, 3.

Breedlove, G. K., Schorfheide, A. M., & Wieczorek, R. R. (2000). *Adolescent pregnancy.* White Plains, NY: March of Dimes Birth Defects Foundation.

Brewer, M. (2008). Colorado's battle over domestic partnerships and marriage equality in 2006. *Journal of GLBT Family Studies,* 4(1), 117–124.

Briggs, G. G., Freeman, R. K., & Yaffe, S. J., (2005). *Drugs in pregnancy and lactation* (7th edition). Philadelphia: Lippincott.

Brindis, C. D., Barenbaum, M., Sanchez-Flores, H., McCarter, V., & Chand, R. (2005). Let's hear it for the guys: California's male involvement program. *International Journal of Men's Health,* 4(1), 29–53.

Broderick, C. B. (1993). *Understanding family process: The basics of family systems theory.* Thousand Oaks, CA: Sage Publications.

Brodzinsky, D. M., & Pinderhughes, E. (2002). Parenting and child development in adoptive families. In. M. H. Bornstein (Ed.), *Handbook of parenting: Children and parenting* Vol. 1 (2nd ed., pp. 279–311). Mahwah, NJ: Lawrence Erlbaum Associates.

Bronfenbrenner, U. (1979). *The ecology of human development.* Cambridge, MA: Harvard University Press.

Bronfenbrenner, U. (1985). The parent-child relationship and our changing society. In L. E. Arnold (Ed.), *Parents, children, and change.* Lexington, MA: Lexington Books.

Bronfenbrenner, U. (1986). Ecology of the family as a context for human development: Research perspectives. *Developmental Psychology,* 22, 723–742.

Bronfenbrenner, U. (1993). Ecological systems theory. In R. H. Wozniak (Ed.), *Development in context* (pp. 44–78). Hillsdale, NJ: Erlbaum.

Brookey, R. A. (2000). Saints or sinners: Sociobiological theories of male homosexuality. *International Journal of Sexuality & Gender Studies,* 5, 37–58.

Brophy-Herb, H. E., & Honig, A. S. (1999). Quality of adolescent mother-infant interactions and clinical determinations of risk status. *Early Child Development & Care,* 152, 17–26.

Brown, H. N., Saunders, R. B., & Dick, M. J. (1999). Preventing secondary pregnancy in adolescents: A model program. *Health Care for Women International,* 20, 5–15.

Brown, R., & Perlesz, A. (2007). Not the "other" mother: How language constructs lesbian co-parenting relationships. *Journal of GLBT Family Studies,* 3(4), 267–308.

Brown, S. L. (2000). Union transitions among co-habitors: The significance of relationship assessments and expectations. *Journal of Marriage and the Family,* 63, 833–846.

Bruckner, H., & Bearman, P. S. (2005). After the promise: the STI consequences of adolescent virginity pledges. *Journal of Adolescent Health,* 36(4), 271–278.

Bryson, K., & Casper, L. M. (1999). Coresident grandparents and grandchildren. *Current Population Reports, P-23-198.* Washington, DC: U.S. Government Printing Office.

Bubolz, M. M., & Sontag, S. (1993). Human ecology theory. In P. Boss, W. J. Doherty, R. LaRossa, W. R. Schumm, & S. K. Steinmetz (Eds.), *Sourcebook of family theories and methods: A contextual approach* (pp. 419–448). New York: Plenum Press.

Budig, M. J., & England, P. (2001). The wage penalty for motherhood. *America Sociological Review,* 66(2), 204–226.

Bulterys, M. (2001). What's new in perinatal research? U.S. and international update from http://www.cdc.gov/hiv/PROJECTS/perinatal/materials/ps2_Bulterys.ppt 08-04-01.

Bundy, D. A. P., Shaeffer, S., Jukes, M., Beegle, A., Drake, L., Saunghee, F., et al. (2006). School based health and nutrition programs. In D. T. Jamison et al. (Eds.). *Disease control priorities in developing countries* (2nd ed., pp. 1091–1108). New York: Oxford University Press.

Bunting, L., & McAuley, C. (2004). Research Review: Teenage pregnancy and parenthood: The role of fathers. *Child & Family Social Work, 9*(3), 295–303.

Burgess, E. (1926). The family as a unity of interacting personalities. *Family, 7*, 3–9.

Burns, D. (1999). *Feeling good: The new mood therapy*. New York: Morrow/Avon.

Buxton, A. P. (1994). *The other side of the closet: The coming-out crisis for straight spouses and families*. New York: Wiley.

Buxton, A. P. (1999). The best interest of children of gay and lesbian parents. In R. M Galatzer-Levy & L. Kraus (Eds.), *The scientific basis of child custody decisions* (pp. 319–356). Chicago: University of Chicago Press.

Buxton, A. P. (2004). Paths and pitfalls: How heterosexual spouses cope when their husbands or wives come out. *Journal of Couple and Relationship Therapy, 3*(2/3), 95–110.

Buxton, A. P. (2005). A family matter: When a spouse comes out as gay, lesbian, or bisexual. *Journal of GLBT Family Studies, 1*(2), 49–70.

Buxton, A. P. (2006). Healing an invisible minority: How the Straight Spouse Network has become the prime source of support for those in mixed-orientation marriages. *Journal of GLBT Family Studies, 2*(3/4), 49–70.

Byrd, M. M., & Garwick, A. W. (2006). Family identity: Black-white interracial family health experience. *Journal of Family Nursing, 12*(1), 22–37.

Cabrera, N. J. (2003). In their own voices: How men become fathers. *Human Development, 46*, 250–258.

Caldwell, M. (2004). *Adoption: Using technology and time-tested techniques to expedite a safe, successful adoption: Your step-by-step guide*. Nevada City, CA: American Carriage House Publishing.

Campbell, D. A., Lake, M. F., Falk, M., & Backstrand, J. R. (2006). A randomized control trial of continuous support in labor by a lay doula. *Journal of Obstetric, Gynecologic, & Neonatal Nursing, 35*(4), 456–464.

Cancian, F. M., & Oliker, S. J. (2000). *Caring and gender*. Walnut Creek, CA: Alta/Mira.

Caplan, N. J., Whitmore, J. K., & Choy, M. H. (Eds.). (1989). Culture values, family life, and opportunity. In *The boat people and achievement in America: A study of family life, hard work, and cultural values* (pp. 94–127). Ann Arbor, MI: University of Michigan Press.

Capps, R., Fix, M., & Reardon-Anderson, J. (2003). *Children of immigrants show slight reductions in poverty, hardship*. Washington, DC: The Urban Institute.

Carlson, B. E. (1986). Children's beliefs about punishment. *American Journal of Orthopsychiatry, 56*, 308–312.

Carlson, C., & Trapani, J. N. (2006). Single parenting and stepparenting. In G. G. Bear & K. M. Minke (Eds.), *Children's needs III: Development, prevention, and intervention* (pp. 783–797). Washington, DC: National Association of School Psychologists.

Cauthen, K. C., & Fass, S. (2007). Measuring income and poverty in the United States. Retrieved July 9, 2007, from http://www.nccp.org/publications/pub_707.html.

Center for Health and Health Care in Schools. (2005). *Childhood overweight: What the research tells us*. Washington, DC: George Washington University Medical Center. Retrieved August 26, 2007 from http://www.healthinschools.org/sh/obesityfs.pdf.

Centers for Disease Control and Prevention. (2002). *School health policies and program study 2000. Fact sheet: Physical education and activity*. Retrieved August 25, 2007, from http://www.cdc.gov/HealthyYouth/shpps/factsheets/pdf/pe.pdf.

Centers for Disease Control and Prevention. (2003). Physical activity levels among children aged 9-13 years-United States, 2002. *MMWR, 52*(33), 785-788. Retrieved August 26, 2007, from http://www.cdc.gov/mmwr/preview/mmwrhtml/mm5233a1.htm.

Centers for Disease Control and Prevention. (2004). Blood mercury levels in young children and childbearing aged women—United States: 1999–2002. *Morbidity and Mortality Weekly Report, 53*(43), 1018–1020.

Centers for Disease Control and Prevention. (2006). *Sexually transmitted disease surveillance, 2005*. Atlanta, GA: U.S. Department of Health and Human Services.

Centers for Disease Control and Prevention. (2007). Child and adolescent mortality by cause: US/state, 2002–2004. Retrieved August 31, 2007, from http://209.217.72.34/HDAA/TableViewer/summary.aspx.

Centers for Disease Control and Prevention. (2008). 2008 National STD Prevention Conference. Retrieved March 12, 2008, from http://www.cdc.gov/STDConference/2008/media/summaries-11march2008.htm.

Chabot, J. M., & Ames, B. D. (2004). "It wasn't 'let's get pregnant and go do it'": Decision making in lesbian couples planning motherhood via donor insemination. *Family Relations, 53*, 348–356.

Chakraborty, R. (2002). Better late than never. *Femina, 43*, 94–96.

Chamberlain, P., & Patterson, G. R. (1995). Discipline and child compliance in parenting. In M. H. Bornstein (Ed.), *Handbook of parenting, Vol. 4: Applied and practical parenting* (pp. 205–225). Hillsdale, NJ: Lawrence Erlbaum.

Cheal, D. (2007). *Families in today's world*. New York: Routledge.

Cherlin, A. (2004). The deinstitutionalization of marriage. *Journal of Marriage and the Family, 66*, 848–861.

Cherlin, A. (2005). American marriage in the early twenty-first century. *Future of Children, 15*(2), 33–55.

Cherlin, A., & Furstenberg, F. F. (1986). *The new American grandparent*. New York, NY: Basic Books.

Chiang, Y.-Y., & Finley, G. E. (2001). Is adoptee status a risk or protective factor for the experience of adoptive parental divorce? Paper presented at the 63rd Annual Conference of the National Council on Family Relations, Rochester, NY.

Children's Bureau. (2006). *The AFCARS report: Preliminary fiscal year 2005 estimates as of September 2006 (13)*. Washington, DC: U.S. Department of Health and Human Services.

Children's Bureau. (2007). *Child maltreatment 2002: Summary of key findings*. Washington, DC: Author.

Children's Defense Fund. (1996). *The state of America's children yearbook, 1996*. Washington, DC: Author.

Children's Defense Fund. (2003). *The state of children in America's union 2002*. Washington, DC: Author.

Children's Defense Fund. (2004). *The state of America's children: 2004*. Washington, DC: Author.

Chinnaiya, A., Venkat, A., Dawn, C., Chee, W. Y., Choo, K. B., Gole, L. A., et al. (1998). Intrahepatic vein fetal blood sampling: Current role in prenatal diagnosis. *Journal of Obstetrics & Gynaecology Research, 24*, 239–246.

Chrisp, J. (2001). That four letter word—sons: Lesbian mothers and adolescent sons. *Journal of Lesbian Studies, 5*, 195–209.

Christian, A. (2005). Contesting the myth of the wicked stepmother: Narrative analysis of an online stepfamily support group.

Western Journal of Communication, 69(1), 27–47.

Christensen, F. B., & Smith, T. A. (2002). What is happening to satisfaction and quality of relationships between step/grandparents and step/grandchildren? *Journal of Divorce & Remarriage, 37*, 117–133.

Ciano-Boyce, C., & Shelley-Sireci, L. (2002). Who is mommy tonight? Lesbian parenting issues. *Journal of Homosexuality, 43*, 1–13.

Cicero, S., Curcio, P. Papageorghiou, A., Sonek, J., & Nicholaides, K. (2001). Absence of nasal bone in fetuses with trisomy 21 at 11–14 weeks of gestation: An observational study. *Lancet, 358*, 1665–1667.

Cicirelli, V. G. (2000). An examination of the trajectory of the adult child's caregiving for an elderly parent. *Family Relations, 49*(2), 169–175.

Clarke, J. I., & Dawson, C. (1998). *Growing up again: Parenting ourselves, parenting our children* (2nd ed.). Center City, MN: Hazelden Information and Educational Services.

Clarke, V. (2002). Resistance and normalization in the construction of lesbian and gay families: A discursive analysis. In A. Coyle & C. Kitzinger (Eds.), *Lesbian and gay psychology: New perspectives* (pp. 98–116). Malden, MA: Blackwell Publishers.

Clarke, V. (2007). Men not included? A critical psychology analysis of lesbian families and male influence in child rearing. *Journal of GLBT Family Studies, 3*(4), 309–350.

Clarke, V., Kitzinger, C., & Potter, J. (2004). 'Kids are just cruel anyway': Lesbian and gay parents' talk about homophobic bullying. *British Journal of Social Psychology, 43*(4), 531–550.

Clarke-Stewart, A., & Brentano, C. (2007). Divorce: Causes and consequences. New Haven, CT: Yale University Press.

Claxton-Oldfield, S., O'Neill, S., Thomson, C., & Gallant, B. (2005). Multiple stereotypes of stepfathers. *Journal of Divorce & Remarriage, 44*(1–2), 165–176.

Coggins, T. E., Timler, G. R., & Olswang, L. B. (2007). A state of double jeopardy: Impact of prenatal alcohol exposure and adverse environments on the social communicative abilities of school-age children with fetal alcohol spectrum disorder. *Language, Speech, and Hearing Services in Schools, 38*(2), 117–127.

Cohen, S. (2007). A long and winding road: Getting the HPV vaccine to women in the developing world. *Guttmacher Policy Review, 10*, Whole Number 3.

Coll, B. (1991). Consider the children: Is parenthood being devalued? *Psychological Record, 41*, 303–314.

Collins, M. E. (2000). Impact of welfare reform on teenage parent recipients: An analysis of two cohorts. *American Journal of Orthopsychiatry, 70*, 135–140.

Collins, W. A., Maccoby, E. E., Steinberg, L., Hetherington, E. M., & Bornstein, M. H. (2000). Contemporary research in parenting: The case for nature and nurture. *American Psychologist, 55*, 218–232.

Coltrane, S. (1990). Birth timing and the division of labor in dual-earner families: Exploratory findings and suggestions for further research. *Journal of Family Issues, 11*, 157–181.

Committee on Obstetric Practice. (2002). ACOG committee opinion: Exercise during pregnancy and the postpartum period. *International Journal of Gynaecology & Obstetrics, 77*, 79–81.

Connolly, C. M. (2005). A process of change: The intersection of the GLBT individual and their family of origin. *Journal of GLBT Family Studies. 1*(1), 5–20.

Connor, J. M., & Dewey, J. E. (2003). Reproductive health. In M. H. Bornstein & L. Davidson (Eds.), *Well-being: Positive development across the life course: Crosscurrents in contemporary psychology* (pp. 99–107). Mahwah, NJ: Lawrence Erlbaum.

Connor, K. A. (2000). *Continuing to care: Older Americans and their families*. New York: Falmer.

Consumer Product Safety Commission (2004). Think toy safety Retrieved from http://www.cpsc.gov/cpscpub/pubs/281.pdf.

Conway, M. B., Christensen, T. M., & Herlihy, B. (2003). Adult children of divorce and intimate relationships: Implications for counseling. *Family Journal, 11*, 364–373.

Cook, A. S., & Oltjenbruns, K. A. (1998). *Dying and grieving: Lifespan and family perspectives*. New York: Harcourt Trade Publishers.

Coontz, S. (1992). *The way we never were: American families and the nostalgia trap*. New York: Basic Books.

Coontz, S. (1998). *The way we really are: Coming to terms with America's changing families*. New York: Basic Books.

Coontz, S. (2006). *Marriage, a history: How love conquered marriage*. New York: Penquin Group (USA).

Correia, A., & Rubin, J. (2002). *Housing and battered women*. Washington, DC: Department of Justice, Office of Violence Against Women.

Covington, S., & Beckett, L. (1988). *Leaving the enchanted forest: The path from relationship addiction to intimacy*. San Francisco: Harper & Row.

Cowan, C. P., Cowan, P. A., & Pruett, M. K. (2007). An approach to preventing coparenting conflict and divorce in low-income families: Strengthening couple relationships and fostering fathers' involvement. *Family Process, 46*(1), 109–121.

Cox, F. D. (2001). *Human intimacy: Marriage, the family, and its meaning*. Belmont, CA: Brooks/Cole.

Cox, M. E., Orme, J. G., & Rhodes, K. W. (2003). Willingness to foster children with emotional or behavioral problems. *Journal of Social Service Research, 29*, 23–51.

Cox, S. M., Werner, C. L., Gilstrap, L. C., & Cunningham, G. F. (2001). *Williams obstetrics* (21st ed.). New York: McGraw-Hill.

Crea, T. M., Barth, R. P., & Chintapalli, L. K. (2007). Home study methods for evaluating prospective resource families: History, current challenges, and promising approaches. *Child Welfare Journal, 86*(2), 141–159.

Crimmins, E. M. (2001). Americans living longer, not necessarily healthier lives. *Population Today, February/March, 1*, 8.

Crouter, A., MacDermid, S., McHale, S., & Perry-Jenkins, M. (1990). Parental monitoring and perceptions of children's school performance and conducting dual- and single-earner families. *Developmental Psychology, 26*, 649–657.

Crouter, A. C., & Manke, B. (1997). Development of a typology of dual-earner families: A window into differences between and within families in relationships, roles, and activities. *Journal of Family Psychology, 11*(1), 62–75.

Cullen, J., & Carr, A. (1999). Codependency: An empirical study from a systemic perspective. *Contemporary Family Therapy, 21*, 505–525.

Current-Juretschko, L., & Bigner, J. J. (2005). An exploratory investigation of gay stepfathers' perceptions of their role. *Journal of GLBT Family Studies, 1*(4), 1–20.

Daly, D. (2003). Trust me—I'm a midwife. *Practising Midwife, 6*, 32–33.

Damewood, M. D. (2001). Ethical implications of a new application of preimplantation diagnosis. *Journal of the American Medical Association, 285,* 3143–3144.

Daniluk, J. C., & Hurtig-Mitchell, J. (2003). Themes of hope and healing: Infertile couples' experiences of adoption. *Journal of Counseling & Development, 81*(4), 389–399.

D'Augelli, A. R. (2005). Stress and adaptation among families of lesbian, gay, and bisexual youth: Research challenges. *Journal of GLBT Family Studies, 1*(2), 115–136.

Davidson, J. K., & Moore, N. B. (1992). *Marriage and family.* Dubuque, IA: W. C. Brown.

Davies, C., & Williams, D. (2002). *The grandparent study 2002.* Washington, DC: American Association of Retired Persons.

Day, R. D., Peterson, G. W., & McCracken, C. (1998). Predicting spanking of younger and older children by mothers and fathers. *Journal of Marriage and the Family, 60,* 79–94.

deAnda, D. (2006). Baby Think It Over: Evaluation of an infant simulation intervention for adolescent pregnancy prevention. *Health & Social Work, 31*(1), 26–35.

DeBlander, T., & DeBlander, D. (2004). *Parents by choice: An insightful guide exploring adoption to build your family.* Lincoln, NE: iUniverse.

DeCaro, J. A., & Worthman, C. M. (2007). Cultural models, parenting behavior, and young child experience in working American families. *Parenting: Science and Practice, 7*(2), 177–203.

deLissovoy, V. (1973a). Child care by adolescent parents. *Children Today, 2,* 22–25.

deLissovoy, V. (1973b). High school marriages: A longitudinal study. *Journal of Marriage and the Family, 35,* 245–255.

Dembo, M. H., Switzer, M., & Lauritzen, P. (1985). An evaluation of group parent education: Behavioral, PET, and Adlerian programs. *Review of Educational Research, 55,* 155–200.

DeNavas-Walt, C., Proctor, B. D., & Lee, C. H. (2006). Income, poverty, and health insurance coverage in the United States: 2005. *Current Population Reports, P60-231.* Washington, DC: U.S. Bureau of the Census.

DeNavas-Walt, C., Proctor, B. D., & Smith, J. (2007). Income, poverty, and health insurance coverage in the United States: 2006. *Current Population Reports, P-60*(233). Washington, DC: U.S. Census Bureau.

Derbort, J. J. (2006). A cultural look at parenting. In K. H Rubin & O. B. Chung (Eds.), *Parenting beliefs, behaviors, and parent-child relations: A cross-cultural perspective* (pp. 25–40). New York: Psychology Press.

Detzner, D. F., & Xiong, B. (1999). Southeast Asian families straddle two worlds. *NCFR Report, June,* 14–15.

Dickerson, J. L., & Allen, M. (2006). *The basics of adoption: A guide for building families in the U.S. and Canada.* Westport, CT: Praeger Publishers/Greenwood Publishing Group.

Didion, J., & Gatzke, H. (2004). The Baby Think It Over-super™ experience to prevent teen pregnancy: A post-intervention evaluation. *Public Health Nursing, 21*(4), 331–337.

Dinkmeyer, D. (1979). A comprehensive and systematic approach to parent education. *Journal of Family Therapy, 7,* 46–50.

Dinkmeyer, D., & Driekurs, R. (2000). *Encouraging children to learn.* New York: Brunner/Mazel.

Dinkmeyer, D., & McKay, G. D. (1981). *Parents' handbook: Systematic training for effective parenting.* Circle Pines, MN: American Guidance Service.

Dipietro, J. A., Millet, S., Costigan, K. A., Gurewitsch, E., & Caulfield, L. E. (2003). Psychosocial influences on weight gain attitudes and behaviors during pregnancy. *Journal of the American Dietetic Association, 103,* 1314–1319.

Dobbs, J., Doctoroff, G. L., Fisher, P. H., & Arnold, D. H. (2006). The association between preschool children's socio-emotional functioning and their mathematical skills. *Journal of Applied Developmental Psychology, 27*(2), 97–108.

Dode, L. (2004). *A history of homosexuality.* Victoria, BC, Canada: Trafford.

Dodge, K. A., McLoyd, V. C., & Lansford, J. E. (2005). The cultural context of physically disciplining children. In V. C. McLoyd, N, E. Hill, & K. A. Dodge (Eds.), *African American family life: Ecological and cultural diversity* (pp. 245–263). New York: Guilford Press.

Doherty, W. J., Kouneski, E. F., & Erickson, M. F. (1998). Responsible fathering: An overview and conceptual framework. *Journal of Marriage and the Family, 60,* 277–292.

Doherty, W. J., Kouneski, E. F., & Erickson, M. F. (2000). We are all responsible for responsible fathering: A response to Walker and McGraw. *Journal of Marriage and the Family, 62,* 570–574.

Dolbin-MacNab, M. L. (2006). Just like raising your own? Grandmothers' perceptions of parenting a second time around. *Family Relations, 55*(5), 564–575.

Dore, M. M., & Lee, J. M. (1999). The role of parent training with abusive and neglectful parents. *Family Relations, 48,* 313–325.

Downs, B. (2003). Fertility of American women: June 2002. *Current Population Reports, P20-548.* Washington, DC: U.S. Census Bureau.

Driekurs, R. (1950). *The challenge of parenthood* (Rev. ed.). New York: Duell, Sloan, & Pearce.

Drum Major Institute for Public Policy. (2006). *Saving our middle class.* New York: Author.

Dumaret, A.-C., Coppel-Batsch, M., & Couraud, S. (1997). Adult outcome of children reared for long-term periods in foster families. *Child Abuse & Neglect, 21,* 911–927.

Dundas, S., & Kaufman, M. (2000). The Toronto lesbian family study. *Journal of Homosexuality, 40,* 65–79.

Duvall, E. M. (1988). Family development's first forty years. *Family Relations, 37,* 127–134.

Duvall, E. M., & Miller, B. C. (1985). *Marriage and family development* (6th ed.). New York: Harper & Row.

Dye, B. (2005). Fertility of American women: June 2004. Current Population Reports, P20-555. Washington, DC: U.S. Census Bureau.

Dyer, E. (1963). Parenthood as crisis: A restudy. *Journal of Marriage and the Family, 25,* 196–201.

Edgar, T. (1985). The little house out back: Key to encouragement. *Individual Psychology, 41,* 483–488.

Edelstein, R. S., Alexander, K. W., Shaver, P. R., Schaaf, J. M., Quas, J. A., Lovas, G. S., & Goodman, G. S. (2004). Adult attachment style and parental responsiveness during a stressful event. *Attachment and Human Development, 6,* 31–52.

Edwards, O. W., & Daire, A. P. (2006). School-aged children raised by grandparents: Problems and solutions. *Journal of Instructional Psychology, 33*(2), 113–119.

Ehrensaft, D. (2005). *Mommies, daddies, donors, surrogates: Answering tough questions and building stronger families.* New York: Guilford Press.

Eichberg, R. (1990). *Coming out: An act of love.* New York: Plume.

Elder, G. (1962). Structural variations in the child rearing relationship. *Sociometry, 25,* 233–245.

Eldridge, H. (1997). *Therapist guide for maintaining change: Relapse prevention for adult male perpetrators of child sexual abuse.* Thousand Oaks, CA: Sage.

Elgar, K., & Chester, A. (2007). The mental health implications of maternal employment: Working versus at-home mothering identities. *Australian e-Journal for the Advancement of Mental Health), 6*(1), 1–9.

Elkin, F., & Handel, G. (1989). *The child and society: The process of socialization* (5th ed.). New York: Random House.

Elkind, D. (1974). *Child development and education.* New York: Oxford University Press.

Ellerman, C. R. (2007). Influences on the mental health of children placed in foster care. *Family & Community Health, 30*(2,Suppl), S23–S32.

Engel, B. (2000). *Families in recovery: Healing the damage of childhood sexual abuse.* New York: McGraw-Hill.

Erel, O., Oberman, Y., & Yirmiya, N. (2000). Maternal versus nonmaternal care and seven domains of children's development. *Psychological Bulletin, 126,* 727–747.

Erera, P. I., & Fredriksen, K. (1999). Lesbian stepfamilies: A unique family structure. *Families in Society, 80,* 263–270.

Erich, S., Leung, P., Kindle, P. (2005). A comparative analysis of adoptive family functioning with gay, lesbian, and heterosexual parents and their children. *Journal of GLBT Family Studies, 1*(4), 43–60.

Erikson, E. (1950). *Childhood and society.* New York: Norton.

Erikson, E. (1964). *Insight and responsibility.* New York: Norton.

Erikson, E. (1982). *The life cycle completed.* New York: Norton.

Erikson, E., Erikson, J., & Kivnick, H. (1986). *Vital involvement in old age.* New York: Norton.

Eshleman, L. (2004). *Becoming a family: Promoting healthy attachments with your adopted child.* Lanham, MD: Taylor.

Evans, J. M., & Aaronson, R. (2005). *The whole pregnancy handbook.* New York: Penguin Group.

Everett, C. A., & Everett, S. V. (2000). Single-parent families: Dynamics and treatment issues. In W. C. Nichols, M. A. Pace-Nichols, D. S. Becvar, & A. Y. Napier (Eds.), *Handbook of family development and intervention* (pp. 323–340). New York: Wiley.

Eyer, D. (1992). *Maternal-infant bondings: A scientific fiction.* New Haven, CT: Yale University Press.

Fagan, J., Bernd, L., & Whiteman, V. (2007). Adolescent fathers' parenting stress, social support, and involvement with infants. *Journal of Research on Adolescence, 17*(1), 1–22.

Fagan, J., Schmitz, M. F., & Lloyd, J. J. (2007). The relationship between adolescent and young fathers' capital and marital plans of couples expecting a baby. *Family Relations, 56*(3), 231–243.

Fagot, B. I., Pears, K. C., Capaldi, D. M., Crosby, L., & Leve, C. S. (1998). Becoming an adolescent father: Precursors and parenting. *Developmental Psychology, 34,* 1209–1219.

Fairchild, B., & Hayward, N. (1989). *Now that you know: What every parent should know about homosexuality* (Updated ed.). New York: Harcourt Brace Javonovich.

Federal Interagency Forum on Child and Family Statistics (2003). *America's children: Key national indicators of well-being: 2003.* Washington, DC: U.S. Government Printing Office.

Federal Interagency Forum on Child and Family Statistics. (2006). *America's children in brief: Key national indicators of well-being, 2006.* Washington, DC: Author.

Federal Interagency Forum on Child and Family Statistics. (2007). *America's children: Key national indicators of well-being, 2007.* Washington, DC: U.S. Government Printing Office.

Feindler, E. L., Rathus, J. H., & Silver, L. B. (2003). *Assessment of family violence: A handbook for researchers and practitioners.* Washington, DC: American Psychological Association.

Feldman, R., Sussman, A. L., & Zigler, E. (2004). Parental leave and work adaptation at the transition to parenthood: Individual, marital, and social correlates. *Journal of Applied Developmental Psychology, 25*(4), 459–479.

Fenwick, J., Gamble, J., & Mawson, J. (2003). Women's experiences of Caesarean section and vaginal birth after Caesarian: A birth rites initiative. *International Journal of Nursing Practice, 9,* 10–17.

Fergusson, D. M., & Woodward, L. J. (2000). Teenage pregnancy and female educational underachievement: A prospective study of a New Zealand birth cohort. *Journal of Marriage and the Family, 62,* 147–161.

Ferrara, F. F. (2001). *Childhood sexual abuse: Developmental effects across the lifespan.* Belmont, CA: Wadsworth.

Fields, J. (2003). Children's living arrangements and characteristics: March 2002. *Current Population Reports, P20-547.* Washington, DC: U.S. Census Bureau.

First, J. A., & Way, W. L. (1995). Parent education outcomes: Insights into transformational learning. *Family Relations, 44,* 104–109.

Fix, M., Zimmerman, W., & Passel, J. S. (2001). *The integration of immigrant families in the United States.* Washington, DC: The Urban Institute.

Flavell, J. H. (1986). The development of children's knowledge about the appearance-reality distinction. *American Psychologist, 41,* 418–426.

Flavell, J. H., Miller, P. H., & Miller, S. A. (2001). *Cognitive development.* Upper Saddle River, NJ: Prentice Hall.

Fleming, A. S., Ruble, D. N., Flett, G. L., & Shaul, D. L. (1988). Postpartum adjustment of first-time mothers: Relations between mood, maternal attitudes, and motherinfant interactions. *Developmental Psychology, 24,* 71–81.

Flora, S. R. (2004). *The power of reinforcement.* New York: State University of New York Press.

Florsheim, P., & Ngu, L. Q. (2006). Fatherhood as a transformative process: Unexpected successes among high risk fathers. In L. Kowaleski-Jones & N. H. Wolfinger (Eds.), *Fragile families and the marriage agenda* (pp. 211–232). New York: Springer Science + Business Media.

Florsheim, P., & Smith, A. (2005). Expectant adolescent couples' relations and subsequent parenting behavior. *Infant Mental Health Journal, 26*(6), 533–548.

Flowers, R. B. (2000). *Domestic crimes, family violence, and child abuse: A study of contemporary American society.* Jefferson, NC: McFarland.

Floyd, N. M. (1985). "Pick on somebody your own size": Controlling victimization. *Printer, 29,* 9–17.

Forrester, M. B., & Merz, R. D. (2007). Risk of selected birth defects with prenatal illicit drug use, Hawaii, 1986–2002. *Journal of Toxicology & Environmental Health Part A, 70*(1), 7–18.

Forward, S. (1989). *Toxic parents: Overcoming their hurtful legacy and reclaiming your life*. New York: Bantam Books.

Fossum, M. A., & Mason, M. J. (1986). *Facing shame: Families in recovery*. New York: Norton.

Fox, G. L., Bruce, C., & Combs-Orme, T. (2000). Parenting expectations and concerns of fathers and mothers of newborn infants. *Family Relations, 49*, 123–131.

Framo, J. L., Weber, T. T., & Levine, F. B. (2003). *Coming home again: A family-of-origin consultation*. Philadelphia: Brunner-Routledge.

Francis-Connolly, E. (2003). Constructing parenthood: Portrayals of motherhood and fatherhood in popular American magazines. *Journal of the Association for Research on Mothering, 5*, 179–185.

Frank, D. A., Augustyn, M., Knight, W. G., Pell, T., & Zuckerman, B. (2001). Growth, development, and behavior in early childhood following prenatal cocaine exposure. *Journal of the American Medical Association, 285*, 1613–1625.

Franke-Clark, M. J. (2003). The father-daughter relationship and its effect on early sexual activity. *Dissertation Abstracts International: Section B: The Sciences & Engineering, 63 (8-B)*, 3957. Ann Arbor, MI: University Microfilms International.

Friel, J., & Friel, L. (1988). *Adult children: The secret of dysfunctional families*. Deerfield Beach, FL: Health Communications.

Fromm, E. (1970). *The art of loving*. New York: Bantam.

Fronczek, P. (2005). *Income, earnings, and poverty from the 2004 American Community Survey*. Washington, DC: U.S. Bureau of the Census.

Fuller, J. A., & Warner, R. M. (2000). Family stressors as predictors of codependency. *Genetic, Social, & General Psychology Monographs, 126*, 5–22.

Funderberg, F. F. (1994). *Black, white, and other*. New York: Morrow.

Furstenberg, F. F., Jr., Levine, J. A., & Brooks-Gunn, J. (1990). The children of teenage mothers: Patterns of early child-bearing in two generations. *Family Planning Perspectives, 22*, 54–61.

Gabbe, S. G., Niebyl, J. R., & Simpson, J. L. (2003). *Obstetrics: Normal and problem pregnancies* (4th ed.). Philadelphia: Elsevier.

Gallimore, T. (2002). Unresolved trauma: Fuel of the cycle of violence and terrorism. In C. E. Stout (Ed), *The psychology of terrorism: Clinical aspects and responses* (Vol. II, pp. 143–164). Westport, CT: Praeger/Greenwood.

Ganong, L., Coleman, M., & Hans, J. (2006). Divorce as prelude to stepfamily living and the consequences of redivorce. In M. A. Fine & J. H. Harvey (Eds.), *Handbook of divorce and relationship dissolution* (pp. 409–434). Mahwah, NJ: Lawrence Erlbaum Associates.

Garbarino, J., Hammond, W. R., Mercy, J., & Yung, B. R. (2004). Community violence and children: Preventing exposure and reducing harm. In K. I. Maton & C. J. Schellenbach (Eds.), *Investing in children, youth, families, and communities: Strengths-based research and policy* (pp. 303–320). Washington, DC: American Psychological Association.

Gelles, R. J., & Cornell, C. P. (1997). *Intimate violence in families* (3rd ed.). Thousand Oaks, CA: Sage.

Gelles, R. J., Loseke, D. R., & Cavanaugh, M. M. (2004). *Current controversies on family violence*. Thousand Oaks, CA: Sage.

George, C., & Solomon, J. (1999). The development of caregiving: A comparison of attachment theory and psychoanalytic approaches to mothering. *Psychoanalytic Inquiry, 19*(4), 618–646.

Gerlach, P. (2003). *Build a co-parenting team: After divorce or remarriage*. Philadelphia, PA: Xlibris Corporation.

Gerson, K. (1993). *No man's land: Men's changing commitments to family and work*. New York, NY: Basic Books.

Glenn, N. D. (1990). Quantitative research on marital quality in the 1980s: A critical review. *Journal of Marriage and the Family, 52*, 818–831.

Gibbs, J. T. (2003). Biracial and bicultural children and adolescents. In J. T. Gibbs & L. N. Huang (Eds.), *Children of color: Psychological interventions with culturally diverse youth* (pp. 145–182). San Francisco, CA: Jossey-Bass.

Gielen, U. P., & Roopnarine, J. L. (2004). *Childhood and adolescence*. Westport, CT: Praeger.

Gilliam, M. L. (2007). The role of Parents and partners in the pregnancy behaviors of young Latinas. *Hispanic Journal of Behavioral Sciences, 29*(1), 50–67.

Ginott, H. (1965). *Between parent and child*. New York: Macmillan.

Ginsburg, G. S., & Bronstein, P. (1993). Family factors related to children's intrinsic/extrinsic motivational orientation and academic performance. *Child Development, 64*, 1461–1474.

Giordano, P. C., Cernkovich, S. A., & DeMaris, A. (1993). The family and peer relations of black adolescents. *Journal of Marriage and the Family, 55*, 277–287.

Glenn, H. S., Erwin, C., & Nelen, J. (2000). *Positive discipline for your stepfamily: Nurturing harmony, respect, unity, and joy in your new family*. New York, NY: Crown Publishing Group.

Glover, G. (2001). Parenting in Native American families. In N. B. Webb (Ed.), *Culturally diverse parent-child and family relationships: A guide for social workers and other practitioners* (pp. 205–231). New York: Columbia University Press.

Gnaulati, E., & Heine, B. J. (2001). Separation-individuation in late adolescence: An investigation of gender and ethnic differences. *Journal of Psychology, 135*, 59–70.

Goldberg, A. E. (2006). The transition to parenthood for lesbian couples. *Journal of GLBT Family Studies, 2*(1), 13–42.

Goldberg, A. E., & Perry-Jenkins, M. (2004). Division of labor and working-class women's well-being across the transition to parenthood. *Journal of Family Psychology, 18*(1), 225–236.

Goldberg, L., Brinkley, G., & Kukar, J. (2005). *Your child's first journey: A guide to prepared birth from pregnancy to parenthood*. Garden City Park, NY: Square One Publishers.

Golding, K. (2003). Helping foster careers, helping children: using attachment theory to guide practice. *Adoption and Fostering, 27*, 64–73.

Goldschneider, F. K., & Goldschneider, C. (1998). The effects of childhood family structure on leaving and returning home. *Journal of Marriage and the Family, 60*, 745–756.

Golombok, S. (1999). New family forms: Children raised in solo mother families, lesbian mother families, and in families created by assisted reproduction. In L. Balter & C. S. Tamis-LeMonda (Eds.), *Child psychology: A handbook of contemporary issues* (pp. 429–446). Philadelphia: Psychology Press/Taylor & Francis.

Golombok, S., Cook, R., Bish, A., & Murray, C. (1995). Families created by the new reproductive technologies: Quality of parenting and emotional development of children. *Child Development, 66*, 285–296.

Golombok, S., & MacCallum, F. (2003). Practitioner review: Outcomes for parents and children following non-traditional conception: What do clinicians need to know? *Journal of Child Psychology & Psychiatry & Allied Disciplines, 44,* 303–315.

Golombok, S., Murray, C., Brinsden, P., & Abdalla, H. (2003). Social versus biological parenting: Family functioning and the socioemotional development of children conceived by egg or sperm donation. In M. E. Hertzig & E. A. Farber (Eds.), *Annual progress in child psychiatry and child development: 2000–2001* (pp. 155–175). New York: Brunner-Routledge.

Golombok, S., Perry, B., Burston, A., Murray, C., Mooney-Somers, J., Stevens, M., & Golding, J. (2003). Children with lesbian parents: A community study. *Developmental Psychology, 39,* 20–33.

Goode, W. J. (1993). *A theory of role strain.* New York: Irvington.

Goodrich, S. M. (1990). *Boundaries: Development of self within a family system.* Dissertation Abstracts International, 50, 4218.

Gordon, S. (2000). Pregnancy and birth: Mother's helper. *Parents, 75,* 157.

Gordon, S. (2004). *When living hurts: For teenagers, young adults, their parents, leaders, and counselors.* New York, NY: U A H C Press.

Gordon, T. (1975/2000). *Parent effectiveness training: The tested way to raise responsible children.* New York, NY: Wyden.

Gorman, J. C. (1988). Parenting attitudes and practices of immigrant Chinese mothers of adolescents. *Family Relations, 47,* 73–80.

Gottlieb, A. R. (2003). *Sons talk about their gay fathers: Life curves.* New York: Harrington Park Press.

Gottman, J. M., Levenson, R. W., Gross, J., Frederickson, B. L., McCoy, K., Rosenthal, L., Ruef, A., & Yoshimoto, D. (2003). Correlates of gay and lesbian couples' relationship satisfaction and relationship dissolution. *Journal of Homosexuality, 45,* 23–43.

Gowen, G. W., & Nebrig, J. B. (2002). *Enhancing early emotional development: Guiding parents of young children.* Baltimore, MD: Brookes.

Grace, D. M. (2003). Should adopted children be granted access to the identity of their birth parents? A psychological perspective. *Australian Journal of Psychology, 55,* 44–45.

Grall, T. S. (2006). Custodial mothers and fathers and their child support: 2003. *Current Population Reports, P60-230.* Washington, DC: U.S. Bureau of the Census.

Granello, D. H., & Beamish, P. M. (1998). Reconceptualizing codependency in women: A sense of connectedness, not pathology. *Journal of Mental Health Counseling, 20,* 344–358.

Gray, M. R., & Steinberg, L. (1999). Unpacking authoritative parenting: Reassessing a multidimensional construct. *Journal of Marriage and the Family, 61,* 574–587.

Graziano, A. M., & Namaste, K. A. (1990). Parental use of physical force in child discipline: A survey of 679 college students. *Journal of Interpersonal Violence, 5,* 449–463.

Green, R.-J. (2002). Coming out to family … in context. In E. Davis-Russell (Ed.), *The California School of Professional Psychology handbook of multicultural education, research, intervention, and training* (pp. 277–284). San Francisco: Jossey-Bass.

Green, R.-J., & Mitchell, V. (2007). Different storks for different folks: Gay and lesbian parents' experiences with alternative Insemination and surrogacy. *Journal of GLBT Family Studies, 3*(2/3), 81–104.

Greenfield, P. M., & Suzuki, L. K. (2001). Culture and parenthood. In J. C. Westman (Ed.), *Parenthood in America* (pp. 20–33). Madison, WI: University of Wisconsin Press.

Greenfield, P. M., Trumbull, E., Keller, H., Rothstein-Fisch, C., Suzuki, L. K., & Quiroz, B. (2006). Cultural conceptions of learning and development. In P. A. Alexander & P. H. Winne (Eds.), *Handbook of educational psychology* (pp. 675–692). Mahwah, NJ: Lawrence Erlbaum Associates.

Greenleaf, P. (1978). *Children through the ages.* New York: McGraw-Hill.

Grever, C., & Bowman, D. (2008). *When your spouse comes out: A straight mate's recovery manual.* New York: Haworth Press-Taylor & Francis Group.

Grogan-Kaylor, A., & Otis, M. D. (2007). The predictors of parental use of corporal punishment. *Family Relations, 56*(1), 80–91.

Groleger, U., Tomori, M., & Kocmur, M. (2003). Suicidal ideation in adolescence—An indicator of actual risk? *Israel Journal of Psychiatry & Related Sciences, 40,* 202–208.

Gunnar, M. R., & van Dulmen, M. H. M. (2007). Behavior problems in postinstitutionalized internationally adopted children. *Development and Psychopathology, 19*(1), 129–148.

Haas, H. L., & Clompton, J. R. (2001). Psychology of an eating disorder. In J. J. Robert-McComb (Ed), *Eating disorders in women and children: Prevention, stress management, and treatment.* (pp. 39–48). Boca Raton, FL: CRC Press.

Haberstroh, C., Hayslip, Bert, Jr., & Wohl, E. (2001). Perceptions of grandparents and stepgrandparents by young adults. *The Gerontologist, 41,* 35.

Hacker, K. A., Amare, Y., Strunk, N., & Horst, L. (2000). Listening to youth: Teen perspectives on pregnancy prevention. *Journal of Adolescent Health, 26,* 279–288.

Haddock, S. A. (2002). A content analysis of articles pertaining to therapeutic considerations for dual-income couples (1979–1999). *American Journal of Family Therapy, 30*(2), 141–156.

Haig, D. (1995). Prenatal power plays. *Natural History, 104,* 9.

Hain, D. (1999). *Stopping stereotypes: Gays, lesbians, and alcoholism.* Tempe, AZ: Do It Now Foundation.

Hall, C. M. (2005). Physical discipline and child externalizing problems in Caucasian and Korean immigrant families. *Dissertation Abstracts International: Section B: The Sciences and Engineering, 65*(8-B), 4320.

Hall, K. J., & Kitson, G. C. (2000). Lesbian stepfamilies: An even more "incomplete institution." *Journal of Lesbian Studies, 4,* 31–47.

Hallahan, D. P., & Kauffman, J. M. (2004). *Introduction to learning disabilities.* Boston: Allyn & Bacon.

Hamilton, B. E, Martin, J. A, & Ventura, S. J. (2007). Births: Preliminary data for 2006. *National Vital Statistics Reports, 56*(7). Hyattsville, MD: National Center for Health Statistics.

Hangal, S., & Aminabhavi, V. A. (2007). Self-concept, emotional maturity, and achievement motivation of the adolescent children of employed mothers and homemakers. *Journal of the Indian Academy of Applied Psychology, 33*(1), 103–110.

Hansen, D. A., & Hill, R. (1964). Families under stress. In H. Christensen (Ed.), *Handbook of marriage and the family* (pp. 355–375). Chicago: Rand-McNally.

Harms, R. W., Johnson, R. V., & Murry, M. M. (2004). *Mayo Clinic guide to a healthy pregnancy.* New York: HarperCollins.

Harper, S. E., & Fine, M. A. (2006). The effects of involved nonresidential fathers' distress, parenting behaviors, inter-parental conflict, and the quality of father-child relationships on children's well-being. *Fathering, 4*(3), 286–311.

Harry, J. (1989). Parental physical abuse and sexual orientation in males. *Archives of Sexual Behavior, 18*, 251–261.

Harway, M. (2000). Families experiencing violence. In W. C. Nichols, M. A. Pace-Nichols, D. S. Becvar, & A. Y. Napier (Eds.), *Handbook of family development and intervention* (pp. 391–414). New York, NY: Wiley.

Harwood, K., McLean, N., & Durkin, K. (2007). First-time mothers' expectations of parenthood: What happens when optimistic expectations are not matched by later experiences? *Developmental Psychology, 43*(1), 1–12.

Hatheway, J. (2003). *Gilded age roots of American homophobia*. New York, NY: Palgrave Macmillan.

Haveman, R., Wolfe, B., & Pence, K. (2001). Intergenerational effects of nonmarital and early childbearing. In L. L. Wu & B. Wolfe (Eds.), *Out of wedlock: Causes and consequences of nonmarital fertility* (pp. 287–316). New York: Russell Sage Foundation.

Hawkins, D. B. (2003). *When you're living in a stepfamily.* Colorado Springs, CO: Cook Communications Ministries.

Hayslip, B., Jr. (2003). The impact of a psychosocial intervention on parental efficacy, grandchild relationship quality, and well-being among grandparents raising grandchildren. In B. Hayslip, Jr., & J. H. Patrick (Eds.), *Working with custodial grandparents* (pp. 163–176). New York, NY, US: Springer Publishing Co.

Heaven, P. C. L. (2001). *The social psychology of adolescence.* Basingstoke, England: Palgrave.

Helton, L. R., & Smith, M. K. (2004). *Mental health practice with children and youth: A strengths and well-being model.* New York: Haworth Press.

Herek, G. M. (1984). Beyond homophobia: A social psychological perspective on attitudes toward lesbians and gay men. *Journal of Homosexuality, 10*, 1–21.

Herek, G. M. (1993). The context of antigay violence: Notes on cultural and psychological heterosexism. In L. D. Garnets & D. C. Kimmel (Eds.), *Psychological perspectives on lesbian and gay male experiences* (pp. 89–107). New York: Columbia University Press.

Herek, G. M. (2006). Legal recognition of same-sex relationships in the United States: A social science perspective. *American Psychologist, 61*(6), 607–621.

Herrmann-Green, L. K., & Gehring, T. M. (2007). The German lesbian family study: Planning for parenthood via donor insemination. *Journal of GLBT Family Studies, 3*(4), 351–396.

Hess, C. R., Papas, M. A., & Black, M. M. (2002). Resilience among African American adolescent mothers: Predictors of positive parenting in early infancy. *Journal of Pediatric Psychology, 27*, 619–629.

Hetherington, E. M. (2006). The influence of conflict, marital problem solving and parenting on children's adjustment in nondivorced, divorced and remarried families. In A. Clarke-Stewart & J. Dunn (Eds.), *Families count: Effects on child and adolescent development* (pp. 203–237). New York: Cambridge University Press.

Heuvaline, P., & Timberlake, J. M. (2004). The role of co-habitation in family formation: The United States in comparative perspective. *Journal of Marriage and the Family, 66*, 1214–1230.

Higginson, J. G. (1998). Competitive parenting: The culture of teen mothers. *Journal of Marriage and the Family, 60*, 135–149.

Hildebrand, V., Phenice, L., Gray, M., & Hines, R. (2008). *Knowing and serving diverse families* (3rd ed.). Upper Saddle River, NJ: Prentice Hall.

Hill, N. E., & Taylor, L. C. (2004). Parental school involvement and children's academic achievement. *Current Directions in Psychological Science, 13*, 1641–168.

Hilton, J. M., & Kopera-Frye, K. (2004). Patterns of psychological adjustment among divorced custodial parents. *Journal of Divorce & Remarriage, 41*(3–4), 1–30.

Himes, C. L. (2001). Social demography of contemporary families and aging. In A. J. Walker, M. Manoogian-O'Dell, L. A. McGraw, & D. L. G. White (Eds.), *Families in later life: Connections and transitions* (pp. 47–50). Thousand Oaks, CA: Pine Forge.

Hobbs, D. (1965). Parenthood as crisis: A third study. *Journal of Marriage and the Family, 27*, 367–372.

Hobbs, F., & Stoops, N. (2002). Demographic trends in the 20th century. *Census 2000 Special Reports, Series CENSR-4.* Washington, DC: U.S. Government Printing Office.

Hobbs, D., & Wimbish, J. (1977). Transition to parenthood by black couples. *Journal of Marriage and the Family, 39*, 677–689.

Hofferth, S. L., Reid, L., & Mott, F. L. (2001). The effects of early childbearing on schooling over time. *Family Planning Perspectives, 33*, 259–267.

Hoffman, L. (1973). Deviation-amplifying process in natural groups. In J. Haley (Ed.), *Changing families* (pp. 135–168). New York: Grune & Stratton.

Hoffman, L. (1986). Work, family, and the child. In M. Pallak & R. Perloff (Eds.), *Psychology and work: Productivity, change, and employment.* Washington, DC: American Psychological Association.

Hoffman, L. W., & Youngblade, L. M. (1998). Maternal employment, morale and parenting style: Social class comparisons. *Journal of Applied Developmental Psychology, 19*, 389–413.

Holland, P., & Gorey, K. M. (2004). Historical, developmental, and behavioral factors associated with foster care challenges. *Child & Adolescent Social Work Journal, 21*, 117–135.

Holmes, T. H., & Rahe, R. H. (1967). The social readjustment scale. *Journal of Psychosomatic Research, 11*, 213–218.

Holyfield, L. (2003). *Moving up and out: Poverty, education, and the single parent family.* Philadelphia: Temple University Press.

Honein, M. A., Paulozzi, L. J., Mathews, T. J., Erikson, J. D., & Wong, L.-Y. C. (2001). Impact of folic acid fortification of the U. S. food supply on the occurrence of neural tube defects. *Journal of the American Medical Association, 285*, 2981–2986.

Honig, A. S., & Morin, C. (2001). When should programs for teen parents and babies begin? Longitudinal evaluation of a teen parents and babies program. *Journal of Primary Prevention, 21*, 447–454.

Howard, K. S., Carothers, S. S., Smith, L. E., & Akai, C. E. (2007). Overcoming the odds: Protective factors in the lives of children. In J. G. Borkowski, J. R. Farris, T. L. Whitman, S. S. Carothers, & K. Weed (Eds.), *Risk and resilience: Adolescent mothers and their children grow up* (pp. 205–232). Mahwah, NJ: Lawrence Erlbaum Associates Publishers.

Howes, P. W., Cicchetti, D., Toth, S. L., & Rogosch, F. A. (2000). Affective, organizations, and relational characteristics of maltreating families: A system's perspective. *Journal of Family Psychology, 14,* 95–110.

Hoyt, H. H., & Broom, B. L. (2002). School-based teen pregnancy prevention programs: A review of the literature. *Journal of School Nursing, 18,* 11–17.

Hughes, D. (2003). Correlates of African American and Latino parents' messages to children about ethnicity and race: A comparative study of racial socialization. *American Journal of Community Psychology, 31,* 15–33.

Hui, P. W., Lam, Y. H., Tang, M. H., Ng, E. H., Yeung, W. S., & Ho, P. C. (2003). Amniotic fluid, human chorionic gonadotrophin, and alpha-fetoprotein levels in pregnancies conceived after assisted reproduction. *Prenatal Diagnosis, 23,* 484–487.

Humphries, N. A., & Parks, C. A. (2006). Seeking a child through international adoption: Lucy's and Robin's story. In L. Messinger & D. F. Morrow (Eds.), *Case studies on sexual orientation & gender expression in social work practice* (pp. 57–59). New York: Columbia University Press.

Hunter, A. E., & Forden, C. (Eds.). (2002). *Readings in the psychology of gender: Exploring our differences and commonalities.* Needham Heights, MA: Allyn & Bacon.

Hyde, J. S., & DeLamater, J. D. (2000). *Understanding human sexuality* (7th ed.). New York: McGraw-Hill.

Ifejika, S. (2003). *Growing pains: A how to manual for parents and young adults.* Frederick, MD: PublishAmerican, Inc.

Ihinger-Tallman, M., & Pasley, K. (1997). Stepfamilies in 1984 and today—A scholarly perspective. In I. Levin & M. B. Sussman (Eds.), *Stepfamilies: History, research, and policy* (pp. 19–40). New York, NY: Haworth Press.

Imber-Black, E. (1993, May-June). Ghosts in the therapy room. *Family Therapy Networker,* 18–29.

Ingersoll-Dayton, B., Neal, M. B., & Hammer, L. B. (2001). Aging parents helping adult children: The experience of the sandwiched generation. *Family Relations, 50,* 262–271.

Institute of Medicine Staff Board. (2002). *Confronting chronic neglect: The education and training of health professionals on family violence.* Washington, DC: National Academy Press.

Isensee, R. (1991). *Growing up gay in a dysfunctional family.* New York: Prentice Hall Parkside.

Ishizawa, H., Kenney, C. T., Kubo, K., & Stevens, G. (2006). Constructing interracial families through intercountry adoption. *Social Science Quarterly, 87,* 1207–1224.

Itzkoff, S. W. (2003). Intervening with mother nature: The ethics of human cloning. *Mankind Quarterly, 44,* 29–42.

Jaffee, S. (2002). Pathways to adversity in young adulthood among early childbearers. *Journal of Family Psychology, 16,* 38–49.

Jaffee, S., Caspi, A., Moffitt, T. E., Belsky, J., & Silva, P. (2001). Why are children born to teen mothers at risk for adverse outcomes in young adulthood? Results from a 20-year longitudinal study. *Development & Psychopathology, 13,* 377–397.

James, M. (2006). Implementing attachment theory in Head Start to enhance social competence: A program development. *Dissertation Abstracts International: Section B: The Sciences and Engineering, 67*(4-B), 2259.

Jarrett, R. L. (1995). Growing up poor: The family experiences of socially mobile youth in low-income African American neighborhoods. *Journal of Adolescent Research, 10,* 111–135.

Jedrychowski, W., Galas, A. S., Flak, E., Jacek, R., Penar, A., Spengler, J., et al. (2007). Increased burden of respiratory disease in the first six months of life due to prenatal environmental tobacco smoke: Krakow birth cohort study. *Early Child Development and Care, 177*(4), 369–381.

Joe, J. R., & Malach, R. S. (1992). Families with Native American roots. In E. W. Lynch & M. J. Hanson (Eds.), *Developing cross-cultural competence: A guide for working with young children and their families* (pp. 89–119). Baltimore: Paul H. Brooks Publishing.

John, R. (1998). Native American families. In C. H. Mindel, R. W. Haberstein, & R. Wright, Jr. (Eds.), *Ethnic families in America: Patterns and variations* (pp. 382–421). Upper Saddle River, NJ: Prentice Hall.

Johnson, J. O. (2005). Who's minding the kids? Child care arrangements: 2002. *Current Population Reports, P70-101.* Washington, DC: U.S. Census Bureau.

Johnson, S. M., & O'Connor, E. (2001). *For lesbian parents: Your guide to helping your family grow up happy, healthy, and proud.* New York: Guilford Publications.

Jones, D. J., Forehand, R., Brody, G. H., & Armistead, L. (2002). Positive parenting and child psychosocial adjustment in inner-city single-parent African American families: the role of maternal optimism. *Behavior Modification, 26,* 464–481.

Jordan, D-L. (2003). *How to succeed as a single parent.* London: Hodder & Stoughton.

Joselevich, E. (1988). Family transitions, cumulative stress, and crises. In C. J. Falicov (Ed.), *Family transitions: Continuity and change over the life cycle.* New York: Bruner/Mazel.

Judges of the 29th Judicial District of Kansas. (1985). *An informational program for separating/divorcing parents with minor children.* Whandotte, KS: Wyandotte County Bar Association.

Julian, T. W., McHenry, P. C., & McKelvey, M. W. (1994). Cultural variations in parenting: Perceptions of Caucasian, African-American, Latino, and Asian-American parents. *Family Relations, 43,* 30–37.

Kagan, J. (1976). The psychological requirements for human development. In N. Talbott (Ed.), *Raising children in modern America.* Boston: Little, Brown.

Kagitecibasi, C. (1990). Family and socialization in cross-cultural perspective: A model of change. In J. J. Berman (Ed.), *Nebraska symposium on motivation, 1989: Cross-cultural perspectives* (pp. 135–200). Lincoln: University of Nebraska Press.

Kalish, S. (1995). Multiracial births increase as U.S. ponders racial definitions. *Population Today, 23,* 1-2.

Kandakai, T. L., & Smith, L. C. R. (2007). Denormalizing an historical problem: Teen pregnancy, policy, and public health action. *American Journal of Health Behavior, 31*(2), 170–180.

Kane, E. W. (2006). 'No way my boys are going to be like that!': Parents' responses to children's gender nonconformity. *Gender & Society, 20*(2), 149–176.

Kaslow, F. W. (2000). Families experiencing divorce. In W. C. Nichols, M. A. Pace-Nichols, D. S. Becvar, & Y. A. Napier (Eds.), *Handbook of family development and intervention* (pp. 341–368). New York: Wiley.

Kazdin, A. E., & Benjet, C. (2003). Spanking children: Evidence and issues. *Current Directions in Psychological Science, 12*(3), 99–103.

Keck, G. C., & Kupecky, R. M. (2004). *Parenting the hurt child: Helping adoptive families heal and grow.* Colorado Springs, CO: Pinon Press.

Kelder, L. R., McNamara, J. R., Carlson, B., & Lynn, S. J. (1991). Perceptions of physical punishment: The relation to childhood and adolescent experiences. *Journal of Interpersonal Violence, 6,* 432–445.

Kelley, M. L., Grace, N., & Elliott, S. N. (1990). Acceptability of positive and punitive discipline methods: Comparisons among abusive, potentially abusive, and nonabusive parents. *Child Abuse and Neglect, 14,* 219–226.

Kellogg, T. (1990). *Broken toys broken dreams.* Santa Fe, NM: BRAT Publishing.

Kendall-Tackett, K. A. (2001). *The hidden feelings of motherhood: Coping with stress, depression, and burnout.* Oakland, CA: New Harbinger Publications.

Kennedy, R. (2004). *Interracial intimacies: Sex, marriage, identity, and adoption.* New York, NY: Knopf.

Kershaw, S. (2000). Living in a lesbian household: The effects on children. *Child & Family Social Work, 5,* 365–371.

Kershaw, T. S., Niccolai, L. M., Ethier, K. A., Lewis, J. B., & Ickovics, J. R. (2003). Perceived susceptibility to pregnancy and sexually transmitted disease among pregnant and nonpregnant adolescents. *Journal of Community Psychology, 31,* 419–434.

Key, J., Barbosa, G. A., & Owens, V. J. (2001). The Second Chance Club: Repeat adolescent pregnancy prevention with a school-based intervention. *Journal of Adolescent Health, 28,* 167–169.

Kim, H. H. (2004). *Learning disabilities.* Farmington Hills, MI: Greenhaven Press.

Kimes, L. M. (2006). Adolescent parents' understanding of the social and emotional development of their very young children. *Dissertation Abstracts International: Section B: The Sciences and Engineering, 67*(6-B), 3483.

Kinnear, K. L. (2007). *Childhood sexual abuse* (2nd ed., revised). Santa Barbara, CA: ABC-CLIO.

Kinsey, A. C., Pomeroy, W. B., & Martin, C. E. (1948). *Sexual behavior in the human male.* Philadelphia: Saunders.

Kinsey, A. C., Pomeroy, W. B., Martin, C. E., & Gebhard, P. H. (1953). *Sexual behavior in the human female.* Philadelphia: Saunders.

Kirby, D. (1999). *Looking for reasons why: The antecedents of adolescent sexual risk-taking, pregnancy, and childbearing.* Washington, DC: National Campaign to Prevent Teen Pregnancy.

Klein, M. (2006). *America's war on sex: The attack on law, lust and liberty.* Westport, CT: Praeger Publishers/Greenwood Publishing Group.

Knoester, C., & Eggebeen, D. J. (2006). The effects of the transition to parenthood and subsequent children on men's well-being and social participation. *Journal of Family Issues, 27*(11), 1532–1560.

Knowles, C. (1997). *Family boundaries: The invention of normality and dangerousness.* Peterborough, ON, CA: Broadview Press.

Knox, D., & Schacht, C. (2008). *Choices in relationships: Introduction to marriage and the family* (9th ed.). Florence, KY: Cengage Learning.

Koerner, S. S., Jacobs, S. L., & Raymond, M. (2000). When mothers turn to their adolescent daughters: Predicting daughters' vulnerability to negative adjustment outcomes. *Family Relations, 49,* 301–309.

Koonce, D. A., & Harper, W., Jr. (2005). Engaging African American parents in the schools: A community based consultation model. *Journal of Educational & Psychological Consultation, 16*(1/2), 55-74.

Kopera-Frye, K., Wiscott, R. C., & Begovic, A. (2003). Lessons learned from custodial grandparents involved in a community support group. In B. Hayslip, Jr., & J. H. Patrick (Eds.), *Working with custodial grandparents* (pp. 243–256). New York, NY: Springer Publishing Co.

Kornhaber, A. (2003). *The grandparent guide: The definitive guide to coping with the challenges of modern grandparenting.* New York, NY: McGraw-Hill.

Kosunen, E., Kaltiala-Heino, R., Rimpela, M., & Laippala, P. (2003). Risk-taking sexual behavior and self-reported depression in middle adolescence—a school-based survey. *Child: Care, Health & Development, 29,* 337–344.

Kourtis, A., Bulterys, M., Nesheim, S., & Lee, F. (2001). Understanding the timing of HIV transmission from mother to infant. *Journal of the American Medical Association, 285,* 709–712.

Krauss, M. W. (2000). Family assessment within early intervention programs. In J. P. Shonkoff & S. J. Meisels (Eds.), *Handbook of early childhood intervention* (2nd ed.). (pp. 290–308). New York, NY: Cambridge University Press.

Kravetz, J. D., & Federman, D. G. (2002). Cat associated zoonoses. *Archives of Internal Medicine, 162,* 1945–1952.

Krebs, L. L. (1986). Current research on theoretically based parenting programs. *Individual Psychology, 42,* 375–387.

Kreider, R. M. (2003). *Adopted children and stepchildren: 2000.* Washington, DC: U.S. Bureau of the Census.

Kreider, R. M. (2005). *Number, timing, and duration of marriages and divorces: 2001.* Current Population Reports, P70-97. Washington, DC: U.S. Bureau of the Census.

Kritzberg, W. (1985). *The adult children of alcoholics syndrome.* Deerfield Beach, FL: Health Communications.

Kropf, N. P., & Burnette, D. (2003). Grandparents as family caregivers: Lessons for intergenerational education. *Educational Gerontology, 29,* 361–372.

Kuczynski, L. (2003). Beyond bidirectionality: Bilateral conceptual frameworks for understanding dynamics in parent-youth relations. In L. Kuczynski (Ed.), *Handbook of dynamics in parent-youth relations* (pp. 3–24). Thousand Oaks, CA: Sage Publications.

Kuczynski, L., & Kochanska, G. (1995). Function and content of maternal demands: Developmental significance of early demands for competent action. *Child Development, 66,* 616–628.

Kufeldt, K., Simard, M., & Vachon, J. (2003). Improving outcomes for children in care: giving youth a voice. *Adoption and Fostering, 27,* 8–19.

Kurdek, L. A. (1995). Lesbian and gay couples. In A. R. D'Augelli & C. J. Patterson (Eds.), *Lesbian, gay, and bisexual identities over the lifespan: Psychological perspectives* (pp. 243–261). New York: Oxford University Press.

Kurdek, L. A. (2003). Differences between gay and lesbian cohabiting couples. *Journal of Social and Personal Relationships, 20,* 411–436.

Kurdek, L. A. (2004). Are gay and lesbian cohabitating couples really different from heterosexual married couples? *Journal of Marriage and the Family, 66,* 880–900.

Kurjak, A., Kupesic, S., Matijevic, R., Kos, M., & Marton, U. (1999). First trimester malformation screening. *European Journal of Obstetrics, Gynecology, and Reproductive Biology, 85,* 93–96.

Kyriacou, C. (2002). A humanistic view of discipline. In B. Rogers (Ed.), *Teacher leadership and behavior management* (pp. 40–52). London: Paul Chapman Publishing.

Laasko, J. S., & Adams, S. (2006). Noncustodial fathers' involvement with their children: A right or a privilege? *Families in Society, 87*(1), 85–93.

Laird, J. (2003). Lesbian and gay families. In F. Walsh (Ed), *Normal family processes: Growing diversity and complexity* (3rd ed., pp. 176–209). New York, NY: Guilford Press.

Lal, S. (2002). Orphaned, adopted, and abducted: Parents and children in twentieth-century America. *Radical History Review, 84*, 174–184.

Lamanna, M. A., & Reidman, A. (2006). *Marriages and families: Making choices in a diverse society* (9th ed.). Belmont, CA: Wadsworth/Thomson Learning.

Lamaze, F. (1958). *Painless childbirth: Psychoprophalactic method*. New York: Harper & Row.

Lambert, W., Hames, J., & Frasure-Smith, N. (1979). *Childrearing values: A cross-national study*. New York: Praeger.

LaRossa, R. (1986). *Becoming a parent*. Thousand Oaks, CA: Sage.

Larsen, E. (1987). *Stage II relationships: Love beyond addiction*. San Francisco: HarperSanFrancisco.

Larzelere, R. E., Klein, M., Schumm, W. E., & Alibrando, S. A. (1989). Relations of spanking and other parenting characteristics to self-esteem and perceived fairness of parental discipline. *Psychological Reports, 64*, 1140–1142.

LaSala, M. C. (2000a). Gay male couples: The importance of coming out and being out to parents. *Journal of Homosexuality, 39*, 47–71.

LaSala, M. C. (2000b). Lesbians, gay men, and their parents: Family therapy for the coming-out crisis. *Family Process, 39*, 67–81.

Laszloffy, T. A. (2002). Rethinking family development theory: Teaching with the systemic family development (SFD) model. *Family Relations, 51*, 206–214.

Lawrence, E., Nylen, K., & Cobb, R. J. (2007). Prenatal expectations and marital satisfaction over the transition to parenthood. *Journal of Family Psychology, 21*(2), 155–164.

Lawrence, F. R., & Blair, C. (2003). Factorial invariance in preventive intervention: Modeling the development of intelligence in low birth weight, preterm infants. *Prevention Science, 4*, 249–261.

Layne, S. L. (2004). *Over land and sea: The story of international adoption*. Gretna, LA: Pelican Publishing Co.

LeMasters, E. E. (1957). Parenthood as crisis. *Marriage and Family Living, 19*, 352–355.

LeMasters, E. E. (1977). *Parents in modern America* (rev. ed.). Homewoood, IL: Dorsey.

Le Poire, B. A., Hallett, J. S., & Giles, H. (1998). Codependence: The paradoxical nature of the functional-afflicted relationship. In B. H. Spitzberg & W. R. Cupach (Eds.), *The dark side of close relationships* (pp. 153–176). Mahwah, NJ: Lawrence Erlbaum Associates.

Leake, V. S. (2007). Personal, familial, and systemic factors associated with family belonging for stepfamily adolescents. *Journal of Divorce & Remarriage, 47*(1/2), 135–155.

Leboyer, F. (1976). *Birth without violence*. New York: Knopf.

Lee, C. D. (2004). A guidebook for raising foster children. *Child & Adolescent Social Work Journal, 21*, 191–194.

Lee, M. M., & Lee, R. E. (2006). The voices of accepting and supportive parents of gay sons: Towards an ecosystemic strengths model. *Journal of GLBT Family Studies, 2*(2), 1–28.

Lee-Baggley, D., Preece, M., & DeLongis, A. (2005). Coping with interpersonal stress: Role of big five traits. *Journal of Personality, 73*(5), 1141–1180.

Lefever, J. B., Nicholson, J. S., & Noria, C. W. (2007). Children's uncertain futures: Problems in school. In J. G. Borkowski, J. R. Farris, T. L. Whitman, S. S. Carothers, & K. Weed (Eds.), *Risk and resilience: Adolescent mothers and their children grow up* (pp. 69–99). Mahwah, NJ: Lawrence Erlbaum Associates Publishers.

Leon, K. (2005). Portrayals of stepfamilies in film: Using media images in remarriage education. *Family Relations, 54*(1), 3–23.

Lester, T. P. (Ed.). (2003). *Gender nonconformity, race, and sexuality: Charting the connections*. Madison, WI: University of Wisconsin Press.

Lev, A. I. (2004). *The complete lesbian & gay parenting guide*. New York: The Berkley Publishing Group.

Levene, M., Tudehope, D. I., & Sinha, S. (2008). *Essential neonatal medicine* (4th ed.). Ames, IA: Blackwell Publishing.

Levine, J. A., & Pitt, E. W. (1998). *New expectations: Community strategies for responsible fatherhood*. New York: Families and Work Institute.

Leviton, A., & Cowan, L. (2002). A review of the literature relating caffeine consumption by women to their risk of reproductive hazards. *Food & Chemical Toxicology, 40*, 1271–1310.

Lewallen, E. (1992, October 30). Early pain transforms into deep appreciation. *Rocky Mountain United Methodist Reporter, 139*, 13.

Lewis, M. (2002). *Child and adolescent psychiatry: A comprehensive textbook*. Philadelphia, PA: Lippincott, Williams, & Wilkins.

Leyden, S. (2002). *Supporting the child of exceptional ability: At home and school*. London: David Fulton.

Lichter, D. T., & Graefe, D. R. (2001). Finding a mate? The marital and cohabitation histories of unwed mothers. In L. L. Wu & B. Wolfe (Eds.), *Out of wedlock: Causes and consequences of nonmarital fertility* (pp. 317–343). New York: Russell Sage Foundation.

Lin, F.-T., & Chen, J. (2006). Custodial fathers—Do they work more or fewer hours? *Journal of Family and Economic Issues, 27*(3), 513–522.

Lindley, N. R., Giordano, P. J., & Hammer, E. D. (1999). Codependency: Predictors and psychometric issues. *Journal of Clinical Psychology, 55*, 59–64.

Lindon, J. (2004). *Working with children and young people in residential and foster care*. Boston, MA: International Thomson Business Press.

Lino, M. (2006). *Expenditures on children by families, 2005. Miscellaneous Publication No. 1528-2005*. Washington, DC: U.S. Department of Agriculture, Center for Nutrition Policy and Promotion.

Locke, J. (1699). *Some thoughts concerning education* (4th ed., enlarged). London: A & J. Churchill.

Longmore, M. A., Manning, W. D., Giordano, P. C., & Rudolph, J. L. (2003). Contraceptive self-efficacy: Does it influence adolescents' contraceptive use? *Journal of Health & Social Behavior, 44*, 45–60.

Lorah, M. A. (2002). Lesbian stepmothers: A grounded theory study of women who cohabit with biological, custodial mothers of children from previous heterosexual relationships. *Dissertation Abstracts International, 62*, 4074.

Love, K. M., & Murdock, B. (2004). Attachment to parents and psychological well-being:

An examination of young adult college students in intact families and stepfamilies. *Journal of Family Psychology, 18*, 600–608.

Lowenstein, L. F. (2002). Joint custody and shared parenting: Are courts listening? *Family Therapy, 29*, 101–108.

Lumeng, J. C., Cabral, H. J., & Gannon, K. (2007). Pre-natal exposures to cocaine and alcohol and physical growth patterns to age 8 years. *Neurotoxicology and Teratology, 29*(4), 446–457.

Luster, T., Bates, L., Fitzgerald, H., Vanderbelt, M., & Key, J. P. (2000). Factors related to successful outcomes among preschool children born to low-income adolescent mothers. *Journal of Marriage and the Family, 62*, 113–146.

Lynch, J. M. (2000). Considerations of family structure and gender composition: The lesbian and gay stepfamily. *Journal of Homosexuality, 40*, 81–95.

Lynch, J. M., & McMahon-Klosterman, K. (2006). Guiding the acquisition of therapist ally identity: Research on the GLBT stepfamily as resource. *Journal of GLBT Family Studies, 2*(3/4), 123–150.

Lytton, H., & Romney, D. M. (1991). Parents' differential socialization of boys and girls: A meta-analysis. *Psychological Bulletin, 109*, 267–296.

Maccoby, E. (1984). Middle childhood in the context of the family. In W. Collins (Ed.), *Development during middle childhood: The years from six to twelve*. Washington, DC: National Academy of Sciences.

Maccoby, E., & Jacklin, C. (1974). *The psychology of sex differences*. Stanford, CA: Stanford University Press.

Maccoby, E., & Martin, J. A. (1983). Socialization in the context of the family: Parent-child interaction. In P. H. Mussen (Ed.), *Handbook of child psychology* (4th ed.), Vol. 4: Socialization, personality, and social development (pp. 1–101). New York: Wiley.

Macmillan, C., Madder, L. S., Brooders, P., Chase, C., Hotelman, J., Laky, T., et al. (2001). Head growth and neurodevelopment of infants born to HIV-1-infected drug-using women. *Neurology, 57*, 1402–1411.

Madden-Derdich, D. A., Herzog, M. J., & Leonard, S. A. (2002). The coparental involvement of teen-aged fathers: The mediating role of mothers' desire to have fathers involved. Paper presented at the 64th Annual Conference of the National Council on Family Relations, Houston, Texas.

Magen, Z., Levin, T., & Yeshurun, D. (1991). Parent counseling as a means of change: A study of an Adlerian approach. *International Journal for the Advancement of Counseling, 14*, 27–39.

Magnuson, K. A., & Waldfogel, J. (2005). Preschool child care and parents' use of physical discipline. *Infant and Child Development, 14*(2), 177–198.

Malinowski, A., & Stamler, L. L. (2003). Adolescent girls' personal experience with Baby Think It Over infant simulator. *American Journal of Maternal/Child Nursing, 28*(3), 205–211.

Mallery, J. G. (2002). Practicing parenting? Effects of computerized infant simulators on teenage attitudes toward early parenthood. *The Journal of Early Education and Family Review, 9*, 18–28.

Malley-Morrison, K., & Hines, D. (2003). *Family violence in a cultural perspective: Defining, understanding, and combating abuse*. Thousand Oaks, CA: Sage.

Mallon, G. P. (2004). *Gay men choosing parenthood*. New York: Columbia University Press.

Mandel, S. (2006). The non-custodial father: His involvement in his children's lives and the connection between his role and the ex-wife's, child's and father's perception of that role. *Journal of Divorce & Remarriage, 45*(1–2), 79–95.

Manlove, J., Mariner, C., & Papillo, A. R. (2000). Subsequent fertility among teen mothers: Longitudinal analyses of recent national data. *Journal of Marriage and the Family, 62*, 430–448.

Mann, J., & Peabody, E. (1863). *Moral culture of infancy and kindergarten guide*. Boston: Plenum.

Manning, W. D., & Smock, P. J. (2000). "Swapping" families: Serial parenting and economic support for children. *Journal of Marriage and the Family, 62*, 111–122.

March of Dimes Foundation. (2002). *Toxoplasmosis* (fact sheet). Wilkes Bare, PA: Author.

Marlow, N., Wolke, D., Bracewell, M. A., & Samara, M. (2005). Neurologic and developmental disability at six years of age after extremely preterm birth. *New England Journal of Medicine, 352*, 9–19.

Marsiglio, W. (2004). *Stepdads: Stories of love, hope, and repair*. Lanham, MD: Rowman & Littlefield.

Marsiglio, W., Hutchinson, S., & Cohan, M. (2000). Envisioning fatherhood: A social psychological perspective on young men with kids. *Family Relations, 49*, 133–142.

Martin, C. (1996). Baby Think It Over: Doll vocal about teen pregnancy. *The Denver Post*, 1G–2G.

Martin J. A., Hamilton, B. E., Ventura, S. J., Sutton, P. D., Ventura, S. J., Menaker, F., et al. (2006). Births: Final data for 2004. *National Vital Statistics Reports, 55*(1). Hyattsville, Maryland: National Center of Health Statistics.

Martin, M. L. (1993, May-June). The silent tyranny. *Family Therapy Networker*, 46–49.

Martin, P., & Midgely, E. (1999). Immigration in the United States. *Population Bulletin 54*(2). Washington, DC: Population Reference Bureau.

Mather, M., Rivers, K. L., & Jacobsen, L. A. (2005). The American community survey. *Population Bulletin, 60*(3). Washington, DC: Population Reference Bureau.

Mattessich, P., & Hill, R. (1987). Life cycle and family development. In M. Sussman & S. Steinmetz (Eds.), *Handbook of marriage and the family*. New York: Plenum Press.

May, E. T. (1997). *Barren in the promised land: Childless Americans and the pursuit of happiness*. Cambridge, MA: Harvard University Press.

Mays, L. C., & Lechman, J. F. (2007). Parental representations and subclinical changes in postpartum mood. *Infant Mental Health Journal, 28*(3), 281–295.

McBride-Chang, C., & Chang, L. (1998). Adolescent-parent relations in Hong-Kong: Parenting styles, emotional autonomy, and school achievement. *Journal of Genetic Psychology, 159*, 421–435.

McCarthy, B. W., & Ginsberg, R. L. (2007). Second marriages: Challenges and risks. *The Family Journal, 15*(2), 119–123.

McClellan, D. L. (2001). The "other mother" and second parent adoption. *Journal of Gay & Lesbian Social Services, 13*, 1–21.

McCranie, E. W., & Simpson, M. E. (1986). Parental childrearing antecedents of Type A behavior. *Personality and Social Psychology Bulletin, 12*, 493–501.

McDonald, Walter R. and Associates. (2004). *Child maltreatment 2002*. Washington, DC: National Clearinghouse on Child Abuse and Neglect.

McDonell, J. R., Limber, S. P., & Connor-Godbey, J. (2007). Pathways teen mother support project: Longitudinal findings. *Children and Youth Services Review, 29*(7), 840–855.

McElderry, D. H., & Omar, H. A. (2003). Sex education in the schools: What role does it play? *International Journal of Adolescent Medicine & Health, 15*, 3–9.

McGuinness, T., & Pallansch, L. (2000). Competence of children adopted from the former Soviet Union. *Family Relations, 49*, 457–464.

McHale, J. P., & Rotman, T. (2007). Is seeing believing? Expectant parents' outlooks on coparenting and later coparenting solidarity. *Infant Behavior & Development, 30*(1), 63–81.

McKay, A., Fisher, W, Maticka-Tyndale, E., & Barrett, M. (2001). Adolescent sexual health education: Does it work? Can it work better? An analysis of recent research and media reports. *Canadian Journal of Human Sexuality, 10*, 127–135.

McKnight, J. (2000). Editorial: The origins of male homosexuality. *Psychology, Evolution & Gender, 2*, 223–228.

McLoyd, V. C., Cauce, A. M., Takeuchi, D., & Wilson, L. (2000). Marital processes and parental socialization in families of color: A decade review of research. *Journal of Marriage and the Family, 62*, 1070–1093.

McLoyd, V. C., Kaplan, R., Hardaway, C. R., & Wood, D. (2007). *Journal of Family Psychology, 21*(2), 165–175.

McNally, S., Eisenberg, N., & Harris, J. D. (1991). Consistency and change in maternal child-rearing practices and values: A longitudinal study. *Child Development, 62*(1), 190–198.

Melody, P. (1989). *Facing codependence.* New York: HarperCollins.

Menaghan, E. G., & Parcel, T. L. (1990). Parental employment and family life: Research in the 1980s. *Journal of Marriage and the Family, 52*, 1079–1098.

Mereu, G., Fa, M., Ferraro, L., Cagiano, R., Antonelli, T., Tattoli, M., et al. (2003). Prenatal exposure to a cannabinoid agonist produces memory deficits linked to dysfunction in hippocampal long-term potentiation and glutamate release. *Proceedings of the National Academy of Sciences, 100*, 4915–4920.

Merighi, J. R., & Grimes, M. D. (2000). Coming out to families in a multicultural context. *Families in Society, 81*, 32–41.

Meyer, D. J. (2003). *Living with a brother or sister with special needs: A book for sibs.* Seattle: University of Washington Press.

Meyer-Bahlburg, H. F. L., Ehrdardt, A. A., Rosen, L. R., Gruen, R. S., Veridiano, N. P.,

Vann, F. H., & Newhalder, H. F. (1995). Prenatal estrogens and the development of homosexual orientation. *Developmental Psychology, 31*, 12–21.

Mezey, M. D., Berkman, B. J., Callahan, C. M., & Mitty, E. L. (Eds.). (2004) *The encyclopedia of elder care.* New York: Prometheus Books.

Michaels, M. L. (2006). Stepfamily enrichment Program: A preventive intervention for remarried Couples. *Journal for Specialists in Group Work, 31*(2), 135–152.

Milic, J. H., & Crowne, D. P. (1986). Recalled parent-child relations and need for approval of homosexual and heterosexual men. *Archives of Sexual Behavior, 15*, 239–246.

Milkie, M. A., & Peltola, P. (1999). Playing all the roles: Gender and the work-family balancing act. *Journal of Marriage and the Family, 61*, 476–490.

Miller, A. (1990). *For your own good: Hidden cruelty in childrearing and the roots of violence.* New York: Noonday Press.

Miller, A. (2002). *The truth will set you free: Overcoming emotional blindness and finding your true adult self.* New York: Basic Books.

Miller, A. (2006). *The body never lies: The lingering effects of hurtful parenting.* New York: Norton.

Miller, B. C., & Coyl, D. D. (2000). Adolescent pregnancy and childbearing in relation to infant adoption in the United States. *Adoption Quarterly, 4*, 3–25.

Miller, J., & Knudsen, D. D. (2006). *Family abuse and violence: A social problems perspective.* Lanham, MD: Alta Mira Press.

Miller, L. G., & Albrecht, K. M. (2004). *The infant and toddler child development guide.* Beltsville, MD: Gryphon House.

Miller-Perrin, C. L., Perrin, R. D., & Barnett, O. W. (2004). *Family violence across the lifespan: An introduction* (2nd ed.). Thousand Oaks, CA: Sage.

Miniño, A. M., Heron, M. P., Murphy, S. L., & Kochanek, K. D. (2007). Deaths: Final Data for 2004. *National Vital Statistics Reports, 55*(19). Hyattsville, MD: National Center for Health Statistics.

Mintz, S. (2006). *Huck's raft: A history of American childhood.* Boston: Harvard University Press.

Minuchin, S. (1974). *Families and family therapy.* Cambridge, MA: Harvard University Press.

Mitchell, B. A. (1998). Too close for comfort? Parental assessments of "boomerang kid"

living arrangements. *Canadian Journal of Sociology, 23*, 21–46.

Mitchell, B. A. (2006). *The boomerang age: Transitions to adulthood in families.* New Brunswick, NJ: Aldine.

Mitchell, B. A., & Gee, E. M. (1996). "Boomerang kids" and midlife parental marital satisfaction. *Family Relations, 45*, 442–448.

Mitchell, V., & Green, R.-J. (2008). Different storks for different folks: Gay and lesbian parents' experiences with alternative insemination and surrogacy. *Journal of GLBT Family Studies, 3*(2/3), 81–104.

Mizes, J. S., & Miller, K. J. (2000). Eating disorders. In M. Hersen & R. T Ammerman, (Eds.), *Advanced abnormal child psychology* (2nd ed., pp. 441–465). Mahwah, NJ: Lawrence Erlbaum.

Mollborn, S. (2007). Making the best of a bad situation: Material resources and teenage parenthood. *Journal of Marriage and Family, 69*(1), 92–104.

Molter, N. C. (2003). Creating a healing environment for critical care. *Critical Care Nursing Clinics of North America, 15*, 295–304.

Money, J. (1987). Sin, sickness, or status? Homosexual gender identity and psychoneuroendocrinology. *American Psychologist, 42*, 384–399.

Monk, C., Fifer, W. P., Meyers, M. M., Sloan, R. P., Trien, L., & Hurtado, A. (2000). Maternal stress responses and anxiety during pregnancy: Effects on fetal heart rate. *Developmental Psychology, 36*, 67–77.

Mooney-Somers, J., & Golombok, S. (2000). Children of lesbian mothers: From the 1970s to the new millennium. *Sexual & Relationship Therapy, 15*, 121–126.

Moore, M. R., & Brooks-Gunn, J. (2002). Adolescent parenthood. In M. H. Bornstein (Ed.), *Handbook of parenting, Vol. 3: Being and becoming a parent* (2nd ed.) (pp. 173–214). Mahwah, NJ: Erlbaum.

Morgan, S. P., Botev, N., Chen, R., & Huang, J. (1999). White and nonwhite trends in first birth timing: Comparisons using vital registration and Current Population Surveys. *Population Research and Policy Review, 18*, 339–356.

Morris, D. (1986). *The illustrated naked ape: A zoologist's study of the human animal.* New York, NY: Crown.

Morris, D. (1996). *The human zoo: A zoologist's classic study of the urban animal.* New York, NY: Kodansha International.

Morse, A. (2003). *SCHIP and access for children in immigrant families*. Washington, DC: National Conference of State Legislatures.

Mosher, C. M. (2001). The social implications of sexual identity formation and the coming-out process: A review of the theoretical and empirical literature. *Family Journal: Counseling & Therapy for Couples & Families, 9*, 164–173.

Moura, B. (2004). The transition to parenthood: Therapy in context. *Dissertation Abstracts International: Section B: The Sciences and Engineering, 65*(3-B), 1558.

Mueller, M. M., & Elder, G. H. (2003). Family contingencies across the generations: Grandparent-grandchild relationships in holistic perspective. *Journal of Marriage & the Family, 65*, 404–417.

Munson, M. L., & Sutton, P. D. (2006). Births, marriage, divorces, and deaths: Provisional data for 2005. *National Vital Statistics Reports, 54*(20). Hyattsville, MD: National Center for Health Statistics.

Murphy, A. (2003). Daddy boot camp: How an increasingly popular program prepares rookie fathers to hit the ground crawling. *Child, 18*, 85–86, 88, 90.

Murphy, M.-K., & Knoll, J. (2003). *International adoption: Sensitive advice for prospective parents*. Chicago, IL: Chicago Review Press.

Nation, M. (2007). Empowering the victim: Interventions for children victimized by bullies. In J. E. Zins, M. J. Elias, & C. A. Maher (Eds.), *Bullying, victimization, and peer harassment: A handbook of prevention and intervention* (pp. 239–255). New York: Haworth Press.

National Center for Chronic Disease Prevention and Health Promotion. (2006). *Assisted reproductive technology success rates: 2004*. Atlanta, GA: Centers for Disease Control and Prevention.

National Coalition for the Homeless. (2006). Who is homeless? Retrieved July 9, 2007, from http://www.nationalhomeless.org/publications/facts/Whois.pdf.

National Institute for Child Health and Human Development (1999). NICHD child care study investigators to report on child care quality: Higher quality care related to less problem behavior. News release, January 26, from http://www.nichd.gov/new/release/daycar99.cfm.

National Institute for Child Health and Human Development (2003). Child care linked to assertive, noncompliant, and aggressive Behaviors: Vast majority of children within normal range. News release, July 16, from http://www.nichd.gov/new/releases/child_care.cfm.

National Institute of Child Health and Human Development. (2006). *The NICHD study of early child care and youth development: Findings for children up to 4½; years*. Washington, DC: Author.

National Institute on Alcohol Abuse and Alcoholism. (2006). National epidemiologic survey on alcohol and related conditions. *Alcohol Alert, No. 70*. Washington, DC: Author.

Neil, E. (2002). Contact after adoption: the role of agencies in making and supporting plans. *Adoption and Fostering, 26*, 25–38.

Nelson, D. B., Grisso, J. A., Joffe, M. M., Brensinger, C., Shaw, L., & Datner, E. (2003). Does stress influence early pregnancy loss? *Annals of Epidemiology, 13*, 223–229.

Nelson, F. (1999). Lesbian families: Achieving motherhood. *Journal of Gay & Lesbian Social Services, 10*, 27–46.

Nelson, F. (2007). Mother tongues: The discursive journeys of lesbian and heterosexual women into motherhood. *Journal of GLBT Family Studies, 3*(4), 223–266.

Newburn-Cook, C. V., White, D., Svenson, L. W., Emianczuk, N. N., Bott, N., & Edwards, J. (2002). Where and to what extent is prevention of low birth weight possible? *Western Journal of Nursing Research, 24*, 887–904.

Nicholson, J. S., & Farris, J. R. (2007). Children's uncertain futures: Socioemotional delays and psychopathologies. In J. G. Borkowski, J. R. Farris, T. L. Whitman, S. S. Carothers, & K. Weed (Eds.), *Risk and resilience: Adolescent mothers and their children grow up* (pp. 101–123). Mahwah, NJ: Lawrence Erlbaum Associates Publishers.

Nissenberg, S. K., & Pearl, B. N. (2002). *Eating right from 8 to 18: Nutrition solutions for parents*. New York: Wiley.

Nitz, K. (1999). Adolescent pregnancy prevention: A review of interventions and programs. *Clinical Psychology Review, 19*, 457–471.

Norwood, R. (1985). *Women who love too much*. New York: Pocket Books.

Noy-Sharav, D. (2002). Good enough adoptive parenting— the adopted child and self-object relations. *Clinical Social Work Journal, 30*, 57–76.

O'Rand, A. M., & Krecker, M. L. (1990). Concepts of the life cycle: Their history, meanings, and use in the social sciences. *Annual Review of Sociology, 16*, 241–262.

Oberlander, S. E., Black, M. M., & Starr, R. H., Jr. (2007). African American adolescent mothers and grandmothers: A multigenerational approach to parenting. *American Journal of Community Psychology, 39*(1–2), 37–46.

Oldham, J. D., & Kasser, T. (1999). Attitude change in response to information that male homosexuality has a biological basis. *Journal of Sex & Marital Therapy, 25*, 121–124.

Olmos, J. E., Ybarra, L., & Monterrey, M. (1999). *Americanos: Latino life in the United States*. New York: Little, Brown.

Olweus, D. (1995). Bullying or peer abuse at school: Facts and intervention. *Current Directions in Psychological Science, 4*, 196–200.

Orme, J. G., & Buehler, C. (2001). Foster family characteristics and behavioral and emotional problems of foster children: A narrative review. *Family Relations, 50*, 3–15.

Ornelas, E. P. (2007). Hispanic and white non-Hispanic adolescent fathers: An exploratory study using socio-cultural variables. *Dissertation Abstracts International: Section B: The Sciences and Engineering, 67*(8-B), 4761.

Orthner, D. K., Bowen, G. L., & Beare, V. G. (1990). The organization family: A question of work and family boundaries. *Marriage and Family Review, 15*, 15–36.

Osborn, S. T. (2004). *A special kind of love: For those who love children with special needs*. Nashville, TN: Broadman & Holman.

Ostrea, C. (2003). *Family bound: One couple's journey through infertility and adoption*. Lincoln, NE: iUniverse, Inc.

Out, J. W., & Lafreniere, K. D. (2001). Baby Think It Over®: Using role-play to prevent teen pregnancy. *Adolescence, 36*(143), 571–582.

Overturf-Johnson, J. (2005). Who's minding the kids? Child care arrangements: 2002. *Current Population Reports, P70-101*. Washington, DC: U.S. Census Bureau.

Paechter, C. (2000). Growing up with a lesbian mother: A theoretically-based analysis of personal experience. *Sexualities, 3*, 395–408.

Palmer, C. A. (2004). Perceived husband support as a couple resource in the transition to parenthood. *Dissertation Abstracts*

International: Section B: The Sciences and Engineering, 64(8-B), 4056.

Papernow, P. L. (1984). The stepfamily cycle: An experimental model of stepfamily development. *Family Relations, 33,* 355–363.

Papernow, P. L. (1993). *Becoming a stepfamily.* San Francisco: Josey-Bass.

Parens, H. (1995). *The development of aggression in early childhood.* Northvale, NJ: Jason Aronson Publishers.

Parra-Cordona, J. R., Wampler, R. S., & Sharp, E. A. (2006). 'Wanting to be a good father': Experiences of adolescent fathers of Mexican descent in a teen fathers program. *Journal of Marital & Family Therapy, 32*(2), 215–231.

Pasley, K., & Ihinger-Tallman, M. (1987). *Remarriage.* Beverly Hills, CA: Sage Publications.

Patterson, C. J. (1992). Children of lesbian and gay parents. *Child Development, 63,* 1025–1042.

Patterson, C. J. (1995). Sexual orientation and human development: An overview. *Developmental Psychology, 31,* 3–11.

Patterson, C. J. (2000). Family relationships of lesbians and gay men. *Journal of Marriage & the Family, 62,* 1052–1069.

Patterson, C. J. (2006). Children of lesbian and gay parents. *Current Directions in Psychological Science, 15*(5), 241–244.

Patterson, C. J., Fulcher, M., & Wainright, J.(2002). Children of lesbian and gay parents: Research, law, and policy. In B. L. Bottoms & M. Bull Kovera (Eds.), *Children, social science, and the law* (pp. 176–199). New York: Cambridge University Press.

Patterson, C. J., & Redding, R. E. (1995). Lesbian and gay families with children: Implications of social science research for policy. *Journal of Social Issues, 52,* 29–50.

Paul, H. A. (2000). *Is my child OK? When behavior is a problem, when it's not, and when to seek help.* New York: Dell.

Pavao, J. M. (2004). *The family of adoption: Completely revised and updated.* Boston, MA: Beacon Press.

Pearcey, M. (2005). Gay and bisexual married men's attitudes and experiences: Homophobia, reasons for marriage, and self-identity. *Journal of GLBT Family Studies, 1*(4), 21–42.

Pellegrini, A. D., Kato, K., Blatchford, P., & Baines, E. (2002). A short-term longitudinal study of children's playground games across the first year of school: Implications for social competence and adjustment to school. *American Educational Research Journal, 39*(4), 991–1015.

Penny, J., Borders, L. D., & Portnoy, F. (2007). Reconstruction of adoption issues: Delineation of five phases among adult adoptees. *Journal of Counseling & Development, 85*(1), 30–41.

Peplau, L. A., & Beals, K. P. (2004). The family lives of lesbians and gay men. In A. L. Vangelisti (Ed.), *Handbook of family communication* (pp. 233–248). Mahwah, NJ: Lawrence Erlbaum Associates Publishers.

Perez, A., O'Neil, K., & Gesiriech, S. (2004). *Demographics of children in foster care.* Washington, DC: Pew Commission on Children in Foster Care.

Perrin, K. K., & DeJoy, S. B. (2003). Abstinence-only education: How we got here and where we're going. *Journal of Public Health Policy, 24,* 445–459.

Perry, J. L. (2004). *Right to be wanted, right to be loved: Telling children about adoption.* Philadelphia, PA: Xlibris Corp.

Peterson, G. W., Steinmetz, S. K., & Wilson, S. M. (2005). Cultural and cross-cultural perspectives on parent-youth relations. In G. W. Peterson, S. K. Steinmetz, & S. M. Wilson (Eds.), *Parent-youth relations: Cultural and cross-cultural perspectives.* Binghamton, NY: Haworth Press.

Peterson, J., Song, X., & Jones-DeWeever, A. (2003). *Life after welfare reform: Low income single parent families, pre- and post-TANF.* Washington, DC: Institute for Women's Policy Research.

Peterson, L. M., Butts, J., & Deville, D. M. (2000). Parenting experiences of three self-identified gay fathers. *Smith College Studies in Social Work, 70,* 513–521.

Pew Charitable Trusts. (2004a). *Voices from the inside.* Washington, DC: Author.

Pew Charitable Trusts. (2004b). *Fostering the future: Safety, permanence, and well-being for children in foster care.* Washington, DC: Author.

Pew Charitable Trusts. (2007). *Time for reform: Too many birthdays in foster care.* Philadelphia: Author.

Pew Hispanic Center. (2007). *The American community: Blacks, 2004.* Washington, DC: U.S. Bureau of the Census.

Philliber, S. (1999). Peer programs to prevent teen pregnancy: what have we learned? *PPFY Network, 2,* 4–5.

Phillips, S. (2003). Adolescent health. In A. M. Nezu & C. M. Nezu (Eds.), *Handbook of psychology: Health psychology* (Vol. 9, pp. 465–485). New York: Wiley.

Piaget, J. (1967). *Six psychological studies.* New York: Random House.

Piaget, J. (1972). Intellectual evolution from adolescence to adulthood. *Human Development, 15,* 1–12.

Piaget, J., & Inhelder, B. (1969). *The psychology of the child.* New York: Basic Books.

Pinsof, W. M. (2002). The death of "'til death us do part": The transformation of pair-bonding in the 20th century. *Family Process, 41*(2), 135–157.

Piper, B., & Balswick, J. C. (1997). *Then they leave home: Parenting after the kids grow up.* Downers Grove, IL: InterVarsity Press.

Pittman, F. S. (1987). *Turning points: Treating families in transition and crisis.* New York: W. W. Norton.

Planck, C. (2006). Connection and community: How the Family Pride Coalition supports parents and children of GLBT families. *Journal of GLBT Family Studies, 2*(3/4), 39–48.

Plotkin, S. A. (2001). Rubella eradication. *Vaccine, 19,* 3311–3319.

Population Reference Bureau (2003a). Diversity, poverty characterize female-headed households from http://www.prb.org/Template.cfm?Section=PRB&template=/ContentManagement/ContentDisplay.cfm&ContentID=8277

Population Reference Bureau (2003b). *Traditional Families Account for Only 7% of U.S. Households* from http://www.ameristat.org.

Price, E. (2004). *Divorce and teens: When a family splits apart.* Berkeley Heights, NJ: Enslow Publishers.

Price, S., Noseworthy, J., & Thornton, J. (2007). Women's experience with social presence during childbirth. *American Journal of Maternal/Child Nursing, 32*(3), 184–191.

Pryor, J., & Rodgers, B. (2001). *Children in changing families: Life after parental separation.* Malden, MA: Blackwell.

Radke-Yarrow, M., Zahn-Waxler, C., & Chapman, M. (1983). Children's prosocial dispositions and behavior. In M. E. Hetherington (Ed.), *Handbook of child psychology* (Vol. 4). New York: Wiley.

Raffaelli, M., & Crockett, L. J. (2003). Sexual risk taking in adolescence: The role of self-regulation and attraction to risk. *Developmental Psychology, 39,* 1036–1046.

Raley, S. B., Mattingly, M. J., & Bianchi, S. M. (2006). How dual are dual-income couples? Documenting change from 1970 to 2001. *Journal of Marriage and Family, 68*(1), 11–28.

Ramey, M. (2004). *Adult children, adult choices: Outgrowing codependency.* Chicago: Sheed & Ward.

Ratcliffe, S. D. (2007). *Family medicine obstetrics* (3rd ed.). St. Louis: Elsevier.

Reichman, N. E., & Teitler, J. O. (2003). Effects of psychosocial risk factors and prenatal interventions on birth weight: Evidence from New Jersey's HealthStart program. *Perspectives on Sexual & Reproductive Health, 35*, 130–137.

Reynolds, G. P., Wright, J. V., & Beale, B. (2003). The roles of grandparents in educating today's children. *Journal of Instructional Psychology, 30*, 316–325.

Rholes, W. S., Simpson, J. A, Campbell, L., & Grich, J. (2001). Adult attachment and the transition to parenthood. *Journal of Personality & Social Psychology, 81*, 421–435.

Richardson, R. W. (1999). *Family ties that bind: A self-help guide to change through family of origin therapy.* Vancouver, British Colombia, Canada: Self-Counsel Press.

Rigazio-DiGilio, S. A., & Cramer-Benjamin, D. (2000). Families with learning disabilities, physical disabilities, and other childhood challenges. In W. C. Nichols, M. A. Pace-Nichols, D. S. Becvar, & A. Y. Napier (Eds.), *Handbook of family development and intervention* (pp. 415–438). New York: Wiley.

Riley, L. (2006). *Healthy eating during pregnancy.* Des Moines, IA: Meredith Books.

Riley, L. A., & Glass, J. L. (2002). You can't always get what you want—Infant care preferences and use among employed mothers. *Journal of Marriage and the Family, 64*, 2–15.

Ring, S. (2001). Use of role playing in parent training: A methodological component analysis of systematic training for effective parenting. *Dissertation Abstracts International: Section B: the Sciences & Engineering, 61* (11-B), 6121.

Ripley, R. J. (2003). *My child has special needs: A journey from grief to joy.* Enumclaw, WA: Pleasant Word.

Roberge, G. D. (2007). The tentacles of bullying: The impact of negative childhood peer relationships on adult professional and educational choices. *Dissertation Abstracts International Section A: Humanities and Social Sciences, 67*(10-A), 3725.

Robi, J. L., & Shaw, S. A. (2006). The African orphan crisis and international adoption. *Social Work, 51*(3), 199–210.

Robinson, M. M., & Wilkes, S. E. (2006). 'Older but not wiser': What custodial grandparents want to tell social workers about raising grandchildren. *Social Work & Christianity, 33*(2), 164–177.

Robinson, P. W., Robinson, M. P. W., & Dunn, T. W. (2003). STEP parenting: A review of the research. *Canadian Journal of Counseling, 37*(4), 270–278.

Rock, E. A. (2002). Empathy in the easily aroused child. *Dissertation Abstracts International: Section B: the Sciences & Engineering, 63*(4-B), 2101.

Rogoff, B. (1990). *Apprenticeship in thinking: Cognitive development in social context.* New York: Oxford University Press.

Rogoff, B. (2003). *The cultural nature of human development.* Oxford: Oxford University Press.

Rolls, B. J., Engell, D., & Birch, L. L. (2000). Serving portion size influences 5-year-old but not 3-year-old children's food intake. *Journal of the American Dietetic Association, 100*, 232–234.

Rose-Jacobs, R., Cabral, H., Posner, M. A., Epstein, J., & Frank, D. A. (2002). Do "we just know"? Masked assessors' ability to accurately identify children with prenatal cocaine exposure. *Journal of Developmental & Behavioral Pediatrics, 23*, 340–346.

Rosenthal, D. A., & Feldman, S. S. (1992). The relationship between parenting behavior and ethnic identity in Chinese-American and Chinese-Australian adolescents. *International Journal of Psychology, 27*, 19–31.

Ross, M. E., & Aday, L. A. (2006). Stress and coping in African American grandparents who are raising their grandchildren. *Journal of Family Issues, 27*(7), 912–932.

Rothblum, E. (2004). Same-sex marriage and legal relationships: I do or do I? *Journal of GLBT Family Studies, 1*(1), 21–31.

Rozie-Battle, J. (2003). Economic support and the dilemma of teen fathers. *Journal of Health & Social Policy, 17*, 73–86.

Runyon, M. K., Deblinger, E., Ryan, E. E., & Thakkar-Kolar, R. (2004). An overview of child physical abuse: Developing an integrated parent-child cognitive-behavioral treatment approach. *Trauma, Violence & Abuse, 5*, 65–85.

Rushton, A. (2003). Support for adoptive families: a review of current evidence on problems, needs and effectiveness. *Adoption and Fostering, 27*, 41–50.

Russell, C. S. (1974). Transition to parenthood: Problems and gratifications. *Journal of Marriage and the Family, 36*, 294–301.

Rust, P. C. (2003). Finding a sexual identity and community: Therapeutic implications and cultural assumptions in scientific models of coming out. In L. D. Garnets, & D. C. Kimmel (Eds.), *Psychological perspectives on lesbian, gay, and bisexual experiences* (2nd ed., pp. 227–269). New York: Columbia University Press.

Ryan, S. D. (2008). Parent-child interaction styles between gay and lesbian parents and their adopted children. *Journal of GLBT Family Studies, 3*(2/3), 105–132.

Ryan, S. D., Bedard, L. E., & Gertz, M. G. (2007). The influence of gender on the placement of children with gay or lesbian adoptive parents. *Journal of GLBT Family Studies, 3*(1), 15–34.

Rys, G. S., & Bear, G. G. (1997). Relational aggression and peer relations: Gender and developmental issues. *Merrill-Palmer Quarterly, 43*, 87–106.

Saadeh, W., Rizzo, C. P., & Roberts, D. G. (2002). Spanking. *Clinical Pediatrics, 41*(2), 87–88.

Sabbagh, S. (2005). An integrative etic-emic approach to portraying the halutzuit system of societal equity: Comparing Israeli Jew and Israeli Arab perceptions of justice. *Journal of Cross-Cultural Psychology, 36*(1), 147–166.

Saleh, M. F., Buzi, R. S., Weinman, M. L., & Smith, P. B. (2005). The nature of connections: Young fathers and their children. *Adolescence, 40*(159), 513–523.

Samar, V. J. (2005). Same-sex marriage: The difficult road ahead. *Journal of GLBT Family Studies, 1*(2), 137–141.

Sandelowski, M., Harris, B. G., & Holditch-Davis, D. (1989). Infertile couples and the quest for change. *Journal of Nursing Scholarship, 21*(4), 220–226.

Santrock, J. (2007). *Adolescence* (10th ed.). Moorpark, CA: Academic Internet Publishers, Inc.

Satir, V. (1972a). Family systems and approaches to family therapy. In G. D. Erikson & T. P. Hogan (Eds.), *Family therapy: An introduction to theory and technique.* Monterey, CA: Brooks/Cole.

Satir, V. (1972b). *Peoplemaking.* Palo Alto, CA: Science and Behavior Books.

Satyen, L. (2003). Rethinking ADHD: Integrated approaches to helping children at home and at school. *Journal of Family Studies, 9*, 276–277.

Saunders, J. A. (2002). African American teen parents and their non-parenting peers: Differences in high school and young adulthood. *DAI-A, 62*, 4335.

Savin-Williams, R. C. (2001). *Mom, Dad. I'm gay. How families negotiate coming out.* Washington, DC: American Psychological Association.

Savin-Williams, R. C., & Dube, E. M. (1998). Parental reactions and self-esteem among gay and lesbian youths. *Journal of Homosexuality, 18*, 1–36.

Savin-Williams, R. C., & Ream, G. L. (2003). Suicide attempts among sexual-minority male youth. *Journal of Clinical Child & Adolescent Psychology, 32*, 509–522.

Schacher, S. J., Auerbach, C. F., & Silverstein, L. B. (2005). Gay fathers expanding the possibilities for us all. *Journal of GLBT Family Studies, 1*(3), 31–52.

Schatz, J. N., & Lounds, J. J. (2007). Child maltreatment: Precursors of developmental delays. In J. G. Borkowski, J. R. Farris, T. L. Whitman, S. S. Carothers, & K. Weed (Eds.), *Risk and resilience: Adolescent mothers and their children grow up* (pp. 125–150). Mahwah, NJ: Lawrence Erlbaum Associates Publishers.

Scher, M. S., Richardson, G. A., & Day, N. L. (2000). Effects of prenatal crack/cocaine and other drug exposure on electroencephalographic sleep studies at birth and one year. *Pediatrics, 105*, 39–48.

Schmitz, C. L., & Tebb, S. S. (2003). *Diversity in single-parent families: Working from strength.* Chicago: Lyceum Books.

Schneider, B. H., Atkinson, L., & Tardif, C. (2001). Child-parent attachment and children's peer relations: A quantitative review. *Developmental Psychology, 37*(1), 86–100.

Schneider, M. L., Roughton, E. C., Koehler, A. J., & Lubach, G. R. (1999). Growth and development following prenatal stress exposure in primates: An examination of ontogenetic vulnerability. *Child Development, 70*, 253–274.

Shultz, S. K. (2001). Child physical abuse: Relationship of parental substance use to severity of abuse and risk for future abuse. *Dissertation Abstracts International: Section B: the Sciences & Engineering, 62*(1-B), 605. Ann Arbor, MI: University Microfilms International.

Schulz, M. S., Cowan, C. P., & Cowan, P. A. (2006). Promoting healthy beginnings: A randomized controlled trial of a preventive intervention to preserve marital quality during the transition to parenthood. *Journal of Consulting and Clinical Psychology, 74*(1), 20–31.

Schutter, L. S., & Brinker, R. P. (1992). Conjuring a new category of disability from prenatal cocaine exposure: Are the infants unique biological or caretaking casualties? *Topics in Early Childhood Special Education, 11*, 84–111.

Schwartz, L. L. (2000). Families by choice: Adoptive and foster families. In W. C. Nichols, M. A. Pace-Nichols, D. S. Becvar, & A. Y. Napier (Eds.), *Handbook of family development* (pp. 255–278). New York, NY: Wiley.

Schwebel, D. C., & Plumert, J. M. (1999). Longitudinal and concurrent relations among temperament, ability estimation, and injury proneness. *Child Development, 70*, 700–712.

Schweingruber, H. A., & Kalil, A. (2000). Decision making and depressive symptoms in black and white multigenerational teen-parent families. *Journal of Family Psychology, 14*, 556–569.

Scommegna, P. (2002, September). Increased cohabitation changing children's family settings. *Research on Today's Issues, 13.* Bethesda, MD: Demographic and Behavioral Sciences Branch, Center for Population Research, National Institute of Child Health and Human Development (NICHD), National Institutes of Health.

Secunda, V. (2004). *Losing your parents, finding yourself: The defining turning point of adult life.* Collingdale, PA: DIANE Publishing Co.

Segal-Engelchin, D., Erera, P. I., & Cwikel, J. (2005). The hetero-gay family: An emergent family configuration. *Journal of GLBT Family Studies, 1*(3), 85–104.

Shultz, S. K. (2001). Child physical abuse: Relationship of parental substance use to severity of abuse and risk for future abuse. *Dissertation Abstracts International: Section B: the Sciences & Engineering, 62*(1-B), 605. Ann Arbor, MI: University Microfilms International.

Siegenthaler, A., & Bigner, J. J. (2000). The value of children to lesbian and nonlesbian mothers. *Journal of Homosexuality, 39*, 73–92.

Simons, R. L., Whitbeck, L. B., Conger, R. D., & Wu, C. (1991). Intergenerational transmission of harsh parenting. *Developmental Psychology, 27*, 159–171.

Sinclair, J. C. (2003). Weighing risks and benefits in treating the individual patient. *Clinics in Perinatology, 30*, 251–268.

Singer, A. (2001). Coming out of the shadows: Supporting the development of our gay, lesbian, and bisexual adolescents. In M. McConville & G. Wheeler (Eds.), *The heart of development* (Vol. 11, pp. 172–192). Cambridge, MA: GestaltPress Book.

Skinner, B. F. (1938). *The behavior of organisms.* New York: Appleton-Century-Crofts.

Skinner, J. H. (2001). Acculturation: Measures of ethnic accommodation to the dominant American culture. *Journal of Mental Health and Aging, 7*, 41–52.

Smith, C., Perou, R., & Lesesne, C. (2002). Parent education. In M. H. Bornstein (Ed.), *Handbook of parenting* (Vol. 4, 2nd ed., pp. 389–410). Mahwah, NJ: Erlbaum.

Smith, L. M., LaGasse, L., Derauf, C., Grant, P., Shah, R., Arria, A., et al. (2006). The infant development, environment, and lifestyle study: Effects of prenatal methamphetamine exposure, polydrug exposure, and poverty on intrauterine growth. *Pediatrics, 118*(3), 1149–1156.

Smith, P. K., Smees, R., Pellegrini, A. D., & Menesini, E. (2002). Comparing pupil and teacher perceptions for playful fighting, serious fighting, and positive peer interaction. In J. L. Roopnarine (Ed.), *Conceptual, social-cognitive, and contextual issues in the fields of play: Play & culture studies* (Vol. 4, pp. 235–245). Westport, CT: Ablex Publishing.

SmithBattle, L. (2007). "I wanna have a 'hood future": Teen mothers' rise in educational aspirations, competing demands, and limited school support. *Youth & Society, 38*(3), 348–371.

Smithgall, C., & Mason, S. (2004). Identified problems and service utilization patterns among kinship families accessing mental health services. *Journal of Human Behavior in the Social Environment, 9*(3), 41–55.

Snow, J. E. (2004). *How it feels to have a gay or lesbian parent: A book by kids for kids of all ages.* New York: Harrington Park Press.

Sobol, M. P., Daly, K. J., & Kelloway, E. K. (2000). Paths to the facilitation of open adoption. *Family Relations, 49*, 419–424.

Sokol, R. J., Jr., Delaney-Black, V., & Nordstrom, B. (2003). Fetal alcohol spectrum disorder. *Journal of the American Medical Association, 290*, 2996–2999.

Solomon, C. R., & Poirier, M.-C. (2007). Parenting styles and attributions and the behavior of children in the 'no' stage in adoptive and biological families. *Adoption Quarterly, 10*(1), 63–83.

Sonenstein, F. L., Stewart, K., Lindberg, L. D., Pernas, M., & Williams, S. (1997). *Involving males in preventing teen pregnancy.* Washington, DC: Urban Institute Press.

Sood, B., Delaney-Black, V., Covington, C., Nordstrom-Klee, B., Ager, J., Templin, T., Janisse, J., Martier, S., & Sokol, R. J. (2001). Prenatal alcohol exposure and childhood behavior at age 6 to 7 years: I. Dose response effect. *Pediatrics, 108,* 461–462.

Spillman, J. A., Deschamps, H. S., & Crews, J. A. (2004). Perspectives on nonresidential paternal involvement and grief: A literature review. *The Family Journal, 12*(3), 263–270.

Spock, B. (2004). *Dr. Spock's baby and child care* (8th ed.). New York: Simon & Schuster.

Springer, C. A., Britt, T. W., & Schlenker, B. R. (1998). Codependency: Clarifying the construct. *Journal of Mental Health Counseling, 20,* 141–158.

Stacey, J. (1998). Dada-ism in the 1990s: Getting past baby talk about fatherlessness. In C. Daniels (Ed.), *Lost fathers: The politics of fatherlessness in America* (pp. 51–84). New York: Palgrave Macmillan.

Stacey, J., & Biblarz, T. J. (2001). (How) does the sexual orientation of parents matter? *American Sociological Review, 66,* 159–183.

Stafford, J. J. (2004). Remembered parental corporal punishment and its relation to attitudes and abuse: A cross national study. *Dissertation Abstracts International: Section B: The Sciences and Engineering, 64*(11-B), 2004. pp. 5769.

Stainer-Person, K. E. (1998). Individual, familial, and parental factors associated with teenage pregnancy. *Dissertation Abstracts-International: Section B: the Sciences & Engineering, 59*(3-B). Ann Arbor, MI: University Microfilms International.

Stang J., & Bayerl, C. T. (2003). Position of the American Dietetic Association: Child and adolescent food and nutrition programs. *Journal of the American Dietetic Association, 103,* 887–893.

Stanley, S. M., Rhoades, G. K., & Markman, H. J. (2006). Sliding versus deciding: Inertia and the premarital cohabitation effect. *Family Relations, 55*(4), 499–509.

Staples, R. (1999). Interracial relationships: A convergence of desire and opportunity. In R. Staples (Ed.), *The black family: Essays and studies* (pp. 129–136). Belmont, CA: Wadsworth.

Staples, R., & Mirande, A. (1980). Racial and cultural variations among American families: A decennial review of the literature on minority families. *Journal of Marriage and the Family, 42,* 887–903.

Stark, E. (2000). *Everything you need to know about family violence.* New York: Rosen Publishing Group.

Stein, M. T., Fennell, J. H., & Fulcher, A. (2004). Benefits of a doula present at the birth of a child. *Journal of Developmental & Behavioral Pediatrics, 25*(5S), S89–S92.

Stein, T. J. (2007). Court-ordered grandparent visitation: Welcome event or unwarranted intrusion into family life. *Social Service Review, 81*(2), 229–243.

Steinberg, L. D. (2004). *Adolescence.* New York, NY: McGraw-Hill.

Steinberg, L., & Silk, J. S. (2002). Parenting adolescents. In M. H. Bornstein (Ed.), *Handbook of parenting* (Vol. 1, 2nd ed., pp. 103–133). Mahwah, NJ: Lawrence Erlbaum Associates.

Steinberg, L., Elmen, J. D., & Mounts, N. S. (1989). Authoritative parenting, psychosocial maturity, and academic success among adolescents. *Child Development, 60,* 1424–1436.

Steinhausen, H-C., Blattmann, B., & Pfund, F. (2007). Developmental outcome in children with intrauterine exposure to substances. *European Addiction Research, 13*(2), 94–100.

Steinmetz, S., Clavan, S., & Stein, K. F. (1990). *Marriage and family realities: Historical and contemporary perspectives.* New York: Harper & Row.

Stern, M., & Alvarez, A. (1992). Knowledge of child development and caretaking attitudes: A comparison of pregnant, parenting, and nonpregnant adolescents. *Family Relations, 41,* 297–302.

Sternberg, R. J. (1988). *The triangle of love: Intimacy, passion, and commitment.* New York: Basic Books.

Stevens, M., Perry, B., Burston, A., Golombok, S., & Golding, J. (2003). Openness in lesbian-mother families regarding mother's sexual orientation and child's conception by donor insemination. *Journal of Reproductive & Infant Psychology, 21,* 347–362.

Stevens-Simon, C. (2000). Participation in a program that helps families with one teen pregnancy prevent others. *Journal of Pediatric and Adolescent Gynecology, 13,* 167–169.

Stevens-Simon, C., Nelligan, D., & Kelly, L. (2001). Adolescents at risk for mistreating their children. Part I: Prenatal identification. *Child Abuse & Neglect, 25,* 737–751.

Stevens-Simon, C., Sheeder, J., & Harder, S. (2005). Teen contraceptive decisions: Childbearing intentions are the tip of the iceberg. *Women & Health, 42*(1), 55–73.

Stewart, S. D. (2005). Boundary ambiguity in stepfamilies. *Journal of Family Issues, 26*(7), 1002–1029.

Stifter, C. A., Coulehan, C. M., & Fish, M. (1993). Linking employment to attachment: The mediating effects of maternal separation anxiety and interactive behavior. *Child Development, 64,* 1451–1460.

Stiles, J. (2008). *Fundamentals of brain development: Integrating nature and nurture.* Boston: Harvard University Press.

Strasburger, V. C. (2006). Is there an unconscious conspiracy against teenagers in the United States? *Clinical Pediatrics, 45*(8), 714–717.

Strassberg, Z., Dodge, K. A., Petit, G. S., & Bates, J. E. (1994). Spanking in the home and children's subsequent aggression toward kindergarten peers. *Development and Psychopathology, 6,* 445–462.

Straus, M. A. (1991a). Discipline and violence: Physical punishment of children and violence and other crime in adulthood. *Social Problems, 38,* 133–154.

Straus, M. A. (1991b). New theory and old canards about family violence research. *Social Problems, 38,* 180–197.

Straus, M. A. (1994). *Beating the devil out of them: Corporal punishment in American families.* New York: Lexington.

Straus, M. A., & Field, C. J. (2003). Psychological aggression by American parents: National data on prevalence, chronicity, and severity. *Journal of Marriage and the Family, 65,* 795–808.

Straus, M. A., & Gelles, R. J. (2006). *Behind closed doors: Violence in the American family.* Piscataway, NJ: Transaction Publishers.

Straus, M. A., & Yodanis, C. L. (1996). Corporal punishment in adolescence and physical assaults on spouses in later life: What accounts for the link? *Journal of Marriage and the Family, 58,* 825–841.

Strickland, B. R. (1995). Research on sexual orientation and human development: A commentary. *Developmental Psychology, 31,* 137–140.

Strommen, E. F. (1989a). Hidden branches and growing pains: Homosexuality and the family tree. *Marriage and Family Review, 14,* 9–34.

Strommen, E. F. (1989b). "You're a what?": Family member reactions to the disclosure of homosexuality. *Journal of Homosexuality, 18,* 37–58.

Strong, B. (2004). *Human sexuality: Diversity in contemporary America.* New York: McGraw-Hill.

Studd, J. W. (2004). *Progress in obstetrics and gynecology.* Philadelphia: Elsevier.

Sullivan, G., & Reynolds, R. (2003). Homosexuality in midlife: Narrative and identity. *Journal of Gay & Lesbian Social Services, 15,* 153–170.

Sullivan, M., & Wodarski, J. S. (2002). Social alienation in gay youth. *Journal of Human Behavior in the Social Environment, 5,* 1–17.

Sullivan-Bolyai, J., Hull, H. F., Wilson, C., & Corey, L. (1983). Neonatal herpes simplex virus infection in King County, Washington: Increasing incidence and epidemiologic correlates. *Journal of the American Medical Association, 250,* 3059–3062.

Sunley, R. (1955). Early nineteenth century American literature on child rearing. In M. Mead & M. Wolfenstein (Eds.), *Childhood in contemporary cultures.* Chicago: University of Chicago Press.

Susman, E. J., Dorn, L. D., & Schiefelbein, V. L. (2003). Puberty, sexuality, and health. In R. M. Lerner & M. A. Easterbrooks (Eds.), *Handbook of psychology: Developmental psychology* (Vol. 6., pp. 295–324). New York: Wiley.

Swinford, S. P., DeMaris, A., Cernkovich, S. A., & Giordano, P. C. (2000). Harsh physical discipline in childhood and violence in later romantic involvements: The mediating role of problem behaviors. *Journal of Marriage and the Family, 62,* 508–519.

Swize, J. (2002). Transracial adoption and the unblinkable difference: Racial dissimilarity serving the interests of adopted children. *Virginia Law Review, 88,* 1079–1118.

Talmadge, L. D., & Talmadge, W. C. (2003). Dealing with the unhappy marriage. In S. B. Levine & C. B. Risen (Eds.) *Handbook of clinical sexuality for mental health professionals* (pp. 75–92). New York, NY: Brunner-Routledge.

Tan, L. H., & Quinlivan, J. A. (2006). Domestic violence, single parenthood, and fathers in the setting of teenage pregnancy. *Journal of Adolescent Health, 38*(3), 201–207.

Tasker, F. (1999). Children in lesbian-led families: A review. *Clinical Child Psychology & Psychiatry, 4,* 153–166.

Tasker, F. (2002). Lesbian and gay parenting. In A. Coyle & C. Kitzinger (Eds.), *Lesbian and gay psychology: New perspectives* (pp. 81–97). Malden, MA: Blackwell Publishers.

Tasker, F. (2005). Lesbian mothers, gay fathers, and their children: A review. *Journal of Developmental & Behavioral Pediatrics, 26*(3), 224–240.

Tasker, F., & Patterson, C. (2007). Research on gay and lesbian parenting: Retrospect and prospect. Journal of GLBT Family Studies, 3(2/3), 9–34.

Taylor, M. K. (2001). *Grandparent visitation rights: A legal research guide.* Buffalo, NY: William S. Hein & Co.

Therrien, M. & Ramirez, R. R. (2000). The Hispanic population in the United States: March 2000. *Current Population Reports, P20-535.* Washington, DC: U.S. Census Bureau.

Thompson, G. L. (2003). *What African American parents want educators to know.* New York: Praeger.

Thompson, J. M. (2002). *Mommy queerest: Contemporary rhetorics of lesbian maternal identity.* Amherst, MA: University of Massachusetts Press.

Thornberry, T. P., Smith, C. A., & Howard, G. J. (1997). Risk factors for teenage fatherhood. *Journal of Marriage and Family, 59,* 505–522.

Thornton, A., & Young-DeMarco, L. (2001). Four decades of trends in attitudes toward family issues in the United States: The 1960s through the 1990s. *Journal of Marriage and the Family, 63,* 1009–1037.

Timmer, S. G., Borrego, J., Jr., & Urquiza, A. J. (2002). Antecedents of coercive interactions in physically abusive mother-child dyads. *Journal of Interpersonal Violence, 17,* 836–853.

Tinsley, B. J., Lees, N. B., & Sumartojo, E. (2004). Child and adolescent HIV risk: Familial and cultural perspectives. *Journal of Family Psychology, 18,* 208–224.

Tinsworth, D., & McDonald, J. (2001). *Special study: Injuries and deaths associated with children's playground equipment.* Washington, DC: U.S. Consumer Product Safety Commission.

Tobin, C. (2002). *The parent's problem solver: Smart solutions for everyday discipline dilemmas and behavior problems.* New York, NY: Crown Publishing Group.

Topolak, R., Williams, V., & Wilson, J. (2001). Preventing teenage pregnancy: A multifaceted review. *Journal of Psychological Practice, 7,* 33–46.

Townsend, L. (2003). Open adoption: a review of the literature with recommendations to adoption practitioners. *Journal of Child and Adolescent Mental Health, 15,* 1–11.

Trosper, T. B. (2002). Parenting strategies in the middle class African-American family. *Dissertation Abstracts International, 63,* 864.

Trumbull, E., Rothstein-Fisch, C., & Greenfield, P. M. (2000). Bridging cultures in our schools: New approaches that work. Retrieved August 3, 2007, from http://www.wested.org/cs/we/view/rs/81.

Tubman, J. G., Wagner, E. F., & Langer, L. M. (2003). Patterns of depressive symptoms, drinking motives, and sexual behavior among substance abusing adolescents: Implications for health risk. *Journal of Child & Adolescent Substance Abuse, 13,* 37–57.

Turkel, A. R. (2007). Sugar and spice and puppy dogs' tails: The psychodynamics of bullying. *Journal of the American Academy of Psychoanalysis and Dynamic Psychiatry, 35*(2), 243–258.

Turnbull, R., & Cilley, M. (1999). *Explanations and implications of the 1997 amendments to the IDEA.* Upper Saddle River, NJ: Prentice Hall.

Turner, R. J., Sorenson, A. M., & Turner, J. B. (2000). Social contingencies in mental health: A seven-year follow-up study of teenage mothers. *Journal of Marriage and the Family, 62,* 777–791.

U.S. Bureau of the Census. (2006). America's families and living arrangements 2006. *Current Population Survey, March 2006.* Washington, DC: Author.

U.S. Bureau of the Census. (2007a). *Statistical abstract of the United States: 2006.* Washington, DC: Author.

U.S. Bureau of the Census. (2007b). Population profile of the United States: Dynamic version (Internet Release). Retrieved July 12, 2007, from http://www.census.gov/population/www/pop-profile/profildynamic.html#notes.

U.S. Department of Health and Human Services. (2004). *How many children were adopted in 2000 and 2001?* Washington, DC: Child Welfare Information Gateway.

U.S. Department of Health and Human Services, Administration on Children, Youth, and Families. (2008). *Child maltreatment 2006.* Washington, DC: Author.

Urban Institute. (1999). *Get organized: A guide to preventing teen pregnancy*. Washington, DC: Author.

Van Egeren, L. A. (2004). The development of the coparenting relationship over the transition to parenthood. *Infant Mental Health Journal, 25*(5), 453–477.

Vanfraussen, K., Ponjaert-Kristoffersen, I., & Brewaeys, A. (2002). What does it mean for youngsters to grow up in a lesbian family created by means of donor insemination? *Journal of Reproductive & Infant Psychology, 20,* 237–252.

Vanfraussen, K., Ponjaert-Kristoffersen, I., & Brewaeys, A. (2003). Family functioning in lesbian families created by donor insemination. *American Journal of Orthopsychiatry, 73,* 78–90.

Van Houten, R., & Hall, R. V. (2001). *The measurement of behavior: Behavior modification* (3rd ed.). Austin, TX: PRO-ED.

van Poppel, F. W. A., Oris, M., & Lee, James Z. (2004) *The road to independence: Leaving home in western and eastern societies, 16th to 20th centuries*. New York: Peter Lang Publishing, Inc.

van Spronsen, F. J., Molendijk, H., Erwich, J. J., & Smit, G. P. (2003). Inherited metabolic diseases and pregnancy: Consequences for mother and child. *Nederlands Tijdschrift voor Geneeskunde, 147,* 235–240.

Van Tonningen-van Driel, M. M., Garbis-Berkvens, J. M., & Reuvers-Lodewijks, W. E. (1999). Pregnancy outcome after ecstasy use; 43 cases followed by the Teratology Information Service of the National Institute for Public Health and Environment (RIVM). *Nederlands Tijdschrift voor Geneeskunde, 143*(1), 27–31.

van Wormer, K., & McKinney, R. (2003). What schools can do to help gay/lesbian/bisexual youth: A harm reduction approach. *Adolescence, 38,* 409–420.

Varon, L. (2003). *Adopting on your own: The complete guide to adoption for single parents*. Collingdale, PA: DIANE Publishing Co.

Vasquez, G. (2006). Decreasing attitudinal support for corporal punishment through education. *Dissertation Abstracts International: Section B: The Sciences and Engineering, 67*(5-B), 2881.

Veevers, J. E. (1973). The social meanings of parenthood. *Psychiatry, 36,* 291–310.

Vink, T., Hinney, A., van Elburg, A. A., van Goozen, S. H. M., Sandkuikl, L. A., Sinke, R. J., et al. (2001). Association between agoui-related protein gene polymorphism and anorexia nervosa. *Molecular Psychiatry, 6,* 325–328.

von Bertalanffy, L. (1968). General systems theory and psychiatry. In S. Arieti (Ed.), *American handbook of psychiatry* (Vol. 1, pp. 247–300). New York: Basic Books.

von Bertalanffy, L. (1974). *General systems theory*. New York: Braziller.

Vontver, L. A. (2003). *Appleton and Lange's review of obstetrics and gynecology*. New York: McGraw-Hill.

Vygotsky, L. S. (1962). *Thought and language*. Cambridge, MA: MIT Press.

Vygotsky, L. S. (1987). Thinking and speech. In R. W. Reiber & A. S. Carton (Eds.), *The collected works of L. S. Vygotsky: Problems of general psychology* (Vol. 1, pp. 37–285). New York: Plenum.

Wainryb, C. (2004). The study of diversity in human development: Culture, urgencies, and perils. *Human Development, 45,* 131–137.

Wakschlag, L. S., & Hans, S. L. (2000). Early parenthood in context: Implications for development and intervention. In C. H. Zeanah, Jr. (Ed.), *Handbook of infant mental health* (2nd ed., pp. 129–144). New York: Guilford Press.

Waldenstroem, U. (1999a). Experience of labor and birth in 1111 women. *Journal of Psychosomatic Research, 47,* 471–482.

Waldenstroem, U. (1999b). Effects of birth centre care on fathers' satisfaction with care, experience of the birth and adaptation to fatherhood. *Journal of Reproductive & Infant Psychology, 17,* 357–368.

Waldner, L. K., & Magruder, B. (1999). Coming out to parents: Perceptions of family relations, perceived resources and identity expression as predictors of identity disclosure for gay and lesbian adolescents. *Journal of Homosexuality, 37,* 83–100.

Wallace, W. (2004). Family violence: Legal, medical and social perspective (4th ed.). Boston, MA: Allyn & Bacon.

Wallace, W. (2007). *Family violence: Legal, medical and social perspective* (5th ed.). Boston: Allyn & Bacon.

Waller, M. A., Brown, B., & Whittle, B. (1999). Mentoring as a bridge to positive outcomes for teen mothers and their children. *Child and Adolescent Social Work Journal, 16,* 467–480.

Wallerstein, J. S., & Blakeslee, S. (2003). *What about the kids? Raising your children before, during and after divorce*. New York: Hyperion Press.

Wallerstein, J. S., Lewis, J. M., & Blakeslee, S. (2001). *The unexpected legacy of divorce: A twenty-five year landmark study*. New York: Hyperion Press.

Walsh, W. (2002). Spankers and nonspankers: Where they get their information on spanking. *Family Relations, 51,* 81–88.

Wark, M. J., Kruczek, T., & Boley, A. (2003). Emotional neglect and family structure: Impact on student functioning. *Child Abuse & Neglect, 27,* 1033–1043.

Warren, E., & Tyagi, A. W. (2004). *The two-income trap: Why middle-class mothers and fathers are going broke*. New York: Basic Books.

Watson, J. B. (1928). *Psychological care of infant and child*. New York: Norton.

Wegar, K. (2000). Adoption, family ideology, and social stima: Bias in community attitudes, adoption research, and practice. *Family Relations, 49,* 363–370.

Wegscheider, S. (1989). *Another chance: Hope and healthy for the alcoholic family* (2nd ed.). Palo Alto, CA: Science and Behavior Books.

Weight, C. E. (2004). *Divorce in America: A reference handbook*. Santa Barbara, CA: A B C-Clio.

Weinberg, G. (1972). *Society and the healthy homosexual*. New York: St. Martin's Press.

Weingartner, P. L. (1999). *ADHD handbook for families: A guide for communicating with professionals*. Washington, DC: Child and Family Press.

Weinhold, B. K. (1991). *Breaking free of addictive family relationships*. Walpole, NH: Stillpoint.

Weinraub, M., Horvath, D. L., & Gringlass, M. B. (2002). Single parenthood. In M. H. Bornstein (Ed.), *Handbook of parenting: Vol. 3. Being and becoming a parent* (2nd ed., pp. 109–140). Mahwah, NJ: Erlbaum.

Weinstock, H., Berman, S., & Cates, W., Jr. (2004). Sexually transmitted diseases among American youth: Incidence and prevalence estimates, 2000. *Perspectives on Sexual and Reproductive Health, 36,* 6–10.

Weir, K. N. (2003). Adoptive family 'leap-frogging' patterns. *Adoption Quarterly, 7*(1), 27–41.

Weiss, M. R., Ebbeck, V., & Horn, T. S. (1997). Children's self-perceptions and sources of physical competence information: A cluster analysis. *Journal of Sport & Exercise Psychology, 19,* 52–70.

Weitoff, G. R., Burström, B., & Rosén, M. (2004). Premature mortality among lone fathers and childless men. *Social Science & Medicine, 59*(7), 1449–1459.

Wells, M., Glickauf-Hughes, C., & Bruss, K. (1998). The relationship of co-dependency to enduring personality characteristics. *Journal of College Student Psychotherapy, 12*, 25–38.

Westheimer, R. K., & Lopater, S. (2004). *Human sexuality: A psychosocial perspective.* New York: Lippincott, Williams, & Wilkins.

Weston, K. (1997). *Families we choose: Lesbians, gays, kinship.* New York: Columbia University Press.

Wharton, A. S. (2004). *The sociology of gender: An introduction to theory and research.* Malden, MA: Blackwell.

Whitam, F. L., & Zent, M. (1984). A crosscultural assessment of early cross-gender behavior and familial factors in male homosexuality. *Archives of Sexual Behavior, 13*, 427–439.

Whiting, J. B., Smith, D. R., Barnett, T., & Grafsky, E. L. (2007). Overcoming the Cinderella myth: A mixed methods study of successful stepmothers. *Journal of Divorce & Remarriage, 47*(1/2), 95–109.

Wiehe, V. R. (1990). Religious influence on parental attitudes toward the use of corporal punishment. *Journal of Family Violence, 5*, 173–186.

Wilcoxon, S. A. (2002). Permission to speak freely: Consent and intervention with the noncustodial parent and children. In R. E. Watts & J. Carlson (Eds.), *Techniques in marriage and family counseling* (Vol. 2, pp. 109–116). Alexandria, VA: American Counseling Association.

Wiley, A. R., Warren, H. B., & Montenelli, D. S. (2002). Shelter in a time of storm: Parenting in poor, rural African-American communities. *Family Relations, 51*, 265–273.

Williams, S. S., Norris, A. E., & Bedor, M. M. (2003). Sexual relationships, condom use, and concerns about pregnancy, HIV/AIDS, and other sexually transmitted diseases. *Clinical Nurse Specialist, 17*, 89–94.

Williamson, D. S. (1998). Disclosure is a family event. *Family Relations, 47*, 23–25.

Wilson, K., & Fyson, R. (2007). Foster fathers: Their experiences and contributions to fostering. *Child & Family Social Work, 12*(1), 22–31.

Winkler, R. (2004). *The family—Where violence begins, recognizing and stopping it.* Lincoln, NE: iUniverse.

Witters-Green, R. (2003). Parental expression of physical intimacy with young children: Influences on subjective norms about what is appropriate. *Dissertation Abstracts International: Section B: the Sciences & Engineering, 64* (3-B), 1556. Ann Arbor, MI: University Microfilms International.

Woo, H., & Raley, R. K. (2005). A small extension to 'costs and rewards of children: The effects of becoming a parent on adults' lives. *Journal of Marriage and Family, 67*(1), 216–221.

Wood, B., & Talmon, M. (1983). Family boundaries in transition: A search for alternatives. *Family Process, 22*, 347–357.

Wood, C., & Davidson, J. (2003). Helping families cope: A fresh look at parent effectiveness training. *Family Matters, 65*, 28–33.

Woodhill, B. M., & Samuels, C. A. (2003). Positive and negative androgyny and their relationship with psychological health and well-being. *Sex Roles, 48*, 555–565.

Wordlaw-Stinson, L. (2003). Unbroken homes: Single parent mothers tell their stories. *Sex Roles, 49*, 190.

Xie, H., Cairns, B. D., & Cairns, R. B. (2001). Predicting teen motherhood and teen fatherhood: Individual characteristics and peer affiliations. *Social Development, 10*, 488–509.

Zabin, L. S., & Cardona, K. M. (2002). Adolescent pregnancy. In G. M. Wingood & R. J. DiClemente (Eds.), *Handbook of women's sexual and reproductive health: Issues in women health* (pp. 231–253). New York: Kluwer Academic/Plenum Publishers.

Zachary, E. M. (2005). Getting my education: Teen mothers' experiences in school before and after motherhood. *Teachers College Record, 107*(12), 2566–2598.

Ziegahn, S. J. (2002). *The stepparent's survival guide: A workbook for creating a happy blended family.* Oakland, CA: New Harbinger Publications.

Index